Game Theory and Economics

Christian Montet and Daniel Serra

First published 2003 by
PALGRAVE MACMILLAN
Houndmills, Basingstoke, Hampshire RG21 6XS and
175 Fifth Avenue, New York, N. Y. 10010
Companies and representatives throughout the world

PALGRAVE MACMILLAN is the global academic imprint of the Palgrave Macmillan division of St. Martin's Press, LLC and of Palgrave Macmillan Ltd. Macmillan® is a registered trademark in the United States, United Kingdom and other countries. Palgrave is a registered trademark in the European Union and other countries.

ISBN 0–333–61846–7 hardback
ISBN 0–333–61847–5 paperback

This book is printed on paper suitable for recycling and made from fully managed and sustained forest sources.

A catalogue record for this book is available from the British Library.

Library of Congress Cataloging-in-Publication Data
Montet, Christian.
    Game theory and economics / Christian Montet and Daniel Serra.
       p. cm.
    Includes bibliographical references and index.
    ISBN 0–333–61846–7
    1. Game theory. 2. Economics. I. Serra, Daniel. II. Title.
HB144.M66 2003
330′.01′5193—dc21   2002030258

10 9 8 7 6 5 4 3 2 1
12 11 10 09 08 07 06 05 04 03

Printed and bound in Great Britain by
Creative Print & Design (Wales), Ebbw Vale

To Brigitte,
Sandrine and Vivian

To Marie-Sylvette,
Caroline and Charles

Contents

List of Figures   x

Acknowledgements   xv

Introduction   xvii

I.1   Why the need for a new textbook?   xvii
I.2   Five distinctive features of the book   xix
I.3   Organization of the book and alternative course design   xx
I.4   Advice to the reader   xxiii

Notation and symbols   xxv

1 Preliminaries   **1**
1.1   Introduction to game theory and outline of the book   1
     1.1.1   Game theory: what it is and where it comes from?   1
     1.1.2   Non-cooperative and cooperative games: the two classical frameworks   2
     1.1.3   Game theory and decision theory: what is the difference?   4
     1.1.4   Rational behaviour, information and equilibrium   4
     1.1.5   'Rationalistic' and 'evolutive' interpretations of an equilibrium   6
     1.1.6   Game theory and empiricism   9
1.2   Detailed description of the book's content   10
1.3   Formal representation of games   13
     1.3.1   Extensive-form games   13
     1.3.2   Strategic-form games   17
     1.3.3   Coalitional-form games   22
Bibliography   26

2 Optimal Decentralized Decisions   **28**
2.1   Dominant strategy equilibrium   29
     2.1.1   Definition   29
     2.1.2   Existence and efficiency   31
2.2   Iterated dominance and backward induction   34
     2.2.1   Iterated dominance   34
     2.2.2   Backward induction   37

2.3	Safety First		39
	2.3.1	Security strategies	39
	2.3.2	Optimal security strategies in strictly competitive games	42
2.4	Applications		45
	2.4.1	Voting game	45
	2.4.2	Implementation theory and public decision making	49
Bibliography			59

3 Non-Cooperative Games with Complete and Perfect Information — **62**

3.1	Nash equilibrium: theory and early applications		63
	3.1.1	Definition and existence	63
	3.1.2	Two classical applications in industrial organization: Cournot and Bertrand duopoly models	68
	3.1.3	Justification and selection of a Nash equilibrium	73
	3.1.4	Failures of NE concept: non-existence, multiplicity, inefficiency	78
3.2	Extensions: randomization and correlation		80
	3.2.1	Mixed strategy equilibrium	80
	3.2.2	Correlated equilibrium	86
3.3	Repeated games		91
	3.3.1	Definition	91
	3.3.2	The folk theorem	94
3.4	Sub-game perfection: refinement 1		97
	3.4.1	Sub-game perfection and backward induction	97
	3.4.2	Stackelberg equilibrium: a classical application in industrial organization	100
	3.4.3	Sub-game perfection in general games	103
3.5	Applications		109
	3.5.1	Sequential games and strategic commitment	109
	3.5.2	Sequential games and hidden actions: moral hazard	120
	3.5.3	Repeated games and credible threats or promises	127

Appendix: Basic topological concepts: convexity, correspondences and fixed point theorems		135
Bibliography		137

4 Non-Cooperative Games with Imperfect or Incomplete Information — **141**

4.1	Games with incomplete information: Bayesian equilibrium		142
	4.1.1	The axiomatic framework of games with complete information	142

4.1.2	Rationalizable strategies	144
4.1.3	The Bayesian game and Nash equilibrium	146
4.1.4	A classical application: auctions	151
4.2	Perfectness and sequentiality: refinement 2	155
4.2.1	Perfectness	156
4.2.2	Sequentiality	161
4.3	Forward induction: refinement 3	170
4.3.1	Forward induction and backward induction	171
4.3.2	Formalizations of forward induction in signalling games	175
4.3.3	Stable sets of equilibria	185
4.4	Applications	188
4.4.1	Repeated games with incomplete information: reputation effects	188
4.4.2	Signalling games	192
Bibliography		203

5   Bargaining: from Non-Cooperative to Cooperative Games   206

5.1	Strategic games of bargaining	207
5.1.1	Indeterminacy or extreme Nash equilibria in simple two-person bargaining games with complete information	208
5.1.2	The Rubinstein model: alternating offers in finite and infinite horizon bargaining games	211
5.1.3	'Outside option' games	218
5.1.4	Non-cooperative theories of bargaining under incomplete information	222
5.2	Axiomatic models of bargaining and Nash program	226
5.2.1	The Nash bargaining solution	226
5.2.2	Other axiomatic bargaining solutions	236
5.2.3	The Nash program: the relationships between the strategic and the axiomatic approaches	239
5.3	Applications	242
5.2.4	Bilateral monopoly	242
5.2.5	Firm–union bargaining over wage and employment	244
Bibliography		246

6   Coalitions: Cooperative and Non-Cooperative Games   248

6.1	Introduction to coalition games	249
6.1.1	General properties of cooperative games	249
6.1.2	Interpretation and classification of solution concepts in cooperative games	255

	6.1.3	Coalition formation: cooperative or non-cooperative framework	258
6.2		The domination approach: the core and related solution concepts	260
	6.2.1	The core	260
	6.2.2	Like-core solution concepts	269
6.3		The valuation approach: the Shapley value and extensions	276
	6.3.1	The Shapley value	276
	6.3.2	Relationships between the Shapley Value and other solution concepts	280
	6.3.3	Extensions	284
6.4		Endogenous coalition structures and formation of coalitions	287
	6.4.1	Endogenous coalition structures: generalities	287
	6.4.2	Non-cooperative games of coalition formation with externalities	296
6.5		Applications	304
	6.5.1	Cost sharing games	304
	6.5.2	Environmental coalitions	311

Appendix: Linear programming   323
Bibliography   323

7   Evolutionary Games and Learning   **329**
7.1		Replicator dynamics and evolutionary stable strategies: the basic biological concepts	330
	7.1.1	The Replicator dynamics	330
	7.1.2	Evolutionary stable strategies	337
	7.1.3	Neutral stability, evolutionary stable sets and robustness against equilibrium entrants	340
	7.1.4	Asymmetrical evolutionary games	343
7.2		Extensions and generalizations to economics: evolution, rationality and efficiency	347
	7.2.1	Connection between Replicator dynamics, evolutionary stable strategy and other equilibrium concepts	347
	7.2.2	Evolution and dominance	351
	7.2.3	Evolutionary stability and efficiency	353
7.3		Learning models	356
	7.3.1	Routine learning	357
	7.3.2	Learning by way of imitation	358
	7.3.3	Belief learning	359
7.4		Applications	363

7.4.1   International trade and the internal
        organization of firms   363
7.4.2   An evolutionary version of the 'chain-store' game   370

Appendix 1: Elements of a dynamic system   379
Appendix 2: The model of Friedman and Fung (1996)   381
Bibliography   382

8   Experimental Games   **385**
8.1   Some methodological remarks and first applications   386
      8.1.1   History and methodology   386
      8.1.2   First applications: strictly competitive games   388
8.2   Cooperation   391
      8.2.1   Cooperation: altruism or strategic reputation
              building behaviour?   392
      8.2.2   Cooperation and backward induction in
              sequential games   398
8.3   Coordination   401
      8.3.1   Classical coordination games   403
      8.3.2   Factors increasing coordination   407
8.4   Bargaining   411
      8.4.1   The ultimatum game   411
      8.4.2   Some other bargaining games   421
      8.4.3   Coalition games   425
8.5   Learning and evolution   428
      8.5.1   Questions explored in experimental
              evolutionary games   428
      8.5.2   Examples of experimental evolutionary game   430
      8.5.3   Learning in games   435
8.6   From experimental evidences to some new
      game theoretic modelling principles   439
      8.6.1   Players' abilities: towards new bounded
              rationality principles   440
      8.6.2   Players' motivations: the new 'social utility' models 444
Bibliography   460

Name Index   469

Subject Index   474

List of Figures

1.1	Examples of game trees	18
1.2	Example of matrix game associated with an extensive-form game	21
1.3	Strategic-form and extended-form representation of the 'rock, scissors, paper' game	22
2.1	Domination between strategies	29
2.2	The Prisoner's dilemma game	33
2.3	Iterated dominance equilibrium	35
2.4	(Weak) dominance and indeterminate outcomes	36
2.5	Iterated dominance with weak strategies	36
2.6	Game in extensive form with its associated strategic form	38
2.7	Security strategies	40
2.8	Zero-sum games	44
2.9	Hurwicz's diagram	51
2.10	Vickrey auction	56
3.1	Nash equilibrium	64
3.2	The Battle of the Sexes	66
3.3	Cournot–Nash equilibrium	71
3.4	Non-existence of NE	78
3.5	Multiplicity of NE	79
3.6	Inefficiency of NE	79
3.7	Matching pennies game	80
3.8	Mixed strategy NE	82
3.9	Correlated equilibrium	87
3.10	Extended game for the second coordination device	88
3.11	Extended game for the third coordination device	89
3.12	Prisoner's dilemma	92
3.13	The principle of backward induction	98
3.14	Backward induction and Pareto-inefficiency	99
3.15	Sub-game perfect equilibrium	103
3.16	NE of the sub-game	104
3.17	SPE and irrational behaviour	108
3.18	The centipede game	109
3.19	Cournot–Nash equilibria	111
3.20	The extensive form of the multinational firm game	112
3.21	An extended form of the multinational firm game	113
3.22	Reaction curves and iso-profit curves of the duopoly game	116

3.23	Taxonomy of the different strategic situations	119
3.24	The payoff matrix	128
3.25	Countries' welfare	129
4.1	A game of incomplete information: strategic form	147
4.2	A game of incomplete information: extensive form	148
4.3	PTHE	157
4.4	PTHE and inefficiency	159
4.5	Proper equilibrium	160
4.6	Assessment equilibrium	163
4.7	Sequential equilibrium	169
4.8	Sequential equilibrium: reduced game trees	170
4.9	Forward induction	172
4.10	Iterated dominance	172
4.11	Payoff matrix of a variant of the Battle of the Sexes game	174
4.12	Forward induction in the Battle of the Sexes game	174
4.13	Forward induction and backward induction in the Battle of the Sexes game	175
4.14	The extensive form of the Beer–Quiche game	180
4.15	Payoff matrix of the Beer–Quiche game with $p = \frac{1}{3}$	181
4.16	Payoff matrix of a game	186
4.17	Best response correspondences	186
4.18	Extensive form of the entry game	189
4.19	Payoff matrix of the 'chain-store' game	190
4.20	Single-crossing condition	196
4.21	Separating equilibria	199
5.1	The ultimatum game in extensive form	209
5.2	Extensive form for the ultimatum game with discrete choices	211
5.3	Extensive form of the alternating offer model (finite horizon)	212
5.4	'Outside option' game tree: case 1	218
5.5	'Outside option' game tree: case 2	219
5.6	A bargaining problem (X, d)	227
5.7	Independence of irrelevant alternatives	229
5.8	Generalized Nash bargaining solution (NBS)	231
5.9	The Raiffa–Kalai–Smorodinsky solution	237
5.10	NBS of the bilateral monopoly	243
6.1	Kernel (K), Nucleolus (NL), Core (C) and Bargaining Set (BS)	275
6.2	TVA cost data	306
6.3	The core and the Shapley Value of the TVA cost game	307
6.4	The core and the Shapley Value of the modified TVA cost game	308
6.5	NL (N) for the modified TVA cost game	310
6.6	Valuation function and profitability function $(P = v - v^0)$	314

6.7	Free-riding function (Q)	315
6.8	Stability function with orthogonal free-riding and low fixed abatement costs	317
6.9	Stability function with orthogonal free-riding and high fixed abatement costs	318
6.10	Stability function with non-orthogonal free-riding	319
6.11	Stability function with non-orthogonal free-riding and humped-shaped valuation function	321
7.1	A coordination game	333
7.2	Phase diagram of the RD in the coordination game	334
7.3	The Hawk–Dove game	335
7.4	Phase diagram of the RD in the Hawk–Dove game	336
7.5	A Prisoner's dilemma	338
7.6	A coordination game	339
7.7	An entry game	344
7.8	Phase diagram of the RD in the entry game	345
7.9	An asymmetric Hawk–Dove game	346
7.10	Phase diagram of the RD in an asymmetric Hawk–Dove game	347
7.11	A game for which the asymptotically stable points of the RD are not ESS	350
7.12	A version of the 'rock, paper, scissors' game	352
7.13	A game with strong losses if the other player deviates from the NE	354
7.14	A game showing the difficulties faced by mutants	355
7.15	Adjustment in Cournot duopoly	361
7.16	A simple non-cooperative game	363
7.17	Profits profiles for different values of s	366
7.18	Phase diagram for different values of the parameters when countries are open to international trade	369
7.19	The 'chain-store' game in both extensive form and strategic form	370
7.20	Equilibria of the 'chain-store' game	371
7.21	Extensive form of the evolutionary version of the 'chain-store' game	372
7.22	Extensive form of the modified 'chain-store' game	373
7.23	Strategic form of the modified 'chain-store' game	374
7.24	Phase diagram of the RD of the 'chain-store' game for particular values of the parameters	375
7.25	Phase diagram for $\delta_I = \delta_{II} = 0.01$	376
7.26	Phase diagram for $\delta_I = 0.01$ and $\delta_{II} = 0.1$	377
7.27	Stable equilibrium of a dynamic system	380
8.1	A constant sum game	389
8.2	Non-constant sum games	390
8.3	Cooperation problem in a symmetric game	391

8.4	The Prisoner's dilemma game	392
8.5	The trust game	398
8.6	Centipede game A	399
8.7	Centipede game B	399
8.8	Coordination problems	401
8.9	Matrix of coordination games	401
8.10	Coordination games' payoffs	403
8.11	Pure coordination game A	404
8.12	Pure coordination game B	404
8.13	Cooperation–coordination game A	406
8.14	Cooperation–coordination game B	406
8.15	Cooperation–coordination game C	407
8.16	Coordination games with recommended plays	408
8.17	Battle of the Sexes game	409
8.18	Selection of each equilibria at the first and last periods	410
8.19	Expected payoff for player 1	419
8.20	Multistage bargaining games	422
8.21	Single-population experimental evolutionary games	430
8.22	Convergence percentage in the Hawk–Dove game (single population)	431
8.23	Convergence percentage in the coordination game (single population)	432
8.24	Convergence percentage in the Prisoner's dilemma game (single population)	432
8.25	Two-population evolutionary games	433
8.26	Convergence percentage in the three standard two-population games	433
8.27	Iterated rationality in the guessing game ($n = 100$, $p = 0.7$)	442
8.28	Prisoner's dilemma payoff matrix	453

Acknowledgements

We have been helped by many people in the long and arduous task of transforming and adapting our teaching notes (most of them in French) into a complete textbook. We are especially grateful to those who have patiently managed and monitored the development of this text at Palgrave Macmillan.

Among our colleagues, we first want to thank David Greenaway (University of Nottingham), who was the first to encourage us to write this book. Without his support, we would not even have thought of venturing into the enterprise of writing a whole textbook in English (which is not our native language). Some parts are the product of common work with Didier Laussel. We are grateful to the colleagues who read some Chapters or the whole text and gave us comments for revisions and improvements. In this regard, we are especially grateful to Valérie Clément, Michel Deshons, Nicolas Gravel, Walter Labys, Didier Laussel, Philippe Mahenc and Marc Willinger.

We would like to thank the reviewers who read a preliminary version of the book and suggested many important changes. We are also grateful to the three reviewers of the final version for their encouraging reports and the suggestions for improvements that they proposed.

Stephane Aymard, former PhD student at the University of Montpellier and now Research Engineer at the University of Poitiers, deserves special thanks. As a specialist in experimental economics, he has made an important contribution to Chapter 8. He also proposed several exercises, especially in the early chapters. He also put a huge effort into a critical reading of the text and in the organization of some sections.

Members of the LAMETA, a French research centre for economics (University of Montpellier 1, CNRS, INRA), provided valuable assistance at different stages of the writing and development of the book. Several of them assisted us on the technical side in writing parts of the text (in particular, equations, tables and figures) or in testing some exercises. We want especially to thank: Cédric Domergue, Nicolas Marchetti, Céline Mermet, Fabrice Yafil and Emmanuel Sol. Thierry Vignolo contributed to parts of Chapter 7.

Many people have provided useful technical advice and have helped us at different stages of our work. Among them we wish to thank: Stephane Ballet and Caroline Beaucousin, and especially for linguistic corrections Asha Neuville, Bénédicte Ricot and Anne Rocca.

Finally, we are grateful to a number of students, especially students of the graduate programme, DEA 'Microéconomie et calcul économique' of the Department of Economics, University of Montpellier I, and PhD students in the same programme. They contributed to the improvements of our teaching notes; they tested many exercises; they even sometimes identified errors or unsatisfactory explanations.

CHRISTIAN MONTET
DANIEL SERRA

Introduction

1.1   Why the need for a new textbook?
1.2   Five distinctive features of the book
1.3   Organization of the book and alternative course design
1.4   Advice to the reader

This book is the result of long years of experience of teaching Game Theory (GT) in various environments. We have both taught courses of GT at undergraduate and graduate level and we have also been involved in teaching game theoretical applications in other courses including Industrial Organization and Managerial Economics for MBA students.

In the early 1990s, when we started teaching GT, the only texts available were either only at a beginner level, as in a number of Microeconomics textbooks, or at a very technical level more suited to advanced graduate students. At the time there was a need for a textbook covering the main sections of GT, in a comprehensive and rigorous style, but which did not go into the hard technicalities at too much length, since the latter are required only by advanced and specialized researchers in the field. Our teaching notes progressively grew in depth and volume in order to bridge the gap facing us. In the meantime of course, since Nature always abhors a vacuum, several texts have been published targeting the advanced undergraduate/beginner graduate level.

1.1   Why the need for a new textbook?

The needs at this core level have also evolved, first as a result of the success of non-cooperative GT in dealing with an increasing number of issues studied in Economics, and secondly under the pressure of the continuous advances of GT itself.

The *success of non-cooperative GT* in pervading all fields of economic theory and sections of other disciplines such as Strategic Management, Law and Political Science is now acknowledged as a central feature of the evolution of thought in the last few decades. The Nobel Prize awarded in 1994 to three of the major developers of GT in the 1950s–1970s: John Nash, John Harsanyi and Reinhard Selten – came as the most visible recognition of this outstanding success. More recent Nobel laureates, such as the specialists of information and contracts – William Vickrey and James Mirrlees in 1998 and Michael Spence, Joseph Stiglitz and Georges Akerlof in 2001 – are also in various ways great users and developers of the applications of game theoretical analysis to economic theory.

Indeed, GT has deeply changed the contents of all the sub-disciplines of Economics. The major changes have occurred in Industrial Organization, International Economics (especially Trade Policy and Macroeconomic Policy coordination), Labour Economics, Macroeconomic Policy, Public Economics and Public Policy. Beyond a mere fashion effect which may explain the pervasive nature of game theoretical analysis, even in cases where this approach may finally not appear to be the most appropriate one, this state of affairs is likely to be lasting. GT is still in a creative, evolutionary phase, evolving according to the relative success and failure of its various applications to economic problems.

Today, the normal curriculum requires that students in Economics learn at least the basics of GT. For those entering graduate programmes and wishing to start a new research project, more advanced knowledge of GT is becoming a prerequisite, in both Microeconomics and Macroeconomics, together with other standard tools such as Econometrics. Even in other fields such as Management studies, Law and Political Science, some basic knowledge of GT is becoming more and more a compulsory requirement, especially at the graduate and Ph D level.

The last few years have seen *continuous advances in GT* and its applications. First, cooperative GT, which had somehow become less fashionable and suffered from the success of non-cooperative models, is now making an interesting comeback, largely in a more integrated way with the non-cooperative approach for the study of coalitional games. Secondly, while research into the refinements of equilibrium seems to be petering out and suffering strong decreasing returns, the great bulk of research has turned to the study of how people play games, how they learn in playing them and how they may finally reach an equilibrium. Evolutionary thinking from the field of Biology has shown interesting features useful for the study of economic and business games, provided one can endow the players with some capacities of learning, thus accelerating in one way or another the access to equilibrium. Evolutionary game theory has thus become an integrated part of a GT course, and the study of learning in games is certainly one of the most active areas of research in the discipline. A third major evolution of GT in the 1990s came from the support provided by experimental methods. Experimental games have not only been able to confirm a series of predictions from game theoretical thinking, but also by revealing some types of behaviour not entirely conforming to the theory, have been able to revolutionize the way games are designed and also the way numerous kinds of games are interpreted and analysed.

Our teaching notes have evolved since the early 1990s in order to respond to these new needs and to incorporate as far as possible the changes occurring in GT. The distinctive features of this book are the result of this continuous process.

1.2 Five distinctive features of the book

First and foremost, the book is very *comprehensive*. It covers non-cooperative games extensively, and also cooperative games, evolutionary games and experimentation. Recent developments of the literature are included, and even in the more traditional parts of the book an effort is made to include neglected topics such as forward induction, or the role of 'outside options' in bargaining. A detailed bibliography is given at the end of each chapter.

The second feature is that a large section of the book, three chapters in fact, is devoted to *special topics*, that are hardly ever discussed or only summarily referred to in other textbooks: a chapter deals with coalition games, another with evolutionary game theory (EGT), and a third with experimental games. A comprehensive survey of cooperative GT seemed welcome at this level, and the inclusion of topics such as the endogenous formation of coalitions helps to link cooperative GT to the more standard framework. The space and emphasis given to new topics such as evolutionary GT and experiments in games reflects the recent trends of research and evolution of the field.

Thirdly, the level of difficulty has been designed to suit advanced-level undergraduates. We have tried to find a compromise between *verbal or intuitive expositions and more rigorous presentations*.

The fourth feature is that the theory is presented together with many *economic applications*, generally with a focus on recent work. Up-to-date examples are given in various fields of economics: Industrial Organization, International Trade and Trade Policy, Public Economics and Labour Economics. An effort has been made to cover different applications of GT in the economics of asymmetric information and contract theory. Special topics belonging to this branch of modern economics, such as moral hazard, signalling or mechanism design, are spread throughout the book in relation to the equilibrium concepts used in each case.

Finally, a series of **exercises** with an answers key is provided free of charge on the following website: **http://www.lameta.univ-montp1.fr/ online/gte/exercises.html**. We have tried to present a complete set of problems, enabling us to treat some theoretical points mentioned in the text as exercises.

1.3 Organization of the book and alternative course design

The book is organized in eight chapters. A justification of this organization and a detailed description of the chapters' content is provided in Chapter 1. As emphasized above, the book is very comprehensive, which also means that it is nearly impossible to cover all the contents, even in a one-year course (or two one-semester courses). Instructors will thus have to choose the parts of the book they wish to cover, depending on the type and the level of course they are teaching. It is possible to select different topics and adapt them to each particular need.

Four alternative syllabuses for a one-semester course are suggested below. The first corresponds to a basic teaching in GT and applications, while the second covers topics of an advanced theoretical level with rather more difficult applications. The third syllabus stresses above all the economic applications of GT. The fourth corresponds to the more recently developed topics in GT.

1.3.1 Syllabus 1: basic GT with some easy applications

Section(s)	Sub-section(s)	Topic(s)
1.1		Introduction to GT
1.3		Formal representations of games
2.1		Dominant strategy equilibrium
2.2		Iterative dominance and backward induction
2.3		Safety first
3.1		Nash equilibrium: theory and early applications
3.2		Extensions: randomization and correlation
3.3		Repeated games
3.4		Sub-game perfection: refinement 1
	3.5.1	Application of SPE: sequential games and strategic commitment (*only the first application: entry deterrence*)
	3.5.2	Repeated games and credible threats or promises
4.1		Games with incomplete information: Bayesian equilibrium
4.2		Perfectness and sequentiality: refinement 2
5.1		Strategic games of bargaining (*except 5.1.4: incomplete information*)

5.2		Axiomatic models of bargaining and the Nash program
5.3		Application of the NBS: bilateral monopoly or firm–union bargaining wage and employment
6.1		Introduction to coalition games
	6.2.1	The core
	6.3.1	The Shapley Value
	6.5.1	Application of the core and the Shapley Value: cost sharing games (*except the passage about the NL*)

1.3.2 Syllabus 2: advanced GT with some more difficult applications

Section(s)	Sub-section(s)	Topic(s)
	2.4.2	Application of the dominant strategy equilibrium: implementation theory and public decision making
	3.5.1	Application of the SPE: strategic trade policy or strategic investment in a model of differentiated goods duopoly
	4.4.1	Application of repeated games with incomplete information: reputation effects
4.3		Forward induction: refinement 3
	4.4.2	Application of forward induction: signalling games (*only the first application: a portfolio management game*)
	5.1.4	Non-cooperative theories of bargaining under incomplete information
	6.2.2	Like-core solution concepts (in cooperative games)
	6.3.2.	Relationships between the Shapley Value and other solution concepts
	6.3.3	Extensions (of the Shapley Value)
6.4		Endogenous coalition structure and formation of coalitions
7.1–7.4		Evolutionary games and learning (*with only one application and without the Remarks*)
8.1–8.5		Experimental games (*except section 8.6 and without the Remarks*)

1.3.3 Syllabus 3: economic applications of GT

Section(s)	Sub-section(s)	Topic(s)
	3.1.2	Applications of the Nash equilibrium concept in industrial organization: Cournot and Bertrand duopoly models
2.4		Applications of dominance: models of voting game, implementation theory and public decision making
	4.1.4	Application of the Bayesian equilibrium: auctions
	3.4.2	Application of backward induction in industrial organization: Stackelberg duopoly model
	3.5.1	Applications of sub-game perfection in sequential games: entry deterrence in the case of multinational firms, strategic trade policy or strategic investment in a model of differentiated goods duopoly
	3.5.2	Applications of sub-game perfection in sequential games with hidden information: moral hazard
	3.5.3	Applications of repeated games with complete information: credible threats or promises
	4.4.1	Application of repeated games with incomplete information: reputation effects
	4.4.2	Applications of forward induction: a portfolio management signalling game or a job market signalling game
5.3		Applications of bargaining games: bilateral monopoly, firm–union bargaining over wage and employment
	6.5.1	Application of cooperative games of coalition: cost sharing games
	6.5.2	Application of non-cooperative games of coalition: environmental coalitions
7.4		Applications of evolutionary games: international trade and the international organization of firms, an evolutionary version of the 'chain-store' game

1.3.4 Syllabus 4: new topics in GT

Section(s)	Sub-section(s)	Topic(s)
6.1		Introduction to coalition games
6.4		Endogenous coalition structures and formation of coalitions
	6.5.2	Environmental coalitions.
7.1–7.4		Evolutionary games and learning
8.1–8.6		Experimental games

1.4 Advice to the reader

If you are reading this book on your own and not as part of a class, then you need to check that you have the necessary mathematics and economics background. In terms of prerequisites one semester each of calculus and optimization, mathematical statistics and intermediate microeconomics are probably required, and if you do not have this you will need to acquire it. When the required mathematical level is higher (as is occasionally the case), an Appendix provides the missing notations.

We would naturally invite the reader to follow the order of the chapters as we have written them. But one may skip some sections, especially the more difficult ones, noted with a *star*, without endangering the understanding of the book. Also, we strongly advise students to try answering the exercises before looking at the answers on the website.

The book includes many Remarks, numbered inside each sub-section, which develop certain points not dealt with or merely referred to in the text, and which also give guidelines for further reading. At a first reading, these Remarks may be skipped.

The perceived 'difficulty' of the text varies, of course, with the student's background. We have tried to keep things as simple as possible, in every part of the book, even in the topics suggested for advanced courses. Only the starred sub-sections or paragraphs should be considered as at all difficult.

Notation and Symbols

For the most part, our use of mathematical notation is standard. The meanings we attach to a few mathematical symbols whose use is somewhat less uniform in the literature are described below:

$x^{-i} = (x_1, \ldots, x_{i-1}, x_{i+1}, \ldots, x_n)$

$X^{-i} = \Pi_{j \neq i} X_j$

$x_S = (x_i)_{i \in S}$

$X \backslash Y = \{x / x \in X \text{ but } x \notin Y\}$

$\dfrac{df}{dx}$ or f', $\dfrac{d^2 f}{dx^2}$ or f''	The first and second derivatives of a function, respectively
$\dfrac{\partial f}{\partial x_i}$ or f_i', $\dfrac{\partial^2 f}{\partial x_i \partial x_j}$ or f_{ij}''	The first-order and second-order partial derivatives of a function, respectively
$D f(x)$	The matrix whose ijth entry is $\partial f_i(x)/\partial x_j$
$\dot{f}$	The derivative of a function with respect to time

We largely use abbreviations for notions which are often used in the book. The main abbreviations are the following (ordered according to their first use in the text):

GT	Game theory
TU	Transferable utility
NTU	Non-transferable utility
VNM	Von Neumann–Morgenstern
DSE	Dominant strategy equilibrium
IDE	Iterative dominant equilibrium
NE	Nash equilibrium
SPE	Sub-game perfect equilibrium
BE	Bayesian equilibrium
PTHE	Perfect trembling hand equilibrium
PE	Proper equilibrium
PBE	Perfect Bayesian equilibrium
SE	Sequential equilibrium
NBS	Nash bargaining solution
SNE	Strong Nash equilibrium
CPNE	Coalition-proof Nash equilibrium
I	Imputations (*used sometimes in a different sense: for instance, for 'Incumbent' in applications*)
C	Core

S	Stable set
BS	Bargaining set
K	Kernel
NL	Nucleolus
SV	Shapley value
SCE	Social coalition equilibrium
EGT	Evolutionary game theory
RD	Replicator dynamics
ESS	Evolutionary stable strategy
EE	Evolutionary equilibrium
TFT	Tit-for-tat
ES	Evolutionary stable
NSS	Neutrally stable strategy
REE	Robust against equilibrium entrants
EES	Equilibrium evolutionary stable (set)
FP	Fixed point (of the dynamics)

Notes:

- These abbreviations sometimes may be understood in the plural: for instance, NE for Nash *equilibria*
- When these abbreviations are set in **heavy type** that means they represent a set: for instance, **NE** for the *set* of NE.

Remark

Throughout the book, we will use the following simple rule concerning the players' identity (sex): if the game is played by two individuals, player 1 will systematically be called 'She' and player 2 will be called 'He'. In other circumstances, we will say who is who or simply write 'she or he' for any player.

Preliminaries

1.1 Introduction to game theory and outline of the book
1.2 Detailed description of the book's content
1.3 Formal representations of games

1.1 Introduction to game theory and outline of the book

1.1.1 Game theory: what it is and where it comes from

Modern game theory (GT) has a very large scope. Although the common usage of the word 'game' refers to parlour games (chess, bridge, poker, . . .), in GT this notion must be understood as situations of *conflict* and *cooperation* between intelligent and rational individuals (or groups of people) for which the objectives are generally more complex than simply to beat their opponent. Usually – and notably in economics – agents can confront each other in some ways and work towards the same end in another respect; for instance, firms have competing interests in market shares while showing a common interest in high prices.

More fundamentally, game theory deals with all real-life situations where *rational* people *interact* with each other, that is when one individual's actions depend essentially on what other individuals may do. In these situations, many of the really interesting questions are concerned with the possibility of cooperation among rational people. In using the language of parlour games, game theorists are simply attempting to indicate that they want to analyse the *logic* of these interactions 'coldly' like a chess player who thinks about all issues that logically may arise during play. Indeed, as Aumann (1987, 461) suggests, '*Interactive decision theory* would perhaps be a more descriptive name for the discipline usually called "*Game theory*"'.

It should not be surprising that economics is the biggest customer for the ideas developed by game theorists: the scarcity of economic resources and the supposed rationality of economic agents both create all the necessary ingredients for a game situation. Besides, from the very beginning economics was presented as the main field of application for game theory. The very nature of the book *Theory of Games and Economic Behavior*, published by the mathematician John Von Neumann and the economist Oskar Morgenstern in 1944, underlines this preoccupation (Von Neumann and Morgenstern, 1944).

Some of the ideas exposed in the book were anticipated in the nineteenth century and in the early twentieth century by a few economists (Cournot, 1838; Bertrand, 1883; Edgeworth, 1881; Zeuthen, 1930; Von Stackelberg, 1934) and a handful of mathematicians (Zermelo, 1913; Borel, 1924; De Possel, 1936; Ville, 1938); Von Neumann (1928) himself had already introduced some basic concepts. However GT as a specific discipline indubitably began only with the publication of Von Neumann and Morgenstern's famous book. A few years later a seminal series of papers published by the mathematician John Nash (Nash, 1950a, 1950b, 1951, 1953) strengthened the foundations of the new discipline. From that time on, history of GT was very chaotic, with periods of excitement and growth alternating with periods of disillusion and stagnation (for a historical survey or a historical framework presentation of the ideas of GT, see for instance, Aumann, 1987; Schmidt, 1990; Weintraub, 1992; or Leonard 1995). The official acknowledgement of game theory as a powerful tool for studying human interaction arose in 1994 with the awarding of the economics Nobel Prize to John C. Harsanyi, John F. Nash and Reinhard Selten, for their noteworthy innovative works in this discipline. It is rather striking to observe that only some ten years ago Ken Binmore was writing about history of GT: 'there are some names that cannot pass unmentioned. The acronym NASH may assist in remembering who they are: Nash himself gets the letter N; A is for Aumann; S is for both Shapley and Selten and H is for Harsanyi' (Binmore, 1992, 13). Today the common feeling of the world scientific community would also include the name of Binmore (among a few others) in this 'honours list'.

1.1.2   Non-cooperative and cooperative games: the two classical frameworks

A classical distinction is made in GT between non-cooperative games and cooperative games; yet the word 'non-cooperative' can be misunderstood. It does not mean that each player always refuses to cooperate with the others. Simply, in a 'non-cooperative' game players' decisions are based only on their *perceived self-interest* because it is supposed that players cannot commit themselves. In a non-cooperative game, players' commitments (agreements, threats, promises) are not enforceable, even if pre-play communication between players is possible. Players are not able to make binding agreements except for those which are explicitly allowed by the rules of the game. Thus, in non-cooperative games all aspects relevant to the situation have to be explicitly modelled by the rule of the game. Yet, it should be emphasized that non-cooperative players motivated only by self-interest can exhibit 'cooperative behaviour' in some circumstances. Indeed, an outstanding result of non-cooperative game theory is to prove that endogenous cooperation can be reached in this framework.

In contrast, 'cooperative' games assume that commitments are fully binding and enforceable: *cooperation is exogenous*. Cooperative game theory studies frictionless negotiation among rational players who can make binding agreements about how to play a game. In some ways, however, cooperative games may be considered as a special case of non-cooperative games in the sense that negotiation and enforcement procedures may be built explicitly into the rule (or structure) of the game (Aumann, 1989; Kreps, 1990).

In non-cooperative games the emphasis is mainly on the *individual* behaviour: what decision should each rational player use (normative viewpoint), or how will rational players actually choose their actions and then, what is the most likely outcome of the game (more descriptive viewpoint)? In cooperative games we are faced with a different problem. Now the emphasis is on the groups or *coalitions* of players (including the grand coalition of all the players). What coalition will form? How would (or will) they share the cooperative payoff between the members? If there are gains from cooperation but the distribution of these gains does not provide enough incentives for all the players to accept the outcome, then the existence of some exogenous 'mechanism' (institution, arbitrator, ...) is supposed to enforce commitment. Some ideas of fairness (equity, justice) must sometimes be added to the arguments of rationality in order to justify a particular outcome for the game, because the outcome of the mechanism will leave none of the concerned players unhappy only if it is perceived as fair.

'Solution' concepts of cooperative games often have both direct and axiomatic characterizations. The direct definitions apply to each game separately whereas most axioms deal with relationships between games. In axiomatic approaches, a set of desirable properties for the solution ('axioms') is first formulated and then one tries to characterize a solution or a class of solutions by its properties. More generally axioms summarize certain primitive relationships among the terms which define a game and knowledge comes from inferring propositions from these axioms that do not obviously follow from them.

Chapters 2, 3 and 4 of the book deal with non-cooperative games. Chapter 5 is devoted to the so-called bargaining problem; it deals with both non-cooperative and cooperative games of pure bargaining and looks for the relationships between the two great classes of games. In Chapter 6 the focus is on coalitions of players; the classical framework for studying this topic is provided by cooperative games, but the more recent analysis of endogenous formation of coalitions uses a mixed setting of both cooperative and non-cooperative games. Chapter 7 tackles non-cooperative games again, but from a very different viewpoint which includes the emergent 'evolutionary game theory' (EGT). Finally Chapter 8 considers experimental studies on the two classes of games.

1.1.3   Game theory and decision theory: what is the difference?

In some sense, GT (that is analysis of interactive decisions of *many* players) can be viewed as a generalization of decision theory (that is analysis of *single* player's decisions); one can think of decision theory as a two-person game in which one of the players is 'nature', a fictitious player who makes decisions based on a random device that determines the 'state of nature'. The utility of the other (active) player is determined jointly by player's decision(s) and by the state of nature. But there is a major difference between GT and decision theory. In a decision problem uncertainty is only about the moves of 'nature' (chance moves) and the agent has exogenous beliefs about the probabilities of chance moves. In contrast, for game situations in which several agents have to make decisions, players' expectations about their opponents decisions are endogenous: there is *'strategic uncertainty'*.

The essential difficulty of GT rests on this property: generally the implications of players' actions depend on others' actions that they cannot observe and must therefore forecast. Strategic uncertainty implies that each player is taking not only the structure of the game but also other players' behaviour into account. A player's *'strategic behaviour'* refers to the extent to which her (or his) actions and beliefs reflect her (or his) grasp of the environment as a non-cooperative game with strategic uncertainty rather than as a decision problem.

Yet, there are particular environments in which this strategic uncertainty of a game may be ignored and for which *optimal decentralized decisions* of players may be defined in a purely normative approach. Chapter 2 presents this first analysis of non-cooperative games. The question is: what behaviour should be prescribed to an isolated player who chooses her (or his) strategy while *totally ignoring* her (or his) opponents' decisions? Only arguments in terms of rationality are used in this decentralized context to determine players' non-cooperative behaviour. Issues not only about 'dominance' but also concerning 'security' (in some particular situations) are of central importance here.

1.1.4   Rational behaviour, information and equilibrium

So far we have spoken about 'rational' players; yet how do we define 'rationality' in an interactive situation? When game theorists describe players as 'rational', they mean no more than that they make choices 'consistently'. It turns out that a *consistent* player can be characterized as one who acts as though maximising her (or his) 'payoff' (or her (or his) 'utility') given their beliefs about 'environment'.

In fact this players' mental reasoning can be decomposed fictitiously into two steps, each implying a distinct form of rationality. *'Cognitive'* rationality deals with consistency between available information to the player and her (or his) beliefs: this notion refers to players' capability of forming beliefs about a relevant environment (i.e. their 'perception' of the game situation). In contrast *'instrumental'* rationality deals with consistency between given opportunities and fixed preference: this notion now refers to players' capability of inferring their strategies from given beliefs (i.e. their 'abilities') (Walliser, 1989). By combining these two forms of rationality players are able to reduce their strategic uncertainty about the other players' strategies given their expectations about the game rules and about the circumstances under which the game is played (the 'environment').

Then, two distinct informational properties must be introduced.

To say a game is with 'perfect' or 'imperfect' information is to say something about its rules: if players know exactly what happened in previous moves when they choose their actions and if there are no simultaneous moves, then the game is with *perfect information*; otherwise it is with imperfect information. On the other hand, to say a game is with 'complete' or 'incomplete' information is to say something about circumstances under which the game is played; that property refers to players' degree of mutual understanding of all the aspects of the game.

An information is said to be 'common knowledge' if everybody knows it, everybody knows that everybody knows it, everybody knows that everybody knows that everybody knows it, and so on. Thus a game is with *complete information* if each element of the game is common knowledge; otherwise it is with incomplete information. The idea of common knowledge is due to the American philosopher David Lewis (1969) and Aumann (1976) gave a first formal rigorous definition of this subtle concept in GT. Of course this notion of common knowledge requires more information than 'mutual knowledge' of an event which requires only that each individual knows the event: common knowledge is an infinite-order mutual knowledge (for a simple introduction to this question see Binmore, 1992, Chapter 10).

There is thus a clearly formal distinction between games of incomplete information and games of imperfect information. Incomplete information refers to an informational characteristic of players while imperfect information is a structural property of a game. Yet, it turns out that analysis of the former practically boils down to analysis of the latter according to Harsanyi's procedure (Harsanyi, 1967/8), any game of incomplete information can be reduced to a game of complete information with imperfect information. Furthermore this distinction is of little significance for applications. Therefore, it is logical to study these two classes of non-cooperative games together.

Chapter 3 of this book will be devoted to non-cooperative games with *complete and perfect information*, while Chapter 4 deals with non-cooperative games with *imperfect or incomplete information*.

With respect to Chapter 2, the descriptive viewpoint tends to have precedence over the normative approach. The analytical framework is enriched by consideration of various kinds of indirect communication between players. In particular, the game is no more necessarily a one-shot game and the repetition of the game over time makes available to the players the use of credible threats of punishments. Players can also observe the past decisions of their rivals and so take advantage of the history of the game. They can even directly communicate, exchange some information and agree to choose a particular outcome of the game.

In that context mutual consistency of players' best responses define a 'Nash equilibrium' (a 'strategic equilibrium', or in short an 'equilibrium') of the game. Strategic uncertainty implies that some knowledge of the opponents' behaviour is required; we cannot say something about a player's rational behaviour without simultaneously studying all the other players' rational behaviour. An outcome is an *equilibrium* if and only if each player anticipates correctly the behaviour of all the agents taking part in the game.

Unfortunately, multiplicity of equilibria is a very common situation. Besides, a core problem of non-cooperative GT can be formulated as follows: *given a game with several equilibria, which one of those should (or will) be chosen by rational players?*

1.1.5 'Rationalistic' and 'evolutive' interpretations of an equilibrium

Modern game theorists have developed several ways of answering this worrying question of selecting the 'right' equilibrium. These answers in fact lead to different interpretations of an 'equilibrium' in a non-cooperative game.

The previously given definition of an equilibrium says nothing about how players can coordinate themselves on such a fixed point. We are sure only that such a state can be rationalized *a posteriori*. Indeed, the problem of defining the strategic properties of equilibria in a game must not be confused with justifying the appearance of a particular equilibrium. Theoretically the search for the 'strategic stability' conditions of an outcome is not the same thing as wondering if players can coordinate themselves on the same outcome.

We will adopt in Chapter 3 and 4 the 'traditional' or 'standard' interpretation which is summarized by what Crawford (1997) called the 'rationalistic' scenario. We also can speak of 'deductive' (Osborne and Rubinstein, 1994), 'introspective' (Kreps, 1990; Fudenberg and Tirole, 1991) or 'eductive' approach (Binmore, 1987). This scenario describes a process by means of which equilibrium is achieved only through careful reasoning by players. This traditional equilibrium analysis assumes an extreme form of strategic behaviour. Each player is supposed to deduce how the other players will behave simply from principles of rationality and postulates of common knowledge. Of course, if there is a preliminary stage of non-binding negotiation between the players and if an agreement comes out of this pre-play communication, players' coordination on that outcome is natural. However there are many situations in which players can communicate only indirectly. So 'traditional' GT supplies a host of equilibrium 'refinements' in order to discriminate between equilibria by defining stronger notions of rationality and introducing 'reasonable' increasing restrictions on players' beliefs. Yet this rationalistic approach was not entirely successful; the problem of multiplicity of equilibria is not solved for many strategic situations. Then how does one explain that players' beliefs are coordinated on the same outcome?

Fortunately in many games an equilibrium appears as compelling due simply to some qualitative facts or principles (symmetry, efficiency, equity, for instance), or more fundamentally with reference to social or cultural norms which encourage people to focus on particular outcomes. This so-called 'focal-point' argument was originally introduced by Schelling (1960) and expresses the view that rational solutions of some games depend on players' 'culture' or 'customs' too. It should be emphasized, however, that this view is different from the traditional 'consequentialist' concept of GT (and more generally, of rational decision theory). Traditional view assumes that a rational player merely chooses an action according to her (or his) expectations of its *consequences*, whereas this view amounts to introducing elements of 'deontological' behaviour with that acknowledgement of leading role of *norms* in rational individual choices. Indeed the heart of the question here is the relationship between rational choice and ethics. It refers to the exciting present-day debate on the possibility of reconciliation between the two old oppositing paradigms developed through social sciences: the rationalist, individualist and consequentialist 'economic' paradigm on the one hand, and the holist norms-oriented 'sociological' paradigm on the other.

Therefore, according to the orthodox rationalistic scenario, the 'equilibriating' processes are purely mental: it describes a world of hyper-rational players in which each of them are simulating the mental reasoning of the other players and going instantaneously to an equilibrium. However we all know that in the real world rationality of people is generally bounded and learning processes by trial and error mechanisms, imitation, experience or routine are common behaviour. The emergent 'evolutive' scenario in GT (the word was first used by Binmore, 1987) champions the point of view that in games in which players are endowed with more or less limited cognitive and instrumental capacities, the time compensates for the weaker rationality. Repetitions take place in real time and time equilibriating processes replace purely mental equilibriating processes. Instead of making predictions by introspection and deduction players are supposed to forecast the behaviour of their opponents by extrapolation: they use past observations of play in 'similar' interactive situations with the same opponents or with 'similar' ones. This justification of an equilibrium is 'extrapolative' (Fudenberg and Tirole, 1991). While the traditional approach treats a game in isolation, with the modeller attempting only to infer the restrictions that players' rationality imposes on the outcome, the evolutive approach treats a game as a model designed to explain some observed regularity when decision makers interact repeatedly in real time. That is why this approach sometimes is also called the 'steady-state' interpretation of an equilibrium (Osborne and Rubinstein, 1994).

The evolutive scenario actually admits two great variants which are becoming closer and closer. The 'learning models' always assume that players can calculate the best response. They typically study learning processes in which 'bounded rational' players revise initial expectations on opponents' future actions after observing their past actions according to more or less pragmatic revision rules. Thus, players' strategic behaviour is limited; restrictions on behaviour (or beliefs) are derived from simple and plausible assumptions from a psychological point of view.

The 'evolutionary' process represents the extreme situation of a world composed of purely passive 'automates' selected in very long-term dynamics. Furthermore the biological origin of this story (Maynard Smith, 1982) explains that each 'player' is now represented by a sub-population of similar agents. Players meet together in an anonymous way and they reproduce according to various 'reproduction' rules. The most efficient players become progressively more numerous by a process of mutation and selection that tends to eliminate players that are relatively less successful. If the dynamic evolutionary process leads to a population whose members are fractionally distributed, then that distribution is an 'equilibrium', provided that the evolutionary process works to maintain and restore this distribution in the face of all sufficiently small arbitrary displacements of the population proportions. The goal of 'evolutionary' game theory (EGT) is simply to identify those locally stable steady states (or rest points) of the dynamics. Thus according to this extreme evolutionary viewpoint the problem of selecting a particular 'equilibrium' is no longer a meaningful one. The equilibrium actually observed results simply from the conjunction of essentially random events in the history of the 'equilibriating' process and of the initial conditions from which the process began.

Interestingly, a remarkable result was proven in EGT: for a large class of evolutionary games, if the dynamics converge, they converge towards a steady state in which the limiting distributions are in 'equilibrium' in the sense of the traditional GT: 'evolutionary' equilibrium have the properties of 'strategic' equilibria. In short, even though players' behaviour is not rational, the population seems to 'learn' the rational equilibrium as its distribution evolves. It should be emphasized incidentally that this basic idea of the evolutionary approach is not totally new in economics; it is in line with a tradition according to which economic agents may not consciously optimize but behave 'as if' they were rational because economic competition selects more performant agents (Friedman, 1953). In the same way, adjustment dynamics towards an equilibrium has a very long history in economics. What is new in EGT is its clear acknowledgement that rationality alone fails to justify equilibrium and that something 'ad hoc' is necessary for explaining players' equilibrium behaviour.

Learning models for game situations and *evolutionary games* has become an active field of research since 1990. This topic will be tackled in detail in Chapter 7.

1.1.6 Game theory and empiricism

Binmore (1990) distinguishes five general tactical purposes for which a game theoretic model might be used: prediction, explanation, description, investigation and prescription. Except when the model is used for prescription from a normative viewpoint, and perhaps also for 'investigation' (i.e. when we abandon the general problem in favour of simple examples that present the problem in a special form more suitable in searching for counterexamples that would prove the conjecture false), the *empirical* content of GT is generally relevant. In this perspective game models have to be submitted to systematic empirical validation, either in laboratory or in field experiments. In particular, there is a need for empirical works that directly test the domain of validity of the 'rationalistic' and 'evolutive' scenarios in non-cooperative games.

Since the 1980s empirical studies of strategic interaction under controlled laboratory conditions have been the subject of intense investigation. There is now a substantial body of experimental results in the GT field. As Crawford (1997, 207) underlines: 'it is the most important source of empirical information we have and it is unlikely to be less reliable than casual empiricism or introspection'. There is nevertheless a history of valuable empirical studies using field data from strategic environments, usually with well-specified readily observable structures. There is even a small, yet growing, literature that employs game theory in economic history and 'cliometrics'. Indeed history provides in some respects another laboratory in which to examine the relevance of the game theoretic approach and its insights into positive economic analysis (on the cliometric revolution, see Goldin, 1995, and for a survey on economic history and game theory, see Greif, 2002).

Chapter 8 of that book is devoted to a presentation of this empirical literature on focusing on *experimental games*.

1.2   Detailed description of the book's content

In order to provide the reader with some guidelines for the use of the book, we will describe in this section the detailed contents of each chapter.

Chapter 2 deals with non-cooperative games in which the 'environment' is such that strategic uncertainty may be ignored. We look at games from the point of view of a single player and the purpose is to determine optimal decentralized decisions for players in such purely conflicting situations. Fundamentals axioms of decentralized non-cooperative behaviour postulates elimination of 'dominated strategies'. Such a dominance argument is intuitively appealing and often applied in economics. This behaviour leads to the 'dominant strategy equilibrium' presented in section 2.1. When a player has a dominant strategy, it is of no use to know the other players' preferences in order to infer their strategies. Yet, if no dominant equilibrium exists, we need precise assumptions about player's mental information possibilities. Section 2.2 studies another type of decentralized behaviour in strategic-form games with complete information, called 'iterated dominance'. But in extensive-form games with perfect information, 'backward induction' plays an equivalent role for describing optimal behaviour. This principle is presented in section 2.3. Section 2.4 treats the opposite case concerning players' information: we look at games with total ignorance. In this framework, the 'safety-first' principle tries to envisage the worst situation and to secure oneself against the maximal risk; it leads us to choose 'security strategies'. Lastly, section 2.5 is devoted to some applications of dominance and security principles.

In **Chapter 3** we leave the normative decision-analysis approach to study a more descriptive approach in order to understand players' behaviour in a non-cooperative game with complete and perfect information. Players' strategic behaviour becomes the main concern in order to define an equilibrium for the game. Section 3.1 is devoted to the chief concept of Nash equilibrium (definition, existence, properties, justifications and selection, failures) and Cournot and Bertrand duopoly models are studied as first very simple applications. Section 3.2 deals with two extensions of Nash equilibrium which allow us to rectify some shortcomings of this concept: mixed strategies (for non-existence) and correlated strategies (for inefficiency in some classes of games). Section 3.3 is devoted to the important class of repeated games, which also allows us to improve efficiency. According to the traditional rationalistic approach, multiplicity of equilibria requires us to elaborate 'refinements' of Nash equilibrium. Section 3.4 presents the less controversial among the various criteria proposed by game theorists: sub-game perfection. A first classical economic application of sub-game perfect equilibrium is given with the presentation of the Stackelberg duopoly model. Finally section 3.5 deals with several economic applications of Nash and sub-game perfect equilibria concepts in sequential games (strategic commitment, moral hazard) and in repeated games (credible threats or promises).

Chapter 4 can be viewed as an extension of Chapter 3 when information is imperfect or incomplete. The Nash equilibrium concept was introduced in games with complete information: each player is supposed to know all data about the structure of the game and about players' rationality. Thus the question is: can we generalize this notion to more general and realistic games of incomplete information? Section 4.1 is devoted to this ticklish question: under some conditions, a 'Bayesian equilibrium' has the properties of a Nash equilibrium in a game with incomplete information. We present the 'Harsanyi procedure' and show that a Bayesian equilibrium is just a Nash equilibrium of a 'Bayesian' game. In games with imperfect information, sub-game perfection is not strong enough to discard some unreasonable equilibria: we need further refinements. 'Perfectness' and 'sequentiality' are two kinds of strong refinements in the same logic as backward induction. Section 4.2 deals with those refinements of Nash equilibrium. Perfectness includes 'perfect trembling hand equilibrium' and 'proper equilibrium'. The main advantage of sequentiality, which includes 'perfect Bayesian equilibrium' and 'sequential equilibrium', is to emphasize explicitly the crucial role of beliefs in the definition of an equilibrium. In section 4.3 we return to refinement in games of incomplete information with a presentation of the 'forward induction' principle. Differences between forward induction and backward induction are underlined and formalizations of the former in the particular class of signalling games are proposed, with emphasis being on the 'intuitive criterion'. Lastly, section 4.4 gives some economic applications of repeated games with incomplete information ('reputation' effects) and some economic examples of signalling games.

Chapter 5 deals with bargaining as a tool for cooperation between players. We first study negotiation in the classical framework of non-cooperative games: cooperation appears as the result of an explicit bargaining procedure where at each stage each player is supposed to choose her (or his) optimal strategy as in any other situation described by non-cooperative games. This 'strategic' approach of bargaining is presented in section 5.1. Unfortunately this first approach often leads to an indeterminacy or to extreme equilibria. Another way consists in the explicit introduction of some desirable properties which allow a comparison of the different outcomes. Formally, this 'axiomatic' approach uses the framework of cooperative games. But this second way of analysing negotiation may be sometimes reconciled with the first viewpoint. Nash himself underlined the need to construct non-cooperative bargaining games for testing axioms. Section 5.2 deals with this axiomatic approach to bargaining and with the so-called 'Nash program' for reconciling the two points of view. Finally, section 5.3 is devoted to some economic applications of both strategic and axiomatic approaches to pure bargaining.

Chapter 6 focuses on the analysis of coalitions in GT. Pure bargaining games introduced in Chapter 5 deal essentially with negotiation problems between *two* players: they both agree or not. For more general settings with n players, we need a theory taking into account the possibility of cooperation among some players only in intermediate coalitions. Generalities about coalitional games are first presented in section 6.1. The classical framework for studying coalitions is cooperative games. Two approaches are followed: the 'domination' and the 'valuation' approaches. Section 6.2 is devoted to the solution concepts defined by the domination approach: the core and related concepts (the stable sets, bargaining set, kernel and nucleolus). Section 6.3 deals with the valuation approach by presenting the Shapley value and its main extensions. Yet, in this classical cooperative framework, only stability of coalitions and the sharing of surplus between players inside each coalition are well analysed. The formation of coalitions cannot be appropriately studied when the coalition structures are assumed exogenous. Section 6.4 deals with the recent topic of endogenous coalition structures in the mixed framework of both cooperative and non-cooperative games. Lastly, economic applications of coalitional games are presented in section 6.5. They illustrate the interest both of classical concepts (notably the core and the Shapley value) and of the recent models of endogenous coalitions formation.

Originally evolutionary games were developed in biology and mathematics. Now, these models are becoming popular among game theorists and the approach appears to be fruitful in the field of economics and business studies. One feels that the kind of adjustment dynamics studied by evolutionary games may be useful for analysing various types of issues where players react slowly through emulation, imitation or learning. Of course the kind of modelling suitable for applications in Economics must be different from the one used in biology. **Chapter 7** presents evolutionary games and learning models. It mainly develops the framework put forward to study biological games but some applications to economic problems also are explored. Section 7.1 introduces us to the basic concepts of 'Replicator dynamics' and 'Evolutionary stable strategies', both in symmetrical and asymmetrical games. Section 7.2 presents extensions of the basic concepts and discuss their relevance for economics. Section 7.3 is devoted to a presentation of learning models. Both the old approach, in the tradition of the Cournot adjustment model, and new developments in relation with evolutionary games, are presented. Lastly, section 7.4 deals with some examples of applications of the concepts of evolutionary games to economic issues.

The purpose of **Chapter 8** is to illustrate how game theoretic solutions have been tested in laboratory experiments In section 8.1, we introduce some methodological remarks explaining what is the goal of experimental methods in economics and what are their limits. We also overview some applications to strictly competitive games. In section 8.2 we present experiments on 'cooperation' problems, which include studies on the Prisoner's dilemma game, the public goods provision game and sequential games (the trust game, the centipede game). Section 8.3 deals with 'coordination' problems, where there are several equilibria and the players have to select one of them. Section 8.4 offers a survey on bargaining problems with experiments on the ultimatum game, on other bargaining games testing strategic and axiomatic solutions and on coalitional games. Section 8.5 deals with learning and evolution by describing some recent experiments in an evolutionary framework but also in the more standard setting of adaptive models. Lastly, in section 8.6, we present some recent progress carried out in GT by the incorporation of new modelling principles more consistent with experimental evidence.

1.3 Formal representations of games

This last section may seem somewhat tedious, yet the knowledge of its content is essential for a good understanding of the whole book. It deals with the various tools usually used for studying an interactive decision problem.

It turns out that the same game situation can be represented by different models whose joint formalisation is often useful, or among which we must choose the most convenient for the analysis. For non-cooperative games two standard representations can be used: the 'extensive-form' and the 'strategic-form' models. For cooperative games the 'coalitional-form' model is the standard tool.

1.3.1. Extensive-form games

The most general model used to describe a non-cooperative game is the 'extensive-form' model, which specifies in detail the progress of the situation by providing an exact description of the players' successive moves in connection with the information at their disposal: 'who knows what and when?' and 'what is the implication of which?' All relevant aspects of the situation might be included in the model.

Von Neumann and Morgenstern (1944) introduced the term 'extensive-form game' but they use a set theoretic approach. The more suitable graph theoretical representation proposed by Kühn (1953) has become the standard model.

A formal description of the extensive form of a game is generally rather tedious while the intuition is straightforward. Let us begin by an informal presentation.

An n-person extensive-form game is represented by a rooted tree, that is a directed acyclic graph with a distinguished vertex. The game starts at the root of the tree. The tree's terminal nodes correspond to the end points of the game, each of them being associated with the players' payoffs that result from that play. The non-terminal nodes correspond to the decision points; for each of them one indicates which of the players is choosing. A maximal set of decision points that a player can not distinguish between is an 'information set'. A decision at an information set associates a unique successor in the tree to every decision point in the set. This formal description of an extensive-form game helps an understanding why it is often called a 'game tree'.

Furthermore, when a 'chance' move intervenes in addition to personal moves, the initial decision point may perform the moves of Nature; the information set of this chance player always is a singleton (a set with one element).

To summarize, the extensive form representation of a game must specify:

- The set of players
- Whose turn it is to move
- What she (or he) can choose at each of her (or his) information sets
- What she (or he) knows when she (or he) takes her (or his) decision
- Each player's payoff for each combination of moves that could be chosen by her (or him).

The extensive-form presentation of a game allows one to reveal particularly important properties of games concerning what a player knows when it is her (or his) turn to move. When the players never forget what they knew or did in the past, a game is said to be one of 'perfect recall'. At each information set of the game tree, every player knows all the preceding information sets as well as the decisions taken then. This characteristic should not be confused with that of a game with 'perfect information'.

Recall that an extensive form game is said to be of perfect information if there are no simultaneous moves and if each player always is perfectly informed about anything that happened in the past; in that case all information sets are singletons. When a player is in a team (such as, for instance, in bridge) a game may fail to have perfect recall. However, by modelling different agents as different players with the same payoff function, perfect recall can be restored. Hence attention will be restricted to this class of games. In contrast a game with 'imperfect information' cannot be so easily reduced to a game with perfect information. Indeed a major part of non-cooperative game theory is concerned with how to expand natural solution principles for games with perfect information to games with imperfect information.

Notice finally that an extensive-form game is said to be 'finite' if its tree contains only a finite number of nodes.

If we take the familiar examples of parlour games, we can say that under this definition: chess or draughts are games with perfect information without chance moves (except for the determination of who shall play first); bridge and poker are games of imperfect information, in which chance plays a much greater part, but skill is still important; roulette is a pure game of chance. Moreover, most parlour games are finite.

We can now describe more precisely the elements used in the extensive form of a game (a complete exposition of the notation involved in an extensive-form game is given in Kreps and Wilson, 1982, section 2 ; we follow here the presentation of Eichberger, 1993, 3–8).

The set of players is denoted by N. In most applications, it is a finite set with an arbitrary player denoted by i. Denote by I the set of nodes of the tree and by o the initial node ('origin'). Let $\sigma: I \rightarrow I$ be the function that associates with each node other than o its predecessor, and, for origin, define $\sigma(o) = o$. For any node $n \in I$ and any positive integer k, $\sigma^k(n)$ indicates the kth iteration of the function σ, that is:

$$\sigma^k(n) \equiv \underbrace{\sigma(\sigma(\sigma(\ldots \sigma(n) \ldots)))}_{k \text{ times}}$$

Definition 1 (Game tree)

A game tree is a set of nodes I and a function $\sigma: I \rightarrow I$, $\sigma(o) = o$, such that, for all nodes $n \in I$, $\sigma^k(n) = o$ holds for some positive integer k.∎

Note that the condition $\sigma^k(n) = o$ for all n is necessary to guarantee that all nodes are connected to the origin (i.e. the graph is a tree).

Nodes are connected to other nodes by the predecessor node function σ. Since players choose actions to move from one node to another, it is necessary to specify how actions lead from one node to another. This goal is fulfilled by the predecessor action function $\alpha: I \backslash \{o\} \longrightarrow A$ which associates with each node n (except o) the action $\alpha(n)$ leading from the predecessor node $\sigma(n)$ to node n.

Several classifications of nodes have to be introduced.

Firstly, one needs to distinguish *decision* nodes and *terminal* nodes. A node is called a terminal node if it is the predecessor of no other node, that is, if $\sigma^{-1}(n) = \emptyset$. And every non-terminal node is a decision node. We denote $T(I)$ and $D(I)$ the sets of terminal and decision nodes, respectively. Remark that $T \cup D = I$ and $T \cap D = \emptyset$, i.e. this classification forms a partition of I.

A second classification of decision nodes has to be operated according to the player who takes the decision. Denote I_i the set of decision nodes at which player i is choosing an action and suppose that in a particular node one and only one player is moving. Then, we can partition D into sub-sets $(I_i)_{i \in I}$ such that $\bigcap_{i \in I} I_i = \emptyset$.

Definition 2 (*Player partition*)

A list of mutually exclusive sets of decision nodes for players $(I_i)_{i \in I}$ is called a *player partition* of $D(N)$.∎

Note that a player partition assigns nodes to players who must take an action at these nodes. Thus, we are able to define the set of all possible actions of some player i:

$$A_i = \bigcup_{n \in I_i} A(n)$$

Lastly, we need to define the players' payoffs at the end of the game. Assuming the game is finite, one simply associates the payoffs with the terminal nodes. The payoff function associates with each node $n \in T$ a payoff vector $[u_i(n)]_{i \in N}$ that gives the payoff for each player i at this terminal nodes.

Definition 3 (*Payoff function*)

The payoff function $u \colon T(N) \to I\!R^N$ associates with each terminal node a vector of real numbers, each one representing the player's payoff for each terminal node.∎

Examples

Let us consider a two-player game where:

- Each player has only one action to make and the order of moving is specified as follows: first, player one and next player two.
- Each player has two possible actions (or moves):

L_1 or L_2 for player 1
R_1 or R_2 for player 2

- The outcomes associated with the various combinations of actions are:

$$\left(u_1^{L_i R_j}, u_2^{L_i R_j} \right), \qquad i, j = 1, 2$$

with the player 1's payoff indicated in this first place (remember that in this book player 1 will be named 'she' and player 2 will be named 'he').

We consider three variants:

  I. When player 2 has to move, he knows player 1's action.
 II. When player 2 has to move, he does not know what player 1 has played.

III. There is a chance move: a random event may arise with a certain probability P and player 2 still does not know what player 1 has played.

The game trees corresponding to these three variants are shown in Figure 1.1. Variant I is a game with perfect information: all information sets are singleton; we denote information sets by enclosing in a dotted ellipse the indiscernible nodes for a player (when information sets are singletons usually the broken line is not explicitly drawn). Variant II is a game with imperfect information: the information set of player 2 includes two nodes. Variant III can also be represented by an extensive form with imperfect information by introducing an additional fictitious player, Nature (N), who moves before player one makes a decision: each action at a chance move is labelled with the probability that it will be chosen (this probability is indicated in brackets).

A possible play of the game is indicated by thickening appropriate edges of the tree: one draws a 'path' starting from the root of the tree (the initial node) and ending in a terminal node. See for instance the path drawn on the tree game corresponding to Variant II which is associated with the play (L_2, R_1) and payoffs $(U_1^{L_2 R_1}, U_2^{L_2 R_1})$.

1.3.2. Strategic-form games

In spite of the great variety of game trees we always can pass from the extensive form of a game to a theoretically more simple presentation: the strategic form of the game.

Strategic-form games are also called 'normal'-form games (the term used by the fathers of game theory) but today the majority of game theorists prefer the former term because it explicitly focuses attention on *strategies* as primitives of the model (This most appropriate terminology was initially proposed by Shapley, 1973). The intuitive meaning of a 'strategy' is that of *a plan for playing a game*. We imagine a player as saying to herself (or himself): 'If such and such a thing happens, I will act in such and such a way.'

A strategy is a complete specification of how a player intends to play in every contingency that might arise. For a player to choose a strategy means to take a *single global decision before playing*, which includes all the elementary decisions she (or he) could have taken during play (but in fact she (or he) will not take necessarily all of them); a strategy is 'mental' while a decision is 'physical'. There is some logical difficulty in understanding that these players' global decisions might be able to describe both the elementary decisions of the players and their sequential connections. This difficulty vanishes if one imagines a strategy as being like instructions given to an agent (or a computing machine) who can then play instead of the player herself (or himself). These instructions must be

Figure 1.1 Examples of game trees

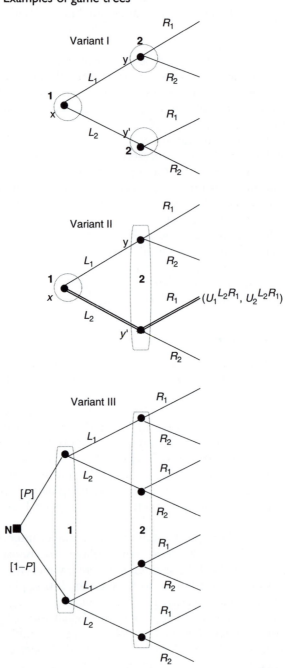

exhaustive, so that whatever the progress of the play the mandatory has only to apply without personal initiative. However, the contingent nature of strategies explains that the number of strategies increases exponentially with the number of moves in the play. This image points out (at the same time) that the simplicity of the structure of the strategic form implies in return a great complexity of strategies and large sets of strategies.

Hence, the strategic-form representation of a game must specify:

- The players of the game
- The strategies available to each player
- Each player's payoff for each combination of strategies that could be chosen by her (or him).

Given strategies $x_1, \ldots, x_n$ of the n players, the rule of the game determines a payoff $u_i(x_1, \ldots, x_n)$ for each player i, and so a unique outcome for the game. The strategic form is simply the function that associates to each vector $x = (x_1, \ldots x_n)$ of feasible strategies $x_i \in X_i$, $i = 1, \ldots, n$, the payoff vector (or players' payoffs): $(u_1(x), \ldots, u_n(x))$.

Definition 4 (*Strategic-form game*)

An n-player game is in strategic form if $(X_1, \ldots, X_n; u_1, \ldots, u_n)$ is specified.■

The definition of a strategy given above is more precisely what is called a 'pure' strategy. Game theorists use also another concept of 'mixed' strategy. To say that a player is choosing a mixed strategy means that she (or he) selects a random device for choosing the pure strategy to be employed among all the feasible strategies. Mixed strategies are a natural generalisation of pure strategies. The set of mixed strategies always includes all pure strategies, since a pure strategy can be viewed as a special mixed strategy for which the respective pure strategy is played with probability one and any other pure strategy with probability zero.

Definition 5 (*Mixed strategy*)

Consider a game in which player i has m pure strategies. Any player's mixed strategy can be represented by the vector:

$$p = (p_1, \ldots, p_j, \ldots, p_m) \text{ where } p_j \geq 0 \text{ and } \sum_j p_j = 1$$

The number p_j represents the probability with which the player will choose her (or his) pure strategy x_j ■

Thus, if the set of pure strategies is finite (for instance, m strategies), the set of probability distributions on the set X_i has the particularly simple form of the unit simplex of dimension m.

Throughout this book we use the term 'strategy' for 'pure' strategy, except when we emphasize the differences between pure and mixed strategies. Only mixed strategies on *finite* pure strategies will be considered.

It is important to notice that if a chance move intervenes in the game, or if the players randomize strategies (whatever the origin of this randomization), the resulting outcome of the game becomes itself a random variable. Hence, players are making decisions *under uncertainty*. The common practice in game theory is to suppose that players maximize their 'expected' payoff, in accordance with the theories of Von Neumann and Morgenstern (1944) and Savage (1954). It follows in particular that the payoff function is a Von Neumann–Morgenstern (VNM) function (i.e. invariant under strictly increasing affine transformations).

Remark I

Recall that in decision theory the curvature of the expected utility function represents the agent's attitude towards risk (for instance, if the agent is risk-averse the function is concave). In GT, in contrast, we suppose usually that the payoffs represent the subjective evaluation of outcomes by a player; so the payoffs reflect directly players' risk attitudes. Consequently, attitudes towards risk are rarely introduced explicitly in game models (the unique exception is in the study of bargaining problem, see Chapter 5, section 5.1). Yet, when designing experiments on game problems, taking into account subjects' attitude towards risk is advised (see Chapter 8, subsection 8.12).■

We saw above that in finite games each player has only a finite number of strategies. Yet, why restrict analysis to that particular case: players' strategy sets may be infinite (or sometimes simply uncountable). We frequently encounter this case in economics, where agents are often supposed to be choosing among a 'continuum' of actions: for instance, firms take decisions about prices or output levels, that is on continuous economic variables. Then, the game is said to be 'infinite'.

Note that in the particular class of two-player finite games, the strategic-form representation is straightforward. One can associate the strategies of a player with the rows of a matrix and the strategies of the other with the columns of this matrix; the payoffs of the players are then written in the boxes (which describe the elements of the cartesian product of the two strategy sets). For three-player games, the representation is less easy: the strategies of the third player must be a matrix. And extension to n-person games ($n > 3$) presents serious practical difficulties.

Example

Let us consider the variant I of the two-player game previously presented in extended form in Figure 1.1. Its associated strategic form can be drawn

Figure 1.2 Example of a matrix game associated with an extensive-form game

2

		(R_1, R_1)	(R_1, R_2)	(R_2, R_1)	(R_2, R_2)
1	L_1	$u_1^{L_1R_1}, u_2^{L_1R_1}$	$u_1^{L_1R_1}, u_2^{L_1R_1}$	$u_1^{L_1R_2}, u_2^{L_1R_2}$	$u1^{L_1R_2}, u2^{L_1R_2}$
	L_2	$u_1^{L_2R_1}, u_2^{L_2R_1}$	$u_1^{L_2R_2}, u_2^{L_2R_2}$	$u_1^{L_2R_1}, u_2^{L_2R_1}$	$u1^{L_2R_2}, u2^{L_2R_2}$

in Figure 1.2 by a bi-matrix where the entries are the payoffs to players 1 and 2, respectively. Notice that player 1 has two strategies (identical to her actions L_1 and L_2), but player 2 has four strategies, since his two actions are conditioned by player 1's actions. Player 2's strategies are written: (Ri, Rj), $i, j = 1, 2$, with the following meaning: if player 1 chooses L_1 then play Ri, and if he chooses L_2, then play Rj.

When passing from the extensive form of a game to its strategic form, mathematical analysis of the game becomes simpler because a game tree is indeed a complicated mathematical object whereas a matrix is easy to formalize. Yet, generally, this gain in simplicity is achieved at a cost: the strategic-form game hides the potential 'dynamics' of the game. The players are supposed to choose their plans of action *once and for all*. Although each player must foresee unlimited contingencies, she (or he) cannot reconsider her (or his) plan of action after possibly being informed of some events in the game.

It is only for one class of game, the *simultaneous-move* games, that nothing is lost by using the strategic form. In these games all the players move simultaneously (or in secret) and independently (that is, no player being informed of the decision of any other players prior to making her own choice). Furthermore, in this 'static' game, the interpretation of a strategy becomes obvious: players' strategies are identical to players' *actions*. It would be false however to believe that simultaneous-moves games can not be represented by an extensive-form game: indeed the notion of *imperfect information* allows one to model that property in the game tree.

Example

The following children's game, called 'rock, scissors, paper', is well known in many countries. The game is played by two players. They start the game with their hands behind their backs. Then, simultaneously, each of them stretches out her (or his) right hand, with the following meaning:

- A clenched fist indicates a preference for the 'rock' (R)
- A flat hand means that the player chooses the 'paper' (P)
- The forefinger and the middle finger forming a V means the choice of the 'scissors' (S).

If both players choose the same object, the game is a draw and the payoff is zero to both of them. Otherwise, one wins a dollar from the other according to the following rule. The 'scissors' cut the 'paper'; the 'paper' envelops the 'rock'; but the 'rock' resists the 'scissors'. In summary the rule is: rock beats scissors, scissors beat paper, paper beats rock.

This game is a simultaneous-moves game in which players' strategies are identical to their actions. The natural representation of the game is the strategic form but two equivalent extended forms with imperfect information can also be used (see Figure 1.3 opposite).

In summary, it is important not to confuse the differences between simultaneous-moves and sequential-moves game on the one hand, and between strategic-form and extensive-form games on the other. The first classification refers to *properties of the game rule* while the second is concerned with *conceptual and formal representation of the game*.

1.3.3 Coalitional-form games

The extended-form representation of a game emphasizes the details of the moves in the play with great attention put on what each player knows when she (he) makes her (his) decision. On the other hand, the strategic-form representation gives a global grasp of game's outcomes according to the various player's strategies. Yet, only the *individual* payoffs are concerned. If players can make binding agreements and they form coalitions (i.e. a sub-group of players), the strategic form is unable to evaluate the global gains of the cooperation among the players. Such is the purpose of the 'coalitional form' of a cooperative game.

Cooperative game models use an important distinction between transferable utility (TU) and not transferable utility (NTU) among players. *Transferable utility* means that each coalition can achieve a certain total amount of utility that it can freely divide among its members in any mutual agreeable fashion. This assumption has played and continues to play a major role in coalitional games. As interactions among $(2^n - 1)$ different intermediate coalitions in an n-player game can be very complex, this assumption highly simplifies the analysis.

In TU cooperative games, the cooperative possibilities of a coalition S can be described by a function v (the 'characteristic function') that assigns it a real number $v(S)$. $v(S)$ represents the *total transferable utility* that coalitions can make effective for their members; it is called the 'wealth', or the 'worth' or else the 'power' of coalition S according to the particular interpretation of utility in the game.

Hence, the coalitional-form representation of a TU cooperative game must specify:

- The players of the game (N)

Figure 1.3 Strategic-form and extended-form representation of the 'rock, scissors, paper' game

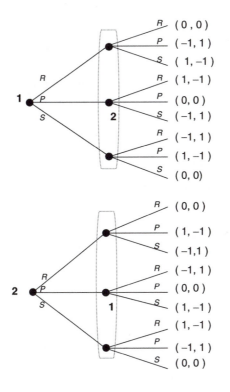

- A characteristic function $v(.)$, that associates $v(S) \in \mathbb{R}$ with each $S \subseteq N$, where by definition $v(\phi) = 0$.

Definition 6 (TU coalitional-form game)

A TU cooperative game is in 'coalitional form' (or 'characteristic function form') if (N, v) is specified.■

Restricting attention to TU cooperative games is tantamount to assuming that players are endowed with quasi-linear utilities – namely, additively decomposable in 'money' and other goods and linear in money – an assumption which implies that utility is fully transferable among players by means of monetary transfers. For that reason TU coalitional games are sometimes called games with 'side payments'. Yet it should be emphasized that the TU assumption actually uses only $(n-1)$ degree of freedom in the utility representation of a general n-person cooperative game. The choice of the side-payment 'numeraire good' (money) is arbitrary and one has still to freely choose a common scale factor (across players) and the origins of the players' VN-M utility functions. It follows that for any positive real number a and any real numbers $b_1, , \ldots, b_n$, the characteristic function w, defined for all coalition S by:

$$w(S) = a(v(S) - \sum_{i \in S} b_i),$$

is 'strategically equivalent' to the characteristic function v.

This observation enables us to introduce a useful normalization. The '(0,1)-normalization' of v is the characteristic function w defined as follows:

$$w(S) = \frac{v(S) - \sum_{i \in S} v(\{i\})}{v(N) - \sum_{i \in N} v(\{i\})} \quad \text{for all } S \subset N$$

Therefore: $w(\{i\}) = 0$ for all $i \in N$ and $w(N) = 1$. That normalisation uses the remaining degrees of freedom in the theoretic derivation of the characteristic function.

Example

A very simple example of a TU coalitional-form game can be provided by voting systems in elections and legislatures. A voting rule is a collective decision problem in which people ('voters' or 'electors') must jointly choose one particular outcome among several possibilities (the 'candidates'). If we suppose that the voters can make *binding agreements,* a voting rule can be modelled by a TU coalitional-form game in which the players are the voters.

We can use the normalisation: $v(N) = 1$, where N is the grand coalition of all the players, $v(\{i\}) = 0$ for every player i in N. We also can introduce the additional normalisation: for each coalition $S \subset N$, $v(S) = 1$ if the coalition is winning or $v(S) = 0$ if it is losing. Such a game is said to be 'simple' (Shapley, 1962).

Among simple games, the easiest one to define is the 'simple majority voting' procedure. For instance, if $N = 3$, then:

$$v(S) = \begin{cases} 0 & \text{if } Card\ S < 2 \\ 1 & \text{if } Card\ S \geq 2 \end{cases}$$

More generally we can define the 'weighted majority game' as follows. Let $w_1, \ldots, w_n$ a vector of non-negative numbers (the 'weights') and q a positive real number (the 'quota'), such that:

$$q \leq \sum_{i=1}^{n} w_i$$

then:

$$v(S) = \begin{cases} 0 \text{ if } \sum_{i \in S} w_i < q \\ 1 \text{ if } \sum_{i \in S} w_i \geq q \end{cases}$$

The NTU cooperative games are actually highly developed, but they are conceptually and technically more complex than TU cooperative games. To assume transferable utility is to require that the payoffs attainable by any particular coalition consist of all individual payoffs that sum to no more than a particular number.

For example, consider a four-player TU game model and the coalition $\{1, 4\}$. Each player has her (or his) own utility scale but there is a number $v(\{1, 4\})$ that describes the payoff possibilities of the coalition. The members of this coalition can achieve any payoff (x_1, x_4) that fulfil the linear constraint: $x_1 + x_4 \leq v(\{1, 4\})$. If we drop the TU assumption it is no longer possible to describe the payoff available to a particular coalition as a sum of utility that the group can guarantee. Instead, each coalition S has a set of s-dimensional payoff vectors in $\mathbb{R}^s$ that it can achieve. The characteristic function must specify all obtainable payoff vectors for each coalition and this must be done by specifying these sets of payoff vectors. For example, the ability of the coalition $\{1, 2, 3\}$ to obtain the payoff $(4, 8, 12)$ does not impart any information on that coalition's ability to achieve, say $(5, 9, 10)$, a payoff vector whose component payoffs also sum to 24. On the one hand, this second payoff vector could be beyond the set of payoffs that $\{1, 2, 3\}$ can reach, or, on the other hand it may be interior to the coalition's attainable set of payoffs even if $(4, 8, 12)$ is on the frontier of that set.

Let $V(S)$ the set of all s-dimensional vectors of payoffs that the coalition S can guarantee to itself. V is called the 'NTU characteristic function' of the game. It is a set valued function that assigns to each coalition $S \subseteq N$ a sub-set $V(S) \subset \mathbb{R}^s$.

We always have $V(\phi) = \phi$ and we impose the following natural technical restrictions: for $S \neq \phi$, $V(S)$ is non-empty, closed and 'comprehensive': if $x \in V(S)$ and $y_i \leq x_i$, for all $i \in S$, then $y \in V(S)$. Comprehensiveness is actually a mild assumption, since $V(S)$ is viewed as a utility possibility set; comprehensiveness can be interpreted simply as the classical 'free disposable' of utility in microeconomics.

Bibliography

Aumann, R.J. (1976) 'Agree to disagree', *Annals of Statistics*, 4, 1236–39.

Aumann, R.J. (1987) 'Game theory', in J. Eatwell, M. Milgate and P. Newman (eds), *Game Theory – The New Palgrave*, 2 (London: Macmillan).

Bertrand, J. (1883) 'Théorie mathématique de la richesse sociale', *Journal des Savants*, 499–508 (in French).

Binmore, K. (1987) 'Modeling rational players, Part I', *Economics and Philosophy*, 3, 9–55.

Binmore, K. (ed.) (1990) *Essays on the Foundations of Game Theory* (Oxford: Basic Blackwell).

Binmore, K. (1992) *Fun and Games* (Lexington, MA: D.C. Heath).

Cournot, A. (1838) *Recherches sur les principes mathématiques de la théorie des richesses* (Paris: Librairie des sciences politiques et sociales, M. Rivière et cie) (English edn: N. Bacon (ed.), *Researches into the Mathematical Principles of the Theory of Wealth* (London: Macmillan, 1897)).

Crawford, V.P. (1997) 'Theory and experiment in the analysis of strategic interaction', in D.M. Kreps and K.F. Wallis (eds), *Advances in Economics and Econometrics: Theory and Applications: Seventh World Congress of the Econometric Society*, 1 (Cambridge: Cambridge University Press), 206–42.

Edgeworth, F.Y. (1881) *Mathematical Psychics* (London: Kegan Paul).

Eichberger, J. (1993) *Game Theory for Economists* (New York: Academic Press) ch. 3.

Friedman, M. (1953) 'The methodology of positive economics', in M. Friedman (ed.), *Essays in Positive Economics* (Chicago: University of Chicago Press).

Fudenberg, D. and J. Tirole (1991) *Game Theory* (Cambridge, MA: MIT Press).

Goldin, C. (1995) 'Cliometrics and the Nobel', *Journal of Economic Perspectives*, 9, 191–208.

Greif, A. (2002) 'Economic history and game theory', in R.J. Aumann and S. Hart (eds), *Handbook of Game Theory with Economic Applications*, 3 (Amsterdam: North-Holland).

Harsanyi, J.C. (1967–8) 'Games with incomplete information played by "Bayesian" players, Parts I, II and III', *Management Science*, 14, 159–82, 320–34, 486–502.

Kreps, D.M. (1990) *Game Theory and Economic Modeling* (Oxford: Clarendon Press).

Kreps, D. and R. Wilson (1982) 'Sequential equilibrium', *Econometrica*, 50, 863–84.

Kühn, H.W. (1953) 'Extensive games and the problem of information', in H.W. Kühn and A.W. Tücker (eds), *Contributions to the Theory of Games*, II (Princeton: Princeton University Press).

Leonard R.J. (1995) 'From parlour games to social science: von Neumann, Morgenstern and the creation of game theory: 1928–1944', *Journal of Economic Literature*, 33, 730–61.

Lewis, D.K. (1969) *Convention: A Philosophical Study* (Cambridge, MA: Harvard University Press).

Maynard Smith, J. (1982) *Evolution and the Theory of Games* (Cambridge: Cambridge University Press).

Nash, J.F. (Jr.) (1950a) 'Equilibrium points in *n*-person games', *Proceedings of the National Academy of Sciences*, 36, 48–9.

Nash, J.F. (Jr.) (1950b) 'The bargaining game', *Econometrica*, 18, 155–62.

Nash, J.F. (Jr.) (1951) 'Non-cooperative games', *Annals of Mathematics*, 54, 289–93.

Nash, J.F. (Jr.) (1953) 'Two-person cooperative games', *Econometrica*, 21, 128–40.

Osborne M.J. and A. Rubinstein (1994) *A Course in Game Theory*, (Cambridge, MA: MIT Press).

Possel, R. de (1936) 'Sur la théorie mathématique des jeux de hasard et de réflexion', reprinted in H. Moulin, *Fondation de la théorie des jeux* (Paris: Hermann, 1979), 85–120 (in French).

Savage, L.J. (1954) *The Foundations of Statistics* (John Wiley, 2nd rev. edn, London: Dover, 1972).

Schelling, T.C. (1960) *The Strategy of Conflict* (Cambridge, MA: Harvard University Press).

Schmidt, C. (1990) 'Game theory and economics: an historical survey', *Revue d'Economie Politique*, 100, 589–619.

Shapley, L.S. (1962) 'Simple games: an outline of the descriptive theory', *Behavioural Science*, 7, 59–66.

Stackelberg, H. Von (1934) *Marktform und Gleichgemicht* (Berlin: Julius Springer) (in German).

Ville, J.A. (1938) 'Sur la théorie générale des jeux où intervient l'habileté des joueurs', in E. Borel (ed.), *Traité du calcul des probabilités et de ses applications*, 4 (Pans: Gauthier Villars), 105–13 (in French).

Von Neumann, J. (1928) 'Zür Theorie der Gesellschaftsspiele', *Mathematische Annalen*, 100, 295–320 (English translation, 'On the theory of game strategy', in A.W. Tücker and R.D. Luce (eds), *Contribution to the Theory of Games*, IV, Princeton: Princeton University Press 1959).

Von Neumann, J. and O. Morgenstern (1944) *Theory of Games and Economic Behavior* (New York: John Wiley).

Walliser, B. (1989) 'Instrumental rationality and cognitive rationality', *Theory and Decision*, 27, 7–36.

Weintraub, E. (ed.) (1992) *Toward a History of Game Theory* (Lanham: Duke University Press).

Zermelo, E. (1913) 'Über eine Anwendung der Mengenlehre auf die Theorie des Schachspiels', in E.W. Hobson and A.E.H. Love (eds), *Proceedings of the Fifth International Congress of Mathematicians*, 2 (Cambridge: Cambridge University Press), 501–4.

Zeuthen, F. (1930) *Problems of Monopoly and Economic Welfare* (London: Routledge).

2 Optimal Decentralized Decisions

2.1 Dominant strategy equilibrium
2.2 Iterated dominance and backward induction
2.3 Safety first
2.4 Applications

In this chapter we consider a non-cooperative game in which each player chooses alone her (or his) strategy while ignoring entirely the other players' decisions. We look at the game from the point of view of a *single* player. Each player takes a decision that does not require knowledge of the decisions taken by her (or his) opponents because the 'environment' is such that strategic uncertainty may be ignored. Any type of communication between the players is precluded. The game has no past. Furthermore, no repetition of the game is conceivable.

In this context, all strategies are *a priori* equally possible. Players' choices are driven only by individual rationality. The approach is a normative one. It can be summarized by the following question: in such a purely conflicting situation how *must* an individual play? We look for *optimal decentralized* decisions.

The fundamental axiom of decentralized non-cooperative behaviour postulates elimination of 'dominated' strategies. Such a dominance argument is intuitively appealing and often applied in economics. Indeed this axiom is equivalent to classical 'admissibility' postulate of decision theory: rational choice must be 'admissible' or undominated. This behaviour leads to the 'dominant strategy equilibrium' presented in section 2.1.

When a player has a dominant strategy, it is unnecessary for her (or him) to know the other players' preferences in order to infer their strategy. Yet, if no dominant strategy equilibrium exists, we need precise assumptions about players' mutual information possibilities. We first study the case where each player knows perfectly all the other players' preferences in addition to his own: we have a game with complete information. In this setting another type of decentralized behaviour can be defined in strategic-form games: 'iterated dominance'. But in extensive-form games with perfect information, 'backward induction' plays an equivalent role for describing optimal behaviour. These two principles are presented in section 2.2. Section 2.3 treats the completely opposite case concerning the player's information: we look at games with total ignorance. The 'safety-first' principle envisages the worst situation and tries to secure oneself against the maximal risk; it leads us to choose 'security' strategies. Yet, except in the particular class of 'strictly competitive games', this decentralized behaviour is rarely optimal. Finally, section 2.4 is devoted to some applications of dominance and security principles in public economics.

2.1   Dominant strategy equilibrium

2.1.1   Definition

Let us consider the game in strategic form represented by the payoff matrix in Figure 2.1.

Is it possible to determine an optimal strategy for each player in this very simple game? It is easy to see that for player 1, it is always preferable to play r_1 rather than r_2, no matter what player 2 does. Similarly, one may note that player 2 is better off playing c_1 rather than c_2, regardless of what player 1 chooses to do. Strategy r_1 is said to 'dominate' strategy r_2 for player 1 and, similarly, strategy c_1 is said to 'dominate' strategy c_2 for player 2. The criterion of dominance consists of comparing the vectors of payoffs:

$(5, 4) > (3, 3)$ and $(2, 2) \geq (2, 1)$

Let us introduce a more rigorous presentation. Consider the game in strategic form $(X_1, \ldots, X_i, \ldots, X_n; u_1, \ldots u_i, \ldots, u_n)$, where X_i and u_i represent the strategy set and the payoff function of player i respectively.

Definition 1 (Dominance)

Player i's strategy $x_i \in X_i$ 'dominates' strategy $x'_i \in X_i$ if:

$u_i(x_i, x^{-i}) \geq u_i(x'_i, x^{-i})$ for all $x^{-i} \in X^{-i}$

with a strict inequality for at least one $x^{-i} \in X^{-i}$. A player i's strategy is 'dominated' if there exists at least another strategy which dominates it.∎

Figure 2.1   Domination between strategies

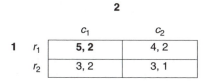

		c_1	c_2
		5, 2	4, 2
1	r_1		
	r_2	3, 2	3, 1

2

In this definition we use the following notational conventions: $x^{-i} = (x_1, \ldots, x_{i-1}, x_{i+1}, \ldots, x_n)$ i.e. the vector of all players strategies *except player i*, and $X^{-i} = \prod_{j \neq i} X_j$, i.e. the Cartesian product of the strategy sets of all other players than i.

A basic rationality assumption in a game in strategic form is to assume that a player will always discard dominated strategies. If x_i^* dominates x_i then, whatever the strategies of the other players are, it never hurts i to choose x_i^* rather than x_i, and it sometimes benefits i.

It should be noticed that this axiom of elimination of dominated strategies is totally consistent with the assumption of decentralization of the players' decisions. When a player selects non-dominated strategies, she (or he) does not need any information about other players' behaviour. She (or he) only has to know their strategy sets.

Definition 2 (*Dominant strategy equilibrium*)

Player i's strategy $x_i^* \in X_i$ is a 'dominant' strategy if:

$$u_i(x_i^*, x^{-i}) \geq u_i(x_i, x^{-i}) \text{ for all } x_i \in X_i \text{ and all } x^{-i} \in X^{-i}$$

Any strategy vector $(x_1^*, \ldots, x_i^*, \ldots, x_n^*)$ of the game such that, for each player i, x_i^* is a dominant strategy for i, is called a 'dominant strategy equilibrium' (DSE). ∎

If x_i^* is a dominant strategy, then whatever the choices of the player i's opponents it is never disadvantageous for her (or him) to choose x_i^* rather than any other strategy. For instance, in the game presented in Figure 2.1, (r_1, c_1) is a DSE.

The principle of elimination of dominated strategies which underlies the notion of DSE actually corresponds to the classical postulate of 'admissibility' in basic decision theory: a rational agent will never choose an inadmissible (i.e. dominated) strategy (see, for instance, Luce and Raiffa, 1957). Yet these scholars were clearly well aware that a more general theory could be obtained using a much restrictive postulate involving 'strict' dominance.

Definition 3 (*Strict dominance*)

Player i's strategy $x_i \in X$ 'strictly dominates' strategy $x_i' \in X_i$ if:

$$u_i(x_i, x^{-i}) > u_i(x_i', x^{-i}) \text{ for all } x^{-i} \in X^{-i} \blacksquare$$

In contrast to dominance (sometimes called 'weak' dominance), 'strict' (or 'strong') dominance requires that a players' payoff be always *strictly increased*, whatever her (or him) rivals' choice. For instance, in the game presented in Figure 2.1, r_1 *strictly* dominates r_2 (5 > 4 and 4 > 3) while c_1 (weakly) dominates c_2 (2 = 2 and 2 > 1).

With strict dominance, Bayesian decision theory and dominance procedure always coincide, since a strictly dominating strategy is a best response to *every* belief whereas a dominating strategy is a best response to only *some* beliefs. Thus it may be argued that strict dominance is more compelling than (weak) dominance: Bayesian rationality alone would require only the elimination of *strictly* dominated strategies. It turns out, however, that for the players there is never some advantage in choosing a (weakly) dominated strategy. It seems therefore natural to discard such strategies in order to simplify complicated games.

2.1.2 Existence and efficiency

Existence

Non-dominated strategies generally exist under standard topological assumptions in microeconomics (compact sets of strategies and continuous payoff functions). It is much more difficult to have a dominant strategy for each player. This is not really surprising when one thinks of the definition of this notion.

If x^* is a DSE, that means that x^* is the optimal solution to n optimization problems parameterized by $x^{-i} \in X^{-i}$ of the following type:

$$\max_{x_i \in X_i} u_i(x_i, x^{-i}), \quad \text{for all } i$$

It is a very strong strategic property that is rarely satisfied. Nevertheless, in the rare games having a DSE, this outcome represents a plausible answer to the problem of the determination of *decentralized non-cooperative behaviour* thanks to the following result:

Theorem I (Moulin, 1986)

If x^* is a DSE, then:

(i) the set of dominant strategies corresponds to the set of non-dominated strategies
(ii) all the non-dominated strategies are equivalent for the player, i.e. they assure the same payoff.∎

On the other hand, if a DSE does not exist, that means that for the player who has no dominant strategy all her (or his) non-dominated strategies are not equivalent. The search for a decentralized non-cooperative behaviour becomes more difficult. In particular, it is then necessary to specify the assumptions concerning the players' mutual information.

Efficiency

We insist on the fact that the *players' independence* is a fundamental assumption of the setting in which we consider non-cooperative behaviour. For a non-cooperative player enjoying a dominant strategy, any information about the other players' strategic decisions is worthless. Yet, this information may be valuable when taken collectively. Indeed the concept of DSE deliberately ignores considerations of collective interest and focuses on *individual rationality* of choices made by *isolated* players unable to coordinate with the others.

In a strategic-form game, Pareto-efficiency (or Pareto-optimality) is defined as follows:

Definition 4 (*Pareto-efficiency*)

A strategy vector x of the game is 'Pareto-dominated' by a strategy vector y if:

$$u_i(y_i) \geq u_i(x_i), \quad \text{for all } i$$

with a strict inequality for at least one player i. A strategy vector is 'Pareto-efficient' if it is not Pareto-dominated by any other strategy vector. ∎

The classical Prisoner's dilemma game is a good illustration of a situation where a DSE may be inefficient.

Example: The Prisoner's dilemma game

The Prisoner's dilemma is one of the most famous examples in game theory (A.W. Tucker is said to have imagined the story). This game has given rise to numerous discussions and multiple applications in the domains of economics, diplomacy and military conflicts.

Originally, the story studied is as follows. Two prisoners are put separately in prison. The police know that they have committed a small offence and they are suspected of having committed a bigger crime. The issue is to make them confess this crime. They are independently submitted to questioning, facing the following choice. If both of them confess they are punished for the big crime; if neither of them confesses they are simply penalized for the small offence; if one of them confesses while the other denies (i.e if one of them denounces his accomplice), the former is released for having cooperated with justice, while the latter is heavily punished (more heavily than if both confess). What will be the decisions of the prisoners?

This Prisoner's dilemma game can be reformulated in a more general way. It is a two-player game in which each player can choose between a 'pacific' strategy P ('to deny' in the original story) and an 'aggressive' strategy *A* ('to confess'). One says also that if a player chooses *P* he 'cooperates' (with his accomplice), while if he chooses *A* he 'defects'. The rule of the game supposes that 'peace' (i.e. outcome (P, P)) is preferred to 'war' (i.e. outcome (A, A)) by the two players. On the other hand, a unilateral aggression (choosing *A* when the other player sticks to *P*) is supposed to be rewarding for the aggressor; one could say that a sudden attack is preferred to peace by the aggressor and more feared than war by the attacked person. This rule explains the ordering of the numerical values given to the payoffs of the game, as it appears in the matrix of the game in strategic form (Figure 2.2).

It is easy to verify that, for each player, pacific strategy *P* is Pareto-dominated by aggressive strategy *A*:

$(3, 1) > (2, 0)$ for both players

This game has a unique DSE (A, A), which means 'open war'. In a pure non-cooperative framework, the two players have a clear interest in being aggressive. However, war (A, A) is less interesting than peace (P, P) for the two players: $(2 > 1)$ and $(2 > 1)$. Therefore, from a general interest point of view, such an outcome is not satisfactory.

We should emphasize that the source of the dilemma is not a lack of direct communication between players but *incentives*. Even if they could talk and agree to play the Pareto-efficient outcome, each player has an incentive to break the agreement.

Remark I

Generalization of the Prisoner's dilemma to the *n*-player case is sometimes referred to as the 'Tragedy of the Commons', because originally the story is concerned with the overgrazing of common land that results when each peasant is free to graze as many cattle as he wants (Hardin, 1968). More generally, the issue is encountered in economics when studying the provision of public goods and 'free-riding' behaviour. Since at least David Hume, political philosophers and economists have understood that if people respond only to private incentives public goods would be underprovided and public resources overused (see Exercise 2.7).■

Figure 2.2 The Prisoner's dilemma game

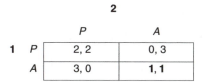

		2 *P*	2 *A*
1 *P*		2, 2	0, 3
A		3, 0	1, 1

For a player with a dominant strategy, it is of no use to know the other players' preferences and to infer their strategy. As long as there is no possibility of coordination between players, her (or his) dominant strategy constitutes her (or his) optimal strategy; but if the game has no DSE, then it is necessary to state precise assumptions about the players' mutual information possibilities.

2.2 Iterated dominance and backward induction

Let us consider the case where each player knows perfectly all the other players' preferences in addition to her (or his) own ones: we have a game with complete information. If we use the strategic form of the game, then we can imagine another type of decentralized behaviour, called 'iterated dominance'.

2.2.1 Iterated dominance

Since information is complete, each player can foresee the other players' behaviour with no need to communicate with them and the solution of the game must take into account these players' mutual strategic expectations.

'Dominance solvability' of a strategic-form game is based on a criterion of 'iterated' elimination of dominated strategies. Since each player knows the other players' preferences, each one is assured of what the others will not do if they are rational: they will never choose dominated strategies. And since everyone is able to discern simultaneously the other players' dominated strategies, strategy sets are simultaneously reduced. In turn, new dominated strategies appear for one player or another and so on.

This principle of resolution of a strategic-form game was first studied by Luce and Raiffa (1957) and developed later by Farqharson (1969) and Moulin (1979), among others.

Definition 5 (Iterated dominance equilibrium)

Iterated dominance consists of building up for each player i the sequence

$$X_i \equiv X_i^0 \supseteq X_i^1 \supseteq X_i^2 \supseteq \ldots \supseteq X_i^{t-1} \supseteq X_i^t \supseteq \ldots$$

which is defined by recurrence:

$$X_i^t = ND_i(u_i; X_1^{t-1}, \ldots, X_n^{t-1}) \text{ for all } t \geq o$$

where ND_i is the set of non-dominated strategies.

The game is said to be 'dominance solvable' if there exists an integer N such that, for each player i and for all $x^{-i} \in (X^{-i})^N$:

$$x_i, x_i' \in X_i^N \text{ implies } u_i(x_i, x_{-i}) = u_i(x_i', x_{-i})$$

that is, if there is a final game in which each player gets the same payoff from all her (or his) remaining strategies. The set of outcomes that survives the iterated procedure is called 'iterated dominance equilibrium' (IDE) (or sometimes 'd-solution' or 'sophisticated equilibrium'). ■

That behaviour is actually a non-cooperative decentralized procedure when information is complete. Each player can individually make calculations of the series X_i^t, according to the following rule:

- From X_i to X_i^1, she (or he) eliminates all the dominated strategies
- From X_i^1 to X_i^2, she (or he) again eliminates all the strategies which have now become dominated, the other players being known to use only non-dominated strategies, and so on.

The game can be solved if, after a limited number of such iterations, each player finds all strategies equivalent; otherwise an IDE does not exist.

Example

Take the game of Figure 2.3 in which one can define a single IDE.
For player 2, strategy c_3 is dominated. Whatever player 1's choice, choosing c_2 is always preferable to choosing c_3: $(4, -1) \geq (4, -2)$. Player 1 is aware of this domination among player 2's strategies and she realizes that her strategy r_1 is then dominated by r_2: $(5, 5) > (4, 2)$. Finally player 2 choose c_1 rather than c_2 because: $5 > -1$. The unique IDE of the game is (r_2, c_1).

Iterated dominance unfortunately is somewhat disturbing: in certain games the set of strategies that survive iterated elimination of dominated strategies may depend upon *the order* in which the strategies are eliminated (i.e. if one begins by the dominated strategies of player 1 or 2). An example is given in Figure 2.4.

Strategy r_1 (weakly) dominates strategy r_2. Strategy c_3 is strictly dominated. If r_2 is eliminated first, the IDE is (r_1, c_2). On the other hand, if c_3 is

Figure 2.3   Iterated dominance equilibrium

		c_1	c_2	c_3
1	r_1	4, 3	2, 4	0, 4
	r_2	5, 5	5, –1	–4, –2

with **2** as the column header above c_1, c_2, c_3.

Figure 2.4   (Weak) dominance and indeterminate outcomes

		c_1	c_2	c_3
1	r_1	10, 0	5, 1	4, –200
	r_2	10, 100	5, 0	0, –100

2

discarded first, then r_1 does not (weakly) dominate r_2: player 1 is indifferent with respect to her two strategies and the IDE may be (r_2, c_1). Yet, it should be emphasized that the difficulty mentioned above disappears if only *strict* dominance is applied in the procedure of iterated elimination of dominated strategies.

Remark I

Introducing *mixed* strategies in a game extends the possibility of defining an optimal decentralized behaviour for the players. As a consequence, a pure strategy non-dominated by any other pure strategy can be dominated by a *mixed* strategy. Consider the example of Figure 2.5.

Strategy r_2 is strictly dominated by strategy r_3. After an iteration, r_2 is eliminated and the payoff matrix is now the one presented in Figure 2.5b. No pure strategy of player 2 is dominated. However, c_2 is strictly dominated by the mixed strategy $p = (½, 0, ½)$. This result comes from the following reasoning. If player 2 plays p and player I chooses r_1, player 2's expected utility is:

$$½ (0) + 0(4) + ½ (9) = 4.5$$

Figure 2.5   Iterated dominance with mixed strategies

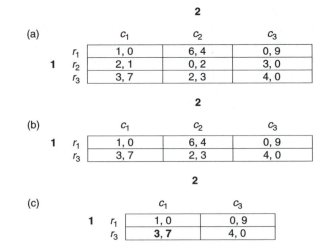

(a)		c_1	c_2	c_3
	r_1	1, 0	6, 4	0, 9
1	r_2	2, 1	0, 2	3, 0
	r_3	3, 7	2, 3	4, 0

2

(b)		c_1	c_2	c_3
1	r_1	1, 0	6, 4	0, 9
	r_3	3, 7	2, 3	4, 0

2

(c)		c_1	c_3
1	r_1	1, 0	0, 9
	r_3	3, 7	4, 0

2

Since $4.5 > 4$, player 2 has a clear interest in choosing p rather than c_2 when player I chooses r_1. Player 2 is also interested in choosing p rather than c_2 when I plays r_3:

$$½ (7) + 0(3) + ½ (0) = 3.5 > 3.$$

Hence, p strictly dominates c_2. And the payoff matrix is reduced to that of Figure 2.5c. In this matrix, r_3 strictly dominates r_1. Once r_1 is eliminated, c_1 strictly dominates c_3. So, the criterion of iterated dominance leads to (r_3, c_1) as the unique IDE of the game.■

Remark 2

Remember that the feasibility of this procedure requires not only that all players know each other's preferences, but also that each knows that the others know that she (or he) has this information, and so on: in other words, information about preferences must be 'common knowledge' (see sub-section 1.1.5 of Chapter 1 for a definition of this notion). The same idea applies for the assumption of rationality: in order to justify the elimination of an arbitrary number of dominated strategies, it is necessary to admit that it is common knowledge that no player will be irrational enough to choose a dominated strategy.■

The IDE of a game in strategic form corresponds to a decentralized and static reasoning from all the players. The game is played once only and each player separately makes her (or his) own expectations about her (or his) rivals' decisions. When these separate expectations are convergent, the game can be solved. Yet, one can draw a parallel between this approach and the principle of backward induction used for solving extensive-form games with perfect information, which brings some kind of dynamics into the analysis.

2.2.2   Backward induction

The criterion of iterated dominance defined in strategic-form games may be compared to an equivalent principle defined in extensive-form games with perfect information.

Consider the game represented in Figure 2.6a. It is a game with perfect information in which player 1 plays first, then player 2 chooses his strategy knowing the strategy chosen by player 1.

The resolution of this game rests on the following reasoning. Suppose that player 1 chooses r_2, then player 2 has a choice between c_1 (with a payoff -1) and c_2 (payoff 1): he will choose c_2. Thus, if player 1 chooses her strategy r_2, player 2 will play his strategy c_2. Player 1 anticipates player 2's behaviour and between her strategies r_1 and r_2, she will choose

Figure 2.6   Game in extensive form with its associated strategic form

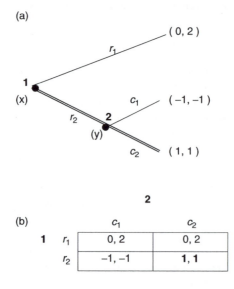

(a)

(b)

		c_1	c_2
1	r_1	0, 2	0, 2
	r_2	−1, −1	1, 1

r_2, which will generate a payoff 1 instead of 0. So, the solution of this game is (r_2, c_2).

It is easy to see that the argument used here is equivalent to iterated elimination of dominated strategies. Figure 2.6b shows the strategic form associated with this game. In the matrix, player 2's strategy c_2 dominates his strategy c_1: $(2, 1) \geq (2, - 1)$. Strategy c_1 can then be eliminated. In that case, the best choice for player 1 is to play r_2 $(1 > 0)$.

The resolution principle just presented can be generalized to all extensive-form games with complete and perfect information when the game is finite (i.e. there must exist a finite number of nodes in the game tree). The algorithm consists of starting from the last node of the game and 'moving back' (or up) in the tree toward the first node (in Figure 2.6a one starts from node (y) and goes back to node (x)). At each iteration, one holds the best strategy for the player concerned (in the example above: at node (y) player 2 chooses c_2, and at node (x) player 1 chooses r_2, knowing that player 2 will choose c_2). This is the reason why this resolution method is called 'backward induction'.

Remark I

This method is very old: the famous mathematician Zermelo (1913) used such an algorithm to analyse the game of chess (a two-player zero-sum game). Incidentally, Zermelo's algorithm sometimes is called Kühn's algorithm because the latter was the first to use this method in the modern literature on game theory (Kühn, 1953). Moreover, the same approach is well known in decision theory where *dynamic programming*, based on the pioneering work of the mathematician R. Bellman (1957), uses a similar algorithm for computing the solution of sequential decision problems.■

Backward induction always provides a solution in all games of *perfect information* but the procedure does not warrant uniqueness. However, in games in which no player is indifferent between any two outcomes, it is clear that backward induction gives a unique solution. Furthermore, if all the players are indifferent between any two outcomes whenever any one player is indifferent, though backward induction provides several solutions, then all players are indifferent between them.

Remark 2

In games with perfect information, the principle of backward induction is equivalent to iterated dominance except when the order of deletion matters in the strategic form of the game In that case, it may be that the IDE does not include the solution which would pass the test of backward induction.■

2.3   Safety first

Let us now consider the completely opposite case concerning the players' information. We suppose that each player, when forced to choose a strategy, ignores entirely the other players' preferences: we have a game with total ignorance. In this context, each player will contemplate the possibility that *all* the strategies could equally be employed by the rivals. Then the 'safety-first' rule envisages the worst situation and one tries to secure oneself against the maximal risk. 'Security' strategies formalize this behaviour, but it is only for the particular class of strictly competitive games that they can be characterized as *optimal* strategies for the players.

2.3.1   Security strategies

Definition and existence

The safety behaviour rests only on a security argument.

Definition 6 (Security strategy)

In the strategic-form game $(X_1, \ldots, X_n; u_1, \ldots, u_n)$, any strategy $\hat{x}_i$, solution of the problem:

$$\max_{x_i \in X_i} \min_{x^{-i} \in X^{-i}} u_i(x_i, x^{-i})$$

is called a 'security' strategy.■

Security strategies also are called 'maximin' strategies (or 'defensive' strategies). When corresponding to a security strategy $\hat{x}_i$, the payoff $\alpha_i = u_i(\hat{x}_i, x^{-i})$ is the *minimal guaranteed payoff* for player i. α_i is the payoff that the player can obtain against any other defensive behaviour from the other players.

Example

Consider the payoff matrix shown in Figure 2.7. Let $R = \{r_1, r_2\}$ and $C = \{c_1, c_2, c_3\}$ be the players' strategy sets.
For player 1, one gets:

$$\min_{c_j \in C} u_1(r_1, c_j) = 0, \ \min_{c_j \in C} u_1(r_2, c_j) = -1$$

thus:

$$\alpha_1 = \max_{r_i \in R} \{\min_{c_j \in C} u_1(r_i, c_j)\} = \max_{r_i \in R} \{0, -1\} = 0$$

For player 2, one gets:

$$\min_{r_i \in R} u_2(r_i, c_1) = 0, \ \min_{r_i \in R} u_2(r_i, c_2) = -1, \ \min_{r_i \in R} u_2(r_i, c_3) = 0$$

so:

$$\alpha_2 = \max_{c_i \in C} \{\min_{r_i \in R} u_2(r_i, c_j)\} = \max_{c_i \in R} \{0, -1, 0\} = 0$$

Player 1 has a unique security strategy, r_1, which guarantees her a minimal payoff 0; player 2 has two security strategies c_1 and c_3, which also guarantee him 0.

It is easy to show that for a finite game, under topological assumptions usually accepted in microeconomics (like X_i being compact and u_i continuous), each player has at least one security strategy. One can also prove that there exist non-dominated security strategies. Yet, generally, the set of non-dominated security strategies appears to be very large. Safety behaviour is too crude to allow discrimination among non-dominated strategies when the game does not display a DSE. Fortunately, in this setting, we can define a more stringent criterion which succeeds in selecting non-dominated security strategies. The notion of 'strong security' is a direct generalization of the concept of dominant strategy.

Figure 2.7   Security strategies

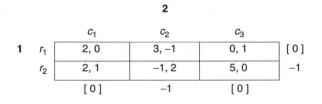

Strong security strategies

Let $x \in \mathbb{R}^n$; we note $x^\#$ the vector whose elements are globally the same as those of z, but reordered according to an increasing ordering. The lexicographic ordering R_L is the one used to classify the words in a dictionary. For R_L defined on $\mathbb{R}^n$, one gets:

$y \, R_L \, z$ if and only if   there is one $j \in \{1, \ldots, n\}$ such that:

for all $i, \, i < j$: $y_i = z_i$ and $y_j > z_j$

Definition 7 (*Strong security strategy*)

Suppose that to each strategy $x_i \in X_i$ corresponds the vector $(u_i(x_i, x^{-i}))_{x^{-i} \in X^{-i}}$. A strong security strategy for player i is a strategy $\hat{x}_i$ which maximizes over X_i, for the lexicographic ordering R_L of $\mathbb{R}^{X^{-i}}$, the application: $x_i \rightarrow \{(u_i(x_i, x^{-i}))_{x^{-i} \in X^{-i}}\}^\#$ ∎

The behaviour described here is very simple indeed. It can be summarised as follows:

- Player i starts maximizing the first element of the payoff vector (i.e. min u_i, since the vector is ordered increasingly); this first step simply means that she (or he) chooses a security strategy.
- Then, among the security strategies, she (or he) will choose one which maximizes the second element of the payoff vector (i.e. the payoff associated with the second-worst outcome); the player uses the same rule of selection over the set of security strategies as for choosing the security strategies over X_i.
- Then again she (or he) uses the same procedure until she (or he) has exhausted all the elements of the payoff vector. The player applies the security behaviour lexicographically.

The following result is then easy to prove:

Theorem 2 (*Moulin, 1986*)

Every strong security strategy for a player is a non-dominated strategy. Moreover, if player i has a dominant strategy, then the set of strong security strategies corresponds to the set of dominant (or non-dominated) strategies. ∎

This result shows that the notion of strict security strategy generalizes the notion of dominant strategy. Nevertheless, it is only in some particular games that safety behaviour can also be considered as optimal behaviour.

2.3.2   Optimal security strategies in a strictly competitive game

A strictly competitive game is a game in which the players cannot hope to improve their payoff through any kind of cooperation. In such a game, the vector of guaranteed minimal payoffs $(\alpha_1, \ldots, \alpha_n)$ cannot be improved. The outcome of the game is necessarily Pareto-efficient: it is impossible to improve one player's payoff without diminishing the payoff of at least one other player. It is just for this particular class of games that a player's security strategy can be considered as optimal.

In a strictly competitive game, the existence of an optimal security strategy allows the player to stop considering the other players' behaviour. She (or he) can surely obtain her (or his) guaranteed minimal payoff and she (or he) cannot expect a better outcome if all the players themselves behave rationally. Hence the existence problem of an equilibrium amounts to the existence problem of a solution to an optimisation problem.

A classic illustration of the notion of 'optimal-security strategy' is given by the study of the special class of two-player games having strictly opposed interest: 'zero-sum games'.

Definition 8 (Two-player, zero-sum game)

A two-player, zero-sum game in strategic form can be described by the triplet $(X_1, X_2; u)$, where u is the payoff function that *player 1* tries to *maximize* and that *player 2* tries to *minimize* (since their preferences are diametrically opposed).∎

Security strategies of player 1 are 'maximin' strategies while security strategies of player 2 can be called 'minimax' strategies. Numbers $\alpha_1 = \max_{x_1 \in X_1} \min_{x_2 \in X_2} u(x_1, x_2)$ and $\alpha_2 = \min_{x_2 \in X_2} \max_{x_1 \in X_1} u(x_1, x_2)$, respectively correspond to the guaranteed minimal *gain* of player 1 and to the guaranteed maximal *loss* of player 2. The following proposition can be easily proven.

Theorem 3

For any two-player zero-sum game: $\alpha_1 \leq \alpha_2$. When equality prevails, the common value is called the 'value' of the game: $v = \alpha_1 = \alpha_2$.∎

One can show that a two-player zero-sum game which has a value is a strictly competitive game. Reciprocally, one can demonstrate that (if X_1 and X_2 are compact sets and u is continuous) a two-player zero-sum game has a value only if it is strictly competitive. Theorem 3 shows that not every game has a value. Indeed, games with a value are named 'inessential' because the only outcome corresponds to the security level for all players.

For a two-player zero-sum game with a value (an inessential game), the 'safety-first' behaviour is optimal. The outcome of the game is an equilibrium characterized by a couple of optimal security strategies $(x_1{}^*, x_2{}^*)$. It is sometimes called 'maximin' or 'minimax' equilibrium of the game.

Theorem 4

A two-player zero-sum game has an equilibrium if and only if it has a value. The equilibrium $(x_1{}^*, x_2{}^*)$ is computed as a saddle-point of the payoff function:

for all $x_1 \in X_1$ and for all $x_2 \in X_2$: $u(x_1, x_2{}^*) \leq u(x_1{}^*, x_2{}^*) \leq u(x_1{}^*, x_2)$. ∎

This twofold inequality shows that $(x_1{}^*, x_2{}^*)$ is the solution of the two optimization problems:

$$\max_{x_1} u(x_1, x_2{}^*) \quad \text{and} \quad \min_{x_2} u(x_1{}^*, x_2)$$

The term 'saddle-point' is used as an analogy with the surface of a saddle which curves upwards in one direction and downwards in the other direction.

On the other hand, if the game has no value (i.e. if the game is not inessential) security strategies are no longer optimal. Each player faces a problem of non-convergent expectations. Player 1 can 'force' the payoff above α_1 and player 2 can 'force' under α_2. Player 1 will win if the payoff is greater than or equal to α_2 and player 2 will win if the payoff is lower than or equal to α_1. Player 1 can then make the following reasoning. She plans to play a security strategy x_1. If player 2 guesses this decision correctly, he would win while playing a better response x_2' to $\hat{x}_1$:

$$u(\hat{x}_1, x_2') = \min_{x_2} u(\hat{x}_1, x_2) = \alpha_1$$

Player 1 can expect this behaviour of player 2 and she can win while playing a better response x_1' to x_2':

$$u(x_1', x_2') = \max_{x_1} u(x_1, x_2') \geq \alpha_2$$

But player 2 can himself have expected this behaviour of player 1 and he can win while playing a better response x_2'' to x_1':

$$u(x_1', x_2'') = \min_{x_2} u(x_1', x_2) \leq \alpha_2$$

and so on. The sequence of strategy expectations built by player 1 does not converge; neither does the sequence of expectations by player 2 (Moulin, 1981, 25).

Figure 2.8   Zero-sum games

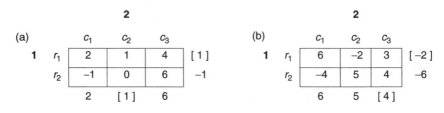

Examples

Figure 2.8 represents two examples of zero-sum games. Note that in zero-sum games, only player 1's payoffs are written in the matrix. We get a 'matrix game' instead of a 'bi-matrix game' for more general two-player non-zero-sum games. The first one (2.8a) is strictly competitive and its value is equal to 1: $\alpha_1 = \alpha_2 = 1$. The second one (2.8b) is such that: $\alpha_1 = -2 < \alpha_2 = 4$. Security strategies are optimal only in the former.

Therefore, in two-player zero-sum games without value, it is impossible to define an optimal behaviour for the players in pure strategies. In such games, the solution may be to choose the strategy at random; this is the idea behind the notion of mixed strategies. Introducing mixed strategies allows the extension of the domain in which a decentralized behaviour can be determined. Indeed, the first famous result in the history of game theory – the *minimax theorem* – is about this issue.

Theorem 5 (*Von Neumann, 1928*)

Each *finite* two player zero-sum game has at least one equilibrium in *mixed* strategies. The outcome of the game corresponds to a pair of optimal security strategies, which are computed as a saddle-point of the bilinear function:

$$\sum_i \sum_j p_i^1 u_{ij} p_j^2$$

where u_{ij} is the payoff function of player 1 when she chooses strategy i while player 2 chooses strategy j, and $(p_1 \ldots, p_i \ldots, p_n)^1$ and $(p_1 \ldots, p_j \ldots, p_m)^2$ are the probability distributions on the strategy sets of players 1 and 2, respectively (in a decentralized context, of course, these probabilities are independent).■

Many examples of zero-sum games can be found in Shubik (1982), Moulin (1986), Binmore (1992), Owen (1995).

Remark I

An appealing feature of a security strategy is the independence of a player's decision from any information about her (or his) opponent's payoff. Notice however that even if the game is strictly competitive, the choice of a security strategy by a player is optimal only if she (or he) believes (rightly) that her (or his) rivals are themselves rational: *players' rationality must be common knowledge.* If one of the players doubts that one of her (or his) rivals will behave rationally, a security behaviour is no longer optimal; she (or he) can take advantage of her (or his) rival by forcing a payoff above her (or his) guaranteed minimal level with a good chance of success.■

Remark 2

A two-player *constant*-sum game (i.e. such that $u_1 + u_2 =$ constant) is equivalent to a two-player zero-sum game ($u = u_1 = -u_2$) by operating a strictly increasing linear transformation of the payoff functions. Thus, for two-player constant-sum games, security strategies (pure or mixed) are optimal for the players. For two-player *non-constant*-sum games and for general games, this proposition is no longer true. Nevertheless, the notions of security strategy (or maximin strategy) and of minimal guaranteed payoff remain well defined and these notions are sometimes used in general *non-cooperative* games (for instance, in the 'Folk theorem' for repeated games – see Chapter 3). The same notion also is used in general *cooperative* games in the definition of the 'worth' of players' coalition (see Chapter 6).■

2.4   Applications

This section presents two applications of dominance and security arguments in economics and politics. Voting games are the first classical field in which DSE and IDE concepts can be appropriately employed. But voting problems provide a very large domain for applications of a lot of other game theoretic concepts which will be presented in the remainder of the book. Implementation theory is another field where the use of game theoretic concepts allows proving stimulating results for public decision making. Again, we focus on application of concepts studied in this chapter.

2.4.1   Voting games

Many collective decisions cannot be left to the market but must be selected from conflicting opinions of a given set of agents by voting systems. Indeed, many public allocation decisions are made by voting (for instance, taxes and public expenses) and this procedure is usually also employed to fill many public offices.

Formally, a voting rule corresponds to the following collective decision problem: several individual agents (the 'voters' or 'electors') must jointly pick one particular outcome amongst several possibilities, about which they have conflicting opinions (the 'candidates').

The election of a candidate by a voting procedure can easily be represented by a non-cooperative game. Electors are the players and the candidates are their strategies. The outcome chosen represents the election winner. The game is non-cooperative in the sense that any communication between the players is forbidden. (This sub-section is based on Moulin, 1981, 10–13 and 31–2.)

Let us assume that the voting procedure is the simplest of all – *simple majority voting* – and consider first the case where each elector totally ignores the other electors' opinions.

Model with incomplete information*

Let C be the set of p candidates and E the set of n electors. The candidate obtaining the largest number of votes wins the election. Assume that player 1 does not vote; she comes into play only to break a tie. Suppose also that each player ranks the candidates according to an increasing ordering (indifference between two candidates is excluded), corresponding to a pay-off function u_i defined on C.

This voting procedure can be formally represented by a strategic-form game. The strategy sets of the players are: $X_2 = \ldots = X_n = C$ and $X_1 \subset C^{(2^C)}$ is the set of applications which associates one element x_1 of S to each part S of C (there are 2^C parts).

If $x = (x_1, \ldots \ldots, x_n)$ represents a strategy vector, since player 1 breaks a possible tie, the elected candidate is: $v(x) = x_1(S(x))$, where $S(x)$ represents the set of candidates tying for the first place in the vote. Thus, the strategic form of the game is: $(X_1, \ldots, X_n; u_1 o v, \ldots, u_n o v)$ where $u_i o v$ means $v[u_i(.)]$.

It is easy to show that, in this game, if there are at least three electors, every strategy is a security strategy. This result shows that, for each player i, one gets:

$$\text{for all } x_i \in X_i, \quad \min_{x^{-i} \in X^{-i}} \{u_i o v(x_i, x^{-i})\} = \min_{c \in C} u_i(c)$$

This result is obvious, since if $\underline{c}$ is the worst candidate (i.e. associated with the lowest value of u_i), and if all the other players vote for $\underline{c}$, then necessarily she (or he) will be elected (by assumption, there are at least three electors and then a majority for c).

In this voting procedure the notion of security strategy does not allow players to discriminate between the candidates. It is too crude for this purpose. Thus, let us consider the stronger notion of a *strong security strategy*. We can then show that playing such strategies will now allow each player to choose a precise candidate.

Let us imagine a player i (any other player than 1 in fact) who prefers candidate $\bar{c}^i$ (the higher value for u_i is associated with $\bar{c}^i$). If she (or he) chooses a strong security strategy, she (or he) must necessarily vote for this candidate, the best according to her (or his) point of view. This proposition can be justified as follows. According to the strong security behaviour, in order to rank her (or his) strategies, player i will examine the vector:

$$z(x_i) = \left\{ \left[u_i ov(x_i, x^{-i}) \right]_{x^{-i} \in X^{-i}} \right\}^{\#}$$

Call $a(c, x_i)$ the number of times that candidate c is chosen and assume that $c_1, \ldots, c_p$ is a ranking of candidates corresponding to an increasing ordering of u_i: $u_i(c_1) < u_i(c_2) < \ldots < u_i(c_p) = u_i(\bar{c})$. The vector $z(x_i)$ can then be written:

$$z(x_i) = \underbrace{(u_i(c_1), \ldots, u_i(c_1)}_{2(c_1, x_i)times}; \underbrace{u_i(c_2), \ldots, u_i(c_2)}_{2(c_2, x_i)times}; \ldots; \underbrace{u_i(c_p), \ldots, u_i(c_p)}_{2(c_p, x_i)times}$$

Now it is obvious that by voting for any candidate c, player i increases the probability of the election of c without changing those of the others. It follows that by voting for her (or his) unique preferred candidate, player i maximizes the vector $z(x_i)$ for the lexicographic ordering.

A similar reasoning can be developed for player 1 who breaks any tie for first place. One can then assert that, in this voting game where each player ignores entirely the other players' opinions, the strong security behaviour corresponds to an unambiguous rational decentralized behaviour: vote for her (or his) own favourite candidate.

Let us now consider the situation where each elector can get the information about the other participants.

Model with complete information

In order to simplify the model let us reduce the set of candidates C and the set of electors E to three units. One also assumes that, in case of a tie for first place, player 1 (the 'president') has a casting vote. The strategy sets are such that: $X_1 = X_2 = X_3 = C$ and for a vote (x_1, x_2, x_3) the chosen outcome is:

$$v(x_1, x_2, x_3) = \begin{cases} x_2 & \text{if } x_2 = x_3 \\ x_1 & \text{if } x_2 \neq x_3 \end{cases}$$

In the first case, there are two votes for x_2 and one for x_1. In the second case, the three candidates get one vote each and player 1 can force the election of her preferred candidate thanks to her casting vote.

Imagine then that the voters' preferences can be represented by the following particular orderings:

$$u_1(c_1) > u_1(c_2) > u_1(c_3)$$

$$u_2(c_3) > u_2(c_1) > u_2(c_2)$$

$$u_3(c_2) > u_3(c_3) > u_3(c_1)$$

In this situation, where no candidate can be ranked in the same position in players' preferences, the collective choice according to a simple majority rule does not correspond to a binary transitive relation; the famous 'voting paradox' or 'Condorcet effect' applies. Information is complete: each player knows the preference ordering of the two other electors. One can then demonstrate that the game is dominance solvable: an IDE exists.

Player 1 has a dominant strategy: playing for c_1. Strategy c_1 dominates the two others for player 1 since, whatever the other players' choices, she obtains by voting for c_1 an outcome which cannot be improved upon. If 2 and 3 choose different candidates, her favourite candidate c_1 will be elected. If 2 and 3 vote for the same candidate, player 1 clearly cannot improve her situation by voting for c_2 or c_3.

For player 2 (hereafter named 'she'), strategy c_2 is dominated by c_1 and c_3: whatever the votes of the other players, she has no interest in voting for c_2. However strategy c_1 is not dominated. If player 1 votes for c_2 and player 3 votes for c_1, then 2 has an interest in voting for c_1 rather than for c_3, since c_1 will then be elected (and she prefers c_1 to c_2).

Finally, player 3 (hereafter named 'he') has a dominated strategy: c_1. It is always better for him to vote for another candidate, since whatever the choice made by the other electors, the outcome will be better in that case.

In summary, after a first round of elimination of dominated strategies, one gets the following results:

- For player 1, c_2 and c_3 are discarded
- For player 2, c_2 is discarded
- For player 3, c_1 is discarded.

At the second round, player 2 and player 3 have a dominant strategy: c_3. Player 3 anticipates that 1 will vote for c_1 (her own dominant strategy) and that 2 will not vote for c_2 (dominated). He infers that c_2 has no chance of being elected. If he nevertheless votes for c_2, his preferred candidate, he incurs the risk of an election of c_1 if 2 votes for c_3. On the contrary, if he falls back on c_3, he may have a chance of election of his second-best candidate.

Player 2 expects that player 1 will vote for c_1 (dominant strategy) and that 3 will not vote for c_1 (dominated). If she votes for c_1, this candidate will be elected, but if she votes for c_3, the latter has a chance to be elected thanks to the vote of player 3. Now remember that player 2 prefers c_3 to c_1. So, after two iterations, the game is solvable. The iterated elimination of dominated strategies leads to the election of candidate c_3, with two votes out of three.

Remark I

Note that the election winner is the worst candidate from the 'President's' point of view. Since the situation is symmetric with respect to the three candidates, one can conclude that in simple majority voting procedure with complete information and when the Condorcet effect is verified, the decentralized rational behaviour leads to the election of the worst candidate for the player with casting vote. This paradox comes from the fact that, with complete information, the supposed privilege turns against its owner, each player being able to anticipate that her (or his) optimal strategy is to vote right away for her (or his) preferred candidate. However, the result would be entirely different if the information was incomplete, since then the 'President's' favourite candidate would be elected. In this context, the strong security behaviour leads everyone to vote for her (or his) preferred candidate. Now, if everyone votes for her (or his) preferred candidate, thanks to the perfect heterogeneity of preferences, the casting vote of the 'President' allows her to assure the election of her preferred candidate.■

Remark 2

The voting procedure used in this application – namely, electing the candidate defeating every other candidate in pair-wise comparison – was first suggested by Condorcet in 1783. Yet this important family of voting systems is challenged by the 'scoring method' initiated by Borda in 1781, in which points are assigned to each candidate (for a comparison between these two classical voting rules see, for instance, Moulin, 1988, Chapter 9).■

2.4.2 Implementation theory and public decision making

From a methodological viewpoint, in this class of economic applications the problem studied is the inverse of the one considered previously. Rather than formulate a game that captures an economic situation and look for the properties of the likely outcome given by some equilibria, we are here fixing a set of outcomes satisfying some desirable properties and look for a game whose equilibria yield that outcome.

Implementation theory and welfare economics

We can imagine a 'planner' who develops criteria for social welfare but cannot enforce the desirable allocation directly, as he lacks information about several parameters of the situation. A mean then has to be found to 'implement' such criteria.

Recall that we noted earlier that a DSE of a non-cooperative game will typically fail to satisfy even the mild condition of efficiency. Hence the planner may try to change the rules of the game in order to attain an efficient outcome.

Much of welfare economics is based on Pareto-efficiency. Yet, efficiency is generally not regarded as sufficient for social optimality. Some economists even question its necessity, arguing that non-welfare information about people can be relevant for evaluating the social desirability of allocations (in particular, people's rights). Indeed such a question of defining the social objective raises many issues, both technical and philosophical. The modern social choice theory and theories of justice are concerned with this problem of justifying some particular 'social welfare functional' or 'principles of justice' (equity, fairness). Some of these approaches will be studied in Chapters 5 and 6. According to this viewpoint, 'implementation theory' can be seen as a particular branch of applied welfare economics in an extended sense. The social objective is supposed given and the basic problem is to *design games* whose equilibria have the desirable properties. This task of implementing social objectives is also called the problem of 'incentive compatibility' (Hurwicz, 1972).

Remark I

The class of economic applications, in which there is an agent who would like to condition her (or his) decisions on certain information that is privately known to other agents, is very large. The first agent usually is called the 'principal' and those who are privately informed on certain characteristics are called the 'agents'. Hence, the principal is not necessarily a 'planner' (or the 'government') but any organization, firm or individual facing such a problem. Examples of economic problems which belong to this class of 'asymmetric information' games include notably provision of public goods, design of auctions, monopolistic price discrimination and optimal taxation (see Chapter 3, sub-section 3.5.2 and Chapter 4, sub-section 4.4.2 for an analysis of two categories of asymmetric information games: games with 'moral hazard' and 'signalling' games.■

The implementation problem: mechanism design*

We consider an economy in which there is a finite set of feasible allocation X and a finite set of individuals N. Each agent i owns a private characteristic $e_i \in E_i$ and we suppose that her (or his) preferences on X are described by an ordinal utility function u_i. Each agent sends a message m_i to the planner. We note $E = \prod_i E_i$ the set of all individual characteristics and $M = \prod_i M_i$ the set of all messages.

We define the 'social choice rule' f as the correspondence (or set-valued function) that assigns a sub-set of X to each vector of characteristic e:

$$f : e \in E \rightarrow f(e) \subseteq X$$

The choice rule selects allocations verifying the social objectives (for instance, the efficient allocations). This notion indicates what the planner would do if he had all the information.

We define also the 'announcement function' as the function that assigns a global message m to each vector of characteristics e:

$$m : e \in E \rightarrow m(e) \in M$$

Finally, the 'outcome function' g is the function that associates sub-set of X with every global message:

$$g : m \in M \rightarrow g(m) \subset X$$

The implementation problem can be summarized in a diagram said to have originated from L. Hurwicz (Figure 2.9).

We call a 'mechanism' (or a 'game form') a pair (M, g). This notion indicates how the planner uses the conveyed information. The objective of the planner is to design a mechanism whose equilibrium allocations, for each vector of utility functions, are also selected by the social choice rule (for instance, efficient allocations). The mechanism and the vector of individual utilities induce a *strategic-form game* $(M_1 \ldots M_i \ldots M_n; u_1 \ldots u_i \ldots u_n)$:

- The players are the agents
- The players' strategies are the messages M_i; each player can reveal or not reveal her (or his) true characteristics

Figure 2.9 Hurwicz's diagram

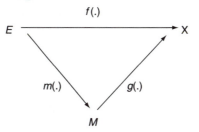

- The players' payoff functions are:

$u_i(g(m), e_i)$

Then we can give the following definition:

Definition

A mechanism (M, g) is said to 'implement' a social choice rule f, for a certain equilibrium concept C of the game $(M_1, \ldots, M_n; u_1, \ldots u_n)$, if:

for all $e \in E$, $g[m^*(e)] \subseteq f(e)$

where $m^* = (m_1{}^*, \ldots m_i{}^*, \ldots m_n{}^*)$ is the equilibrium messages vector, and we assume non-emptiness of the set of equilibrium allocations. When equality is imposed, there is *full* implementation: *every* equilibrium has to produce an outcome which is acceptable according to the social choice rule being implemented. We say also that f is C-implementable in this environment.∎

It turns out that often, for each agent, her (or his) set of *messages* is supposed to coincide with her (or his) set of individual *characteristics*: $M_i = E_i$, for all i. In that case, the mechanism is said to be 'direct'. Since the social choice of a mechanism by the planner has to consider the strategic behaviour of all the agents facing the choice rule, indeed it may be a long and complex iterative procedure. So it is best to restrict attention to simple mechanisms like direct (or one-step) mechanisms.

In this class of *direct mechanisms*, it is possible to give another definition of the implementation in an environment similar to the classical social choice theory (Arrow, 1951). We suppose now that the set of messages of each player is restricted to the set of possible *preference profiles* (that is, the vector $u = (u_1(e_1), \ldots, u_i(e_i), \ldots, u_n(e_n))$. In this framework, we can say that a direct mechanism is 'truthful' (or 'strategy-proof') if the possibility of strategic misrepresentation of their preference by players is discarded. The notion of 'manipulation' of a choice rule by a player allows the formalization of this idea.

Let U be the set of all possible orderings on X (condition of 'Unrestricted domain' in Arrow's axiomatic model). We say that agent i can manipulate the social choice rule f for preference profile $u \in U$, if a profile $u' \in U$ exists such that:

$u_i(f(u'_i, u^{-i})) > u_i(f(u))$

Therefore agent i has an incentive to manipulate f for profile u by misrepresenting her (or his) preferences to be u'_i rather than u_i.

Then, a direct mechanism is truthful if no admissible preference profile exists at which f is manipulable. Roughly speaking, for each agent, every utility-maximizing choice of which preference to announce must depend only on her (or his) own preferences and not her (or his) expectations about the preferences that other agents will announce. So, each agent can straightforwardly announce her (or his) true preference ordering (i.e. that maximizes her (or his) utility).

Definition

A direct mechanism g is said to 'truthfully implement' the social choice rule f, for some equilibrium concept C, if:

- The direct mechanism is truthful and 'truth-telling' is consistent with the equilibrium of the game
- When every player announces the true preference profile, the outcome belongs to $f(u)$:

$$g(u^*) \subseteq f(u),$$

assuming non-emptiness of the set of equilibrium allocations.
We also say that the choice rule f is C-truthfully implementable in this environment.■

Notice that this second notion of implementation is weaker than the first because it allows some equilibria (non truth-telling) of the game to yield outcomes that are inconsistent with the choice rule. However, the incentive strength of implementation depends above all on the *equilibrium concept* that we use for solving the game.

Implementation in dominant strategy equilibrium[*]

The notion of implementation in DSE is strong, since the choice of dominant strategy by a player is optimal *whatever the other players do*. It is for this concept of equilibrium that the implementation procedure is the more significant in strategic-form games. Unfortunately it can be proved that it is hard to implement a social choice rule in DSE.

We say that a social choice rule is 'dictatorial' if there is an agent such that her (or his) preferred allocation always corresponds to the outcome selected by the choice rule.

Theorem (*Gibbard, 1973; Satterthwaite, 1975*)

If X contains at least three allocations, U is the set of all possible preference profiles and for every allocation in X there exists a preference profile such that the social choice rule f is single value, then f is 'truthfully implementable' in DSE and efficient if and only if it is dictatorial.■

This result is a milestone in implementation theory. It uses the classical assumption of social choice theory in requiring agents to announce directly their preference orderings as the inputs of the choice rule. One may wonder about the generality of this assumption. There is, however, a result which shows that in fact this model is not restrictive.

Theorem (*Gibbard, 1973*)

Any social choice rule implementable in DSE is also '*truthfully* implementable' in DSE.■

From this theorem it follows that if a social choice rule cannot be 'truthfully implementable', then it cannot be implementable in DSE. Furthermore, in the particular case in which only *strict* preferences are allowed, it can be proved that the correspondence between the two notions of implementation is one-to-one.

This result is called 'revelation principle'. It says that, in considering what outcome is implementable, we need to consider only outcomes that are implementable by *direct* mechanisms. Therefore, this application of the 'revelation principle' allows us to conclude that the impossibility theorem of Gibbard–Satterthwaite is a proposition whose scope is very general.

Remark 2

The revelation principle is a general result in implementation theory which was discovered more or less independently during the 1970s by many researchers including, Gibbard (1973), Green and Laffont (1977), Dasgupta and Maskin (1979) and Myerson (1979). We discuss here the revelation principle for DSE but the same reasoning holds for other equilibria concepts, notably for 'Bayesian equilibria' (see Chapter 4, sub-section 4.1.4 for a definition of this notion and the use of implementation in Bayesian equilibrium).■

The Gibbard–Satterthwaite theorem states that, in a general environment, strategizing cannot be taken out of economic behaviour by cleverly designing the allocation mechanism. During the 1970s and 1980s, a great deal of research was done to identify environments in which a non-dictatorial efficient social choice rule is truthfully implementable in DSE. The seminal problem is the search for a mechanism whereby every agent, no matter what her (or his) preferences are, has an incentive to reveal it sincerely to the public decision maker. Unfortunately, the results of these approaches have been uniformly discouraging (Muller and Satterthwaite (1985)). Indeed, the impossibility theorem seems to apply to a very wide class of environments.

In order to escape from the nihilistic tone of the impossibility theorem, one could think of restricting the preferences that the players can have. Two such restrictions have been extensively studied in the literature. First, preferences can be restricted to be 'single-peaked'. If this is done, then generalizations of the classical 'majority' voting rule are efficient and truthful. Another such restriction, which concern preferences over elements of the 1-dimensional Euclidian space, would be to assume that admissible preferences are quasi-linear. If this second restriction is assumed, then a particular class of mechanism, the so-called Groves–Clarke–Vickrey pivotal mechanism, can be shown to be truthful.

The Groves–Clarke–Vickrey mechanism

We can intuitively discern the main properties of truthfully-implementable social choice rules in such a restricted environment in describing first the 'Vickrey auction'.

When people wish to sell objects, sometimes, they can choose a set of rules fixing how the object will be sold: such a set of rules is a mechanism for selling the object. Usually the seller (hereafter named 'he') hopes to sell the object for the highest expected price: he looks for an 'optimal' mechanism. Yet, before choosing an optimal mechanism the seller must wonder what the feasible rules are. In a very extensive meaning, these mechanisms are 'auctions'.

A 'Vickrey auction' is a particular mechanism: the object is sold to the highest bidder, but at the highest price bid by a loser. Unless there is a tie for first place, this corresponds to the second-highest price. Each potential buyer (hereafter named 'she') privately writes her bid on a piece of paper and seals it in an envelope. Then the winner is chosen at random from those who make the highest bid and pay only the second-highest bid. This rule has the appealing property that it is the interest of each bidder to seal her true valuation (or reservation price) in the envelope: truth-telling is a dominant strategy for each buyer. Thus, a Vickrey auction is an optimal mechanism (Vickrey, 1961)

This proposition is very easy to prove. Let us consider an auction with two bidders. For bidder 1, for instance, two cases arise: her true valuation v_1 is the highest bid or it is not.

In the first case (see Figure 2.10a), she wins the object and pays the second-highest bid w_2. She can never benefit from bidding below her true valuation. If she writes $w_1 > w_2$, no change arises. If she writes $w_1 < w_2$, she loses the object and pays nothing. Yet she loses the opportunity of gaining $v_1 - w_2$, if she had written her true valuation: she was ready to pay v_1, but she has to pay only $w_2 < v_1$.

In the second case (see Figure 2.10b) she does not win the object and pays nothing. Once again she can never benefit from bidding above her true valuation. If her misrepresented valuation is less than the highest bid, $w_1 < w_2$, no change arises: she does not win the object. If she writes

Figure 2.10 Vickrey auction

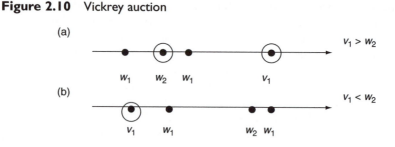

$w_1 > w_2$, then she wins the object but she sustains the loss $w_2 - v_1$, since she was ready to pay only v_1 and she must pay $w_2 > v_1$ for winning the object. Therefore, using a Vickrey auction guarantees the seller the second-highest price among the potential buyers and he cannot hope to do better (for instance, with a first-price sealed bid auction), as long as he does not know all the buyers' true reservation prices.

Remark 3

In fact, this property of the Vickrey auction requires that utility of the object is only a function of bidders' tastes ('private value auction'). When utility depends both on personal tastes and object data ('common value auction'), the object is won by the bidder with the highest over-evaluation ('winner's curse') (see, for instance, McAfee and McMillan, 1987).∎

It should be emphasized that a Vickrey auction is efficient since the highest bidder wins the object and the price corresponds to the loss that she imposes on the other bidders. The mechanism studied now represents a generalization of this powerful idea. The rule was discovered by Groves (1973) and Clarke (1971) who show that any efficient provision of indivisible public goods can be truthfully implemented in DSE.

Notice that, in contrast to an auction where the problem (the choice function) is to defined a *rule of attribution* (who wins the object?) and the *price* that the winner has to pay, in the public goods demand-revealing problem we must define a *rule of production* (for instance, should a bridge be built ?) and a rule of *cost sharing*.

Suppose that the agents have quasi-linear preferences (that is utility is additively separable in the public decision and in money, and linear in money). Thus, the agent i's preferences are described by the transferable utility function:

$$u_i(x, v_i, t_i) = v_i x - t_i, \, i = 1, \ldots, n$$

where x corresponds to the public decision (the good is produced or not), v_i is agent i's valuation or willingness to pay for the public good ($v_i \in \mathbb{R}$) and t_i agent i's monetary transfer (agent i's payment for the provision of the public good). Notice that under these assumptions we can identify the set of preference profiles with the set $\mathbb{R}^n$ of profiles of real numbers. We normalize x as follows: $x = 1$ if the project is executed or 0 otherwise.

Consider the mechanism $g = (x(w_i), t(w_i))$ where $t = (t_i)_{i=1}^n$ with $c > 0$ denoting the cost of supplying the public good; the efficient production rule is:

$$
x^*(w_1 \ldots w_i \ldots w_n) = \begin{cases} 1 & \text{if } \sum_{i=1}^{n} w_i \geq c \\ 0 & \text{otherwise} \end{cases}
$$

with w_i agent i's announcement.

The aim of the mechanism is to implement social choice functions: $f : \mathbb{R}^n \rightarrow X$ which verifies this requirement. Not all such social choice functions are implementable in DSE.

The Groves–Clarke mechanism is the only one that truthfully implements f in DSE. In the particular problem studied, the Groves–Clarke mechanism is such that:

$$
t_i^*(w) = x(w)\left(c - \sum_{j \neq i} w_j \right) + h_i(w^{-i}), \text{ for all } w_i \in R^n
$$

where $h_i(.)$ is an arbitrary function independent of agent i's announcement (the Clarke mechanism corresponds to the particular case $h_i(.) = 0$).

Thus, the mechanism used to implement f can be summarized as follows: the project is executed if and only if the announced sum that the individuals are willing to pay covers the costs; the payment made by agent i is equal to an arbitrary price (independent of her (or his) announcement) and, if the project is carried out, plus an additional amount corresponding to the difference between the cost of the project and the sum of the announcements made by the other agents. To summarize, this optimal mechanism has two general properties: first, it links the collective decision to the set of all individual announcements; secondly, the share of each agent i in the eventual cost is independent of her (or his) announcement except where agent i's announcement changes the collective decision (for instance, not to build the bridge when all the other agents' announcements would have led to the bridge being built), that is, when agent i is 'pivotal'.

We see easily that the Groves–Clarke mechanism is a generalization of the Vickrey auction to the discrete public goods provision problem. In the Vickrey auction, when a bidder wins (i.e. when she prevents the other bidders from getting it), she must pay the cost they bear (i.e. the second-highest bid). In the same way, in the Groves–Clarke mechanism, when an agent by her (or his) announcement changes the collective decision, then her (or he) must pay the cost she (or he) imposes on the others.

Remark 4

There is a large literature on Groves–Clarke–Vickrey mechanisms (see, for instance, Green and Laffont, 1979; Moulin, 1988, Chapters 8 and 9). Among the additional results, two are very important:

- *First proposition*: these mechanisms are the only truthfully dominant strategy implementable mechanisms in the presence of transferable utility, when no restriction is put on the domains of agents' characteristics.
- *Second proposition*: for dominant strategy implementation, efficiency is not consistent with budget balance; the mechanism necessarily induces a collective cost (the cost of 'telling the truth'); consequently, a first-best Pareto-optimality is not compatible with the strategy proofness requirement.■

Remark 5

How do we interpret these rather negative results on truthfully dominant strategy implementable mechanisms? Several viewpoints may be defended.

On one hand, we can try to use weaker equilibrium concept than DSE. Rationality based on dominance requires no assumption regarding the agents' information about each other. Iterated dominance is appropriate only if it is common knowledge among the agents which preferences they have, and that all agents are rational. For this more restrictive case, Farqharson (1969) and Moulin (1979, 1980) have proved that non-dictatorial social choice functions can be implemented. Unfortunately, a paper by Borgers (1995) shows simple impossibility results on implementation both in dominated and iteratively dominated strategies when rationality is based on *strict* dominance. Since rationality based on strict dominance is less restrictive than rationality notion based on (weak) dominance, these impossibility results are more general.

Another way to escape the negative results on truthfully dominant strategy implementable mechanisms is to use equilibrium notions that assume more coordination of agents' behaviour than definitions of rationality based on dominance notions. Whenever agents' preferences are *a priori* uncertain to other agents, then they are engaged in a game with *incomplete* information for which we can define a weaker notion of equilibrium named 'Bayesian equilibrium' (see Section 4.1 of Chapter 4 for a presentation of this equilibrium concept in a game with incomplete information). If agents' preferences are supposed known to other agents, we can even claim that the less restrictive notion of Nash equilibrium can also be used in implementation theory (see Section 3.1 of Chapter 3 for a formal presentation of this notion). These approaches have been broadly explored in the literature on implementable mechanisms (see for instance d'Aspremont and Gerard-Varet (1979) and Myerson (1985) for Bayesian equilibrium implementable mechanisms and Maskin (1985) for Nash equilibrium implementable mechanisms).

Yet another more philosophical lesson can be drawn from the general impossibility result mentioned above. From an ethical viewpoint a lie can be defined as an intentionally misleading statement. When a collective decision can be represented by a particular allocation mechanism, an agent who misrepresents her (or his) preferences may sometimes legitimately be termed a 'liar'. Then, the impossibility results about truthful mechanisms should simply reflect the inevitable imperfectability of society. Whatever the qualities of social institutions, we cannot prevent some people from lying because the incentives to lie are in fact intrinsic to social mechanisms. Indeed 'an individual decision to be honest and not to lie is truly an ethical decision because, even in principle, society cannot be designed so that honesty is self-enforcing' (Muller and Satterthwaite, 1985, 169).■

Bibliography

Arrow, K. (1951) *Social Choice and Individual Values* (2nd corrected edn, 1963) (New York: John Wiley).

Aspremont, C.d' and L.A. Gerard-Varet (1979) 'Incentives and incomplete information', *Journal of Public Economics*, 11, 25–45.

Bellman, R. (1957) *Dynamic Programming* (Princeton: Princeton University Press).

Binmore, K. (1992) *Fun and Games* (Lexington, MA: D.C. Heath), Chapter 6.

Borgers T. (1995) 'A note on implementation and strong dominance', in W. Barnett, H. Moulin, M. Salles and W.J. Schofield (eds), *Social Choice, Welfare and Ethics* (Cambridge: Cambridge University Press).

Clarke, E.H. (1971) 'Multipart pricing of public goods', *Public Choice*, 11, 17–33.

Dasgupta, P. and H. Maskin (1979) 'The implementation of the social choice rule: some general results on incentive compatibility', *Review of Economic Studies*, 46, 85–216.

Farqharson, M. (1969) *Theory of Voting* (Newhaven, Yale University Press).

Gibbard, A. (1973) 'Manipulation of voting schemes: a general result', *Econometrica*, 41, 587–601.

Green, J. and J.J. Laffont (1977) 'Characterization of a satisfactory mechanism for the revelation of preferences for public goods', *Econometrica*, 45: 427–38.

Green, J. and J.J. Laffont (1979) *Incentives in Public Decision Making* (Amsterdam: North-Holland).

Groves, T. (1973) 'Incentives in teams', *Econometrica*, 41, 617–63.

Hardin, G. (1968) 'The tragedy of the commons', *Science*, 162, 1243–8.

Hurwicz L. (1972) 'On informationally decentralized systems', in C.B. McGuire and R. Radner (eds), *Decision and Organization. A Volume in honor of Jacob Marschak* (Amsterdam: North Holland), 297–332.

Hurwicz, L., D. Schmeidler and H. Sonnenschein (eds) (1985) *Social Goals and Social Organization – Essays in Memory of Elisha Pazner* (Cambridge: Cambridge University Press).

Kohlberg, E. and J.-F. Mertens (1986) 'On the strategic stability of equilibria', *Econometrica*, 54, 1003–37.

Kühn, H.W. (1953) 'Extensive games and the problem of information', in H.W. Kühn and A.W. Tücker (eds), *Contributions to the Theory of Games*, 2 (Princeton: Princeton University Press).

Luce, R.D. and H. Raiffa (1957) *Games and Decisions* (New York: John Wiley).

McAfee P. and McMillan J. (1987) 'Auctions and bidding', *Journal of Economic Literature* 25, 699–738.

Maskin E. (1985) 'The theory of implementation in Nash equilibrium: a survey', in L. Hurwicz, D. Schmeidler and H. Sonnenschein (eds), *Social Goals and Social Organization – Essays in Memory of Elisha Pazner* (Cambridge: Cambridge University Press).

Moulin, H. (1979) 'Dominance solvable voting schemes', *Econometrica*, 47, 1337–51.

Moulin H. (1980) 'Implementing efficient, anonymous, and neutral social choice functions', *Journal of Mathematical Economics*, 7, 249–69.

Moulin, H. (1981) *Théorie des jeux pour l'économie et la politique* (Paris: Hermann) (in French).

Moulin, H. (1986) *Games Theory for Social Sciences*, 2nd rev. edn (New York: New York University Press).

Moulin, H. (1988) *Axioms of Cooperative Decision Making* (Cambridge: Cambridge University Press).

Muller E. and M.A. Satterthwaite (1985) 'Strategy-proofness: the existence of dominant strategy equilibrium', in L. Hurcwicz D. Schmeidler and H. Sonnenschein (eds), *Social Goals and Social Organization – Essays in Memory of Elisha Pazner* (Cambridge: Cambridge University Press).

Myerson, R. (1979) 'Incentive compatibility and the bargaining problem', *Econometrica*, 51, 1767–97.

Myerson, R. (1985) 'Bayesian equilibrium and incentive compatibility', in L. Hurwicz, D. Schmeidler, and H. Sonnenschein (eds), *Social Goals and Social Organization – Essays in Memory of Elisha Pazner* (Cambridge: Cambridge University Press).

Osborne, M.J. and A. Rubinstein (1994) *A Course in Game Theory* (Cambridge, MA: MIT Press).

Owen, G. (1995) *Game Theory*, 3rd edn (San Diego: Academic Press), Chapter 2.

Satterthwaite, M.A. (1975) 'Strategy-proofness and Arrow's conditions: existence and correspondance theorems for voting procedures and social welfare functions', *Journal of Economic Theory* 10, 187–217.

Satterthwaite M.A. (1987) 'Strategy-proof allocation mechanisms', in J. Eatwell, M. Milgate and P. Newman (eds), *Game Theory – The New Palgrave*, 2 (London: Cambridge, MA: Macmillan).

Shubik, M. (1982) *Game Theory in the Social Science: Concepts and Solutions* (MIT Press).

Vickrey, W. (1961) 'Counterspeculation, auctions and competitive sealed tenders', *Journal of Finance*, 16, 8–37.

Von Neumann, J. (1928) 'Zür theorie der Gesellschaftsspiele', *Mathematischen Annalen*, 100, 295–320 (English translation 'On the theory of game strategy', in A.W. Tücker and R.D. Luce (eds), *Contribution to the Theory of Games*, 4, Princeton: Princeton University Press, 1959).

Zermelo, E. (1913) 'Über eine Anwendung der Mengenlehre ant die Theorie der Schachspiers', in E.W. Hobson and A.E.H. Lore (eds), *Proceedings of the Fifth International Congress of Mathematicians*, 2 (Cambridge: Cambridge University Press).

3 Non-Cooperative Games with Complete and Perfect Information

3.1 Nash equilibrium: theory and early applications
3.2 Extensions: randomization and correlation
3.3 Repeated games
3.4 Sub-game perfection: refinement I
3.5 Applications

We now leave the normative decision-analysis approach to study a more descriptive approach to try to understand the behaviour of all the players in a game. The problem becomes: how will players actually choose? One does not look here for an unambiguous optimal behaviour for a player in a perfectly decentralized context. One rather tries to guess what are the outcomes which are likely to appear as solutions in a non-cooperative interacting situation. Players are still unable to make binding agreements with their rivals, so the game basically remains strictly non-cooperative. Yet, players are allowed to communicate with each other. They can, for instance, directly exchange information and agree to choose a particular outcome of the game, but none of these eventual agreements can be enforceable. In another aspect, the game is no longer necessarily a one-shot game; the conflicting relations may be repeated over time and this possibility of repetition creates new strategic interactions between players.

In this new context, we can claim that the only obvious outcomes of non-cooperative games are 'Nash equilibria' (or, in short, 'equilibria'). This notion is really the cornerstone of non-cooperative GT, so this chapter develops and applies this concept to games with complete and perfect information.

In section 3.1 we introduce the notion of Nash equilibrium, with emphasis placed on several important theoretical topics: definition, existence, justification and selection, and failures; we also review early classical economic applications. In section 3.2 we consider extensions and generalizations of Nash equilibrium in two directions: 'mixed' strategies equilibria and 'correlated' equilibria. We show in particular that these generalizations play a great part in correcting (to a certain extent) two of the main shortcomings of the initial notion, namely non-existence and inefficiency. If we preclude any communication between the players before taking their decisions, is it possible to find another way allowing some kind of indirect coordination likely to improve the final outcome? Section 3.3, devoted to the important class of repeated games, gives a precise answer to this question. The last difficulty that can arise with Nash equilibrium lies in the multiplicity of outcomes verifying the required properties. Any set of Nash equilibria is too large, so that we need stronger additional restrictions to discard some of them by 'refining' equilibrium. Section 3.4 is devoted to the first and most popular refinement of Nash equilibrium: sub-game perfection. We show that in extensive-form games with perfect information, the use of the sub-game perfect equilibrium concept is effective to reduce significantly the number of equilibria by extending the normative principle of backward induction. Nevertheless, one should be aware of the limits of this refinement when applied to more general games and, at the same time, of the existence of paradoxical results in some contexts as regards to intuition and empirical findings. Several economic applications of Nash equilibrium and sub-game perfect equilibrium concepts are also given in section 3.5. In the first sub-section (3.5.1), we study models where commitment is the main strategic move used by economic agents. The next sub-section (3.5.2) is devoted to models of 'moral hazard', a class of asymmetric information games with hidden action. The last sub-section (3.5.3) analyses more general repeated games in which emphasis is placed on the credibility of threats or promises.

3.1   Nash equilibrium: theory and early applications

3.1.1   Definition and existence

Definition

It is well known that Nash (1950) identified a fundamental solution of non-cooperative games, which he called an 'equilibrium point'. Today this concept is known as a 'Nash equilibrium' (NE), or sometimes a 'strategic' equilibrium, or more simply, an 'equilibrium'.

This concept poses the following question: does there exist an 'obvious' or 'reasonable' way to play a non-cooperative game? Does there exist an outcome such that everyone believes it is more likely to be realized than any other outcome? If such an outcome exists, it must necessarily correspond to the best response of every player to the prospective plays of all the others. It must be such that it is in everyone's interest that it is realized. The NE notion fits these requirements.

In a two-player game, the outcome (x_1^*, x_2^*) is a NE if and only if x_1^* is a best response to x_2^* and, simultaneously, x_2^* is a best response to x_1^*; a NE is a *best mutual response* criterion. Thus, if player 1 anticipates that 2 will choose his strategy x_2^*, and if player 2 expects that 1 will play x_1^*, then none of them will have an interest in deviating from the rival's expectation. In that sense, their predictions constitute 'an equilibrium'.

Definition 1 (*Nash equilibrium*)

An outcome $(x_1^*, \ldots, x_n^*)$ of the game $(X_1, \ldots, X_n; u_1, \ldots, u_n)$ is a NE if it verifies:

$$u_i(x_i^*, x^{-i*}) \geq u_i(x_i, x^{-i*}) \quad \text{, for all } x_i \in X_i \text{ and all } i$$

If the inequalities are strict, it is a *strict* NE.∎

The strategy x_i^* is a 'strategy of best response' for player i, facing the strategies chosen by her opponents; and this is true for all the players. The outcome of the game is 'stable' in the sense that none of the players has an incentive unilaterally to deviate from this choice; in a sense, a NE is a 'no-regret' solution of a game.

The following restatement of the definition of a NE is sometimes useful. For any $x^{-i} \in X^{-i}$, we define the set of player i's best responses:

$$B_i(x^{-i}) = \{x_i \in X_i : u_i(x_i, x^{-i}) \geq u_i(x_i', x^{-i}) \text{ for all } x_i' \in X_i\}$$

B_i generally is a 'correspondence' or 'set-valued function' (see the Appendix at the end of this chapter). It is called the 'best response function' of player i. So we can define a NE as a strategy vector $(x_1^*, \ldots, x_2^*)$ for which:

$$x_i^* \in B_i(x^{-i*}) \text{ for all } i$$

$$(3.1)$$

Example

In the payoff matrix drawn in Figure 3.1, the outcome (r_1, c_1) is the unique NE.

The following reasoning is used to find the solution. If player 1 anticipates that 2 will play c_1, her best response is r_1 ($\underline{5} > 4$). If she

Figure 3.1 Nash equilibrium

		2 c_1	c_2
1	r_1	**$\underline{5}, \underline{5}$**	$-1, 4$
	r_2	$4, \underline{1}$	$\underline{0}, 0$

anticipates that 2 will play c_2, her best response is r_2 ($\underline{0} > -1$). Take then player 2's position. If he anticipates that 1 will choose r_1, his best response is c_1 ($\underline{5} > 4$). Facing r_2, he would also choose c_1 ($\underline{1} > 0$). The equilibrium between best responses is obtained for (r_1, c_1) with the payoff ($\underline{5}$, $\underline{5}$).

This reasoning illustrates an interpretation of Nash behaviour: a NE reflects *self-confirming* players' beliefs. In other words, rational players will choose equilibrium strategies if they correctly anticipate each other's strategies.

The second definition of NE given above points us to a method of finding equilibria in a game. In a first time, calculate a best response function of each player, then find a strategy vector for which (3.1) holds. Moreover, when the sets of strategies X_i correspond to continuous spaces (infinity of strategies), the payoff functions u_i are differentiable and the best response functions are 'functions' (i.e. singleton-valued), this method amounts to:

(i) Search the solutions x_i^* of the n optimization problems:

$$\max_{x_i \in X_i}, \ u_i(x_i, x^{-i*}), \text{ for all } i$$

(ii) Solve the n equations system in the n unknowns x_i^*.

Sometimes the NE concept is still described today as an outcome such that each player acts in her (or his) own best interest against the *given* strategies of the other players. One must take carefully this definition, because it may be misleading. It conveys the impression that players follow a rather naive behaviour when adopting the non-cooperative behaviour which supports a NE. In fact, the opposite is true. We will see that this behaviour may be very sophisticated (sub-section 3.3). It turns out, however, that this kind of non-cooperative behaviour is less precise than the one supported by the dominance argument.

In some way Nash behaviour generalizes dominance and iterative dominance. For any player the choice of a dominant strategy does not require any information on the other players' opinions. That is no longer true for the non-cooperative behaviour defined in games with complete information. So, it is clear that every DSE is also a NE but the reverse is not true (for instance, in the Prisoner's dilemma described above, the DSE is also the unique NE of the game). A NE can even involve dominated strategies (but not *strictly* dominated strategies, of course). Moreover the criterion of iterated dominance always selects an outcome which is a NE, but a given NE is not necessarily an IDE. Besides, using iterated dominance represents a way for selecting a particular NE when there is multiplicity of equilibria (see sections 4.2 and 4.3 of Chapter 4 on 'refinement' of NE).

In summary, if we denote by **DSE** the set of dominant strategy equilibria in a given strategic-form game, and by **IDE** and **NE** the sets of iterated dominance equilibria and Nash equilibria, respectively (of course, these sets may be void), the relationship between these sets is as follows:

DSE ⊆ IDE ⊆ NE

In other respects NE always yields a payoff for each player at least as good as her (or his) minimal guaranteed payoff, but security strategies are generally not Nash strategies. Safety behaviour and non-cooperative behaviour coincide only in strictly competitive games. For instance, for a two-player zero-sum game with a value, every optimal security strategy equilibrium is also a NE.

The following well known 'toy game' illustrates these properties.

Example: the Battle of the Sexes

Let us consider a couple who decide to spend an evening out together but the man and the woman have different preferences about where to go. They have ruled out all possible entertainment except a boxing match and a ballet performance. Preferences are assumed to fit the traditional stereotypes: the husband prefers to watch the boxing match (M), whereas the wife would like to go to the ballet (B). Of course, they would rather go to either of these events together than to spend the evening separately; but in the latter case they are slightly better off if the man watches the match and the woman goes to the ballet, than if they do the opposite. Figure 3.2 describes the resulting pay-off matrix.

Clearly there is neither a DSE nor an IDE in that game. However (M, M) and (B, B) are two NE. If one goes to the match the best response for the other is to follow, and if one goes to the ballet the other does best to make the same choice. Naturally the man would prefer equilibrium (M, M) while the woman would like equilibrium (B, B). In this 'coordination' game, it is not easy to predict which of these two NE will actually be chosen.

On the other hand, if players followed a safety behaviour, the outcome is (M, B) with outcome $(\frac{1}{2}, \frac{1}{2})$, one of the worst outcomes for the two

Figure 3.2 The Battle of the Sexes

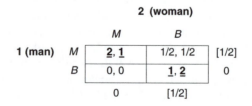

players. In that case no player would be choosing a best response relative to the decision of the other. However the two could alternatively experience 'team' satisfaction.

The previous definition of NE is given for a strategic-form game, but the same basic concept also applies to extensive-form games. A simpler way to extend the definition is to say that the outcome of an extensive-form game is a NE if it corresponds to a NE according to the definition given above in the associated strategic-form game. With each extensive-form game there is associated a *unique* strategic-form game. In contrast, a given strategic-form game may be associated with *more than one* extensive-form games. But an important property holds: the set of NE in the associated strategic form and the extensive form of a game always coincide.

Existence

It is important that a solution concept for a game logically exists under very many circumstances. Indeed, the popularity of NE arises partly from its existence in many games. Nevertheless, there exists some situations without *pure* strategy NE.

In order to prove that a game has at least one NE it is sufficient to show that there exists x^* such that relation (3.1) can be verified. Define the correspondence $B: X \to X$ by:

$$B(x) = \prod_i B_i(x^{-i})$$

with the notation: $X = \prod_i X_i$. This relation can be written in vector form:

$$x^* \in B(x^*)$$

Therefore we can see that a game has a NE if and only if B has a 'fixed point'.

Conditions that guarantee existence of a fixed point for a correspondence are studied in mathematical theory. The most notorious among fixed point theories is the Kakutani theorem (see the Appendix at the end of this chapter).

Nash first demonstrated the following existence theorem by using this particular fixed point theorem.

Theorem I (Nash 1950, 1951)

A game in strategic form $(X_1, \ldots, X_n; u_1, \ldots, u_n)$ has at least one NE in pure strategies, if for each player i:

- The strategy set X_i is a (non-empty) compact and convex subset of an Euclidean space
- The payoff function u_i is continuous and quasi-concave in x_i.■

Proof: For every $i \in N$ the set $B_i(x^{-i})$ is non-empty since u_i is continuous and A_i is compact, and it is convex since u_i is quasi-concave on X_i; B is upper semi-continuous since each u_i is continuous. Thus by Kakutani's theorem B has a fixed point.■

Remark I

Sometimes in economic applications two-person games are symmetric:

$$X_1 = X_2 = X \text{ and } u_1(x_1, x_2) \geq u_1(x'_1, x'_2)$$

if and only if $u_2(x_2, x_1) \geq u_2(x'_2, x'_1)$ for all $x, x' \in X$.

It is easy to prove by using Kakutani's theorem that there is a strategy $x^*_1 \in X$ such that (x^*_1, x^*_1) is a NE of the game. Such an equilibrium is called a 'symmetric' equilibrium.■

3.1.2 Two classical applications in industrial organization: Cournot and Bertrand duopoly models

A solution very similar to NE was first used by Cournot as early as 1838 in the context of duopoly model. This model is considered rightly as one of the major classic examples of applied game theory in economics. In this model, the firms are supposed to choose simultaneously their volume of output. In 1883, Bertrand developed another model of duopoly where the strategic variables are the product prices. Let us present those two classic models of industrial organization as first applications of the NE concept.

Cournot–Nash equilibrium: quantity competition

Two firms produce and sell a homogeneous good. Let us call q_1 and q_2 the quantities produced by firm 1 and firm 2, respectively. To simplify matters, assume that there are no fixed costs and that marginal cost is constant and equal to c, so that the total cost is:

$$C_i = cq_i$$

Firms face an inverse demand function given by:

$$p = \max\{a - Q, 0\}$$

where $Q = q_1 + q_2$, p is the price of the good and a is a positive constant; in order to avoid a 'corner solution', assume that: $a > c$.

Firms are supposed to choose simultaneously the quantities q_1 and q_2. In this model those variables are thus the players' strategies. The strategy sets of the players are identical and given by:

$$X_1 = X_2 = [0, a - c]$$

The players' payoff functions are here the profit functions of the firms:

$$u_1(q_1, q_2) = p(q_1, q_2)q_1 - cq_1$$
$$u_2(q_1, q_2) = p(q_1, q_2)q_2 - cq_2$$

Or, more generally, after a clear change of notations:

$$u_i(q_i, q_j) = \begin{cases} \lfloor a - (q_i + q_j) - c \rfloor q_i & \text{if} \quad 0 \le q_i \le a - c - q_j \\ 0 & \text{if} \quad 2 - c - q_j \le q_i \le a - c \end{cases}$$

If (q_i^*, q_j^*) is a NE of this game, then for any i:

$$u_i(q_i^*, q_j^*) \ge u_i\left(q_i, q_j^*\right), \text{ for all } q_i \in X_i$$

It should be emphasized that in the games we have looked at so far players' strategies were discrete. We have here a first example of a game where the sets of strategies correspond to *continuous* spaces (*infinity of strategies*) and where payoff functions possess the property of differentiability. In this case we know (sub-section 3.1.1) that the computation of NE amounts to a search for the solutions of a very simple mathematical problem. For each player i, q_i^* must be a solution of:

$$\max_{q_i} u_i = \lfloor a - (q_i + q_j) - c \rfloor q_i$$

It is easy to check that in this game there always exists at least one NE.

Proof: Evidently, u_i is continuous in (q_i, q_j). Moreover, $u_i > 0$ and is strictly concave when $q_i < a - c - q_j$ and $u_i = 0$ otherwise. So, on the interval $[0, a - c]$, u_i is quasi-concave. The sufficient conditions for existence of a NE are fulfilled.■

With the assumption that $q_i^* < a - c$, the first-order conditions of this optimization problem are necessary and sufficient:

$\partial u_i / \partial q_i = 0$, $i = 1, 2$

which gives:

$$q_i^* = \left(a - q_j^* - c\right)/2, \ i = 1, 2$$

Solving this pair of equations leads finally to the outcome of the game:

$$q_1^* = q_2^* = (a - c)/3$$

The solution verifies $q_i^* < a - c$, as was required. It is the 'Cournot–Nash solution' of the duopoly model.

The intuition supporting this 'reasonable' solution is easy to set out. Each firm, of course, would like to behave as a monopolist. Should it succeed in doing so, it would choose q_i so that it maximizes $u_i(q, 0)$. It would then obtain monopoly profit $u_i(q_m^*, 0) = \dfrac{(a - c)^2}{4}$ for the optimal quantity $q_m^* = (a - c)/2$. Since there are two firms on the market, the aggregate monopoly profit would be obtained by equating $q_1 + q_2$ to q_m^*. It would be the case, for instance, if each firm were producing $q_i = q_m^*/2$. Nevertheless, this solution cannot be accepted, because each firm has an incentive to deviate from it. Since the monopoly output is low, the associated price $p_m(q_m^*)$ is high, and, at this price, each firm would like to increase its output, despite the decrease in price that may ensue. On the contrary, at the Cournot–Nash equilibrium, no firm has an incentive to deviate.

We should emphasize that this assumed behaviour of firms is quite sophisticated. Each firm is fully conscious of the market interdependence with its rival and it takes this interdependence into account when choosing its production strategy. Each firm knows the profit function and the strategy set of its rival. It can thus anticipate its rational behaviour. In particular, it can 'reasonably' expect that its rival j will choose q_j^*. So, by choosing q_i^*, firm i acts in its own interest. Once the outputs are chosen according to this reasoning, each firm can verify that its expectations were correct and that the choice is actually profit-maximizing.

Remark I

Let us examine a graphical presentation of the Cournot duopoly model. Equation $q_i^* = \left(a - q_j^* - c\right)/2$ represents firm i's best response to the equilibrium strategy of its rival. The same reasoning leads to the best response of firm 2 to any arbitrary strategy of firm 1, and to the best response of firm 1 to an arbitrary strategy of firm 2. Under the assumption: $q_1 < a - c$, the best response function of firm 2 is:

$$B_2(q_1) = (a - q_1 - c)/2$$

Figure 3.3 Cournot–Nash equilibrium

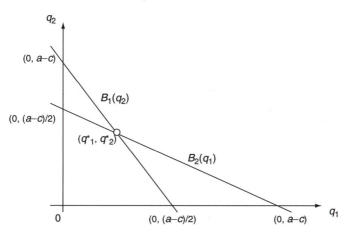

while, under the assumption $q_2 < a - c$, the best response function of firm I is:

$$B_1(q_2) = (a - q_2 - c)/2$$

Figure 3.3 shows that these best response functions have a unique intersection, corresponding to the pair of equilibrium outputs (q_1^*, q_2^*).■

Remark 2

In the Cournot duopoly game one can also obtain a NE by applying the iterated dominance criterion. But the complete procedure of convergence requires an infinite number of iterations during which at each step part of the output levels included in the strategy set can be discarded.■

Bertrand equilibrium: price competition

In the Bertrand model of duopoly, firms choose prices instead of output levels. Players' strategy sets are now the (non-negative) prices: $X_1 = X_2 = [0, +\infty]$.

Consumers are supposed to buy the product from the firm offering the lowest price. If the offered prices are identical, then a particular assumption is required to know how demand will be split between the two suppliers; one generally admits that half of total demand goes to each firm, though such an assumption is not crucial here. The total demand function is:

$$q = D(p)$$

Demand facing each firm i is given by:

$$q_i(p_i, p_j) = \begin{cases} D(p_i) & \text{if } p_i < p_j \\ \frac{1}{2}D(p_i) & \text{if } p_i = p_j \\ 0 & \text{if } p_i > p_j \end{cases}$$

Costs are as previously designated: no fixed costs, and constant marginal cost. As usual the payoff functions of this game correspond to the profit functions of the firms:

$$u_i(p_i, p_j) = p_i q_i(p_i, p_j) - cq_i = (p_i - c)q_i(p_i, p_j)$$

Both firms choose their price simultaneously, without any communication. Not being able to observe the price offered by its rival, each firm anticipates this price while it decides its product price.

If (p_i^*, p_j^*) is a NE of this game, then necessarily for any i:

$$u_i(p_i^*, p_j^*) \geq u_i(p_i, p_j^*), \text{ for all } p_i \in X_i$$

This solution is often called 'Bertrand–Nash equilibrium' because it corresponds exactly to the NE of the Bertrand duopoly model. One can easily show that the conditions required to assure the existence of an equilibrium are verified. Here again, the computation of NE is equivalent to finding solutions of a simple mathematical problem. For each player i, p_i^* must be a solution of:

$$\max_{p_i} u_i = (p_i - c)q_i(p_i, p_j)$$

which can be solved algebraically once the demand function is analytically specified.

However, in this case, an elementary reasoning leads to a classic result known as the 'Bertrand paradox'. The outcome of the game is such that the two firms choose a price equal to their marginal cost: $p_1^* = p_2^* = c$. So, they finally get zero profit at equilibrium. This result is paradoxical since it is hard to believe that two firms in a duopoly would not find a way to manipulate the price in order to benefit from their potential market power and get some supranormal profits.

The proof of this result depends on the following reasoning. Let us consider any situation different from $p_1^* = p_2^* = c$, and verify that this cannot be an equilibrium. Assume first that $p_1^* = p_2^* > c$. Firms share equally the market and individual profits are:

$$\frac{p^* - c}{2}D(p^*) = u_1 = u_2$$

Then each firm has an incentive to slightly underprice its rival. For instance, if firm 1 slightly lowers its price to $(p_1 - \varepsilon)$, it will conquer the whole market and increase its profit since: $u_1^\varepsilon = (p_1^* - \varepsilon - c)$ $D(p_1^* - \varepsilon) > u_1$. But in turn, firm 2 facing this situation would have an incentive to underprice firm 1, and so on. The situation cannot be an equilibrium until one reaches $p_1^* = p_2^* = c$. Even $p_1^* > p_2^* = c$ cannot be an equilibrium since then firm 2 could slightly increase its price, obtain the whole market, and make positive profits; this is impossible since firm 1 would then underprice until finally $p_1^* = p_2^* = c$.

Remark 3

This model highlights a surprising property of NE. A strategy consisting of playing $p_i^* = c$ actually is (weakly) dominated for each player by any other strategy $p_i^* > c$. Strategy $p_i^* = c$ gives a zero payoff whatever the choice of the other player. Strategy $p_i^* = c + \varepsilon, \varepsilon > 0$ would give a positive payoff, subject to the condition that the rival also chooses the same price or a higher one and it never leads to a negative payoff. Of course, choosing this strategy gives a zero profit outcome if the rival chooses the equilibrium strategy $p_j^* = c$. This characteristic of NE is sometimes verified in games allowing an *infinite* number of strategies, as is the case of the Bertrand model. Fortunately this technical property does not have strong repercussions in economics.■

Remark 4

The Bertrand paradox can be solved by dropping one of the three crucial assumptions of the model and by choosing more realistic assumptions concerning pricing behaviour:

- The first solution, suggested by Edgeworth in 1897, consists of considering capacity constraints. More generally, this approach implies technologies with decreasing returns.
- The second solution relies on dropping the assumption of homogeneity of the products in favour of an assumption of differentiation.
- Introducing certain dynamics in the model also evades the paradox. The potential reactions by each firm may generate tacitly collusive behaviour sustained by a credible threat of future losses in case of a 'price war'. However, the proof of this result requires a change of the framework and the use of 'repeated games' (see section 3.3 for a presentation of that class of games).■

3.1.3 Justification and selection of a Nash equilibrium

So far the major idea developed is the following: if there is an obvious (or reasonable) way to play a non-cooperative game, then the outcome necessarily must be a NE. Yet nothing was said about the way players are supposed to act to lead them to such an issue of the game. We are sure only that this issue can be rationalized *a posteriori*. Now, the question is: how to justify the coordination of players to reach such a fixed point? Indeed, various stories can be used in order to explain appearance of a NE. We present now the most often-quoted explanations.

Pre-play negotiation

This first story refers to *direct communication* between players. A common justification for NE analysis holds that such a solution is useful for making predictions when there is a preliminary stage of non-binding negotiation between players. They can gather beforehand to seek to coordinate their plans. Each player, separately and secretly, will thus choose her (or his) strategy. Nothing assures us, of course, that an agreement will come out of this pre-play negotiation stage. Yet, if they agree on a certain outcome, one would expect that this outcome be 'self-enforcing', in the sense that if each player thinks that the other will stick to the agreement, it is in her (or his) own interest to behave accordingly. So, such an agreement generally corresponds to a NE of the game.

It should be emphasized that these agreements are not binding; once the negotiation stage is over, players part and any communication between them is excluded. Each agent chooses her (or his) strategy secretly. She (or he) can then stick or not to the agreed behaviour: nobody will control an eventual defection. Therefore, the game clearly remains non-cooperative.

Following this reasoning, the selection of equilibrium strategies has to occur during pre-play negotiations. The only claim is that any outcome of the game must be a NE; otherwise it will not be *self-enforcing*.

Remark I

Nash (1951) suggested another natural way of treating the pre-play negotiation between the players. In so far as equilibria are interpreted as potential outcomes of pre-play negotiation, it appears natural to extend the initial game to a game in which the negotiation is formalized by the use of explicit moves in the non-cooperative game. Nash names as a 'contest' any game without pre-play negotiation or communication. Today this name is still used by some game theorists (for instance Binmore and Dasgupta, 1986, 13). Moreover, any pre-play negotiation constitutes a 'bargaining game' whose analysis requires an extensive-form description. Those bargaining games will be studied in Chapter 5.■

This first interpretation of a NE as a self-enforcing outcome was supported in the 1980s. Yet it cannot be considered as a realistic representation of many situations of conflict between players who cannot communicate except indirectly. If the players never meet, they cannot directly exchange information and so they cannot explicitly coordinate their strategies. Several reasons can explain this situation: it may be that the material conditions preclude any communication (for instance, if the game involves a large number of players), or that the minimum level of mutual trust required for a dialogue may not be present or, more simply, that some rules may prevent a meeting of the players. How, in this setting, can an outcome of the game about which the players have a great chance of agreement emerge? Several arguments can be proposed to justify the existence of some way of *indirect communication* between players.

Focal-point principle and social conventions

Although Schelling's book *The Strategy of Conflict* was written in 1960, it is surprisingly modern. Schelling examines in detail things such as threats, promises and commitments, which he named 'strategic moves' (these strategic moves will be studied in a formal way in the remainder of the book), but he is also known for his 'coordination games' and the focal-point principle that he introduced for solving these games.

In certain situations, players do seem to 'know', or at least have a good idea, how to choose an action. If we ask them to explain the origins of this choice, we are likely to hear: 'it's just obvious'. The focal-point principle is supposed to express this idea that, very often, the outcome of a game may be selected through a certain number of self-evident reasons.

In many cases, a solution appears as compelling thanks to some qualitative facts or principles like symmetry, efficiency, uniqueness, equity or 'risk-dominance' (see sub-section 7.2.3 of chapter 7 for a definition of this property defined by Harsanyi and Selten, 1988, and based on comparisons of 'riskiness' of equilibria).

Closely related to this argument is the idea of 'social conventions'. Actually, cultural and social norms are supposed to act as focal or salient points, insofar as they incite people to focus on particular equilibria. So, rational solutions of some games depend largely on the culture of the players and a NE can be interpreted as some kind of 'standard of behaviour' (Kreps, 1990a). Therefore, according to this point of view, multiplicity of equilibria just means that there are many 'customs' among the players.

Coordination by an exterior entity

A third scenario often is proposed to justify an equilibrium. It refers to the so-called 'Nashian regulator', a fictitious entity which achieves an outer compatibility between players' actions. This kind of 'mediator' exterior to the game is like the Walrasian auctioneer who provides agents with an equilibrium price vector in a competitive economy. In a preliminary step of the game, this fictitious agent is supposed to be computing and suggesting to the players an equilibrium strategies' set. And this outcome of the game is such that no player has an incentive to unilaterally deviate from this choice.

It should be emphasized, however, that fundamentally this scenario represents a very formal viewpoint: it resorts to an artificial method expressing necessary conditions leading to the emergence of an equilibrium. A more realistic justification for mutual adjustment of players' strategies needs to care more about the 'equilibriating' processes.

Mental equilibriating processes and full rationality of players

Recall that according to the standard 'rationalistic' game theory, equilibrium is achieved only through careful reasoning by the players. The game describes a world of hyper-rational players, in which each player is simulating the mental reasoning of the others. In fact, when considering the whole strategic situation, each player simulates her (or his) own behaviour at the same time that she (or he) simulates the rivals'. Hence, each player simultaneously simulates the Nashian regulator.

Notice that according to this scenario the non-cooperative behaviour which supports a NE is very sophisticated. Each player uses all the relevant information, and correctly perceives the interactions existing between all the players, she (or he) makes right expectations about her (or his) opponents' decisions and she (or he) is fully conscious of the fact that her (or his) own decision influences the other players' choices. In this respect, the concept of a NE can be compared with the notion of *rational expectations equilibrium* (Johansen, 1982). However, like the indeterminate origin of the agents' rational anticipations, the real convergence process towards the equilibrium is not clarified.

The basic assumption is that players' rationality is common knowledge. And according to the scope of players' common knowledge about various elements of the game, several variants of a NE may be studied. But in many games, rationality requires us to impose supplementary restrictions on players' beliefs ('refining' NE) in order to discriminate between multiple equilibria. Notice incidentally that this approach is somewhat disturbing because it introduces a confusion of the problem of *defining* an equilibrium with the problem of *selecting* an equilibrium by reducing the latter to the former. This important topic of 'equilibrium refinement' will be studied later (section 3.3 of Chapter 3 and sections 4.2 and 4.3 of Chapter 4).

Time equilibriating processes and bounded rationality of players

The 'evolutive' scenario of a game describes a dynamic process by means of which equilibrium is achieved through time mechanisms. Repetitions take place in real time and include not only very long-run processes such as the natural selection mechanisms studied by biologists, but also medium and short-run processes of learning, not necessarily based on genetic considerations. In contrast with the rationalistic scenario, in the evolutive scenario players are endowed with more or less limited cognitive and computational capacities, but time is supposed to compensate for the weaker rationality. Some learning processes correspond to bounded rational players who revised initial expectations of opponents future strategies after observing their past actions, according to pragmatic revision rules; but they act more or less myopically since they re-optimize at each step. Other learning processes correspond to still weaker cognitive rationality, since the players are supposed to summarize their experience by a payoff index aggregating the outcomes of each strategy in the past and they apply ameliorating rules which reinforce winning strategies and weaken losing ones. Imitation, experience, routine and trial-and-error mechanisms are very important tools in analysing an equilibrating process.

The 'evolutionary' process represents the extreme situation of a world composed of purely passive automatons selected in very long-term dynamics. In evolutionary GT, each player has no cognitive capacities and acts as an automaton according to behaviour of type: if context C, then strategy S. Furthermore, the biological origin of this story explains that each player is now represented by a sub-population of similar agents. Players meet together in an anonymous way and they reproduce according to various 'reproduction' rules. Players are assimilated to strategies, and players' payoffs are interpreted as fitness. The most efficient players become progressively more numerous by a process of mutation and selection that tends to eliminate players that are relatively less successful. If the dynamic evolutionary process leads to a population, whose members are fractionally distributed, then that distribution is an equilibrium, provided that the evolutionary process works to maintain and restore this distribution in the face of all sufficiently small arbitrary displacements of the population proportions.

When pre-play negotiation is not a realistic representation of a game, the rationalistic and the evolutive scenarios are two conflicting viewpoints of players' coordination on a particular equilibrium. In any case, the equilibrating processes give justifications to a NE or some variants by substituting for the Nash regulator a more plausible individual behaviour and/or collective interaction rules. Indeed they provide two alternative ways of thinking about games. Whereas the first approach assumes that each player deduces how other players will behave from principles of rationality and postulates of common knowledge, the second approach treats a game as a model designed to explain some observed regularity when decision makers interact in real time. This last point of view, opposed to the orthodox and still dominant rationalistic conception, will be explored in Chapter 7, in which evolutionary games and learning models are studied in greater depth.

3.1.4 Failures of the NE concept: non-existence, multiplicity and inefficiency

Even in the simplest non-cooperative games, utilization of a NE as a solution concept raises several difficulties. A pure strategy NE may be non-existent or, on the contrary, there may be too many equilibria. In that case, how should it be possible to predict the most likely outcome of a game? On the other hand, how should we treat the eventual inefficiency of an equilibrium – i.e. the fact that the payoff vector can be improved? Doesn't this inefficiency sound unlikely in a context where players can communicate directly or indirectly before choosing their respective strategy?

Let us illustrate the difficulties mentioned above in a simple example.

Example: the advertising game

Consider two rival firms producing an identical product (or two perfect substitutes) and contemplating launching a promotional campaign for this product. If neither one of them takes the risk of launching such a campaign, their revenues will remain low. If only one of them decides to start advertising, it bears the costs alone and thus gets a lower return than the rival. The problem is to ask what decisions the firms are most likely to take. Are they going to work jointly in the promotional activity?

This situation corresponds to a non-cooperative game in which each of the two players has two strategies: participate in the promotional campaign (P), or not participate (NP). Different cases can be envisaged depending on the numerical values of the payoffs (in that case each player's payoff corresponds to the net revenue of the firm).

First case

Assume that when firm 1 spends alone on advertising, it faces higher costs and gets lower returns than firm 2 in the same situation. Figure 3.4 represents the payoff matrix in that case.

This game has no NE in pure strategy. The situation can be interpreted as follows. If firm 1 decides to launch its advertising campaign, firm 2 has an interest in standing aside. However, firm 1 should also refrain from spending, since it would then end up losing. Yet if firm 1 does not

Figure 3.4 Non-existence of NE

		2	
		P	NP
1	P	$\underline{5}, 5$	$-1, \underline{6}$
	NP	$4, \underline{1}$	$\underline{0}, 0$

participate, firm 2 finds it profitable to advertise. The promotional campaign appears first attractive to firm 1, and then to firm 2. A kind of cycle
appears in this reasoning, and there is no clear solution to the game.

Second case

Assume now a perfectly symmetric outcome. Figure 3.5 describes the
payoff matrix.

There are now two NE in this game, which lead to opposite results for
the players. Firm 1 prefers (NP, P) while firm 2 prefers (P, NP). What
would be the chosen outcome then? Even if the players could communicate, the problem of coordination is not easy to solve, since the two firms
do not identically rank the two equilibria. The matrix of this game is
similar to the one for the Battle of the Sexes (see sub-section 3.1.1 above).

Third case

A symmetric payoff structure still exists here, but now it is more costly for
each firm to spend alone than it is for both of them to remain inactive. The
corresponding payoff matrix is shown in Figure 3.6.

The game now has a single NE (NP, NP). This outcome is indeed very
bad for both firms. The outcome (P, P) would improve their situation and
it is clear that the equilibrium solution is not Pareto-efficient. But there is
no chance of (P, P) being chosen by the firms. Notice that, for each player,
strategy NP is a dominant strategy. Therefore the NE of this game is also a
DSE. The stability property is reinforced, although the outcome is collectively unsatisfactory. Indeed the matrix of this game displays a structure
identical to the one of the Prisoner's dilemma (see sub-section 2.1.2
above).

Figure 3.5   Multiplicity of NE

		2	
		P	NP
1	P	5, 5	**1, 6**
	NP	**6, 1**	0, 0

Figure 3.6   Inefficiency of NE

		2	
		P	NP
1	P	5, 5	−1, **6**
	NP	**6**, −1	**0, 0**

The difficulties for finding the NE of games may seem severe; fortunately there are various extensions and generalizations of this notion which allows us to mitigate these difficulties.

3.2 Extensions: randomization and correlation

3.2.1. Mixed strategy equilibrium

The first difficulty, namely the non-existence of a solution, can be circumvented thanks to the very old procedure dating back to the pioneering works by Von Neumann (1928) on two-player zero-sum games, and to the fundamental article of Nash (1950) on general n-player games. The trick here is to extend the strategic possibilities of the players through the introduction of mixed strategies.

Definition and first interpretation

Consider the game described by the payoff matrix of Figure 3.7. This game is named 'Matching pennies'. In this game, players' strategies are 'heads' and 'tails'. Imagine that each player has a penny and must choose whether to display it with heads or tails facing up. If the two pennies match (i.e. both are heads or both are tails), then player 1 wins player 2's penny; and vice versa when they don't match.

This game has no pure strategy NE. The particular feature of Matching pennies is that each player strives to outguess her (or his) opponent. Several versions of this game also arise in games like poker, battle or baseball, for instance. In such games, there is no NE. However, it is possible to assert that they have a solution when considering mixed strategy.

Imagine that players in the Matching pennies game perceive the game in such a way that they can compute probabilities about the strategies likely to be chosen by the rivals. Consider player 2: he has a clear incentive to keep player 1 uncertain about his own choice of strategy. Keeping player 1 uncertain is equivalent to assuming that 1 has no interest in playing one strategy rather than another. In other words, player 2 will

Figure 3.7 Matching pennies game

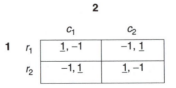

want to choose c_1 with a certain probability p, and c_2 with a probability $(1 - p)$, so that player 1's expected payoff will be identical with strategy r_1 or r_2:

$$p - (1 - p) = -p + (1 - p)$$

or:

$$p = 1 - p = \tfrac{1}{2}$$

In terms of expected payoff, this randomization of strategies by player 2 leads to an undetermined choice for player 1.

Of course, the same reasoning applies to player 1. She can instil doubts into her rival's mind by choosing strategy r_1 with a probability q and strategy r_2 with a probability $(1 - q)$, so that player 2's choice becomes undetermined:

$$-q + (1 - q) = q - (1 - q)$$

or:

$$q = 1 - q = \tfrac{1}{2}$$

This evasive behaviour tends to make each player's choice unforeseeable. In order to avoid having her (or his) choice correctly anticipated by her (or his) rival, each player makes her (or his) play partly 'blind'. Each player creates an uncertainty about her (or his) own decision by randomizing her (or his) strategy choice. *Strategies* should be chosen *at random* (or irrationally) but the *randomization scheme* should be chosen *rationally*. We know that the strategies so designed are named mixed strategies, as opposed to 'pure' strategies which correspond to the actual decisions that the player has to choose (see Definition 5 in 1.3.2, Chapter 1).

The main advantage of this procedure is to solve the existence problem of a NE. In the previous example, although there is no pure strategy NE, there is a mixed strategy NE: $p = (\tfrac{1}{2}, \tfrac{1}{2})$ for the first player and $q = (\tfrac{1}{2}, \tfrac{1}{2})$ for the second. Here, the two players have the same expected payoff: $\tfrac{1}{2}(1) + \tfrac{1}{2}(-1) = 0$. That is an example of a zero-sum game with *zero value* (a game of pure chance or 'fair' game). Nash first established this important result in the case of finite games.

Theorem 2 (Nash, 1950)

Every finite game possesses at least one NE, possibly in mixed strategies.

This result is proved by again using a fixed point theorem. It can actually be considered as a corollary of the theorem proving existence of a pure strategy NE under special conditions, since these conditions are always fulfilled for mixed strategies. Formally the major point is not the introduction of probabilities. Basically what makes a change is the *extension of strategic possibilities* generated by this procedure.

Let us come back to the advertising game studied above, and consider the case where there is no pure strategy NE (Figure 3.4 reproduced on Figure 3.8a).

This game has a mixed strategy NE: $p = (\frac{1}{2}, \frac{1}{2})$ and $q = (\frac{1}{2}, \frac{1}{2})$ which leads to an expected payoff 2 for player 1 and an expected payoff 3 for player 2. The 'payoff region' is represented on Figure 3.8b, where player 1's payoff and player 2's payoff are on the horizontal axis and the vertical axis, respectively. This region is obtained as the convex hull of the set formed by the four points corresponding to the outcomes of the game. In this non-cooperative game, no point in the region can be reached. Introducing mixed strategies makes point (2, 3) accessible.

The previous theorem is concerned only with games in which there is a *finite* set of strategies for each player. Yet, for conceptual or computational reasons it is seldom easy to formalize conflict situations in economics as finite games. Generally agents are supposed to choose among a 'continuum' of strategies (i.e. an infinite set). For instance, firms generally take decisions about prices or output levels, all continuous economic variables (as in Cournot or Bertrand duopoly models). In this case, the

Figure 3.8 Mixed strategy NE

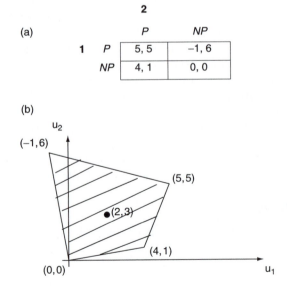

Nash theorem (see sub-section 3.1.1.) states sufficient conditions for existence of at least one pure strategy equilibrium: compactness and convexity of strategy sets, and continuity and quasi-concavity of payoff functions. If we allow for mixed strategies, NE indeed exist in a much wider range of games.

Theorem 3 (*Glicksberg, 1952*)

A game in strategic form $(X_1, \ldots, X_n; u_1, \ldots, u_n)$ has at least one mixed strategy NE if for each player i:

- The strategy set X_i is a (non-empty) compact subset of $\mathbb{R}^n$
- The payoff function u_i is a continuous function.■

These properties are *a priori* straightforward in economics. However, there are some economic situations of games where the assumption of discontinuity of the payoff function is required (it is in particular the case for situations of imperfect competition in industrial organization). Fortunately, Dasgupta and Maskin (1986) were able to solve this difficulty. They proved a theorem of existence for *discontinuous infinite* games.

Remark 1

Technically, computation of NE in a game is greatly simplified by extension to mixed strategies. For the class of two-player zero-sum games computation of mixed strategy equilibria is generally equivalent to resolution of two dual linear programs. For any two-player game, one has to solve two complementary linear programs for which there are well established solution algorithms. For games involving more than two players, it is necessary to use methods of non-linear 'complementarity' and computations become more difficult. However, a number of particular cases have been identified where linear methods can be employed (for a good introduction to computation of an equilibrium by applying linear programming, see Owen, 1995, Chapters 2 and 3).■

Another interpretation of mixed strategies: equilibrium in beliefs

The classical interpretation of mixed strategy equilibrium introduces an element of trickery in the game. Each player strategically creates an uncertainty about her (or his) own behaviour by designing a probability distribution over her (or his) pure strategies. In some real-game situations, this interpretation may seem likely (for instance in certain parlour games, like poker). However, in other games, the procedure can only be an artifice without clear empirical relevance.

There is another interpretation of a mixed strategy equilibrium which gives more empirical credit to the assumption of mixed strategies. It originates from the following fact: in a mixed strategy NE, every player is indifferent with respect to the pure strategies assigned with a *positive* probability. While playing against her (or his) rivals' equilibrium strategies, a player can actually choose any of her (or his) pure strategies. It follows that a mixed strategy equilibrium can just be conceived as an equilibrium situation in which the players are *uncertain* about the actual choices of their rivals. And according to Bayesian logic, this uncertainty gives rise to the introduction of probability distributions over players' pure strategies as their '*beliefs*'. In games with complete information these beliefs are common knowledge, like players' rationality and the structure of the game. Thus, any two players' beliefs about a third player's strategy must be the same and these common beliefs (viewed as mixed strategies) must be in equilibrium.

To summarize, according to this beliefs-based interpretation of equilibrium, a player's mixed strategy represents other players' beliefs about her (or his) realized pure strategy and players' beliefs determine their best response strategies and their optimal expected payoffs. Equilibrium becomes an *equilibrium in beliefs* rather than an *equilibrium in actions*. Here, the concept of mixed strategy contains the idea that even in situations of complete information players are not limited to building certain expectations over their rivals' choices. It would be for simplifying motives that one would like to consider pure strategy equilibria only.

Remark 2

Taking this Bayesian viewpoint has allowed us to improve the knowledge of the epistemic conditions for NE. It was proved that common knowledge of rationality is not really a necessary condition but only a sufficient condition. What is necessary is *common* knowledge of *beliefs* and *mutual* knowledge of *rationality* only (and of the structure of the game, of course). Furthermore, common knowledge of beliefs can be relaxed to 'approximate' common knowledge for 'strict' equilibrium and to mutual knowledge for two-player games. Remember that mutual knowledge is one-order common knowledge, and as such, a very weak condition (for overviews of this belief-based interpretation of equilibrium see for instance Aumann and Brandenburger, 1995, and Dekel and Gul, 1996).■

Remark 3

There is another possible interpretation of mixed strategy equilibrium which also corresponds to an equilibrium *in beliefs* rather than an equilibrium *in actions*. However this interpretation requires a repeated game framework in learning models (these games will be studied further in section 7.3 of chapter 7). When the same game is repeated over time in a long sequence of plays, mixed strategy equilibrium may appear as a result of the learning process of players. Agents choose *pure* strategies which maximize their expected payoffs, given their beliefs. But their beliefs are changing when they observe the decisions of their rivals. In the long run, their beliefs converge towards the NE of the game. And for an external observer *players seem to randomize their choices* but they actually behave in a deterministic way.■

Harsanyi (1973) has proposed another different interpretation of a mixed strategy equilibrium. In his view, a game is a frequently occurring situation in which players' preferences are subject to small random variations. In each event players know only their payoff functions. Then we can rationalize a mixed strategy equilibrium as a kind of summary of the frequencies with which each player chooses her (or his) action. Harsanyi has shown that, if the random variations of payoffs are small, almost any mixed strategy equilibrium of the game is close to a *pure strategy* equilibrium of what is called the associated 'Bayesian game' (this notion will be defined in section 4.1 of chapter 4 for games with incomplete information). Such an interpretation comes to 'purify' the notion of mixed strategy NE.■

Behavioural strategies

When a game is represented in its extensive form, it is possible to considerably simplify the analysis by reasoning with players' 'behavioural strategies' instead of their mixed strategies. In fact, such a simplification can be realized only for games with 'perfect recall'.

In this case, a pure strategy determines a specific decision for every player in each of her (or his) information sets. For instance, if the game involves four information sets and if each time two decisions l and r are possible, one player has a total of $2^4 = 16$ pure strategies. A mixed strategy is a lottery over the set of pure strategies. In the previous game the determination of the mixed strategies requires the specification of 16 probabilities $p_1, p_2, \ldots, p_{16}$.

A behavioural strategy looks like a pure strategy since it shows a player's decision at each of her (or his) information sets. Yet, instead of determining a particular action, it assigns a probability to each of the possible actions. In the previous game, a behavioural strategy required only the specification of four probabilities $q_1, \ldots, q_4$, where q_h, for instance, is the probability that decision l be chosen when the information set h is reached.

The following analogy often is quoted to help understand the relationship between mixed and behavioural strategies. A pure strategy is like a book of instructions in which each page tells us how to play at a particular information set. A library of these books corresponds to the set of strategies. Then a mixed strategy is a probability distribution over books; it provides a random way of choosing from the library. In contrast a behavioural strategy is a single book but it prescribes a random way of choosing an action on each page (Kreps, 1990b).

Choosing a behavioural strategy is thus entirely different from choosing a mixed strategy. In the former case a player postpones her (or his) randomization to the very last moment (until the information set in question is actually reached). In the latter, randomization is done before the games starts. A mixed strategy corresponds to *prior* randomization whereas a behaviour strategy requires *local* randomization. Surprisingly enough, one can show that in games with perfect recall, these two kinds of strategies are equivalent. That is what Kühn's theorem states.

Theorem 4 (*Kühn, 1953*)

In extensive-form games with perfect recall, each mixed strategy can be associated with a behavioural strategy and inversely, each behavioural strategy can be associated with an equivalent mixed strategy (generally several mixed strategies). These strategies are equivalent in the sense that they lead to the same distribution of payoffs between the players.■

From now on, when a game is represented in an extensive form, perfect recall will be assumed and we will use the term 'mixed strategy' to refer to the mixed and behavioural formulations interchangeably.

3.2.2. Correlated equilibrium

The problem of non-existence of a NE can thus be solved in a natural way. We now examine the question of inefficiency. Recall that in the definition of NE, it is supposed that players choose their strategy independently. However, if they engage in pre-play discussion and decide to build a 'signalling device', in some situations players may reach better collective outcomes than those associated with certain NE. This first mechanism of indirect coordination rests on a procedure of randomization which is external to the game. It allows players to partly correlate their strategies. For that reason Aumann (1974) named 'correlated equilibria' the outcome that can be reached thanks to this procedure.

Let us come back to the example of the advertising game presented above, focusing here on the case where there are two NE (Figure 3.5 reproduced as Figure 3.9a).

This game has two pure strategies NE: (*P, NP*) offering the payoffs (1, 6) and (*NP, P*) offering the payoffs (6, 1) But there is also a mixed strategy equilibrium: $p = (\frac{1}{2}, \frac{1}{2})$ and $q = (\frac{1}{2}, \frac{1}{2})$, with an expected payoff (3, 3). The outcome (*P, P*), corresponding to a payoff (5, 5), appears as a good compromise between the different possibilities, but it is not an equilibrium of the game. Nevertheless, we can show that there exist coordination devices leading closer to this solution (we borrow from d'Aspremont, Forges and Mertens, 1989, the description of the coordination devices presented below).

Figure 3.9 Correlated equilibrium

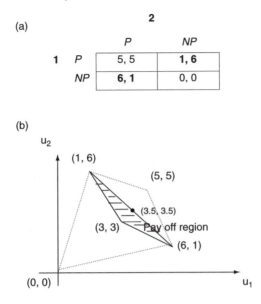

(a)

		2	
		P	NP
1	P	5, 5	**1, 6**
	NP	**6, 1**	0, 0

(b)

First coordination device

The marketing managers of the two companies have a meeting before a decision is to be taken. They agree to base their decisions on the realization of a random event E external to the game and which happens with a probability $\frac{1}{2}$ (for instance, tossing a coin). This event can be observed by the two players. However, before they discover it, they agree to the following strategies:

- If E happens, they will choose the outcome (P, NP)
- If E does not happen, they will choose (NP, P)

(for instance, if heads is drawn, firm 1 alone launches the advertising campaign, and if tails is drawn, firm 2 alone bears the risk).

The final payoff $(3\frac{1}{2}, 3\frac{1}{2})$ results from a convex combination of the two pure strategy NE: $\frac{1}{2}(6, 1) + \frac{1}{2}(1, 6)$. The resulting payoff is not as good as the payoff $(5, 5)$ corresponding to the strategies (P, P); nevertheless it is better than the payoff $(3, 3)$ associated with the mixed strategy NE. The set of all payoffs that can be reached through this procedure is shown in Figure 3.9b inside the shaded region at the 'payoff region' of the game. This set is built as the convex hull of the three points corresponding to the three NE of the game.

The important point to notice here is that the players' strategies defined in the 'extended game' (i.e. the game in which players observe if event E

happens before acting) set up a NE. If *E* happens, firm 1 expects that firm 2 will choose *NP*, and is thus incited to play *P* (1 > 0). If *E* does not happen, firm 1 expects that firm 2 will choose *P*, and is this time interested in playing *NP* (6 > 5).

Second coordination device

Let us now assume that the marketing managers of the two companies meet before taking their decisions, and that they make a joint public announcement. More precisely, assume that they announce two messages: for instance 'yes' or 'no'. Those announcements are simultaneous (in any case, when a firm has to make its own announcement, no one knows in advance the message that will be proposed by its rivals). This procedure represents the first step of the extended game. The second step is the play of the initial game: knowing the other player's proposal, each firm chooses *P* or *NP*.

Player 1 adopts the following behaviour: choose at random 'yes' or 'no', with probabilities ($\frac{1}{2}$, $\frac{1}{2}$); then if the two messages of the first step coincide (yes/yes or no/no), choose *P*; if they don't, choose *NP*. Player 2 adopts a similar behaviour, but he decides to choose *P* when the messages differ (yes/no, no/yes). The strategic form of the extended game is represented in Figure 3.10.

The resulting payoffs are again: ($3\frac{1}{2}$, $3\frac{1}{2}$). This corresponds to a random choice between the two pure strategy NE with probabilities ($\frac{1}{2}$, $\frac{1}{2}$);. Again it is easy to see that the final outcome is a NE of the extended game. Imagine that player 2 does not deviate. Whatever player 1 did during the first step, the probability that the announcements lead player 2 to play *P* is $\frac{1}{2}$. At the second step, player 2 chooses *P* or *NP*. He cannot do better than in each of the initial NE. The same reasoning can be applied to player 1.

Third coordination device

Figure 3.10   Extended game for the second coordination device

		2	
		(1/2) yes	(1/2) no
1	(1/2) yes	P, NP	NP, P
	(1/2) no	NP, P	P, NP

The communication framework now becomes more sophisticated. We assume that the two marketing managers can privately observe some aspects of an external random event. More precisely, three mutually exclusive events E_1, E_2, and E_3 are supposed to be equally probable (i.e. each one has a probability ($\frac{1}{3}$) before players choose. The coming of these events has no *a priori* influence on the strategies chosen by the players. Firm 1 can observe only if E_1 happens and firm 2 has knowledge of event E_2 only. In the game extended by these pre-play events, the two firms can decide to base their choice between P and NP on their preliminary observations.

Consider the following strategies for the players:

- 1 chooses P only if she does not observe E_1
- 2 chooses P only if he does not observe E_2.

The consequences of these strategies are shown in Figure 3.11.

If E_1 happens, player 1 sees it and chooses NP; player 2 learns only that E_2 did not occur and he chooses P. Therefore, E_1 is linked to the outcome (NP, P). Similarly, E_2 is associated with the outcome (P, NP). Finally, if E_3 happens, 1 learns that E_1 did not occur, and 2 learns that E_2 did not occur. Both of them will then play P. The resulting outcome is (P, P), with the associated payoff $(4, 4)$. This outcome results from the convex combination of the payoffs corresponding to the pure strategy NE and the 'cooperative' outcome (P, P):

$$\tfrac{1}{3} (1, 6) + \tfrac{1}{3} (6, 1) + \tfrac{1}{3} (5, 5) = (4, 4)$$

Players' payoffs are improved since they approach the 'cooperative' payoff $(5, 5)$.

In order to verify that these strategies are properly NE, let us imagine that player 2 actually plays according to the rule described above and let us verify if player 1 has no incentive to deviate. The probability that player 2 will choose P if E_1 does happen is 1, while it is $\tfrac{1}{2}$ if E_1 does not happen. Player 1 has a clear interest in choosing NP in the first case $(6 > 5)$, and she has nothing to lose in playing P in the latter. If she chooses P, she would get $\tfrac{1}{2} (5) + \tfrac{1}{2} (1) = 3$; if she chooses NP she would also obtain $\tfrac{1}{2} (6) + \tfrac{1}{2} (0) = 3$.

The major characteristic of this third coordinating device is that players receive *private* correlated signals that are extrinsic to the initial game. Notice however that in this case the fact that the signals are private requires the intervention of a mechanism external to the game.

Figure 3.11 Extended game for the third coordination device

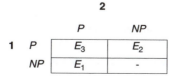

To summarize, the different situations studied above underline the influence that certain variables can exert on players' decision although they have no relation to the initial game. Analysis of the various coordination devices shows that this influence may be beneficial to players in the sense that it allows them to reach payoffs near 'cooperative' ones. During the pre-play negotiation stage, players can exchange messages and observe signals. Those signals and messages represent variables which do not change the payoff functions of the initial game, but they can modify the way players choose between the different strategies. These phenomena are outside the initial game but they are integrated in an extended game for which the solution concept remains NE. The main advantage of such an approach is that it allows one modelling of some kind of cooperation between players in the framework of a non-cooperative game through various coordination devices. The more sophisticated the communication devices during the pre-play stage, the stronger the chances of the players to approach the best outcome. If, on the contrary, no possibility of coordination is available, the players' strategies are totally independent and the only likely outcomes are NE. In that respect, a NE resembles a kind of 'degenerated' correlated equilibrium (For more developments on 'correlated and communication equilibrium', see Forges, 1986, and Forges, 1992).

Remark I

So far, in the presentation of the correlated equilibrium concept, we took the view that correlation is the result of pre-play communication during which players are able to design particular correlated devices. Furthermore, except for the last coordination device, correlation of strategies should be conceived as provided by 'endogenous' correlated signals. It turns out, however, that we can give another interpretation of correlated equilibria. According to the Bayesian approach of GT (Aumann, 1987; Brandenburger and Dekel, 1987; Brandenburger, 1992), even if players do not meet or do not observe exogenous random signals, it is plausible that a correlated equilibrium arises. The usual assumption of statistical independence of beliefs is not at all obvious. In games with more than two players, correlation may result from reasoning as follows: player 3, for instance, thinks that player 2's choice is a function of players 1's beliefs on player 2's choice. There is no collusion between players 1 and 2. Their choices are completely independent but it might be possible to infer information about player 2's choice by observing the strategy used by player 1, so that the traditional independence of strategies vanishes. Notice incidentally that according to this interpretation *mixed strategy equilibria* are just *particular correlated equilibria*: those in which beliefs are independent of strategies.

Remark 2

When we refer to endogenous or exogenous correlated signals in order to classically justify the existence of correlated equilibrium, it is natural to assume that the probabilities assigned to the external event are common knowledge: each player has the same priors. If we agree with the above-mentioned Bayesian interpretation, then the 'common prior' assumption may be more easily removed. In the case where players are allowed to disagree on prior beliefs, one gets a generalization of the initial correlated equilibrium notion that Aumann (1987) called a 'subjective correlated equilibrium' in contrast to the initial 'objective' concept.∎

3.3   Repeated games

If we preclude any communication between players before they take their decisions, is it possible to find other ways permitting some kind of indirect coordination likely to improve the final outcome? In fact, until now we have considered situations in which a very common property of conflicting relations was omitted: very often those relations are *repeated over time*. The study of repeated games precisely examines the new strategic properties resulting from repetition of the game. The essential result is that, under precise conditions, a tacit collusion between players seems perfectly likely to develop. In other words: *repetition facilitates cooperation*. Some outcomes which would require an explicit cooperation between players in a one-shot game can emerge as NE of the repeated game. By allowing repetitions, those games are well adapted for the study of threats of retaliations and their effects in conflicting situations.

3.3.1. Definition

An intuitive presentation of the issue can be given by using the classical game of the Prisoner's dilemma (see the presentation of this game in sub-section 2.1.2 and Figure 3.12).

We see easily that this game has a unique NE in pure strategies (A, A) giving the payoffs $(1, 1)$. Moreover we could say that this equilibrium is particularly robust since it is also a DSE (see sub-section 2.1.1 of Chapter 2, p. 30). However the fact that the players cannot reach the cooperative outcome $(2, 2)$ is often perceived as a kind of paradox. Intuitively, people are convinced of the reasonableness of this outcome only after stressing the fact that the game correctly sums up all aspects of the conflict and it is played only once. People generally think that if for instance the game were played several times, rational players would very likely find a way to agree indirectly to choose the 'cooperative' outcome (P, P). This is

Figure 3.12   Prisoner's dilemma

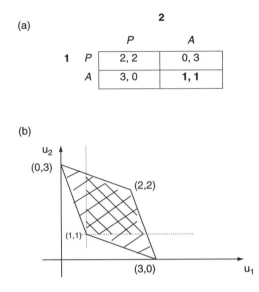

(a)

(b)

precisely the result obtained by analysis of repeated games, first observed in the research of Luce and Raiffa (1957).

Definition 2 (Repeated game)

A repeated game results from finite or indefinite repetition of a game G, called a 'constituent' game or 'stage' game. In the repeated game $G(T)$, a strategy mentions player's decisions at the first stage $t = 1$ and all the decisions that she (or he) will choose at the subsequent stages $(2 \leq t \leq T)$ taking into account the history of the game. At each stage, every player knows the past decisions taken by all her (or his) rivals and all the payoffs of the game for the past stages. Once each player has chosen her (or his) strategy, the game is over.■

Basically, the definition of a NE for a repeated game is not different from what we have seen before; it is just a bit more complex since players' strategies are sequences of *contingent* actions (for each player, strategies take account of all other feasible actions). In games with a *finite* horizon (T finite), the payoff function is equal to the sum of the payoffs at each of the T stages of the repeated game. In games with an *infinite* horizon ($T = \infty$), sometimes called 'supergame', one can not keep this simple criterion (for instance, a uniform payoff 5 at each stage seems preferable to a uniform payoff 1 but both sum up to infinity).

Two measures are then generally used to serve as long-run pay-off functions:

- The limit of average payoffs:

$$\bar{U}_i = \lim_{T \to +\infty} u_i^T = \frac{1}{T} \sum_{t=1}^{T} u_i(t)$$

- The discounted sum of the payoffs:

$$\sum_{t=1}^{\infty} \delta^{t-1} u_i(t) = u_i(1) + \delta u_i(2) + \delta^2 u_i(3) + \dots$$

where $0 \le \delta = 1/(1+a) \le 1$ is the discount factor and $a > 0$ is the corresponding rate of discount, featuring the players' preference for the present. Notice incidentally that the 'limit of average payoffs' criterion treats the periods differently since the value of a given payoff decreases in the time. On the contrary, the 'discount sum of payoffs' criterion treats all periods symmetrically. For the latter, a change in the payoff in a single period can matter while for the former differences in any finite number of periods do not matter. This last property is especially relevant when players put overwhelming emphasis on the long run at the expense of the short run.

On the other hand, very often the sum of the discounted payoffs is replaced by the following formula:

$$U_i^\delta = (1 - \delta) \sum_{t=1}^{\infty} \delta^{t-1} u_i(t)$$

Since the change amounts only to a re-scaling of the measure, maximizing U_i^δ is equivalent to maximizing the discounted sum of payoffs. The advantage of this new normalization is that it gives a long-run payoff directly comparable to the payoffs of each stage by exploiting the stationary structure of the game.

Let us define $G_T(\infty)$ and $G_\delta(\infty)$ as the repeated games respectively associated with the long-run payoff functions $\bar{U}_i$ and U_i^δ.

Remark I

There is another way to conceive the payoff function of a repeated game. One can assume that the game is finite but *indeterminate* (the game is repeated a finite number of times without a precise knowledge of when the end will come). Formally, in this case, we can use the 'discounted sum of payoffs' criterion. Let p be the probability that the game will continue at least for another stage and $(1 - p)$ the probability that the game will end once the decision for the current stage is taken. Then, the expected payoff is:

$$\sum_{t=1}^{\infty} p^{t-1} u_i(t)$$

And for $0 \le p \le 1$, maximizing the expected payoff is formally equivalent to maximizing the discounted payoff over a finite horizon with just δ being replaced by p.■

Remark 2

Another criterion is sometimes introduced to measure the long-run payoff functions in repeated games. According to the 'overtaking criterion' a sequence $\{u_i; (t)\}$ is preferred to the sequence $\{v_i(t)\}$ if and only if:

$$\liminf \sum_{t=1}^{T} u_i(t) - v_i(t) > 0$$

This criterion is interesting because it treats all periods symmetrically and puts emphasis on the long run, but *at the same time* it is sensitive to a change in payoff in a single period (see Osborne and Rubinstein, 1994, 138–9, 149–50).■

The most famous result of the theory of repeated games is the so-called 'folk theorem'.

3.3.2   The folk theorem

Aumann called 'folk theorem' something that game theorists and economists feel they 'knew' all along. Consider the infinite repetition of the Prisoner's dilemma. At each stage, every player can observe her (or his) rival's decision at the previous stage. Thus each agent can render her (or his) choice dependent on what her (or his) rival did previously. This property facilitates a cooperative outcome.

Assume that the two players choose the following strategies:

- Play P as long as the rival plays P
- If the rival plays A, play A forever.

A player who deviates from the outcome (P, P) obtains at this deviation stage a payoff equal to $3 - 2 = 1$. Thereafter, she (or he) will incur a relative loss equal to $2 - 1 = 1$ at each stage. In game $G_T(\infty)$, it is obvious that no player has an interest in deviating. In game $G_\delta(\infty)$ as well, players will stick to the cooperative outcome provided that they are not too impatient (i.e. δ is high enough). Those strategies are thus a NE of the repeated game. Tacit collusion is supported by a threat of retaliation in the future. And this threat is credible, since once her (or his) rival chooses to deviate, it is in the player's self-interest to deviate also $(1 > 0)$.

The strategies so defined are called 'trigger' or 'grim' strategies. They have two properties:

- Players anticipate a repetition of the cooperative outcome as long as all of them chose this solution in the earlier stages
- Strategies include a possibility of punishment for any deviant: infinite reversion to the NE of the stage game G; this punishment would harm all the players, but the dissuasive effect of the threat is strong enough to prevent any deviation by any one.

The most commonly quoted version of the folk theorem was suggested by Friedman (1971). Another notion must be introduced in order to correctly formulate the theorem. Let α_i be the lowest payoff attainable by player i facing a coalition of all her (or his) rivals – i.e. her (or his) security strategy. Any payoff vector u such that: $u_i > \alpha_i$, for all i, is called an 'individually rational'(or sometimes 'enforceable') payoff vector. The folk theorem can then be stated as follows.

Theorem 5 (*Friedman, 1971*)

In repeated game $G_\delta(\infty)$, if u represents a vector of individually rational payoffs in the constituent game, the indefinite repetition of this payoff vector can be generated by some strategies forming a NE of the repeated game (provided that players are not too impatient, i.e. δ is high enough).■

In the Prisoner's dilemma game, we have: $\alpha_1 = \alpha_2 = 1$. The cooperative outcome (P, P) ensures a vector of individually rational payoffs: $(2, 2) > (1, 1)$. The theorem says that the repetition of the outcome (P, P) can be obtained as a NE of the repeated game (provided δ is close enough to 1).

Formal statements and proofs of the folk theorem can be a bit complex but the intuition is clear and obvious. Cooperation of a given sort is held together by a threat to punish those who transgress. As long as the future looms large relative to the present time, such implicit punishments are effective. Part of the complexity of mathematical proofs of the result comes from showing that the threats can be made credible.

In the Prisoner's dilemma, repetition of the outcome (P, P) is only one particular case. Many equilibria can actually be supported by credible threats of retaliation. For the repeated play of the Prisoner's dilemma all the outcomes represented in the double shaded area of Figure 3.12b (p. 92) are NE for game $G_\delta(\infty)$ (the quadrant having its origin at the NE of game G limits the set of individually rational payoff vectors). This set notably includes the cooperative outcome (P, P) but also the one-shot NE (A, A). All the equilibria of game $G_\delta(\infty)$ Pareto-dominate the equilibrium of game G, but this property is not always true.

Another example of a strategy leading also to a NE in $G(\infty)$ can be given. Assume that player 1 chooses the following strategy:

- Play P and A alternatively as long as player 2 chooses P
- Play A forever if player 2 deviates and plays A.

This strategy offers to player 2 the choice between on the one side a payoff equal alternatively to 2 or 0, and on the other side, a payoff equal to 3 (at best, in case of deviation in facing P) and equal to 1 thereafter. For a player patient enough, the 'cooperative' response will be chosen. Player 2 can then propose the following credible threat:

- Play P as long as player 1 plays alternatively P and A
- Play A forever if player 1 deviates from her alternate strategy.

Such players' strategies represent a NE for the repeated game, even if the corresponding outcome is not as good from a collective point of view as the 'cooperative' outcome (P, P).

Another very simple strategy of retaliation often invoked in this context is the so-called 'tit-for-tat' (TFT) strategy (Axelrod, 1984). It requires that a player begin by playing P and then copies whatever move the opponent made at the previous stage. Thus, a player is deviating if and only if the other player herself (or himself) deviated at the previous stage.

It should be emphasized that if the game is repeated over a *finite* number of times set in advance, the reasoning leading to the folk theorem collapses. At the fixed horizon players know that they will be making their last decision. The argument in favour of collusion based on a threat of future retaliation does not work any more. At the penultimate round, they will still have to make a decision in the future. Yet they know that they will choose the non-cooperative solution at the last stage, so there is again no incentive to cooperate at the penultimate stage; and so on back to the first stage. Players never find an incentive to cooperate.

Fortunately this negative result can be mitigated somewhat. In various finite repeated games, modified versions of the folk theorem can be obtained, such as in the case where there are multiple equilibria in the constituent game (Benoit and Krishna, 1985) or in the presence of incomplete information (Kreps *et al.*, 1982; Fudenberg and Maskin, 1986). More details on this topic will be provided later when we present economic applications of repeated games with complete information (sub-section 3.4.2) and with incomplete information (sub-section 4.4.1). On the one hand, some experiments conducted by Axelrod (1984) have shown that a cooperative outcome may emerge from a finitely repeated game, when players adopt a tit-for-tat strategy. Axelrod underpins the interesting properties of tit-for-tat with regard to communication and human relations; it is a simple, clear and forgiving strategy.■

> **Remark 1**
>
> The theory of automata is used to introduce some kind of extreme bounded rationality in repeated games. In a 'machine game', a player is viewed as a stimulus–response machine with (generally) finite memory. Originally the goal was to derive theoretical results from limits on strategic complexity. Yet finite automata games also examine processes of out-of-equilibrium behaviour and search for robust strategies. Aumann (1981) was among the first game theorists to mention this notion (see Marks, 1992, and Osborne and Rubinstein, 1994, Chapter 3, for surveys).■

The last but not the least difficult problem that can arise with a NE lies in the *multiplicity* of outcomes verifying the required properties. Unfortunately there are many games with several NE. In that context, how should we predict a reasonable outcome of a game? It can be argued that this equilibrium selection problem is perhaps the Achilles' heel of non-cooperative GT. Sometimes, the focal-point principle can be very useful for explaining why a particular outcome is chosen. An equilibrium can be singled out by specific properties of the issues (symmetry, efficiency, 'riskiness') or, more generally, by salient features (past experience, background knowledge, anchored habit) acting as conventions. When referring to the rationalistic equilibrium interpretation, this issue falls under the 'refinements' of NE.

3.4 Sub-game perfection: Refinement 1

The main idea is that the properties of a NE are *necessary but not sufficient conditions* for explaining why a particular outcome of a game is chosen in a non-cooperative context. The set of NE is too large and one feels the need to use a stronger criterion in order to discard some of them; we need to 'refine' equilibrium. The literature on equilibrium refinement flourished during the 1980s but unfortunately it is very controversial. Undoubtedly sub-game perfection is the less controversial of the various criteria proposed by game theorists.

The concept of 'sub-game perfect equilibrium'(SPE) is defined for extensive-form games. It comes from a combination of the idea of self-enforcing and stable equilibrium with the normative principle of backward induction by rational players. It lends itself to a clear and illuminating interpretation: sub-game perfection consists of discarding NE associated with players' threats and promises that are not credible. It turns out that 'credibility' is a central issue of any dynamic game.

3.4.1 Sub-game perfection and backward induction

The concept of SPE rests on an extension of the principle of backward induction that was examined above as a normative criterion of resolution of extensive-form games with perfect information. More precisely one may view sub-game perfection as a combination of *backward induction* and *Nash equilibrium*.

Consider the extensive form game described in Figure 3.13.

This game has two NE in pure strategies: (l_1, r_2) and (r_1, l_2). Applying backward induction leads to the selection of one of them. At the node (y) of the game tree, player 2 has a choice between l_2 and r_2. He will choose l_2 which provides a larger payoff $(1 > 0)$. At the node (x), player 1 has a choice between l_1 and r_1. Anticipating player 2's choice at node (y), she chooses r_1 which gives her a higher payoff $(3 > 2)$. Only one of the two NE, namely (r_1, l_2), passes the test of backward induction.

The argument leading to the rejection of (l_1, r_2) goes as follows. Assume that the two players had agreed to play this pair of strategies. If player 1 expects that player 2 will stick to the agreement, then it is actually optimal for her to play l_1 (since $(2 > 0)$). However is it sensible to imagine that player 1 will believe in player 2's promise to abide by the agreement? The answer is unambiguously negative. Indeed, since l_2 secures a higher payoff than the one obtainable with r_2, if node (y) is reached $(1 > 0)$ player 2 will rather play l_2 if he is allowed to choose. Hence, player 1 will prefer to play r_1, also breaking the agreement. The only self-enforcing agreement corresponds to outcome (r_1, l_2).

To summarize, equilibrium (l_1, r_2) is discarded because it implies an *irrational* behaviour of player 2 at an *out-of-equilibrium* node. Hence, what this phenomenon reveals is that NE requires that players have a rational behaviour only at nodes of the tree actually reached when they play their equilibrium strategies. At any other node their behaviour can be more or less arbitrary. The strategy chosen by a player does not have any effect on her (or his) payoff, but the choice made by a player at an out-of-equilibrium node may have an effect on the equilibrium strategies of the other players. While searching to evaluate the expected payoffs corresponding to other possible strategies, these players must take into account the consequences

Figure 3.13   The principle of backward induction

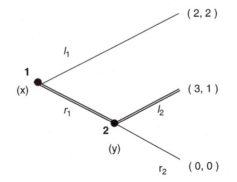

of their decisions (out-of-equilibrium node becoming an in-equilibrium node).

Equilibrium (l_1, r_2) can be interpreted as a 'threat equilibrium'. Player 2 threatens to punish player 1 by playing r_2, if she does not play l_1. Yet this threat is not credible since player 2 will not implement it when the moment comes. Once player 1 has chosen r_1, player 2 will prefer to play l_2.

The principle of backward induction is actually a criterion of refinement of NE: it imposes a supplementary notion of rationality which allows us to pick a particular NE.

Remark I

It should be emphasized that the principle of backward induction does not improve efficiency: a NE passing the test of backward induction may be Pareto-dominated by a rejected NE. The extensive-form game presented in Figure 3.14 illustrates this difficulty.

This game has three NE: (L_1l_1, R_2), (L_1r_1, R_2), and (R_1l_1, L_2). The corresponding payoffs are $(1, 1)$ for the first two and $(2, 2)$ for the third. The only NE resisting backward induction is (L_1r_1, R_2) giving $(1, 1)$. At node (z), player I chooses $r_1 (0 > -1)$. At node (y), player 2 chooses R_2 knowing that I will choose r_1 at (z) $(3 > 2)$. At node (x), I chooses L_1 knowing that 2 will choose R_2 at (y) and that she herself will choose r_1 at (z) $(1 > 0)$. This equilibrium is Pareto-dominated by equilibrium (R_1l_1, L_2) giving $(2, 2)$. However the latter is discarded since player I cannot commit herself to play l_1 as her second decision. Both players know that I will play r_1 if node (z) is reached. It is thus illusory to imagine that they could both obtain a payoff equal to 2. If player I chooses R_1, she will end up with a zero payoff. She will then prefer to choose L_1 at (x) $(1 > 0)$. Therefore (R_1l_1, L_2) is a non-credible threat equilibrium.■

Figure 3.14   Backward induction and Pareto-inefficiency

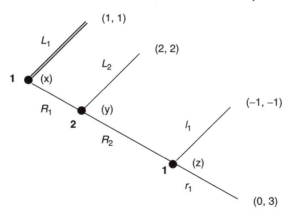

A particular class of non-cooperative games, often encountered in economic situations, offers an illustration of this first criterion of refinement of NE.

3.4.2 Stackelberg equilibrium: a classical application in industrial organization

We envisage a game in which the players choose sequentially (i.e. at different stages of the game), each player taking only one decision. One of the rules of the game specifies the order of intervention of the players. The fundamental characteristic of this class of games lies in the *asymmetry between the players*. To simplify matters, we will consider only the case of two players. This category of games is sometimes called the 'Stackelberg game'. Thus a Stackelberg game is simply a sequential game with perfect information in which players in turns make only one decision (that is, a two-stage game in the case of two players). One can also solve Stackelberg games by working backward, i.e. with the help of backward induction.

Backward induction and Stackelberg games

In a Stackelberg game, player i, who plays first, behaves as a 'leader'. She anticipates the reactions of her rival and takes them into account before choosing her own strategy. The other player j chooses his strategy after the leader's strategy has been revealed. He takes as given this strategy and behaves accordingly as a 'follower'. The game of Figure 3.13 (p. 98) is an example of a Stackelberg game (player 1 is the leader), in which the outcome (r_1, l_2) is a NE which passes the test of backward induction. In a Stackelberg game, such a NE is called 'Stackelberg equilibrium'.

The conditions of existence for a pure strategy Stackelberg equilibrium are weaker than those required for the existence of a NE in a simultaneous game. The usual assumptions in microeconomics (compactness of the strategy sets, continuity of the payoff functions) are sufficient. Hence, the existence of a pure strategy Stackelberg equilibrium is ensured in a sequential game, without the need of assumptions like convexity of the strategy sets and quasi-concavity of the payoff functions.

When the order of intervention of players is no longer given *a priori*, a Stackelberg game gives rise to specific forms of behaviour, which can be analysed in terms of *strategic exchange of information*.

Let L_i be player i's maximal payoff when she (or he) is leader. If payoffs (L_1, L_2) are incompatible, each player has an incentive to move first, forcing the rival to face this commitment. This phenomenon reflects what is known as the 'competition for the first move'. Both players will try to let their rival know their planned strategy before the latter actually plays. Bidding and higher bidding takes place, in terms of commitment results. In the competition for the first move, the leader is the winner. However, in certain games, the leader may have a disadvantage. It is the follower who benefits from the strategic interdependence. One can then talk of a 'competition for the second move'.

Let F_i be the maximal payoff of player i, when she (or he) is a follower. If payoffs (F_1, F_2) are incompatible, each player has an incentive to discover her (or his) rival's strategy before choosing her (or his) own. Each player wants to keep her (or his) own choice secret, while searching to guess the choice of her (or his) rival. So there is a climate of mutual distrust. Everyone tries to deceive the rival by sending false information. Every player tries to spy on the rival, while fearing being spied upon by her (or him). As the competition for the first move, the critical element is the real level of commitment of the players. In the competition for the first move, each player wants to commit herself (or himself) as quickly as possible. In the competition for the second move, each player wants to delay her (or his) choice as long as possible, in order to play in the last position and use all the information available on the rival's choice. Two-player zero-sum games with no value are good examples of Stackelberg games giving rise to competition for the second move ($\alpha_1 < \alpha_2$). In this type of game, the player choosing second wins whereas the player choosing first loses.

Of course, a Stackelberg game cannot simultaneously be in a situation of competition for the first move and competition for the second move. Only if $L_1 = F_1$ and $L_2 = F_2$ are the players indifferent between the position of leader and of follower. This kind of situation happens, for instance, when the game has a DSE.

Remark 1

The choice between the position of a leader or a follower can be considered as the first step of an extended game in which the order of intervention of the players is not exogenous any more. One can also imagine that, in this first step, the players have a larger set of options, in the sense that they can also choose between simultaneous or sequential actions.■

Stackelberg first used this concept of equilibrium to study a dynamic model of duopoly. Let us consider its classical application in industrial organisation.

Application: Stackelberg model of duopoly

Two firms produce a homogeneous good with a constant marginal cost and without fixed costs. The cost function is:

$$C_i = cq_i, \ i = 1, 2$$

As in the Cournot duopoly, the firms choose the quantities, that are continuous strategies. Yet here, their decisions are sequential. Firm 1 chooses first a quantity q_1, then, firm 2, knowing q_1, decides about q_2.

It is clearly a Stackelberg game with two players, and player 1 acting as the leader. The payoff of firm i corresponds to its profit function:

$$u_i(q_i, q_j) = q_i[p(q_1, q_2) - c]$$

where $p(q_1, q_2) = a - (q_1 + q_2)$ is the equilibrium market price.

The Stackelberg equilibrium of this game is given by applying the backward induction principle. The best response of firm 2 to any quantity chosen by the leader is first computed. It is given by $\bar{q}_2(q_1)$, which is a solution of the problem:

$$\max_{q_2} u_2(q_1, q_2) = q_2[a - q_1 - q_2 - c]$$

which gives:

$$\bar{q}_2(q_1) \quad = \frac{1}{2}(a - q_1 - c) \text{ if } q_1 < a - c$$

Notice that this expression is very similar to the best response of player 2 in the simultaneous move model of Cournot duopoly. The difference is that, in the simultaneous game, the expression represents the best response of 2 to a *hypothetical* quantity simultaneously chosen by 1, while in the sequential game, it is really the best response of 2 to the quantity *actually* chosen by 1.

Firm 1 (the leader) anticipates this behaviour of firm 2 (the follower) and determines its production level q_1 according to $\bar{q}_2(q_1)$. So, at the first stage of the game, q_1 is the solution of the problem:

$$\max_{q_1} u_1(q_1, \bar{q}_2(q_1)) = q_1[a - q_1 - \bar{q}_2(q_1) - c] = q_1\left[\frac{a - q_1 - c}{2}\right]$$

which gives:

$$q_1^* = \frac{a - c}{2}$$

Substituting this value in the previous equation, yields the equilibrium strategy of firm 2:

$$q_2^* = \frac{a - c}{4}$$

It is then easy to calculate the corresponding profits for each firm at Stackelberg equilibrium:

$$u_1^* = \frac{(a-c)^2}{8}, \; u_2^* = \frac{(a-c)^2}{16}$$

In this Stackelberg game, the leader gets a higher payoff than does the follower.

3.4.3 Sub-game perfection in general games

The argument used to find the equilibrium in the Stackelberg duopoly model applies quite generally to all games with perfect information. For games with imperfect information, (i.e. when the game has several stages during which the players can make possibly simultaneous choices), the principle defined above no longer applies. The concept of sub-game perfection attempts to generalize this principle to general games in extensive form.

Definition and existence

This criterion of refinement of NE was introduced by R. Selten (1965). Let us introduce it with a simple example. Consider the game represented in Figure 3.15.

It is a game with imperfect information since player 1 cannot discriminate between nodes (z) and (z') in her information set. She does not know if player 2 chose L_2 or R_2 when she takes her decision concerning the choice between l_1 and r_1. The principle of backward induction cannot be applied since at (z), player 1 would chose $l_1(1 > 0)$ while she would chose r_1 at $(z')(5 > 0)$.

The method suggested by Selten exploits the fact that the branch of the game tree starting at node (y) is itself a game: it is called a 'sub-game' starting at (y). A sub-game can also be interpreted as reflecting some features of the decisions taken by the players, in particular simultaneous

Figure 3.15   Sub-game perfect equilibrium

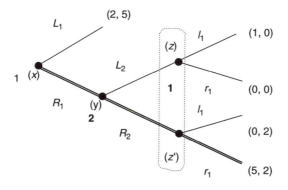

actions. Since it is not possible to firmly commit oneself in a non-cooperative game, the behaviour of the players in a sub-game must be determined independently of the rest of the game. Consequently, a NE of the game must induce a NE in a sub-game. If this proposition were not true, at least one of the players would have an incentive to deviate, once the branch of the game tree corresponding to this sub-game were reached.

The sub-game beginning in (y) can be represented by the bi-matrix game in Figure 3.16.

This sub-game has a single NE: (r_1, R_2). Once this equilibrium is determined, it is easy to calculate the equilibrium for the *whole* game by applying the principle of *backward induction*. At node (x), player 1 chooses R_1, knowing that at node (y), player 2 will choose R_2 and that she will herself choose $r_1 (5 > 2)$. Equilibrium $(R_1 r_1, R_2)$ is called the 'sub-game perfect equilibrium' (SPE) of the game.

Notice that $(R_1 r_1, R_2)$ is not the unique NE of this game. The outcome $(L_1 l_1, L_2)$ is also a NE. However this equilibrium implies a *non-credible threat* from player 2 (who threatens to play L_2 if player 1 chooses R_1), and thus it cannot hold.

Until now, the notion of sub-game has been loosely introduced as corresponding to any branch of the game tree which remains to be explored, each time that a node is reached for which the history of the game leading to this node is common knowledge. A more rigorous definition of the notion is now required.

Definition 3 (*sub-game*)

A sub-game of an extensive-form game has the following properties:

- It begins at a node of the tree corresponding to an information set reduced to a singleton (the set contains only one node)
- It encompasses all parts of the tree following the starting node
- It never divides an information set (if y is a node following x, which belongs to the sub-game starting at x, any other node of the information set to which belongs y must also be a part of the given sub-game).■

It is then possible to give a rigorous definition of a SPE.

Figure 3.16 NE of the sub-game

		L_2	R_2
1	l_1	1, 0	0, 2
	r_1	0, 0	5, 2

(column header label: **2**)

Definition 4 (*Sub-game perfect equilibrium*)

A NE is a SPE if the strategies of the players yield a NE in every sub-game, whether these sub-games are reached with a positive probability at the equilibrium or not.■

It follows immediately from this definition that in extensive-form games a SPE is necessarily a NE but the inverse is false. If we define **NE** as the set of Nash equilibria and **SPE** as the set of sub-game perfect equilibria in a game, the relationship between these sets is as follows:

SPE ⊆ NE

We should emphasize that this concept is defined in *general* games. Unfortunately the following result can be proved only for games of *perfect* information.

Theorem 6 (*Selten, 1965*)

Every finite extensive-form game of perfect information has at least one pure strategies SPE, and if no ties occur in players' payoff, then there is a unique SPE.■

In this class of game, the concept of sub-game perfection actually coincides with backward induction. Yet notice that SPE are defined without reference to terminal nodes; therefore this concept can be applied to *infinite* games too.

Remark 1

In a NE each player chooses a strategy of best response to the strategies of the other players, so that no single player ever uses a strictly dominated strategy. The criterion of sub-game perfection extends this principle to all the sub-games: in a SPE, no player ever uses a strictly dominated strategy in every sub-game.■

Remark 2

In many examples of games, this criterion appears effective to significantly reduce the number of NE by eliminating the more unlikely ones. However it is still ineffective in the class of repeated games, which are so important in economic applications.

For repeated games, there is an obvious division in sub-games, since at the end of each repetition, players can observe what their rivals had played. If $G(T)$ is the game corresponding to the T times repetition of the same constituent game G, then for any $t < T$, $G(t)$ is a sub-game of $G(T)$. Every NE of the one-shot game is also a NE of the repeated game and every SPE of the one-shot game is also a SPE of the repeated game: it simply repeats the equilibrium strategies in every repetition. Thereby, repetition of a game can not restrict the set of equilibrium outcomes. On the contrary, repetition typically gives rise to a proliferation of outcomes. Indeed it is what the 'folk theorem' teaches. This famous result, which was proved originally for NE, applies to SPE too.

'Perfect folk theorems' were proved in the literature about infinitely repeated games with complete information for the three generally used forms of the payoff function, which are based on the 'limit of means', 'discounting' or 'overtaking' criterion (see sub-section 3.3.1 of Chapter 3, pp. 93–4, for a definition of these payoff functions; Sorin, 1992, Pearce, 1992, and Osborne and Rubinstein, 1994, Chapter 8, give surveys of this literature).∎

Remark 3

In repeated games, the past influences current decisions and future actions only because all players believe that past play matters. The more complex games with a changing 'physical environment' have to be modelled as 'dynamic systems' in which the past has a direct influence on current opportunities. In the particular class of 'Markovian' (or 'transitive') systems, the whole history at each period can be summarized in the game by a 'state'. So players' current payoffs are a function only of this state and of current actions. In this framework, we focus on 'Markov' or 'state–space' strategies.

When we use a continuous-time model, we obtain a particular class of games named 'differential games'. As the moves are continuous in these games, the strategies are generally thought of as defining a differential motion for the payoffs. At each moment of time, players make choices (the 'control variables') and the motion of the outcomes (the 'state variables') is influenced by these choices according to a system of differential equations. The differential game continues until termination, which is assumed to occur when the state variables reach some values, called the 'terminal states'. It is then possible to work backward from the terminal state to an initial state by differential equations and one can define an exact version of a SPE in the differential game called a 'closed-loop' NE. As with Cournot, Bertrand and Stackelberg equilibria, this is not really a new equilibrium concept but rather a way of describing the equilibria of a particular class of games.

Differential games distinguish another type of strategy called 'open-loop'. An open-look strategy refers to the case where players commit themselves at the beginning of the game to a path that is not supposed to change in the future, while a closed-loop strategy is a decision rule which prescribes an action as a function of time and of the state variable (i.e. at each point in the time each agent can observe the value of the state variable and choose her (or his) best action accordingly). An open-loop NE is then a set of open-loop strategies such that every player has committed herself (or himself) to the best response to the paths to which the other players have committed themselves. A closed-loop NE is a set of closed-look strategies such that for every initial condition each strategy is a best response to the other players' strategies.

There are many economic situations where such a modelling is required. For instance, the state variable can be capacity (Fudenberg and Tirole 1983, Reynolds 1987), or product price in a situation of price stickiness (Fershtman and Kamien, 1987). (For a good introduction to differential games see Fudenberg and Tirole (1991, Chapter 13) and Owen (1995, Chapter 5). Dockner et al. (2000) offers a more recent and complete presentation of differential games with economic applications)■

Limits of sub-game perfect equilibrium

One reason why SPE is a good solution concept for a multi-stage game is because out-of-equilibrium behaviour is irrational in a non-perfect equilibrium. It turns out, however, that this criterion is not always sufficient to discard irrational behaviour in all games with imperfect information. In this general class of games, sub-game perfection loses much of its selection ability. Consider for instance the classic 'Selten's horse' game.

The Selten's horse game

This three-player game is represented in Figure 3.17 in both extensive form and strategic form. Notice incidentally that in the strategic-form game, strategies of player 3 are *matrices*.

This game has two pure strategies NE: (R_1, R_2, L_3) and (L_1, R_2, R_3). These two equilibria are marked both in the strategic-form game (Figure 3.17c) and in the extensive-form game (Figure 3.17a and 3.17b, respectively). We can show that the latter implies an irrational behaviour of player 2 at the node (y), which is not reached in equilibrium.

If the information set of player 2 were actually reached, this player would have an incentive to renege on any agreement on this equilibrium. If player 2 chooses L_2, instead of R_2, player 3, being in the impossibility of discriminating between (z) and (z') in her information set, will not notice that the agreement has been violated and will continue in playing R_3. It follows that by playing L_2, player 2 obtains a larger payoff than by playing $R_2(4 > 1)$, and thus 2 will play L_2 (and not R_2) if (y) is reached. Correctly anticipating this behaviour, player 1 will play R_1 (and not L_1) since she expects in this case a higher payoff $(4 > 3)$. Finally, the equilibrium (L_1, R_2, R_3) represents a non-credible threat by player 2. This equilibrium is not rejected by the criterion of sub-game perfection because simply there exists no 'proper' sub-game (that is a sub-game *different from the game itself*). Trivially one could say that in this game any NE is a SPE.

The difficulty which arises when a game has no 'proper' sub-game is that players have no way of knowing the node at which play begins. They accordingly have no way of assessing the effects their choices have on the

Figure 3.17   SPE and irrational behaviour

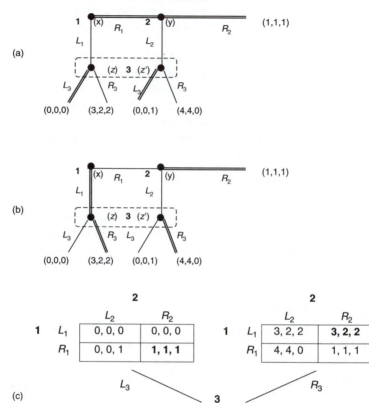

terminal node. As a result, they cannot evaluate the payoff implications of their choices.

It should be emphasized that this negative result is quite general for all games with *incomplete* information. In this class of games even if the players can observe the decisions of all their rivals at each stage of the game (multi-stage games with observed actions), since they don't know the type of the others, the branch of the game tree starting at a particular node cannot be a sub-game.

These limits of sub-game perfection call for the definition of additional refinements of NE in games of imperfect information. Before outlining this problem with the help of stronger refinement criteria in Chapter 4, we will illustrate another weakness of the SPE by examining a well-known 'toy game'.

The centipede game

The centipede game is a perfect information game imagined by Rosenthal (1981). It offers a good illustration of weakness of sub-game perfection by

Figure 3.18 The centipede game

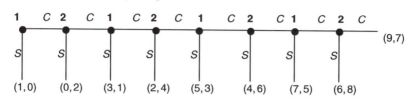

enlightening the conflict between common sense and empirical evidence on the one hand and by zealous application of this theoretic concept solution on the other.

Two players are involved in a process that they alternately have the opportunity to stop. Each prefers the outcome when she (or he) stops (S) in any stage to that in which the other player does so in the next stage if she (or he) continues (C), although each player may obtain a still better payoff if the process is not halted in either of these stages. After a finite number of stages, the process ends. An eight-stage particular version of this game is presented in Figure 3.18. Of course, the name 'centipede' comes from the shape of the game tree.

It is easy to see that the game has a unique SPE in which each player chooses S at each stage. At the last node, player 2 will choose S, because that gives him 8 instead of 7. Thus, in the next-to-last node, if 1 chooses C she will gain 6, whereas if she chooses S her payoff is 7; therefore 1 prefers S. At the next-to-next-to-last node, 2 chooses S, getting 6 instead of a payoff 5 if he continues, and so on. Finally, sub-game perfection predicts that player 1 will begin the game by choosing to stop immediately, getting 1 and giving 0 to player 2.

In the equilibrium each player believes that the other player will choose to stop at the next stage, even if she (or he) has chosen to continue many times in the past. Evidently such beliefs are not intuitively appealing, except perhaps if the number of stages is very small. Moreover, it turns out that experimental evidence disproves this prediction: no player ever stops in the first stage (see section 8.2 of Chapter 8). Notice however that this paradoxical outcome may be deleted when we lightly reduce the condition of common knowledge towards players' rationality (Aumann, 1995). But this modification implies that we study games with *incomplete* information.

3.5 Applications

3.5.1 Sequential games and strategic commitment

Commitment is a very subtle form of strategic move which lends itself to rich applications in economics. According to Schelling 'the essence of these tactics is some voluntary but irreversible sacrifice of freedom of choice. They rest on the paradox that the power to constrain an adversary may depend on the power to bind oneself...' (Schelling, 1960, 22). Everyone has experienced in real life the fact that a threat is more credible if there is no choice but to carry it into effect when the moment comes. Therefore it may often be worthwhile to suppress any exit from an announced plan of action.

There are many applications of this argument in economics. For instance, a firm enjoying a monopolistic position can credibly deter a potential entrant by building irreversible extra capacity which implies that a threat of flooding the market (and thus rendering entry unprofitable) would be executed in the case of entry (Spence, 1977; Dixit, 1980; Fudenberg and Tirole, 1984). A government may change an international oligopolistic market outcome to favour a domestic firm by announcing a subsidy policy in its favour. In this case the credibility of the threat, which would not be rational in general to carry into effect, comes from the nature of the political decision process: ratification by votes in representative assembly and slowness in making a new decision (Krugman, 1984; Brander and Spencer, 1985).

Most models built along these lines have the same basic structure. For simplicity and tractability the time structure is generally reduced to two periods. In the first period, the agents take 'strategic' decisions about variables whose influence lasts over the second period: capacity, research and development (R & D), advertisement and so on. In the second stage, the agents compete on 'tactical' issues, i.e. shorter-run decisions like price or quantity choices. The concept of sub-game perfection is used for solving these games, so that the second-period equilibrium must be a NE whatever actions have been chosen before. First, the second-period game is solved for any value of the strategic variable and then, by backward induction, we get the SPE.

We will consider below three examples of models sharing the same logic stated above. We chose to increase the level of technical complexity from the first model to the third.

Entry deterrence: the case of a multinational firm

'Entry deterrence' is a classical question in industrial organization (this topic in general is summarized in Tirole, 1988, Chapter 8). We present here a less well-known particularisation of entry-deterrence in the case of a multinational firm.

Let us consider a situation in which a domestic firm serves as a monopolist in a foreign country (the following model owes a lot to Smith, 1987). It operates a plant in the domestic country, after having sunk a firm-specific cost F and could have started a new plant abroad requiring it to sink plant-specific costs f. On the other hand, the firm could serve the foreign market by exporting, which would have required no further sunk costs but only supplementary variable costs like transportation costs or other obstacles to trade (like tariff, exchange, and non-tariff barriers (NTBs)). We assume that the profit of becoming multinational is below that of exporting. Formally let us call Π_{ME} the domestic firm's profits abroad when it exports the goods and Π_{MI} its profit when it becomes multinational:

$$\Pi_{ME} = P(x)x - (c + t)x > \Pi_{MI} = P(x)x - cx - f$$

Notice that c is assumed to be the same in the two cases, but the optimal level of x will not be identical. From the concavity of the revenue function it is clear that: $x_E < x_I$ (Smith, 1987, 91).

Now, let us imagine that the domestic firm fears the entry of a potential rival in the foreign country (a foreign firm whose variables are noted with a *). This potential entrant would have to incur both sunk costs, firm-specific costs F, and plant-specific costs f.

In the case of entry, two types of duopoly are possible, one with the domestic firm still exporting, and another with the domestic firm becoming multinational. Since the marginal cost function would differ for the domestic firm, the two Nash–Cournot equilibria would be different (see Figure 3.19 where $R(.)$ are the reaction functions of the two firms).

Let us call $\Pi_{DE}, \Pi^*_{DE}, \Pi_{DI}, \Pi^*_{DI}$ the profits of the domestic and of the foreign firm respectively in case of an exporting domestic firm and in the case of a multinational:

$$\Pi_{DE} = P(x_E + x^*_E)x_E - (c + t)x_E$$

$$\Pi^*_{DE} = P(x_E + x^*_E)x^*_E - cx^*_E - (F + f)$$

Figure 3.19 Cournot–Nash equilibria

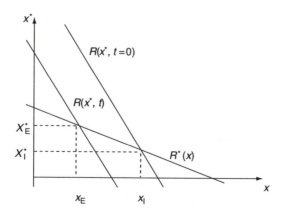

$$\Pi_{DI} = P(x_I + x_I^*)x_I - cx_I - f$$

$$\Pi_{DI}^* = P(x_I + x_I^*)x_I^* - cx_I^* - (F + f)$$

Let us assume that $\Pi_{DE} > \Pi_{DI}$, which is a reasonable assumption to make when, as noted above, $\Pi_{ME} > \Pi_{MI}$. In other words, we assume that the presence of a competitor for our domestic firm does not change the ordering of its profits between the option export and the option investment. So it seems that whatever the choice of the potential entrant (enter or not) the best choice of the domestic firm is still to export rather than to become multinational. However we have to consider more deeply the extensive form of the game to analyse the equilibrium.

The domestic firm is exporting abroad because $\Pi_{ME} > \Pi_{MI}$. Now it contemplates a potential entrant who can either enter (strategy E) or not enter (strategy N) and it can itself either accommodate it (strategy A) or fight it (strategy F). Let us call Π_{WE} and Π_{WE}^* the payoffs in case of a price war between the two firms. Of course, these profits are inferior to the duopoly Cournot profit, that is $\Pi_{WE} < \Pi_{DE}$ and $\Pi_{WE}^* < \Pi_{DE}^*$. The extensive form of the game is shown in Figure 3.20.

The game is solved by backward induction. The issue (N, F) is a NE of the game but it is not sub-game perfect because it rests on a non-credible strategy. It is not in the domestic firm's interest to fight if the foreign firm enters. The only SPE is (E, A). So in the case of exporting, the outcome would be: Π_{DE}, Π_{DE}^*.

Now consider a broader view of the extensive game by reintroducing the possibility of becoming multinational, which had been discarded on the grounds of being dominated by the export strategy (Figure 3.21).

A possibility of strategic deterrence appears here. Becoming multinational involves spending an irreversible cost f on the one hand and reduces the marginal cost from $(c + t)$ to only c on the other. The latter change moves the NE in favour of the domestic firm (see Figure 3.9), the former diminishes the domestic firm's profit. The shift of NE along the

Figure 3.20   The extensive form of the multinational firm game

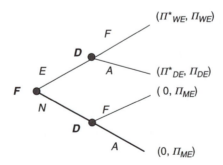

Figure 3.21   An extended form of the multinational firm game

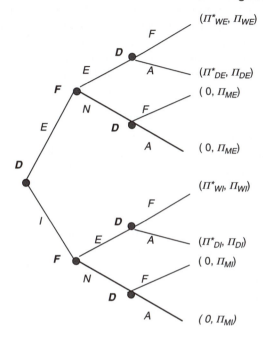

foreign firm reaction function may be enough to cause negative profits in case of entry. If this is the case, that is if $\Pi^*_{DI} < 0 < \Pi^*_{DE}$, then the new SPE is $(\Pi_{MI}, 0)$. By investing abroad and becoming a multinational the domestic firm deters the entry of the potential foreign rival. Note however that this result requires two basic conditions:

$$\Pi^*_{DI} < 0 < \Pi^*_{DE}$$

$$\Pi_{DE} < \Pi_{MI}$$

If $\Pi^*_{DI} > 0$, then the previous result is no longer true because the foreign firm would then enter and the domestic firm would then prefer to export in order to get Π_{DE} rather than Π_{DI}. Yet even in this case, it may happen that becoming multinational is still an entry-deterrent strategy. This would be the case if the sunk costs f could help the domestic firm in case of a price war (for instance, by facilitating a flood of the market through less expensive exports) and diminish the duopoly profits so that $\Pi_{DI} < \Pi_{WI}$. The threat of fighting after entry would then become credible.

An interesting implication of the above outcome is that starting with a situation where $\Pi_{MI} < \Pi_{DE}$, and where the equilibrium is a duopoly with exports of the domestic firm, any increase in the obstacles to trade t, like an increase in a tariff rate or an administrative obstacle to crossing the border may reverse the relation between Π_{MI} and Π_{DE} and thus shift the equilibrium from (Π_{DE}, Π_{DE}^*) to a monopoly $(\Pi_{MI}, 0)$. The loss of the foreign country in such a protectionist policy would be obvious: loss of the foreign firm's profits and decrease in their consumer's surplus owing to the increase in price after the move from a duopoly to a monopoly.

Strategic trade policy (Laussel and Montet, 1994)[*]

Let us consider here the case where the domestic firm and the foreign firm are both incumbents and compete in quantities (Brander and Spencer, 1985). In the first stage the domestic government chooses unilaterally a constant export subsidy s per unit of output. Then, in the second stage, a NE in quantities between the two firms (Cournot equilibrium) takes place.

For the sake of simplicity, let the two firms produce a homogeneous product. Assume that the inverse demand function is $p(Q)$ where Q is total industry output and $p'(Q)$ is negative. Suppose, moreover, that the two firms have the same total cost functions $C(Q)$ with $C'(Q) > 0$ and $C''(Q) \geq 0$. Finally let $p'(Q) + Qp''(Q) \leq 0$. The Cournot–Nash equilibrium of the second stage of the game then satisfies the following first-order conditions (corresponding to the equalities of marginal revenues and marginal costs):

$$p(Q) + s + Q_1 p'(Q) - C'(Q_1) = 0 \tag{3.2}$$

$$p(Q) + Q_2 p'(Q) - C'(Q_2) = 0 \tag{3.3}$$

Given the above-mentioned assumptions, the second-order conditions are satisfied and the reaction functions implicitly defined by (3.2) and (3.3) are downward sloping (i.e. the quantities are strategic substitutes according to Bulow, Geneakoplos and Klemperer, 1985): the marginal profitability of one firm's output is a decreasing function of the other firm's output) and the NE values Q_1^* and Q_2^* are, respectively, increasing and decreasing functions of s.

In the first stage of the game the domestic government is assumed to choose s in order to maximize the domestic firm's profits net of export taxes or subsidies (the assumption that transfers between the firms and the government are wholly in lump-sum form is implicit). The domestic firm's net profits may be written as:

$$\Pi_1^N = \Pi_1\big(Q_1^*(s), Q_2^*(s), s\big) - sQ_1^* \tag{3.4}$$

where Π_1 denotes firm 1's profits including export subsidies, and Π_1^N firm 1's profits net of subsidies. The equilibrium condition for the first stage of the game now is:

$$\frac{\partial \Pi_1^N}{\partial s} = \frac{\partial \Pi_1}{\partial Q_1}\frac{\partial Q_1^*}{\partial s} + \frac{\partial \Pi_1}{\partial Q_2}\frac{\partial Q_2^*}{\partial s} - s\frac{\partial Q_1^*}{\partial s} = 0 \tag{3.5}$$

From the envelope theorem, the first term on the right-hand side of (3.5) equals zero (this is because Q_1^* is chosen in stage 2 in order to maximise Π_1). Equation (3.5) can equivalently be written as:

$$p'(Q)Q_1^* R_2'(Q_1^*) - s = 0 \tag{3.6}$$

where R_2' is the slope of the foreign firm's reaction function (implicitly (3.3) defines the foreign output Q_2 as a function of Q_1 which is called the 'reaction function' of the foreign firm).

From (3.6) we conclude that if the two incumbent firms compete in quantities, the domestic government should subsidize exports (in other words, the optimal level of s is positive); this is a 'top-dog' strategy according to Fudenberg and Tirole (1984)'s 'animal terminology' (we will develop more thoroughly the definition of 'top dog', 'fat cat', and similar strategic behaviour in the next application of this sub-section). One way to look at this result is to consider the second term on the right-hand side of (3.5). This term may be called the 'strategic effect' and through a development of the comparative strategic effects, it may be written as:

$$\frac{\partial \Pi_1}{\partial Q_2}\frac{\partial^2 \Pi_1}{\partial Q_1 \partial s}\frac{\partial^2 \Pi_2}{\partial Q_1 \partial Q_2} \tag{3.7}$$

In this case, this strategic effect is positive because the first part is obviously negative, the second part is positive because, in Fudenberg and Tirole's terminology, subsidizing domestic exports make the domestic firm tough ($\partial^2 \Pi_1/\partial Q_1 \partial s > 0$) and the third part is negative because quantities are strategic substitutes ($\partial^2 \Pi_2/\partial Q_1 \partial Q_2 < 0$).

These results are illustrated by Figure 3.22 below where we have drawn in the (Q_1, Q_2) space the iso-profit curves of the domestic firm and the reaction function of the foreign firm. Note that successive iso-profit curves correspond to increasing profit levels as one approaches the Q_1 axis.

$R_1(Q_2)$ is the domestic reaction function in the *laissez-faire* case where a NE occurs at point N where the two reaction functions intersect. The Stackelberg equilibrium point is where the foreign firm's reaction function is tangent to one iso-profit curve of the domestic firm, i.e. at S. The Stackelberg equilibrium is the equilibrium of a two-stage game in which

Figure 3.22   Reaction curves and iso-profit curves of the duopoly game

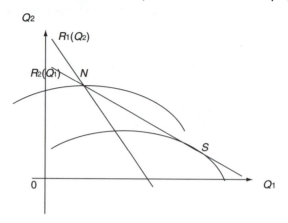

the domestic firm would choose its output level in the first stage, before the foreign firm (the first mover is the leader and the second mover is the follower in such a game). Along NS, domestic net profits increase as one moves from N to S. Subsidizing domestic exports shifts the domestic firm's reaction function outwards and moves the Cournot Nash-equilibrium down along R_2. Trade policy is optimal when the NE point coincides with point S where domestic net profits are at their maximum, given the foreign firm's reaction function.

Another example will now show how the structure of this type of game can be advanced further.

Strategic investment in a model of differentiated goods duopoly (Montet, 1991)*

Consider a duopoly producing two differentiated but similar products in quantities x_1 and x_2. The inverse demand functions are $p^i(x_1, x_2)$, $i = 1, 2$. We assume that they satisfy the usual properties expressed by the following inequalities (*using simply subscripts to denote partial derivatives*): $p^i_i < 0$, $p^1_2 < 0$, and $p^2_1 < 0$. Assuming that the utility function $U(x_1, x_2)$ is concave in (x_1, x_2) and that $p^i = \partial U/\partial x_i$, we have: $p^1_2 = p^2_1$, $p^1_1 p^2_2 - p^1_2 p^2_1 \geq 0$.

Costs are functions of quantities and functions of a long-run strategic variable denoted by K for capital: $C^i(x_i, K_i)$. Marginal costs are noted as $C^i_i(x_i, K_i)$.

The firms compete in a two-stage game. In the first period they choose a level of capital expenditure K_i measured in period 1 money units. An increase in K leads to a marginal cost reduction, i.e. $C^i_{xK} < 0$.

In the second period, the firms choose the quantities to be produced (and sold). We shall model this second stage as a 'conjectural variation' equilibrium. The concept of conjectural variation is often used for modelling the way that agents anticipate their rivals' reactions without having recourse to a fully dynamic framework. Many commentators have stressed the logical flaw in this model which remains static in nature and whose strategies cannot be described as an extensive-form game. However, it constitutes a useful tool for cataloguing various kinds of equilibrium (for example, in oligopoly theory two nice values of the conjectural variation parameters give the Cournot–Nash equilibrium in quantities and the Bertrand–Nash equilibrium in prices, respectively). Each firm tries to maximise its total profit:

$$\Pi_i = \beta[p^i(x_1, x_2)x_i - C^i(x_i, K_i)] - K_i \tag{3.8}$$

where β is again a positive discount factor. We are looking for the SPE of the game. First, we solve the second-stage sub-game for given values of K_1 and K_2, and then, knowing how x_1 and x_2 depend on K_1 and K_2, we solve the first-stage game.

Firms can make credible threats only concerning their planned levels of production. However, they are also aware of the fact that irreversible investment in the first stage modifies the initial conditions of the game in the second stage. Therefore they take into account all the effects of the investments: reduction of costs and modification of the second-stage game. The sunk-cost nature of capital expenditures is of course a crucial condition of the strategic effect of K. By choosing a certain level of K, each firm commits itself irreversibly to certain behaviour in the second stage. The first-order conditions of the second-stage equilibrium are, as usual:

$$H^i(x_1, x_2, K_i) = p^i(x_1, x_2) + [p_i^i(x_1, x_2)$$
$$+ p_j^i(x_1, x_2) v_i]x_i - C_i^i(x_i, K_i) = 0 \tag{3.9}$$

where $v_i = (dx_i/dx_j)_c$ is the conjectural variation relation. Differentiating (3.9) gives in matrix form:

$$\begin{bmatrix} H_1^1 & H_2^1 \\ H_1^2 & H_2^2 \end{bmatrix} \begin{bmatrix} dx_1 \\ dx_2 \end{bmatrix} = - \begin{bmatrix} H_K^1 & dK_1 \\ H_K^2 & dK_2 \end{bmatrix} \tag{3.10}$$

A few additional assumptions are needed to obtain precise results:

$$H_1^1 < 0, \; H_2^2 < 0 \tag{3.11a}$$

$$H_1^1 H_2^2 - H_2^1 H_1^2 > 0 \tag{3.11b}$$

$$H_2^1 < 0, \; H_1^2 < 0 \tag{3.11c}$$

Assumptions (3.11a) and (3.11b) are conditions of uniqueness and 'stability' of the static equilibrium (Dixit, 1986). Assumption (3.11c) is a necessary and sufficient condition for having downward sloping 'reactions curves' (or equilibrium loci of firms). By setting the right-hand side in (3.10) equal to zero, we can obtain the following expressions for the slopes of the firms' reaction functions:

$$r_1 = -\frac{H_2^1}{H_1^1} \quad r_2 = -\frac{H_1^2}{H_2^2} \tag{3.12}$$

Now let us study the comparative static effects of an increase in K_1, with K_2 kept constant. Solving (3.10) for dx_1 and dx_2 gives:

$$dx_1 = -\frac{H_2^2 H_K^1 dK_1}{\Delta}$$

where $\Delta > 0$ is the determinant of the matrix in (3.10) and

$$dx_2 = \frac{H_1^2 H_K^1 dK_1}{\Delta}$$

or using r_2 as in (3.12)

$$dx_2 = -\frac{r_2 H_2^2 H_K^1 dK_1}{\Delta}$$

(in fact $dx_2 = r_2 dx_1$, which means that the equilibrium is shifted along firm 2's reaction function). The signs of r_2 and H_2^2 are determined by assumptions (3.11a) and (3.11b), but $H_K^1 dK_1$ may be positive or negative.

Consider the case where $H_K^1 > 0$, i.e. where the increase in K_1 leads to an increase in firm 1's marginal profit. Then dx_1 and dx_2 can be unambiguously signed: $dx_1 > 0$ and $dx_2 < 0$. More generally, in this case the output level of each firm is an increasing function of its capital stock and a decreasing function of the rival firm's capital stock. Now let us go back to the first stage of the game: each firm chooses its level of capital, taking into account the direct effects on costs and indirect effects on the initial conditions of the second-period game. We are looking for a NE of this game. The equilibrium conditions are:

$$\beta[p^i(x_1, x_2) + p_i^i(x_1, x_2)x_i - C_i^i(x_i, K_i)]\frac{dx_i}{dK_i}$$
$$+ \beta p_j^i(x_1, x_2)x_i \frac{dx_j}{dK_i} - (1 + \beta C_K^i) = 0$$

Using the second-stage equilibrium condition (3.9) and the expressions for the slopes of the reaction functions in (3.12), we obtain:

$$\beta x_i p_j^i(x_1, x_2)(r_j - v_i)\frac{dx_i}{dK_i} - (1 + \beta C_K^i) = 0 \tag{3.13}$$

The second term in (3.13) represents the direct effect of K and the first term is the indirect or strategic effect. The sign of the strategic effect depends on the sign of $(r_j - v_i)$ and the sign of dx_i/dK_i, which itself depends on the sign of H_K^1 (given assumptions (3.11a) and (3.11b)). If, as we have assumed so far, $H_k^1 > 0$, firm i will overinvest in the case where $(r_j - v_i)$ is negative, which encompasses the normal Cournot situation (with $r_j < 0$ and $v_i = 0$), and will underinvest in the case where $(r_j - v_i)$ is positive (which encompasses the normal Bertrand case). If $r_j = v_i$, a case known as 'consistent conjectures' (and which can be justified in such a framework only as a shortcut for representing a particular dynamic equilibrium), the variable K has no strategic effect at all. In the case where $H_K^1 < 0$, the results would simply be reversed.

Using the zoological taxonomy suggested by Fudenberg and Tirole (1984), we represent in Figure 3.23 the different strategic situations.

If the game in the second stage is Cournot with downward sloping reaction curves–that is, a case of 'strategic substitutes', we obtain the results of column (3). If the game in the second stage is Bertrand with upward sloping curves (in the price space), that is a case of 'strategic complements', we obtain the results of column (4). In the case discussed above we assumed $H_K^1 > 0$, that is that the investment was making firm 1 tough, or in other words that an increase in K was leading firm 1 to behave more competitively an the last stage of the game. However, other types of investments, such as advertising, could make the incumbent softer, that is less likely to act competitively in the second stage. If competition is of the Bertrand type, firm 1 should then overinvest to look like a 'fat cat' in order to avoid too rough competition in the second stage.

Figure 3.23 Taxonomy of the different strategic situations

(1)	(2)	$(r_j - v_j) < 0$ (3)	$(r_j - v_j) > 0$ (4)
$H_K^1 > 0$	Investment by firm 1 makes it tough	Overinvestment: firm 1 wants to look like a 'top dog'	Underinvestment: firm 1 wants to look like a 'puppy dog'
$H_K^1 < 0$	Investment by firm 1 makes it soft	Underinvestment: firm 1 wants to have a 'lean and hungry look'	Overinvestment: firm 1 wants to look like a 'fat cat'

We can only repeat here the qualifications made at the beginning of this model: the concept of conjectural variation is logically flawed since the values of the parameter v generally cannot be consistent with an extensive form of a game. The model must simply be understood as a device to present in a compact way different oligopoly solutions (Cournot, Bertrand, and others including more or less collusive solutions of a true dynamic game), although purists may prefer to write explicitly alternative models for Cournot, Bertrand or other solutions (such as tacit collusion in a repeated game).

Despite this problem of interpretation, this general framework can be applied to a variety of economic problems. The case put forward by Brander and Spencer (1985) for strategic trade policy (and presented previously in this sub-section) is a good example: government subsidies act as a commitment like the variable K above. Brander and Spencer assume $H_K^1 > 0$ and a Cournot second-stage game, they find that subsidies have a positive strategic effect, but a different type of second-stage game, such as Bertrand, may entirely reverse the result (see Eaton and Grossman, 1986, for a discussion of Brander and Spencer's argument in the general framework presented above).

3.5.2   Sequential games and hidden actions: moral hazard

There are in economic and business life a number of situations where an individual or an organization, usually called the 'principal' or the 'contractor', proposes a 'contract' to another individual or organization, called an 'agent' or a 'contractee', in order to have some task accomplished. A contract may be either an explicit written agreement or an unwritten, implicit agreement which is assumed to govern the relationship. These *principal–agent* relationships involve a sequence of decisions which can be analysed as a game and solved by using the solution concept of SPE as studied in this chapter.

The typical contract can be described as having the following order of moves:

(1)   In a first stage, the principal designs a contract
(2)   Then, the agent can accept or reject it
(3)   Assuming the contract is accepted, the agent can choose an amount of effort in accomplishing her (or his) task
(4)   Nature plays at this stage and determine a state of the world influencing the outcome.

Informational asymmetries between the principal and the agent raise a series of interesting issues in this particular framework, which covers a wide variety of economic and business relationships. The focus of principal–agent models is on establishing the form of the *optimal contract* for the principal to offer the agent given their private information, and on identifying potential difficulties in implementing the optimal contract. Different forms of asymmetries raise different types of problems. We will focus here on a classic problem, called 'moral hazard with hidden actions'.

There is a moral hazard problem when the agent's *action* is not observable. At the time the contract is signed, both parties have the same information. But, once the agent begins executing the contractual assignments, her (or his) actions are not seen perfectly by the principal. Real-life examples include contracts between firms and workers, a manager and her (or his) commercial people, a government and regulated firms, a patient and a doctor, a client and her (or his) lawyer. In all these classical examples, the level of effort actually put forth by the agent cannot completely be verified by the principal.

It may also be possible that once the task is being accomplished by the agent, the latter learns some private information, not directly observable by the principal. This situation also raises issues of moral hazard ('moral hazard with hidden information') In the following, we will concentrate the analysis on the classical case of non-observable actions.

A simple example

Consider a risk-neutral manager (principal, thereafter named 'she') who wants to hire a risk-averse employee (agent, thereafter called 'he'). If the employee accepts the proposed contract, he will have a choice to perform his task by exerting a high effort $e_H = 3$ or a low effort $e_L = 1$. This level of effort is not verifiable by the manager. The latter can observe only a final result x, which for simplicity is reduced to two levels: $x \in \{300, 900\}$. The manager obtains a payoff from the employee's work equal to:

$$\Pi = x - w$$

where w is the employee's wage. The employee's utility is measured by the difference between the utility from receiving the wage w, $(u(w) = \sqrt{w})$ and the disutility of effort noted $v(e) = e^2$:

$$u(w, e) = \sqrt{w} - e^2$$

The labour market offers the employee an opportunity to obtain at least a level of utility: $\bar{u} = 8$.

Nature decides the state of the world when the agent accomplishes his task. There can be a good state or a bad state. This uncertainty has a considerable influence on the employee's output, whatever his effort level. When the employee exerts a high effort, the high level of output $x_2 = 900$ occurs with probability 0.75, whereas the low level of output $x_1 = 300$ could still occur with probability 0.25. When the exerted effort is low, the probability are reversed:

$$p_2(e_H) = 0.75 \text{ and } p_1(e_H) = 0.25$$

$$p_2(e_L) = 0.25 \text{ and } p_1(e_L) = 0.75$$

Symmetric information

Before solving this game, we can check as a reference case what the optimal solution would be if information were symmetric. The manager would then be in a position enabling her to verify the employee's effort and thus, when seeing a particular output, she would be able to disentangle what results from the employee's efforts and what results from random events.

If the manager envisages that the agent puts forth a low effort, a fixed wage contract w_1 offering only the reservation utility level $\bar{u}$ would be high enough to have the task accomplished. This constraint is called the 'participation constraint' (PC) (or sometimes the 'reservation utility' or 'individual rationality' constraint):

$$\sqrt{w_1} - e_L^2 = \bar{u}, \tag{PC}$$

or:

$$\sqrt{w_1} - 1 = 8$$

and so:

$$w_1^* = 81$$

The manager's payoff would then be:

$$\Pi_1 = \tfrac{3}{4}\,(300 - 81) + \tfrac{1}{4}\,(900 - 81) = 369$$

Now if the manager wishes that the employee exert a high effort, a fixed wage contract w_2 is required; such that:

$$\sqrt{w_2} - e_H^2 = \bar{u}, \tag{PC}$$

or:

$$\sqrt{w_2} - 9 = 8$$

and so:

$$w_2^* = 289$$

The manager's payoff would be:

$$\Pi_2 = \tfrac{1}{4}\,(300 - 289) + \tfrac{3}{4}\,(900 - 289) = 459$$

Asymmetric information

Now let us come back to the case of asymmetric information. The principal will have to check whether the implementation of a high effort level is not too costly compared to the case where the employee exerts only a low effort.

In the latter case, things are simple. A fixed wage adjusted to the reservation utility level will be high enough to convince the agent to participate and to have him choose the low effort level.

Implementing a high effort level is now more tricky since the agent can shirk. Another constraint called the 'incentive compatibility constraint' (ICC) must be fulfilled. It states that the contract must give a higher utility to the employee when he puts forth the high effort than when he shirks. Formally here:

$$0.25\sqrt{w(300)} + 0.75\sqrt{w(900)} - 9 \geq 0.75\sqrt{w(300)} + 0.25\sqrt{w(900)} - 1$$

The principal must solve the following maximization problem:

$$\begin{cases} \max\,[0.25(300 - w^*(300)) + 0.75(900 - w^*(900))] \\ \text{s.t.: } 0.25\sqrt{w(300)} + 0.75\sqrt{w(900)} - 9 \geq 8 \hspace{2cm} \text{(PC)} \\ 0.25\sqrt{w(300)} + 0.75\sqrt{w(900)} - 9 \geq 0.75\sqrt{w(300)} + 0.25\sqrt{w(900)} - 1 \text{ (ICC)} \end{cases}$$

The optimal solution is:

$$w^*(300) = 25, \quad w^*(900) = 441$$

And the manager's payoff is:

$$\Pi^* = 413$$

It must be noticed that in this case, the principal's payoff is lower than in the case of symmetric information when the employee is paid to exert the high effort level: $\Pi^* = 413 < \Pi_2 = 459$. But Π^* is still higher than

$\Pi_1 = 289$. So it pays the principal to implement the incentive wage leading the employee to put forth a high effort level.

In the rest of this sub-section we shall present a more general principal–agent model. Another particular case, the linear principal–agent model, is presented as an exercise (see exercise 3.12).

The general model

At the final stage of the game, the agent chooses an amount of effort e in the set of available actions $e \in \{e_1, \ldots, e_n\}$. Notice that the agent's effort might be a continuous variable, $e \in [0, 1]$. Since the continuous effort case raises some technical difficulties of its own, we will stick here to cases of discrete choices.

The principal observes the outcome of the agent's action. This outcome depends not only on the agent's effort but also on a random component, the state of the world determined by Nature.

Assuming a finite set of outcomes $x \in \{x_1, \ldots, x_m\}$, one can write the probability of outcome x_j conditional on action e_i:

$$p_j(e_i) = \text{prob } \{x = x_j / e = e_i\} \quad i = 1, \ldots, n \text{ and } j = 1, \ldots, m$$

We must have

$$\sum_{j=1}^{m} p_j(e_i) = 1 \text{ for } i = 1, \ldots, n$$

We shall assume $p_j(e_i) > 0$ for all e_i, $i = 1, \ldots, n$.

This means that any outcome is possible for a given effort. Notice that, since uncertainty plays an important role in the problem, both agent and principal's utility functions must reflect their respective attitude toward risk; so we will use VNM utility functions.

The agent's utility is given by:

$$u(w, e) = u(w) - v(e)$$

where w is the wage or agent's payoff . It is assumed that the utility is additively separable in the components w and e:

$$u'(w) > 0, \ u''(w) \leq 0, \ v'(e) > 0, \ v''(e) \geq 0$$

For a given contract, the agents expected utility is:

$$Eu(w, e) = \sum_{j=1}^{m} p_j(e_i) u(w(x_j)) - v(e_i)$$

The principal's expected payoff, or expected profit, can be written:

$$\sum_{j=1}^{m} p_j(e_i)\Pi(x_j - w(x_j)).$$

Both agent and principal can be either risk-neutral or risk-averse. However, the most appealing assumption is to have a risk-neutral principal facing a risk-averse agent. The assumption of additive separability for the agent's utility implies that his risk aversion does not vary with the effort he supplies. This assumption is a bit restrictive, but it does not represent a great loss of generality.

The principal–agent problem can then be summarized by the following optimization problems (this presentation follows Wolfstetter, 1999).

At the last stage, the agent chooses the effort which maximizes his expected utility:

$$e \in \arg\max_{e} \left\{ \sum_{j=1}^{m} p_j(e_i)u(w(x_j)) - v(e_i) \right\}$$

This condition defines the incentive compatability constraint ICC. At the second stage of the game, the agent decides whether to participate or not. The expected utility to the agent must be at least equal to a reservation level (outside option) $\bar{u}$. Formally:

$$\sum_{j=1}^{m} p_j(e_i)u(w(x_j)) - v(e_i)) \geq \bar{u}$$

This condition is the participation constraint (PC).

In the first stage, the principal designs the contract, anticipating what the agent's behaviour will be at the following stages. The principal thus maximizes her expected payoff:

$$\begin{cases} \max_{\{e_i, w(x_j)\}} \sum_{j=1}^{m} p_j(e_i)\Pi(x_j - w(x_j)) \\ \text{s.t (a) ICC} \\ \quad\;\; (b) \text{ PC} \end{cases}$$

The ICC is used because we know from the revelation principle that the equilibrium payoffs of a game induced by a contract that is not incentive-compatible can be replicated by an incentive-compatible contract (see subsection 2.4.2 of chapter 2 for a more general presentation of the revelation principle).

The principal's problem can be decomposed into (i) the optimal implementation of a given effort e_i; and (ii) the choice of the effort level that maximizes the principal's expected payoff.

Part (i) of the problem can be written formally as the minimization of expected wage costs for obtaining a particular effort level e_i (it should be noticed that the minimization is transformed below into a maximization problem):

$$
\begin{cases}
\max_{\{w(x_j)\}} \left[-\sum_{j=1}^{m} p_j(e_i) w(x_j) \right] \\
\text{s.t:} \quad E(u(w, e_i)) \geq \bar{u} & \text{(PC)} \\
E(u(w, e_i)) \geq E(u(w, e_k)), \text{ for all } k, k \neq i = 1, \ldots, n & \text{(ICC)}
\end{cases}
$$

The first-order conditions are:

$$
\frac{1}{u'(w_j)} = \lambda + \sum_{k=1}^{n} \mu_k \left(1 - \frac{p_j(e_k)}{p_j(e_i)} \right) \quad j = 1, \ldots, m \tag{3.14}
$$

where λ and μ_k are the (non-negative) Kühn–Tücker multipliers, respectively, on the PC and the ICC.

The ratio of probabilities in (3.14) may have a property of monotonicity called the 'monotone likelihood ratio condition' (MLRC), which states that:

$$
\text{if } e_i > e_k, x_j > x_h \text{ then } \frac{p_j(e_i)}{p_j(e_k)} \geq \frac{p_h(e_i)}{p_h(e_k)}
$$

When this condition holds, one can show that the wage schedule implementing the effort level e_i is monotone non-decreasing:

$$
w_m \geq w_{m-1} > \ldots \geq w_1
$$

In other words, the wage must be greater if the principal wants the agent to put forth a higher effort.

Remark I

As mentioned at the start of the sub-section, moral hazard with hidden action is just one among the different types of asymmetric information on which economic research has concentrated. A taxonomy of asymmetric information into 'pre-' and 'post-contractual' has been proposed by Milgrom (1985). The problem of moral hazard arises when there exists 'post-contractual' asymmetry of information which affects decisions made after a contract is agreed. The second classical problem of 'adverse selection' arises when there exists a 'pre-contractual' asymmetry in information between parties to a contract. Prior to 'signing' a contract with the principal, agents observe some information that will affect the outcome of the contractual relationship. A special class of adverse selection problem, named 'signalling', will be presented in sub-section 4.3.2 of chapter 4 (for a classical survey of the principal–agent literature, see Hart and Holmstrom, 1987; for a more detailed presentation of the different classes of asymmetrical information games see, for instance, Rasmusen, 1989).■

3.5.3   Repeated games and credible threats or promises

In most of the situations where game theory can be applied to economic problems, the agents meet repeatedly. In general, firms compete not only once for the share of a set of potential customers. They face each other regularly over time, very often over an indefinite period of time. Negotiators in international trade know that their countries will have other occasions of discussing, arguing and retaliating in the future.

In those circumstances, the set of strategic moves is enriched. Agents can promise to be nice if their rivals are nice and threaten to retaliate if a bad action is attempted. This interaction of threats and promises may give rise to cooperation among the players who can obtain a better outcome. The intuition of this result is quite clear and does not need any sophisticated reasoning. What game theory brings is precisely the identification of the conditions under which a cooperative result can be achieved. It basically shows that the number of equilibria may be very large, corresponding to different levels of cooperation. It also shows that there is a dramatic difference in the results if one assumes that the game is repeated infinitely or if it is ending after a certain number of plays. Cooperation is much more difficult to assess theoretically in the latter case.

The best way to illustrate these issues is to consider a standard static game and to see what happens when the agents repeat the same game over time. The most standard game would be a duopoly, but in order to show the versatility of NE and its dynamic versions, we prefer to consider a tariff game between two countries (but the logic is basically the same). Let us first introduce the static NE in the constituent game.

The constituent game

We assume that the world is composed of two countries whose governments have only one choice concerning trade: let it be free or put a specified tariff on imports. This binary choice is sufficient to show the kind of Prisoner's dilemma arising in this situation. If both governments choose a non-interventionist strategy, the countries will enjoy the advantages of free trade. If both of them put a tariff on imports, in general their

Figure 3.24   The payoff matrix

		Country 2	
		FT	OT
Country 1	FT	8, 8	2, 10
	OT	10, 2	4, 4

situation would deteriorate compared to the previous case. However, the worst case would certainly be for a country to do nothing, while the other influences the terms of trade in its favour through the tariff policy. Figure 3.24 gives the payoff matrix of this simple static game (where FT is used for free trade and OT for optimal tariff).

This game has a DSE (which is also a NE). The choice of free trade is more efficient for both countries, but it is not an equilibrium of the non-cooperative game. If a pre-play agreement were settled between the two governments, each would be interested in reneging on it and could do so in the absence of a supranational institution with coercive power.

Of course, the choice of strategies need not be so limited as in this extreme example. One can consider a more general situation where two countries produce two products 1 and 2, country 1 exports product 1 and imports product 2, and each country can levy various tariffs on imports. Let us call t and t^*, respectively, the domestic and foreign *ad valorem* tariffs so that the national prices of the two goods are related by: $p_2^1 = p_2^2(1 + t)$ and $p_1^2 = p_1^1(1 + t^*)$ with p_j^i the price of product j in country i. Each tariff can be positive or negative and take any value in between -1 (imports would then be free) and $\bar{t}$ (prohibition of any imports). The relative price on the world market is $p = p_2^2/p_1^1$.

Let $M_i(p, t)$ denote country's i import demand as a function of the terms of trade and the tariff level; $i = 1, 2$. The trade balance condition is:

$$pM_1(p, t) = M_2(p, t^*) \tag{3.15}$$

This determines a function $p(t, t^*)$, which we assume to be continuous and differentiable. We assume that raising the tariff improves the terms of trade:

$$\frac{\partial p}{\partial t} < 0, \ \frac{\partial p}{\partial t^*} > 0$$

This is true if the Marshall-Lerner conditions hold (i.e. the sum of the elasticity of export demand and the elasticity of import demand exceeds one), and if all tariff revenues are redistributed to consumers.

The payoffs of the game are the values derived from the collective utility functions: $U = U(p, t)$, $U^* = U^*(p, t^*)$ which from (3.15) can be rewritten as functions of t and t^* only: $W(t, t^*)$ and $W^*(t, t^*)$. With the assumptions stated above, each country is hurt by increases in the other country's tariff. We also assume that each country gains from a slight increase in its tariff starting from a zero tariff. The functions W and W^* give welfare contours as illustrated on Figure 3.25 (see McMillan, 1986, and Dixit, 1987, for a more detailed presentation).

Country 1's welfare increases as we move down and to the right and country 2's welfare increases when moving up and to the left. The locus of the maxima of these curves for country 1 – that is the points corresponding to $\partial W / \partial t = 0$ – is RR on Figure 3.25. It is called the home country's reaction function (as Dixit argued, the term 'equilibrium locus' would be a better name since in a one-shot game there is not strictly such a thing as 'reaction'). The corresponding locus for country 2 is $R^* R^*$ We assume here that they are negatively sloped and that they cross only once. The intersection point N represents the NE of this game (in fact, autarky could be another NE; see Dixit, 1987).

As in the case of the Prisoner's dilemma, the equilibrium is not Pareto-efficient. Efficiency would require the same relative price in the two countries, that is:

$$p_2^1 / p_1^1 = p_2^2 / p_1^2$$

or:

$$p(1 + t) = p/(1 + t^*)$$

or finally:

$$t + t^* + tt^* = 0 \tag{3.16}$$

Figure 3.25 Countries' welfare

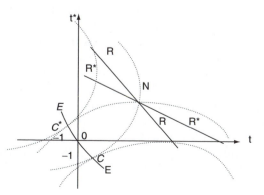

The locus of (t, t^*) verifying condition (3.16) is the curve EE on Figure 3.25. The points between C and C^* are preferred by both countries to the NE and in this case, the free-trade solution lies on this segment (this is not always true, see for instance Kennan and Riezman, 1988, for a different case). The problem is that the countries cannot reach the free-trade solution or a point on CC^* without being constrained by an external force (like a powerful sort of WTO).

Remark I

In the presentation above, the governments use *ad valorem* tariffs as their strategic instruments. Horwell (1966) has shown that the NE in specific tariffs between the two countries differs from the NE in *ad valorem* tariffs. Tower (1975) proved that the NE in quotas is yet another thing. The classical equivalence results cease to be valid when both governments are active. In this case, one encounters problems which are very much like the problem of divergence between Cournot and Bertrand equilibria in oligopoly (on these questions see Laussel, 1991). However, the above discussion remains qualitatively valid, whatever the strategic variables chosen by the governments.■

Infinite repetition

It is then worth considering the effect of the repetition of the game concerning dynamic non-cooperative equilibrium. As seen above, it is now well established in oligopoly theory and other applications of game theory that strategic moves such as threats and promises offer serious possibilities of tacit cooperation in dynamic games. The same logic is easily applicable to tariff games.

Consider first that the two governments expect an *infinite repetition* of the constituent game. Each period's choices will depend on the history of the game and the memory of prior moves. A strategy in the supergame is a plan of actions for each period and it is natural to plan different actions according to the rival's prior move. Does this infinitely repeated game admit a SPE? There is an obvious solution: the repetition of the static NE. Yet, there are other solutions, eventually more 'collusive'.

Let us revert again to the assumption that there are only two strategies in the stage game: free trade (F) and the static NE (N). A country may promise to be a free trader as long as the other country has not defected from the efficient solutions and threatens to permanently revert to the Nash tariff-ridden equilibrium. The threat is credible since after having observed a rival country's defection a reversion to the static Nash point constitutes a SPE. If the losses induced by the collapse of the 'colluding' behaviour are sufficiently high compared to the gains from a unilateral defection, the promise to be friendly is also credible. The intertwined

threats and promises would then generate self-enforcing cooperative behaviour.

Let us briefly state the conditions under which the promises are credible. Each country is supposed to maximize the sum of its discounted total
welfare. Let W^F denote the total welfare for one period in the case of free
trade, W^d the welfare that could be obtained by unilateral defection and
W^N the welfare which can be reached in the static NE. Consider a country
contemplating the choice of remaining at free trade or defecting in order
to get transitory benefits.

If the two countries stay in free trade, the total welfare on the infinite
horizon will be: $\sum \beta^t W^F$, with β a positive discount factor $0 < \beta < 1$.
When the horizon is infinite β can be written as $\beta = 1/(1+r)$: it is the
present value of a unit received one stage later, when the interest rate per
stage is r. However, notice that β may receive another interpretation if we
assume that the game will end at an indefinite period. Let us call q the
probability that the game will continue after a given period. The payoff of
the game at the next stage is $qW^F/(1+r)$ and at the following stage
$q^2 W^F/(1+r)^2$ and so on. Then if β is defined as $q/(1+r)$, it would reflect
both the pure interest component and the possibility of having an end of
the game. The rest of the argument works with both hypotheses.

We know from simple algebra that:

$$\sum \beta^t W^F = W^F/(1-\beta)$$

If a country unilaterally defects it will obtain during the first period a
welfare level $W^d > W^F$, thereafter the sum of the W^N until infinity. So its
total welfare would be:

$$W^d + [\beta W^N/(1-\beta)]$$

It is clear that this country will remain a free trader if:

$$\beta \geq [(W^d - W^F)/(W^d - W^N)]$$

or:

$$(W^d - W^F) \leq (W^F - W^N)/r \tag{3.17}$$

(with r, the rate of discount; $\beta = 1/1+r$) that is, if the discounted future
losses more than offset the immediate gains. Condition (3.17) will be met if
the transitory gains from defection are bounded ($W^d < \infty$), if the reversion to the static NE constitutes a true punishment ($W^N < W^F$) and if β is
high enough (close enough to unity).

Remark 2

One problem with the previous analysis is the multiplicity of equilibria of the supergame. In our presentation above we restricted the choices at each period to two actions: the static NE or the Pareto-efficient outcome (free trade). However, there may be a lot of other tariff policies. The perfect folk theorem (see sub-section 3.3.2 and Remark 2 in sub-section 3.4.3), tells us that, for a discount factor close enough to one, any outcome between the static Nash point and free trade can be sustained as a SPE of the supergame. A pre-play negotiation between the governments to find an agreement on the Pareto-efficient outcome(s) does not solve the multiplicity problem since it conveys the idea that the agents could renegotiate after a defection in order to avoid the mutually costly punishments. This possibility of renegotiations crucially undermines the credibility of the threats supporting the efficient outcome. The adoption of one equilibrium among the set of possible candidates may lie in communication and behavioural rules like simple rules of thumb between players or the convergence to a focal point , which in this case may be the free-trade point. A great deal has still to be learned from experimental games in this area (for further details on this issue see Chapter 8)∎

Remark 3

It is also worth noting that the choice of an optimal punishment strategy along the lines suggested by Abreu (1988) for oligopoly theory could increase the likelihood of an outcome close to free trade. The idea is that to achieve free trade, for a given discount rate, the players must design the most severe punishment for defectors. Reversion to the static NE is in general not the most severe punishment and so it is insufficient to sustain free trade. Fortunately here, as Dixit (1987) noted, autarky could be used as a credible threat since it is also an equilibrium of the static game.∎

Finite repetition

Another problem with the previous analysis is the assumption of an infinite (or an indefinite) repetition of the game. Governments may perceive their relations as limited in time. When the stage game is repeated only over a *limited number of periods,* it would seem that the only SPE is the simple repetition of the static game NE. This result is easily deduced by checking each period equilibrium, starting with the last one and going back to the previous ones. At the last round there is no other credible action than the static Nash strategy. Yet a threat to punish defection at the penultimate round is worthless and not credible. So the static NE will result also at this stage; and so on back to the first round.

On the other hand, some experiments conducted by Axelrod (1984) have shown that an efficient outcome may emerge from a non-cooperative *finitely* repeated game when agents adopt a 'tit-for-tat' strategy. Each agent simply reproduces what its rival did at the previous stage: defect if it defected, cooperate if it cooperated. Axelrod underpins the interesting properties of tit-for-tat with regard to communication and human relation: it is a simple, clear and forgiving strategy. Although it raises interesting questions about the relationships between formal GT and experimental studies of human behaviour, this argument is not too serious in our case since there are two static NE: the point called N (representing an equilibrium with trade and tariffs) and autarky. The mutual threat to play autarky at the last stage is credible. Each government understands that if it does not play nicely in the penultimate round, the other country will retaliate by choosing autarky at the end. A straightforward application of Benoit and Krishna (1985) would illustrate the possibilities of improvement in cooperation in the previous stages of the game.

Remark 4

Formal GT and its various applications to oligopoly offer some other reasons why tacit cooperation may emerge from a repetition of the game with a finite horizon. In particular, the introduction of *incomplete* information can bring some level of collusion. This was first suggested by Dixit (1987) who used the model of Kreps and Wilson (1982) to describe governments playing Bayesian strategies to learn about the nature of the other government. A long phase of free trade may be rational before a collapse of the tacit coordination in the last phase of the play.∎

Remark 5

All these models can explain how countries are normally able to sustain a larger level of trade (freer trade) than with static NE tariffs. However, they cannot explain why, in certain periods, there are reversals to a higher level of protection or why countries use special measures like Voluntary Export Restraints (VERs) or Orderly Market Arrangements (OMAs). Bagwell and Staiger (1990) have studied a repeated game model in the presence of volatility in the trade volume. This trade war model, clearly inspired by the work of Rotemberg and Saloner (1986) on price wars in oligopoly, shows that episodes of 'special protection' might be viewed as part of a tacit agreement to sustain a level of trade higher than the static non-cooperative outcome. In a repeated game situation with volatile trade swings, increases in the volume of trade create incentives for each government to defect unilaterally from a collusive equilibrium. A limited level of protection called 'managed trade' is then required to lessen the effects of the increase in the trade volume and to sustain a level of tacit cooperation.∎

Remark 6

In another extension of repeated game analysis, Riezman (1991) proposed a model focusing on the effects of uncertainty and of the *observability* of protectionist measures. If protection is not observable, the outcome depends on the trigger strategies (see sub-section 3.3.2) used to punish eventual defections from the cooperative agreement. Countries can use an import trigger strategy. Cheating on the tacit agreement would then be detected by observing home imports since an increase in the foreign country's tariff rate would lead to a fall in *home imports* (given some restrictions on offers curve's elasticity). So, if home imports fall under some predetermined critical level, this might with some probability reveal foreign country cheating. A period of punishment (high tariffs) would then follow. Riezman shows that, in this case, some level of cooperation can be supported. However, countries can also use a terms of trade trigger strategy, that is to try to detect cheating by observing the *terms of trade changes*. When the terms of trade are too low, this might probabilistically indicate cheating and be followed by a reversion to a high tariff period. But, in this case, tacit cooperation cannot occur. This is so because reversions to high tariffs are also triggered by terms of trade being too high (contrary to the case of oligopoly rivalry, Green and Porter, 1984) or to the case of import trigger strategy above, here each agent's cheating moves the observed variable in opposite directions). Each country thus has an incentive to cheat because from an individualistic point of view it reduces the probability of reversion to high tariffs. This result shows clearly the crucial importance of the choice of the mechanism used to induce cooperation.■

Some other refinements of this approach may be expected in the near future. In the long term, one may hope to have a better understanding of the emergence of *focal points* to solve the problem of the multiplicity of equilibria. One particular question of interest in our case is the study of the motivations for protection. In reality tariff wars rarely correspond to terms of trade objectives and it is more than doubtful that governments ever have optimal tariff objectives. Fortunately most of the previous analysis applies to situations where governments have other motivations, such as employment or responses to lobbying activities. A mixture of this theory of strategic protectionism and the political economy of trade policy constitutes an interesting approach to tackle these issues. This more 'realistic' view of tariff conflicts and tacit cooperation requires a good understanding of the functioning and outcomes of games between governments when the other agents, essentially firms, have some market power.

Appendix: Basic topological concepts – convexity, correspondences and the fixed point theorems

A.1   Basic topological concepts

- The *norm* of a vector $x = (x_1, \ldots, x_i, \ldots x_n)$ is $\|x\| = (\sum_i x_i^2)^{\frac{1}{2}}$
- A sequence of vectors $x_0, x_1, \ldots x_k$ denoted $\{x_k\}$, is said to *converge* to the limit x if $\|x_k - x\| \to 0$ as $k \longrightarrow \infty$. In this case, we write: $x_k \to x$
- A *sphere* around x is a set of the form $\{y/\|y - x\| < \varepsilon\}$ for some $\varepsilon > 0$
- A sub-set X of $\mathbb{R}^n$ is *open* if for every point in X there is a sphere centred at that point and contained in X
- A sub-set X of $\mathbb{R}^n$ is *closed* if every point that is arbitrarily close to X belongs to X
- A sub-set X of $\mathbb{R}^n$ is *bounded* if it is contained in a sphere of finite radius
- A sub-set X of $\mathbb{R}^n$ is *compact* if it is closed and bounded.

A.2   Convexity

- *Convex set*: a set X in $\mathbb{R}^n$ is said to be 'convex' if for every $x_1, x_2 \in X$ and every real number α, $0 < \alpha < 1$, the point $\alpha x_1 + (1 - \alpha)x_2 \in X$
- *Convex hull*: the convex hull of a set Y is the smaller convex set containing Y
- *Concave function*: Let f be a real-valued function defined on a convex sub-set X of $\mathbb{R}^n$; then f is said to be 'concave' if for any $x_1, x_2 \in X$ and α, $0 \le \alpha \le 1$, there holds:

$$f(\alpha x_1 + (1 - \alpha)x_2) \ge \alpha f(x_1) + (1 - \alpha)f(x_2)$$

If for every $x_1 \ne x_2$ and $0 < \alpha < 1$ there holds:

$$f(\alpha x_1 + (1 - \alpha)x_2) > \alpha f(x_1) + (1 - \alpha)f(x_2)$$

thus the function is said to be 'strictly concave'

- *Convex function*: A function g defined on a convex $X \subset \mathbb{R}^n$ is 'convex' if $-g$ is concave.
- *Quasi-concave function*: Let f be a real-valued function defined on a convex set X of $\mathbb{R}^n$, then f is quasi-concave if the set: $\{x : x \in X, f(x) \ge c\}$ is convex for all real numbers c; quasi-concavity is somewhat weaker than concavity.

A. 3.   *Correspondences and fixed point theorems*

- *Correspondence* (or set-valued function, or point-to-set mapping): Suppose $X \subset \mathbb{R}^n$ and $Y \subset \mathbb{R}^m$ are sets; a correspondence T from X to Y assigns to every point $x \in X$ a sub-set $T(x)$ of Y, the set $T(x)$ is called the image of x (Figure 3A.1).
- *Upper semicontinuity*: Let $T: X \to Y$ be a correspondence from X into Y and assume that Y is compact. T is 'upper semicontinuous' (usc) if for any sequences $\{x_k\}$ and $\{y_k\}$ from X and Y, respectively, such that $x_k \to x$, $y_k \in T(x_k)$, and $y_k \to y \in Y$, it follows that $y \in T(x)$ (Figure 3A.2). In Figure 3A.1, T is usc at x' and not usc at x.

If a correspondence T is usc at each $x \in X$, it is said 'upper semicontinuous'. A correspondence is usc at each point if its graph is a closed subset of $X \times Y$.

Figure 3A.1   Correspondence

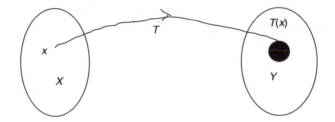

Figure 3A.2   Upper semicontinuity

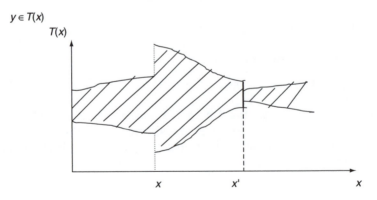

The correspondence $T(x) = \arg\max\limits_{z \in Z} f(x, z)$ is usc if f is continuous and Z is compact.

- *Fixed point theorem* (Kakutani)
  Let X be a compact convex subset of $I\!R^n$ and let $T\colon X \to X$ be a correspondence for which:

  – for all $x \in X$ the set $T(x)$ is non-empty and convex
  – T is usc.

Then there exists $x^* \in X$ such that $x^* \in T(x^*)$.

Bibliography

Abreu, D. (1988) 'On the theory of infinitely repeated games with discounting', *Econometrica*, 56: 383–96.

Aumann, R.J. (1974) 'Subjectivity and correlation in randomized strategies', *Journal of Mathematical Economics*, 1, 67–96.

Aumann, R.J. (1981) 'Survey of repeated games', in *Essays in Game Theory and Mathematical Economics in Honor of Oskar Morgenstern*, (Mannheim, Wien and Zurich: Wissenschaftsverlag, Bibliographisches Institut.).

Aumann, R.J. (1987) 'Correlated equilibrium as an extension of Bayesian rationality', *Econometrica*, 55, 1–18.

Aumann, R.J. (1995) 'Backward induction and common knowledge of rationality', *Games and Economic Behavior*, 8, 6–19.

Aumann, R.J. and A. Brandenburger (1995) 'Epistemic conditions for Nash equilibrium', *Econometrica*, 63, 1161–80.

Axelrod, R. (1984) *The Evolution of Cooperation* (New York: Basic Books).

Bagwell, K. and R. Staiger (1990) 'A theory of managed trade', *American Economic Review*, 80, 779–95.

Balwin, B. and G. Meese (1979) 'Social behavior in pigs studied by means of operant conditioning', *Animal Behavior*, 27, 947–57.

Benoit, J.P. and V. Krishna (1985) 'Finitely repeated games', *Econometrica*, 53, 890–904.

Benoit, J.P. and V. Krishna (1996) 'The folk theorems for repeated games: a synthesis', Working Paper, C.V. Starr Center, New York University and Institute of Economics, University of Copenhagen, February.

Binmore, K. (1987) 'Modeling rational players, Parts I and II', *Economics and Philosophy*, 3, 179–214; 9, 9–55.

Binmore, K. and P. Dasgupta (1986) 'Introduction-game theory: a survey', in K. Binmore and P. Dasgupta (eds), *Economic Organizations and Games* (Oxford: Basil Blackwell).

Brandenburger, A. (1992) 'Knowledge and equilibrium in games', *Journal of Economic Perspectives*, 6, 83–101.

Brandenburger, A. and E. Dekel (1987) 'Rationalizability and correlated equilibrium', *Econometrica*, 55, 1391–402.

Brander, J. and B. Spencer (1985) 'Export subsidies and international market share rivalry', *Journal of International Economics*, 18, 83–91.

Bulow, J., J. Geneakoplos and P. Klemperer (1985) 'Multimarket oligopoly: strategic substitutes and complements', *Journal of Political Economy*, 93, 488–511.

d'Aspremont, C., F. Forges and J.-F. Mertens (1989) 'Stratégies d'entreprises et avantages de la coopération: l'apport de la théorie des jeux', in CORE, *Gestion de l'économie et de l'entreprise* (Brussels: De Boeck) (in French).

Dasgupta, P. and E. Maskin (1986) 'The existence of equilibrium in discontinuous economic games, 1: theory', *Review of Economic Studies*, 53, 1–26.

Dekel, E. and F. Gul (1997) 'Rationality and knowledge in game theory', in D. Kreps and K.F. Wallis (eds), *Advances in Economics and Econometrics: Theory and Applications: Seventh World Congress of the Econometric Society*, 1 (Cambridge: Cambridge University Press).

Dixit, A. (1980) 'The role of investment in entry deterrence', *Economic Journal*, 90, 95–106.

Dixit, A. (1986) 'Comparative statics for oligopoly', *International Economic Review*, 27, 107–22.

Dixit, A (1987) 'Strategic aspects of trade policy', in T.F. Bewley (ed), *Advances in Economic Theory – Fifth World Congress* (Cambridge: Cambridge University Press).

Dockner, E., S. Jorgensen, N. Van Long and G. Sorder (2000) *Differential Games in Economics and Management Science* (Cambridge: Cambridge University Press).

Eaton, J. and G. Grossman (1986) 'Optimal trade and industrial policy under oligopoly', *Quarterly Journal of Economics*, 101, 383–406.

Fershtman, C. and M.I. Kamien (1987) 'Dynamic duopolistic competition with sticky prices', *Econometrica*, 55, 1151–64.

Forges, F. (1986) 'An approach to communication equilibria', *Econometrica*, 54, 65–82.

Forges, F. (1992) 'Repeated games of incomplete information: non-zero sum' in R.J. Aumann and S. Hart (eds), *Handbook of Game Theory with Economic Applications*, 1, (Amsterdam: North-Holland).

Friedman, J.W. (1971) 'A non-cooperative equilibrium for supergame', *Review of Economic Studies*, 38, 1–12.

Friedman, J.W. (1990) *Game Theory with Applications to Economics*, 2nd edn (Oxford: Oxford University Press), Chapters 2 and 3.

Friedman, J.W. (1971) 'A non-cooperative equilibrium for supergames', *Review of Economic Studies*, 38, 1–12.

Fudenberg, D. and E. Maskin (1986) 'The folk theorems in repeated games with discounting and with incomplete information', *Econometrica*, 54, 533–54.

Fudenberg, D. and J. Tirole (1983) 'Capital as commitment: strategic investment to deter mobility', *Journal of Economic Theory*, 31, 227–56.

Fudenberg, D. and J. Tirole (1984) 'The fat-cat effect, the puppy-dog ploy and the lean and hungry look', *American Economic Review, Papers and Proceedings*, 74, 361–6.

Fudenberg, D. and J. Tirole (1991) *Game Theory* (Cambridge, MA: MIT Press), Chapters 4, 5, 13.

Glicksberg, I.L. (1952), 'A further generalization of the Kakutani fixed point theorem with application to NE points', *Proceedings of the National Academy of Sciences*, 38, 170–4.

Green, E. and R. Porter (1984) 'Non-cooperative collusion under imperfect price information', *Econometrica*, 52, 87–100.

Harsanyi, J. (1973) 'Games with randomly disturbed payoffs: a new rationale for mixed strategy equilibrium points', *International Journal of Game Theory*, 2, 1–23.

Harsanyi, J. and R. Selten (1988) *A General Theory of Equilibrium Selection in Games* (Cambridge, MA: MIT Press).

Hart, O. and B. Holmstrom (1987) 'The theory of contracts', in T. Bewley (ed.), *Advances in Economic Theory* (Cambridge: Cambridge University Press), 71–115.

Horwell, J.D. (1966) 'Optimum tariffs and tariff policy', *Review of Economic Studies*, 33, 147–58.

Johansen, L. (1982) 'On the status of the Nash type of non-cooperative equilibrium in economic theory', *The Scandinavian Journal of Economics*, 84, 421–42.

Kennan, J. and R. Riezman (1988) 'Do big countries win tariff wars?', *International Economic Review*, 29, 81–5.

Kreps, D. (1990a) *Game Theory and Economic Modeling* (Oxford: Clarendon Press).

Kreps, D. (1990b) *A Course in Microeconomic Theory* (London: Harvester Wheatsheaf), Chapter 12.

Kreps, D. and R. Wilson (1982) 'Reputation and imperfect information', *Journal of Economic Theory*, 27, 253–79.

Kreps, D, F. Milgrom, J. Roberts and R. Wilson (1982) 'Rational cooperation in the finitely-repeated prisoner's dilemma', *Journal of Economic Theory*, 27, 245–52.

Krugman, P.R. (1984) 'Import protection as export promotion: international competition in the presence of oligopoly and economics of scale', in H. Kierzkowski (ed.), *Monopolistic Competition and International Trade* (Oxford: Oxford University Press).

Kühn, H.W. (1953) 'Extensive games and the problem of information', in H.W. Kühn and A.W. Tücker (eds), *Contribution to the Theory of Games*, 2 (Princeton: Princeton University Press).

Laussel, D. (1991) 'Strategic commercial policy revisited: a supply function equilibrium model', *American Economic Review*, 82, 84–99.

Laussel, D. and C. Montet (1994) 'Strategic trade policies', in D. Greenaway and L.A. Winters (eds), *Surveys in International Trade* (Oxford: Blackwell).

Laussel, D. and C. Montet (1995) 'La dynamique des guerres commerciales', *Revue économique*, 46, 911–19 (in French).

Luce, R.D. and H. Raiffa (1957) *Games and Decisions* (New York: John Wiley).

Marks, R. (1992) 'Repeated games and finite automata', in J. Creedy, J Borland and J. Eichberger, *Recent Developments in Game Theory* (Cheltenham: Edward Elgar).

McMillan, J. (1986) *Game Theory in International Economics, 1: Fundamentals of Pure and Applied Economics* (New York: Harwood).

Mertens, J.F. (1987) 'Repeated games', in *Proceedings of the International Congress of Mathematicians*, Berkeley, 1528–76.

Milgrom, P. (1985) 'Economies with asymmetric information', Yale University, unpublished.

Montet, C. (1991) 'Game theory and strategic behavior', in M. Bleaney, D. Greenaway and I. Stewart (eds), *Companion to Contemporary Economic Thought* (London: Routledge).

Nash, J.F. (Jr) (1950) 'Equilibrium points in n – person games', *Proceedings of the National Academy of Sciences*, 36, 48–9.

Nash, J.F. (Jr) (1951) 'Non-cooperative games', *Annals of Mathematics*, 54, 289–93.

Osborne, M.J. and A. Rubinstein (1994) *A Course in Game Theory* (Cambridge, MA: MIT Press), Chapters 8, 9.

Owen, G. (1995) *Game Theory*, 3rd edn (San Diego: Academic Press), Chapters 2, 3, 5.

Pearce, D. (1992) 'Repeated games: cooperation and rationality', in J.J. Laffont (ed.), *Advances in Economic Theory: Sixth World Congress*, 1, (Cambridge: Cambridge University Press), Chapter 4.

Rasmusen, E. (1989) *Games and Information: An Introduction to Game Theory* (Oxford: Blackwell).

Reynolds, S. (1987) 'Capacity investment, preemption, and commitment in an infinite horizon model', *International Economic Review*, 28, 69–88.

Riezman, R. (1991) 'Dynamic tariffs with asymmetric information', *Journal of International Economics*, 30, 267–84.

Rosenthal, R.H. (1981) 'Games of perfect information, predatory pricing and the chain store paradox', *Journal of Economic Theory*, 25, 92–100.

Rotemberg, J. and G. Saloner (1986) 'A supergame-theoretic model of price wars during booms', *American Economic Review*, 76, 390–407.

Samuelson, L. (1992) 'Subgame perfection' in J. Creedy, J. Borland and J.Eichberger (eds), *Recent Developments in Game Theory* (Cheltenham: Edward Elgar).

Schelling, T.C. (1960) *The Strategy of Conflict* (Cambridge, MA: Harvard University Press).

Selten, R. (1965) 'Spieltheoretische Behandlung eines Oligopolmodells mit Nachfrageträgheit', *Zeitschrift für die gesamte Staatswissenschaft*, 121, 301–24, 667–89 (in German).

Smith, M.A.M. (1987) 'Strategic investment, multinational corporations, and trade policy', *European Economic Review*, 31, 89–96.

Spence, M. (1977) 'Entry, capacity, investment and oligopolistic pricing', *Bell Journal of Economics*, 6, 163–72.

Sorin, S. (1992) 'Repeated games with complete information', in R.J. Aumann and S. Hart (eds), *Handbook of Game Theory with Economic Applications*, 1, (Amsterdam: North-Holland), Chapter 4.

Tirole, J. (1988) *The Theory of Industrial Organization*, (Cambridge, MA: MIT Press).

Tower (1975) 'The optimum quota and retaliation', *Review of Economic Studies*, 42, 623–30.

Von Neumann, J. (1928) 'Zur theorie des Gesellschattsspiele', *Mathematische Annalen*, 100, 295–320 (English translation, 'On the theory of game strategy', in A.W. Tücker and R.D. Luce (eds), *Contributions to the Theory of Games*, 4, Princeton: Princeton University Press, 1959).

Wolfstetter, E. (1999) *Topics in Microeconomics, Industrial Organization, Auctions and Incentives* (Cambridge: Cambridge University Press).

4 Non-Cooperative Games with Imperfect or Incomplete Information

4.1 Games with incomplete information: Bayesian equilibrium
4.2 Perfection and sequentiality: refinement 2
4.3 Forward induction: refinement 3
4.4 Applications

Most non-cooperative games have a NE but, very often, they have many equilibria. Additional restrictions are then necessary in order to discard some of them: we need 'refinements' of the NE concept. For extensive-form games with perfect information, sub-game perfection provides a powerful and seemingly natural refinement: this criterion eliminates equilibria sustained by incredible threats or promises off the equilibrium path. Unfortunately in games with *imperfect* information, the SPE concept loses much of its selection power, particularly in games with no proper sub-game, where every NE is also sub-game perfect. Therefore, stronger refinements have to be defined for general games with imperfect information.

In other respects, the NE concept was introduced in games with *complete* information: each player is supposed to know all data about the structure of the game and about the rationality of players; in particular each one knows the exact preferences of her (or his) opponents in order to anticipate their behaviour and calculate her (or his) best response. Yet, such a requirement is very demanding; there are in fact many economic conflicting situations in which some information is private. Thus the question is: can we generalize the notion of NE to more general and realistic games of *incomplete* information? The answer is 'yes', though under some rather strong conditions. For games in which players are incompletely informed about the characteristics of their opponents, the 'Bayesian equilibrium' (BE) has the properties of NE after transforming the initial incomplete information game into an *imperfect* information game by a 'Harsanyi procedure'. Ignorance about players' characteristics is analytically captured by introducing several 'types' of players together with an exogenously given probability distribution on the set of possible types, which is supposed common knowledge of all players. Unfortunately, multiplicity is the rule for Bayesian equilibria, too, so that we still need refinements in order to eliminate unreasonable equilibria. It is an especially crucial question since in games with incomplete information sub-game perfection never applies.

The number of refinements that have been proposed for games with imperfect information is indeed staggering. Yet we can claim that all these refinements represent attempts to formalize a few intuitive ideas. Backward induction and forward induction, in connection with iterated dominance, are the two great principles of 'strategic stability' in the background of the different refinement criterions. An equilibrium might not only be consistent with deductions based on the opponents rational choices in the *future* ('backward induction'), but also with inferences based on the opponents' rational choices in the *past* '(forward induction'). This chapter is devoted to the analysis of this difficult theoretical topic and at the same time, we present economic applications of the main defined concepts.

In section 4.1 we present a generalization of the NE notion for incomplete information games; we show in particular that those games may be analytically treated as games with complete but imperfect information. Section 4.2 is concerned with refinements in the spirit of backward induction: 'perfectness' and 'sequentiality'. In section 4.3 we tackle the second great logic of refinement, namely forward induction. Finally, section 4.4 studies some economic applications of these refinements. Economic applications of perfectness and sequentiality in repeated games with incomplete information are first described. These models mainly illustrate the leading role of 'reputation effects' in this framework. Emphasis is next placed on signalling games as economic applications of forward induction, in section 4.3.

4.1 Games with incomplete information: Bayesian equilibrium

The extension of the NE concept to games with incomplete information was first proposed by Harsanyi (1967–8). In order to understand the full implications of this approach, it is necessary to precisely recall the set of assumptions characterizing a game with complete information and to emphasize those which are dropped in the procedure imagined by Harsanyi.

4.1.1 The axiomatic framework of games with complete information

Remember that in a complete information game players know all the information which is not explicitly excluded by the game rule. Five main assumptions impose conditions on the rationality implicit in a non-cooperative Nash behaviour:

H1   Players know everything about the game rule: the circumstances under which they are led to choose a strategy, the different possible decisions and the information available about the history of the game before the time they are to take their decision; and this information is common knowledge.

H2   Players know everything about the characteristics of the participants: their preferences and their beliefs. Players' preferences are perceived through their payoff functions defined on the action possibility sets of all players. When chance moves intervene in the game, players' beliefs are formally represented by subjective probability distributions on the set of 'states of nature'. These beliefs on the 'states of nature' are common knowledge, but of course players' beliefs about the strategies chosen by the other players remain determined by an analysis of the game.

Rationality implies that anyone puts herself (or himself) in the other's place and tries to examine things from the other's point of view. Everyone makes the same reasoning, which gives rise to a phenomenon of crossed expectations of the type: 'If I think that you think that I think that you think ...'. There is nothing *a priori* to stop these reasoning chains until all the strategies can ultimately be considered as reasonable. The only way to escape this kind of infinite retrogression is to add supplementary conditions. Usually three additional assumptions are implicitly agreed upon (Binmore and Dasgupta, 1986):

H3   Every rational player behaves as a Bayesian agent: she (or he) weighs *all* uncertainties by introducing subjective probability distributions, then she (or he) maximizes her (or his) expected payoff. Each of these beliefs is common knowledge.

H4   Every rational player is able to reproduce the reasoning conducted by any other rational player provided she (or he) knows the same information; thus the difference in players' beliefs can be traced to differences in information (it is not possible to 'agree to disagree').

H5   Rationality of players is common knowledge.

Under these five assumptions, the reasonable solution of a game with complete information is necessarily a NE, or possibly a correlated equilibrium if players have non-independent beliefs about the strategies played by their rivals (Indeed *H*1 and *H*5 may be slackened: what is necessary is simply *mutual* knowledge of the game rule and of players' rationality, see sub-section 3.2.1 of Chapter 3).

Consider a two-player game and assume that the pair (x_1, x_2) is not a NE. Then, under the five preceding assumptions, this outcome of the game would not be chosen. If players were playing (x_1, x_2), this would mean that at least one strategy, say x_1, is not the best reply to the other, x_2.

Why then would player 1 choose x_1? He would not have chosen it if he had anticipated that player 2 were going to play x_2. So x_1 must be a best response strategy to the strategy of player 2 that player 1 had expected, for instance $\hat{x}_2$, and this belief is common knowledge. However, since, by assumption, player 2 chose x_2, this means that player 1 makes an error in reasoning. It follows that assumptions $H4$ and $H5$ are not fulfilled. So, this outcome cannot be chosen.

In this reasoning, however, the role of assumption $H5$ is not entirely clear. Yet, without $H5$, assumption $H4$ would be purposeless. Luce and Raiffa (1957) raised this issue. Indeed it is legitimate to call 'irrational' a player who does not follow a Nash non-cooperative behaviour but it is more difficult to also call her (or his) rivals irrational, since it can be perfectly rational for them to behave irrationally in this case. Similar considerations developed the notion of 'rationalizable strategies'.

4.1.2   Rationalizable strategies

This notion was introduced separately by Bernheim (1984) and Pearce (1984). They defend the idea that there is no *a priori* reason that Nash strategies are necessarily chosen by players on the sole base of 'rationality' and 'common knowledge' postulates. They suggest a weaker concept of 'rationalizable' strategic behaviour which relies on a minimal assumption: it is just common knowledge that each player is *rational in a Bayesian sense*. In this more restrictive axiomatic framework non-Nash strategies can eventually be reasonably chosen by players. Thus, this work questions the idea that any reasonable outcome of a non-cooperative game with complete information should be a NE.

How can the choice of an outcome (x_1, x_2), which is not a NE, be justified? Player 1 chooses strategy x_1 because she believes that player 2 will choose $\hat{x}_2$. This belief is justified by an infinite sequence of crossed expectations like: '1 believes that 2 believes that 1 will choose $\hat{x}_1$, and $\hat{x}_2$ is a best response to $\hat{x}_1$; 1 believes that 2 believes that 1 believes that 2 will play $\tilde{x}_2$, against which $\hat{x}_1$ is a best response, and so on. However – and this is the essential point – 2 is not supposed to play $\hat{x}_2$. In particular, 2 is authorized to believe that 1 believes that 2 will choose a strategy other than $\hat{x}_2$, while 1 believes in reality that 2 will choose $\hat{x}_2$.

This reasoning is perfectly consistent with the assumption of common knowledge on players' Bayesian rationality. Each player is uncertain about the strategy which will be chosen by her (or his) rival. She (or he) assigns subjective probabilities to these different possible strategies and she (or he) determines her (or his) actions by maximizing her (or his) expected payoff. She (or he) behaves as if she (or he) were choosing a best response to one of the mixed strategies of her (or his) rival. But how are the beliefs formed? Generally, one assumes that the probabilities assigned by each player to her (or his) rival's strategies are based on what she (or he) knows about this rival. The essential assumption here is that the player knows that her (or his) rival is rational in a Bayesian sense.

While Nash strategies require that each player knows the other player's *equilibrium* behaviour, rationalizable strategies do not assume that players' beliefs about each other's actions are correct. The crucial feature of common expectations is relaxed. Predictions are based only on the assumptions that the game structure and players' rationality are common knowledge. The difference is that not all players need to have the same beliefs, nor need their beliefs be consistent: it is a 'non-equilibrium' notion. In this framework rational behaviour means simply choosing a mixed strategy of best response to different mixed strategies.

Furthermore, like iterated dominance presented previously (section 2.2), rationalizability looks at a game from the point of view of a *single* player. Each player takes an action based on reasoning that does not require knowledge of the rivals' actions. Iterated dominance and rationalizability are in fact two closely related notions. In some way, the latter is the 'contra-positive' of the former when dominance is *strict*. Iterated strict dominance rests on the following axiom: a rational player will never play a strictly dominated strategy. Rationalizability asks the complementary question: what are *all* the strategies that a rational player could play? The answer is that she (or he) cannot play a strategy that is not a best response to some beliefs about her (or his) rivals' strategies. Since a strictly dominated strategy is never a best response, rationalizable strategies form a subset of those strategies that survive iterated deletion of a *strictly* dominated strategy; in two-players' games the two are identical (see Pearce, 1984; Tan and Werlang, 1988 for an overview on the subject).

In many games where there are no strictly dominated strategies, all strategies are rationalizable. It follows that this approach has a rather weak predictive power. Nevertheless, it has the advantage of stressing the restrictiveness of 'common rational expectations' assumptions behind Nash behaviour and exploring the logical implications of weaker assumptions about players' knowledge.

Remark 1

The notion of rationalizable strategy supposes a statistic independence of players' beliefs. That is the reason for which in general games (more than two players) an IDE (with strict dominance) is not always a rationalizable strategy. Allowing *correlated* beliefs about the others players' strategies make more strategies rationalizable, of course. Indeed it weakens rationalizability, so that it becomes 'correlated rationalizability' (Brandenburger and Dekel, 1987) and it was even proven that this notion is then equivalent to iterated deletion of strictly dominated strategies (Fudenberg and Tirole, 1991, Chapter 2, for instance).

Remark 2

Limiting players' common knowledge to their 'Bayesian' rationality is probably too restrictive. There are few situations in economics where agents cannot anticipate the behaviour of their rivals from another viewpoint. This argument partly refers to an issue already raised when we examined the different scenarios that can explain justification of an equilibrium (see subsection 3.1.3 of chapter 3). The role of conventions was especially mentioned. It can be legitimate to admit that, in certain circumstances, the ruling conventions are common knowledge. From a more general point of view, the approach in terms of 'rationalizability' offers the advantage of underlining the limits of the rationalistic scenario, that is the approach which bases the equilibrium of a game on consideration of *ex ante* reasoning of players only. It should be recalled that this is not the only way to rationalize an equilibrium in a game. The evolutive approach is an alternative way. For instance, one can admit that an equilibrium is reached through an adjustment process reflecting an adaptive behaviour of trial and error by myopic players during a long enough repetition of the game in real time rather than through the effect of prior crossed expectations of the players (see Chapter 7 for a discussion of this alternative approach).∎

According to Harsanyi, the fundamental assumption in the axiomatic approach of complete information games is H2, because uncertainties concerning the game rules can in fact be formulated in terms of uncertainties about the payoffs. In particular he has shown how one can transform a game with incomplete information about strategy sets into a game with incomplete information about payoffs by expanding the strategy spaces of the players appropriately. The approach suggested is then to find a means of getting rid of assumption H2. The notion of 'Bayesian game' offers the advantage of keeping NE as a solution concept.

4.1.3   The Bayesian game and Nash equilibrium

Dropping assumption H2 means that there is an uncertainty about the 'characteristics' of the players. Let us consider first a simple game in order to present the procedure imagined by Harsanyi.

Example (Fudenberg and Tirole, 1991a, 209–11)

A firm (player 1) contemplates the possibility of producing a new product, while simultaneously another firm (player 2) seeks to enter the market. Player 1 knows the cost of producing the product, while player 2 hesitates between two cost levels: a high one (HC) and a low one (LC). The payoffs of the game are shown in Figure 4.1. Player 2's payoffs are independent

Figure 4.1 A game of incomplete information: strategic form

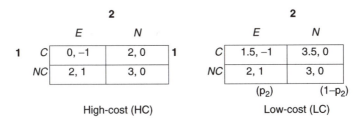

		2	
		E	N
1	C	0, –1	2, 0
	NC	2, 1	3, 0

High-cost (HC)

		2	
		E	N
1	C	1.5, –1	3.5, 0
	NC	2, 1	3, 0
		(p_2)	($1-p_2$)

Low-cost (LC)

of the production costs of firm 1. But they are indirectly a function of this cost (uncertain for player 2), since they differ according to the decision taken by firm 1 to create the new product or not, and since for player 1 the payoffs depends on the costs when production is chosen.

Figure 4.1 describes the strategic form of this game with two strategies for player 1: create the new product (C) or non-create (NC) and two strategies for player 2: enter the market (E) or not enter (N).

If the production cost is high, for player 1 strategy NC dominates strategy C. On the other hand, if the cost is low, player 1's choice depends on his belief about the probability of entry of firm 2. Let p_2 be this probability. Then for player 1, C is preferable to NC if:

$$1.5p_2 + 3.5(1 - p_2) > 2p_2 + 3(1 - p_2)$$

or:

$$p_2 < 1/2$$

Hence, in this game, player 1 will try to anticipate the behaviour of player 2 in order to choose his own strategy, while player 2 cannot anticipate the behaviour of player 1 as a function of the sole knowledge of this player's payoffs. We have a game of incomplete information owing to the uncertainty about the cost of production of firm 1 for firm 2.

The device imagined by Harsanyi to solve this game consists of introducing a 'chance move' which determines the 'type' of the player (i.e. here his production cost). In the modified game, the *incomplete* information of player 2 concerning player 1's characteristics becomes *imperfect* information about the chance move of Nature, and the modified game becomes tractable with the concept of NE. Figure 4.2 illustrates the extensive form of the transformed game, after the introduction of the supplementary player – Nature **N** – which chooses the type of player 1 (P being the probability of high costs and (1-P) the probability of low costs).

Figure 4.2   A game of incomplete information: extensive form

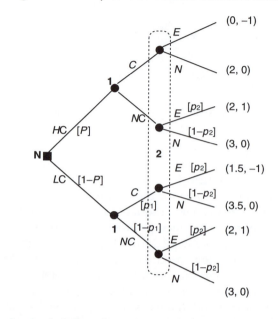

Let p_1 be the probability that player 1 will choose C when the cost is low (when the cost is high, he never plays C which is dominated by NC). An equilibrium is reached if there is a pair (p_1, p_2) such that p_1 is a best response to player 2's choice when the cost is low and p_2 is a best response to player 1's choice, for a given belief P.

Player 2's expected payoff is: $P + (1 - P)[-p_1 + (1 - p_1)]$ when he chooses E and 0 when he chooses N. It follows that player 2's best response is:

- Play E (i.e.: $p_2 = 1$) if: $P(1) + (1 - P)[p_1(-1) + (1 - p_1)(1)] > 0$ or:
$$p_1 < \frac{1}{2(1 - P)}$$

- Play N (i.e. $p_2 = 0$) if: $p_1 > \dfrac{1}{2(1 - P)}$

- Play one or the other strategies if: $p_1 = \dfrac{1}{2(1 - P)}$

Player 1's best response is:

- Play C (i.e. $p_1 = 1$) if: $p_2 < \frac{1}{2}$
- Play NC (i.e. $p_1 = 0$) if: $p_2 > \frac{1}{2}$
- Play one or the other strategies if: $p_2 = \frac{1}{2}$

It is clear then that, for instance, $(p_1^*, p_2^*) = (0, 1)$ (i.e. player 1 chooses NC and player 2 chooses E) is an equilibrium whatever the value of P. In this case, $p_1 = 0$ is always consistent with the condition $p_1 < \dfrac{1}{2(1 - P)}$

(imposed by $p_2 = 1$) since $0 \le P \le 1$, and $p_2 = 1$ verifies $p_2 > \frac{1}{2}$ (imposed by $p_1 = 0$). In the same way, $(p_1^*, p_2^*) = (1, 0)$ (i.e. player 1 chooses C and player 2 chooses N) is also an equilibrium, but only for some value of P. In this case indeed, $p_2 = 0$ is consistent with the condition $p_2 < \frac{1}{2}$ (imposed by $p_1 = 1$), but $p_1 = 1$ verifies

$$p_1 \ge \frac{1}{2(1 - P)}$$

(imposed by $p_2 = 0$) only if $P \le \frac{1}{2}$. There is also in this case a mixed strategy equilibrium:

$$(p_1^*, p_2^*) = \left(\frac{1}{2(1 - P)}, \frac{1}{2} \right)$$

In the previous example, players' 'types' are simply different costs. More generally the 'type' of a player encompasses all kinds of private information likely to influence players' choices. To know the type of a player means to possess a complete description of this player (preferences and beliefs).

Assume that it is common knowledge that each player i belongs to one of the possible types $t \in T_i$ (to simplify suppose that the sets T_i, $i = 1, \ldots, n$, are finite). Each player knows only her (or his) own type t_i. The beliefs embodied in the description of a type $t \in T_i$ must include subjective probability distributions over the sets T^{-i}. These probabilities $p_i(t^{-i}/t_i)$ represent uncertainty about players' type against whom i is playing. If these players' types are independent (which is mostly the case in economics), then p_i is independent of t_i.

This uncertainty is taken into account in the game by the introduction of a 'chance move' preceding the play. This initial move of Nature (or this 'state of the world') selects a vector of 'types' $(t_1, \ldots, t_n)$ which are going to play the game according to a prior probability distribution $p(t_1, \ldots, t_n)$ that one assumes to be common knowledge. Consequently, each 'type' determines her (or his) own belief about other players' 'types', assuming that she (or he) was herself (or himself) selected by Nature.

Proceeding this way, one gets a *Bayesian game in strategic form*. The initial chance move linked with the original game with incomplete information generates a game with complete but imperfect information. In this game the 'players' (or agents) are represented by the *types* and no longer by the actual players. There is one 'player' for every possible type of every player in the given game. The type t_i of a player (known by herself (or himself) only) determines her (or his) payoff function $u_i(a_1, \ldots, a_n; t_i)$, where $a_i \in A_i$ is player i's action. Note that to avoid confusion, in a strategic-form Bayesian game, the object of choice is called an 'action' rather that a 'strategy'.

Sometimes, the private information of the players concerns not only their own payoff function, but also the other players' payoff functions. In order to take this possibility into account, the payoff function of player i is written down with a more general form: $u_i(a_1, \ldots, a_n; t_1, \ldots, t_n)$. If a player is not selected by the initial chance move, she will get a zero payoff.

Definition 1 (Bayesian game in strategic form)

The strategic-form representation of a Bayesian game specifies the players' action sets A_i, their type sets T_i, their beliefs p_i and their payoff functions u_i. We denote this game by $G = \{A_1, \ldots, A_n; T_1, \ldots, T_n; p_1, \ldots, p_n; u_1, \ldots, u_n\}$. ■

A last technical point needs to be covered to complete the presentation of a Bayesian game. Recall that we assume that initially Nature draws a vector of types $(t_1, \ldots, t_n)$ according to the prior probability distribution $p(t_1, \ldots, t_n)$. Once Nature reveals t_i to player i, she is able to compute the belief $p_i(t^{-i}/t_i)$ using Bayes' rule:

$$p_i(t^{-i}/t_i) = \frac{p(t^{-i}, t_i)}{p(t_i)} = \frac{p(t^{-i}, t_i)}{\sum\limits_{t^{-i} \in T^{-i}} p(t^{-i}, t_i)}$$

Of course, if players' types are independent, $p_i(t^{-i})$ does not depend on t_i, but the belief is still derived from the prior distribution $p(t_1, \ldots, t_n)$.

Once this transformation of the original game is accomplished, one can develop an argument similar to the one leading to a NE in a game with complete information.

We know that generally speaking in a strategic-form game a player's strategy must include all the decisions that she might be induced to take in all kinds of circumstances. In a Bayesian game, a strategy for player i is thus a *function* $x_i(t_i)$, which specifies, for each t_i of T_i, the action that type t_i would choose from the set A_i, assuming she (or he) had been selected by Nature. Hence the set of *strategies* is constructed from the sets of *types* and *actions*. The pure strategies set of player i, X_i, is the set of all the functions with domain T_i and range A_i. Assume that type $t \in T_i$ chooses strategy $x_i(t_i)$ when the initial chance move allows her (or him) to play. This strategy tells player i how to play according to her (or his) type. Notice, however, that, unlike games of complete information, in a Bayesian game the strategy sets are not given in the strategic-form game.

Definition 2 (Bayesian equilibrium)

In the Bayesian game $G = \{A_1, \ldots, A_n; T_1, \ldots, T_n; p_1, \ldots, p_n; u_1, \ldots, u_n\}$ the outcome $(x_1^*, \ldots, x_n^*)$ is a BE if no player has an incentive to change her (or his) strategy x_i^* after knowing her (or his) type $t \in T_i$

unless another player j herself (or himself) deviated from her (or his) own strategy x_j^*. That is: if $x^* = (x_1^*, \ldots, x_i^*, \ldots, x_n^*)$ is a BE for all i, for all $t_i \in T_i$, x_i^* is solution of the optimization problem:

$$\max_{a_i \in A_i} \sum_{t^i \in T^{-i}} p_i(t^{-i}/t^i) u_i(x_1^*(t_1), \ldots, x_{i-1}^*(t_{i-1}), a_i, x_{i+1}^*(t_{i+1}), \ldots,$$

$$x_n^*(t_n); t_1, \ldots, t_n). \blacksquare$$

This definition points out that a BE is nothing but a NE applied to a Bayesian game. Harsanyi's merit was to show that this concept could also be useful in studying incomplete information games after a proper modification of the original game.

Remark I

It should be emphasized that in the study of incomplete information games presented here, assumptions H3, H4 and H5 of complete information games are maintained. Moreover, the probabilities with which the types are chosen by Nature (the priors) are common knowledge. Therefore, a large amount of common information still remains in the model. Note however that equilibrium *actions* – of course – are not common knowledge; otherwise asymmetric information would play no role.

4.1.4 A classical application: auctions

Auctions are one of the most famous applications of the BE concept.

Auctions as Bayesian games

An auction model is a useful description of a 'thin market' where the fundamental characteristics is the asymmetry of market position. In contrast to the model of perfect competition which supposes that buyers and sellers are sufficiently numerous so that agents have no degree of market power, in auction models there is competition on only one side of the market. Typically, we suppose there is a simple seller of an indivisible object who face a certain number n of potential buyers. Competition among the buyers takes place according to a particular scheme specifying how to submit bids from the buyers, who win the object, and what is the price paid by the winner.

Auctions can be viewed as games of incomplete information for two reasons. First, there is a problem of hidden types: the seller does not know the valuation (that is the reserve price) that the buyers place on the object that she want to sell. Secondly, these valuations are supposed to be independently and identically distributed, drawn from a common distribution over a certain interval.

Auction models represent a class of principal–agents problem with 'adverse selection' whose analysis is especially interesting when assuming that it is common knowledge that everybody is risk-neutral. Most commonly, the choice of auction scheme used rests with the seller who is viewed as the 'principal' and the potential buyers are viewed as the 'agents'. If we wonder about the more profitable auction scheme for the seller (that is, on the means which allow the seller to best exploit her (or his) monopoly position), we face the problem of *designing* games (or implementation theory). Recall that we have already met this question (see sub-section 2.4.2 of chapter 2) to illustrate applications of DSE.

It was proved that in the case of 'private' value auctions (i.e. when the valuations depend merely on individual tastes), using a 'Vickrey auction' (that is a sealed-bid auction in which the object is sold to the highest bidder but at the highest bid by a loser) guarantees the seller the second-highest valuation among the set of buyers. It is a 'second-best' outcome because the seller has not extracted the whole surplus from the situation.

There is a large literature on the 'optimal auction' whose purpose is to find the best auction scheme from the seller's viewpoint notably with the help of the revelation principle in the context of a Bayesian game. (The proof of the revelation principle for BE is due to Myerson, 1979.) (See Fudenberg and Tirole, 1991a, Chapter 7 for a survey of Bayesian games and mechanism design.)

However, before wondering about the optimal auction, a natural first question is to seek how a sale price is determined in each particular auction procedure. We now deal with this question in a straightforward auction model.

A particular first-price sealed-bid auction model

Let us consider what is called a 'first-price' sealed-bid auction. In this bidding procedure bidders simultaneously submit their bids, and the highest bidder gets the object and pays the price he announces.

We focus on a particular model whose BE is easy to compute (this model is borrowed from Gibbons, 1992, 155–8). There are only two bidders ($i = 1, 2$) with a valuation v_i for the object. These valuations are independently and uniformly distributed on the interval [0,1]. The bidders are risk-neutral. Furthermore, we impose the reasonable requirements that no bidder bids more than her (or his) valuation and bids are constrained to be non-negative. All of these assumptions are common knowledge.

This problem can be viewed as a strategic-form Bayesian game $G = \{A_1, A_2; T_1, T_2; p_1, p_2; u_1, u_2\}$. Players' actions are their bids b_i, so the action sets are: $A_i = [0, v_i]$. The player's valuation v_i represents her (or his) type: $T_i = [0, 1]$. Furthermore, since the valuations are independent, each player believes that the other's valuation is uniformly distributed on $[0, 1]$, whatever her (or his) own valuation. Finally, the payoff functions are such that:

$$u_i(b_1, b_2; v_1, v_2) = (v_i - b_i)w_i$$

with $w_i = \text{prob}\{b_i > b_j\}$, that is the probability to win.

In order to compute a BE of this game, we have to define the players' strategy sets. A strategy indicates the bid that each type would announce: $b_i = b_i(v_i)$. The higher v_i, the more likely b_i is high; thus, we restrict ourselves to strictly increasing strategies. Furthermore, since the types are continuously distributed, we assume that the strategies are differentiable functions. Finally, since the model is symmetric, we consider only symmetric BE in which players' strategies are identical; that means that two players with a same valuation will submit the same bid:

$$b_i(v_i) = b(v_i) \text{ for } i = 1, 2 \tag{4.1}$$

In a BE of the game, by definition, player 1's strategy $b(v_1)$ is a best response to player 2's strategy $b(v_2)$, and inversely. For a given value of v_i, player i's optimal strategy is a solution of the optimization problem:

$$\max_{b_i} (v_i - b_i)w_i \tag{4.2}$$

with $w_i = \text{prob}\{b_i > b(v_j)\}$

Let $b^{-1}(b_j)$ be the valuation which allows bidder j to win the object. That is:

$$b^{-1}(b_j) = v_j \text{ if } b_j = b(v_j)$$

and:

$$w_i^{-1} = \text{prob}\{b^{-1}(b_i) > v_j]$$

Since v_j is uniformly distributed on $[0, 1]$, we have:

$$w_i = w_i^{-1} = b^{-1}(b_i)$$

And the optimization problem [4.2] becomes:

$$\max b_i(v_i - b_i)b^{-1}(b_i)$$

The first-order necessary condition for this problem is:

$$(v_i - b_i)\frac{db^{-1}(b_i)}{db_i} - b^{-1}(b_i) = 0$$

Or, equivalently, according to [4.1]:

$$(v_i - b(v_i))\frac{db^{-1}(b(v_i))}{db_i} - b^{-1}(b(v_i)) = 0 \tag{4.3}$$

Now, it is clear that:

$$b^{-1}(b(v_i)) = v_i$$

and so:

$$\frac{db^{-1}(b(v_i))}{db_i} = \frac{1}{\dfrac{db(v_i)}{dv_i}}$$

Consequently, (4.3) is also equivalent to:

$$(v_i - b(v_i))\frac{1}{\dfrac{db(v_i)}{dv_i}} - v_i = 0$$

Finally, we conclude that the strategy $b(.)$ must satisfy the first-order differential equation:

$$\frac{db(v_i)}{dv_i}v_i - b(v_i) = v_i \tag{4.4}$$

Since the left-hand of this equation is precisely the derivative of $b(v_i)v_i$ with respect to v_i, integrating both sides of (4.4) yields:

$$b(v_i)v_i = \frac{1}{2}v_i^2 + c \tag{4.5}$$

where c is a constant of integration.

A boundary condition is necessary to eliminate the constant c. This condition is provided here by the initial requirement that we impose to reasonable bids:

$$0 \leq b(v_i) \leq v_i, \text{ for all } v_i$$

This assumption implies in particular:

$$b(0) = 0$$

and so:

$$c = 0$$

Therefore the solution of (4.5) is:

$$b(v_i) = v_i/2$$

We conclude that in this very simple auction model, there exists a unique symmetric BE in which each bidder submits a bid equal to half her (or his) true valuation. Such a result illustrates what the stakes are in this auction scheme. The bidder faces a trade-off: the higher the bid the more likely she (or he) is to win; the lower the bid the larger the payoff she (or he) gets when winning. (For a survey on auctions, see in particular McAfee and McMillan, 1987; Wilson, 1992; Klemperer, 1999.)

4.2 Perfectness and sequentiality: refinement 2

Recall that multiplicity of equilibria means that there are several strategy vectors which are consistent with rational behaviour of all players. Under these circumstances, of course, 'putting oneself in the other player's shoes' does not help to anticipate what will occur in the game. Therefore, for games with multiple equilibria, the rationality assumption has to be supplemented by other selection criteria in order to predict the outcome of a game. Sub-game perfection is a good one because out-of-equilibrium behaviour is irrational in a non-perfect equilibrium. But we saw that there are some potential difficulties with this notion. Indeed the failure of sub-game perfection is not that it is too restrictive but rather that it still allows too many outcomes to be solutions in imperfect information games and specifically in incomplete information games where sub-games fail to exist.

For games with multiple equilibria, a theory of social co-ordination would thus have to use additional structural information. The flourishing literature on refinements of NE deals with this controversial topic of selection of an equilibrium according to the *'rationalistic' scenario*.

Though the issue is rather complex, we can follow Binmore (1992) who proposed an easy way of looking at refinement theory. The ideal framework in which the orthodox game theory is developed is in fact only one of the 'possible worlds' in the logicians' sense. In this world, rational players do not ever deviate from their equilibrium strategies. Their behaviour is dictated by their expectations about what would happen should they deviate from the equilibrium, but if they are rational the probability of the advent of out-of-equilibrium outcomes is equal to zero. But how to say something sensible about what happens at equilibrium, without contemplating what might happen *outside* equilibrium? One can then claim that an event E with a probability *zero* in the world of game theory, can perfectly correspond to an event E' with a *positive* probability in one of the other possible 'neighbouring' worlds. The players' behaviour in the latter world if event E' does happen can be considered as good approximations of their behaviour in the world of game theory if E materializes. Any interest in this approach depends of course closely on the possible neighbouring world called upon. In turn, this choice determines the choice of the criterion of refinement.

The neighbouring world which has been the most extensively explored until now is a world where a certain amount of *uncertainty* or a kind of *irrationality* always is present. Players are never sure about the behaviour of their rivals and they are never in a position to allow them to discard entirely some of their decisions.

In strategic-form games the question arises of how a player will choose her (or his) strategies facing decisions which have a probability zero of being chosen by the rivals at equilibrium. It is necessary to argue about the relative likelihood of events about which the feeling is that they are unlikely to materialize. In extensive-form games the phenomenon takes a different form: the purpose is to take into account players' behaviours in nodes of the game tree never reached in equilibrium. Introducing these considerations justifies various refinement criteria in strategic-form games or in extensive-form games.

We have already seen that sub-game perfection is a natural generalization of backward induction to games with imperfect information (and also to infinite games). 'Perfectness' and 'sequentiality' are two kinds of stronger refinements in the same logic: they extend the possibilities of discarding non-credible threats or promises equilibria.

4.2.1 Perfectness

This kind of refinement treats players' rationality with respect to out-of-equilibrium events as the result of each player taking into account that the other players could make 'mistakes' that lead to these unexpected outcomes. The basic idea is that each player's actions are a best response not only given her (or his) equilibrium beliefs but also given a 'perturbed' belief that allows for the possibility of small 'trembles'. The 'neighbouring' world in which the reasoning is placed is a world where the players cannot exclude the possibility of slight mistakes in the choice of strategies; hence, the metaphor of the 'trembling hand'.

Perfect trembling hand equilibrium

This concept was proposed by Selten (1975) who called it simply 'perfect equilibrium'. Yet the same author had previously proposed the concept of SPE. So, in order to distinguish the two concepts the second generally is called 'perfect trembling hand equilibrium' (PTHE). It can be introduced through the study of the strategic-form game presented in Figure 4.3.

This game has two pure strategies NE: (r_1, c_1) and (r_2, c_2). But it may be claimed that the latter will be discarded. The argument goes as follows. If player 2 chooses c_2, then player 1 has nothing to win but also nothing to lose in playing r_1 (since $0 = 0$). If player 2 chooses by mistake c_1, 1 will get a higher payoff by choosing r_1 rather than r_2 ($1 > 0$). Similarly, player 2 cannot but win in playing c_1 rather than c_2. Consequently, even if the two players agree to choose outcome (r_2, c_2), it is likely that both of them deviate: that NE is unstable.

In the example presented above, notice that strategy c_2 for player 2 is weakly dominated by strategy c_1. Similarly for player 1, strategy r_2 is weakly dominated by strategy r_1. Note that it is a general result: a PTHE is a NE and attaches zero probability to weakly dominated strategies. Moreover, in a two-player game, a NE which attaches zero probability to weakly dominated strategies is a PTHE, but this latter statement for games with more than two players turns out to be false.

Formally, the selection of a PTHE was done through a transformation of the initial game into an auxiliary 'perturbed' game. This game has the same basic structure as the initial game, except for one particular property: all the strategies must be used with a minimal positive probability $\epsilon > 0$. In other words, this perturbed game is a game in which each player can choose only *mixed strategies* (i.e. which attach positive probabilities to each pure strategy).

Definition 3 (*Perfect trembling hand equilibrium*)

A strategy vector x is a PTHE (for a strategic-form game) if, for each player i, there exists a completely mixed strategy sequence $\{x_i^n\}$ such that:

(a) $x_i = \lim_{n \to +\infty} x_i^n$, for all i

(b) x_i is a best response of player i to the strategy vector of the other players $(x^{-i})^n$ for all n and all i.∎

The major point in this definition is that the strategies of the other players are assumed to be completely mixed, the probability distributions

Figure 4.3 PTHE

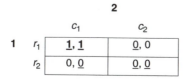

		c_1	c_2
		2	
1	r_1	**1, 1**	0, 0
	r_2	0, 0	0, 0

being independent of each other (non-correlated mistakes). Player i intends to play x_i and she (or he) assumes that her (or his) rivals intend to play x^{-i}. Yet the players can make some errors. While trying to play x^{-i}, they actually play $(x^{-i})^n$, a strategy vector such that all actions of i's rivals are possible but in which they are 'almost sure' to play according to their plans (condition a). Moreover, the equilibrium is such that the strategy chosen by player i (if she (or he) makes no error) is a best response to the strategies *actually* chosen by her (or his) rivals (condition b) and not simply to the strategies they plan to play (as is assumed in a NE). Note, however, that 'perfectness' in this sense is a relatively weak criterion: the definition requires only that *some* sequence of perturbed equilibria converge; it is not necessary that all such sequences converge.

Selten (1975) demonstrated the existence of such an equilibrium for any finite game and he proved that this notion has another attractive property, as the following result shows.

Theorem 1 (*Selten*)

Every strategic-form game with finite pure strategy sets has at least one PTHE. Moreover in a PTHE no player uses a dominated strategy.■

Note that the definition of a PTHE implies that there exists a particular relation between the solution of the initial game and the solution of the perturbed game. The PTHE of the initial game is the limit of the NE of the perturbed game when ε approaches zero. In other words, a NE of the initial game is a PTHE if each of its components remains optimal when the rivals' hands 'tremble' at the moment of choosing their strategies, that is when they are slightly mistaken.

Remark 1

The definition of a PTHE given here applies to strategic-form games. It cannot be immediately transposed to extensive-form games. The difficulty comes from the fact that in the extensive-form game directly built on the strategic form, the criterion of sub-game perfection can lead to the selection of an outcome which is different from the PTHE in the strategic form. In order to solve this difficulty, Selten uses a special procedure, called 'agent normal form', to construct the associated extensive form of the game. Each information set belongs to a particular player. So there are as many information sets as agents. Let h be a particular information set (i.e. a player in this new extensive form). The payoff for h is exactly equivalent to the payoff for player $i(h)$ in the original game. One can imagine that a player i holds more than one information set, but then she (or he) appoints an agent responsible for the decision at each set. These agents of i all have the same payoff function as player i, and therefore they act according to her (or his) interests. Yet, each of these agents is considered as a different player in this modified version of the extensive form of the original game. It is then possible to show that in this context any 'agent normal form' PTHE corresponds to a SPE, but the reverse is not true.■

Remark 2

We interpreted PTHE as the result of the recognition that players can be mistaken in choosing their strategies. However, another interpretation can be attached to the 'trembles'. This solution concept could be considered as a BE of an incomplete information game in which each player is almost – but not totally – sure of the rationality of the other players. Alternatively, for some game theorists, 'trembles' are just a calculation device that carry no significance of their own.■

Remark 3

It should be emphasized that the criterion of perfect equilibrium is not necessarily a good one from a collective point of view. It can lead us sometimes to discard an efficient NE. Consider the strategic form game represented in Figure 4.4.

This game has two pure strategies NE: (r_1, c_2) and (r_2, c_1). But only (r_1, c_2) is a PTHE. Notice that r_2 is weakly dominated by r_1: player 1 is indifferent with respect to r_1 and r_2 as long as player 2 chooses c_1 or c_2, and she prefers r_1 to r_2 if player 2 chooses c_3. Since r_2 is not a best response for 1 when 2 tries to play c_1 (if 2 by mistake plays c_3, r_1 is a best response), equilibrium (r_2, c_1) is not a PTHE, although this NE gives higher payoffs to the two players.■

This criterion of refinement has another limitation: it does not allow the deletion of *all* the intuitively unreasonable equilibria. The difficulty is that no restriction is placed on the 'trembles' in the perturbed games which support a PTHE. One response to this weakness would be to use an equilibrium notion about the particular 'trembles' chosen. In particular, we can define a 'strict' PTHE if for *every* sequence of perturbed equilibria the two conditions of the previous definition are fulfilled. Clearly, any strictly perfect equilibrium is a perfect equilibrium. Thus the concept is definitely stronger. Unfortunately, it may be too strong, because it suffers from non-existence (Samuelson, 1992, 24). An alternative approach was designed to deal with this drawback of the PTHE.

Figure 4.4   PTHE and inefficiency

		2		
		c_1	c_2	c_3
1	r_1	50, 0	5, 5	1, −1000
	r_2	50, 50	5, 0	0, −1000

Proper equilibrium

The idea is to construct theories in which 'trembles' are most likely or most plausible. For strategic-form games, this idea appears initially in the concept of 'proper equilibrium' (PE), which assumes that more costly 'trembles' are arbitrarily less likely than less costly ones.

Considers the game in strategic form in Figure 4.5.

This game was obtained by adding a new strategy to each of the games presented in Figure 4.3 for studying the PTHE. Furthermore one may note that for each player this new strategy is *strictly dominated*. Thus, it seems reasonable to claim that these strategies are without influence on the outcome of the game resulting from application of the perfection criterion. The outcome (r_1, c_1) is expected to appear again as the PTHE of this game. Yet the set of PTHE actually does not coincide in the two games. In the new game the outcome (r_2, c_2) also is an equilibrium. If players agreed to play (r_2, c_2), but if each player thinks that the error on the third strategy is more important than the error on the first, then it is truly optimal for her (or him) to choose the second. Therefore, adding a strictly dominated strategy may change the solution of the game.

In order to eliminate this kind of undesirable property of the perfection criterion, Myerson (1978) suggested the stronger criterion of 'properness'. The idea supporting this notion is that a player, although not immune to errors, generally tries to avoid the *most costly* of them. So, we admit that there is a kind of rationality in the process generating the errors. Formally this assumption materializes in terms of probabilities attached to the errors. A very costly error (in terms of payoffs) will be assigned a lower probability than a less costly one.

In the previous example only (r_1, c_1) is a PE. According to the logic of this refinement criterion, players should not expect that the errors concerning r_3 and c_3 have higher probabilities than the errors on r_1 and c_1. Owing to the fact that r_3 and c_3 are strictly dominated by r_1 and c_1, respectively, each player will try to avoid making mistakes on r_3 (or c_3) rather than on r_1 (or c_1). The consequence of this rational behaviour is thus that the outcome (r_2, c_2) is less likely to be realized than the outcome (r_1, c_1). The NE (r_2, c_2) is then discarded by the criterion of the trembling hand. Only the equilibrium (r_1, c_1) resists a deviation.

Figure 4.5   Proper equilibrium

		2		
		c_1	c_2	c_3
	r_1	1, 1	0, 0	−1, −2
1	r_2	0, 0	0, 0	0, −2
	r_3	−2, −1	−2, 0	−2, −2

It can be proved that any finite game in strategic form has a PE (Myerson, 1978).

Remark 4

PTHE are outcomes which are stable against some slight perturbations of the equilibrium strategies. PE require an outcome to be stable against perturbations of the equilibrium strategies which are more or less rational, since they assign the preponderance of weight to the better strategies. These two criteria do not exhaust the proposed refinements of NE for strategic-form games but the goal is always to focus on the most likely or more plausible 'tremble': 'robust' equilibria, 'persistent' equilibria,... (see Van Damme, 1991, Chapter 2, for a complete presentation).■

In summary, if we denote by **NE** the set of Nash equilibria in a given strategic-form game and by **PTHE** and **PE** the sets of perfect trembling hand equilibria and proper equilibrium, respectively (of course, these sets may be void), the relationship between these sets are the following:

PE ⊆ PTHE ⊆ NE

4.2.2 Sequentiality

The difficulty which arises when an extensive-form game has no subgame is that players are not able to know the node of the tree at which the play begins; so they have no way of calculating the effects of their decisions on terminal nodes. Solving this indeterminate situation requires the adoption of a theory on players' beliefs which allows one to select the correct node among the several initial ones.

Sequentiality is a kind of refinement based on the idea that a game between Bayesian players should be defined not only in terms of *actions* available to the players (as for sub-game perfection) but also in terms of their *beliefs*. Any definition of an equilibrium must in fact involve two types of assumptions. The first deals with what the players *do*, while the second bears on what they *believe*. The logic of 'assessment' reflects the relation of circularity existing between the actions and the beliefs of players.

Assessment equilibrium: strategies and beliefs

The first concern leads to the introduction of a *strategy vector* x (a strategy x_i for each player i). The second concern leads to the introduction of a *system of beliefs* μ, which assigns a probability measure μ_h to each information set h in the game tree.

When a player must decide in advance the action she (or he) will implement when the information set h is reached, she (or he) generally does not know which node will be reached in this set. She (or he) thus assigns subjective probabilities to each node of h. These priors represent players' beliefs.

The pair (x, μ) can be called an *'assessment'* of the game. Therefore an assessment is defined as the simultaneous consideration of a strategy vector and a system of beliefs for the players.

The equilibrium of a game must necessarily take the form of an *assessment equilibrium* (Binmore 1992, 536–7). The players' beliefs play a role as important as their strategies in the definition of the equilibrium (x^*, μ^*). The main advantage of this approach is to enlighten us as to the necessity of requiring some specific conditions upon players' beliefs. We need to discard complete arbitrariness of these beliefs. The criterion of sub-game perfection requires a condition of *credibility* on the *strategies*; it is also necessary to constrain the players to adopt *'reasonable' beliefs*.

The differences between the main refinement criteria of SPE rest on the more or less demanding assumptions placed upon players' beliefs. The weakest requirement just imposes two conditions: beliefs have to be consistent with equilibrium strategies and they have to be up to date with the Bayes' rule on any information set reached at equilibrium with a positive probability.

Each time a player reaches an information set, he must revise his priors, and thereby adopt posteriors taking into account any new information. So, at each information set, the beliefs are determined by the Bayes' rule and players' equilibrium strategies. Following the suggestion made by Kreps and Wilson (1982) we call 'consistency' this condition placed upon beliefs and 'sequential rationality' the condition concerning strategies. Yet, in order to formulate this last condition, we must introduce beforehand the notion of a 'continuation game' which is a generalization of the notion of a sub-game previously defined.

Definition 4 (*Continuation game*)

A continuation game corresponds to a sub-game, but it can start from *any* information set in the game tree and not only from the set reduced to singletons.■

Sequential rationality requires that, for any continuation game in the game tree, the players always plan to play the optimal strategies. More precisely, a player who takes a decision at a particular information set h assumes that in the continuation of the game the play will be in conformity with the vector of equilibrium strategies x^*.

Definition 5 (*Sequential rationality*)

Sequential rationality is verified if in each information set h, the actions decided by each player must be best responses simultaneously taking into account her (or his) beliefs in h and the other players' strategies in the continuation game starting from h.■

We must stress the link between strategies and beliefs. The beliefs are consistent between themselves and with the strategies, while the latter are optimal for given beliefs. Owing to this circularity, it is impossible to determine the equilibrium by backward induction only.

A simple example will illustrate how this approach allows us to select a particular equilibrium among NE.

Example

Consider the game with imperfect information presented previously in Figure 3.17 and reproduced in Figure 4.6 below. We saw that this game had two NE and one of them (L_1, R_2, R_3), although associated to a non-credible threat, resisted the test of sub-game perfection because of non-existence of a proper sub-game.

Consider the strategy vector $x = (L_1, R_2, R_3)$. The problem is to determine the system of beliefs μ likely to be associated with this vector of strategies, in order that assessment (x, μ) satisfies the two conditions defining the equilibrium: sequential rationality and consistency.

The information sets of players 1 and 2 are singletons. So, obviously, beliefs must assign a probability 1 to each of the nodes (x) and (y) of the game tree. On the other hand, the probabilities that μ must assign to nodes

Figure 4.6   Assessment equilibrium

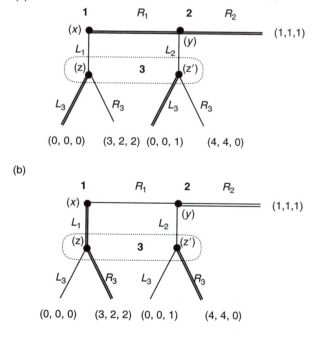

(z) and (z') in player 3's information set must satisfy the consistency condition. One adopts here the weakest expression for this assumption: the respect of Bayesian inference. When she has to take her decision, player 3 knows that player 1 chooses L_1 (see Figure 4.6b). She infers that node (z) is reached and μ must assign a probability 1 to (z) and 0 to (z') in player 3's information set.

Yet, a problem arises. While assessment (x, μ) does verify the condition of sequential rationality (player 1 and 3 each choose an optimal action, for given beliefs), the same is not true for player 2. Although his information set is not reached at equilibrium, notice that, should it be reached for any reason, player 2 would play L_2 and not R_2 ($4 > 1$). It follows that the strategy vector (L_1, R_2, R_3) can not be one of the components of equilibrium. So, while the criterion of SPE was not capable of discarding this non-credible equilibrium, the new approach succeeds in this task.

It is now necessary to show that this approach can justify the choice of the strategy vector $x^* = (R_1, R_2, L_3)$ as one of the components of the equilibrium of the game. Beliefs μ always must assign a probability 1 to (x) and (y). However, now, the consistency condition does not allow one to speak about player 3's information set (see Figure 4.6b). This set is not reached with a non-zero probability at equilibrium, and so Bayes' rule cannot apply. One can then turn to the condition of sequential rationality. This condition restricts the acceptable domain of probabilities μ_3 and $(1 - \mu_3)$ assigned to nodes (z) and (z'), respectively, in player 3's information set. If L_3 is an optimal decision for player 3 for given beliefs, this decision must lead to an average payoff at least as high as the one corresponding to R_3. Hence, the following inequality must hold:

$$0.\mu_3 + 1.(1 - \mu_3) \geq 2\mu_3 + 0.(1 - \mu_3)$$

or:

$$\mu_3 \leq \frac{1}{3}$$

Consequently, as long as player 3 believes that her probability of reaching node (z) is at most $\frac{1}{3}$ (and thus, at least $\frac{2}{3}$ to reach node (z')) in her information set, (x^*, μ^*) is an assessment equilibrium of the game.

In order to explain why player 3 believes that she has a higher probability of reaching (z') than (z), it is necessary to add stronger requirements about reasonableness of the players' beliefs.

Perfect Bayesian equilibrium

In games with *incomplete information*, the criterion of sub-game perfection never can apply since there is no proper sub-game in that case. In this class of games, the SPE concept can be replaced by the concept of 'perfect

Bayesian equilibrium' (PBE) as a criterion of perfection. On the other hand, since in games with incomplete information BE are just a generalization of NE, PBE also is a *refinement of BE*.

The concept is based directly on the principle of 'assessment', but the consistency condition is generally slightly stronger: the Bayesian revision of beliefs also applies at any information set reached at equilibrium with a zero probability, when possible. This simple version of PBE was proposed by Fudenberg and Tirole (1991b) for the class of 'multi-stage games with observed actions' (sometimes named 'games of almost-perfect information').

In these extensive-form games two properties are verified:

- In each stage, each player knows the history of the game (i.e. all the actions previously taken by everybody)
- No information set contained in a stage provides any knowledge of play in that stage (i.e. players' moves are simultaneous).

For instance, an incomplete information game in which the types of players are the unique root of strategic uncertainty corresponds to a multistage game with observed actions before transformation into a game with imperfect information by Harsanyi's procedure.

Many simple economic applications can be studied with the help of this class of game, for which the condition of sequential rationality and this slightly stronger consistency condition are sufficient to determine PBE.

On the whole, this concept rests on three basic principles:

1. *Harsanyi's procedure* which gives rise to the concept of BE, by changing a game with incomplete information into a game with complete but imperfect information.
2. The principle of *backward induction*. That is the basic idea supporting both SPE and PBE. However, this principle cannot be directly implemented (because of the circular relationship linking actions and beliefs). A condition of *sequential rationality* expresses the general validity of this principle for each continuation game: every PBE must induce a BE in each continuation game.
3. *Bayes' rule* for the revision of beliefs after any acquisition of information: this rule is imposed by the condition of *consistency*.

In spite of the good properties of PBE, it is not always effective in eliminating equilibria based on non-credible threats or promises because beliefs can be assigned arbitrarily at information sets not reached at equilibrium. Thereby, imposing stronger restrictions on out-of-equilibrium beliefs may be necessary.

Sequential equilibrium

The concept of 'sequential equilibrium' (SE) was defined by Kreps and Wilson (1982). It requires stronger assumptions that PBE regarding the condition of consistency. The imposed condition about the revision of beliefs on events with probability zero at equilibrium rests on the following principle: one cannot entirely discard the possibility of a *mistake* by a player choosing her (or his) action. As a consequence one must assign a *positive* probability to all the nodes in information sets and then Bayes' rule always applies. More precisely, this refinement of NE lays down the following assumption: in each information set players' beliefs are such that there is always a slight probability of error, with these errors being statistically independent (in each information set) and the probability of error depending only on the available information of the concerned information set.

Hence, the SE concept links the condition of *sequential rationality* with a condition of *consistency* defined as follows:

Definition 6 (Consistency)

An assessment (x^*, μ^*) is consistent if:

$$(x^*, \mu^*) = \lim_{n \to +\infty} (x^n, \mu^n)$$

for *some* sequence $\{x^n, \mu^n\}$ of the set of all the assessments (x, μ) such that:

- The strategy vector x is defined in players' mixed strategy sets
- The system of beliefs μ is defined unambiguously by Bayes' rule, taking into account the strategy vector.■

Strategies x^* are not necessarily *mixed* strategies, but, like beliefs μ_h^*, we need to think of the components of x^* as being the limits of totally mixed strategies and of their associated beliefs.

Note, however, that in incomplete information games the definition of the consistency condition does not impose a possibility of error on the initial move played by Nature, since the distribution of probability on the move of Nature is not represented by a strategy.

Definition 7 (Sequential equilibrium)

A sequential equilibrium is a strategy vector x^* and a system of beliefs μ^* that are consistent with each other in the sense above and that satisfy sequential rationality at every information set.■

The foundations of SE are thus slightly different from those of PBE:

1. The principle of backward induction remains the major idea that is reflected in the condition of sequential rationality of the assessment: every SE must induce a NE in each continuation game.

2. The Bayes' rule of revision of beliefs according to acquired information is imposed by the condition of consistency of the assessment.

3. The view of a 'neighbouring' world to the world of the theory of the game in which nothing is absolutely certain (each player has a potential for mistaken behaviour) introduces an additional restriction on players' beliefs. This idea, implicit in the expression of the condition of consistency, allows the assignment of a *positive* probability (albeit possibly small) to any event. Then, Bayes' rule of revision of beliefs applies in any circumstances.

Of course, if there is incomplete information, Harsanyi's procedure (transformation in a game with imperfect information) has to be added as one of the foundations of the concept.

We conclude that in SE, out-of-equilibrium beliefs have to be consistent with some small deviation (the 'trembles') from the equilibrium strategy vector. And therefore, we can interpret SE as PBE in which, *in addition*, out-of-equilibrium beliefs are 'justified' by a small deviation from the equilibrium strategy vector.

Notice, however, that in many applications to economics SE and PBE are very similar, or even totally equivalent. For instance, for multi-stage games with observation of actions, the condition of sequential rationality is identical and the conditions of consistency are very similar (the condition concerning SE being however slightly more restrictive). In games with incomplete information and at most two stages, or in which each player has at most two types, there is a complete equivalence (Fudenberg and Tirole, 1991b).

Existence of at least one SE for any *finite* game has been proved by Kreps and Wilson (1982); but there is no corresponding existence theorem for the infinite game. We can also infer from this result the existence of a PBE. Moreover, for this weaker notion a general existence theorem is proved for an *infinite* game.

Remark 1

It is easy to see the close relationship between SE and PTHE: both refer to the same kind of 'story' in restricting players' beliefs. Only a minor difference distinguishes perfectness and sequentiality. Perfectness requires best replies to beliefs which arise in the perturbed games (that is for *all the converging sequences* of completely mixed strategies). Sequentiality requires best replies only to the *limits* of these beliefs. In some ways SE have to be optimal with respect to mistakes made in the past only, whereas PTHE have also to be optimal with respect to mistakes that might occur in the future. Yet, generically, there is little difference between the two kinds of equilibria. In economic applications the two sets of equilibria coincide in almost all games.■

Remark 2

SE may be independently justified by elimination of *strictly* dominated strategies: if there are no beliefs for which x_i is a best response to x_j, then x_i is strictly dominated by some mixture of strategies. Thus, as regards to the criterion of dominance, an informal link can be drawn between NE, SPE and SE. In a NE no player uses a *strictly* dominated strategy. The same property is true for games with incomplete information in a BE. However, no restriction is imposed on the out-of-equilibrium nodes of the tree. Sub-game perfection extends this condition to the out-of-equilibrium sets of information: for any sub-game no player uses a strictly dominated strategy. Yet, this criterion is ineffective when there are no sub-games, in particular in games with incomplete information. Sequentiality succeeds in extending more widely the same idea: for any continuation game, players never use a strictly dominated strategy; players cannot threaten to play strictly dominated strategies from any out-of-equilibrium information set.■

To summarize, if we denote by **NE** the set of Nash equilibria of an extensive-form game and by **SPE**, **PBE**, **SE** and **PTHE** the sets of sub-game perfect equilibria, perfect Bayesian equilibria, sequential equilibria and (agent normal form) perfect trembling hand equilibria, respectively (of course, these sets may be void), then the following relationships between these sets are true:

$$\textbf{PTHE} \subseteq \textbf{SE} \subseteq \textbf{PBE} \subseteq \textbf{SPE} \subseteq \textbf{NE}$$

We now provide a simple example to illustrate how the concept of SE allows us to choose a particular outcome among NE.

Example

Consider the three-player game of imperfect information presented in Figure 4.7 in both strategic form and extensive form.

It is easy to see that (*CEG*) and (*ADF*) are two NE for this game (Figure 4.7a), but it may be argued that the first one must be discarded.

We begin with the continuation game starting at h_3 (player 3's information set) (Figure 4.7b). There are only four possibilities according to player 3's beliefs:

- *Belief* 1: 1 chose A and 2 chose D; then 3 will prefer F
- *Belief* 2: 1 chose A and 2 chose E; then 3 will prefer F
- *Belief* 3: 1 chose B and 2 chose D; then 3 will prefer F
- *Belief* 4: 1 chose B and 2 chose E; then 3 will prefer G

Next we work backwards in the tree and consider the continuation game starting at h_2 (player 2's information set). Anticipating the behaviour of player 3, player 2 will reason as if the game were reduced to the tree of

Figure 4.7 Sequential equilibrium

(a)

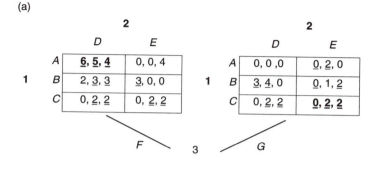

(b)

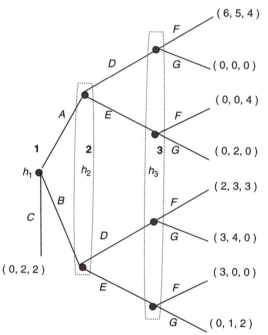

Figure 4.8a. It is easy to see then that player 2 will choose D whatever the choice of player 1 (E is dominated by D). Finally, at the first node of the game, anticipating the behaviour of players 2 and 3, player 1 will reason as if the game were reduced to the Figure 4.8b. And clearly player 1 will choose A.

Thus in this game (ADF) is a SE: in each information set, the actions decided by each player are best responses simultaneously taking into

Figure 4.8 Sequential equilibrium: reduced game trees

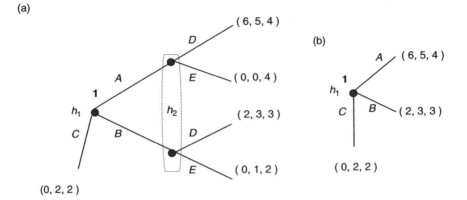

account her (or his) beliefs and the other players' strategies in the continuation game, and furthermore all players' beliefs are consistent.

On the other hand, it is easy to verify that (CEG) is not a SE. If player 3 believes that player 1 chooses B and player 2 chooses E, then it is optimal for her to prefer G (belief 4). In the same way, if 2 believes that 1 chooses A and 3 will choose G, his rational choice is to prefer E (if 2 believes that 1 chose B, D strictly dominates E whatever the choice of 3 and so, only this belief is consistent with the choice of E by 2). Nevertheless, in this case, the beliefs of player 2 and 3 cannot be consistent.

The SE concept appears to capture the rationality properties of backward induction in a form that is convenient to use. On the strength of this confirmation, SE is now the standard equilibrium concept used in extensive-form games with imperfect information in economic applications.

4.3 Forward Induction: Refinement 3

Some NE are thought to be unintuitive. By imposing a requirement of backward induction rationality, the closely related concepts of sequentiality and perfectness rule out equilibria supported by non-credible threats or promises. However in some classes of games, particularly those with incomplete information, some equilibria generate behaviour that is thought to be unreasonable even though the equilibria are sequential. The notion of SE essentially bases beliefs on equilibrium strategies and imposes only 'structural' restrictions on out-of-equilibrium beliefs. The refinements of SE take new strategic considerations into account. In the 1980s, there were considerable discussions about this topic (in particular, McLennan, 1985; Grossman and Perry, 1986; Kohlberg and Mertens, 1986;

Banks and Sobel, 1987; Cho, 1987; Cho and Kreps, 1987; Cho and Sobel, 1990). Although each of these papers proposes a different refinement of SE, all of them incorporate some elements of what Kohlberg and Mertens (1986) have called 'forward induction', because this principle reasons from past behaviour forward.

4.3.1 Forward induction and backward induction

Backward induction implies that a player making a decision at a particular information set will consider the effects of his decision on the equilibrium behaviour of players who will have to move subsequently in the game tree. In a game with a finite number of stages, sub-games in the last stage are analysed before decisions in the second-to-last stage can be evaluated, and so forth, in a process of backward induction. The difference between this notion and that of forward induction is summarized by Kohlberg and Mertens (1986, 1013): 'A subgame should not be treated as a separate game, because it was preceded by a very specific form of pre-play communication – the play leading to the subgame.' At any specific information set, players who made decisions previously could have led the game in a different direction; this fact may have some bearing on the assessment of the likelihood of the different moves that led to this information set. In other words, forward induction takes into account players' incentives for actions that led to particular information sets and it requires players to draw inferences on how future play will proceed on the basis of the past play of the game. This forward induction reasoning restricts the beliefs that can be held at information sets that are never reached in equilibrium by discarding incredible inferences.

Example *(Brandts and Holt, 1992, 120–1)*

Consider the two-stage Entry game represented in Figure 4.9. In the first stage, the potential entrant (player 1) decides to enter (E) or stay out (S); then if entry occurs, both entrant and incumbent monopolist (player 2) decide simultaneously whether to choose a high price (p_H) or a low 'discount' price (p_L) in the second stage.

The post-entry sub-game has two NE: (p_H, p_H) and (p_L, p_L); that results in two pure strategy SE for the game. The first corresponds to entry (E) and no discounting (p_H, p_H); the second involves the potential entrant staying out (S) in order to earn normal profits, because if she decides to enter players' strategies specify discounting (p_L, p_L). Note that this latter equilibrium is sequential because (p_L, p_L) is a NE in the post-entry sub-game; the no-entry outcome is supported by beliefs that discounting will follow a decision to enter.

In this example, forward induction requires that the sub-game cannot be analysed independently of the history of the game in the first stage. The incumbent can make the following inference: he should not expect the

Figure 4.9   Forward induction

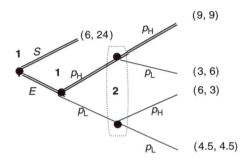

entrant to discount in the post-entry sub-game since by entering she renounces normal profits. By the decision to enter the firm gives to the incumbent certain information: the entrant would not enter if she anticipated sub-normal profits, so the incumbent should not expect that she will choose a low price if she enters. Thus this reasoning suggests that the out-of-equilibrium beliefs with no entry are unreasonable. The only SE consistent with the forward induction argument is $(E; p_H, p_H)$: the potential entrant decides to enter and both firms simultaneously choose a high price.

The above example shows that for an equilibrium to be reasonable, it must not only be consistent with deductions based on the players' rational behaviour in the *future* (principle of backward induction) but also with deductions based on the players' rational behaviour in the *past* (principle of forward induction).

Remark I

It should be emphasized that the same conclusion would result from application of iterated dominance. The associated strategic-form game is represented in Figure 4.10

We can see that Ep_L is dominated by S for player I and then, for player 2, p_L is dominated by p_H. Finally, for player I, Ep_H is preferred to S and the IDE is $(E, p_H; p_H)$. However, in more complex games, forward induction and iterated dominance arguments do not necessarily have equivalent effects, as will be apparent in the example presented in p. 173■

Figure 4.10   Iterated dominance

		2	
		p_H	p_L
1	S	6, 24	6, 24
	$E\,p_H$	**9, 9**	3, 6
	$E\,p_L$	6, 3	4.5, 4.5

Opposition between backward induction and forward induction rests on the interpretation of players' deviation from the equilibrium strategies they provide. According to backward induction any deviation is the result of a passing irrationality with a null probability of repetition in future because of non-correlation of 'mistakes'. So possibly future deviations cannot be inferred from present deviations. In this 'inverted' time logic the current actions are based on expectations about future actions. In contrast, according to forward induction a deviation from equilibrium strategies has to be interpreted as a player's strategic move with the intention of giving some information about his type or his future behaviour. Indeed the original intuition underlying forward induction is that a player's deviation from equilibrium can be interpreted as a kind of *signal*. Past actions are interpreted as signals of future intentions even though those actions may not influence payoffs in the continuation game. Thus the principle of forward induction rules out the 'non-correlated trembling' assumption in order to make players' deviations play a strategic role. This new equilibrium refinement requires that at each stage of the game players are taking into account all inferences from past rational strategies of opponents. An equilibrium which depends on players' supposed inability to interpret such signals is viewed as unreasonable: forward induction discards *incredible inferences* by the players.

In some way, for backward induction in an extensive-form game, a player is imagined as being like a different player at each information set. By contrast, forward induction focuses on relationships between the different outcomes of the same player at each stage of the game; incidentally this property explains why the strategic form of the game often is more relevant for studying forward induction.

As the preceding example shows, the conjunction of forward and backward induction can be powerful for solving a game of imperfect information. However the logic of these two kinds of refinement are so different that one may wonder whether they are ever mutually consistent. Unfortunately it turns out that this concern is well founded.

Example *(adapted from Van Damme, 1989, and Kohlberg, 1991)*

Consider the following variant of the Battle of the Sexes, with its two pure strategy NE (4, 1) and (1, 4) and a mixed strategy NE ($\frac{4}{5}$, $\frac{4}{5}$). In this example we assume that payoffs are dollar amounts and that players are risk-neutral in money (Figure 4.11).

Suppose that before playing the game, player 1 can burn 2 dollars and that player 2 observes what he does. Then the game can be represented by the tree of Figure 4.12.

It would seem logical that, since the burned money is like a 'sunk cost', the equilibria of this game ought to be identical to those of the original game. Yet this conclusion is wrong: now, only the outcome (4, 1) corresponds to a reasonable equilibrium.

Figure 4.11   Payoff matrix of a variant of the Battle of the Sexes game

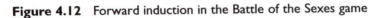

		M	B
1	M	4, 1	0, 0
	B	0, 0	1, 4

Figure 4.12   Forward induction in the Battle of the Sexes game

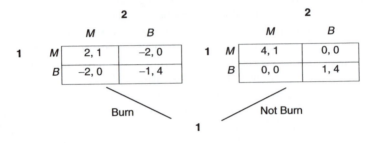

If player 1 burns the money, by forward induction, player 2 ought to think that player 1 is going to play *M* in the sub-game, because if she had a plan to choose B, she would have done better to avoid burning (*B* after having burned the money is dominated by *B* without burning). Therefore, player 2 should play *M*, and player 1 would then get a payoff of 2. Yet, if player 1 chooses not to burn, then by backward induction player 2 understands that player 1 is giving up an opportunity to get a payoff of 2. So, by forward induction again, it appears that player 1 is planning to choose *M* in the sub-game, since *B* without burning yields less than 2. Finally, player 2, ought to choose *M*, and the final outcome is (4, 1). We conclude that if before playing the Battle of the Sexes, player 1 had refused the opportunity of getting 2, the outcome of the game had to be her preferred issue.

But what happens if both players had refused the same opportunity? Figure 4.13 provides such a situation.

Since player 1 could have received a payoff of 2 dollars if she chose to burn, by forward induction player 2 must anticipate her intention to play *M* when she decides not to burn. Yet, for exactly the same reason, player 2 indicates his intention to play *B* and in this case by backward induction player 1 must play herself *B*. Hence in this game the conjunction of forward and backward induction seems to lead to a contradiction.

Fortunately we may claim that such a contradiction can occur only *off the equilibrium path* in the tree. In order to show this, let us analyse the nature of the difficulty in Figure 4.13.

Figure 4.13   Forward induction and backward induction in the Battle of the Sexes game

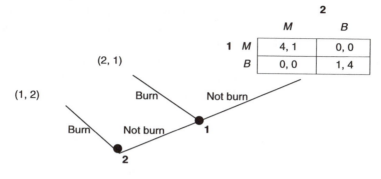

Player 2 can do the following reasoning: if I choose not to burn, then my opponent would either choose to burn or not to burn and then to choose M, knowing that the third possibility (not to burn and B) is dominated by the choice to burn (2 > 1). In either case, I would obtain a lower payoff than I could obtain by choosing to burn (2 > 1). Thus, if player 2 had agreed to choose to burn, it is in his interest to abide by his agreement. It follows that outcome (1, 2) can be viewed as a self-enforcing norm of behaviour for player 2, but in this case we do not need a precise determination of players 1's strategy.

Of course we must wonder if all contradictions between forward induction and backward induction can always be resolved in this way. An attempt to answer this question was made by Kohlberg and Mertens (1986) with the notion of a 'stable set' of equilibria. Before presenting this concept and analysing refinement criteria in general games, we restrict the topic to a particular class of games with several important economic applications: signalling games.

4.3.2 Formalizations of forward induction in signalling games

It is in fact rather difficult to find an appropriate formalization of the forward induction principle in general games with imperfect information. This difficulty becomes less hard when the game gets the structure of a 'signalling game'.

Signalling games

In many economic situations, agents are asymmetrically informed: for instance, workers may be better informed about their ability than the firm, a firm may know more about its own costs of production than about its competitors' costs, purchasers of insurance have better information about their own risk characteristics than the insurance agent, and so on. It may be however that the agent with private information decides to do an action before the uninformed agent does. For example: the worker may choose to acquire some education before applying it to a job and this action may well be informative about the worker's ability. Or, if we consider an incumbent monopolist and potential entrants to this market which do not know the cost structure of the firm, the pricing decision of the incumbent might be informative about costs. Indeed these two situations correspond to two seminal economic models: the model of job market signalling in labour (Spence, 1973) and the model of limit pricing in industrial organizations (Milgrom and Roberts, 1982). Signalling games allow one to analyse these kind of models with asymmetric information. Game theoretic concepts have helped to sharpen considerably the predictions of those models; they have been also used to better understand the difference between 'signalling' strictly speaking (as in the education model of Spence, 1973) and 'screening' (as in the insurance model of Rothschild and Stiglitz, 1976).

Signalling games have a very simple structure. Generally, there are only two players who move just once. Player 1 is supposed to have private information about some characteristic and move first: her action is interpreted as a 'signal' or a 'message' (from which it is called the 'sender' S). Next, player 2, who does not know this information but observes the action of the first player (from which it is called the 'receiver' R), chooses in his turn an action or 'response'. Therefore a signalling game is a particular Bayesian extensive game with observable actions. In a first stage Nature is supposed to choose the senders' 'type' $t \in T$ (supposed finite) with a certain probability distribution p (assumed to be common knowledge); she is informed of her type but the receiver is not. In a second stage, the sender chooses an action $m \in M$ (supposed finite) which the receiver can observe. In a third stage, the receiver himself chooses an action $r \in R$ (supposed finite). Players' payoffs depend on senders' types as well as on both players' actions: $u_S = u_S(t, m, r)$, $u_R = u_R(t, m, r)$.

Notice that this last assumption differentiates clearly signalling games from 'cheap talk' games or games with pre-play negotiation. In those games, players' payoff functions are independent of exchange messages.

Therefore in signalling games moves of the sender – the signal – may reveal her type or may not reveal it. For the sender's private information to be revealed in equilibrium, it is necessary that observing an equilibrium message m of the sender be equivalent to observing the private information t. The sender's strategy must be one-to-one: if $t \neq t'$, then $m(t) \neq m(t')$. In other words, each type of the sender chooses a different action. If m is one-to-one, the equilibrium is called 'separating' (or 'fully revealing'). If m is not one-to-one, that is if some types choose different actions and others the same, then the equilibrium is called 'semi-pooling' (or 'partially revealing' or 'hybrid'). At last, if m is a constant function, that is if each type chooses the same action, the equilibrium is 'pooling'. In the last two cases, the responder is not able to infer precisely the characteristics of the sender from the signal.

The tension in signalling games arises from the asymmetry between the two players: the *receiver* controls the *action* while the *sender* controls the *information*.

Remark 1

In a signalling game, the informed player moves first and this action possibly may reveal her (or his) private information. If she (or her) moves second, after the non-informed player, this situation corresponds to a 'screening' game. In a screening game beliefs no longer need to be specified. Since the uninformed agent is playing first, her (or his) beliefs after seeing the move of the informed player are irrelevant. The informed player is fully informed, so her (or his) beliefs are not affected by what she (or he) can observe. Screening is much like a simple 'adverse selection' problem in 'information economics' (Rasmusen, 1989).■

Remark 2

'Cheap talk' games are a class of games with incomplete information close to signalling games, but in the former the sender's messages are just talk, that is costless and non-verifiable claims. Such talk can not be informative in all contexts of asymmetric information. Three conditions are necessary: (1) different sender types have different preferences over the receiver's actions; (2) the receiver's preferences over actions depend on the sender's type (like in signalling games, of course); (3) the receiver's preferences over actions are not completely opposed to the sender's. (See notably Crawford and Sobel, 1982, for an analysis of an abstract model that verifies these three necessary conditions)■

The intuitive criterion: a formalization of forward induction in signalling games

This particular refinement of a SE was introduced by Cho and Kreps (1987). It is the best-known formalization of forward induction in a signalling game. The 'intuitive criterion' lies in taking a particular equilibrium as an initial point for the reasoning of the player, then using iterated dominance in order to evaluate the receiver's beliefs after he observes out-of-equilibrium messages. It is a direct generalization of the dominance argument to a situation in which we suppose that a given equilibrium is common knowledge of the players, in addition to common knowledge of the game rule and players' rationality. Cho and Kreps chose this name because it is simply a non-cooperative game theoretic unifying formulation of various intuitive criteria used previously in information economics.

Definition 8 (*Intuitive criterion*)

A SE satisfies the intuitive criterion if it is stable towards elimination of strategies which yield less than equilibrium payoffs whatever the other players' choices may be.∎

In other words, under the intuitive criterion, if there is a type of informed player who could not benefit from the out-of-equilibrium action, no matter what beliefs were held by uninformed players, the uninformed players' beliefs must assign zero probability to that type.

A bit of additional notation is necessary in order to give a formal definition of this criterion. Let $\sigma_S(m/t)$ be the probability that the sender of type t chooses the message m (her strategy), $\sigma_R(r/m)$ the probability that the receiver chooses the response r if the message is m (his strategy) and $\mu_R(t/m)$ the probability that the sender's type is t when she chooses m according to the receiver (his beliefs).

The set of players' best responses are defined as follows:

$$BR_S(t, \sigma_R) = \arg\max_{m \in M} \sum_{r \in R} u_S(t, m, r)\sigma_r(r/m)$$

$$BR_R(m, \mu_R) = \arg\max_{r \in R} \sum_{t \in T} u_R(t, m, r)\mu_R(t/m)$$

with:

$$\mu_R(t, m) = \frac{p(t)\sigma_S(m/t)}{\sum_{t \in T} p(t)\sigma_S(m/t)}$$

for all m such that the denominator is non-zero (the receiver is updating his beliefs by applying Bayes' rule).

The message m is said to be 'equilibrium dominated' in a particular SE $(\sigma_S^*, \sigma_R^*, \mu_R^*)$ for the type t if:

$$u_S^*(t) > \max_{r \in BR_R(m, \mu_R)} u_S(t, m, r)$$

Then, the intuitive criterion requires that:

$$\mu_R^*(t/m) = 0$$

if m is 'equilibrium dominated' in the equilibrium $(\sigma_S^*, \sigma_R^*, \mu_R^*)$ for the type t and not for some type $t' \in T$.

Remark 3

There are a lot of related criteria of refinement which require more and more restrictions on out-of-equilibrium beliefs. Cho and Kreps (1987) have themselves proposed a stronger test with the 'criterion D_1'. The message m is said 'equilibrium D_1-dominated' for a type t if, for all the receivers' responses to m that justify the deviation of t, there is some type t' whose strict interest is to deviate. Then, the criterion D_1 is satisfied in a particular equilibrium $(\sigma_S^*, \sigma_R^*, \mu_R^*)$ if, for all 'equilibrium D_1 dominated' messages m for a type t: $\mu_R^*(t/m) = 0$.

The 'divine criterion' introduced by Banks and Sobel (1987) is weaker than the criterion D_1 in the sense that it requires simply that $\mu_R^*(t/m)$ be superior to the beliefs level justifying a profitable deviation (i.e. not necessarily a zero probability). In contrast, the concept of 'perfect sequential equilibrium' proposed by Grossman and Perry (1986), is a bit stronger than the criterion D_1. It requires that the receiver's response justifying a deviation be supported by a belief in which the weight is focused (via the Bayes' rule) on the only type whose interest is to deviate for such a response.

All these classical criteria based on forward induction in signalling games are in some way unsatisfactory in so far as they lack consistency considering the identification of deviating players. Several new refinements were introduced in the literature in order to restrict the set of SE. These criteria propose a more consistent interpretation following a deviation by confronting the beliefs supporting the tested SE with the beliefs of another SE (see in particular the 'undefeated equilibrium' of Mailath, Okuno-Fujiwara and Postlewaite, 1993).∎

It should be emphasized that the intuitive criterion, like the related criteria previously mentioned, is a condition of *local* stability, in contrast to the iterated dominance which is a condition of *global* stability, because the latter can be used to restrict receivers' beliefs *without* reference to a particular equilibrium. It is easy to verify that for signalling games any equilibrium which satisfies the intuitive criterion also passes the test of iterated dominance.

Cho and Kreps (1987) have proven that in all signalling games there is at least one SE which satisfies the intuitive criterion.

We can illustrate this particular refinement of SE in the spirit of forward induction with the famous Kreps' Beer–Quiche game.

Example: the Beer–Quiche game (adapted from Binmore, 1992, 463–4, 541–4)

In the Beer–Quiche game, Nature begins by choosing the type of player 1: he will be a Tough (T) or a Wimp (W) with a particular probability. Then, player 1 has to face player 2 who may decide to Fight (F) player 1 or Defer (D) to him (we suppose here that the two players are men). Of course, player 2 would defer to him if he anticipates that he is Tough and he would fight him if he believes that he is Wimpish. Only player 1 knows his nature, but he can send signals to player 2 by behaving like a Tough or a Wimp. These signals are very stylized; player 1, is supposed to enter a tavern to order either beer (B) or quiche (Q). If he is Tough, he prefers to drink a beer and if he is Wimpish he prefers to eat a quiche. However, player 1 will not necessarily order the item that he prefers between beer and quiche; he may strategically disguise his taste. For example, a Wimp may decide to order a beer in the hope of passing for a Tough.

Thus the Beer–Quiche game is a signalling game with the following properties: there are two types of player 1 (the sender), T and W, the probabilities of these types being P and $1-P$ respectively. The sender has the set of messages (B, Q) at his disposal; player 2 (the receiver) has two possible actions: F or D

We suppose that players' payoffs are evaluated in this way. Player 1's payoff is the sum $x + y$, where $x = 1$ if he orders the item that he prefers between beer and quiche and $x = 0$ otherwise, $y = 2$ if he does not fight with player 2 and $y = 0$ otherwise. Player 2's payoff is 1 if he fights a Wimp or if he defers to a Tough and 0 otherwise. Figure 4.14 represents the extensive form of the Beer–quiche game.

Player 1 has four pure strategies:

$$(Q_T, Q_W), (Q_T, B_W), (B_T, Q_W), (B_T, B_W)$$

For instance, the meaning of (Q_T, B_W) is: if 1 knows he is T, he sends the message Q, if 1 knows he is W, he sends the message B.

Player 2 also has four pure strategies:

$$(F_Q, F_B), (F_Q, D_B), (D_Q, F_B), (D_Q, D_B)$$

Figure 4.14   The extensive form of the Beer–Quiche game

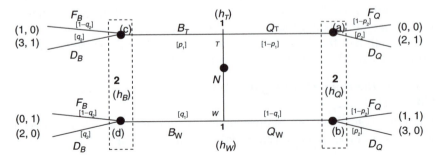

For instance, the meaning of (F_Q, F_B) is: if 2 observes the message Q, he chooses the action F; if 2 observes the message B, he chooses still the action F.

According to the value of the parameter P (i.e. the probability distribution of player 1's types chosen by Nature), this game is more or less interesting for illustrating the forward induction principle.

Let us first examine briefly the less interesting case, for which the game has a unique mixed strategy BE. Suppose that $P = \frac{1}{3}$, i.e. there is a probability $\frac{1}{3}$ that player 1 was a Tough and $\frac{2}{3}$ that he was a Wimp. The payoff matrix corresponding to this case is traced in Figure 4.15. The expected payoffs are calculated as follows: for the first row and the first column, for instance, for player 1, $\frac{1}{3}(0) + \frac{2}{3}(1) = \frac{2}{3}$, for player 2, $\frac{1}{3}(0) + \frac{2}{3}(1) = \frac{2}{3}$.

It is easy to see that there are no equilibria in pure strategies. Yet the Nash theorem assures us that at least one mixed strategy equilibrium can be computed. We search for such an equilibrium in the extensive-form game (of course, here, 'mixed' strategies are behavioural strategies).

We note p_1 and $(1 - p_1)$ as the probabilities with which player 1 will choose B and Q, respectively, at his information set h_T (i.e. B_T and Q_T). The corresponding probabilities for B and Q at his information set h_W (i.e. B_W and Q_W) are q_1 and $(1 - q_1)$. Furthermore, we note p_2 and $(1 - p_2)$ as the probabilities with which player 2 will choose D and F, respectively, at his information set $h_Q = \{a, b\}$ (i.e. D_Q and F_Q), and the corresponding probabilities for D and F are q_2 and $(1 - q_2)$ at his information set $h_B = \{c, d\}$ (i.e. D_B and F_B).

Consider first the information set h_Q of player 2. In this set the probability that node a will be reached is: $\text{prob}(a) = \frac{1}{3}(1 - p_1)$ and the probability that node b will be reached is: $\text{prob}(b) = \frac{2}{3}(1 - q_1)$.

Thus, at h_Q, player 2's posteriors are:

$$\text{prob}(T/Q_T) = \frac{\text{prob}(a)}{\text{prob}(a) + \text{prob}(b)} = \frac{\frac{1}{3}(1 - p_1)}{\frac{1}{3}(1 - p_1) + \frac{2}{3}(1 - q_1)}$$

Figure 4.15   Payoff matrix of Beer–Quiche game with $P = \frac{1}{3}$

		F_QF_B	F_QD_B	D_QF_B	D_QD_B
				2	
1	Q_TQ_W	2/3, 2/3	2/3, 2/3	8/3, 1/3	8/3, 1/3
	Q_TB_W	0, 2/3	4/3, 0	2/3, 1	2, 1/3
	B_TQ_W	1, 2/3	5/3, 1	7/3, 0	3, 1/3
	B_TB_W	1/3, 2/3	7/3, 1/3	1/3, 2/3	7/3, 1/3

$$\text{prob}(W/Q_W) = \frac{\text{prob}(b)}{\text{prob}(a) + \text{prob}(b)} = \frac{\frac{2}{3}(1 - q_1)}{\frac{1}{3}(1 - p_1) + \frac{2}{3}(1 - q_1)}$$

Player 2 defers if he believes it is more likely that player 1 is Tough and he fights if he anticipates it is more likely that he is a Wimp. Hence, player 2's best response is:

- Play D_Q if: $\text{prob}(T/Q_T) > \text{prob}(W/Q_W)$ or: $1 - p_1 > 2(1 - q_1)$
- Play F_Q if: $\text{prob}(T/Q_T) < \text{prob}(W/Q_W)$ or: $1 - p_1 < 2(1 - q_1)$
- Play D_Q or F_Q if: $\text{prob}(T/Q_T) = \text{prob}(W/Q_W)$ or: $1 - p_1 = 2(1 - q_1)$

The same reasoning applies at the information set h_B. There is no difficulty in showing that player 2's best response is then:

- Play D_B if: $p_1 > 2q_1$
- Play F_B if: $p_1 < 2q_1$
- Play D_B or F_B if: $p_1 = 2q_1$

Finally, as it can only be optimal to randomize among a set of actions if the player is indifferent about which action is chosen, player 2's best response in mixed strategies must be such that: $1 - p_1 = 2(1 - q_1)$ or $p_1 = 2q_1$ (or both).

The first possibility in fact is impossible. If $1 - p_1 = 2(1 - q_1)$, then $2q_1 = 1 + p_1 > p_1$ and player 2 chooses F_B at h_B. In this circumstance, player 1 has no interest in drinking beer at h_W and so he will eat quiche for certain $(1 - q_1 = 1)$, but then: $1 - p_1 = 2(1 - q_1) = 2 > 1$.

Thus the only possibility is: $p_1 = 2q_1$. This equality implies that $1 - p_1 = 1 - 2q_1$. So, $1 - p_1 < 1 + (1 - 2q_1) = 2(1 - q_1)$. It follows that player 2 chooses F_Q at h_Q. In this circumstance, player 1 has no interest in eating quiche at h_T and so he will drink beer for certain $(p_1 = 1)$, but then: $q_1 = \frac{1}{2}$, $p_1 = \frac{1}{2}$. That means that at h_W, player 1 is randomizing between Q and B (he chooses Q_W and B_W with a probability $\frac{1}{2}$). He must get an identical payoff from eating quiche and from drinking beer. Insofar as he obtains a payoff 1 at h_Q (since player 2 is fighting him), at h_B it must be true that: $0(1 - q_2) + 2q_2 = 1$. Therefore, $q_2 = \frac{1}{2}$ and player 2 must be randomizing at h_B, too (he chooses D_B and F_B with a probability $\frac{1}{2}$).

Finally, the unique BE is characterized as follows:

- Player 1 drinks beer for certain if he is Tough
- Player 2 fights for certain if he observes that player 1 is eating quiche
- If player 1 is Wimpy, he randomizes his message: he eats quiche with probability $\frac{1}{2}$, in accordance with his nature, but he also drinks beer with probability $\frac{1}{2}$ in the hope of being mistaken for a Tough. Player 2 is not able to guess his true nature and if he observes that he is drinking beer, he randomizes himself: he fights player 1 with probability $\frac{1}{2}$ and he defers to him with probability $\frac{1}{2}$.

In short: $(p_1^*, (1-p_1)^*, q_1^*, (1-q_1)^*) = (1, 0, \frac{1}{2}, \frac{1}{2})$ and $(p_2^*, (1-p_2)^*, q_2^*, (1-q_2)^*) = (0, 1, \frac{1}{2}, \frac{1}{2})$

In this version of the Beer–Quiche game, every information set in the tree is reached in equilibrium with a *positive* probability and the signalling issues are straightforward. A Tough is signalling his type by sending the message 'beer-drinking'. The receiver is sure that it is the 'right' signal, and so he fights a player who sends the message 'quiche-eating'. It follows that for a Wimp it is not optimal to eat quiche all the time. By sending a 'wrong signal' (i.e. 'beer-drinking'), he hides his true type and introduces uncertainty in his opponent's mind.

If we modify the value of the probability distribution of player 1's type chosen by Nature (recall that it is common knowledge), the matter may be much less simple. Suppose for instance that: $P = 0.9$, i.e. there is a probability of 0.9 that player 1 was a Tough and of 0.1 that he was a Wimp ($P \geq \frac{1}{2}$ is enough for modifying the story). Problems about incredible plans off the equilibrium path then complicate the analysis of the game, which requires the use of SE as solution concept (or PBE, since the two concepts are equivalent in finite signalling games). Henceforth, what constitutes an equilibrium is powerfully affected by the interpretation that would be given by the receiver to messages that the sender might have sent, but in equilibrium does not send.

In this game, the belief vector is: $\mu = (\mu_T, \mu_W, \mu_Q, \mu_B)$, corresponding to the four information sets h_T, h_W, h_Q and h_B, respectively. Since player 1 knows his type (h_T and h_W contains only one node): $\mu_T^* = \mu_W^* = 1$. In order to support a SE, the distribution of probability μ_Q^* and μ_B^* must satisfy the condition of consistency.

In this game, in fact, two kinds of SE can be found.

1. Consider the strategy vector $x^* = (B_T, B_W; F_Q, D_B)$. Both types of player 1 choose B and player 2 fights if he observes Q and not if he observes B. Consistency requires that: $\mu_B^*\{c\} = 0.9$ and $\mu_B^*\{d\} = 0.1$, because the signal 'beer-drinking' conveys no information. Whatever her type, player 1 will choose to drink beer. So, at h_B player 2's priors are unchanged. Furthermore, if player 1 plays according to x^*, h_Q will be reached with zero probability; so, consistency claims no restriction on beliefs at h_Q. However, in order to satisfy sequential rationality, $\mu_Q^*\{b\} \geq \mu_Q^*\{a\}$ is required; that is, to make such a scenario a SE, player 2 must assign a probability of at least $\frac{1}{2}$ that player 1 is Wimpish.

2. Consider the strategy $x^* = (Q_T, Q_W; D_Q, F_B)$. Both types of players 1 choose Q and player 2 fights if he observes B and not if he observes Q. Consistency requires that: $\mu_Q^*\{a\} = 0.9$ and $\mu_Q^*\{b\} = 0.1$, because the signal 'quiche-eating' provides no information about the type of player 1. On the other hand, consistency says nothing about how the beliefs vector μ should assign probabilities to the nodes c and d in h_B.

Yet, again, sequential rationality requires that: $\mu_B^*\{d\} \geq \mu_B^*\{c\}$; that is player 2 must assign a probability of at least $1/2$ that player 1 is Wimpish.

Notice that these two kinds of SE are *pooling* equilibria: both types of player 1 send the same message, so that player 2 cannot exploit this action to deduce the sender's private information.

Among these two types of equilibrium, the second may not seem very reasonable. The argument followed in order to justify this suggestion rests on the intuitive criterion.

In the second kind of pooling equilibrium, player 2's belief that player 1 is Wimpish with positive probability when he observes B is not reasonable. When he is Wimpish, whatever player 2's beliefs on his type, player 1 could not gain in sending the message B; his optimal action always is to send Q (his equilibrium payoff is 3 whereas the most he can get if he deviates is 2). Indeed, if player 1 plans to drink beer (i.e. if he plays an out-of-equilibrium action), that means that he is Tough, because it is his interest to persuade player 2 not to fight him (his payoff would be 3 instead of 2).

Since the seminal work of Spence (1973), *continuous* signalling games (i.e. games with continuous strategic sets) were often used in economics in order to study the functioning of markets with asymmetric information. Most of continuous signalling games satisfy the following assumptions:

H1   The sender and the receiver choose their actions in a subset of $\mathbb{R}_+$

H2   For a given message, the sender's payoff is increasing in the receiver's response; for instance, in Spence's job market signalling model, the worker prefers a high wage

H3   The marginal cost of signalling is decreasing in sender's type: this assumption is named 'single-crossing' condition, in Spence's model, education is less costly for a worker if his ability takes a high value.

H4   For a given message, the receiver's best response is increasing in the sender's type, in Spence's model, the more the firms believe that the workers ability is high, the more they are willing to pay a high wage.

For models verifying H1–H4, with a finite number of types for the sender, there is generally an infinity of SE. One separating equilibrium outcome of interest is the outcome that is *efficient* for the informed player among all separating outcomes; after Riley (1979), the literature refers to this outcome as the 'Riley equilibrium'. Note that if the set of the sender's type is a compact interval (i.e. there is an infinity of types), in contrast, the game has a *unique* separating SE, whose Riley equilibrium is the 'obvious' analogue in the finite case.

For the case of two types, the intuitive criterion is strong enough to rule out all equilibria (pooling and separating) other than the Riley equilibrium. Unfortunately, it is no longer true for three or more types.

4.3.2   Stable sets of equilibria*

For signalling games, the forward induction idea is well captured by the intuitive criterion. But this refinement criterion is defined with reference to the particular structure of this class of games. It is impossible to apply directly the intuitive criterion to other types of games. A lot of alternative criteria have been proposed in the literature in order to formalize the forward induction idea in more general games. Three concepts seem to capture some aspects of this principle:

- 'Admissibility' (A): equilibrium strategies shall be undominated in the strategic form of the game
- 'Iterated dominance' (ID): deletion of dominated strategies from a game does not change the equilibrium
- 'Equilibrium domination' (ED): deletion of strategies that are not a best response to any equilibrium strategy does not change the equilibrium

All these requirements for an equilibrium are based on the following idea: an equilibrium *should not depend on dominated strategies*. The first criterion (A) demands that the equilibrium strategies be undominated. The second criterion (ID) rules out that equilibria may be sustained by beliefs that some player chooses a dominated strategy off the equilibrium path. The third criterion (ED) requires that no player shall believe that another player would prefer a strategy that cannot yield for her (or him) a higher payoff than the equilibrium strategy. Note that this last condition captures best the logic of the intuitive criterion, but this formalization can be applied to general games.

Unfortunately, there does not seem to exist a *unique* criterion that formalizes the forward induction principle in *all* classes of games. For signalling games, the intuitive criterion (interpreted as a variant of ED) is particularly relevant, while in others classes of games the ID criterion appears to be the most appropriate.

Kohlberg and Mertens' work (1986) deals with this insistent question: is it possible to find a concept that verifies *all* the relevant properties for *general* games. For that purpose they move from Selten's basic programme of perfecting *individual* equilibria to a consideration of 'perfect' *sets* of equilibria. They develop a number of criteria for NE and sets of NE that fit under the general heading of 'strategic stability' (in their vocabulary 'perfection' becomes 'stability'), in particular the above-mentioned criteria A, ID and ED.

They demonstrate with many examples that in general it is impossible to find an equilibrium strategy vector that satisfies *both* sequentiality and forward induction. However we can find *sets of equilibria* with the same equilibrium payoff distribution and the same equilibrium path that include equilibria some of whose satisfy the forward induction principle whereas others respect the backward induction principle (in what follows we are greatly inspired by the very clear presentation of this topic given in Eichberger, 1993, sub-section 7.2).

Let us show in a simple example how multiple equilibria can have the same payoff and the same equilibrium path. Consider the strategic-form game in Figure 4.16.

Denote the mixed strategies of both players by $(p, 1 - p)$ and $(q, 1 - q)$, respectively. The best response correspondences are drawn as solid lines in Figure 4.17.

Typically the set of NE consists of several sets of strategy vectors called 'components'. For this game there are two components: $E_1 = \{(p, q): p = 1, q = 1\}$ and $E_2 = \{(p, q): p = 0, 0 \leq q \leq 0.5\}$. The equilibrium paths are the same on each component:

- Component E_1 holds a single equilibrium with payoffs $(1, 1)$ and the equilibrium path 'r_1 followed by c_1'
- All equilibria in component E_2 yield the payoffs $(0, 3)$ and have the equilibrium path 'r_2'; equilibria differ only in a different probability of player 2 choosing c_2.

The particular structure of the equilibrium set in this example is a characteristic of games with *finite* strategy sets: all stable equilibria have the same payoff if they lie in one component.

Figure 4.16 Payoff matrix of a game

		2	
		c_1	c_2
1	r_1	1, −1	−1, 1
	r_2	0, 4	0, 4

Figure 4.17 Best response correspondences

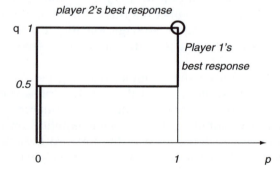

Definition 9 (*Stable set of equilibria*)

A set of equilibria is 'stable' if it is a sub-set of a single component and if it includes equilibria that verify the backward induction principle and equilibria that satisfy the forward induction principle in the form of A, ID and ED. Generally these equilibria are characterized by the same equilibrium vector and the same equilibrium path.■

Note that Kohlberg and Mertens (1986) actually introduce supplementary conditions. In particular, equilibria in a stable set must be invariant to transformations of the game tree that they consider strategically irrelevant. In this setting they develop an argument for studying *strategic-form* games only.

Roughly speaking, stability of a set of equilibria for strategic-form games is then defined as follows: there is a class of perturbations of the strategic-form game such that for every perturbation in this class, there is an equilibrium close to this stable set of equilibria.

Some properties of equilibria in a stable set are interesting because they allow one to identify these solutions in many games.

Theorem 2 (*Mertens, 1989*)

(i) For every game, there exists a stable set of equilibria
(ii) Every equilibrium in a stable set is a PTHE in the strategic form of the game
(iii) A stable set of equilibria contains a stable set of equilibria of any game derived by deletion of dominated strategies
(iv) A stable set of equilibria contains a stable set of equilibria of any game derived by deletion of strategies that are not a best response to any equilibrium strategy in the set
(v) A stable set of equilibria contains a SE.■

This theorem proves that sets of stable equilibria exist and that they include equilibria that verify both backward and forward induction principles. The former is captured by properties (ii) (iii) and (iv), while property (v) guarantees the latter (property (ii) implies that A is verified since every PTHE is undominated). Note however that this result does not say that a *single* equilibrium verifies always (iii), (iv) and (v): it may be that no equilibrium satisfies both backward and forward induction. Moreover, uniqueness of the stable set is not proved.

Let us come back to the above example for illustrating the application of this theorem. It is easy to see that in this game all equilibria included in component E_2 are such that player 2 uses a dominated strategy: $q = 1$ dominates $0 \leq q \leq \frac{1}{2}$. It follows that equilibria in components E_2 are not stable since property (ii) is not satisfied. Yet, by property (i), existence of a stable set of equilibria is guaranteed and therefore E must be a stable set (restricted here to a singleton).

4.4   Applications

4.4.1   Repeated games with incomplete information: reputation effects

We showed in sub-section 3.3.2 of Chapter 3 that cooperation can occur in an infinitely repeated game with complete information and we illustrated such an equilibrium based on credible threats and promises by a tariff game between two countries (sub-section 3.5.2). On the other hand, for *finitely* repeated games in which the stage game has a *unique* NE, this theoretical result vanishes. The literature about 'reputation effects' proves that the introduction of a bit of incomplete information in finitely repeated games makes cooperation between players plausible again.

In this framework, each player is supposed to entertain doubts about the intentions of her (or his) opponents: at the very beginning of the game, there is a small probability that they are 'irrational' or 'crazy'. And the 'rational' or 'normal' types may consider it profitable to imitate the crazy types insofar as the short-term loss that follows may be more than balanced by the long-term gain from 'building a reputation'. Thus, this way of modelling asymmetric information expresses the idea that players may behave as if they are crazy because such a behaviour incites their opponents to choose responses which, even according to their real preferences, ultimately get better payoffs for them.

A rich variety of strategic behaviour often observed in economic life can be analysed along these lines: predatory pricing or limit pricing in industrial organizations (see Kreps and Spence, 1985; Roberts, 1987) or the building of a reputation for anti-inflation toughness by a government (Blackburn, 1992). Formal games of asymmetric information use the concepts of PBE or SE.

A simple example taken from Kreps and Wilson (1982) will give an illustration of this kind of modelling and of the equilibrium concept generally used. In industrial organization it is frequently claimed that a firm might find it worthwhile to resist any entry into its market, even if this is costly, in order to build a reputation for toughness and thus discourage future potential entrants. Let us first put this story in terms of the famous 'chain-store paradox' (Selten, 1978).

Denote by I an incumbent firm operating on a given number of markets N. For each market there is a potential entrant E_i, $i = 1, \ldots, N$. E_i has to decide whether to enter (E) or stay out (O) and I must then respond either aggressively, i.e. he fights (F), or non-aggressively, i.e. he accommodates (A). The payoffs to E_i depend on firm I's reaction: +1 if I

cooperates, -1 if it reacts negatively and 0 in the case of non-entry. The corresponding payoffs to I are $+1$, -1 and $+2$, respectively. The overall payoff to i is the sum of the payoffs obtained on each market. The entry decision is sequential, beginning with $i = N$ and ending with $i = 1$ (time is indexed backward).

When information is perfect, the result of this game depends strongly on the number of markets. If there is only *one* market, the game can be described in extensive form as in Figure 4.18 where the payoffs of E_1 and of I are given in parentheses: the 'chain-store' game is simply the 'entry' game. The outcome 'E_1 does not enter, I fights' is a NE of this game. However it is no sub-game perfect, since the threat to fight announced by 1 is not credible. Once E_1 has entered, it is in I's interest to accommodate.

However, the story says that when there is a *larger number* of markets the incumbent has a strategic incentive to prey upon early entrants in order to deter future ones. This is typically true in the case of an infinite number of markets. It will resist any entrant and since any potential entrant knows that the incumbent will have many further periods to recover its present expenses, the threat is credible and entry is actually deterred.

On the other hand, for any finite N there is a unique SPE with accommodation at each stage. At the final stage entry is inevitable, as in the one-period game shown in Figure 4.18. Therefore E_N will necessarily enter. E_{N-1} knows that I has no means of deterring E_N from entering, so that I has no incentive to fight in the penultimate round. E_{N-1} will enter, and so on back to E_1.

In the perfect information case, it is common knowledge that fighting is a dominated strategy for I at each stage. Therefore the story of predatory pricing to deter entry would seem to be without rational foundations. However, a major achievement of the new models of game theory with imperfect information is to show that predatory behaviour may be

Figure 4.18 Extensive form of the entry game

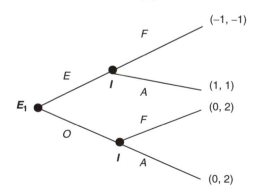

rational once there is some asymmetric information between the incumbent and the potential entrant. Firm I can credibly commit itself with some probability to prey upon each entrant (Milgrom and Roberts, 1982), or fighting may be better for I than cooperating at certain stages (Kreps and Wilson, 1982). In any case, each potential entrant faces the risk of being confronted with a firm committed to fighting or loving to fight (even if this is an irrational behaviour – 'a crazy type of firm') and it will try to infer which type it is from past experience.

The results of the Kreps–Wilson model can be stated as follows: 'for any given (small but positive) prior probability that cooperating is not the best response to entry in the stage game there is an n^* such that if $N > n^*$ then both the normal and the crazy types of I prey on any entry into markets $n^*, \ldots, N'$ (Roberts, 1987).

Let us give a simple illustration of this argument. Consider a case where $N = 2$. The incumbent firm may be a tough firm I^T or a weak firm I^W. The prior probability on the tough incumbent is P. The tough firm will prey on any entrant (probability equal to unity); the weak incumbent may want to prey on E_1 with a probability $(1-p)$, but it has no interest to prey on E_2 (p is of course the probability of accommodation).

The per period payoffs are presented in the two matrixes in Figure 4.19 corresponding to the cases of a tough incumbent (a) and a weak incumbent (b).

Π_M is the monopoly profit. Π_{IF}^T and Π_{IF}^W are the incumbent's profits in case of a fight, respectively, when it is a tough and a weak firm. Π_{IN} and Π_{EN} are, respectively, the incumbent's profit and the entrant 1 profit in case of accommodation of entry (N is for static NE profits). We assume that $\Pi_{IF}^T > \Pi_{IN} > \Pi_{IF}^W$.

Figure 4.19   Payoff matrix of the 'chain-store' game

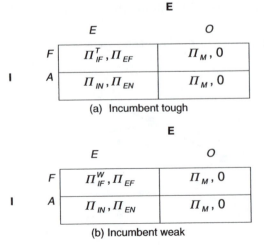

(a) Incumbent tough

(b) Incumbent weak

The two potential entrants are supposed to be identical and get the same payoffs in case of entry. In case of fight the entrants' payoffs would be negative:

$$\Pi_{EF} < 0 < \Pi_{EN}$$

Two assumptions are needed concerning the profitability of fighting for the incumbent or entering for the potential entrant:

(i)   Whether weak or tough, the incumbent would prefer to fight the first entrant and keep the monopoly in the second round rather than accommodate both entrants:

$$\Pi_{IF}^W + \delta\Pi_M > (1 + \delta)\Pi_{IN} \tag{4.6}$$

where δ is a discount factor.

(ii) Using the prior probability of facing a tough incumbent the potential entrant would still prefer to enter:

$$P\Pi_{EF} + (1 - P)\Pi_{EN} > 0 \tag{4.7}$$

The last assumption means that a potential entrant would certainly enter if the game was only one stage.

This game has no pure strategy equilibrium. This first result can be easily checked. First suppose that a weak incumbent decides to fight. Then when entrant 2 (in the second stage) contemplates the possibility of entering, he has no new information regarding the type of the Incumbent. So from Assumption (4.7) above, potential entrant 2 will actually enter. In that case the weak incumbent would do better to accommodate in the first stage since fighting has no entry deterrence effect.

Now, if the weak incumbent prefers accommodation in the first round, entrant 2 knows that if a fight occurs the incumbent is a tough one. Entrant 2 would not enter. So in that case the weak incumbent should fight in the first round (because of Assumption (4.6)). No pure strategy can constitute an equilibrium of this game. However there is a mixed strategy which can be a SE of the game.

Let us see how entrant 2 mixes actions between E and O at his information set h and how the incumbent chooses to mix A and F when he is weak. Call q the probability of entry at h and p the probability of accommodation when the incumbent is weak. I would be indifferent between A and F at that node if and only if:

$$\Pi_{IN} + \delta\Pi_{IN} = q(\Pi_{IF}^W + \delta\Pi_{IN}) + (1 - q)(\Pi_{IF}^W + \delta\Pi_M) \tag{4.8}$$

or

$$q = 1 - \frac{\Pi_{IN} - \Pi_{IF}^{W}}{\delta(\Pi_M - \Pi_{IN})} \tag{4.9}$$

Since we are searching for a SE, the beliefs must be consistent. Entrant 2's beliefs about facing a weak incumbent or a tough one after observing a fight in stage 1 must be consistent with the probability priors and I's strategy. Therefore, 2 will use a mixed strategy if and only if:

$$P^* \Pi_{EF} + (1 - P^*)\Pi_{EN} = 0 \tag{4.10}$$

where

$$P^* = \frac{P}{P + (1 - P)(1 - p)}$$

is the updated probability of facing a tough firm after observing a fight in stage 1. From (4.10) one gets:

$$p = 1 + \frac{P\Pi_{EF}}{(1 - P)\Pi_{EN}} \tag{4.11}$$

With the probability computed in (4.8) and (4.10), the mixed strategies at node where I is weak in information set h constitute a SE of the game.

A final condition is needed to confirm that we are in a situation where potential entrant 1 does enter:

$$[P + (1 - P)(1 - p)]\Pi_{EF} + (1 - P)p\Pi_{EN} \geq 0$$

where p is given by (4.10).

In this simplified version of the Kreps–Wilson model, a weak incumbent will fight with a positive probability in order to create a reputation of toughness. Of course considering a higher number of rounds would simply increase the advantage of reputation building

4.4.2. Signalling games

We consider two economic examples of signalling games: the first is concerned with a portfolio management problem and the second deals with a job market problem.

A portfolio management signalling game

The following game studies the properties of financial investment contracts, in which groups of share owners (pools of investors) ask specialized professionals to manage their funds. Over a period, the gross return of a portfolio depends on the investment fund manager's capability, which is not observable by investors. Contracts may involve warranties, offered by the fund managers before the contract is signed. A fee will compensate the fund manager when the warranty is accepted. We suppose here that there are two investment funds and only one manager. The two investment funds compete in a Bertrand game. They give an identical *a priori* probability on the manager's quality (low or high).

In this game the fund manager is the informed player. Nature chooses a particular quality, then the manager has the opportunity to send a signal, through the warranty proposal G, in order to reveal information on the given quality. Warranties work here as a pure signal, since they are not productive as such.

At the beginning of the game, the investors know that the fund manager may be of high ability with probability $\pi = \frac{1}{2}$ and may be of low ability with probability $(1 - \pi) = \frac{1}{2}$. These probabilities can be revised after receiving a signal, through a belief function applying Bayes' rule: $\mu(\theta/G)$.

The game has the following steps:

(i)   Nature chooses the fund manager's ability. We consider here only two types: low ability θ_1 leading to gross returns $R(\theta_1) = 2$, and high ability θ_2 leading to gross returns $R(\theta_2) = 5, 5$.

(ii) The fund manager learns his type and can choose a level of warranty in order to signal his ability: $G_1 = 0$ or $G_2 = 1$, for example.

(iii) The investment funds, having received this signal, offer contracts to the manager.

(iv) The fund manager accepts or refuse the contract. If the contract is accepted, the outcome is a certain level of gross return and corresponding payoffs.

A contract $(G, F(G))$ specifies the compensation fees $F(G)$ for a given level of warranty G. The fund manager's payoff function is:

$$u_0(G, F(G), \theta) = F(G) - c(G, \theta)$$

where $c(G, \theta)$ is the cost of providing the warranty: $c(G, \theta) = 8G/R(\theta)$ He will choose the signal accordingly, knowing that that level of warranty will influence the amount of fees. The investor's payoff function is:

$$u_1 = (G, F(G), \theta) = \begin{cases} R(\theta) - F(G), & \text{if the manager accepts the contract} \\ 0 & , \text{ otherwise} \end{cases}$$

It is assumed that the investors will try to maximize the difference between the gross return of funds and the compensation fees given to the manager.

Since the investment funds compete in a Bertrand fashion, at equilibrium, they will offer identical compensation fees, equal to the gross return of their investment:

$$F_1^* = R_1^*(\theta_1)$$
$$F_2^* = R_2^*(\theta_2)$$

This game has plenty of PBE. The pure strategy equilibria are either separating or pooling equilibria.

Separating equilibrium

In a separating equilibrium, different types of fund managers signal their ability at different levels of warranty. The investors can then infer their ability from the signal sent. High-ability managers will choose a signal $G_2 = 1$, while low-ability managers will offer a warranty $G_1 = 0$. At equilibrium, the compensation fees are:

$$F_1^* = F_1^*(G_1^*(\theta_1)) = R_1^*(\theta_1) = 2$$
$$F_2^* = F_2^*(G_2^*(\theta_2)) = R_2^*(\theta_2) = 5,5$$

A system of beliefs supporting this separating equilibrium is, for instance:

$$\begin{cases} \mu(\theta_2/G) = 1 \; if \; G = G_2^* \\ \mu(\theta_2/G) = 0 \; if \; G \neq G_2^* \end{cases}$$

We must now check if the incentive compatibility constraints are satisfied, that is if the low-ability manager is not attracted to the high-ability contract and if the high-ability manager has no interest for the low-ability contract. These constraints are, respectively:

$$F_1 - \frac{8G_1}{R(\theta_1)} \geq F_2 - \frac{8G_2}{R(\theta_1)}$$

$$F_2 - \frac{8G_2}{R(\theta_2)} \geq F_1 - \frac{8G_1}{R(\theta_2)}$$

The incentive compatibility constraint is satisfied for the low-ability manager since:

$$2 - 0 \geq 5,5 - \frac{8}{2}$$

For the high-ability manager, we have:

$$5,5 - \frac{8}{5,5} \geq 2 - 0$$

The constraint is also satisfied.

Pooling equilibrium

In a pooling equilibrium both types of managers provide the same level of warranty (i.e. they send the same signal). This equilibrium can be supported by the following system of beliefs:

$$\begin{cases} \mu(\theta_2/G) = 1/2 \ if \ G = G^* \\ \mu(\theta_2/G) = 0 \quad if \ G \neq G^* \end{cases}$$

In that case, the investors will offer a compensation fee such that:

$$c^* = \frac{1}{2}R_1^*(\theta_1) + \frac{1}{2}R_2^*(\theta_2) = 3,75$$

It is important to specify the belief function $\mu(\theta_2/G)$ for levels of warranties which will never be reached in equilibrium. Fund managers have a clear incentive to provide no warranty (that is $G_1 = 0$) since they realize that even with a warranty G_2, investors would still believe that the manager has a low ability with probability $\frac{1}{2}$.

The concept of PBE (equivalent here to SE) does not restrict the investors' beliefs about the warranty choices which never occur. The 'intuitive criterion' proposed by Cho and Kreps (1987) allows us to restrict these beliefs. For all out-of-equilibrium choices of G, it puts a zero probability on the type who would lose by choosing a level of G relative to what he can get in the assumed equilibrium. All the pooling equilibria can be discarded by this criterion. Among the separating equilibria, the most efficient will be selected.

A job market signalling game

The following game is a variant of the model of job market signalling by Spence (1973) (This part of the section is based on Donze, 1995, 68–83).

There are three players: two firms and a worker. The worker may have a high ability or a low ability. For simplicity we restrict attention to the case of only two types of workers: workers with high productivity θ_H and workers with low productivity θ_L ($\theta_H > \theta_L > 0$). We will call p the probability of θ being equal to θ_H:

$p = \text{prob}(\theta = \theta_H) \in (0, 1)$

The game has four stages:

(i)   The first move is made by Nature which determines worker type
(ii) In a second stage, the worker learns his type and chooses a level of education accordingly: $e \geq 0$.
(iii) In a third stage, the firms simultaneously make a wage offer w, conditional on the observed level of education (but not of the worker's type)
(iv) Finally, the worker accepts the higher of the two wage offers, flipping a coin in case of a tie; we denote w the wage accepted by the worker.

In order to specialize the example, we need to define the players' cost and utility functions. The objective of each firm is to maximize a 'profit function': $\theta e - w$. However, following Spence (1973), we assume that competition among firms will drive expected profits to zero. One way to build this assumption into the model consists in replacing the two firms in the third stage with a single player called 'the firm', whose payoff is given by:

$$\Pi(\theta, e, w) = -(\theta e - w)^2$$

i.e. when the expected ability of the worker is θ_H the firm proposes the wage $\theta_H e$.

On the other hand the payoff of a worker of ability θ is:

$$U(\theta, e, w) = w - e^2/2\theta$$

i.e. we assume that in order to acquire e units of education the worker with utility θ incurs a cost noted $e^2/2\theta$.

Figure 4.20   Single-crossing condition

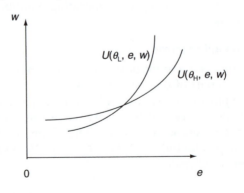

This payoff function verifies the 'single-crossing' condition: the higher is the type of the sender, the lower is the marginal cost associated with sending a message. The property is illustrated in Figure 4.20, where indifference curves for a high-ability worker and a low-ability worker are drawn.

Here, the single crossing property means that the marginal cost of acquiring education is lower for the high-ability worker than for the low-ability worker. Equivalently: for all education levels e and e' such that $e > e'$ and for all wages w and w':

$$U(\theta_L, e, w) \geq U(\theta_L, e', w') \Rightarrow U(\theta_H, e, w) > U(\theta_H, e', w') \qquad (4.12)$$

The worker θ_H is more inclined to send high-level messages than the worker θ_L.

If information was complete, that is if the firm knows the worker type, the firm would offer a wage θe (which maximizes $\Pi(\theta, e, w)$). In that case the worker would choose a level of education maximizing $U(\theta, e, w)$. It is then easy to verify the following result.

Proposition 1 If information was complete, a type θ_H worker would choose a level of education θ_H^2 and a type θ_L worker would choose a level of education θ_L^2.

More interesting (as it is also more realistic) is the case of incomplete information. Then the firm has a belief function $\mu(\theta/e) \in [0,1]$, which defines a probability of facing a type θ worker after seeing a choice of education e by the worker.

We are interested in finding an equilibrium of this particular game with incomplete information game. We employ the SE concept and its refinements.

The sequential equilibrium

A SE for this game is a set of strategies (e, w) and a belief function $\mu(e)$ satisfying:

(i)   the worker's strategy is optimal given her (or his) type and the firm's strategy
(ii) the firm's strategy maximizes its payoff function given the worker's strategy and the belief function $\mu(\theta/e)$
(iii) the belief function $\mu(\theta/e)$ is derived from the worker's strategy using Bayes' rule whenever possible.

From condition (ii) it must be true that the wage offered by the firm is a best response to the belief about the workers' productivity based on the observation of e and the function $\mu(\theta/e)$. The belief function has a support $\{\theta_L, \theta_H\}$, so the firm would not offer a wage lower than the one proposed to a θ_L type worker after an education level e. Thus in any SE, any type can get a payoff (utility-based) at least equal to the maximum payoff that she (or he) could obtain when the firm thinks it is facing a type θ_L worker.

Lemma 1: In any sequential equilibrium, a θ type worker will get a payoff higher than (or equal to) $U_L(\theta) \equiv \max_e U(\theta, e, \theta_L e) = \theta_L^2 \theta/2.$ ∎

Two different SE may arise in this game: separating equilibria, in which workers of different types would choose different education levels, and pooling equilibria, in which the two types of workers would choose the same education level.

In a separating equilibrium, the two types of workers acquire different education levels $e^s(\theta_H)$ and $e^s(\theta_L)$. Then the firm can infer their types after observing e^s. From Lemma 1, we know that the type θ_L worker's payoff must be greater than $U_L(\theta_L)$. Also, this worker cannot get more than $U_L(\theta_L)$ since after having chosen $e^s(\theta_L)$, the firm can infer her (or his) low ability. For the type θ_L worker the utility $(U(\theta_L, e, \theta_L e))$ is maximized only by choosing $e^s(\theta_L) = \theta_L^2$. The high-ability worker must chose an education level high enough so that the θ_L type worker would not find it worthwhile to choose it as well. Formally:

$$e^s(\theta_H) \in S^L \equiv \{e/U(\theta_L, e, \theta_H e) \leq U(\theta_L, e^s(\theta_L), \theta_L e^s(\theta_L))\}$$

Moreover, the type θ_H worker's payoff must be greater than $U_L(\theta_H)$, the maximum payoff that he could obtain when facing the most unfavorable belief of the firm. Formally:

$$e^s(\theta_H) \in S^H \equiv \{e/U(\theta_H, e, \theta_H e) \geq U_L(\theta_H)\}$$

It can then be shown that:

$$S \equiv S^L \cap S^H = [\theta_H\theta_L + \theta_L\sqrt{\theta_H^2 - \theta_L^2}, \theta_H^2 + \theta_H\sqrt{\theta_H^2 - \theta_L^2}] \neq \phi$$

The following proposition summarizes these results.

Proposition 2 For any $p \in]0, 1[$, there exist separating equilibria, and at equilibrium, the type θ_L worker chooses an education level $e^s(\theta_L) = \theta_L^2$ and the type θ_H worker chooses an education level $e^s(\theta_H) \in S.$ ∎

For example, the following pessimistic beliefs can sustain such separating equilibria:

$$\mu(\theta_H/e) = 1 \text{ if } e = e^s(\theta_H) \text{ and } \mu(\theta_H/e) = 0 \text{ otherwise.}$$

Figure 4.21   Separating equilibria

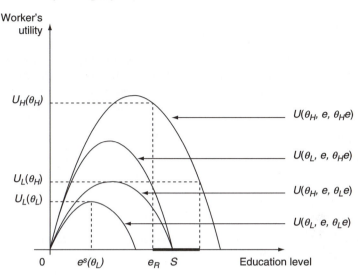

Figure 4.21 shows the set of separating equilibria as defined above. The low-ability worker choses $e^s(\theta_L)$ and the high-ability worker chooses an education level in S.

Notice that the lowest level of education e_R is supposed to be higher than the level that would maximize $U_H(\theta_H)$ in the perfect information case.

Assumption 1: $\theta_H^2 < e_R \equiv \theta_H\theta_L + \theta_L\sqrt{\theta_H^2 - \theta_L^2}$

This assumption is simply made to make the signalling model more interesting: high-ability workers choose an otherwise useless level of education to distinguish themselves from low-ability workers.

The minimum level of education in S is noted e_R because it is a Riley equilibrium (Riley, 1979). We saw above that in such a game the Riley equilibrium will be the unique SE surviving the intuitive criterion. We will check this result below. But before that, let us present the pooling equilibria.

Pooling equilibria

In the pooling equilibrium, the two types of workers choose the same level of education: $e^*(\theta_L) = e^*(\theta_H) = e^*$. The firm's beliefs must in that case be equal to the *a priori* probabilities p and $(1 - p)$ of facing, respectively, a high-ability worker and a low-ability worker. The expected productivity of the worker is thus:

$$E(\theta) \equiv p\theta_H + (1 - p)\theta_L$$

And the offered wage is then:

$$w^*(e^*) = E(\theta)e^*$$

We know from Lemma 1 that both types of workers must obtain a higher payoff than the payoff they would obtain when the firm conjectures that it is facing a low-ability type. Formally, the previous condition means that e^* must belong to the sets $P^L(p)$ and $P^H(p)$, defined as:

$$e^* \in P^L(p) \equiv \{e : U(\theta_L, e, E(\theta)e) \geq U_L(\theta_L)\}$$

and

$$e^* \in P^H(p) \equiv \{e : U(\theta_H, e, E(\theta)e) \geq U_L(\theta_H)\}$$

Let us call $P^*(p) = P^L(p) \cap P^H(p)$ the set of pooling equilibria (which can be void). It can be proven that , when p is greater than

$$p^* = \frac{(\theta_H + \theta_L)\sqrt{\theta_H\theta_L} - 2\theta_H\theta_L}{2(\theta_H - \theta_L)\theta_H} \in [0,1]$$

the set $P^*(p)$ is not void and is equal to:

$$P^*(p) = [\theta_H E(\theta) - \theta_H\sqrt{E(\theta)^2 - \theta_L^2}, \theta_L E(\theta) + \theta_L\sqrt{E(\theta)^2 - \theta_L^2}]$$

So there may exist pooling equilibria, where the two types of workers choose the same level of education e^*. For instance, beliefs $\mu(\theta_H/e) = p$ if $e = e^*$ and $\mu(\theta_H/e) = 0$ if $e \neq e^*$ can sustain such a pooling equilibrium.

Equilibrium refinements

The multiplicity of SE may leave the reader worried about the predictive power of such models. However, it may be reasonable to discard many, and in some cases all but one of these equilibria which are founded on unlikely out-of-equilibrium beliefs. As we saw above, various criteria have been developed to select reasonable equilibria.

Let us apply here first a simple test of weak dominance. We can say that an education level e is weakly dominated for a type θ worker if:

$$U(\theta, e, \theta_H e) \leq \max_{e'} U(\theta, e', \theta_L e') \equiv U_L(\theta)$$

In other words, the education level e is weakly dominated for a type θ worker if e can allow him a lower payoff than the optimal payoff which he could obtain under the most unfavorable belief of the firm.

A SE (e^*, w^*, μ^*) is undominated if $\mu(\theta_H/e) = 0$ (respectively $\mu(\theta_H/e) = 1$) for any education level e weakly dominated for the type θ_H worker (respectively, θ_L), but not for the type θ_L worker (respectively θ_H).

The application of the weak dominance criterion to the SE of labour market signalling leads to a significant reduction of the set of equilibria. In particular, all but one separating equilibria violate the criterion. However, several pooling equilibria may resist.

Let us check first for the separating equilibria. The following result can be proved.

Lemma 2 In any undominated SE, the equilibrium payoff for a type θ_H worker must be higher than or equal to $U_H(\theta_H) = U(\theta_H, e_R, \theta_H e_R)$ and $U_H(\theta_H) > U_L(\theta_H)$. ∎

Proof: $D_H \equiv \{e: U(\theta_H, e, \theta_H e) \leq U_L(\theta_H)\}$ is the set of weakly dominated education levels for a type θ_H worker. $D_L \equiv \{e: U(\theta_L, e, \theta_H e) \leq U_L(\theta_L)\}$ is the set of weakly dominated education levels for a type θ_L worker. Undominated equilibria are sustained by beliefs that must satisfy the following condition: $\mu(\theta_H/e) = 1$ if $e \notin D^H$ but $e \in D^L$, and $\mu(\theta_H/e) = 0$ if $e \in D^H$ but $e \notin D^L$. Some calculations lead to $\mu(\theta_H/e) = 1$ if $e \in S$ and $\mu(\theta_H/e) = 0$ if $e \in S'$ $[\theta_H\theta_L - \theta_L\sqrt{\theta_H^2 - \theta_L^2}, \theta_H^2 - \theta_H\sqrt{\theta_H^2 - \theta_L^2}]$. In every undominated equilibrium a type θ_H worker must get at least $U_H(\theta_H) = \max_{e \in S} U(\theta_H, e, \theta_H e)$. Since $U(\theta_H, e, \theta_H e)$ is strictly decreasing in e over S and $e_R < \theta_H^2 + \theta_H\sqrt{\theta_H^2 - \theta_L^2}$, one gets:

$$U_H(\theta_H) = U(\theta_H, e_R, \theta_H e_R) > U(\theta_H, \theta_H^2 + \theta_H\sqrt{\theta_H^2 - \theta_L^2},$$

$$\theta_H(\theta_H^2 + \theta_H\sqrt{\theta_H^2 - \theta_L^2}) = U_L(\theta_H). ∎$$

From this result, it is easy to infer that:

Proposition 3: For any $p \in [0, 1]$, the only undominated separating SE is the Riley equilibrium. ∎

Proof: From the previous result, a type θ_H worker gets at least a payoff equal to $U_H(\theta_H)$. Then, the only undominated separating equilibrium is such that $e^S(\theta_L) = \theta_L^2$ and $e^S(\theta_H) = e_R$. This equilibrium is sustained by the following admissible beliefs: $\mu(\theta_H/e) = 1$ if $e \in S$, $\mu(\theta_H/e) = 0$ if $e \in S'$ and e.g. $\mu(\theta_H/e) = 0$ otherwise. ∎

So far, so good, but the result is a bit less interesting as far as pooling equilibria are concerned. Let us call $P^{**}(p) \equiv \{e \in P^*(p): U(\theta_H, e, E$

$(\theta)e) \geq U_L(\theta_H)\}$, the set of undominated pooling equilibria (of course the set could be empty).

Proposition   4: Let $p^{**} = \arg\min_p \{\max_e U(\theta_H, e, E(\theta)e) \geq U_H(\theta_H)\}$. Then, $p^* < p^{**} < 1$ and for any $p \in [p^{**}, 1[, P^{**}(p) \neq \phi.\blacksquare$

Proposition 4 means that when the firm's beliefs are favourable enough, the set of undominated pooling equilibria is non-empty.

Proof: Let $Q^{**}(p) \equiv \{e: U(\theta_H, e, E(\theta)e) \geq U_H(\theta_H)\}$ be the set of education levels which allow a type θ_H worker to get payoff higher than $U^H(\theta_H)$ when the firm has a belief $\mu(\theta_H/e) = p$. First of all, one can show that $P^{**}(p) = Q^{**}(p)$. For any undominated pooling equilibrium we must have: $e^* \in P^L(p)$, $e^* \in P^H(p)$ and $e^* \in Q^{**}(p)$. From Lemma 2 we know that $U^H(\theta_H) > U^L(\theta_H)$, which implies that $Q^{**}(p) \in P^H(p)$. Now we can check that $Q^{**}(p) \in P^L(p)$. Suppose that the opposite is true: there is an education level e^* in $Q^{**}(p)$ which does not belong to $P^L(p)$. By definition of a Riley equilibrium, $U(\theta_L, e_R, \theta_H e_R) = U_L(\theta_L)$. Since by assumption $e^* \notin P^L(p)$, one can write:

$$U(\theta_L, e_R, \theta_H e_R) > U(\theta_L, e^*, E(\theta)e^*)$$

Since $e_R > e^*$, and using the single crossing property one gets:

$$U(\theta_H, e_R, \theta_H e_R) = U_H(\theta_H) > U(\theta_H, e^*, E(\theta)e^*)$$

However $e^* \in Q^{**}(p)$, which implies a contradiction with the previous inequality. It is then clear that $e^* \in Q^{**}(p)$ implies that $e^* \in P^L(p) \cap P^H(p)$, so that $P^{**}(p) = Q^{**}(p)$.

Now one has to verify if $Q^{**}(p)$ is non-empty when p is high enough. Since p^{**} is such that: $p^{**} = \arg\min_p \{\max_e U(\theta_H, e, E(\theta)e) \geq U_H(\theta_H)\}$, clearly $p^* < p^{**}$. From Assumption 1, we know that: $U(\theta_H, \theta_H^2, \theta_H\theta_H^2) > U(\theta_H, e_R, \theta_H e_R) \equiv U_H(\theta_H)$, so we have $p^* < p^{**} < 1$.

Finally what are the beliefs which can sustain the undominated pooling equilibria? Every pooling equilibrium e^* in $P^{**}(p)$ can be sustained by the beliefs $\mu(\theta_H/e) = p$ if $e = e^*$, $\mu(\theta_H/e) = 1$ if $e \in S$, $\mu(\theta_H/e) = 0$ if $e \in S'$ and e.g. $\mu(\theta_H/e) = 0$ otherwise.$\blacksquare$

Intuitive criterion

The intuitive criterion put forward by Cho and Kreps (1987) is specially interesting because it is able to select only one equilibrium in this kind of models with two types of informed players (see above 4.3.2, Definition 8). For a given equilibrium (e^*, w^*, μ^*), an education level e is equilibrium-dominated for the type θ worker if: $U^*(\theta, e^*, \theta e^*) \geq U(\theta, e, \theta_H e)$. So a SE (e^*, w^*, μ^*) would pass the intuitive criterion test when: $\mu(\theta_H/e) = 1$ (respectively $\mu(\theta_H/e) = 0$) for all education level e equilibrium dominated for a type θ_L worker (respectively θ_H) but not for a type θ_H worker (respectively θ_L). In this model, it can be proven that:

Proposition 5: For all $p \in \,]0, 1[$, the only SE which does not violate the intuitive criterion is the Riley equilibrium.■

Proof: First for the case of separating equilibria, one can easily show that any equilibrium other than the Riley equilibrium cannot pass the intuitive criterion test. The proof uses here the same kind of argument as for the weak dominance above. The case of pooling equilibria is trickier. Two cases must be distinguished.

Suppose first that $p < p^{**}$. In any pooling equilibrium, the type θ_H worker is assured to get a payoff strictly lower than $U_H(\theta_H)$. The out-of-equilibrium education level e_R is equilibrium-dominated for the low-ability worker but not equilibrium-dominated for the high-ability worker. Then the firm should attribute a level of education e_R to type θ_H and offer a wage $\theta_H e_R$, which indeed destabilizes the pooling equilibrium.

Now suppose that $p \geq p^{**}$ and consider a pooling equilibrium where the two types of workers choose a level e^*. Let $\bar{e}$ be defined as follows: $\bar{e} = \max_e H$, where: $H \equiv \{e : U(\theta_L, e, \theta_H e) \geq U^*(\theta_L) \equiv U(\theta_L, e^*, E(\theta)e^*)\}$. Notice that since $U(\theta_L, e^*, \theta_H e^*) > U(\theta_L, e^*, E(\theta)e^*) \equiv U^*(\theta_L)$, the set H is not empty. It is also easy to see that the set H has a highest bound. There is a solution to the maximization problem defining $\bar{e}$, and $\bar{e}$ must be such that: $U(\theta_L, \bar{e}, \theta_H \bar{e}) = U(\theta_L, e^*, E(\theta)e^*)$. Since $\bar{e} > e^*$ (see that $U(\theta_L, e^*, \theta_H e^*) > U^*(\theta_L)$) and using the single crossing property, one gets: $U(\theta_H, \bar{e}, \theta_H \bar{e}) = U(\theta_H, e^*, E(\theta)e^*) = U^*(\theta_L)$. The education level is then equilibrium-dominated for a type θ_L worker, but not for a type θ_H. The firm should offer a wage $\theta_H \bar{e}$ after a level $\bar{e}$, which destabilizes the pooling equilibrium.■

Bibliography

Banks, J. and J. Sobel (1987) 'Equilibrium selection in signaling games', *Econometrica*, 55, 647–62.

Bernheim, B.D. (1984) 'Rationalizable strategic behavior', *Econometrica*, 52, 1007–28.

Binmore, K. (1992) *Fun and Games* (Lexington, MA: D.C. Heath), Chapter 11

Binmore, K. and P. Dasgupta (1986) 'Introduction-game theory: a survey', in K. Binmore and P. Dasgupta (eds), *Economic Organizations and Games* (Oxford: Basic Blackwell).

Blackburn, K. (1992) 'Credibility and time consistency in monetary policy' in K. Dowd and M.K. Lexis (eds), *Current Issues in Financial and Monetary Economics* (London: Macmillan).

Brandenburger, A. and E. Dekel (1987) 'Rationalizability and correlated equilibrium', *Econometrica*, 55, 139–1402.

Brandts, J. and C. Holt (1992) 'An experimental test of equilibrium dominance in signaling games', *American Economic Review*, 82, 1350–65.

Cho, I.K. (1987) 'A refinement of sequential equilibrium', *Econometrica*, 55, 1367–89.

Cho, I.K. and D. Kreps (1987) 'Signaling games and stable equilibria', *Quarterly Journal of Economics*, 102, 179–221.

Cho, I.K. and J. Sobel (1990) 'Strategic stability and uniqueness in signalling games', *Journal of Economic Theory*, 50, 381–413.

Crawford, V. and J. Sobel (1982) 'Strategic information transmission', *Econometrica*, 50, 1431–51.

Donze, J. (1995) *Raffinements dans les jeux bayesiens dynamiques*, PhD, University of Toulouse (in French).

Eichberger, J. (1993) *Game Theory for Economists* (New York: Academic Press), Chapters 5, 6, 7.

Fudenberg, D. and J.Tirole (1991a) *Game Theory* (Cambridge, MA: MIT Press), chapters 9, 11.

Fudenberg, D. and J. Tirole (1991b) 'Perfect Bayesian equilibrium and sequential equilibrium', *Journal of Economic Theory*, 53, 236–60.

Gibbons R. (1992) *A Primer in Game Theory* (Hemel Hempstead: Harvester-Wheatsheaf), Chapters 3, 4

Grossman, S.J. and M. Perry (1986) 'Perfect Sequential Equilibrium', *Journal of Economic Theory*, 39, 97–119.

Harsanyi J.C. (1967–8) 'Games with incomplete information played by "Baysian" players, Parts I, II and III', *Management Science*, 14, 159–82, 320–34, 486–502.

Hillas, J. and E. Kohlberg (2002) 'Foundations of strategic equilibrium', in R.J. Aumann and S. Hart (eds), *Handbook of Game Theory and Applications*, 3 (New York: Elsevier).

Klemperer P. (1999) 'Auction theory: a guide to the literature', *Journal of Economic Surveys*, 13, 227–86.

Kohlberg, E. (1991) 'Refinement of Nash Equilibrium: the main ideas', in A. Ichiishi and Y. Tauman (eds), *Game Theory and Applications* (New York: Academic Press), 3–45.

Kohlberg, E. and J-F. Mertens (1986) 'On the strategic stability of equilibria', *Ecochometrica*, 54, 1003–37.

Kreps, D. (1990) *A Course in Microeconomic History* (London: Harvester Wheatsheaf), Chapter 12.

Kreps, D. and M. Spence (1985) 'Modelling the role of history in industrial organization and competition', in G. Feiwel (ed.), *Issues in Contemporary Microeconomics and Welfare* (London: Macmillan).

Kreps, D. and R. Wilson (1982) 'Sequential equilibrium', *Econometrica*, 50, 863–84.

Luce, R.D. and H. Raiffa (1957) *Games and Decisions* (New York: John Wiley).

McAfee P., and J. McMillan (1987) 'Auctions and bidding', *Journal of Economic Literature*, 25, 699–738.

McLennan, A. (1985) 'Justifiable beliefs in sequential equilibrium', *Econometrica*, 53, 889–904.

Mailath, G. (1993) 'Signaling games', in J. Creedy, J. Borland and J. Eichberger, *Recent Developments in Game Theory* (Cheltenham: Edward Elgar).

Mailath, G., J. Okuno-Fujuwara and A. Postlewaite (1993) 'Belief based refinements in signaling games', *Journal of Economic Theory*, 60, 241–76.

Mertens J.-F. (1989) 'Stable equilibria – a reformulation, I. Definition and basic properties', *Mathematics of Operations Research*, 14, 575–624.

Mertens J.-F. and S. Zamir (1985) 'Formulation of Bayesian analysis for games with incomplete information', *Industrial Journal of Game Theory*, 14, 1–29.

Milgrom, P. and J. Roberts (1982) 'Predation, reputation and entry deterrence', *Journal of Economic Theory*, 27, 280–312.

Milgrom, P. and J. Roberts (1986) 'Price and advertising signals of product quality', *Journal of Political Economy*, 94, 796–821.

Myerson, R. (1978) 'Refinements of the Nash equilibrium concept', *International Journal of Game Theory*, 7, 73–80.

Myerson, R (1979) 'Incentive compatibility and the bargaining problem', *Econometrica*, 51, 1767–91.

Myerson, R. (1991) *Game Theory-Analysis of Conflict* (Cambridge, MA: Harvard University Press), Chapters 4, 5.

Pearce, D. (1984) 'Rationalizable strategic behavior and the problem of perfection', *Econometrica*, 52, 1029–50.

Rasmusen, E. (1989) *Games and Information: An Introduction to Game Theory* (Oxford: Blackwell).

Riley, J. (1979) 'Informational equilibrium', *Econometrica*, 47, 331–59.

Roberts, J. (1987) 'Battles for market shares: incomplete information, aggressive strategic pricing, and competitive dynamics', in T.F. Bewley (ed.), *Advances in Economic Theory–Fifth World Congress* (Cambridge: Cambridge University Press).

Rothschild, M. and J.E. Stiglitz (1976) 'Equilibrium in competitive insurance markets', *Quarterly Journal of Economics*, 80, 629–49.

Samuelson, L. (1992) 'Subgame perfection', in J. Greedy, J. Borland and J. Eichlier-ger (eds), *Recent Developments in Game Theory* (Cheltenham: Edward Elgar).

Selten R. (1978) 'The chain-store paradox', *Theory and Decision*, 9 127–59.

Selten, R. (1975) 'Reexamination of the perfectness concept for equilibrium points in extensive games', *International Journal of Game Theory*, 4, 25–55.

Spence, M. (1973) 'Job market signalling', *Quarterly Journal of Economics*, 87, 355–74.

Tan, T.C.C. and S.R.C. Werlang (1988), 'The Bayesian Foundation of solution concept of games', *Journal of Economic Theory*, 45, 370–91.

Van Damme, E. (1983) *Refinement of the Nash Equilibrium Concept* (Berlin: Springer-Verlag).

Van Damme, E. (1989) 'Stable equilibria and forward induction', *Journal of Economic Theory*, 48, 476–96.

Van Damme, E. (1991) *Stability and Perfection of Nash Equilibria* (Berlin: Springer-Verlag) (1st edn, 1987).

Van Damme, E. (1992) 'Refinements of Nash Equilibrium', in J.-J. Laffont (ed.), *Advances in Economic Theory: Sixth World Congress* (Cambridge: Cambridge University Press), 32–75.

Van Damme, E. (2002) 'Strategic equilibrium', in R.J. Aumann and S. Hart (eds), *Handbook of Game Theory and Applications*, 3 (New York: Elsevier).

Wilson, R. (1992), 'Strategic analysis of auctions' in Aumann, R. and S. Hart, editors, *Handbook of Game Theory*, Vol. I (New York: Elsevier Science).

Wolfstetter, E. (1999) *Topics in Microeconomics, Industrial Organization, Auctions and Incentives* (Cambridge: Cambridge University Press).

5 Bargaining: From Non-Cooperative to Cooperative Games

5.1 Strategic games of bargaining
5.2 Axiomatic models of bargaining and the Nash program
5.3 Applications

The concept of cooperation is central in GT, but it is a complex notion. The previous chapters have already shown the existence of mechanisms or devices which act to promote some kind of tacit or indirect cooperation between the players in the framework of non-cooperative games. A true cooperation between the players implies a formal arrangement and a common action in order to achieve a common goal. The most natural way to represent in theory the existence of this common interest between the players would be to introduce a kind of 'social welfare function'. However this approach leads to abandoning one of the major foundations of GT, namely its basic link with the theory of individual decision making.

In order to avoid this difficulty, Nash (1951) suggested at the very beginning the need to study cooperation between players with the same analytical tools as those used in the determination of equilibrium in a non-cooperative game. Cooperation then appears as the result of an explicit procedure of negotiation and during the stage of bargaining each agent is supposed to choose her (or his) cooperative strategy as in any other situation described by non-cooperative games. Remember that such non-cooperative games in which any pre-play negotiation or communication between the player is excluded were named 'contests' by Nash. The search for an agreement between the players in contests can thus be modelled in a classic way through an extensive form or a strategic form of the game, and the most likely outcomes are given by the set of equilibria of the game. This 'strategic' approach of bargaining is presented in section 5.1.

Unfortunately, in many instances, this 'strategic' approach of bargaining, through a detailed analysis of all the actions that the players can choose when they negotiate, leads to an indeterminacy: there are too many equilibria. Interestingly, in important classes of games, one can apply previous analysis of equilibrium refinements to find that only one equilibrium is sub-game perfect (in games with complete information) or sequential (in games with incomplete information).

Another way to remove the difficulty consists in the explicit introduction of some desirable formal properties which allow a comparison of the different outcomes; it is then an 'axiomatic' approach. Formally the game now takes a *cooperative form*. This axiomatic approach of bargaining has also been introduced by Nash (1950b) (1953), who realized at the same time the tension between the two approaches: in the strategic approach the outcome of the negotiation depends on the specification of the bargaining procedure, while in the axiomatic approach the acceptability of the axioms is what matters. So, he suggested reconciling these two viewpoints in what is today called the 'Nash programme': any axiomatic model that prescribes a particular outcome should be associated with a strategic bargaining model whose equilibrium corresponds to this outcome; in other words, we need to construct non-cooperative bargaining games for testing the axioms. Section 5.2 is concerned with this topic: the axiomatic approach of bargaining and the Nash programme are successively presented. Finally, section 5.3 is devoted to some economic applications of both the strategic and the axiomatic approach of bargaining.

5.1 Strategic games of bargaining

The recent non-cooperative bargaining models all start from a particular specification of the 'institutional framework' in which the game is embedded. By 'institutional framework' we mean a structure of moves by the players. Do they make simultaneous offers? Do they alternate their moves? When a player acts, can she (or he) only answer 'yes' or 'no' to the other player's proposal or can she (or he) also make another offer in turn? A strategy in such a game is a rule specifying what offer (or reply) the player should make at each point, as a function of the history of offers and replies made up to that point.

The basic idea of the non-cooperative approach is to search for the equilibrium of the game once the institutional framework is defined. Applying what we learned in Chapters 3 and 4 we are interested first in searching for NE. Yet, since the game has a dynamic structure – that is, a sequence of moves – one is primarily interested in some kind of refinement of NE. It is clear that the nature of information available to the players is a crucial aspect. So it is necessary to distinguish between the situations with complete information and those where information is incomplete; we study first the easier games with complete information.

5.1.1   Indeterminacy or extreme Nash equilibria in simple two-person bargaining games with complete information

Many simple bargaining games do not allow one to get out of the fundamental indeterminacy illustrated by Edgeworth's contract curve. Dividing a cake, or for this purpose anything of value, i.e. sum of money – typically 1 dollar – between two players choosing simultaneously results in a whole set of NE, without any clues for choosing between them.

A division game leading to indeterminacy: 'dividing the dollar'

Let us first verify this rather sad state of affairs by studying an extremely simple game. Two people are faced with the following problem. They must divide between them a sum of money: say, 1 dollar. They propose simultaneously a share x_1 and x_2, respectively. If $x_1 + x_2 \leq 1$, they get their money, but they get nothing if $x_1 + x_2 > 1$.

We assume that they care only about the money they can get. By assumption, we thus rule out a situation where one player would prefer to receive nothing, like the other one, rather than to get a very small amount when a large part of the sum of money is left to the other. In order to keep things simple, we also assume that utility and sums of money are equivalent.

In this situation, we can check that there is an infinity of NE. In fact, any division of the dollar is a NE of this bargaining game. Consider as an example, the proposal $x_1 = 0.7$, no less and $x_2 = 0.3$, no less. Clearly player 2's proposal is a best response to player 1's strategy and reciprocally. However, the same is true for the strategies: $x_1 = 0.4$ and $x_2 = 0.6$. There are too many NE in this game and unfortunately there is no way to get out of this plethora of solutions.

Slightly different protocols of bargaining would reveal the same indeterminacy. One can easily check that it would also be the case in the following games:

(i)   Players 1 and 2 choose simultaneously a share of the dollar; if the proposed shares are compatible they get their money; if the payoffs are not feasible they make another simultaneous set of proposals; and so on up to five rounds; then if the shares are still above 1 dollar the players get nothing.

(ii)   Player 1 makes a proposal, then 2 says 'yes' or 'no', if he says 'yes' the game ends, if he says 'no', he can in turn make his own proposal which can either be accepted or rejected by player 1; and so on for ten rounds; then, if no agreement has been reached, the players must try a final simultaneous move and get nothing if their claims are too high.

One could give still other extensions of the previous bargaining games. However in all these cases of simultaneous offers, or cases where there is no cost in waiting and where the last offer is of the simultaneous type, as in (ii) above, there are a lot of NE among which it is not possible to choose. More generally in this kind of game, NE are all the divisions of the cake (dollar, etc.) which are feasible (that is, they do not go beyond the given amount), efficient (that is, they give the maximum amount to one player for a given amount to the other), and individually rational (that is, they give to each agent at least as much as what she (or he) can get otherwise)

Remark

As we will see in Chapter 8, experiments in the laboratory reveal in fact the frequent appearance of 'focal equilibria', such as equal sharing or other attractive issues (according to various criteria of attraction: fairness, conventions, ...) (see sub-section 3.1.3 of Chapter 3 for an introduction to this notion).∎

An extreme equilibrium: the ultimatum game

The preceding games all show the famous indeterminacy noted in the contract curve discussion. Some other simple bargaining games lead to a unique solution but a very extreme one: a typical example is the 'ultimatum game'. Player 1 proposes a share of the dollar, say x for herself and $(1 - x)$ for player 2. Then the latter accepts this offer or rejects it and the game ends. In case of agreement the players receive $(x, 1 - x)$. In case of rejection, both of them receive zero. This 'take it or leave it' kind of bargaining is very simple indeed; yet it is very common in reality since it describes exactly the situation that we face every day when we are confronted with fixed 'written' prices in most shops.

The tree of this game can easily be constructed, as in Figure 5.1.

As we noted above, each player is supposed to care only about money. Moreover, we can admit that player 2 will accept player 1's proposal if he is indifferent between saying 'yes' or 'no', that is when he will receive a zero payoff in both cases. If this assumption looks strange, it can easily be transformed into: player 2 will accept any sum ε close to zero, rather than nothing at all (the only required assumption here is that payments can be made infinitely small).

Figure 5.1 The ultimatum game in extensive form

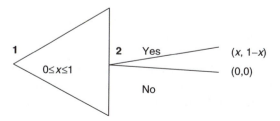

Now let us look at the NE of this game. For instance, the following pair of strategies is a NE:

(a) player 1 first demands 0 for herself
(b) player 2 will say 'no' to any proposal offering him less than the whole dollar and 'yes' when the whole dollar is proposed for him.

Actually each strategy is a best response to the other. This fact is particularly clear for player 2. Player 1's position is a little more critical. However once player 1 recognizes that player 2 will reject any offer lower than the whole dollar, then there is nothing better that she can do. Any other strategy would get a zero payoff. So, proposing 0 in the first place is a best response to player 2's strategy.

Yet it should then be clear that any division of the dollar can be supported as a NE. If player 2 uses the strategy 'accept only if 1 demands x or less' and if 1 uses the strategy 'demand x', each strategy is an optimal reply to the other and the couple $(x, 1 - x)$ is a NE.

This multiplicity of NE seems to replicate the indeterminacy of bargaining presented above. However, if we limit ourselves to the strategies which generate NE in the sub-game, then we can dramatically reduce the number of equilibria. In fact, there is only one SPE in this game. If player 2's strategy is as noted above, this player would not behave optimally in the sub-game following a demand of $x + \varepsilon$ by player 1. Player 2 would do better to accept and get $(1 - x - \varepsilon)$ rather than refuse and get 0.

As backward induction shows, the unique SPE in this case is:

(a) player 1 demands 1 (possibly less ε)
(b) player 2 accepts.

The payoffs are then: $(1, 0)$. There is no way to escape this extreme result, giving player 1 a strong first-mover advantage in this institutional framework. One can add that a fundamental indeterminacy remains here, because there is nothing natural in giving player 1 the first move. However, in 'real institutional frameworks' where this 'take it or leave it' kind of bargaining does happen, conventions or habits give one player the leading move (as in the case of the shopkeeper writing her (or his) prices).

Remark I

If the division of the dollar can only be in finite amounts, then there can be more than one SPE. Suppose, for instance, that there only exist units of 10 cents (see the game tree in Figure 5.2).

Player 2 will say 'yes' to any positive amount left for him. He may or may not say 'yes' when 0 cents are offered, since he will receive 0 in any case. If player 2 says 'no' when offered 0 cents, player 1 has to propose 90

Figure 5.2 Extensive form for the ultimatum game with discrete choices

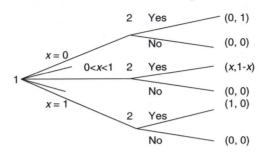

cents instead. So there are two SPE: one in which player 1 proposes 90 cents for herself and the other player says 'yes', one in which player 1 proposes 100 for herself and the other says 'yes'. Of course, if the division can be done in smaller amounts, the two equilibrium outcomes converge toward a single number. For instance, if they can divide each cent, the two equilibria are 99 cents and 100, and so on if smaller amounts are still allowed.■

The non-cooperative approach of bargaining has been regenerated by Rubinstein (1982) who constructed a model in which the result is neither indeterminacy nor necessarily an extreme solution (first-mover extreme advantage, for instance). The result is interesting because it illuminates a lot of related issues, especially the relationship with the 'Nash bargaining solution' (corresponding to the axiomatic approach that we are going to study in section 5.2 of this chapter). It may also show the rationality of certain outcomes, like a division of the cake or sum of money close to fifty-fifty, which appears as a frequent outcome in controlled experiments (although, as we will see in Chapter 8 the observed outcomes do not always conform to the predicted rational solutions).

We consider again the simple problem of dividing 1 dollar but now the bargaining is modified as follows: player 1 and player 2 alternate in making offers, and know that they both are impatient to get their money.

5.1.2 The Rubinstein model: alternating offers in finite and infinite horizon bargaining games

The finite horizon game

Let us first restrain the bargaining procedure to a finite number of 'periods', say 2 periods. Player 1 makes a first proposal: x_1 for herself and $x_2 = (1 - x_1)$ for the other person. Then player 2 decides whether to accept or reject this proposal. In case of acceptance the game ends, while in case of rejection player 2 in turn makes his own proposal. If player 2 chooses to reject player 1's proposal and to make his own offer, then it is up to player 1 to accept or reject. In case of rejection both players then get 0 and the game ends. In case of acceptance, they get what player 2 proposed. Both players are impatient and have thus an incentive to end the game rapidly. Formally their impatience is translated into a discounting of future payoffs.

Let us name 'period' the time corresponding to each offer. Payoffs are discounted by a factor δ per period, where $0 \leq \delta \leq 1$. It is of course likely that the degrees of impatience differ from one agent to another. In the latter case, there would be two discount factors δ_1 and δ_2, one for each player. The significance of δ is clear. One may note that it corresponds to $1/1 + a$, when one calls a the discount rate or, more generally, $\delta = e^{-rt}$, calling r the *instantaneous* discount rate and t the time period (with $r \approx a$ for low values of a).

So when in the second period, player 2 makes his proposal, say y_2 for himself and $(1 - y_2)$ for the other person, these shares correspond to the following present values of payoffs: δy_2 for player 2 and $\delta(1 - y_2)$ for player 1.

The game tree is shown in Figure 5.3.

Again there are many NE. Applying backward induction shows that there is only one SPE: $(1 - \delta, \delta)$. At the very beginning, player 1 knows that if she proposes an amount of money x_2 lower than δ to player 2, the latter will say 'no' and will be able to obtain that amount by choosing $y_2 = 1$ in the second round. The best proposal at the beginning is thus $(1 - \delta, \delta)$, and this is the only SPE. Increasing the number of periods in this game would not change the basic result that there is only one SPE, whose outcome is built on the value of δ.

Figure 5.3   Extensive form of the alternating offer model (finite horizon)

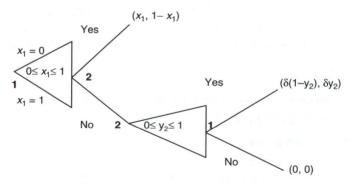

> **Remark 1**
>
> In a sequential model of bargaining, the players' attitudes towards time are of crucial importance. They are summarized by a series of axioms that the 'temporal' preference functions must satisfy.
>
> The time of the bargaining procedure is described by periods corresponding to the set of natural numbers $T = \{1, 2, 3, \ldots\}$. If players agree at period t, the agreement is notated (x, t), where $x \in [0, 1] = X$. Perpetual disagreement is notated D. Player i's preferences are represented by a binary relation R (with P and I for strict preference and indifference, respectively) on the set of possible outcomes: Y. They satisfy the following axioms:
>
> A1   The object of bargaining is desirable: if $x > y$ then: $(x, t)P(y, t)$
> A2   Time is valuable: for all $x > 0$ and $t_1 < t_2$: $(x, t_1)P(x, t_2)$
> A3   Continuity: the graph of R is closed in the product topology $Y \otimes Y$
> A4   Stationarity: $(y, t+1)P(x, t)$ if and only if $(y, 1)P(x, 0)$
> A5   Increasing compensation for delay: if $(x + \varepsilon(x), 1)I(x, 0)$ then $\varepsilon(x)$ is an increasing function of x
> A6   Existence of present value: for all $x \in X$, there exists $v(x) \in X$ such that: $(x, 1)I(v(x), 0)$.
>
> Assumptions 1–4 above guarantee the existence of a utility function $u(x)\delta^n$ for all arbitrary δ (Fishburn and Rubinstein, 1982). They are sufficient for proving the existence in Rubinstein's theorem stated below. The uniqueness part of the theorem also requires Assumptions 5 and 6.∎

The infinite horizon game

It is particularly interesting to extend the previous model to the infinite horizon case. Rubinstein (see also Shaked and Sutton, 1984, and Binmore, 1986, for different presentations and proofs) showed that with an infinite horizon, this game has also a unique SPE.

> **Theorem 1 (*Rubinstein*)**
>
> The infinite horizon bargaining game of alternating offers has a unique SPE.∎

The infinite horizon model is still more interesting for a new investigation of the 'Nash program', i.e. the relationship between the axiomatic approach and the non-cooperative approach. We will focus here on the first result and leave the relation with the 'Nash bargaining solution' for sub-section 5.2.3 of the chapter.

Equilibrium determination and proof of Rubinstein's result

Consider again two players who bargain over the division of a fixed amount of money. We want to study the non-cooperative equilibria of such a game. Rubinstein's theorem states that there is a unique SPE of this game. We will verify it, using the proof put forward by Shaked and Sutton (1984). There is a game G_1 when player 1 starts and a game G_2 when player 2 starts. As previously, the two games are entirely similar, except for the identity of the player starting the game. In principle, it is very difficult to solve this infinite horizon game by backward induction. Yet here one can exploit the stationarity of the structure of the game.

Imagine that there are several SPE outcomes. Let H_1 be the highest payoff to player 1 and L_1 be the smallest one. Similarly call H_2 and L_2 the corresponding values for game G_2. For the Rubinstein theorem (stated above) to be verified, we must have:

$$H_1 = L_1 \text{ and } H_2 = L_2$$

First notice that any SPE of game G_1 will be proposed by player 1 at the first round (time 0) and will be accepted immediately by player 2. Notice also that there is a strong interaction between the highest and smallest payoffs of our players. Indeed at time 0, when game G_1 begins, if player 1 proposes less than $\delta_2 L_2$ to player 2, the latter will refuse and be sure to get his minimum payoff of game G_2, that is the present value of L_2, or $\delta_2 L_2$. So any SPE for game G_1 will give to player 2 at least $\delta_2 L_2$, and so to player 1 not more than $(1 - \delta_2 L_2)$. That is:

$$H_1 \leq 1 - \delta_2 L_2 \tag{5.1}$$

Then one can use also the maximum sub-game perfect outcome for player 2 in game G_2, to infer something about the minimum outcome for player 1 in game G_1. If player 1 starts game G_1 by proposing to the other player a payoff greater than his maximum in game G_2, player 2 would immediately accept. Formally, player 2 would immediately accept any proposal by player 1 greater than the discounted value of H_2, that is $\delta_2 H_2$. This proposal by player 1 cannot thus be one of her sub-game perfect outcomes. By offering a bit less, she would be better off and find the other player accepting. So in any case the smallest sub-game perfect outcome for player 1, that is L_1, cannot be lower than $1 - \delta_2 H_2$. Formally:

$$L_1 \geq 1 - \delta_2 H_2 \tag{5.2}$$

Now it is clear that the same reasoning applies if we consider first the game begun by player 2. So similar inequalities would be obtained:

$$H_2 \leq 1 - \delta_1 L_1 \tag{5.3}$$

and

$$L_2 \geq 1 - \delta_1 H_1 \tag{5.4}$$

Now substitute (5.4) into (5.1) to get:

$$H_1 \leq 1 - \delta_2 L_2 \leq 1 - \delta_2(1 - \delta_1 H_1)$$

And finally, we get:

$$H_1 \leq \frac{1 - \delta_2}{1 - \delta_1 \delta_2} \tag{5.5}$$

The same manipulation of (5.2) and (5.3) gives:

$$L_1 \geq 1 - \delta_2 H_2 \geq 1 - \delta_2(1 - \delta_1 L_1)$$

and finally:

$$L_1 \geq \frac{1 - \delta_2}{1 - \delta_1 \delta_2} \tag{5.6}$$

From (5.5) and (5.6) we get:

$$H_1 \leq \frac{1 - \delta_2}{1 - \delta_1 \delta_2} \leq L_1 \tag{5.7}$$

However we know by definition that the lowest outcome L_1 cannot be greater than the highest outcome H_1, that is:

$$L_1 \leq H_1 \tag{5.8}$$

Clearly (5.7) and (5.8) give:

$$L_1 = H_1 = \frac{1 - \delta_2}{1 - \delta_1 \delta_2} \tag{5.9}$$

Similarly:

$$L_2 = H_2 = \frac{1 - \delta_2}{1 - \delta_1 \delta_2} \tag{5.10}$$

So the game has a unique SPE.

We must emphasize that this outcome is reached immediately (at the first round of negotiation). What the two players will actually receive depends on which one starts the game. When player 1 starts she will get:

$$\frac{1 - \delta_2}{1 - \delta_1\delta_2}$$

and player 2 will get

$$\frac{\delta_2(1 - \delta_1)}{1 - \delta_1\delta_2}$$

Notice also that if the two players share the same impatience, their discount rate is common, let us say δ. Player 1's share becomes

$$x_1 = \frac{1}{1 + \delta}$$

and player 2 gets

$$x_2 = \frac{\delta}{1 + \delta}$$

Comments and interpretations

In this case, it is clear that a strong impatience, represented by a high discount rate r, or a discount factor δ close to 0, gives a large share to player 1. For example, with a discount rate equal to 5000 per cent, we have $\delta = 0.0196$ and finally $x_1 = 0.98$. The intuition behind this result is clear: when impatience is so strong, the game collapses in a kind of one-period ultimatum game. The strong first-mover advantage is then nothing of a surprise.

When the players are not impatient, δ is close to one and player 1's share is close to $\frac{1}{2}$. The intuition here is that with a low discount rate r, the second player has an incentive to reject any unequal offer by player 1. The latter would suffer more in case of delay. Note that the discount rate must not be equal to zero, because then the game admits a continuum of SPE. For a removal of the indeterminacy one must be sure that the player has some incentives to come to an early agreement.

Another situation where the first-mover advantage observed above is removed is when there is no time interval between an offer and a counteroffer. Denote the time delay between two periods Δ. The discount factor can then be written δ^Δ. Then when $\Delta \to 0$, the equilibrium share of player 1 becomes:

$$x_1 = \lim_{\Delta \to 0} \frac{1 - \delta_2^{\Delta}}{1 - \delta_1^{\Delta} \delta_2^{\Delta}} = \frac{\ln \delta_2}{\ln \delta_1 + \ln \delta_2} = \frac{r_2}{r_1 + r_2}$$

When the discount factors are equal, the outcome in the limit is $x_1 = x_2 = \frac{1}{2}$. In that case, the solution depends only on time preferences, not on who moves first.

Now when the players have different discount rates, their relative magnitude influences the outcome. If player 1 is more impatient than player 2, that is if $\delta_1 < \delta_2$, then from (5.9) and (5.10): $x_2 > x_1$, i.e. player 2's share is larger than player 1's share. This result reflects a very intuitive idea about bargaining: *part of the 'bargaining power' is due to a capacity or willingness to wait.*

Similar variations in the protocol of the negotiation will bring other changes in the equilibrium outcomes. For example, one can imagine that the players have different *speeds of response*, instead of assuming, as we have done until now, that the interval between each offer is uniform and equal to 1. If player 2 takes a longer time to respond, it is clear that the cost of disagreement is larger for him than for player 1. This is logically equivalent to a higher discount rate r_2 for player 2 and it brings an advantage in terms of bargaining power for player 1. This is hardly a surprise, but what is really a source of discussion is the large shift in the outcome resulting from a slight change in the protocol.

Consider the case put forward by Kreps (1990). Start from a situation where the time interval is common and equal to 1 and where the discount rate r is also the same and equal to, say, 10 per cent. The dollar would be split according to the previous results:

$$x_1 = \frac{1}{1 + \delta}, \; x_2 = \frac{\delta}{1 + \delta}$$

which gives here something like: a little more than fifty cents to player 1 (52.50 cents) and a little less than fifty cents to player 2. Now, suppose that each player can agree instantaneously to the other player's offer but that it takes player 1 two seconds to propose her counteroffer to player 2's proposal, while it takes player 2 six seconds to makes his own counteroffer. Then the equilibrium outcome is $x_1 = 0.75$ and $x_2 = 0.25$. The shift is quite impressive.

Similarly another slight change in the protocol could move the outcome in the other direction. Suppose now that any answer, either positive or negative in the form of a counteroffer, takes a different time interval between the players. For instance, it again takes two seconds for player 1 to give any answer and six seconds for player 2. But, as opposed to the previous case, player 2 has not to wait another six seconds after having said 'no'. Then somewhat surprisingly, the equilibrium outcome changes in favour of player 2, who would get $x_2 = 0.75$ while player 1 would only get now $x_1 = 0.25$. The reason here is that since saying 'yes' or making another proposal takes the same time interval, the waiting costs are reversed compared to the previous example. The waiting cost of player 2 is not six seconds which he must spend anyway before answering, but the two seconds necessary for getting an answer from player 1. Clearly here player 1 has a larger cost of waiting.

One interesting interpretation of these results has been proposed by Kreps (1990b, 565): 'The key to bargaining power, in Rubinstein's model and in other variations, comes from the ability to put the onus of waiting on the other party.' In Rubinstein's model, when one proposal has been made by one player, the other player has in hand the task of avoiding to wait, knowing that waiting may bring a better deal but is also costly. That is why, when the cost of waiting is slightly higher for one player the equilibrium outcomes shifts dramatically in favour of the other player.

This interpretation raises another interesting point. Do these results strictly depend on the structure of alternating offers suggested by Rubinstein? The answer is 'no'. The same kinds of results should appear in every game where 'each player has the ability to put the onus of waiting entirely on the other party'.

5.1.3 'Outside option' games

A first example

We consider now a game very similar to the one described in Rubinstein's simplest model, except that we will assume that player 2 has an 'outside option': worth share x_2^0 of the cake. As in the game studied previously, player 2 will have to say 'yes' or 'no' to any proposal by player 1, but he can now also say 'I am quitting'. This game can be represented by the tree drawn in Figure 5.4.

It can then be shown that the unique SPE is:

$$x_1 = \min\left(1/1 + \delta, 1 - x_2^0\right); \quad x_2 = \max\left(\delta/1 + \delta, x_2^0\right)$$

Figure 5.4 Outside option' game tree: case I

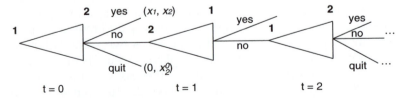

Proof: Imagine first that player 2's option exceeds what he would get in the bargaining game without outside option: $x_2^0 > \delta/1 + \delta$. Player 1 knows that if she offers less than x_2^0 at the very beginning, then player 2 will say 'no' and obtain the assured amount. The best choice for player 1 is clearly to offer immediately $x_1 = 1 - x_2^0$ and $x_2 = x_2^0$. The case where $x_2^0 < \delta/1 + \delta$ is also easy to check. In that case, the presence of an outside option does not influence the final outcome ∎

The previous example is indeed a particular case of a general model of the influence of outside options. An interesting aspect is the study of the level of credibility of threats outside the game. Small threats are not credible and so do not really influence the outcome (we will comment further this issue in the following section in relation with the 'Nash bargaining solution', since it has to do with the 'status quo' position, the question being if any outside option shifts the status quo position and then the agreed outcome).

Other examples

Let us study here the game proposed by Sutton (1986). The problem is again the division of a dollar (any cake of size 1). The players have a common discount factor $\delta < 1$. As in the previous games player 2 is invited to say 'yes' or 'no' after any proposal by player 1 at time $t = 0$. If he says 'yes' the game ends. But if he says 'no', a random event occurs with probability p. If the event occurs, player 2 can choose to quit the game. In that case, he would receive a share of the cake x_2^0, while player 1 would receive x_1^0. This opportunity of quitting is not available if the event fails to occur. Then the game could continue by a counteroffer made by player 2. In turn, 1 will say 'yes' or 'no'. If she says 'yes', the game stops. If she says 'no', an event may come with probability p again, and in this case player 1 can quit and receive a discounted payoff δx_1^0, while player 2 will receive a discounted payoff δx_2^0. And so on, as depicted in Figure 5.5.

Of course if the game is to be played at all, both players must have a gain to share in the process. This remark rules out the possibility that the sum of the outside options be larger than 1. This is true not only for $x_1^0 + x_2^0$ but also for the sums of the security levels that could be achieved if both players simply waited for their options to become available, that is:

Figure 5.5   Outside option' game tree: case 2

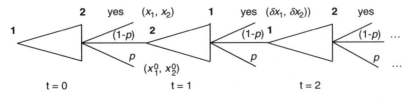

$$\pi_1^0 + \pi_2^0 < 1$$

where: $\pi_1^0 = px_1^0 + p(1-p)\delta x_1^0 + \ldots = px_1^0/[1-(1-p)\delta]$, and similarly: $\pi_2^0 = px_2^0/[1-(1-p)\delta]$.

This game can be solved by using the method studied above. It has a unique SPE division of the fixed amount of money (or cake). When the outside options are small compared to what the players can get in negotiating, the equilibrium outcome is the same as in Rubinstein's model, that is:

$$x_1 = \frac{1}{1+\delta} \text{ and } x_2 = \frac{\delta}{1+\delta}, \quad \text{when: } x_1^0, x_2^0 \leq \frac{\delta}{1+\delta}$$

The opposite case is when both players want to take their options when available. The equilibrium outcome is then:

$$x_1 = \frac{1 - px_2^0 - (1-p)\delta + p(1-p)\delta \, x_1^0}{1-(1-p)^2\delta^2}$$

for player 1 and of course $(1 - x_1)$ for player 2.

Proof: The result comes easily from the application of the Shaked and Sutton proof. Calling M, the supremum of player 1's payoffs, the minimum that player 2 should propose when his turn comes if he wants player 1 to accept is the maximum expected payoff of player 1, that is:

$$px_1^0 + \delta(1-p)M$$

So the maximum that player 2 can obtain at time $t = 1$ is:

$$[1 - px_1^0 - \delta(1-p)M]$$

Then when player 1 considers her first proposal at time $t = 0$, she knows that she can get an acceptance from player 2 only if she offers him his expected payoff, that is:

$$px_2^0 + \delta(1-p)[1 - px_1^0 - \delta(1-p)M]$$

Finally, the maximum payoff of player 1 is:

$$M = 1 - px_2^0 - \delta(1-p)[1 - px_1^0 - \delta(1-p)M]$$

from which we get:

$$M = x_1 = \frac{1 - px_2^0 - (1-p)\delta + p(1-p)\delta x_1^0}{1-(1-p)^2\delta^2}$$

There are, of course, two intermediate cases corresponding to the situations where one player has a good outside option but the other player has only a small one (see exercise 5.4).■

A 'limit version' of the previous result gives interesting insights. Suppose (as in sub-section 5.1.2) that offers and counteroffers follow each other immediately. The time interval between successive offers is then Δ and the discount factor is written δ^{Δ}. Finally, replace the probability p by $(1 - e^{\lambda\Delta})$, so as to keep constant the probability per unit of time that bargaining is interrupted by the appearance of an outside option. In the limit, $\Delta \to 0$ and the equilibrium outcomes becomes:

$$x_1 = \frac{1}{2}, \quad \text{when } x_1^0, x_2^0 \leq \frac{1}{2}$$

and when the players prefer to take their option when it is available:

$$(1 - \omega)\frac{1}{2} + \omega[x_1^0 + \frac{1}{2}(1 - x_1^0 - x_2^0)]$$

where: $\omega = 1/(1 - \ln\delta/\lambda \ln\lambda)$. Again there are two intermediate cases.

Notice that the final outcome depends not only on the relative importance of the outside option with respect to what can be obtained by continuing the bargaining process, but also on the relative importance of the probability of availability of the option with respect to the discount factor (as expressed by the factor ω). If ω tends towards 0, player 1 will get $\frac{1}{2}$, just as in the Rubinstein game. On the other hand, if the probability of taking the option is very high, that is if ω tends towards 1, then the amount of money is shared according to the 'split the difference' rule. Each player gets an amount of money corresponding to the sum of the outside option and half of the difference between 1 (the total to be shared) and the sum of the two outside option values.

The preceding framework helps to understand when and how some outside options constitute empty threats. This is confirmed by considering another game, very similar to the previous one, except that if the random event occurs the players must automatically receive their outside options. For all values of the outside options, the formula $(1 - \omega)\frac{1}{2} + \omega[x_1^0 + \frac{1}{2}(1 - x_1^0 - x_2^0)]$ applies. If $\omega \to 1$, we get the 'split the difference' rule:

$$x_1 = x_1^0 + \frac{1}{2}(1 - x_1^0 - x_2^0)$$

This result illustrates the *importance of credibility of threats*. When they are chosen voluntarily, small options have no effect on the outcome. Yet in the second game, where options are imposed exogenously, even small threats are made credible.

All these results will appear important when we discuss the link between the non-cooperative and the axiomatic approaches.

Remark 2

A crucial issue in bargaining process is the number of players. Unfortunately Rubinstein's result does not extend to the case when there are more than two players. With three or more than three players, there is a multiplicity of SPE. The Rubinstein result is thus limited to situations of *bilateral* bargaining.∎

5.1.4 Non-cooperative theories of bargaining under incomplete information*

Until now, we assumed that the players knew all the aspects of the game. These games of complete information implied an immediate agreement between the players. However it is well known that in real bargaining experiments, agreements are often delayed. Introducing explicitly incomplete information may help to understand such delays or even failures of agreement despite the existence of significant gains from trade.

Players often lack information and need time to acquire at least part of it. Also a kind of signalling argument may explain the delay. A player may want to signal that she (or he) is relatively strong by making a proposal that a weaker player would not want to sustain. Waiting before an agreement is reached can then be part of this signalling strategy. The occurrence and lasting time of strikes can be interpreted according to these lines.

There are many ways to introduce incomplete information into bargaining models. The equilibrium concept is then the PBE and its refinements. In most cases, there are a large number of PBE, which is not something really surprising (see sub-section 4.2.2 of chapter 4). Particular equilibria can be selected through the use of various refinement criteria. However, the selection of equilibria looks more like a series of examples than like generally accepted results.

We consider here a two-period sequential bargaining model (see Fudenberg and Tirole, 1983). A seller and a buyer (risk-neutral) bargain over the price of an indivisible good. The opportunity cost for the seller (hereafter named 'she') is c, which is thus her valuation for this good, known by each player. For simplicity, we will assume that $c = 0$. However, the buyer (hereafter named 'he') may have a low valuation $\underline{v}$ or a high valuation $\bar{v}$ for the good, and this information is not known by the seller.

At date $t = 0$, the seller makes a price offer p_0. The buyer says 'yes' or 'no' and if he says 'no' there is another trial at date $t = 1$. Then the game ends in any case. (Remark that the model may also be interpreted as a monopoly (durable good monopoly) selling to a continuum of infinitesimal consumers.) The payoffs are p_0 and $(v - p_0)$, respectively, for the seller and the buyer $(v = \{\underline{v}, \bar{v}\})$ if an agreement is reached in the first round. Assuming common discount factors $\delta_s = \delta_b = \delta$, the payoffs would be, respectively, δp_1 and $\delta(v - p_1)$ if an agreement is reached only in the second round. In case of disagreement the payoffs would be 0 for both players.

We look for the PBE of the game. The seller has *a priori* probabilities on the buyer's type. Let say that $\bar{\Pi}$ and $\underline{\Pi}$ are the probabilities of facing in period 0, respectively, a buyer who has a high valuation and a buyer who has a low valuation. After observing the buyer's reaction to the first price offer, the seller can revise the probabilities according to Bayes' rule. Let $\bar{\mu}(p_0)$ be the posterior belief that $v = \bar{v}$, after observing a rejection of p_0 in the first round:

$$\underline{\mu}(p_0) = 1 - \bar{\mu}(p_0)$$

If the game reaches the second round, what are the best pricing policies for the seller? Notice first that only two prices are optimal pure strategies: $p_1 = \underline{v}$ and $p_1 = \bar{v}$. Any price lower than $\underline{v}$ would be accepted by the buyer but that is also true for $p_1 = \underline{v}$, which is obviously better for the seller. Above $\bar{v}$, nobody would buy. And between $\underline{v}$ and $\bar{v}$, only a high-valuation buyer would buy, but he would buy as well if $p_1 = \bar{v}$. A mixed strategy is also feasible: it would be a randomization between $\underline{v}$ and $\bar{v}$. If the buyer charges $p_1 = \underline{v}$, the expected (second-price) payoff is $\underline{v}$ for sure. If he charges $p_1 = \bar{v}$, then the expected second-price profit is: $\bar{\mu}(p_0)\bar{v}$. The optimal pricing strategy in stage 2 is thus:

$$p_1^* = \underline{v} \text{ if } \bar{\mu}\bar{v} < \underline{v}$$
$$p_1^* = \bar{v} \text{ if } \bar{\mu}\bar{v} > \underline{v}$$
$$p_1^* = \text{any randomization between } \underline{v} \text{ and } \bar{v} \text{ if } \bar{\mu}\bar{v} = \underline{v}$$

The buyer's optimal strategies are clear enough. Notice that the low-valuation type can never get a surplus, while the high-valuation type gets a surplus only if the seller thinks that his valuation is $\underline{v}$.

Now let us turn to the first round of the bargaining game. The seller offers a price such that $p_0 \in [\underline{v}, \bar{v}]$. How does the buyer react? If $p_0 = \underline{v}$, both types agree and buy, because they cannot hope for a better deal. If $p_0 > \underline{v}$, the low-valuation buyer rejects the offer, which would imply a negative surplus. The high-valuation buyer's behaviour is more interesting.

If a rejection of p_0 leads to a revised probability $\bar{\mu}(p_0)$ such that $\bar{\mu}(p_0)\bar{v} > \underline{v}$, the seller should charge $p_1 = \bar{v}$ in the second period. Then the buyer would not obtain any positive surplus. In that case, he would be better off in buying in the first round.

Clearly this case leads to a contradiction, since the low-valuation buyer always rejects a price offer such that $p_0 > \underline{v}$, and applying Bayes' rule gives $\bar{\mu}(p_0) = 0$ (while $\bar{\mu}(p_0)\bar{v} > \underline{v}$ is assumed here). Now if $\bar{\mu}(p_0)\bar{v} < \underline{v}$, the seller should charge $p_1 = \underline{v}$ in the second period. A high-valuation buyer would get a payoff $(\bar{v} - p_0)$ if he agrees in the first round and a payoff equal to $\delta(\bar{v} - \underline{v})$ if he waits until the second period. Obviously he would prefer to agree immediately if $(\bar{v} - p_0) \geq \delta(\bar{v} - \underline{v})$.

Let $\tilde{v}$ be the highest price that the high-valuation buyer is ready to accept in period 0 (knowing that p_1 is going to be $\underline{v}$). The seller will sell in the first round if p_0 is such that: $p_0 \leq \tilde{v} \equiv (1 - \delta)\bar{v} + \delta\underline{v}$. If $p_0 > \tilde{v}$, the optimal strategy of the high-valuation buyer is to reject the price offer and wait. Applying Bayes' rule gives: $\bar{\mu}(p_0) = \bar{\Pi}$.

Two cases can be distinguished: $\bar{\Pi}\tilde{v} < \underline{v}$ or $\bar{\Pi}\tilde{v} > \underline{v}$.

First case: $\bar{\Pi}\tilde{v} < \underline{v}$

In that case, for any $p_0 > \underline{v}$, the seller must charge $p_1 = \underline{v}$ in the second round, because $\bar{\mu}(p_0)\bar{v} \leq \bar{\Pi}\tilde{v} < \underline{v}$. In the first round, the seller could charge $p_0 = \underline{v}$ or $p_0 = \tilde{v}$. The latter strategy would yield a total payoff equal to $\bar{\Pi}\tilde{v} + \delta\bar{\Pi}\underline{v}$, the former would give $\underline{v}$. Of course, if $\underline{v} > \bar{\Pi}\tilde{v} + \delta\bar{\Pi}\underline{v}$, the seller offers $p_0 = \underline{v}$ and the buyer agrees immediately, whatever its type. The assumption $\bar{\Pi}\tilde{v} < \underline{v}$ rules out $\underline{v} < \bar{\Pi}\tilde{v} + \delta\bar{\Pi}\underline{v}$ (since $\bar{\Pi}\tilde{v} + \delta\bar{\Pi}\underline{v} = \bar{\Pi}\tilde{v} + \delta(\underline{v} - \bar{\Pi}\tilde{v}) < \underline{v}$).

Second case: $\bar{\Pi}\tilde{v} > \underline{v}$

Then, if $p_0 = \underline{v}$, the buyer will buy the good in the first round whatever its type may be. The seller's payoff is $\underline{v}$. If $p_0 \in]\underline{v}, \tilde{v}[$, a type $\underline{v}$ buyer will reject the offer in the first round. A high-valuation buyer would buy in the first period if $p_0 \leq \tilde{v}$, since it does not pay him to wait until the second round. The best choice for the seller is then $p_0 = \tilde{v}$ and $p_1 = \underline{v}$, which yields a total payoff: $\bar{\Pi}\tilde{v} + \delta\bar{\Pi}\underline{v}$. The last possibility is: $\tilde{v} < p_0 < \bar{v}$. Then both players should randomize. Always rejecting p_0 cannot be an equilibrium strategy for the $\bar{v}$-type buyer. The revised probability would then be: $\bar{\mu}(p_0) = \bar{\Pi}$. The seller does not gain any information when the buyer rejects. Since here we are considering $\bar{\Pi}\tilde{v} > \underline{v}$, the seller would charge $p_1 = \bar{v}$ and clearly, the high-valuation buyer would be better off in agreeing immediately.

A probability 1 of a high-valuation player agreeing to such a deal in the first round can not be an equilibrium either (as we already noted above). A mixed strategy is the only equilibrium strategy for the buyer in that case. This strategy is consistent with the seller's beliefs and behaviour only if the revised probability $\bar{\mu}(p_0)$ is such that the seller is indifferent between charging $\underline{v}$ or $\bar{v}$ in the second round, or else: $\bar{\mu}(p_0)\bar{v} = \underline{v}$. Let us call $\beta(p_0)$ the probability that the high-valuation buyer accepts the offer p_0. Bayes' rule yields:

$$\bar{\mu}(p_0) = \frac{\bar{\Pi}[1 - \beta(p_0)]}{\bar{\Pi}[1 - \beta(p_0)] + \underline{\Pi}}$$

We must have:

$$\frac{\bar{\Pi}[1 - \beta(p_0)]}{\bar{\Pi}[1 - \beta(p_0)] + \underline{\Pi}} \bar{v} = \underline{v},$$

which defines a unique value for $\beta(p_0)$:

$$\beta(p_0) = \frac{\bar{v} - \underline{v}/\bar{\Pi}}{\bar{v} - \underline{v}}$$

Since the seller can randomize between $\underline{v}$ and $\bar{v}$ in the second period, it is necessary to know the equilibrium mixed strategy. The high-valuation buyer is indifferent between buying in period or waiting only if:

$$(\bar{v} - p_0) = \delta\gamma(p_0)(\bar{v} - \underline{v})$$

where $\gamma(p_0)$ is the probability that the seller charges $\underline{v}$ in the second round. The probability $\gamma(p_0)$ is also uniquely defined. So when $\bar{\Pi}\bar{v} > \underline{v}$, there is also a unique PBE.

Depending on the values of the parameters this equilibrium takes one of the three following forms:

(a)   The seller chooses $p_0 = \underline{v}$ and the buyer agrees whatever his type
(b)   The seller offers $p_0 = \tilde{v}$, which is accepted only by a high-valuation buyer, then the seller offers $p_1 = \underline{v}$, always accepted
(c)   The seller offers $p_0 = \bar{v}$, accepted with a certain probability by a $\bar{v}$-type buyer, then $p_1 = \bar{v}$ again always accepted by a $\bar{v}$-type buyer in the second round (it is easy to verify that when the parameters make this case more favourable and $p_0 = \bar{v}$, the probability $\gamma(p_0)$ for the seller to charge $p_1 = \underline{v}$ is equal to zero).

In the previous model there is only one PBE and the equilibrium strategies are in conformity with the so-called Coasian dynamics: the seller becoming more pessimistic over time offers decreasing prices in the different rounds. The problem is that many PBE exist in more complex bargaining environment. The multiplicity of equilibria is especially worrying when both the seller and buyer have two potential types (two-sides incomplete information) (see Fudenberg and Tirole, 1983). Incomplete information in

Rubinstein's model of bargaining also leads to a multiplicity of PBE. Various selection criteria can then be used (see section 4.3 of Chapter 4) but, unfortunately, the solutions found so far rest on too specialized assumptions and cannot be considered as fully satisfactory.

5.2 Axiomatic models of bargaining and the Nash program

While the non-cooperative approach seeks the equilibria of games defined in certain 'institutional frameworks', the axiomatic approach tries to develop some general features which might be expected to hold good over a broad range of 'institutional arrangements'.

In two celebrated papers, Nash (1950b, 1953) proposed a series of axioms which the bargaining solution should verify. He then showed that, under well-specified conditions, only one outcome could verify these axioms. This outcome is known today as the 'Nash bargaining solution' (NBS).

This axiomatic approach can be applied to a variety of economic situations. It should be clear that it does not claim to describe real aspects of negotiation processes. Its announced aim is to shed some light over what a desired solution should be, once it verifies the reasonable properties represented by the axioms. Other axiomatic solutions have been suggested: in particular the Raiffa–Kalaï–Smorodinsky solution and the egalitarian solution.

We will see, however, that an especially interesting property of the NBS is that, in certain circumstances, it appears to be the limit solution of a non-cooperative model of the Rubinstein type.

5.2.1 The Nash bargaining solution

Characterization of the bargaining problem

A bargaining problem according to Nash (1950b) is defined from the set of feasible payoffs in terms of utility on one side and the particular payoff that the players can obtain in case of disagreement on the other. Formally, a bargaining problem is thus characterized by a couple (X, d), where $X \subset \mathbb{R}^2$ is the set of feasible payoff pairs (jointly attainable by the two bargaining agents) and d is a point in X representing the 'status quo' if the players disagree (the 'disagreement', 'threat' or 'impasse' point). It is worth noticing that this representation does not use any information on the object or the nature of possible agreements but only on their consequences in terms of *utility*. No essential information is lost by so doing if we suppose that the players are basically interested in the outcome of the bargaining process in terms of utility; accordingly, we suppose 'welfarism' (Sen, 1970).

Figure 5.6   A bargaining problem (X, d)

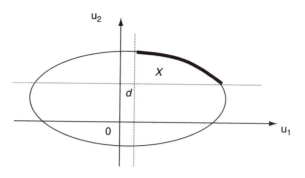

Some classical technical assumptions are made about the feasible sets concerned: X is a convex, compact (closed and upper bounded) and comprehensive sub-set of $\mathbb{R}^2$.

As a consequence of these assumptions, a bargaining problem must look like the diagram in Figure 5.6.

Nash axioms

A bargaining solution is defined as an axiomatic method assigning to each bargaining problem a unique outcome: the payoffs pair on which players will agree.

Definition I

Let B be a set of bargaining problems. A bargaining solution is a function $f: B \to \mathbb{R}^2$ that associates with each bargaining problem $(X, d) \in B$ a particular outcome $(u_1^*, u_2^*) = f(X, d)$.∎

Given this definition, we easily understand that different systems of axioms will lead to different bargaining solutions.

Let us consider the following axioms.

A1 - Individual rationality:

$$f(X, d) \geq d, \text{ for all } (X, d) \in B$$

A2 - Weak Pareto-efficiency:

$$(u_1, u_2) > (u_1^*, u_2^*) = f(X, d) \text{ implies } (u_1, u_2) \notin X$$

A3 - Invariance (with respect to utility scale):

If $(X, d) \in B$ and $(Y, d') \in B$ are such that:

$$(v_1, v_2) = (a_1 u_1 + b_1, a_2 u_2 + b_2)$$

for all $(u_1, u_2) \in X$ and $(v_1, v_2) \in Y$, and for all $a_1, a_2 \in \mathbb{R}_+^2$ and $b \in \mathbb{R}$
then: $(v_1^*, v_2^*) = f(Y, d') = (a_1 u_1^* + b_1, a_2 u_2^* + b_2)$

A4 - Independence of irrelevant alternatives:
   For any convex compact set Y, $Y \subseteq X$:

$$f(Y, d) = f(X, d)$$

A5 - Symmetry.
   If (X, d) is such that:

$$d_1 = d_2$$
$$(u_1, u_2) \in X \text{ implies } (u_2, u_1) \in X$$

   then $(u_1^*, u_2^*) = f(X, d)$ satisfies $u_1^* = u_2^*$

Axiom *A1* says that each player, if she (or he) is rational, will accept a negotiated outcome only if it gives to her (or to him) as much utility as she (or he) would get in case of disagreement. This axiom thus implies that $u_1^* \geq d_1$ and $u_2^* \geq d_2$. Axiom *A2* indicates that the negotiated outcome must be rational from the point of view of the players as a whole. This collective rationality is evaluated through the weak Pareto efficiency. The players will not agree on a couple of payoffs in X if there is another one better for each of them. This two first axioms, defining the sub-set of all individually rational efficient payoffs in the set of feasible payoff pairs, is sometimes called the 'bargaining set' (thick part of the frontier of X in Figure 5.6).

Axiom *A3* says that the agreed payoff should be invariant with respect to utility scale. Any linear transformation of the utility measure of any player (or of both of them) must lead to a corresponding transformation of the outcome in terms of utility, which means an agreement on the same real amount. This property of the Nash bargaining solution implies that the outcome is independent of interpersonal comparison of utilities between the two players. So the axiom can be interpreted as a way of focusing on the pure aspects of bargaining, while leaving clearly aside ethical concerns. Of course, this choice does not mean that the concerns about fairness cannot be associated with interpersonal comparisons of utilities in real experiments of bargaining.

Axiom *A4* is called 'independence of irrelevant alternatives' by Nash. It tells us that the withdrawal of feasible pairs of utilities, which would not be chosen as solutions of the bargaining process, must not change the final outcome. To avoid confusion with Arrow's axiom with the same name in

Figure 5.7 Independence of irrelevant alternatives

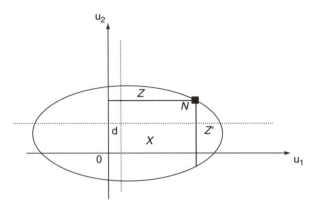

social choice theory (Arrow, 1963), Axiom $A4$ is sometimes called 'contraction consistency'. A simple graph (Figure 5.7) may help to understand this axiom.

If a point such as N is the NBS when the set of feasible utilities is X, then it must also be the solution for the set Y when areas such as Z and Z' have been withdrawn from the feasible set. This axiom leads us to consider as essentially equivalent a large number of bargaining problems; notably, all bargaining problems in which X has a linear frontier are equivalent in this sense.

Axiom $A5$ introduces an element of symmetry. It says that the positions of the two players are perfectly symmetric, in the sense that the solution does not depend on the precise identification of the player called 1 and the player called 2.

Nash products: the regular and the generalized Nash solutions

Nash (1953) showed that the unique bargaining solution which verifies the set of axioms $A_1 - A_5$, also called the 'regular' solution, is such that:

$$(u_1^*, u_2^*) = f(X, d) = \arg \max \ (u_1 - d_1)(u_2 - d_2)$$

The product in this expression is called the 'Nash product'.

It can be shown in fact that the proof of this result requires only axioms A_1, A_3, A_4 and A_5, because axiom A_2 (weak Pareto-efficiency) is an implication of the three first postulates (Roth, 1979).

We should note that the regular NBS is consistent with the more restrictive axiom of Pareto-efficiency:

A_2'-Pareto-efficiency:

If

$$(u_1, u_2) \geq (u_1^*, u_2^*) = f(X, d) \text{ and } (u_1, u_2) \neq (u_1^*, u_2^*), \text{ then } (u_1, u_2) \notin X$$

If we restrict the initial set of axioms by discarding axiom of symmetry A5, a more general result can be proven (Roth, 1979)

Theorem 2 (Nash, Roth)

If the bargaining solution satisfies the set of axioms $A_1 - A_4$, there exists a unique outcome such that:

$$(u_1^*, u_2^*) = f(X, d) = \arg \max (u_1 - d_1)^\alpha (u_2 - d_2)^\beta$$
where $\alpha > 0$, $\beta > 0$ and $\alpha + \beta = 1$

If the bargaining solution also satisfies Axiom A5, then: $\alpha = \beta = \frac{1}{2}$. ∎

The product is now a 'generalized' Nash product. The theorem characterizes the 'generalized' (or 'asymmetric') NBS. The parameters α and β can be viewed as a 'bargaining power' for the players. The larger a player's bargaining power, the more she (or he) will get when we use the generalized NBS. Nash considered only the particular case when two players have equal bargaining powers.

Remark I

Contrary to the regular solution, the generalized Nash solution does not verify the consistency property with Axiom A'2. It can be shown that A_2 (weak Pareto-efficiency), A_3 (invariance) and A_4 (independence) no longer are consistent with A_1 (individual rationality). Yet, by refining the solution by some lexicographic procedure, the Pareto-efficiency property can be restored (see Peters, 1992, 17–25, for instance).■

What this theorem shows is that the solution of a bargaining problem can be found by solving an optimization problem. A graphical representation throws light on the properties of the NBS. Graphically, the NBS corresponds to a point of tangency between the bargaining set and the hyperbola representing $(u_1 - d_1)^\alpha (u_2 - d_2)^\beta = c$ (see Figure 5.8).

Define $(u_1^*, u_2^*) = f(X, d)$ to be the point N in Figure 5.8. In this diagram, N is a boundary point of X and the line through R, N and T is a supporting line to X at N (recall that X is supposed convex). Then, the point N and this supporting line are such that:

$$N = \alpha R + \beta T$$

Figure 5.8 Generalized Nash bargaining solution (NBS)

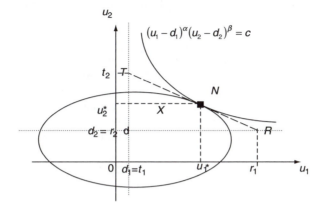

Proof (Binmore, 1992, 189–90) Assuming differentiability, the equation of the tangent line to the curve $g(u_1, u_2) = c$ at the point N is:

$$g'_{u_1}(N)(u_1 - u_1^*) + g'_{u_2}(N)(u_2 - u_2^*) = 0$$

For $g(u_1^*, u_2^*) = (u_1^* - d_1^*)^\alpha (u_2^* - d_2)^\beta$ this equation can be written:

$$\alpha \frac{u_1 - u_1^*}{u_1^* - d_1} + \beta \frac{u_2 - u_2^*}{u_2^* - d_2} = 0$$

Since $d = (d_1, d_2) = (t_1, r_2)$, this equation becomes:

$$\alpha \frac{u_1 - u_1^*}{u_1^* - t_1} + \beta \frac{u_2 - u_2^*}{u_2^* - r_2} = 0$$

The fact that R and T lie on the tangent line implies:

$$\alpha \frac{r_1 - u_1^*}{u_1^* - t_1} - \beta = 0, \quad -\alpha + \beta \frac{t_2 - u_2^*}{u_2^* - r_2} = 0, \text{ respectively}$$

If we solve these two equations for u_1^* and u_2^*, we obtain:

$$u_1^* = \alpha r_1 + \beta t_1, \ u_2^* = \alpha r_2 + \beta t_2$$

that is: $N = \alpha R + \beta T$.∎

Example: the 'split the difference' rule

The NBS can be also characterized by using the 'bargaining set' (i.e. the Pareto-frontier of the set X). This frontier is the graph of a concave function denoted by h since X is convex. At the NBS the graph of the function $(u_1 - d_1)(u_2 - d_2)$ is tangent to the graph of h. From this tangency property comes the following proposition (assuming again that h is differentiable):

> **Proposition 1 (Muthoo, 1999)** The NBS solution is the unique solution to the following pair of equations: $-h'(u_1) = \frac{u_2 - d_2}{u_1 - d_1}$ and: $u_2 = h(u_1)$.∎

Proof From the proposition above one can then infer the so-called 'split the difference' rule which applies in some applications of the bargaining problem when the Pareto-frontier of X is a linear function $h(u_1) = s - u_1$ where $s > 0$; in that case: $-h'(u_1) = 1$.
Hence:

$$u_1^* = u_2^* - d_2 + d_1 \text{ and } u_2^* = s - u_1^*$$

And finally:

$$u_1^* = d_1 + \frac{1}{2}(s - d_1 - d_2) \text{ and } u_2^* = d_2 + \frac{1}{2}(s - d_1 - d_2)∎$$

The outcome of such a bargaining is equivalent to an agreement on giving to each player her (or his) status quo utility level augmented by an equal split of the remaining utility $(s - d_1 - d_2)$. The same reasoning applied to the generalized NBS gives:

$$-h'(u_1) = \frac{\alpha(u_2 - d_2)}{\beta(u_1 - d_1)} \text{ and } u_2 = h(u_1)$$

where α and β are the bargaining powers in the generalized NBS.

Variable threat games

We now consider a situation in which binding agreements are possible but in which each player has great scope for decision if non-agreement arises, and such that the decision of each player affects both of them. This class of games also was studied by Nash (1953), who proved a justification for a revised version of his bargaining solution. The originality of this approach is in combining arbitration with a non-cooperative game.

Each player is supposed to have a strategy set X_i (compact and convex) and $d_i(x_1, x_2)$ is the payoff function for player i in the absence of an agreement. Thus the game (X_1, X_2, d_1, d_2) is a 'default' non-cooperative game that players must play if they cannot agree. Suppose also that there exists a set $X \subset \mathbb{R}^2$ consisting of all the payoffs that the players can reach by means of binding agreement (of course X includes all those payoffs attainable in the default game).

Definition 3 (*Variable threat two-person cooperative game*)

The game $(X_1, X_2, d_1, d_2; X)$ is a variable threat two-person cooperative game where (X_1, X_2, d_1, d_2) is a two-person non-cooperative
game that is played if non-agreement is reached and X is the cooperative attainable payoff set (compact and convex). We have
$\{d(x) \in \mathbb{R}^2 : x_1 \in X_1, x_2 \in X_2\}$. ∎

The Nash arbitration game consists in having the players simultaneously choose strategies for the default game, $x_i^T \in X_i$, which are used to
determine a threat point $d(x^T)$. The arbitrated outcome to the game is
the NBS to $(X, d(x^T))$. In this setting the players are not interested in the
payoffs $d_i(x^T)$ for their own sakes, but they care about the effect on the
final outcome that is due to their choices of x_i^T. Any point on the Pareto-
frontier of X could be an arbitrated outcome. With the help of a graphic
showing the relationship between points on the Pareto-frontier and the
points in X which could serve as threat points, and observing further that
the non-cooperative game whose outcome is the cooperative solution is
strictly competitive, one can prove the following result (see, for instance,
Friedman, 1989, 178–9 or Owen, 1995, 198–200).

Theorem 3 (*Nash, 1953*)

Let $(X_1, X_2, d_1, d_2; X)$ a two-person variable threat game. If u^* is the
NBS to the game and d^T is the optimal threat strategy vector, then:

$$\frac{u_2^* - d_2(x_1^T, x_2)}{u_1^* - d_1(x_1^T, x_2)} \geq \frac{u_2^* - d_2(x^T)}{u_1^* - d_1(x^T)} \geq \frac{u_2^* - d_2(x_1, x_2^T)}{u_1^* - d_1(x_1, x_2^T)}$$

Furthermore, all cooperative Nash variable threat solutions yield the
same payoffs. ∎

Note that the existence of a Nash cooperative solution is not guaranteed,
except if the strictly competitive game whose payoff function is $d^*(x)$
satisfies the usual concavity conditions.

Nash solution and risk aversion: more on 'dividing the dollar'

Let us consider one more time the problem of sharing a fixed amount of
money (which can be in fact any kind of surplus, cake, you name it...)
between two players, 1 dollar will again be the amount to be divided.
The physical set at stake is any couple of cents x_1 and x_2 such that:
$x_1 + x_2 \leq 1$. The frontier of such pairs in the space of x_i is: $x_1 + x_2 = 1$.
Remember, however, that in a bargaining problem we are interested in
the effects of the sharing in terms of *utilities*, the players having VN-M
utility functions.

We know that the solution depends on the bargaining powers of the players, given exogenously. But another aspect of the NBS can be stressed through this example: the solution also depends on the relative degree of *risk aversion* of the two players. This point is true even if there is no particular element of risk involved in the negotiation.

In order to verify this point let us assume that the bargaining powers of the two players are equal:

$$\alpha = \beta = \frac{1}{2}$$

and consider the following *VN-M* utility functions:

$$u_1(x_1) = x_1 \quad \text{and} \quad u_2(x_2) = x_2^{1/4}$$

These functions are chosen so that player 1 is risk-neutral and player 2 is risk-averse (concave *VN-M* utility function).
The NBS (u_1^*, u_2^*) is such that:

$$\begin{cases} \max (x_1)^{1/2}(x_2^{1/4})^{1/2} \\ x_1 + x_2 = 1 \end{cases}$$

Solving this problem gives:

$$x_1^* = \frac{4}{5} \text{ and } x_2^* = \frac{1}{5}$$

So, even if the players have equal bargaining powers ($\alpha = \beta = \frac{1}{2}$), the division of the dollar is unequal. The risk-averse player gets a lower share than the risk-neutral agent.

This property of the NBS reflects the attitude of the players facing the risk of collapse of the negotiation. Fear of disagreement puts the risk-averse agent in a relative weak position with respect to the other. Since in this kind of game the information is complete, this fear cannot be concealed from the risk-neutral player, who can then take advantage of the situation.

Remark 2

Nash (1950b) was the first to use the axiomatic method in deriving a solution of a game with applications in economics. Although the publication date of the famous Arrow 'impossibility theorem' in social choice theory (Arrow, 1963, 1st edn 1951) suggests that these two works were carried out essentially simultaneously, neither Arrow nor Nash mentions the other's study. Thanks to the axiomatic method the great insight of Arrow and Nash was to change the focus of the social choice problem or the bargaining problem: from a single society to the 'social welfare functional' that would give an answer for *all* societies on the one hand, from a single bargaining problem to the 'solution' that would lead to an answer for *all* problems on the other. Today the axiomatic method has considerably expanded its scope: general equilibrium theory, social choice theory, welfare economics and theories of justice, decision theory and cooperative game theory are some of the main topics where this tool is commonly used for elaborating elegant formal constructions encompassing a host of axioms into unified frameworks.

Axiomatic bargaining theory entertains relationships with several of these different topics, notably social choice theory and welfare economics.

A social welfare functional F (or a social choice rule in Arrow's word) is defined on a quite abstract space of utility vectors. Let U denote the set of *all* utility vectors $u = (u_1, \ldots, u_n)$ on a finite set of alternative social states X. Then F is a mapping from a sub-set $V \subseteq U$ into the set of all orderings over X. In contrast, in welfare economics, a Bergson–Samuelson social welfare function W is defined on a more concrete Euclidian space. W associates with any vector of utility number $(u_1, \ldots, u_n) \in \mathbb{R}^n$ a real number. 'Utilitarianism' (maximizing the sum of individual utilities) and 'egalitarianism' (seeking to equalize individual utilities by lexicographically maximizing the weakest level of individual utilities) represents two among the most popular social welfare functionals when interpersonal comparisons of utilities are allowed (see, for instance, Moulin 1988 and Mongin and d'Aspremont, 1998).

A bargaining solution f is a more complex collective choice rule than a social welfare function W, but less general than a social welfare functional F, since f is a mapping from the set of all objects (S, d) into $S \subset \mathbb{R}^2$ (i.e. points in S).

In bargaining theory, the goal is to take into account the whole feasible set of utility vectors to select the best one. Hence, we cannot compare two utility vectors independently of the context (namely, the actual set of feasible utility vectors), as is the case with a social welfare function. Furthermore, a bargaining solution includes one additional 'primitive' – the disagreement point – that we can interpret as a Pareto-inferior utility vector.

On the other hand, a bargaining solution is less general than a social welfare functional. In the social choice framework, the 'primitives' are *individual utilities* and *social states*; and under certain assumptions it can be proved that analysis can be restricted to utility possibilities only. In contrast, in the bargaining problem framework the 'primitives' are directly the set of utility possibilities X. No consideration about the actual utilities of players and the objects being distributed are included in the analysis.

Finally, beyond differences about their domains of definition, F and f differ in one important way: while a social welfare functional induces an *ordering* of allocations, a bargaining solution always chooses just *the best*.

Yet there exists a common property of these notions of social welfare functional, bargaining solution and social welfare function: they are all 'welfarist'. They systematically ignore any aspect of the problems that is not conveyed by the utilities. Some theories of justice elaborated in Rawls' wake (Rawls, 1971) have been freed from this somewhat restrictive framework (see for surveys on 'post welfarist' approaches, Fleurbaey, 1995; Kolm, 1996; Roemer, 1996).■

Remark 3

A great number of alternative axiomatic characterizations of the NBS have been given in the literature on axiomatic bargaining games (see, in particular, Peters, 1992; Thomson, 1994 or Young, 1994, for surveys). Yet, an interesting result was proved by Roberts (1980) in the social choice framework: the 'Nash product' can emerge as a *social welfare functional*. In a sense this result may be viewed as more complete than Nash theorem: whereas Nash simply *assumes* welfarism, Roberts proves that welfarism can be *deduced* from primitive postulates.■

Remark 4

Originally, Nash axioms were intended to have only 'positive' content: the goal was to predict the resulting outcome on which rational bargaining agents are supposed to agree when binding agreements are allowed. The axiomatic bargaining models are often called 'normative' approaches in contrast to strategic bargaining games which should reflect a more 'positive' approach. Indeed, as Roemer underlines, 'there is an ambiguity in the word "normative" as it is used by economists: it can mean either "should" in the sense of *ethically* mandated or "should" in the sense of what *pure rationality* requires' (Roemer, 1986, 52). According to the traditional view, axiomatic bargaining models can be called 'normative' only in the second sense.

Yet, in recent years some game theorists have followed the idea suggested by Luce and Raiffa (1957) to confer an *explicitly ethical content* upon the axioms; so that there now exists another interpretation of axiomatic bargaining games as a 'normative' approach in the first sense. Here, axioms must reflect some specific idea of fairness or equity and axiomatic bargaining games can be viewed as particular theories of distributive justice.■

If we maintain the traditional viewpoint, the test of axioms in bargaining games can follow two ways: either we discuss the axioms directly by estimating their accuracy as characterization of bargaining, or we follow the 'Nash program'. Before exploring this last approach, we present some other axiomatic solutions for the bargaining problem.

5.2.2   Other axiomatic bargaining solutions

The Raiffa–Kalai–Smorodinsky solution

Among the set of axioms put forward by Nash, axiom *A4* (Independence of irrelevant alternatives) is certainly the most disputed. Reference to introspection or to experimentation conveys the idea that an enlargement of the opportunities given to the players leads to a revision of the hierarchy of preferences concerning the previous feasible utility set. This line of criticism has given birth to other attempts to formulate axiomatic solutions in the spirit of NBS, but with a realistic change of axiom A4.

In particular Kalai and Smorodinsky (1975), following a suggestion made by Raiffa, have proposed a solution resting on a weak version of axiom A4 that they called 'individual monotony'. This axiom requires that if the set of feasible utility is extended for the benefit of a particular player, the bargaining solution has also to increase the utility of this player. The basic idea maintained by the Raiffa–Kalai–Smorodinsky (RKS) solution is that each player would like to get the most she (or he) can possibly hope for when the other player is rational (that is when she (or he) never agreed on a payoff under her 'threat point' level). Yet, the resulting outcome is not feasible; it is called the 'ideal point'. The solution consists of selecting a feasible payoff pair such that the utility gain of each player beyond the threat point is proportional to her (or his) maximal utility level in the 'ideal' (or the 'utopian') point.

Formally, the ideal point $a(X, d)$ is such that:

$$a_i(X, d) = \max \{u_i : u \in X, u \geq d\}$$

and we can write the new axiom as follows:
A'_4 Individual monotony:
Let (X, d) and (Y, d) be two bargaining problems in B with $X \subset Y$. If $a_1(X, d) = a_1(Y, d)$, then $u_2^* \geq v_2^*$, where $(u_1^*, u_2^*) = f(X, d)$ and $(v_1^*, v_2^*) = f(Y, d)$. Similarly, if $a_2(X, d) = a_2(Y, d)$, then $u_1^* \geq v_1^*$.

Then, graphically the RKS solution for the bargaining problem (X, d) is the point on the bargaining set that lies at its intersection with the line joining the threat point d and the ideal point $a(X, d)$ (see the diagram in Figure 5.9 in which the regular NBS also is indicated).

Figure 5.9 The Raiffa–Kalai–Smorodinsky solution

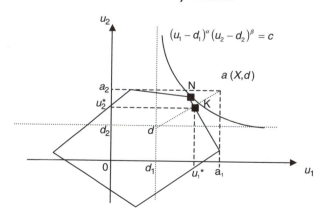

It can be seen easily in Figure 5.9 that the following conditions are verified:

$$\frac{u_2^* - d_2}{u_1^* - d_1} = \frac{u_2 - d_2}{u_1 - d_1} = \frac{a_2 - d_2}{a_1 - d_1}$$

The utility gain of each player beyond the threat point is proportional to her (or his) maximal utility in the ideal point, the factor of proportionality is the same for the two players and its value is maximal, with the constraint that the payoff pairs belongs to the bargaining set. Denote $(u_1^*, u_2^*) = f^{KS}(X, d)$ the outcome that satisfies this condition.

Theorem 4 (Kalai–Smorodinsky)

Let $f(X, d)$ satisfy A_2 (Pareto-efficiency), A_3 (Invariance), A_5 (Symmetry) and A_4^1 (Individual monotony). Then: $f = f^{KS}(X, d)$. ∎

The egalitarian solution

This bargaining solution can be regarded as representing compromises between the independence axiom (verified by the NBS) and the monotony axiom (verified by the RKS solution). It is based on a stronger property than individual monotony, according to which no player should lose when the utility set is enlarging:

A_4^n Strong monotony:
  For any bargaining problem (X, d) and (Y, d) in B with $X \subset Y$: $f(Y, d) \geq f(X, d)$.
  In general, strong monotony is inconsistent with Pareto-efficiency. The RKS solution requires Pareto-efficiency and assumes the weaker individual monotony condition. This new bargaining solution requires only weak Pareto-efficiency. Yet, as for the generalized NBS, thanks to refinement of these solutions by some lexicographic procedure, the Pareto-efficiency property can be restored (see for instance Peters, 1992, 84–87). Furthermore, this solution has two notable differences with respect to the previous bargaining solutions: it does not involve axiom A_3 (invariance), but it respects utility information which is fully comparable among players.
  The egalitarian solution was initially proposed by Kalai (1977) as a particular case of a more general class of 'proportional' solutions. The idea is to equalize the gains of each player with respect to the disagreement point.
  A bargaining solution $(u_1^*, u_2^*) = f(X, d)$ is egalitarian if it picks up a point on the bargaining set such that:

$$u_1^* - d_1 = u_2^* - d_2$$

Several characterizations of the egalitarian solution exist. In particular, the following result can be proved.

Theorem 5 (*Kalai*)

For any bargaining problem (X, d) with $d = 0$, the unique solution that verifies A_2 (Weak Pareto-efficiency), A_5 (Symmetry) and A_4'' (Strong monotony) is the egalitarian solution.∎

Remark I

As the NBS, the RKS solution and the egalitarian solution can be interpreted as a criterion of distributive justice. Barry (1989) distinguishes two classical views of justice in political philosophy: 'justice as mutual advantage' and 'justice as impartiality'. According to the first tradition (Hobbes, Hume), 'justice is simply rational prudence pursued in contexts where the cooperation of other people is a condition of our being able to get what we want' (Barry, 1989, 6). By contrast, according to the second tradition (Aristotle, Kant, Rousseau, Locke), 'a just state of affairs is one that people can accept not merely in the sense that they cannot reasonably expect to get more, but in the stronger sense that they cannot reasonably *claim* more' (Barry, 1989, 8). If we try to articulate what the first 'reasonably' means, we need a theory of *bargaining*, and the second 'reasonably' requires a theory of *fairness*.

The prime contemporary example of the second view is Rawls' theory. (Rawls, 1971). We have already seen (Remark 4 of sub-section 5.2.1) that the NBS may be ethically defended as a justice criterion. Indeed it was the *single* bargaining solution with which the two above views of justice may be conciliated. The Nash program can be interpreted in this way. On the other hand, the RKS solution can be viewed as the realization of distributive justice, but from the sole viewpoint of justice as mutual advantage (see Gauthier, 1986) and the egalitarian solution can be interpreted as a just distributive principle from the sole viewpoint of justice as impartiality (Thomson and Lensberg, 1989; Roemer, 1996).∎

5.2.3 *The Nash program: the relationships between the strategic and the axiomatic approaches*

We have already noted the differences between non-cooperative GT and cooperative GT. Axiomatic theories of bargaining look much like models with a cooperative flavour. However, Nash himself did not consider the two approaches as rivals. He even envisaged that the complementary feature of the two lines of research could be used to verify the plausibility of the axiomatic solutions. What has come to be known as the 'Nash program' can be described as follows: starting from an axiomatic solution having plausible properties, is it possible to design a particular bargaining process that would naturally lead 'rational' negotiators to the outcome prescribed by the axiomatic solution?

The idea is to model the various plays open to the players when they are negotiating as strategies within a bargaining game whose rules are explicitly specified in detail. If the equilibrium outcomes of a sufficiently wide class of such bargaining games turn out to satisfy the Nash axioms, then the Nash bargaining theory will be vindicated; otherwise it has to be abandoned.

Fortunately the non-cooperative approach leads to the Nash bargaining outcome in many interesting situations. This results can especially be obtained in the Rubinstein framework. There are different ways to verify this important result. We reproduce a few of them here (for a presentation of several other non cooperative bargaining games in which equilibrium corresponds to the NBS, see Binmore, Rubinstein and Wolinski, 1986); Binmore and Dasgupta, 1987; Rubinstein, Safra and Thomson, 1992).

Nash demand game

Historically, this is the first model used by Nash himself to implement the so-called Nash program (Nash, 1953). It would be too long to develop the whole model here, but the intuition of the result is along the following lines.

Consider a non-cooperative bargaining game in which two players simultaneously announce demands x and y. If the sum is lower than or equal to 1, they receive their demanded amounts, if not, they get zero.

As we already noticed in sub-section 5.1.1, such a game has a lot of NE. In fact any pair such that $x + y = 1$ is a NE. Nash suggested a 'smoothing' device permitting the limitation of the number of equilibria. He introduces a function $h(x + y)$ which takes the value 1 on the set $\{(x, y): x + y \leq 1\}$ and falls rapidly to zero outside this set.

The possible outcome is modified in the following way. When players demand x and y, player 1 gets x with probability $h(x + y)$ and gets an amount s_1 otherwise. Similarly, agent 2 receives y with probability $h(x + y)$ and s_2 otherwise.

By considering a suitably defined family of functions $h(.)$ which fall off more and more rapidly to zero outside the set $\{(x, y): x + y \leq 1\}$, it can be shown that any NE of this game will at the limit coincide with the NBS (see Binmore, 1984, for details).

The intuition underlying this result can be seen as follows: given any demand by agent 2, player 1 will raise her demand to the point where the marginal utility she obtains from an increment to her share is just offset by the rise in the probability $(1 - h)$ of failure to agree.

Player i's payoff is:

$$hu_i(x) + (1 - h)u_i(s_i)$$

Optimization of the payoff yields:

$$\frac{dh}{dx}[u_i(x) - u_i(s_i)] + hu_i' = 0$$

This equation implies:

$$x^* = \arg \max [u_1(x) - u_1(s_1)][u_2(1 - x) - u_2(s_2)]$$

that is the NBS.

Sequential bargaining converging to the Nash bargaining solution (impatience)

In sub-section 5.1.2 we noticed that when the time delay between two periods $\Delta \to 0$ in the limit, the Rubinstein bargaining solution is:

$$x_1 = \frac{r_2}{r_1 + r_2}, \; x_2 = \frac{r_1}{r_1 + r_2}$$

where r_i is the instantaneous discount rate of player i. This is also the NBS of a bargaining over one monetary unit when $h(u_1) = 1 - u_1$, when the status quo is $d = (0, 0)$ and when the bargaining powers are, respectively:

$$\alpha = \frac{r_2}{r_1 + r_2}, \text{ and } \beta = \frac{r_1}{r_1 + r_2}$$

There is a straightforward interpretation of this result. The strong first-mover advantage that we noticed in the Rubinstein model seems to make the result very different from the NBS which verifies an axiom of symmetry. Even the generalized NBS may involve too much symmetry to fit the Rubinstein framework. But when the time delay between two periods goes to 0 in the limit, the non-cooperative bargaining does not present any longer the strong first-mover advantage, and in case of asymmetry between the players, their bargaining power is clearly linked to the discount factors.

Finally, in sub-section 5.1.3, we also noticed that a Rubinstein model with outside options yields the 'split the difference' rule, as does the NBS, when there is a serious risk of breakdown of the negotiation (imposed from outside, for example).

The links between the Rubinstein non-cooperative model and the NBS also help to understand the role of the status quo in Nash bargaining theory. Suppose that two agents with linear utilities bargain over one dollar. Imagine that in case of disagreement player 1 gets a sum x_0, his outside option, while in the same circumstances, player 2 would receive nothing. Applying directly the NBS gives an equal share of the surplus, that is:

$$u_1^* = x_0 + \frac{1}{2}(1 - x_0) \quad u_2^* = \frac{1}{2}(1 - x_0)$$

Now, when one uses the Rubinstein model and looks for the SPE of the game, taking into account the outside option of player 1, it appears that the NBS is valid only if $x_0 > \frac{1}{2}$. If the threat by player 1 to exercise her option is empty, or if $x_0 < \frac{1}{2}$, one gets the solution:

$$u_1 = u_2 = \frac{1}{2}$$

This simple example may not seem very informative, but in various other cases of utilization of the NBS the role played by the status quo may sometimes be rather dubious.

Remark 2

According to Harsanyi (1977,149–53), the idea of a bargaining process in which players make alternating offers goes back to Zeuthen (1930). Harsanyi shows that the equilibrium of Zeuthen's process is the NBS. But the weakness of this proof of the NBS is the ad hoc feature of the concession rule used by Zeuthen.■

5.3 Applications

5.3.1 Bilateral monopoly

A typical real-life example of bargaining is the negotiation of a price between a unique seller and a unique buyer. In such a bilateral monopoly situation both agents are conscious of their power on the market price and wish to exercise it. The only obstacle is the other participant's power.

Let us consider a numerical example of a producer A selling to a unique buyer B which in turn sells the product, slightly transformed to a lot of final buyers (the consumers). Firm A can be conceived as the producer and firm B as the distributor of the product. We know from the study of vertical relations in modern industrial organization theory that various problems linked to vertical structure may hamper firms in their quest for the maximization of joint profit (see for instance Tirole, 1988, Chapter 4, 169). But there do exist ways for the two firms to maximize the joint profit, that is to obtain the same amount of profit as that which could be obtained by a single integrated company (the devices to do so are extensively described in Tirole).

Now imagine that our firms A and B use one of these devices to actually get this maximum joint profit. Then we can consider the problem of allocating it between the two players. The problem is then analogous to sharing a cake of given size or sharing a dollar.

The profit functions are respectively for firm A and for firm B:

$$\Pi^A = (w - C_A)x$$
$$\Pi^B = (p - w - C_B)x$$

where C_A is the marginal (constant) cost of production of firm A; C_B is the marginal (constant) cost of distribution; and w is the price asked by A when it sells the good to the resaler. Market demand is represented by the demand function: $x = 24 - p$. Joint profit maximization is done over:

$$\Pi^T = \Pi^A + \Pi^B = (p - C_A - C_B)(24 - p)$$

We assume for simplicity that the average costs are constant (and thus equal to marginal costs): $C_A = 3$ and $C_B = 1$. The integrated structure maximizes joint profits when:

$$d\Pi/dp = 0 = -2p + 28$$

So $p = 14$ and $x = 10$. Now bargaining is over total profit $\Pi^T = 100$, through the choice of w. We will assume that the firms have the same bargaining powers: $\alpha = \beta = 1/2$. Graphically the problem is to find the optimal point on the line MN in Figure 5.10.

Point M corresponds to the situation where all the (maximum) joint profit goes to firm B. The reader can check that this is done by fixing

Figure 5.10   NBS of the bilateral monopoly

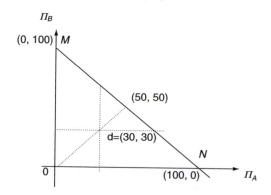

$w = 3$. On the other hand fixing $w = 13$ would allocate the whole profit to firm A and give point N in Figure 5.10.

Suppose that the firms have no other option available but to trade between themselves. In other word the status quo point is the origin 0 in Figure 5.10, where both profits are zero. Then, applying the NBS gives: $\Pi^A = \Pi^B = 50$. The solution in that case is to split equally the total profit.

Now if the firms have outside options, the threat point is no longer the origin. For instance, if firm A can find a seller at $w = 6$ in any case and if firm B can assure on its own a profit of 30 by buying the product at the price $w = 10$, then the threat point is point d in Figure 5.10. The optimal solution is then: $\Pi^A = \frac{1}{2}\, 70 + \frac{1}{2}\, 30 = 50$ and $\Pi^B = \frac{1}{2}\, 70 + 1/2\, 30 = 50$. Again this solution splits equally the difference between the total profit and what can be got by the firms on their own. Each firm here can assure a profit of 30. The difference is then $100 - (30 + 30) = 40$. Splitting it gives 20 for each on top of their assured 30, that is 50 in the end.

In this respect, Nash bargaining illustrates an intuitive property of outside options. In the previous example the outside options maintain the equal outcome. But what if they look more advantageous for one firm, say for firm A, if it can obtain on its own $w = 9$ when firm B has only an outside price of $w = 11$ available ? The reader can verify that the outcome switches then to $\Pi^A = 70$ and $\Pi^B = 30$. Of course any change in the exogenous bargaining talents α and β would also change the outcome in the expected direction.

5.3.2   Firm–union bargaining over wage and employment

Consider bargaining over wage and employment in a firm where for specific reasons wages can be set up above a competitive level w_0 that any worker could get outside the firm, in the absence of any union (for a general presentation and more details on such models see, for instance, McDonald and Solow, 1987, Malcomson, 1987). Now if w is the wage rate in the firm and n is the number of people employed, one can represent the firm's profit function by $\Pi(w, n)$ and the union utility function by $U(w, n)$, if we assume that the union cares both about wages and employment.

An agreement (w^*, n^*) must verify the three following constraints:

$$w^* \geq w_0$$
$$\Pi(w, n) = R(n) - wn \geq 0$$
$$n \leq L$$

where $R(n)$ is the firm's revenue when it employs n workers and L is the union's size. If the players fail to reach an agreement, the firm leaves the business and all the union members (L) can obtain a wage (or un-employment benefit) w_0 elsewhere. We assume here that the union utility function is linear and corresponds to the total income received by its members:

$$U(w, n) = w.n + (L - n)w_0$$

The status quo point when the players fail to reach an agreement corres-ponds to $\Pi = 0$ (since $R(0) = 0$) for the firm and $u^0 = w_0L$ for the union: $d = (w_0L, 0)$.

In this example, the Pareto-frontier of the set of attainable utilities can be derived from the maximization problem:

$$\begin{cases} \max_{(w, n)} \Pi(w, n) \\ s.t. u(w, n) \geq w_0L \end{cases}$$

The solution to this problem is unique and yields an optimal employ-ment level n^* such that $R'(n^*) = w_0$. The Pareto-frontier is thus the graph of the function:

$$h(u) = s - u(.)$$

where:

$$s = R(n^*) + (L - n^*)w_0$$

We can apply here the 'split the difference' rule and verify that the NBS is:

$$\Pi^*(w, n) = \frac{1}{2}(s - w_0L)$$

and:

$$u^*(w, n) = w_0L + \frac{1}{2}(s - w_0L) = \frac{1}{2}(s + w_0L)$$

The NBS gives a level of employment $n = n^*$ and the wage w^* is obtained from:

$$\Pi^* = R(n^*) - w^*n^*$$

so:

$$w^* = \frac{1}{2}\left(w_0 + \frac{R(n^*)}{n^*}\right)$$

The wage rate is equal to the average of the competitive wage w_0 (equal to the marginal revenue of the firm) and the average revenue.

Bibliography

Arrow, K. (1963) *Social Choice and Individual Values*, 2nd edn (New York: Wiley (1st ed; 1951).

Barry, B. (1989) *Theories of Justice*, 1 (Berkeley: University of California Press).

Binmore, K. (1987), 'Perfect equilibria in bargaining models', in K. Binmore and P. Dasgupta (eds), *The Economics of Bargaining* (Oxford: Blackwell) 77–105.

Binmore, K. (1992) *Fun and Games* (Lexington, MA: D.C. Heath), Chapter 5.

Binmore, K.G. and P. Dasgupta (eds) (1987) *The Economics of Bargaining* (Oxford: Blackwell).

Binmore, K, M.J. Osborne and A.Rubinstein (1992) 'Non cooperative models of bargaining', in R.J. Aumann and S. Hart (eds), *Handbook of Game Theory with Economic Applications*, 1 (Amsterdam: North-Holland), Chapter 7.

Binmore, K., A. Rubinstein and A.Wolinsky (1986) 'The Nash bargaining solution in economic modelling', *Rand Journal of Economics*, 17, 176–88.

Buchanan, J. and G. Tullock (1962) *The Calculus of Consent* (Ann Arbor: University of Michigan Press).

Fishburn, P.C. and A. Rubinstein (1982) 'Time Preference', *International Economic Review*, 23, 677–94.

Fleurbaey, M. (1995) 'Three solutions for the compensation problem', *Journal of Economic Theory*, 65, 505–21.

Friedman, J. (1989) *Game Theory with Applications to Economics* (Oxford: Oxford University Press), Chapter 5.

Fudenberg, D. and J.Tirole (1983) 'Sequential bargaining with incomplete information', *Review of Economic Studies*, 50, 221–47.

Gauthier, D. (1986) *Moral by Agreements* (Oxford: Oxford University Press).

Harsanyi, J. (1977) *Rational Behavior and Bargaining Equilibrium in Games and Social Situations* (Cambridge: Cambridge University Press).

Hart, S. and A. Mas-Colell (1992) 'A model of n-person non-cooperative bargaining', *Economic Theory Discussion Paper*, 7, Harvard Institute of Economic Research.

Kalai, E. (1977) 'The bargaining game', *Econometrica*, 18, 155–62.

Kalai, E. and M. Smorodinsky (1975) 'Other solutions to Nash's bargaining problem', *Econometrica*, 43, 513–18.

Kolm, S.C. (1996) *Modern Theories of Justice* (Cambridge, MA: MIT Press).

Kreps, D. (1990) *A Course in Microeconomic Theory* (London: Harvester Wheatsheaf, Chapter 15.

Luce, R.D. and H. Raiffa (1957) *Games and Decisions* (New York: John Wiley).

Malcomson, P. (1987) 'Trade union labour contracts', *European Economic Review*, 31.

McDonald I.M. and R.M. Solow (1987) 'Wage bargaining and employment', *American Economic Review*, 75.

Mongin, P. and C. d'Aspremont (1998) 'Utility theory and ethics', in S. Barbera, P.J. Hammond and C. Seidle (eds), *Handbook of Utility theory*, 1: *Principles* (Boston: Kluwer Academic Publishers).

Moulin, H. (1988) *Axioms of Cooperative Decision Making* (Cambridge: Cambridge University Press).

Muthoo, A. (1999) *Bargaining Theory with Applications* (Cambridge: Cambridge University Press).

Nash, J.F. (Jr) (1950a) 'Equilibrium points in *n*-person games', *Proceedings of the National Academy of Sciences*, 36, 48–9.

Nash, J.F. (Jr.) (1950b) 'The bargaining game', *Econometrica*, 18, 155–62.

Nash, J.F. (Jr.) (1951) 'Non-cooperative games', *Annals of Mathematics*, 57, 289–93.

Nash, J.F. (Jr.) (1953) 'Two-person cooperative games', *Econometrica*, 21, 128–40.

Osborne, M.J. and A. Rubinstein (1990) *Bargaining and Markets* (San Diego: Academic Press).

Osborne, M.J. and A. Rubinstein (1994) *A Course in Game Theory* (Cambridge, MA: MIT Press), Chapters 7, 15.

Owen, G. (1995) *Game Theory*, 3rd edn (San Diego: Academic Press), Chapter 9.

Peters, H.J.M. (1992) *Axiomatic Bargaining Game Theory* (Boston: Kluwer Academic Publishers).

Rawls, J. (1971) *A Theory of Justice* (Cambridge, MA: Harvard University Press).

Roberts, K. (1980) 'Interpersonal comparability and social choice theory', *Review of Economic Studies*, 47, 409–20.

Roemer, J.E. (1996) *Theories of Distributive Justice* (Cambridge, MA: Harvard University Press).

Roth, A. (1979) *Axiomatic Models of Bargaining* (Berlin: Springer-Verlag).

Roth, A. (ed.) (1988) *The Shapley Value; Essays in Honour of Lloyd Shapley* (Cambridge: Cambridge University Press).

Rubinstein, A. (1982) 'Perfect equilibrium in a bargaining model', *Econometrica*, 50, 97–109.

Rubinstein, A., Z. Safra and W. Thomson (1992) 'On the interpretation of the Nash bargaining solution', *Econometrica*, 60, 1171–86.

Sen, A. (1970) *Collective Choice and Social Welfare* (London: Oliver & Boyd).

Shaked, A. and J. Sutton (1984) 'Involuntary unemployment as a perfect equilibrium in a bargaining model', *Econometrica*, 52 1351–64.

Sobel, J. and I. Takahashi (1983) 'A multi-stage model of bargaining', *Review of Economic Studies*, 50, 411–26.

Sutton, J. (1986) 'Non-cooperative bargaining theory: an introduction', *Review of Economic Studies*, 53, 709–24.

Thomson, W. (1994) 'Cooperative models of bargaining', in R.J. Aumann and S. Hart (eds), *Handbook of Game Theory with Economic Applications*, 2 (Amsterdam: North-Holland), Chapters 35.

Thomson, W. and T. Lensberg (1989) *Axiomatic Theory of Bargaining with a Variable Number of Agents* (Cambridge: Cambridge University Press).

Tirole, J. (1988) *The Theory of Industrial Organization* (Cambridge, MA: MIT Press).

Young, H.P. (1994) *Equity in Theory and Practice*, (Princeton: Princeton University Press).

Zeuthen, F. (1930) *Problems of Monopoly and Economic Welfare* (London: Routledge).

6 Coalitions: Cooperative and Non-Cooperative Games

6.1 Introduction to coalition games

6.2 The domination approach: the core and related solution concepts

6.3 The valuation approach: the Shapley value and extensions

6.4 Endogenous coalition structures and formation of coalitions

6.5 Applications

The study of coalitions in GT is one of the knottiest problems. Three factors at least have played a great part in this fuzziness. First, classical coalitional games deal simultaneously with several questions: the process of coalition formation, the stability of coalitions facing the entry or the exit of players, and the sharing of surplus from cooperation between players into each coalition via the disbursement of payoffs. Secondly, though the classical framework for studying coalitions is provided by cooperative games, this dominant view has been challenged by the use of a non-cooperative framework for the same purpose by some game theorists. Thirdly, the dual positive/normative (in the sense of ethically justifiable) potential interpretation of solution concepts in cooperative games has been obscured for a long time by many exclusively formal works with little thought given to this question of methodology. In section 6.1 we attempt to unravel the skein somewhat. Then, the two main approaches commonly followed in the setting of cooperative games are presented: the domination approach, with the core and related solution concepts (the stable sets, the bargaining set, the kernel, the nucleolus) in section 6.2, and the valuation approach, with the Shapley Value and its extensions, in section 6.3. Section 6.4 deals with a more recent topic: the analysis of coalition formation and endogenous coalition structures in a mixed framework of both cooperative and non-cooperative games. Finally, economic applications of coalitional games are studied in section 6.5. They illustrate the interest of both classical solution concepts (notably, the Shapley Value) and recent models on endogenous coalitions formation.

6.1   Introduction to coalition games

6.1.1   General properties of cooperative games

The limits of pure bargaining games

In Chapter 5, we analysed axiomatic bargaining and cooperation in two-player games only. It seems at first sight easy to generalize the bargaining problem, and notably the NBS, to games with more than two players. But this approach of *pure bargaining* is not widely used because it ignores the possibility of cooperation among some players in coalitions (see, however, Harsanyi, 1977, Chapters 10–13). Indeed analysing a game in coalitional form is going beyond the simple model of a n-person bargaining problem.

Let $N = \{1, \ldots, n\}$ be the set of players and let X be the set of feasible payoffs that players can get if they all work together. Let $(d_1, \ldots, d_n)$ be the disagreement payoff allocation that players would expect if they did not cooperate. Then, for all i, the pair $(X, (d_1, \ldots, d_n))$ may be interpreted as a *n-person bargaining model*. The NBS for such a model can be defined as being the unique outcome such that:

$$(u_1^*, \ldots, u_n^*) = \arg \max_{x_i} \prod_{i \in N} (u_i - d_i), \text{ for all } x \in X \text{ and } u_i \geq d_i, \text{ for all } i$$

It is easy to prove that this solution can be derived from a generalized version of Nash' axioms. This n-person NBS, however, ignores completely the possibility of cooperation among sub-sets of players. A general approach for studying cooperative games must propose a theory of 'intermediate' coalitions, i.e. coalitions containing at least two but no more than $(n - 1)$ players.

For an introduction to the question of coalitional analysis, let us consider the following two examples (Myerson, 1991, 418).

Example: game A

The game is initially given in strategic form. The set of players is $N = \{1, 2, 3\}$ and the set of strategies for each player i is:

$$X_i = \{(x_1, x_2, x_3) \in \mathbb{R}^3 : x_1 + x_2 + x_3 \leq 300 \text{ and } x_j \geq 0, \text{ for all } j\}$$

In game A, the three players get 0 unless they all propose the same allocation, in which case they get that allocation; that is, we let:

$$u_i(y_1, y_2, y_3) = \begin{cases} x_i & y_1 = y_2 = y_3 = (x_1, x_2, x_3) \\ & \text{if} \\ 0 & y_j \neq y_k, \text{ for some } j \text{ and } k \end{cases}$$

Example: game B

In game B, the set of players and the set of strategies are the same as in game A, but now players get 0 unless players 1 and 2 propose the same allocation, in which case they get that allocation. That is, we let:

$$u(y_1, y_2, y_3) = \begin{cases} x_i & y_1 = y_2 = (x_1, x_2, x_3) \\ & \text{if} \\ 0 & y_1 \neq y_2 \end{cases}$$

Notice that in the two games, players can jointly achieve any allocation in which their payoffs are non-negative and sum to 300 or less, and the minimal guaranteed payoff for each player is 0.

Thus, we could describe the two games as a *three-person bargaining model* $(X, (d_1, d_2, d_3))$ with:

$$X = \{(x_1, x_2, x_3) \in \mathbb{R}^3 : x_1 + x_2 + x_3 \leq 300 \text{ and } x_j \geq 0, \text{ for all } j\}$$
$$\text{and } (d_1, d_2, d_3) = (0, 0, 0)$$

It is easy to find that the NBS would select the outcome (100, 100, 100) for the two games. For game A, this might be a reasonable outcome. Yet this is no longer true for game B, into which players 1 and 2 can set together the payoff allocation while player 3 does not intervene. In that game, it is reasonable to assume that players 1 and 2 simply would share the payoff between themselves. If players 1 and 2 behaved as if they were in a two-person cooperative game, then the NBS would prescribe dividing equally between themselves the maximum total payoff that they can get and the outcome would be (150, 150, 0).

Notice, however, that this argument for dismissing the outcome (100, 100, 100) for game B requires that players 1 and 2 can negotiate effectively in order to focus on an outcome that they both prefer before choosing their strategies. Indeed, one of the two assumptions that distinguishes cooperative GT from non-cooperative GT is that assumption of *actual negotiation*. It follows that the n-person NBS might be relevant if the *only* coalition that can negotiate effectively is the *grand* coalition. Instead, in general n-person cooperative models, one generally assumes that *all intermediate coalitions* can effectively negotiate and that they are also able to correlate their strategies. Therefore the possibility for some players forming a cooperative coalition without others must be explicitly introduced in the models.

In game A, no coalition smaller than the grand coalition can guarantee more than 0 to its members. On the other hand, in game B, the intermediate coalition $\{1, 2\}$ could guarantee its members any payoff allocation that they could get in $\{1, 2, 3\}$. Therefore the n-person pure bargaining model is an irrelevant representation of a cooperative game with more than two players because it does not take into account all information about the role of intermediate coalitions.

Recall that the second assumption that distinguishes cooperative from non-cooperative games is that coalitions are able to commit to a course of actions once an agreement has been reached. Thus a way for evaluating the global gains of intermediate coalitions is to model the game in coalitional form, that is by introducing a 'coalitional' or 'characteristic' function (see sub-section 1.3.3 of Chapter 1 for the definition of this formal representation of a cooperative game).

The coalitional function of cooperative games

Let us consider first a TU cooperative game (N, v) (i.e. a game with transferable utility). In axiomatic bargaining games, we specify the feasible utility set for the *grand* coalition N and for each coalition containing only a *single* player. We can interpret a player's disagreement utility d as her (or his) opportunity cost for joining the grand coalition. Therefore in n-player cooperative games the 'worth' $v(S)$ of a coalition S corresponds to the opportunity cost of that intermediate coalition.

In theory, the number v may be derived from a strategic-form game. The worth of the grand coalition can be written:

$$v(N) = \max_{y} \sum_{i \in N} u_i(y)$$

But several ways can be thought up to derive the value of the characteristic function of proper coalitions $v(S)$.

Definitions

A first approach consists in supposing that the number $v(S)$ represents the maximal payoff that members of S could earn *independently of actions taken by outside members*. In the previous examples, we get:

Game A — $v(\{1, 2, 3\}) = 300$, $v(\{1, 2\}) = v(\{1, 3\}) = v(\{2, 3\}) = 0$,
$$v(\{1\}) = v(\{2\}) = v(\{3\}) = 0$$

Game B — $v(\{1, 2, 3\}) = 300$, $v(\{1, 2\}) = 300$,
$$v(\{1, 3\}) = v(\{2, 3\}) = v(\{1\}) = v(\{2\}) = v(\{3\}) = 0$$

This interpretation of coalition worth may be opposed to the one initially proposed by Von Neumann and Morgenstern (1944). A coalition worth $v(S)$ is based on what a coalition can guarantee its members *when the remaining players act to minimize their payoff* (see Shubik, 1982, or

Mas-Colell, 1989, for more developments on this interpretation of coalition worth). While this 'minimax' formulation of the characteristic function is unambiguous in zero-sum games, it is twofold in non zero-sum games (Aumann, 1967).

If the members of the coalition are supposed to move second, the characteristic function can be defined as what they cannot be prevented from getting. This *β-characteristic function* is:

$$v_\beta(S) = \min_{y_{N\backslash S}} \ \max_{y_S} \sum_{i \in S} u_i(y_S, y_{N\backslash S})$$

with $N\backslash S$ denoting the set of all players in N out of coalition S and $y_S = (y_i)_{i \in S}$

If the members of the coalition are supposed to move first, the *α-characteristic function* is defined more strictly as what they can guarantee themselves when they are ready for retaliatory behaviour on the part of the complementary coalition:

$$v_\alpha(S) = \max_{y_S} \ \min_{y_{N\backslash S}} \sum_{i \in S} u_i(y_S, y_{N\backslash S})$$

Generally the following inequality is satisfied:

$$v_\alpha(S) < v_\beta(S), \text{ for all } S \subset N$$

This is identical to players' security payoffs in two-person zero-sum games. In the definition of v_α and v_β, coalitions S and $N\backslash S$ are regarded as the two players in the zero-sum game, where the players' payoff in S is $\sum_{i \in S} u_i(y)$ and the players' payoff in $N\backslash S$ is the opposite.

Notice incidentally that both α- and β-characteristic functions correspond to a quite pessimistic appraisal of what the complementary coalition may do. Therefore, although this formulation might be adequate for strictly competitive situations (such as two-person zero-sum games), it is less convincing for general games where players' interests may coincide. Indeed, why should players in $N\backslash S$ behave in such an aggressive way if it is against their own interest?

Another approach takes into account the possibility that coalition S and players out of coalition $N\backslash S$ might have some common interest. It was initially suggested by Harsanyi (1959), who proposes a different conversion of non-cooperative games based on the NBS. Recall that $v(N)$ denote the total gains from cooperation of the grand coalition. Then define $v(S)$ to be the maximizer of the Nash product:

$$\left(y_S - \min_{y_{N\setminus S}} \max_{y_S} \; u_s(y_S, y_{N\setminus S}) \right) \left(v(N) - y_S - \min_{y_S} \max_{N\setminus S} \; u_{N\setminus S}(y_S, y_{N\setminus S}) \right)$$

It should be emphasized that in 'orthogonal' games (according to Shubik's 1982 terminology), where each coalition's worth is genuinely *independent* of other players' actions, all these coalitional form representations of games coincide. Games with this property often arise in economic applications, where the worst way for members of $N\setminus S$ to hurt S is to refuse the trade with members of S and force them to employ their own resources.

More generally, in many economic applications, the number $v(S)$ arises in a direct and natural way from the situation being modelled. For instance, in a normative analysis, $v(S)$ may simply describe a reference set of utilities that plays a focal role (see Moulin, 1995b, for such an interpretation).

Properties

Many economic applications of cooperative games fulfil an important property: they are 'superadditive' games. Superadditivity means that whatever two disjoint coalitions can independently do, a union of these two coalitions can do as well. This property can be written in the following way:

If for all $S, T \subset N, S \cap T = \phi$ then $v(S \cup T) \geq v(S) + v(T)$

In superadditive games, the merger of disjointed coalitions improves their prospects.

It should be noticed that this property actually concerns 'equivalence classes' of TU games: if a game is superadditive, then all strategically equivalent games are too. We also know that a game is 'essential' if players have something to gain through cooperation; that is formally:

$$v(N) > \sum_{i \in N} v(\{i\})$$

Moreover, if we introduce the $(0, 1)$-normalization (see sub-section 1.3.3 of Chapter 1), each equivalent class of essential strategy-equivalent games is formed by a *unique* game (Weber, 1994).

An important inference of the superadditivity property is that every Pareto-efficient allocation can be found in the feasible utility set of the grand coalition. Thus, in superadditive games, the efficiency principle forces overall cooperation and the problem raised by n-person TU cooperative superadditive games can be summarized in the following question: how to use the utility sets open to intermediate coalitions in order to restrict, and possibly determine, the choice of an outcome in the feasible set of the grand coalition?

A stronger property than superadditivity is that of 'convexity' (Shapley, 1971). A convex game fulfils the following inequality:

$$v(S) + v(T) \leq v(S \cup T) + v(S \cap T), \text{ for all } S, T \subseteq N$$

Roughly speaking a game is convex if we have increasing returns to co-operation: the larger a coalition becomes, the greater is the marginal contribution of new members. This is an interesting and important class of games.

Remark 1

Superadditivity is not always required for proving results in GT; sometimes a condition of 'weaker superadditivity' (or zero-monotonicity) is sufficient. If the game (N, w) is $(0,1)$-'strategically equivalent' to the game (N, v), then:

for all $S, T \subset N$, $T \supset S$ implies $w(T) \geq w(S)$

Notice that the class of games that verifies this mild property contains the class of superadditivity games.■

Remark 2

The superadditivity property defined initially in TU games can be easily translated into NTU games (non-transferable utility):

If $S \cap T = \phi$, then: $x \in V(S) \cap V(T)$ implies $x \in V(S \cup T)$

This condition still means that coalition $S \cup T$ can give its members any allocation that they could get in the disjoint coalitions S and T separately. NTU cooperative games actually are generalizations of TU games. Any TU game (N, v) is equivalent to the NTU game (N, V) such that:

$$V(S) = \left\{ x \in \mathbb{R}^S : \sum_{i \in S} x_i \leq v(s) \right\}$$

When this condition holds, NTU games are superadditive if and only if (N, v) are superadditive. Incidentally, it should be noticed that the two-person Nash bargaining game studied in Chapter 5 is just a particular case of NTU games in coalitional form with $v(\{1, 2\}) = X$, the set of feasible payoff allocations that players can get if they work together, and $v(\{i\}) = d_i$ (with $i = 1, 2$), the disagreement payoffs of each player.■

6.1.2   Interpretation and classifications of solution concepts in cooperative games

Given a model of game, what outcome may be expected or prescribed? A large part of GT, in one way or another, is directed at this fundamental question. In a cooperative game, a 'solution concept' is a function (or a correspondence, in the multivalued case) that associates outcomes (or sets of outcomes) with cooperative games. Indeed there is no *a priori* straightforward way for choosing such a solution concept. Each one represents a different approach or point of view.

Neutral, positive or normative viewpoints

Different methodological points of view may be envisaged here. First, one may consider that solution concepts are only 'indicators', not really predictions or prescriptions. They depict or illuminate the situation from different angles, each one stresses certain aspects at the expense of others. Solution concepts of cooperative games may be compared with indicators of statistical distributions (this analogy is developed by Aumann, 1989, 11). Like a game, a distribution contains a lot of hidden information. For example, the median and the mean summarize the information in different ways, but it is difficult to say how. The definitions themselves do have a certain clear intuitive content; furthermore, working with various specific examples and classes of examples highlights the relations between a distribution and its median and mean. The relationship of solution concepts to games is similar. Like the median and the mean, in some sense, they summarize the large amount of information present in the formal description of a game. Finally, the relations between a game and its various solution concepts is best revealed by analysing where they lead in specific games and classes of games.

Another viewpoint amounts to interpreting solution concepts of cooperative games according to the two distinct paths commonly followed in economics: either we confer a *positive* nature to solution concepts by focusing on the strategic stability properties of coalitions, or we look for *normative* prescriptions by emphasizing the ethically appealing properties of solutions.

According to the first viewpoint, cooperative games can be considered as part of the general study of *direct agreements* among rational agents who freely *negotiate*. The question is: what efficient agreements are likely to occur if transaction costs of all kinds are negligible? In contrast, according to the second perspective, cooperative games are regarded as tools for building *equity* (or *distributive justice*) criteria. The purpose is to inform the decision of an *arbitrator* who looks for equitable rules in decision making in democratic contexts.

We again meet the dual positive–normative interpretation proposed for a bargaining solution in *pure bargaining* axiomatic models (see section 5.2

of Chapter 5). Though being useful, this dichotomy may be misleading. On the one hand, it does not mean that fairness or equity considerations are absolutely absent in the positive approach. On the other hand, symmetrically, it does not imply that strategic considerations are not playing a role in the normative approach. This distinction based on the purpose followed by the game theorist is useful only from a *methodological* viewpoint. In particular, it may be argued that equity plays a leading role for reconciling the two viewpoints in the sense that 'the predictions of a positive theory of cooperative game in which the players have equal negotiating ability should coincide with the prescriptions of a normative impartial arbitrator' (Myerson, 1991, 374).

From another outlook, solution concepts of cooperative game often have both *direct* and *axiomatic* characterisations. While the direct definition applies to each game separately, most axioms deal with relationships between games. Generally speaking, the axiomatic method serves several useful purposes: it sheds additional light on the solution concept and it clarifies the similarities and differences between concepts. Another important function of the axiomatic approach relates to counterintuitive examples: solution concepts have to be consistent with certain desirable properties but they also must be thought of as a means to avoid counterintuitive results.

Domination and valuation: the two classical approaches

Finally it may be useful to classify the various solution concepts which have been suggested for cooperative games into two great families: the 'domination' approach and the 'valuation' approach (see, for instance, Mas-Colell, 1989, for such a distinction).

The first approach deals with 'domination' or 'objection' as main principles for deriving results concerning stability and coalition formation. The core and the like-core concepts (the stable sets, the bargaining set, the kernel, the nucleolus) attempt to evaluate the deterrent power of different kind of threats by groups of players. The aim of this dominance approach for cooperative games is to look into deviation possibilities of coalitions for delimiting the set of outcomes which are 'unobjectionable'. A necessary condition for a coalition to credibly object to a proposed outcome is that it can render each of its members better off. Notice that this ability of coalitions to use 'credible threats' in cooperative games is quite similar to the use of credible threats by *single* players in non-cooperative games.

In contrast, like bargaining solutions in pure bargaining games, the valuation approach attempts to associate with every cooperative game a unique *'reasonable'* outcome taking into account – and compromising among – all the conflicting claims. The Shapley value (or its various extensions) picks out of every cooperative game a unique outcome which answers the question: how to share 'reasonably' the surplus from cooperation between players?

In cooperative games all players can effectively negotiate among themselves in forming coalitions and members of a coalition are free to commit to a course of action once an agreement has been reached. In the dominance approach, 'objecting' and 'counterobjecting' are tools of cooperation. This 'deterrent scheme' is not a binding agreement *per se*. However the dissuasion is really effective only if players cannot secretly deviate; so, a watching process is required to prevent players from keeping information. The credibility of threats greatly depends on this watching process. In the valuation approach, the players' strategic behaviour is supposed to be transferred into the hands of an arbitrator who employs it to assess the sharing. Here, the power of individuals and coalitions no longer plays a direct role in reaching outcomes of games.

Remark 1

It should be emphasized that such a goal of computing a value (or a bargaining solution) for a game may be *a priori* not compelling for everybody. According to this approach, one assumes that there is some arbitrator (a referee, a social planner, the state, and so on) who selects a particular outcome guided by some reasonable principles and then, enforces this outcome. This *centralized* view is thus resolutely opposed to the libertarian view of society (for instance Buchanan and Tullock, 1962, or Hayek, 1976). Yet, as Moulin (1995a, 628) pertinently observes: 'the autonomy of the two positions would be only superficial if the determination of the unique solution/value resulted from positive equilibrium analysis: the computation of the value would reflect, then, a better understanding of the strategic parameters of the bargaining situation under consideration.' Indeed, that is precisely the purpose of the 'Nash program' for pure bargaining games. Therefore, a similar approach should be extended to *coalitional* games (pioneering works in this direction have been carried out by Gul, 1989, and Hart and Mas-Colell, 1992, who study the Shapley value implementation in strategic non-cooperative games; for a survey on *implementation* of cooperative solution concepts, see Greenberg, 1994).

To summarize, as for bargaining solutions, there are two ways for choosing a value in cooperative games: either we refer to ethically appealing properties of the solution concept (usually via its axiomatic foundations) from a normative viewpoint, or we can look for strategic decentralized foundations from a positive viewpoint.■

Remark 2

The domination approach is often presented as more descriptive than the valuation approach which would be essentially normative. The previous observation shows that this usage should be avoided. Concept solutions belonging to the two classes may be in fact used for the two purposes of prediction and prescription.∎

6.1.3   Coalition formation: cooperative or non-cooperative framework

The revival of interest in cooperative GT has allowed us to re-examine some parts of this theory. The starting point of classical n-player cooperative games is that each player has a clear idea of the possibility of joint actions in any sub-group of players and can negotiate freely before the play. In other words, the classical viewpoint does not attempt to model how a group of players may communicate among themselves in order to form a coalition. The purpose of this drastic assumption is to focus the analysis on the implications of actual or potential alliance formation. Yet, this way of thinking has a drawback: the meaning of forming a coalition in this framework is not entirely clear. This point is well summarized by Greenberg (1994, 1307): 'Is it a binding commitment of the players to remain and never leave a coalition once it forms? Or is it merely a "declaration of intent" which can be revised and if so, then under what conditions? That is, under what circumstances can a coalition form or dissolve?'

Asking such questions leads us to wonder whether it is legitimate to use a cooperative framework in order to study the formation of coalitions in games. In fact, it turns out that *non-cooperative models* of coalition formation have been offered by game theorists for a long time. The most notable attempt carried out in this direction is the notion of 'strong Nash equilibrium' (SNE) suggested by Aumann (1959).

The idea is that in strategic-form games coalitions form in order to correlate strategies of their members. Thus, by analogy with NE, a SNE is such that no *coalition S* has an incentive to deviate 'in a cooperative way' when the strategy of complementary coalition $N \backslash S$ is supposed fixed. The phrase 'in a cooperative way' means that all the members of a coalition play correlated strategies.

Definition I (*Strong Nash equilibrium*)

A SNE of the strategic-form game $(X_1, \ldots, X_n; u_1, \ldots, u_n)$ is an outcome $x = (x_1, \ldots, x_n)$ such that there is no coalition $S \subset N$ with strategies y_s such that:

$$u_i(y_s, x_{N \backslash S}) > u_i(x), \text{ for all } i \in S$$

Indeed, it is a strong definition, so that such an equilibrium seldom exists. Furthermore, this notion involves – at least implicitly – a condition of 'binding agreements': into each coalition, players have to comply with the strategies they have agreed upon, even if some of them have an interest to deviate.

A more compelling notion of cooperative equilibrium in a non-cooperative framework was later proposed by Bernheim, Peleg and Whinston (1987). In a SNE, no restriction is imposed to the deviating coalition. In contrast, a 'coalition-proof Nash equilibrium' (CPNE) involves *self-enforcing* agreements among members of a coalition by analogy with the requirements imposed on players in a NE. In a CPNE the only coalition deviations which are considered are those which verify a 'consistency' requirement: the coalition deviations must themselves be immunized against further deviations by sub-coalitions.

In order to formally define a CPNE some preliminary notation is needed. For any strategic-form game $G = \{N, \{X_i\}_{i \in N}, \{u_i\}_{i \in N}\}$ and any fixed strategy profile $\bar{x}$ define the reduced game for coalition S given $\bar{x}$ as follows:

$$G_{\bar{x}}^S = \{S, \{X_i\}_{i \in S}, \{\bar{u}_i\}_{i \in S}\}$$

where $\bar{u}_i(x_s) = u_i(x_S, \bar{x}_{N \setminus S})$; i.e. the reduced game is obtained by fixing the strategies of all players outside S, and defining the utility of every player given this fixed strategy choices. A CPNE is then defined recursively.

Definition 2 (*Coalitional-proof Nash equilibrium*)

For $n = 1$, x_i is a CPNE if and only if x_i is a maximizer of u_i over X_i. Let $n \neq 1$ and assume that CPNE have been defined for every coalition size. Then:

- x is self-enforcing for G if and only if, for all $S \subset N$, $S \neq N$, x_s is a CPNE of $G_{\bar{x}}^S$.
- x is a CPNE if and only it is self-enforcing and there does not exist another self-enforcing strategy y such that $u_i(y) \succ u_i(x)$ for all $i, i \in S$. ∎

The introduction of this new cooperative equilibrium has opened the door to an abundant literature on this topic with close connections with the previously mentioned literature on implementation of solution concepts.

The non-cooperative framework can also play a role in coalitional games in another very interesting way. The idea was suggested by Luce and Raiffa (1957) but it was introduced explicitly a few years later by Aumann, Davis and Maschler when they defined the 'bargaining set' as a solution concept (Davis and Maschler, 1963; Aumann and Maschler, 1964).

Definition 3 (*Coalition structure*)

Consider a group of players N who face a TU game (N, v) and suppose that players end up forming disjoint coalitions B_k which form a partition of N: $\beta = (B_1, B_2, \ldots, B_m)$ with $\bigcup_k B_k = N$ and $B_k \neq B_j$, for $k \neq j$. Such a partition is called a 'coalition structure'. ∎

Thus, in a game with a 'coalition structure', we require that players initially belong to such and such a coalition; we are clearly concerned with *actual* coalitions that might form. The motivation is that empirical evidence shows that some coalitions are more likely to form than others, for reasons not directly related to payoffs. This asymmetry may arise, for instance, from exogenous factors (such as historical, geographical, socio-logical, or political factors) which favour the appearance of some actual coalitions.

In order to apply the 'bargaining set' as a solution concept to this coalition structure rather than to the game itself, these game theorists gave rise to an ambitious program whose ultimate goal is to identify 'stable coalition structures' as a solution of a new game called a 'game of coalition formation'. In this way a clear distinction can be traced between two separate elements in coalitional games: a first stage of 'com-munication' or 'negotiation' among the players, in which *agreements are not binding* and a second stage of 'bargaining' (strictly speaking) in a *cooperative* framework. It turns out, however, that the early works on coalition structures avoided the first question (which coalition structures are likely to form?) in order to focus the analysis on the disbursement of payoffs in coalitions for a *fixed* coalition structure.

Aumann and Drèze (1974) were the first authors to explicitly investigate the problem of *endogenous* coalition formation in a non-cooperative frame-work and to extend classical concept solutions in 'coalitional structure' games. Since that seminal paper, research on this topic has been carried out by many scholars and today the program is really flourishing.

We now present the main solution concepts for coalitional games, following the previously mentioned distinction between the domination approach, which includes the core but also the related solution concepts of the stable sets, bargaining set, kernel and nucleolus, and then the valuation approach, with essentially the Shapley value and some of its extensions. The subsequent section will deal with the endogenous formation of coalitions by presenting an outline of these more recent coalitional games which marry cooperative and non-cooperative frame-works.

6.2   The domination approach: the core and related solution concepts

6.2.1   The core

Among all the solution concepts of cooperative games, the core (C) is probably the most intuitive one and the easiest to understand. Once an agreement in the core has been reached, no individual and no group can gain by regrouping. The concept (though not the term) appeared in the writings of Edgeworth (1881) who used the term 'contract curve'. But as a general solution concept for cooperative GT, it was developed by Gillies in the early 1950s (Gillies, 1959).

Imputation and domination principle

Some payoff vectors are naturally singled out for analysis as the set containing all reasonable outcomes for a cooperative game: this is called the set of 'imputations'.

Definition 4 (Imputation)

An imputation (I) in the game (N, v) is a payoff vector x which satisfies the two following conditions of rationality:

$$\sum_{i \in N} x_i = v(N) \quad \text{(group rationality)}$$

$$x_i \geq v(\{i\}), \forall_i \quad \text{(individual rationality)}$$

The set of imputations will be denoted $I(N, v)$. ∎

The 'group rationality' condition incorporates both the requirement that the members of the grand coalition N can actually achieve the outcome x, that is: $\sum_{i \in N} x_i \leq v(N)$ (feasibility) and cannot achieve more, that is: $\sum_{i \in N} x_i \geq v(N)$ (Pareto-efficiency). The 'individual rationality' condition means that no individual can achieve more than the amount allocated to her (or him) as a payoff. We can note that individual rationality and feasibility are not necessarily compatible; clearly the condition:

$$\sum_{i \in N} v(\{i\}) \leq v(N)$$

is needed. If equality holds, we are left with the trivial case: $x_i \equiv v(\{i\})$, which characterizes 'inessential' games (or strictly competitive games) in which no coalition can possibly achieve more than the individual members do on their own (see sub-section 2.3.2 in Chapter 2). Hence, we will assume that this inequality is strict and games are 'essential'.

Imputations constitute the stage on which most of cooperative GT is played out. The outcomes associated with most cooperative solutions are imputations. Sometimes, however, individual rationality is not imposed and we get 'pre-imputations' instead of 'imputations'.

The definition of the core can be derived from the *domination* principle, which refers to the power a coalition can exert through its ability to get along on its own. We say that x is dominated by y via the coalition S if y gives more to the members of S than does x and y_s is feasible for S.

Definition 5 (*Domination relation*)

For $x, y \in I(N, v)$, y dominates x via S if:

$$y_s > x_s \text{ and } \sum_{i \in S} y_i \leq v(s)$$

The payoff vector y dominates the payoff vector x if, for some coalition $S \subset N$, y dominates x via S.∎

When y dominates x via S, we see that the members of S can improve their payoffs by their own efforts; it is said that S can 'improve' on x. Sometimes S is called a 'blocking' coalition and it is said to be 'blocking' or 'objecting' payoff vector x. If we analyse the game in terms of this domination relation an obvious idea is to focus on undominated imputations.

Definition 6 (Core)

The core of the game (N, v), denoted $C(N, v)$, is a sub-set of the set of imputations $I(N, v)$ that are not dominated.∎

Thus the core is the set of all feasible payoffs upon which *no individual and no group can improve*. It is in some sense the set of imputations impervious to countervailing power: no sub-set of players can effectively claim that they could obtain more by acting by themselves.

The following result is then easy to prove.

Theorem I

An imputation $x_i \in C(N, v)$ if and only if:

$$\sum_{i \in S} x_i \geq v(s), \text{ for all } S \subset N \blacksquare \tag{6.1}$$

Notice that individual rationality and Pareto-optimality are in fact special cases of condition (6.1), when S is the singleton or the grand coalition, respectively. On the contrary, feasibility requires an opposite inequality; thus $v(N)$ plays a dual role in this approach. Furthermore, this theorem shows that $C(N, v)$ is a closed convex set, since it is characterized by a set of loose linear inequalities.

The core is a very appealing solution concept in view of the assumption that any coalition can negotiate effectively.

Example I

Let us come back to games A and B presented in sub-section 6.1.1. For game A, in which players can get 300 only if they all cooperate, the core is the set:

$$C(3, v) = \{x \in \mathbb{R}^3: x_1 + x_2 + x_3 = 300, x_1 \geq 0, x_2 \geq 0, x_3 \geq 0\}$$

The core treats the three players symmetrically and it includes all imputations of the game.

For game B, in which player 1 and 2 can get 300 together without player 3, the core is:

$$C(3, v) = \{x \in \mathbb{R}^3: x_1 + x_2 + x_3 = 300, x_1 \geq 0, x_2 \geq 0, x_3 = 0\}$$

So player 3's weakness in this game is reflected in the core, where she always gets 0. A great difficulty with the core is that it may not exist; that is, the core may be empty.

Example 2

Consider game C which differs from previous games A and B in the following way. Players get 0 unless there is a pair of players ($\{1,2\}$, $\{2,3\}$, $\{1,3\}$) who proposes the same payoff, in which case they get that payoff vector. That is, we let:

$$u_i(y_1, y_2, y_3) = \begin{cases} x_i & y_j = y_k = (x_1, x_2, x_3) \text{ for some } j \neq k \\ & if \\ 0 & y_1 \neq y_2 \neq y_3 \end{cases}$$

This game underlines the difficulties which follow from the possibility of competition between overlapping coalitions. In this game, when any player i gets a positive feasible payoff, the other two players must get less than the worth that they could get by themselves (i.e. 300). The emptiness of the core notably explains why the dynamics of coalitional negotiations is so complicated for this game. No matter what outcome may ultimately occur, there is always a coalition that could gain if it could get one more final opportunity to negotiate effectively against this payoff vector.

Remark I

There are also some games in which the core is non-empty but corresponds to rather extreme payoff vectors. However this instability of the core for a large game can be mitigated by considering approximate ε-cores. This solution concept is defined by slightly modifying the definition of the core. For any number ε, a payoff vector x is in the ε-core of the coalitional game $C(N, v)$ if:

$$\sum_{i \in N} x_i = v(N) \text{ and } \sum_{i \in S} x_i \geq v(S) - \varepsilon|S|, \forall S \subseteq N$$

That is, if x is in the ε-core then no coalition would be able to guarantee all its members more than ε above what they get in x (see Kannai, 1992, for more details on approximate cores).■

The 'equivalence principle'

In economic theory it is generally assumed that individuals (or a small set of individuals) are free to negotiate the terms of trade among themselves, but they perceive that the general market equilibrium offers them terms of trade that are fixed independently of their own trading decisions. In this framework several economists proved in the early 1960s the classical conjecture made by Edgeworth according to which for large market games the core is essentially 'equivalent' to the set of competitive equilibria (Walrasian equilibria). This 'equivalence principle', which underlines the relationship between the core and the price equilibria of a competitive market economy, is perhaps one of the most remarkable results in GT and economic theory.

Intuitively this principle says that the institution of market price arises naturally from the basic forces at work in a market no matter what we assume about the way in which these forces work. It highlights the role of prices as a tool of coordination between traders when the population is very large. So the notion of price is not at all artificial but is imposed by the internal necessities of cooperation.

The equivalence principle was essentially modelled by two approaches: the 'asymptotic' and the 'continuum' models.

The *asymptotic model* was initiated by Shubik (1959) who proves in the particular two-dimensional case that the set of Walrasian allocations W is contained in the core: $W \subset C$. This result was generalized by Debreu and Scarf (1963) for large finite dimensional economies. Letting the number of agents replicate identically to infinity, they show that in an appropriate sense the core tends to the set of competitive allocations. More precisely, in replica sequences of economies, the intersection of the core of the replications coincides exactly with the set of Walrasian equilibria:

$$W = \bigcap_{k=1}^{\infty} C_k$$

This convergent result is an important strengthening of the so-called 'First theorem of welfare economics', which asserts that Walrasian allocations are Pareto-optimal. Indeed it is a strong stability property of general competitive equilibrium: no group of individuals would choose to upset the equilibrium by recontracting among themselves. The core convergence theorem has a further normative significance. If we agree on the distribution of initial endowments, no coalition can object that it is treated unfairly at a core allocation. Since Walrasian allocations belong to the core, they necessarily own this group fairness property.

The *continuum model* was introduced by Aumann (1964). An economy with a *continuum* of agents is an idealization of an economy with a very large number of agents, such as continuum models that are used in physics to describe properties of large systems of interacting molecules or particles. We assume that the set of traders is an atomless probability space such as the unit interval [0, 1], endowed with the Lebesgue measure structure. Indeed the model of a large economy with a measure space of agents does express the idea that if the number of traders is very large one can not distinguish any more 'who is who'. This model gives a clear sense to one of the fundamental assumptions of perfect competition, namely that the influence of every one is insignificant. In this setting, it is proved that, under only minimal assumptions, the core coincides with the set of Walrasian equilibria: $W = C$.

Remark 2

The equivalence principle applies not only to the core but holds for all but one of the major solution concepts of cooperative games. The single exception is the 'stable set' (see sub-section 6.2.2 for a presentation of the 'stable set').■

Existence*

Although the logical appeal of the core is self-evident, its possible emptiness encourages us to question its meaning. This solution concept implicitly is based on the following assumptions: when a coalition S objects to an outcome x by negotiating for some outcome y, three conditions are fulfilled:

- The members of S are not prevented from deviating by prior agreements
- Their agreement on y would be final (one-step deviation)
- If they do not agree as a coalition on y, then they really will get x.

Such assumptions are similar to the kinds of conditions made in games with large number of players, especially in the analysis of large competitive markets; but they may seem questionable in cooperative games with *small* numbers of players.

Fortunately, it is possible to give a general characterization of games in which the core is non-empty. This characterization is due to Bondareva (1963) and Shapley (1967). It is based on the concept of a *'balanced game'*.

We already saw that condition

$$\sum_{i \in N} v(\{i\}) \leq v(N)$$

is necessary for the compatibility of *individual rationality* and *feasibility*. It is clear that additional superadditivity conditions are required for the existence of elements in the core. Let $S_1, \ldots, S_k$ be a partition of N. It follows from *group rationality* and inequality (6.1) defining the core that the following condition has to be satisfied for the non-emptiness of the core:

$$\sum_{i=1}^{k} v(S_i) \leq v(N) \tag{6.2}$$

Unfortunately, this condition is far from being sufficient. The necessary and sufficient condition for the core existence considerably strengthens this property.

The suitable generalization of the concept of partition is the notion of a '*balanced*' collection of coalitions, defined as follows.

Definition 7 (*Balanced collection of coalitions*)

A collection of coalitions $\{S_1, \ldots, S_k\}$ of a set N is balanced if there exist positive numbers $\lambda_1, \ldots, \lambda_k$ such that for every $i \in N$: $\sum_{j;\, i \in S_j} \lambda_j = 1$. The numbers λ_j are called 'balancing weights'.■

Every partition is a balanced collection of coalitions with weights equal to 1. If for every j, $S_j = N \backslash \{j\}$, then $\{S_j\}$ is a balanced collection with

$$\lambda_j = \frac{1}{n-1}$$

Indeed the set of all balanced collection of coalitions is very large. It turns out that a substantially smaller sub-set is sufficient for proving the existence of games with non-empty core.

Definition 8 (*Minimal balanced collection of coalitions*)

The balanced collection of coalitions $\{S_1, \ldots, S_k\}$ is said to be a 'minimal' if a non-proper sub-coalition is balanced.■

Games with a non-empty core are then characterized by the following result.

Theorem 2 (*Bondareva, Shapley*)

The core of a TU game (N, v) is non-empty if and only if for every balanced collection of coalitions $\{S_1, \ldots, S_k\}$ with balancing weight $\lambda_1, \ldots, \lambda_k$, the following inequality holds:

$$\sum_{j=1}^{k} \lambda_j v_j(S_j) \leq v(N) \blacksquare \tag{6.3}$$

Note that inequality (6.3) is just a generalization of (6.2). A game satisfying inequality (6.3) for all balanced collections is called a 'balanced' game.

Proof: (i) Necessity. Let $\{S_j\}_{j=1}^{k}$ be a balanced collection with balancing weight $\lambda_1, \ldots, \lambda_k$ and x a payoff vector in $C(N, v) \neq \phi$. By definition of the core:

$$\sum_{i \in S_j} x_i \geq v(S_j), j = 1, \ldots, k$$

We can multiply both sides of this inequality by λ_j and, summing from 1 to k, we get:

$$\sum_{j=1}^{k} \lambda_j \sum_{i \in S_j} x_i \geq \sum_{j=1}^{k} \lambda_j v(S_j)$$

By balancedness and group rationality, the left-hand side is equal to $v(N)$ and inequality (6.3) follows.

(ii) *Sufficiency*. The proof is based on duality theory of linear programming. Let $I_s(i)$ be the indicator function of S:

$$I_s(i) = \begin{cases} 1 & \text{if } i \in S \\ 0 & \text{otherwise} \end{cases}$$

Consider the linear program (P):

$$\begin{cases} \max \sum_{S \subset N} v(S) y_s \\ \text{s.t.: } \sum_{S \subset N} I_S(i) y_s = 1, i = 1, \ldots, n \\ \qquad y_s \geq 0, S \subset N \end{cases}$$

Then, the validity of inequality (6.3) for all balanced collections amounts to the statement that the value v_P of (P) satisfies $v_P = v(N)$.

Let (D) be the dual of (P):

$$\begin{cases} \min \sum_{i=1}^{n} x_i \\ \text{s.t.: } \sum_{i=1}^{n} I_s(i) x_i \geq v(S), S \subset N \end{cases} \tag{6.4}$$

By the Duality theorem the value v_D of this dual program satisfies: $v_D = v_P = v(N)$. Thus there exists a vector $x = (x_1, \ldots, x_i, \ldots, x_n)$ satisfying constraints (6.4) and the core $C(N, v)$ is not empty since (6.4) are actually equivalent to (6.1) in the definition of the solution concept.∎

This balancedness property indeed is not easy to interpret. Yet one can advance that it shows that the worth of intermediate coalitions $v(S)$ must not be too large with respect to the worth of the grand coalition $v(N)$.

Extension to NTU games[*]

The definition of the core extends straightforwardly to NTU games. The core was among the first solution concepts to be investigated in that context. In both situations of TU or NTU the core is based on the domination principle.

Just as for TU games the core of a NTU game (N, V) is the sub-set of undominated imputations; it includes all the feasible payoff vectors that cannot be improved upon by any coalition.

Coalition S can improve upon payoff vector x, if there exists $y \in V(S)$ with $x_S < y_S$. By comprehensiveness, S can improve upon x, if $x \in \text{int} V(S)$. Therefore the core $C(N, V)$ coincides with $V(N) \setminus \bigcup_{S \subset N} \text{int} V(S)$. It is clear that $V(N)$ has to be sufficiently large for the core to be non-empty.

By analogy with the terminology used in TU games, we define a 'balanced' game to be a game (N, V) in which the following relation holds for every balanced collections $\{S_1, \ldots, S_k\}$ of sub-sets of N:

$$\bigcap_{i=1}^{k} V(S_i) \subset V(N) \tag{6.5}$$

Comparing (6.3) and (6.5) shows that a TU game (N, v) is balanced, in the sense that all inequalities (6.3) hold, if its canonical representation as NTU game (N, V) is balanced.

The previous theorem of existence then generalizes into a weaker result proven initially by Scarf (1967, 1973) and Shapley (1973).

Theorem 3 (Scarf, Shapley)

Every balanced game has a non-empty core.∎

Note that unlike the TU case, balancedness of the game is no longer necessary for non-emptiness of the core (for the demonstration see, for instance, Owen, 1995, Chapter 15).

The definition of the core does not restrict a coalition deviation beyond imposing a feasibility condition. In particular, it is assumed that any deviation is the end of the story (one-step deviation). Several 'like-core' solution concepts consider various restrictions on deviations that are motivated by the fact that a deviation may trigger a reaction that leads to a different final output: coalitions are supposed to look beyond the one-step deviation possibilities.

6.2.2 Like-core solution concepts

Stable sets

When economic problems are formulated as an n-person cooperative game, they often have a non-empty core, and the core typically is a satisfactory solution concept. Yet there are many games with an empty core. This difficulty often arises in modelling politics and voting systems but also in models of industrial organization. In these situations 'stable set' theory often is more informative than other solution concepts for analysing coalition formation, competition and distribution of power.

The 'stable set' (S) was initially introduced as a solution concept in cooperative games by Von Neumann and Morgenstern (1944). It is also known as the 'Von Neumann–Morgenstern solution'. This notion is closely related to the core. Since by definition the core is the set of undominated imputations, an allocation in the core is never dominated by another allocation in the core, nor outside of the core.

Let X be a sub-set of the set of imputations $I(N, v)$. Then, roughly speaking, X is a 'stable set' if no allocation *in* X is dominated by any allocation in X, and each allocation *outside of* X is dominated by an allocation in X. Thus, like the core, the stable set is defined in terms of the *domination* principle. But, here, coalitions choose to deviate on the basis of the *ultimate* effect of their action (via some sequence of events) and not just by looking at the proximate effect.

Definition 9

Let (N, v) be a TU cooperative game. A *stable set* is any set of imputations $S(N, v)$ such that the two following properties hold:

$S \cap D(S) = \phi$ and $S \cup D(S) = I(N, v)$

where the domination function D is defined for any sub-set X of I by:

$D(X) = \{y \in I: y \text{ is dominated by some } x \in X\}$ ∎

These two conditions are called *internal stability* and *external stability*, respectively. They state that no element in a stable set S can dominate another element of S, and any element in I-S is dominated by at least one element in S. In other words, set S is 'domination-free', and 'setwise dominates' all elements not in S. The two conditions can be expressed by the one equation:

$S = I - D(S)$

which describes S as a fixed sub-set under the mapping $f(X) = I - D(X)$, where $X \subset I$.

Remember that the core is the set of imputations maximal with respect to the dominance relation; it can then be expressed by the relation:

$$C = I - D(I)$$

The core of a given game is a unique set whereas a game typically does not have only one stable set. Indeed, the definition of a stable set guarantees neither existence nor uniqueness. A game may have many stable sets, or it may have none. From the previous definition we get:

$$C \subset S \text{ and } S \cap D(C) = \phi \text{ for any stable set}$$

Thus, the core is contained in every stable set and it will be the unique stable set whenever $D(C) = I - C$.

Convex games are an interesting class of games with a non-empty core coinciding with the unique stable set (see sub-section 5.3.1 for a definition of convex games). When C is not a unique stable set by itself, then one attempts to enlarge C by adding elements from $I - (C \cup D(C))$ to reach a stable set S. That is, elements are added to C in such a manner as to maintain internal stability at each step in hope of eventually also obtaining external stability (see Lucas, 1992, for this presentation of stable sets and several variations, extensions and generalizations).

Example

In game C previously given as an example for emptiness of the core, there are many stable sets. One of them is $\{(150, 150, 0), (150, 0, 150), (0, 150, 150)\}$. But, for any player i and any scalar α, $0 \leq \alpha \leq 150$, the set $\{x \in I(N, v): x_i = \alpha\}$ also is a stable set. Hence, although the core of this game is empty, every imputation is in at least one stable set.

Remark I

We saw above that the definition of the core is essentially the same for NTU games as for TU ones. The same holds for the stable set.∎

Remark 2

It is interesting to notice a characteristic qualitative feature of the theory of stable sets. By definition, a stable set is just a set of imputations where nothing is explicit about underlying social structures. Yet the mathematical description of a given stable set often may be understood in terms of an implicit social structure (or form of organization) of players. The use of a stable set in 'market games' leads to emergence of subtle organizational forms such as cartels, systematic discrimination, or groups within groups. These special organizational forms are not imposed by definition, they are endogenous. In contrast to other solution concepts, in particular, the stable set theory predicts the formation of cartels in fully competitive economies. That is an important exception to the equivalence principle.■

The bargaining set

Like the concept of stable sets, the 'bargaining set' may be seen as a way of correcting the shortcomings of the core. The stable set hints at taking into account coalitions that might actually form, but such an interpretation is only implicit. In contrast the bargaining set is clearly concerned with the *actual* coalitions that might form, because an outcome is defined in relation to a particular partition of players.

Consider a group of players N who face a game (N, v) and suppose that players end up forming disjoint coalitions which form a partition of N: we know that such a partition is called a *coalition structure* (see sub-section 6.1.3). Then bargaining set theory answers the question: how would or should players share the proceeds, given that a certain coalition structure has formed?

The bargaining set was introduced by Aumann, Davis and Maschler in the early 1960s (Davis and Maschler, 1963; Aumann and Maschler, 1964). Like the stable sets, the bargaining set includes the core. But unlike the core and the set of stable sets, the bargaining set for TU games is never empty.

The idea behind this solution concept is that a player might not make an objection to a proposed payoff vector if he feared that his objection might prompt a counterobjection by another player.

It is important to see that the purpose of claiming an objection for a player is not actually to defect from the coalition structure. During the course of negotiations between all players there is a moment when a certain coalition structure is 'crystallized'. Players will no longer listen to players outside their coalition but each coalition still has to adjust the final share of its proceeds. For player k (hereafter named 'she'), the purpose of claiming an objection is to point out to player l that she can get more by taking her business someplace else, and perhaps l (hereafter named 'he') is getting too much and should transfer some of his share to k. Note that k can object against l only if they both belong to the same coalition of the coalition structure. Player l should not yield, if he can protect his share, namely if he has a counterobjection (see Maschler, 1992, for a defence of that interpretation).

In order to give a rigorous definition of these notions, we need to introduce the '*excess of a coalition*'.

An imputation for a coalition structure β is a payoff vector x satisfying the *rationality group* condition for all coalitions in β and the *individual rationality* condition. The excess of coalition S at x is the quantity:

$$e(S, x) = v(S) - \sum_{i \in S} x_i \text{ if } S \neq \phi \text{ and } e(S, x) = 0 \text{ if } S = \phi$$

It represents the total gain (or loss, if $e < 0$) that members of S will obtain if they depart from the imputation x and form their own coalition.

Definition 10 (*Justified objection*)

Let x be an imputation in a TU cooperative game (N, v) for a coalition structure β. Let k and l be two distinct players in a coalition B of β.

   An *objection* of k against l at x is a pair (y, S) such that:

$y \in \mathbb{R}^n, S \subseteq \mathbb{N}, k \in S, l \notin S$

$e(S, y) = 0$ and $y_s > x_s$

That is, players in S can jointly achieve their share of y, which is strictly better than allocation x for every player in S, including player k.

- A *counterobjection* to k's objection (y, S) against l is any pair (z, T) such that:

$z \in \mathbb{R}^n, T \subseteq \mathbb{N}, l \in T, k \notin T, T \cap S \neq \phi$

$e(T, z) = 0, z_T \geq x_T$ and $z_{T \cap S} \geq y_{T \cap S}$

That is, in the counterobjection, player l claims that he can protect his share by forming a coalition T. He does not need the consent of k, he can give each member of T her (or his) initial payoff, and if some members of T were offered some benefits from k, he can match the offer.

- An objection is said to be '*justified*' if it has no counterobjection.■

This notion of justified objection allows us to define the bargaining set.

Definition 11 (*Bargaining set*)

Let (N, v) be a TU cooperative game. The bargaining set for a coalition structure β is the set of imputations to which there exists *no justified objection;* this set will be noted the bargaining set (BS) (β). The bargaining set of the game (N, v) is got when considering BS($\{N\}$). Moreover, if we take pre-imputations instead of imputations, the solution is called the pre-bargaining set.■

Thus, roughly speaking, an imputation is in the *core* if there is *no objection* to it and it is in the *bargaining set* if there is *no justified objection* (i.e. that has no counterobjection). The use of a BS, like the core and the stable sets, amounts to eliminating some imputations, narrowing the predictions to a smaller set of imputations. But generally players will look at imputations in the BS as a starting point for further bargaining, leading to outcomes that deviate by a second-order magnitude – hence the title 'bargaining set'.

Clearly the BS includes the core for each coalition structure because at core imputations there is no objection and *a fortiori* no justified objection. In general, the BS may contain imputations outside the core. The core, however, is empty in many cases, so that one advantage of the BS over this concept solution is in the following result.

Theorem 4

For every TU game (N, v), if the set of imputations is not empty for a certain coalition structure β, then the BS (β) is not empty. ∎

Closely related to the bargaining set are the 'kernel' and the 'nucleolus'. All these solution concepts are based on an 'objecting' principle, which is essentially the same as the 'domination' principle. Unlike the stable set, the chain of events that a deviation unleashes is cut short after two stages: roughly speaking, the stability coalition is that for every objection to an outcome there is a 'balancing' counterobjection. The BS, kernel and nucleolus actually differ in the nature of the objections and counterobjections.

The kernel

The kernel (K) is due to Davis and Maschler (1965). It differs from the BS in the nature of objections and counterobjections that are effectively considered. Indeed the kernel was originally introduced as an auxiliary solution concept; its main task was for illuminating properties of the bargaining set and for computing at least some part of this set.

Consider $e(S, x)$, the excess of a coalition S at x. If $e > 0$, then it measures the amount that S has to forgo in order for the imputation x to be implemented. If $e < 0$, then its absolute value measures the amount over and above the worth of S that this coalition obtains when the imputation x is implemented.

A player k objects to an imputation x by forming a coalition S that excludes some player l for whom $x_l > v(\{l\})$ and pointing out that she is dissatisfied with the sacrifice or gain of this coalition. Player l counterobjects by pointing to the existence of a coalition that contains l but not k and sacrifices more or less gains. Then, we can define the '*surplus of k against l*' as the most player k can hope to gain or the least to lose (i.e. if $e(S, x) > 0$ or < 0, respectively) if she departs from the imputation x and forms a coalition that does not need the consent of l, assuming that the other members of this coalition are happy with their payoff in x. This surplus can be thought of as a measure of the bargaining power of player k relative to player l. In comparing k and l in this way, one can also look at the surplus of l against k. And the two players are in a kind of balance, relative to x, if these two surpluses are equal. This balance is the base of the kernel; it picks up the idea of symmetry or *equalization of bargaining pressure*.

Definition 12

Let (N, v) be a TU cooperative game and let β be a coalition structure. The surplus of k against l at an imputation x is:

$$s_{k,l}(x) = \max_{\substack{k \in S \\ l \notin S}} e(S, x)$$

The kernel $K(\beta)$ for β is the set of imputation such that:

$$S_{k,l}(x) > S_{l,k}(x) \Rightarrow x_l = v(\{l\}) \text{ for all } k, l \in B \in \beta, k \neq l$$

The pre-kernel for β is the set of pre-imputations such that:

$$S_{k,l}(x) = S_{l,k}(x) \text{ for all } k, l \in B \in \beta, k \neq l$$

The kernel of the game (N, v) is got when considering $K(\{N\})$.∎

Remark

Definitions of the core and the BS do not require to compare the payoffs of different players, while definition of the kernel does. It follows that the kernel is an appropriate solution only in situations in which utilities of different players can be meaningfully compared. However Maschler (1992, 608–9) gives an interesting normative interpretation of the kernel which does not directly use interpersonal comparison of utilities. According to this interpretation, outcomes in the intersection of the kernel and the core satisfy a kind of *fair division* scheme.∎

The nucleolus

Like the bargaining set, the kernel can have many outcomes, whereas the 'nucleolus' (NL) consists of *just an outcome* for a very large class of games. Indeed it is with the aim of picking a unique outcome in the kernel of TU cooperative games that Schmeidler (1969) introduced the NL. Though mathematically complicated, the idea behind this solution concept is very simple: a payoff vector is the nucleolus if the excess of all coalitions for that payoff vector are made as small as possible. Roughly speaking, the NL is the imputation for which *the maximal excess is minimal*. The excess of a coalition may be regarded as a measure of dissatisfaction and then, intuitively, the NL is the point that *minimizes dissatisfaction*. This property also will increase stability. A coalition with a high positive excess will gain a lot by departure and, even if the excess is negative, defection still is less liable if the excess is smaller.

The definition of the NL rests on comparisons among the excesses associated with various payoff vectors. We consider again a TU game (N, v) and a closed set X of vectors of $\mathbb{R}^n$. For each x in X, we define a 2^n-vector $\theta(x)$ to be:

$$\theta(x) = (e(S_1, x), e(S_2, x), \ldots, e(S_{2^n}, x))$$

whose components (the excesses of the 2^n coalitions $S \subset X$) are arranged in decreasing order. Then we compare two arbitrary vectors $\theta(x)$ and $\theta(y)$ using the lexicographic ordering R_L (see sub-section 2.3.1 in Chapter 2, for the definition of the lexicographic ordering).

Definition 13

Let X be an arbitrary non-empty closed *set* in $\mathbb{R}^n$. The $NL(N, v, X)$ is the set of vectors in X whose θs are lexicographically least, i.e.:

$$NL(N, v, X) = \{x \in X : \theta(x) R_L \theta(y), \text{ for all } y \in X\}$$

If $X = I(\beta)$, the NL is called the NL of the game for coalition structure β. If $X = I(\{N\})$, it is called the NL of the game. Finally, if we consider pre-imputations instead of imputations, we get the pre-nucleolus of the game.■

Since the NL is a point in the kernel, it possesses all the nice properties of this solution. When the core is non-empty, the NL belongs to the core. But if the core is empty, the NL can be imagined as the 'latent position' of the core (Shubik, 1982, 340). Figure 6.1 illustrates these properties and shows interesting relationships between BS, C, K and NL for TU games.

Remark I

A more normative interpretation of the NL often is suggested. Like the kernel, this solution concept may be viewed as based on some consideration of equity between players: the NL is defined by an 'egalitarian' arbitration among coalitions (see Moulin, 1988, for such a normative interpretation).■

Figure 6.1   Kernel (K), Nucleolus (NL), Core (C) and Bargaining set (BS)

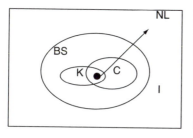
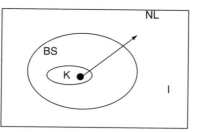

Remark 2

Generalization of concepts of 'objection' and 'counterobjection' to NTU games is straightforward. Therefore it is easy to define the BS for NTU games. Unfortunately, it may be empty even for three-person games. Another definition of that solution concept is then required. Several non-empty BS over the class of NTU cooperative games were introduced (see Maschler, 1992, for a survey). In contrast results concerning extension of the kernel and the NL to NTU games are scarce. The main problem is deciding what should be the analogue of the excess functions. There have been several suggestions, but theses studies are as yet exploratory.■

6.3   The valuation approach: the Shapley value and extensions

As it had proved so useful to represent each alternative facing a player by a single number expressing its expected utility and then to summarize the opportunities facing a coalition in a game by a single number expressing its worth in units of transferable utility, Shapley (1953) suggested to summarize the complex possibilities facing each player in a game in coalitional form by a single number representing the *'value' of playing the game*.

The particular function he derived for this purpose – which will be called hereafter the Shapley value (SV) – was the focus of sustained interest and this solution concept of cooperative games has proved very useful in a wide range of economic and political models. The SV is perhaps the most useful of all cooperative solution concepts, and very often gives results with significant intuitive content. There are very general existence theorems, which cover essentially all the applications that one might want to consider. Lastly, a very important point is that the SV is mathematically tractable (Shubik, 1982, in particular, helped to show the usefulness of the SV in economics and political science).

6.3.1   The Shapley value

The value of a game (N, v) is defined as a vector of n numbers representing the value of playing the game in each of its n-positions:

$$\phi(N, v) \equiv [\phi_i(N, v)]_{i \in N}$$

Thus, for each game in coalitional form, the value predicts a *unique* payoff allocation for the players.

Characterization

The standard characterization is axiomatic. Before stating axioms we need some definitions

First define the *'marginal contribution of player i'* to any coalition S in the game (N, v) to be: $\Delta_i(S) = v(S) - v(S \setminus \{i\})$ Then, player i is named a *'dummy'* if $\Delta_i(S) = v(\{i\})$ for every coalition S that excludes i. Furthermore, players i and j are said *'interchangeable'* if $\Delta_i(S) = \Delta_j(S)$ for every coalition S that contains neither i nor j.

Shapley proposed that the payoff allocation $\phi(N, v)$ verifies three axioms:

A1   Group rationality:
The payoff allocation (N, v) distributes the total payoff of the game:

$$\sum_{i \in N} \phi_i(N, v) = v(N)$$

A2   Symmetry (or equal treatment):
If players i and j are interchangeable in (N, v), then:

$$\phi_i(N, v) = \phi_j(N, v)$$

A3   Dummy player condition (or null player condition):
If player i is a dummy in (N, v), then:

$$\phi_i(N, v) = v(\{i\})$$

These three axioms can be easily justified. The group rationality axiom classically requires both feasibility and efficiency. The symmetry axiom asserts that only the role of a player in the game should matter, not her (or his) specific name or label in N. So the value should be sensitive only to how the characteristic function responds to the presence of a player in a coalition. In particular, players who are treated identically by v should be treated identically by the value ϕ. Given the focus on a player's contribution to various coalitions, axiom *A3* also appears quite natural: a player who contributes to the outcome of any coalition exactly her (or his) individual payoff $v(\{i\})$ should be assigned that payoff in the value allocation. In particular, a player that contributes nothing to any coalition receives nothing.

For some games those three axioms are sufficient to uniquely determine the payoff allocation $\phi(N, v)$, but in general for getting a unique value allocation a *consistency* requirement is necessary. While previous axioms impose conditions on *single* games, the last one links outcomes of *different* games.

A4   Additivity:
For any two games (N, v) and (N, w) we have $\phi_i(N, v + w) = \phi_i(N, v) + \phi_i(N, w)$ for all $i \in N$, where $(N, v + w)$ represents the game defined by $(v + w)(S) = v(S) + w(S)$ for every coalition S.

This last axiom is mathematically convenient but harder to justify than the three first axioms. The first critic of the Additivity axiom was formulated by Luce and Raiffa (1957), who underline the fact that the structure of the game $(N, v + w)$ may induce behaviour unrelated to that induced games (N, v) and (N, w) separately (see, however, Myerson, 1991, 437–8, for a defence of a closely related axiom of Linearity).

Remarkably, Shapley (1953) showed that there is a *unique* payoff function ϕ (N, v) that satisfies these four axioms.

Theorem 5 (*Shapley*)

The unique value $\phi = [\phi_i]_{i \in N}$ satisfying assumptions *A1, A2, A3* and *A4* is:

$$\phi_i(N, v) = \sum_{S \subset N} q(s) \Delta_i(s)$$

with

$$q(s) = \frac{(s - 1)!(n - s)!}{n!}$$

and s representing the number of players in coalition S.∎

Interpretation

This formula expresses the SV for player i as a weighted sum of her (or his) marginal contributions to all coalitions she (or he) can join.

It can be interpreted as the *expected marginal contribution* of each player when she (or he) enters a coalition. Specifically, suppose we decide to assemble the grand coalition N in a room but the door to the room is large enough for only one player to enter at a time, so that players randomly line up in a queue at the door. There are $n!$ orderings of the players in N that are supposed equally likely. Then $\phi_i(N, v)$ is the expected marginal contribution made by player i as she (or he) enters the room. To prove this, consider any coalition S containing i and observe that the probability that player i enters the room to find precisely players in $S \backslash \{i\}$ already there is $(s - 1)!(n - s)!/n!$ (Roth, 1988, 7)

The SV is a powerful tool for *evaluating the power structure* in a coalitional game. It may be thought of as an index of power – or, what comes to the same thing, an index of social productivity.

Examples

Let us come back first, for example, to the three games presented above in sub-sections 6.1.1 and 6.2.1.

For game A, where all three players must agree to get 300, the outcome given by the SV is (100, 100, 100). For game B, where only players 1 and 2 need to agree to get 300, it is (150, 150, 0). And for game C (the 'three-person majority game') where any pair of players can divide 300, by symmetry, the SV gives (100, 100, 100).

Another interesting example is provided by the '*apex game*'(Maschler, 1992). That game is a five-person cooperative game with:

$v(S) = 1$ if player $1 \in S$ and Card $S \geq 2$

$v(S) = 1$ if Card $S \geq 4$

$v(S) = 0$ otherwise

Player 1 is called the 'big player' while the other four are the 'small players'. Associated with one or more of the small players, the big player can earn 1; the four small players can together also earn a worth of 1. It is easy to see that the core of this game is empty. On the other hand, the game has a unique SV. In the randomly ordered entry process the big player will have a marginal contribution of 1 unless she (or he) enters first or last, which happens with probability $\frac{2}{5}$. It follows that: $\phi_1(5, v) = \frac{3}{5}$. By A2, the four small players must get the same values. By A1 and A3 the values of all five players must sum to 1. Therefore, the payoff allocation which corresponds to the SV in the game is:

$$\phi(5, v) = (\frac{3}{5}, \frac{1}{10}, \frac{1}{10}, \frac{1}{10}, \frac{1}{10})$$

Remark 1

Young (1985) showed that one may replace axioms A3 (Dummy player) and A4 (Additivity) with the following requirement: the value of a player depends only on her (or his) marginal contributions. This 'marginal contribution' axiom can be stated as follows: given two games (N, v) and (N, w) and a player $i \in N$, if $v(S) - v(S\backslash\{i\}) = w(S) - w(S\backslash\{i\})$ for all coalitions S, then: $\phi_i(N, v) = \phi_i(N, w)$. Young's result states that a solution concept satisfies 'group rationality', 'symmetry' and 'marginal contribution' if it is the SV.■

Remark 2

Hart and Mas-Colell (1989) suggested a simple way to compute the SV: associate with each game (N, v) just one real number $P(N, v)$, called the '*potential*' of the game, and compute marginal contributions of players according to these numbers. More precisely, put $P(\phi, v) = 0$ and recursively, associate with every game (N, v) a number $P(N, v)$ such that:

$$\sum_{i \in N} [P(N, v) - P(N \setminus \{i\}, v)] = v(N)$$

that is, the sum of marginal increments of P equals $v(N)$. It turns out that the marginal increments of P are precisely Shapley valuations:

$$\phi_i(N, v) = P(N, v) - P(N \setminus \{i\}, v) \text{ for all } (N, v) \text{ and } i \in N. \blacksquare$$

Remark 3

Other extended values were proposed in the literature, notably the Owen value (1977, 1985). Some of these extensions will be presented in section 6.4 which focuses on games with *endogenous* coalition structures. ∎

6.3.2 Relationship between the Shapley value and other solution concepts[*]

The SV is easy to compute and it exists for all cooperative games. The relationship between the SV and other solution concepts has been extensively studied in the literature (see notably Moulin, 1988).

In particular it was proved that the SV and the core are not always compatible solution concepts for games in coalitional form; the value allocation may or may not be part of the core. The reason is that the value allocation is not necessarily stable against any secession of coalitions. But, since the value allocation is not necessarily in the core, we can ask the question: is the value payoff at least an imputation? By *A1* it verifies *group* rationality, but individual rationality is not required directly. Hence, generally, the value allocation is simply a *pre-imputation*. However, if the game is *superadditive*, the SV also satisfies *individual* rationality in the sense that:

$$\phi_i(N, v) \geq v(\{i\}), \, \forall i \in N$$

For verifying this relation, remark that superadditivity implies that:

$$v(S) \geq v(S \setminus \{i\}) + v(\{i\}), \, \forall S \subseteq N$$

In contrast to the core and the bargaining set, definitions of the kernel and the NL make intuitively little sense in reflecting goals that some people may have in some cases. Yet we know that a solution concept can also be justified by providing an axiomatic foundation and by convincing the reader that these properties are desirable. It is remarkable that a particular axiom – the 'reduced game property' or 'consistency' – plays a key role in axiomatization of most previously introduced solution concepts.

Consistency was first noticed by Harsanyi (1959) for the NBS in an n-person bargaining game (see Thomson, 1990, 1994, and Peters, 1992, for detailed analysis of the role of consistency in axiomatic bargaining models). But that property in one form or another is common to just about all cooperative games. Consistency-like conditions are even used in frameworks that are not strictly game theoretic as social choice, equity or distributive justice theories (see for instance Moulin, 1995b; Young, 1994; Roemer, 1996).

Let us consider a cooperative game (N, v) and assume that players believe in a *valued point* solution concept φ, which yields only Pareto-efficient payoffs.

In this setting the consistency principle means as follows: if members of a sub-set S of N gather together and observe what they have received under φ, they will decide that they have no motivation to defect because what they have received is a payoff vector in the solution for 'their own game'.

Definition 14 (Consistency)

φ is consistent if for all $S \subset N$ and every payoff x:

$x = \varphi(N, v)$ implies for all $S \subseteq N$, $(x_i)_{i \in S} = \varphi(S, v_s)$

where (S, v_s) represents the game that players in S call 'their own game' and is also called the 'reduced game on S'. ∎

Roughly speaking, consistency implies that it is not too important how the player set is chosen. We can focus attention to a 'small world', and the outcome for players of this world will be the same as if we had looked at them in a 'big world'. In some way consistency is thus a requirement of 'stability among games'.

This property also can be adapted to a *multivalued* solution concept. If φ is not a consistent solution, there will be games (N, v) with payoffs in φ (N, v), and coalitions S whose members will disagree with x, claiming that for their own game φ yields a payoff vector different from x. Consistency is a rather natural requirement. What is not so obvious is how to define the reduced game (S, v_s). Two definitions have so far proved fruitful.

The first solution is the following:

$$v_s(T) = \begin{cases} 0 & \text{for } T = \phi \\ x(T) & \text{for } T = S \\ \max_{Q \subseteq S} [v(T \cup Q) - x(Q)] & \text{for } T \subset S, T \notin \{\phi, S\} \end{cases}$$

where $\bar{S}$ denotes the complementary coalition $(N \setminus S)$. This formula was first suggested by Davis and Maschler (1965) and later studied by Aumann and Drèze (1974) for games with endogenous coalition structures. The core, the pre-bargaining set, the pre-kernel and the pre-nucleolus are all consistent solutions under that equation. Notice that this result concerns the 'pre-solutions' and not the BS, the kernel and the NL themselves.

The second fruitful definition of a reduced game is:

$$v_s(T) = v(T \cup \bar{S}) - \sum_{i \in \bar{S}} \varphi_i(v/T \cup \bar{S}), \ T \subseteq S$$

where $v/T \cup \bar{S}$ is the sub-game of (N, v), restricted to $T \cup \bar{S}$. This formula was given by Hart and Mas-Colell (1987). The SV is consistent under that second equation.

Notice that there are two basic differences between the two equations. In the first, T is allowed to choose partners Q from $\bar{S}$. In the second, T is stuck with $\bar{S}$. Furthermore, in the second each player in $\bar{S}$ asks for her (or his) payment in the solution of the new game $(T \cup \bar{S}; v/T \cup \bar{S})$ whereas in the first each player asks for her (or his) payment x, which is supposed to be the solution of the original game (N, v).

The rich results concerning reduced games, as well as their intuitive appeal, raised the question whether consistency could be used to compare some of the above solution concepts. Concerning this point, an astonishing result was proved by Hart and Mas-Colell (1989).

Theorem 6 (Hart and Mas-Colell)

The pre-nucleolus and the SV can be axiomatized by the same axioms; only the consistency axiom differs.∎

Axiomatization of the pre-nucleolus was first given by Sobolev (1975). Later, axiomatization of the NL for some classes of game was proposed by Maschler, Potters and Tijs (1992). They make use of the reduced game property. However, instead of 'reducing' the game to a sub-set of players, they 'reduce' the game to a smaller set of permissible coalitions. Thus, in a deep sense, the difference between SV and the pre-nucleolus lies in the way the sub-sets of N want to evaluate 'their own game'. If one of them makes more sense for the particular case, the corresponding solution should be preferred. If one has to decide between the SV and the pre-nucleolus in a concrete application, one should examine both reduced games and see which of them is more appropriate to that application.

In a *convex game*, the SV is always a member of the non-empty core; indeed, it occupies a central position. The marginal contribution vectors are the extreme points of the convex core and the SV represents the barycentre of these extreme points, with the qualification that an extreme point is counted twice if it corresponds to the marginal contribution vectors of two different orderings. All important solution concepts agree on that class of games.

Proposition I Convex games have a unique stable set coinciding both with the core and the BS and for these games, the kernel coincides with the NL.∎

Generally however the NL differs from the SV (see Moulin, 1988, 112–13) and Maschler, 1992, 628–9). Previously, we compared solution concepts of cooperative games to indicators of distribution, like the mean and median. In fact, the SV is in many ways analogous to the mean, whereas the median corresponds to something like the NL (Aumann, 1989, 25).

Remark I

It should be emphasized that the opposition between the 'domination' approach and the 'valuation' approach is just a convenient way to interpret cooperative games. It turns out that the SV may also be characterized in terms of objections and counterobjections. However, in contrast with previous solution concepts, these objections and counterobjections are defined with reference to other games – the 'sub-games' – and not to single games in isolation.

For each coalition S, the sub-game (S, v) of game (N, v) is the coalitional game in which $v^s(T) = v(T)$ for any $T \subseteq S$. Then, an objection of player k against player I to the allocation x of $v(N)$ may take the following form: 'give me more since otherwise I will leave the game, causing you to obtain $\phi_1^{-k} = \phi_1(N\backslash\{k\}, v^{N\backslash\{k\}})$ rather than the larger payoff x, so that you will lose the positive amount $x_1 - \phi_1^{-k}$.' And a counterobjection by player I to an objection of that type is an assertion: 'it is true that if you leave then I will lose, but if I leave then you will lose at least as much': $x_k - \phi_k(N\backslash\{I\}, v^{N\backslash\{I\}}) \geq x_1 - \phi_1(N\backslash\{k\}, v^{N\backslash\{k\}})$. These objections and counterobjections differ from those used to define the BS, the kernel and the NL in that they refer to the outcomes of *smaller games*. These outcomes are derived from the same logic as the payoff of the game itself: they are given by the value.

The SV is required to satisfy the property that every objection of any player k against any other player I is 'balanced' by a counterobjection of player I:

$$\phi_k(N, v) - \phi_k^{-I} = \phi_1(N, v) - \phi_1^{-k}, \ \forall k, \forall I \in N$$

One can prove that the unique value that satisfies this property is the SV (see Osborne and Rubinstein, 1994, 289–90).∎

6.3.3 *Extensions*

Two extensions of the SV are checked: for NTU games and for non-atomic games.

The Shapley value in NTU games[*]

The SV admits several generalizations for NTU games (N, V), with the supplementary restriction that $V(S)$ are convex sets. Perhaps the most natural, although not necessarily the simplest to work with, was proposed by Harsanyi (1959, 1963). An interesting property of the NTU Harsanyi value is that it coincides with SV in the TU case, and with NBS in the two-person case.

Another value for general NTU games was introduced by Shapley (1969). The details of Harsanyi's model are formidable, which accounts for some of the appeal of Shapley's much simpler formulation. Shapley borrows from Harsanyi the concept of 'λ-transfer value' but the two approaches differ with respect to the rules defining how the value is characterized. The basic device suggested by Shapley is to define a family of TU games that can be associated with the original NTU game. Each such game is based on giving weights to players. Each game has a SV, but for most of these games it cannot be achieved in that suitably weighted version of the original game. Roughly speaking, a λ-transfer value for a NTU game is the SV of a member of this family that can be attained in the original game.

Let us consider the unit simplex

$$\left\{ \lambda \in R^n \colon \lambda_i \geq 0,\ \forall i\ \text{and}\ \sum_{i \in N} \lambda_i = 1 \right\}$$

For each profile and each outcome x of the NTU game, define the 'weight outcome' λx by $(\lambda x)_i = \lambda_i x_i$. Let $v_\lambda(S)$ be the maximum total weight that the coalition S can achieve:

$$v_\lambda(S) = \max\left\{ \sum_{i \in S} \lambda_i x_i,\ x \in V(S) \right\},\ S \subset N$$

This represents the characteristic function of the TU game (N, v).

Definition 15 (λ-transfer value)

An outcome x is called a λ-*transfer value* of NTU game (N, V) if $x \in V(N)$ and there exists a profile with: $\lambda x = \phi(N, v_\lambda)$; that is, if x is feasible and corresponds to the value of a member of TU games (N, v_λ). ∎

Weights assign a relative importance to each player and they are chosen so that the resulting value is feasible; an infeasible result would indicate that some people are overrated or underrated. Weight λ_i can also be used for making *interpersonal comparisons* of utility (for an application of this methodology in theories of distributive justice, see Yaari, 1981). Intuitively, $v_\lambda(S)$ is a numerical measure of this coalition's total worth and hence, the value $\phi_i(N, v_\lambda)$ may be viewed as a measure of player i's social productivity.

The NTU SV of a coalitional game does not need to be unique. This may at first sound strange, since unlike stability concepts, one might expect an index of social productivity to be unique. But perhaps it is not so strange when one thinks that even an economic agent's net worth depends on the prevailing prices, which are not uniquely determined by the exogenous description of the economy.

The Harsanyi and Shapley NTU values have been axiomatized by Hart (1985) and Aumann (1985), respectively. Axioms are exact analogues, except that in the Shapley model they refer to payoff profiles, and in Harsanyi model to 2^n-tuples of payoff profiles, one for each of the 2^n coalitions. This underscores the basic difference in outlook between those two concepts: the SV assumes that the grand coalition eventually forms, intermediate coalitions are important only for bargaining talks and threats, whereas the Harsanyi value takes into account a real possibility of intermediate coalitions actually forming (for a recent survey on NTU values see McLean, 2002).

The Aumann–Shapley value of non-atomic games*

Aumann and Shapley (1974) extended the SV to games with infinitely many players that are individually insignificant. Their results are both mathematically elegant and rich in economic intuition. To avoid the measure theoretic prerequisite of their study, we present only an overview of this approach by considering a small part of the range of games that they analyse. We follow here the presentation given by Myerson (1991, 442, 443)

Let H be a finite set which represents the set of classes of players, and suppose that there are infinitely many players of each class. Here we describe coalitions by the fraction of the players of each class who belong to the coalition. So we say that $r = (r_h)_{h \in H}$ is a 'fractional coalition' if r is in the closed interval $[0, 1]^H$, where each component r_h is interpreted as the fraction of all class-h players who are in the coalition. If we view this infinite player model as an approximation of a very large finite player game, then we can also interpret r_h as the number of class-h players in the coalition divided by the total number of class-h players in the game. Thus an *infinite* game in coalitional form can be formalized by a function $v: [0, 1]^H \to \mathbb{R}$, where, for each r in $[0, 1]^H$, $v(r)$ denotes the worth of a fractional coalition r in the game. We pose the following assumptions:

- $v(\mathbf{0}) = 0$, where $\mathbf{0} = (0, \ldots, 0)$
- v is continuous on $[0, 1]^H$
- for each $h \in H$, $v'_h(r) \geq 0$ and continuous at every r such that $r_h > 0$.

The set $\{\alpha \mathbf{1} : 0 < \alpha < 1\}$ is called the main diagonal of the set $[0, 1]^H$, with $\mathbf{1} = (1, \ldots, 1)$. In a large finite game, when the players form coalitions according to the model of randomly ordered entry described previously, the set of players who precede any specific player should be, with high probability, a statistically large sample randomly drawn from the overall population. Here we apply the statistical principle from which the statistical properties of a sample depends on the size of the sample but not on the size of the population.

Thus, by the law of large numbers, the relative numbers of the various classes in the sample that precedes the player should, with very high probability, be very close to the game as the relative numbers of these classes in the set of all players in the game. In other words, the fractional coalition that precedes any given player in the formation process of the coalition is very likely to be close to the main diagonal, where the game is large. When a class-h player enters a fractional coalition r, her (or his) marginal contribution is proportional to $v'_h(r)$. Because the coalition that precedes any player is almost surely on the main diagonal in large games but might be drawn from anywhere on this diagonal according to the uniform distribution, the value of the class-h player in the game should be:

$$\int_0^1 v'_h(\alpha \mathbf{1}) d\alpha$$

Actually this expression should be interpreted not as the value of a single class-h player but as the total value or sum of the values of all class-h players in the game. By symmetry, each class-h player must get an equal share of this value. That is, if the infinite game is an approximation to some large finite game in which there are N players of each class, then the value of each class-h player in the large finite game should be approximately equal to:

$$\phi_h(v) = \frac{1}{N} \int_0^1 v'_h(\alpha \mathbf{1}) d\alpha$$

We can say that v is 1-homogeneous if, for every r in $[0, 1]^H$ and every α in $[0, 1]$, $v(\alpha r) = \alpha v(r)$, so the worth of a coalition is proportional to its size (when the ratios between the numbers of different classes of players are kept constant). If v is 1-homogeneous, then its partial derivatives are constant along the main diagonal. Thus, if v is 1-homogeneous, then the value of the class-h players is just $v'_h(1)$, i.e. their marginal contribution in the grand coalition.

The main argument underlying this approach is called the 'diagonal principle': roughly speaking it asserts that the Aumann–Shapley value is determined by those coalitions S which are close in composition to the whole population (i.e. the proportion of each type of player in S is almost the same as in the grand coalition).

Remark

In this game with infinitely many players, an allocation $x \in \mathbb{R}^H$ is in the core if and only if

$$\sum_{h \in H} r_h x_h \geq v(r)$$

for every r in $[0, 1]^H$. If we accept the additional assumption that v is concave, then it can be shown that this value allocation is also the unique point in the core of the game. It follows that there is a wide and important class of games with infinitely many players in which the core and the value coincide. More generally (notably, if the utilities are not smooth), the SV of large games lies approximately in the core. (for a survey on this topics see Neyman, 2002).∎

6.4 Endogenous coalition structures and formation of coalitions

In this section we leave the classical cooperative setting in which the analysis of coalitions is generally conducted, in order to study the formation of coalitions in a mixed framework of both cooperative and non-cooperative games. First, generalities about endogenous coalition structures are displayed, and then we focus on non-cooperative games of coalition formation with externalities, because in many fields of economics where coalition formation is an important topic externalities between coalitions play a leading role.

6.4.1 Endogenous coalition structures: generalities*

The three basic questions of endogenous formation of coalitions were clearly posed by Von Neumann and Morgenstern themselves: the purpose of game theory is to 'determine everything that can be said about coalitions between players, compensations between partners in every coalition, mergers or fights between coalitions' (Von Neumann and Morgenstern, 1944, 240). In other words the questions are: which coalitions will be formed? How will the coalitional worth be divided among coalition members? How does the presence of other coalitions affect the incentive to cooperate? Traditional cooperative games focus mostly on the second question. Even the bargaining set, which was introduced to study the formation of coalitions, assumes an exogenous coalition structure. The third question, dealing with competition between coalitions, is outside the framework of traditional cooperative game theory, since coalitional games cannot introduce externalities among coalitions.

Aumann and Drèze (1974) were among the first to investigate explicitly solution concepts for coalition structures in the framework of TU games; so they laid the foundations of this important research programme on endogenous formation of coalitions.

The agenda of this programme is normally composed of three elements (Kurz, 1988, 156):

(i) One first defines an extension of the game (N, v) to a game with coalition structure $\beta = (B_1, B_2, \ldots, B_n)$. This requires the specification of restrictions on payoff vectors and the set of coalitions that are allowed to form. Such games will be identified by the notation (N, v, β).

(ii) Having defined the extension of (N, v), one then extends the solution concepts of cooperative game theory to the game (N, v, β).

(iii) Finally, one studies the stability of coalition structure. To this end, one needs to specify a 'coalition formation game' and then define the stable structures to be the solution of that game.

Aumann and Drèze (1974) carried out the first two items of the agenda with respect to the six common solution concepts: the core, stable sets, BS, kernel, NL and SV. Most of the subsequent research on coalitional structures focused on the study of the core and the SV for games with coalitional structures.

Yet, before defining these concept solutions, we can discuss what is a 'feasible' payoff for a given coalition structure. Aumann and Drèze (1974) suggested that the set of feasible payoffs for a coalition structure β be given by:

$$X(\beta) = \left\{ x \in \mathbb{R}^n \colon \forall B_k,\, B_k \in \beta,\, \sum_{i \in B_k} x_i \le v(B_k) \right\}$$

that is, each coalition should distribute among its members the total payoff accruing to that coalition. Thus the major novel assumption introduced by the coalition structure β lies in the condition:

$$x(B_k) = v(B_k)$$

This restriction implies that each coalition is in autarky. In particular, no transfer among coalitions are allowed. Although this feasibility restriction might have some unappealing consequences, most studies on coalition structures adopt it.

Why do coalitions form?

Among the very first questions that come to mind when studying coalition structures is the following one: why do individuals form intermediate coalitions rather than the grand coalition?

Aumann and Drèze (1974) provide several reasons for the existence of social environments that give rise to games that are not superadditive. The first and most straightforward reason is the possible 'inherent' inefficiency of the grand coalition: 'Acting together may be difficult, costly, or illegal, or the players may, for various "personal" reasons, not wish to do so' (Aumann and Drèze, 1974, 233). A second source of subadditivity is related to 'moral hazard': the difficulty in observing players' performance might induce them to exert efforts which lead to suboptimal outcomes. Normative considerations can also explain why an initially superadditive game might become a subadditive game (for example, taking the social norm of 'equal treatment' or 'non-discrimination' into account).

Owen (1977) and Hart and Kurz (1983) offer a quite different reason for coalitions to form. They assume that the game is superadditive and that society operates efficiently. It follows that it is the grand coalition that will actually and eventually form. In their framework, the formation of coalitions is thus a strategic action that players use in order to increase their share of the total social 'pie'. Coalitions must be imagined as tools of bargaining at the players' disposal.

Value of a coalition structure

Aumann and Drèze (1974) defined the notion of SV for a given coalition structure β (or *the β-value*) by extending axioms that define the SV for the grand coalition N in a rather natural way.

Given N and β, the β-value is a function Φ_β defined on the set of all games with a finite 'carrier' N, that satisfies the following axioms:

A1 Relative efficiency:

$$(\Phi_\beta v)(B_k) = v(B_k), \ B_k \in \beta, \text{ for all } k$$

A2 Symmetry:
For all permutations π of N under which β is invariant:

$$(\Phi_\beta(\pi v))(S) = (\Phi_\beta v)(\pi S)$$

A3 Additivity:

$$\Phi_\beta(v + w) = \Phi_\beta v + \Phi_\beta w$$

A4   Null player condition:
If player i is a 'null' player, then:

$$(\Phi_\beta v)(i) = 0$$

Remark that when $\beta = \{N\}$, then $\Phi_\beta(v) = \Phi(v)$; i.e. the β-value is the SV (for simplicity, we denote $\Phi(N, v) = \Phi(v)$).

If for each $S \subset N$, we denote by $v|S$ the game on S defined for all $T \subset S$ by $(v|S)(T) = v(T)$, then we can prove the following result.

Theorem 7 (Aumann and Drèze)

For N and $\beta = (B_1, B_2, \ldots, B_m)$ fixed, there is a unique Aumann–Drèze value (or β-value), given for all $k = 1, \ldots, n$ and all $i \in B_k$ by:

$$(\Phi_\beta v)(i) = \Phi(v|B_k)(i)\blacksquare$$

This result asserts that the restriction to B_k of the value Φ_β for the game (N, v) is the SV Φ for the game $(B_k, v|B_k)$. In other words, the value of a game with a coalition structure has the 'restriction property': the restriction of the value is the value of the restriction of the game. This property is important since it means we can compute Φ_β by computing $\Phi(v|B_k)$ separately for each k. Indeed, the Aumann–Drèze value is easy to compute. Yet, because of Axiom 1 (Relative efficiency) the payoff to any player does not depend upon her (or his) contribution to any coalition outside the coalition to which she (or he) belongs. It follows that if real coalition bargaining is to be an important factor in the value of a coalition structure, then Axiom 1 is not likely to be satisfied in many situations.

Owen (1977), and later Hart and Kurz (1983), proposed another value for games with coalition structures which in fact is based on a modification of Axiom 1. According to the authors a 'coalition structure value' (or *CS value*) is an operator Φ that assigns to every game v with a finite carrier, every coalition structure β, and every player i, a real number $\Phi_i(v, \beta)$. Equivalently, we may imagine $\Phi(v, \beta)$ as an additive measure defined by:

$$\Phi(v, \beta)(S) = \sum_{i \in S} \Phi_i(v, \beta), \text{ for all } S$$

The following axioms on Φ are assumed to hold for all games v and v' and all coalition structures β and β':

A1   Carrier:
Let N be a carrier of v. Then:

(i) $\Phi(v, \beta)(N) \equiv \sum_{i \in N} \Phi_i(v, \beta) = v(N)$

(ii) If $\beta_N = \beta'_N$, then $\Phi(v, \beta) = \Phi(v, \beta')$

This axiom actually contains three parts. If i is a null player in a game, then her (or his) value is 0 in all coalition structures. Moreover, if such a player 'moves' from one coalition to another, it does not affect anyone's values. Last, for all coalition structures the value is efficient. Note that the efficiency of the CS value is an essential feature, it differs from the β-value, where each coalition gets only its worth. This difference arises from the quite different reasons for coalitions to form in Aumann–Drèze and Hart and Kurz models.

A2 *Symmetry*:
Let π be a permutation of the players. Then:

$\Phi(\pi v, \pi \beta) = \pi \Phi(v, \beta)$

A3 *Additivity*:

$\Phi(v + v', \beta) = \Phi(v, \beta) + \Phi(v', \beta)$

Given a game v and a coalition structure $\beta = (B_1, B_2, \ldots, B_m)$, we can say that the game among coalitions is 'inessential' if:

$v\left(\bigcup_{k \in K} B_k\right) = \sum_{k \in K} v(B_k)$

for all sub-sets K of $\{1, 2, \ldots, m\}$; that is, v restricted to the field generated by β is additive.

A4 *Inessential games*:
Let v and β be such that the game among coalitions is inessential. Then:

$\Phi(v, \beta)(B_k) = v(B_k)$, for all k

When the game is inessential, each coalition gets only its worth and there is no surplus to be bargained over.

Let N be a finite set of players and β a coalition structure. A complete linear order on N is said to be consistent with β if, for all $k = 1, \ldots, m$ and all $i, j \in B_k$ all elements of N between i and j also belong to B_k. A random order on N consistent with β is a random variable whose values are the orders on N that are consistent with β, all equally probable. For understanding this property we can imagine that players arrive randomly but such that all members of the same coalition do so successively. This is the same as randomly ordering first, the coalitions and then, the members within each coalition.

Theorem 8 (Hart and Kurz)

The unique Hart and Kurz (CS value) $\Phi(v, \beta)$ satisfying Axioms 1–4 is:

$\Phi_i(v, \beta) = E[v(P_i \cup \{i\}) - v(P_i)]$, for all i

where the expectation E is over all random orders on a carrier N of v that are consistent with β, and P_i denotes the random set of predecessors of i.∎

This value summarizes by a unique real number all the probabilities of playing in all the situations, that is in any coalition structure, for each player i. The CS value is related to the SV thanks to the following corollary.

Corollary

For all $B_k \in \beta$: $\Phi(v, \beta)(B_k) = \Phi(v_\beta)(B_k)$
where (v_β, β) is the game v restricted to the field generated by β (i.e. each $B_k \in \beta$ is a 'player'). Moreover:

$\Phi(v, \{N\}) = \Phi(v)$.∎

In the Aumann–Drèze coalition model, members of each coalition B_k bargain only among themselves to divide $v(B_k)$. In the Hart–Kurz coalition model a more subtle two-stage bargaining is imagined. In the first stage, each coalition acts as one unit, and the negotiations among these 'augmented players' determine the worth of the coalitions. The second stage involves the bargaining of the players within each coalition over the pie received in the first stage. An important feature of this model is that in both stages the same solution concept is employed, namely the SV. Hence the CS value enjoys the following 'consistency' property: the bargaining procedure within coalitions may be derived from the one among coalitions. And the payoffs of a coalition are subordinate to the coalition structure itself. This result underlines the specificity of the approach followed by Hart and Kurz (1983) with regard to the Aumann–Drèze (1974) approach, since for these latter authors, the payoff of each coalition is fixed by its value (i.e., is independent of the coalition structure except itself).

This observation provides a hint for the role played by superadditivity in these coalitional games. Recall that Aumann and Drèze (1974) suggest that non-superadditivity is the most compelling explanation for the formation of intermediate coalitions, whereas in Owen, Hart and Kurz's opinion superadditivity is a plausible assumption and coalitions form only for the sake of bargaining, realizing that the grand coalition (i.e. the most efficient partition) will eventually form.

Remark I

In contrast to these models dealing with coalition structures, Myerson (1977) uses 'cooperation structures'. A 'cooperation structure' is a graph whose vertices are identified with the players. A link between two players means that these players can carry on meaningful direct negotiation with each other. Notice that a coalition structure is a special kind of cooperation structure where two members are linked if and only if they are in the same coalition. Yet Aumann and Myerson (1988) give examples of negotiation situations which can be modelled by cooperation structures, but not by coalition structures.

Myerson defined in this new setting an extension of the SV: the 'Myerson value'. Let (N, v) be a coalitional-form game and let L be the set of links between players. We denote by $n \perp m$ the link between players n and m. Let $g(N)$ be the complete graph on the set of players N:

$$g(N) = \{n/m \perp n \in N, m \in N, n \neq m\}$$

We consider G, the set of all graphs on N, and we identify the set of cooperation structures $g = (N, L)$ with G. The relationship between player payoffs and cooperation structures is represented by a solution function Y: $Y: G \rightarrow I\!R^n$ such that:

$$\sum_{i \in S} Y_i(g) = v(s), \forall g \in S, \forall S \in N/g$$

with $N/g = \{i/i$ and j are linked in S by $g, j \in S\}$. Such a function may be defined as an application to the restricted graph (N, v^g) of an usual value concept, v^g being such that:

$$v^g(S) = \sum_{T \in S/g} v(T), \forall S \subseteq N$$

For instance, for any $g = (N, L)$, the SV of the game associated with g, (N, v^g), is a solution of the game (N, v, L). It is named the 'Myerson value' (see Nouweland, 1993, for a survey of games with cooperation structures).■

Stability of coalition structures

As a first step towards a more general stability analysis, it is useful to focus on games in which only a single player is allowed to deviate and the only coalitions which may have a say are the coalitions left and joined by the player.

Individual stability

Formally there exists a variety of *individual stability* concepts depending on which coalitions can object to the player's move. Perhaps the most immediate notion is that of an 'individual stable equilibrium' (ISE) proposed by Greenberg (1977): in an ISE no player can change coalitions in a way that is beneficial to herself (himself) and to all the members of the coalition which she (he) joins. The concept of 'individual stable contractual equilibrium' proposed later by Drèze and Greenberg (1980) is stronger since agreement both from the coalition left and the coalition joined by the player is required. A special case of individual stability also was defined by Yi (1997). A coalition structure verifies 'stand alone stability' if no player is encouraged to leave her (his) coalition to form a 'singleton coalition' with the remaining coalition structure kept unchanged. Existence of individually stable coalition structures can be proved for a large class of games (see in particular Greenberg, 1994).

Remark 2

Stability when only single players contemplate deviations may be linked to alternative institutional arrangements sometimes encountered in the real world. For instance, in the United States, university departments may be viewed as coalitions of professors who are allowed to move when they receive an attractive offer (whatever the potential loss – or gain – faced by the department left by the professor). In contrast, in all countries, soccer teams 'own' their players, who are not allowed to move to another team unless a proper compensation is paid (Greenberg, 1994, 1315).

Furthermore, individual stability of coalition structures is particularly relevant in the analysis of *cartels*: a cartel is stable if and only if firms inside do not find it desirable to exit (*internal stability*) and firms outside do not find it desirable to enter (*external stability*) (the cartel formation game was first studied by d'Aspremont et al. (1983).

Group stability

The most commonly used concept of a *group stability* is directly derived from the cooperative concept of the core: a coalition structure is 'core stable' if there does not exist a group of agents who would obtain a better payoff by forming another coalition.

Consider a coalition structure game (N, v, β) and a sub-set of players $S \subset N$ who wonder if they should form a coalition. This coalition will actually form if each member anticipates a higher payoff in the new coalition structure. So, in order to foresee the formation of coalitions we have to know the factors determining their values. Yet we know that these determining factors are different according to the approach followed.

In the Aumann-Drèze model the value of a coalition depends only on its members. Hence a coalition S will get its worth $v(S)$ whatever the behaviour of the complementary coalition $N \backslash S$. In that framework the 'core of a coalition structure' is a relevant stability concept.

On the other hand, in the Hart–Kurz model, the value of a coalition is no longer independent of the complementary coalition behaviour. And in that framework, we have to distinguish various games of coalition structures, each one being associated with a particular assumption about the reaction of the complementary coalition N/S to S deviation. Now, not only the relevance of the core stability is questionable but also we can wonder about the appropriateness of the classical characteristic function form representation of the game.

Indeed the presence of *externalities* in this framework requires the use of a more general formal representation. We will bring up this issue again in the next sub-section by introducing 'games in partition form', where the worth of a coalition depends on the entire coalition structure.

For analysing stability in an Aumann–Drèze model, we may refer to Shenoy (1979), who proposes a stability criterion in relation to the β-value Φ_β. Let θ denote a solution concept for a game (N, v, β) and denote by $x^\theta = x^\theta(N, v, \beta)$ the vector of players' payoffs under β and θ. Now let (x^θ, β_1) and (y^θ, β_2) be two such pairs. We then define a 'domination relation' by the following statement.

Definition 16

(x^θ, β_1) dominates (y^θ, β_2) if there exists a coalition $S \in \beta_1$ such that: $x_i^\theta > y_i^\theta,\ i \in S.$■

Relative to this domination relation, Shenoy (1979) defines in particular the 'core' as a stability criterion of a pair (x^θ, β) among alternative coalition structures and payoffs (he also defines the 'dynamic solution'). Yet we should emphasize that an important aspect of this construction is that the solution concept θ adopted for the game (N, v, β) for fixed β may be different from the core concept adopted for the game of coalition formation where β is allowed to vary. So, in relation to the Aumann–Drèze value we may identify x^θ with Φ_β.

Given the domination relation among coalition structures, Shenoy introduces the following notion of stability.

Definition 17 (Core stability)

Coalition structure β is said to be 'core stable' if it is undominated by any other coalition structure.■

Remark 3

Almost all game theorists who study the core of a coalition structure implicitly assume that non-emptiness of that core represents a stability result; so they have no need to make use of a core-stability analysis in the Shenoy sense. For instance, the core of a coalition structure was defined by Aumann and Drèze (1974) to be the core of the game (N, v, β); that is the set of all payoff vectors x^c that are undominated subject to $x^c(B^k) = v(B^k)$, for all $B^k \in \beta$. But every coalition S that deviates from β induces a new coalition structure β', so it is clear that if S can block the imputation x^c then β' will dominate β via S. It follows that the core of a coalition structure, when non-empty, is equivalent to the core in the Shenoy sense (Kurz, 1988, 169).■

6.4.2 Non-cooperative games of coalition formation with externalities*

In many fields of economics where coalition formation is an important question, the coalitions formed are smaller than the grand coalition and the externalities between coalitions play a leading role. Think for instance of the following topics: in international trade, the formation of competing customs unions and the question of 'regionalism' in trade; in industrial organization, the formation of cartels and the study of strategic alliance between firms; in environmental economics, international negotiations to control cross-border pollution and the possibility that cooperation will be accepted by only a small group of countries; in local public finance, the study of spillovers and taxation of neighbouring communities for local public goods provided by a large city. An important feature of all these economic applications is that they create *externalities* for non-members. In these settings, the presence of externalities between coalitions and the subadditivity of the coalition game require the use of a more general model than the classical coalitional-form model. The relevant framework are games in 'partition function form' (for a survey of non-cooperative games of coalition formation with externalities see Bloch, 1997, and Ray and Vohra, 1999).

Partition function form-games

The original definition of a partition function-form game was given by Thrall and Lucas (1963). They simply proposed to extend coalitional-form functions by requiring the worth of a coalition to be function of *all* the coalitions formed in the game.

Definition 18 (Partition function-form game)

A TU cooperative game is in partition function form if (N, β, v) is specified with: N, the set of players, β the coalition structure and v, the 'partition function' of the game. A partition function is a mapping which associates with each coalition structure β a vector in $\mathbb{R}^{|\beta|}$, representing the worth of all the coalition in β. ∎

Notice that partition function-form games actually are a generalization of coalitional function-form games. If the worth of a coalition is independent of the coalition formed by the other players, the two definitions are the same. Otherwise, a game in partition function form carries more information about the underlying situation.

Yet 'the theory of games in partition function form raises substantial technical difficulties' (Aumann and Drèze, 1979). Bloch (1997) summarizes these difficulties in the definition and use of partition functions.

First, partition functions have proved difficult to handle. Secondly, and more importantly, the derivation of partition functions from strategic-form games raises some problems. With more than two coalitions being formed, the classical minimax or bargaining conversions (see section 6.1 of this chapter) are no longer relevant. One needs to answer the question: how do the various coalitions compete with one another?

The most natural way to deal with this question (Ichiishi, 1981; Bloch, 1995; Ray and Vohra, 1997) is to adopt the following assumption.

Assumption: Inside each coalition, players behave *cooperatively* in order to maximize the coalitional surplus, whereas coalitions compete in a *non-cooperative* way.

The partition function is then obtained as a *non-cooperative equilibrium payoff* of the game played by the coalitions. A particular definition, based on the idea of SNE, was initially proposed by Ichiishi (1981). He called this concept 'social coalition equilibrium'.

Definition 19 (*Social coalition equilibrium*)

For a fixed coalition structure $\beta = (B_1, B_2, \ldots, B_m)$, let x^* be a vector of strategies such that:

$$\sum_{j \in B_k} u_j(x^*_{B_k}, x^*_{NIB_k}) \geq \sum_{j \in B_k} u_j(x_{B_k}, x^*_{NIB_k}), \ \forall x_{B_k} \in \underset{j \in B_k}{X} X_j, \ \forall B_k \in \beta$$

Then the partition function is defined by:

$$v(B_k, \beta) = \sum_{j \in B_k} u_j(x^*)$$

and x^* is the social coalition equilibrium (SCE) of the game. ∎

Two particular cases are studied by Ichiishi: the first corresponds to singletons coalition structures where the SCE is just a NE; the second amounts to a NTU coalitional-form cooperative game with the grand coalition as coalition structure, and where the set of SCE is the core.

This approach is more satisfactory than the classical conversions based on *ad hoc* assumptions about the behaviour of the complementary coalition. Yet it also raises new difficulties. In particular, if the equilibrium of the game played by coalitions is not unique, the partition function is not well defined.

According to Bloch (1997), a third difficulty of models of games in partition function form is linked to the interpretation of TU. By definition utility is supposed to be transferable inside each coalition but not across coalitions. This lack of transferability of utility across coalitions then needs to be justified on either institutional or conceptual grounds.

The classical properties on coalitional functions can be extended to the partition function.

Definition 20 (*Superadditivity, monotonicity*)

A partition function v is *superadditive* if and only if for any coalition structure β and two coalitions A and B in β:

$$v(A \cup B, \beta \setminus \{A, B\} \cup \{A \cup B\}) \geq v(A, \beta) + v(B, \beta)$$

The coalition structure formed by players in $N \setminus (A \cup B)$ has to remain constant. A partition function v is *monotonic* if for any two coalitions A and $B \subset A$, for any partition β containing A and any partition β' containing B such that β and β' coincide on $N \setminus A$:

$$v(A, \beta) \geq v(B, \beta'). \blacksquare$$

It can be proved that if v is superadditive, then it is monotonic.

On the other hand, one may notice that the monotonicity of partition functions implies that the grand coalition is always an efficient coalition structure. It follows that, in any game of coalition formation, the formation of a fragmented coalition structure is an inefficient outcome.

The new property of positive or negative externalities also can be defined in this class of coalition games In particular, the effect of the formation of a coalition on external players must be precisely described.

Definition 21 (*Positive or negative externalities*)

A partition function v exhibits positive (negative) externalities if, for any partition v, and any two coalitions A and B in β:

$$v(C, \beta \setminus \{A, B\} \cup \{A \cup B\}) \geq (\leq) v(C, \beta), \text{ for any coalition } C \neq A, B \text{ in } \beta. \blacksquare$$

Valuations

The presence of externalities among coalitions implies that players must take into account the non-members' reactions when they decide to form a coalition to increase their payoffs. However, in order to make the analysis more tractable and to concentrate on the role played by externalities in the formation of the coalition structure, most economic applications do not model the allocation of the coalition surplus among members of a coalition. They rather assume that the coalition worth is distributed according to an *exogenous* sharing rule which specifies the distribution of payoffs corresponding to each pattern of cooperation. The gains from cooperation are then represented by a 'valuation'.

In contrast to a partition function, a *valuation* maps coalition structures into vectors of *individual* payoffs instead of vectors of coalitions' worth. The term 'valuation' means that each player is able to evaluate directly her (his) payoff in different coalition structures (the term 'per-member' payoff is sometimes used rather than 'valuation' (see Yi, 1997).

Definition 22 (*Valuation*)

A valuation v is a mapping which associates with each coalition structure β a vector of individual payoffs in $\mathbb{R}^n$. ∎

The use of a valuation to describe gains from cooperation amounts to deflecting the original problem of coalition analysis: the share of the coalition surplus among coalition members. We should be aware that it is a very restrictive assumption. On the other hand, this restrictive formulation allows us to focus analysis on the role of externalities between coalitions.

It should be noticed that superadditivity and monotonicity are not necessarily verified by valuations. The reasoning that claims that players necessarily get higher payoffs in the coalition $A \cup B$ than in each separate coalition A and B does not hold. It follows that a player might obtain a lower payoff in a coalition rather than in some sub-set of that coalition. Hence, in a coalitional game described by a valuation, the grand coalition is not necessarily efficient and the game of endogenous coalition formation might give birth to a fragmented coalition structure. In this setting, of course, the lack of superadditivity of valuations is a direct consequence of the existence of a fixed sharing rule inside coalitions.

Stability of coalition structures in games with valuations

Shenoy (1979) and Hart and Kurz (1983) were the first to propose games of coalition formation with a valuation function in order to identify stable coalition structures. Aumann and Myerson (1988) also use this structure for games with 'cooperation structures' rather than coalition structures (see Remark 1 in subsection 6.4.1 for a definition of this notion). But the valuations employed by these authors differ: Shenoy considers the Aumann–Drèze value Φ_β, Hart and Kurz adopt the CS-value $\Phi(N, \beta)$ and Aumann and Myerson use the Myerson value.

We will discuss mainly in this sub-section *simultaneous* games of coalition formation, i.e. games in which all players announce at the same time their wish to form coalitions. In such games, it turn out that there is a multiplicity of NE, so that the use of some refinements is necessary to isolate the most likely among them. But these refinements have usually a cooperative nature since they imply correlated strategies by players inside the same coalition. Hence, 'the study of simultaneous games of coalition formation is at the frontier between cooperative and non-cooperative game theory' (Bloch, 1997).

These games can be separated into two types (Yi and Shin, 1995): 'open membership' games and 'exclusive membership' games.

In open membership games, players are supposed to be free to join or leave any coalition. Accordingly they cannot specify beforehand the coalition they want to form. In Yi and Shin's (1995) model, players announce a message (i.e. her (or his) strategy) and coalitions are formed by all players who have announced the same message (for instance, their wish to participate in a coalition).

Let m_i be the message chosen by player i in the message space X, then coalitions are defined by:

$$S(m) = \{i \in N \backslash m_i = m\}, \text{ for all } m \in X$$

And the coalition structure is given by:

$$\beta = \{S(m) \backslash S(m) \neq \varnothing, \text{ for all } m\},$$

with each player getting a payoff $v_i(\{S(m)\})$.

In this model, since entry into a coalition is free, one obtains easily a rather mild monotonicity requirement under which the only NE outcome of the game is the grand coalition.

In exclusive membership games outsiders are not free to join any coalition. The composition of coalitions is supposed to be announced in advance and only those coalitions which are announced can be formed. Two situations are precisely analysed in that setting by Hart and Kurz (1983): either the formation of a coalition requires a unanimous agreement among all its members (this is the case in game Γ), or coalitions are formed as soon as only some of their members agree to join (this is the case in game Δ). In both game, NE are multiple and refinements need to be imposed.

In game Γ, the message space (i.e. the strategy space) of any player i is the set of all coalitions to which she (he) belongs:

$$X_i = \{S \subset N, i \in S\}$$

A coalition S is formed if and only if all members i of S have chosen $x_i = S$. Intuitively, membership is exclusive in that game because all members announce in advance the set of potential coalition members. One problem is: what happens to those coalitions when one or more players depart? Do they 'fall apart' or do they still 'stick together'? The definition of the game Γ implies that, whenever a member leaves a coalition, the coalition breaks down, and the rest of the members become singletons.

In game Δ, a player's strategy space is the same as in game Γ, but the outcome function is different. Coalitions are formed by players who have announced the same coalition, even if not approved unanimously by all its members. For any possible message (i.e. coalition) m, let $S(m) = \{i \backslash x_i = m\}$ represent the coalition formed by players who have announced m. In open membership games messages are used as coordination devices by players. In game Δ, messages play an identical role. Yet, in this setting, they also carry an important restriction on the coalitions that can be formed: only those coalitions announced by the players are feasible. Again, in game Δ, membership is exclusive because players announce in advance the list of coalition members. However, the participation of *all* listed members is not necessary for a coalition to form. This definition implies that, in contrast to game Γ, the fact that a (small) number of players leaves a coalition does not influence the other players' agreement to act together. As in the open membership games, whenever a member departs from a coalition, all other coalition members remain together and form a new coalition.

It is easy to understand that in both games Γ and Δ the trivial coalition structure with singletons is a NE outcome: if all other players announce singletons, it is a best response for each player also to announce a singleton. Hart and Kurz (1983) propose to adopt SNE in order to refine the set of NE.

Definition 23 (γ-stability and δ–stability)

The coalition structure β is γ-stable (δ-stable) in the game (v, N) if the vector of strategies $(S_1, S_2, \ldots, S_n)$ is a SNE in game Γ (Δ, respectively).∎

Do stable coalition structures always exist? Hart and Kurz (1983) prove only, by a counterexample, that a SNE may fail to exist. Yi and Shin (1995) use the less strong notion of CPNE rather than SNE. But they do not prove any general result. In their original study, Hart and Kurz (1983) also suggest broadening the definition of stability and using cooperative concepts: for example, using the *core* concept instead of the *strong equilibrium*.

A coalition structure will be stable if no group of players can *certainly* become better off by transforming the partition. Two new concepts of stability may be defined, depending upon the meaning of 'certainly'. In one case, its means 'not to be prevented from'; in the other 'to guarantee'. Indeed these notions correspond to the α-core and the β-core defined initially by Aumann (1967) in the traditional cooperative GT.

In an 'α-stable' coalition structure, we assume that there does not exist a group of players who could get a higher payoff irrespective of the behaviour of external players. In a 'β-stable' coalition structure, there is no group of players who are assured of getting higher payoff whatever the external players' behavior. The formal definitions given below are borrowed from Bloch (1997).

Definition 24 (α-stability and β-stability)

A coalition structure β is α-stable if there does not exist a group S of players and a partition β_S' of S such that, for all partitions $\beta_{N\setminus S}$ formed by external players:

$$v_i(\beta_s' \cup \beta_{N\setminus S}) > v_i(\beta), \quad \text{for all } i \in S$$

A coalition structure is β-stable if there does not exist a group S of players such that for all partition $\beta_{N\setminus S}$ of external players, there exists a partition β_S of S such that:

$$v_i(\beta_S \cup \beta_{N-S}) > v_i(\beta), \quad \text{for all } i \in S \blacksquare$$

It is clear from the definition that deviations occur more frequently under β-stability than under α-stability: β-stability implies α-stability.

In order to compare this with γ- and δ-stability, it should be noticed that if a coalition structure is *not* β-stable, there exists a group of players S who cannot be prevented from getting better off, despite anything the rest do. Since in the definition of γ- and δ-stability, it is assumed that the complement of S does not change its strategies, it follows that β-stability is implied both by γ-stability and by δ-stability (Hart and Kurz, 1983).

For a given game (N, v), let β_α, β_β, β_γ and β_δ denote the set of all α-, β-, γ- and δ-(respectively) stable coalition structures. Then, for every game:

$$(\beta_\gamma \cup \beta_\delta) \subset \beta_\beta \subset \beta_\alpha$$

The notions of α- and β-stability may be useful whenever the players are 'careful', that is whenever they take into account the possible reactions of the others, when deciding upon a change in the coalition structure. Unfortunately, even for the largest solution concept (the α-stability), the α-stable coalition structure β_α may be empty (Hart and Kurz, 1984).

Remark 1

The analysis of endogenous formation of coalitions in simultaneous games presents several weaknesses. First, the set of NE is usually very large, and this property requires the use of refinements which might be too stringent. Secondly, and more importantly, in this setting, the individual deviations cannot be countered by subsequent decisions since members of coalition left by the deviator react in an *ad hoc* way: to remain together or to break apart. In context of *sequential* games, these difficulties weaken thanks to an explicit analysis of foresighted players' behaviour, who take into account the ultimate consequences of their choices. Sequential processes have initially been proposed in coalitional games *without externalities* (Selten, 1981; Chatterjee *et al.*, 1993; Perry and Reny, 1994, among others). The basic structure is an extension to *n* players of Rubinstein's (1982) alternative-offers bargaining model (see Section 5.1, Chapter 5). This framework was extended to coalitional games *with externalities* by Bloch (1996).

Bloch (1996) studies an infinite-horizon sequential game of coalition formation when the underlying cooperation structure is represented by a valuation (i. e. there is an exogenously fixed sharing rule of surplus inside coalitions). This model must be interpreted as a 'coalition unanimity' game, since a coalition is supposed to form if and only if all potential members agree to form the coalition. Its main characteristics are twofold. First, an exogenous rule of order imposes a fixed order of moves by players. Secondly, once a coalition has been formed, the game is played only among the remaining players. Thus a high degree of commitment by the players is assumed: when agreeing to join a coalition, players are bound to remain is that coalition. In order to restrict the set of SPE (multiplicity of equilibria is a classical property of this bargaining game), 'stationary' strategies (which depend only on the current state of the game) are considered. A first result is that a stationary SPE may fail to exist. And even when existence is proved, stationary SPE of the sequential game differ in general from the SNE of the simultaneous game. However, there exists a specific class of valuations for which stationary SPE exist and are easily characterized: when valuations are *symmetric*, i.e. when the value of a coalition structure depends only on the size of coalition and not on the identity of coalition members (all players are *ex ante* identical).■

Remark 2

Ray and Vohra (1996) were the first to introduce an *endogenous* distribution of coalition gains in the context of coalitional games with externalities. Their study represents a very important step in the analysis of endogenous coalition formation since they tackle simultaneously the three questions underlying this problem. The setting is a TU partition function game rather than a valuation. In their bargaining game, players simultaneously are supposed to announce a coalition *and the division of the coalition worth*. They prove the existence of a stationary SPE in mixed strategies, but an important feature is that players need only to play a mixed strategy when they choose *coalitions* and not when they propose a division of the coalition worth. Furthermore, they show that in symmetric games the assumption of equal sharing of surplus in coalitions can be supported by a non-cooperative bargaining game.■

6.5 Applications

6.5.1 Cost sharing games

N-person cooperative games are the central analytical tools of cooperation by direct negotiation among the parties when the grand coalition of people is no longer the sole possibility. Cost sharing and output sharing problems are two very similar classes of economic problem which can be studied by using n-person cooperative games.

These models of cooperative games are very useful because they allow the study of stable direct agreements in these situations from an axiomatic perspective. Furthermore they provide a unified reduced model for the analysis of all specific resource allocation whose ultimate goal is the allocation of a cost or the division of a surplus. The following presentation deals mainly with the cost allocation problem.

The standard model of cost sharing game

The data of this problem are the total costs to be allocated, the 'objects' to which costs are to be assigned (their identity varies from one situation to the next: projects, products, services,...) and estimation of the costs associated with each sub-set of these cost objects. So, the specification of these data defines a 'cost sharing game' with *cost objects* as 'players' of the game and a *joint costs function* as 'coalitional-form function'.

An important problem in provision of goods and services by a public enterprise or a municipality is the determination of an allocation of the common costs of production. Many facilities such as airports, transit systems, communication networks and reservoirs, are concerned with this common cost allocation problem.

For such enterprises (whether strictly public or publicly regulated) prices must generally be set to exactly cover costs (with possibly a mark-up to cover the costs of capital). Yet, because of declining average costs in these industries, the marginal cost pricing – the economic 'ideal' pricing – does not fit this goal, except in very special cases.

When demands for the service are known, the well-known Ramsey–Boiteux pricing (or average cost pricing), or the Feldstein pricing (taking into account distributional equity) are interesting methods for the common cost allocation problem. Otherwise, we must develop a general cost allocation method with only cost data.

Many of the salient features of cost allocation in this framework can be captured in the following simple model.

Let N be a set of n potential customers of a public facility or a public service. Each of them will either be served at some target level or not served at all (for instance, a customer $i \in N$ will either get a telephone or not , she (he) will hook up to the local water supply or not). The problem is: how much should be charged for the service, based on the costs of providing it?

For each potential sub-group of customers $S \subset N$, the joint cost is summarized by a 'joint cost function' $c(S) \in \mathbb{R}$, with the convention that the cost of serving no one is zero: $c(\Phi) = 0$. $c(S)$ represents the lowest cost of serving the customers in S in the most efficient way. A 'cost allocation method' is then a function ϕ defined for all N and all c on N such that:

$$\phi(N, c) = (x_1, \ldots, x_i, \ldots, x_n) \in \mathbb{R} \text{ and } \sum_{i=1}^{n} x_i = c(n)$$

where x_i represents the charge assessed to customer i.

One of the most known examples of joint cost allocation is provided by the 'multipurpose reservoir' problem (the discussion is based on Young (1991, Chapter 1, and 1994).

The 'multipurpose reservoir' problem

Suppose that a dam on a river is planned to serve several regional interests: for instance, flood control, navigation, irrigation, hydroelectric power and municipal water supply. The height of the dam is supposed to depend mainly on which purposes are to be included in the project. For such a problem the cost function exhibits first decreasing marginal costs per acre-foot of water impounded and, from some critical height of the dam, marginal costs increase because of technological limitations.

The common cost-benefit analysis of such a project consists, first, in deciding whether the project should be undertaken at all, and if so on what scale. Then, the second question is how to apportion the costs of the optimal-scale enterprise among the different purposes. In practice, however, information about the demand for jointly produced services is unavailable (or subject to very large evaluation errors). Thus the approach consists in focusing the analysis on 'target levels' of the planning variables (supposed approximately optimal) and looking for a 'point' estimation of costs for each objective. The unique problem is: how should costs be allocated among the different objectives? More precisely, the problem is: how should costs be apportioned among the different purposes?

This water resource planning problem was first analytically studied in the 1930s on the occasion of the creation of the Tennessee Valley Authority (TVA). The TVA was an ambitious redevelopment project undertaken by the US federal government for planning the Tennessee River Basin through a series of multipurpose reservoirs. The ideas developed by the economists who were commissioned to analyse the costs and benefits of this project have since become standard principles in assessment of the cost of public works projects when demand is unknown.

In a first step they determined the target levels at which the three main aspects of the project: navigation (n), flood control (f), and power generation (p), should be provided.

In a second step, they evaluated the lowest cost of building a dam that would meet the different targets. More precisely, for each combination S of the three objectives $\{n, f, p\}$ they estimated the stand alone cost $c(S)$ of fulfilling those objectives at the targeted levels: $c(n)$, $c(f)$, $c(p)$, $c(n, f)$, $c(n, p), \ldots$ Figure 6.2 reproduces the 'joint cost function' estimated by the TVA (Ransmeier, 1942).

With the previous notations, the 'stand alone cost' condition is:

$$\sum_{i \in S} x_i \leq c(S) \text{ for all } S, S \subset N \tag{6.6}$$

Its rationale is straightforward: because cooperation among the parties has to be voluntary, rationality requires that no group of participants (including each participant herself (or himself)) be charged more than their 'stand alone' costs (i.e. their 'opportunity cost'); otherwise nobody would have an incentive to agree with the allocation $\phi(c) = (x_1, \ldots, x_i, \ldots x_n)$.

Yet there exists an equivalent formulation of this condition with a different justification when we impose the full cost allocation: $\sum_{i \in N} x_i = c(N)$. Whereas the stand alone condition reflects the existence of incentives for voluntary cooperation, the 'no subsidizing cost' (or 'incremental cost') test arises from the introduction of equity considerations:

$$\sum_{i \in S} x_i \geq c(N) - c(N \backslash S), \text{ for all } S, S \subset N \tag{6.7}$$

Figure 6.2   TVA cost data

Services (S)	ϕ	{n}	{f}	{p}	{nf}	{np}	{fp}	{nfp}
Cost (c) $000	0	163,520	140,826	250,096	301,607	378,821	367,370	412,584

This related condition states that no participant should be charged less than the incremental cost of including her (or him) with $c(N) - c(N\backslash S)$, defined as the incremental cost of any coalition S. For instance, in the TVA water resource planning problem (Figure 6.2), the cost of including n at the margin is:

$$c(\{nfp\}) - c(\{fp\}) = 412,584 - 367,370 = 45,214$$

If (6.7) is not verified, then we can say that coalition $N\backslash S$ is 'subsidizing' S.

The core of c is the set of allocations $x \in \mathbb{R}^n$ such that condition (6.6) (or equivalently condition (6.7)) holds for all coalitions S. But the core may be empty, even if c is 'subadditive'; the subadditivity condition is similar to the classical superadditivity condition in games where the focus is on the 'gains' rather that on the costs each coalition can realize.

Figure 6.3 gives an illustration of the core of the TVA cost game.

The top vertex x_n represents the case where all costs are allocated to navigation (n); the left-hand vertex x_f the situation where all costs are allocated to flood control (f), and so on. Note that the core is fairly large, because of rapidly decreasing marginal costs of building higher dams.

In order to illustrate other possibilities, let us follow Young (1994, 1204) and suppose that in the TVA cost game the total costs c ($\{nfp\}$) increase to 515,000 owing to a cost overrun, whereas the other costs are invariant. Figure 6.4 illustrates the core of this modified TVA cost game.

Figure 6.3   The core and the Shapley value of the TVA cost game

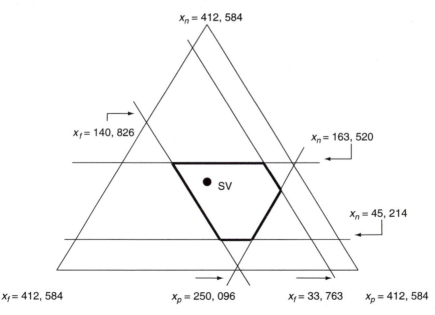

Figure 6.4   The core and the Shapley value of the modified TVA cost game (enlarged)

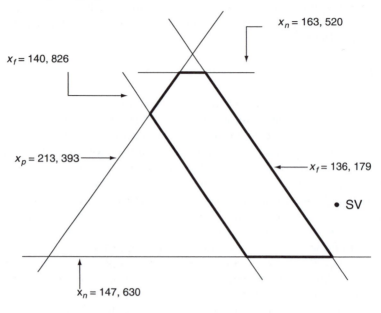

$x_n = 163, 520$

$x_f = 140, 826$

$x_p = 213, 393$

$x_f = 136, 179$

• SV

$x_n = 147, 630$

The civil engineers who suggested allocations of joint costs for the TVA system asserted that the method was not based on any one mathematical formula, but on 'judgement'. Nevertheless, according to Ransmeier (1942, 270–5), these engineers did in fact use a method called the 'alternative justifiable expenditure method'. After further refinements, it has become the main reference method used to allocate the costs of multipurpose reservoirs, known as the 'separable costs remaining benefits method'. But the use of the SV formula also gives near-identical allocations.

For each agent i, the expected cost assessment is given by the formula:

$$\phi_i(c) = \sum_{\substack{S \subseteq N \\ i \in S}} \frac{|s-1|! |N \backslash S|!}{|N|!} (c_i(S) - c_i(S \backslash \{i\}))$$

when $c_c(S)$ is the marginal cost of i relative to S, and the sum is over all sub-sets containing i.

In the TVA cost game, the SV is then:

$$\phi = (117, 829; 100, 756.5; 193, 998.5)$$

which is inside the core (cf. Figure 6.3). However, there are perfectly plausible situations where the cost function has a non-empty core and the SV fails to be in it. For the modified TVA cost game, for instance, the SV is:

$$\phi = (151,\ 967.667; 134,\ 895.167; 228,\ 131.167)$$

This allocation is not inside the core because the total costs for navigation (n) and power generation (p) exceed the stand alone cost:

$$x_n + x_p = 380,\ 098.834 > 378,\ 821 = c(\{np\})$$

If we consider that the core conditions are very important (for instance, as in public utility pricing), then the NL (or the pre-nucleolus) seems better than the SV for solving the cost sharing game. Recall that the NL selects an allocation that makes the least-well-off coalition as well-off as possible, with 'well-off' meaning larger 'excess of the coalition relative to that allocation':

$$e(x,\ S) = c(S) - \sum_{i \in S} x_i$$

The allocation x^* that minimizes the maximum excess $e(x,\ S)$ over all proper sub-sets are found as solutions of the following linear programming problem:

$$\begin{cases} \max \varepsilon \\ e(x, S) \geq S, \forall S \subset N \\ \sum_{i \in N} x_i = c(N) \end{cases} \tag{6.8}$$

If there is a unique solution x^* to (6.8), this is the 'maximin' allocation of c. If not, the following tie-breaking rule may be used: order the excess $e(x, S)$ from lowest to highest, and denote this 2^n-vector by $\theta(x)$. We know that the NL is the vector x that maximizes lexicographically $\theta(x)$.

The NL is inside the core by definition since the idea is to find a solution in the core that is 'central' in the sense of being as far away from the boundaries as possible. For the modified TVA cost game the NL is:

$$(x_n = 155,\ 367.2,\ x_f = 138,\ 502.5,\ x_p = 221,\ 130.25)$$

This allocation is drawn in Figure 6.5.

Remark

Many concepts introduced for discrete cost functions carry over to the *continuous* case. The quantities to be produced q^* is given exogenously and

Figure 6.5 NL (N) for the modified TVA game

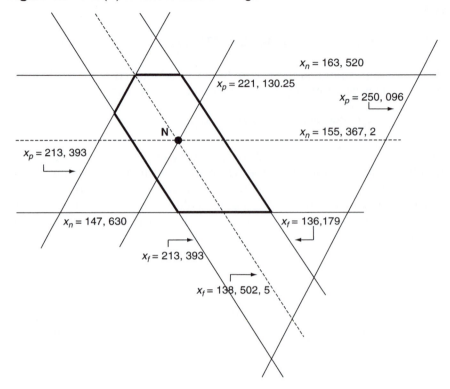

the goal is to allocate the cost $C(q^*)$ among n products. A cost allocation method is a function $f(C, q^*) = p$ where p is a non-negative vector of prices satisfying $\sum p_i q_i^* = C(q^*)$. Under suitable assumptions, one proves that there exists a unique cost allocation method f such that:

$$p_i = f_i(C, q^*) = \int_0^1 (\partial C(tq^*)/\partial q_i)dt$$

In other words, the price of each product is its marginal cost *averaged* over all vectors $tq^*: 0 \le t \le 1$, that define the ray from O to q^*. These prices are called Aumann–Shapley prices and are based on the Aumann–Shapley value for non-atomic games (see sub-section 6.3.3). A lot of economic applications use the Aumann–Shapley method. Among the first classical applications described in the literature, Billera, Heath and Ranaan (1978) explain how this method was used to price telephone calls at Cornell University. For an introduction to this class of games, see Billera and Heath (1982), Mirman and Tauman (1982).■

6.5.2 Environmental coalitions

This sub-section presents an economic application of games with endogenous formation of coalitions borrowed from environmental economics.

It turns out that most economic situations where the role of coalitions is an important topic can be classified into two classes: games with negative or positive externalities (or spillovers) (see Yi, 1997, for this distinction).

In games with *negative* externalities the formation of a coalition decreases the payoffs for agents who are not members of the coalition, while in games with *positive* externalities the formation of a coalition by other players increases an agent's payoff. Negative spillovers arise naturally in many oligopolistic situations; for instance, the formation by the firms of associations or of research joint ventures, which lead to decreasing production costs and a more aggressive behaviour of the joint firm on the market. Similarly, the formation of customs unions enables firms of member states to benefit from increasing returns to scale and to exploit cost advantages on the world market. On the other hand, the two most studied situations of coalition formation with positive spillovers are the formation of cartels on oligopolistic markets and coalitions providing pure public goods (see Bloch; 1997, for examples of each category of economic applications).

In economics with pure public goods, agents have an incentive to form coalitions in order to benefit from increasing returns to size in the production of public goods. Yet, they also have an incentive to leave the coalition and adopt free-rider behaviour on the provision of public goods by coalition members. We focus here on environmental coalition games inspired by pure good economies.

Games of environmental coalition formation

In many cases, environment quality is a public good. When the dimension of the environment problem is global (the greenhouse effect, the ozone layer, biodiversity, and so on), there is no supranational authority that can enforce the provision of the environment good. Sovereign countries must thus decide voluntarily whether or not to provide the public good and thereby to decide the level of emission abatement. In practice, states negotiate on an international environmental agreement whose goal is to define emission targets for each signatory country and often also the way of achieving these targets. Yet, 'how can we explain that some countries decide to sign the agreement even when they could enjoy the same environmental benefit by letting other countries to abate' (Carraro and Moriconi, 1998)? In other words, when the environment is a public good, why countries do not free-ride?

The literature on international environmental agreements shows that cooperation can emerge, even when each country decides independently, voluntarily and without any form of commitment to cooperate (Chander and Tulkens, 1992; Carraro and Siniscalco, 1993; Barrett, 1994). Games of endogenous coalition formation with positive externalities have been built for proving this general result. In these models, formation of coalitions (i.e. *cooperation*) is the outcome of a *non-cooperative* strategic behaviour of the players involved in the negotiations (a survey of this literature is provided by Barrett, 1997; Carraro, 1997; Carraro and Moriconi, 1998).

The standard game is a two-stage game: in the first stage, countries decide non-cooperatively whether or not to sign the agreement (i.e. to join the coalition) given the burden sharing rule which is accepted by the signatory countries; in the second stage, countries determine their emission levels by maximizing their social welfare function, given the decision taken in the first stage and the burden sharing rule adopted. Indeed, each stage may itself be interpreted as a particular game: a first *non-cooperative* game of coalition formation, called the 'coalition game', and a second game in which the countries which signed the agreement play as a single player and divide the resulting payoff according to a given rule derived from *cooperative* game theory, called the 'emission game'.

The ultimate purpose is to determine the equilibrium coalition structures (or stable coalition structures) of the game and whether at the equilibrium at least one non-trivial coalition emerges. This can be either the grand coalition or, more frequently, a partial coalition. But it is also important to know how the equilibrium coalition structures change when the assumptions put on the negotiation rules are modified.

A very interesting property of this environment game is that, under suitable assumptions, its second stage can be reduced to a partition function and, therefore, the study of coalition formation consists of the analysis of the 'coalition game' only, i.e. the negotiation process between the countries (the remaining sub-section is largely based on Carraro and Moriconi, 1998).

Three assumptions are necessary for justifying the standard simultaneous game:

A1   The 'coalition game', in which all players decide simultaneously, has a unique NE for any coalition structure.
        This assumption is necessary for the second stage of the game to be reduced to a partition function.

A2   Inside each coalition, players act cooperatively for maximizing the coalitional surplus, whereas coalitions or singletons compete with one another in a non-cooperative way.
        This assumption allows us to convert the initial strategic-form game in a partition-form game. The partition function is obtained as a NE payoff of the 'coalitional game'.

A3   All players are *ex ante* identical; that is, we consider *symmetric valuations*, where the payoff received by the players depends only on coalition sizes and not on the identities of the coalition members.

This assumption allows us to simplify the derivation of the partition function: the gains from cooperation in each coalition are represented by a 'valuation'.

In this setting a coalition B_k can be identified with its *size* b_k. A coalition structure can be denoted by $\beta = (b_1, b_2, \ldots, b_k)$, and the valuation function of the game can be denoted by $v(b_k, \beta)$, which represents the payoff of a country belonging to the size-b_k coalition in the coalition structure β.

The coalitional game

For many environmental issues (for instance, in the case of global warming and climate change), countries propose to sign a *single* agreement. Therefore, only *one* coalition can be formed, with the remaining countries playing as singletons. In this setting, the 'coalition game' is simplified. The player strategies consist in a binary choice: joining the coalition or acting as a lone free-rider, and the outcome of the game amounts to a single coalition structure:

$$\beta = \left\{ b, \underbrace{1, \ldots 1,}_{n-b \text{ times}} \right\}$$

For simplicity we will denote

$$\underbrace{1, \ldots, 1}_{n-b \text{ times}} \text{ by } 1_{n-b} \ldots$$

In this model the existence of positive externalities implies that the valuation of any player outside the coalition $v(1, \beta)$ is an increasing function of b. Thus, there is an incentive to free-ride on the coalition action. Actually two different types of *free-riding behaviour* may appear according to the pattern of interdependence among countries, as described by the slope of their best-reply functions in the 'emission game'.

The first case corresponds to *orthogonal* (or near-orthogonal) players' reaction function. This situation is particularly important in environment models because it means that free-riders take advantage of cleaner environment as a result of emission abatement by some countries without expanding their own emissions. In second case, by contrast, players' reaction functions are *negatively sloped*. Free-riders benefit twice from the countries' cooperation by getting a cleaner environment and by increasing their own exploitation of natural resources. When market mechanisms induce a so-called 'leakage' problem, free-riding can lead to decreasing returns from cooperation, in particular for small coalitions.

Notice incidentally that in the case of climate change both situations are possible.

Given these properties of the environment game, its equilibrium can be characterized.

Since players are supposed to be absolutely free to join the coalition or not, their decisions are completely self-interested and an obvious necessary condition for the existence of a coalition is its *profitability*. Each cooperating player must obtain a payoff larger than the one it would get if no coalition forms:

$$v(b, \beta) > v(1_n) \tag{6.9}$$

for all players in the coalition b. The value of the minimal profitable coalition size b_m can be derived from inequality (6.9). It depends on the strategic interaction between the coalition and the singleton players. The *profitability function* $P(b) = v(b, \beta) - v(1_n)$ for the two types of free-riding is drawn in Figure 6.6. Notice that, for non-orthogonal free-riding, $P(b)$ is positive for values of b above b_m. We can also define the free-riding function $Q(b)$ as the gain got from free-riding on the coalition emission abatement if a coalition b forms:

$$Q(b) = v(1, \beta) > v((1_n))$$

Figure 6.6   Valuation function and profitability function $(P = v - v^0)$

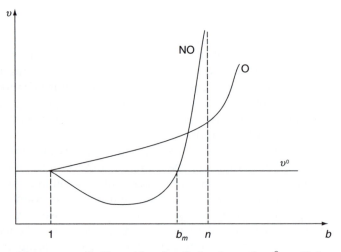

Note: $v = v(b, \beta)$ with $\beta = \{b, 1_{n-b}\}$ and $v^0 = v\{1_n\}$
NO: Non-orthogonal free-riding, O: Orthogonal free-riding.

Figure 6.7 Free-riding function (Q)

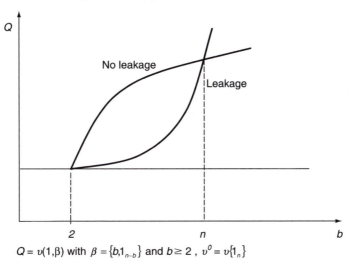

$Q = v(1,\beta)$ with $\beta = \{b,1_{n-b}\}$ and $b \geq 2$, $v^0 = v\{1_n\}$

This is shown in Figure 6.7, where the case with no leakage and the case with large leakage (inducing decreasing returns from free-riding) is identified.

Figure 6.6 shows that, with orthogonal free-riding, any coalition size is profitable and b_m is simply 1. By contrast, we see in Figure 6.7 that, with non-orthogonal free-riding, the coalition has to reach a minimal size for offsetting the damaging free-riders' behaviour (this size is generally larger than 2).

Profitability is a necessary condition for the existence of a coalition but it is not sufficient. In particular, we have to define the *membership rule*. Since we assume a simultaneous environment game, all players decide simultaneously whether or not to join the coalition. Yet, do we suppose absolutely free entry and exit from the coalition? We have already seen (sub-section 6.4.2) that two general alternative rules may be considered: in 'open membership' games, players are free to join or leave the coalition, whereas in 'exclusive membership' games outside members are not free to join the coalition.

Open membership

Open membership is the context adopted originally in the environment literature on international agreements (Carraro and Siniscalco, 1993; Barrett, 1994). The equilibrium of the coalition game is a NE, completely characterized by the following conditions.

Stability of coalitions in the open membership game

A coalition is stable if it is both internally and externally stable. It is internally stable if no cooperating player is better off by defecting in order to form a singleton (we have seen in sub-section 6.4.2 that Yi (1997) calls this condition 'stand alone stability'). It is externally stable if no singleton is better off by joining the coalition.

Let us now introduce a useful tool to identify the size of a stable coalition: the stability function.

Definition 25 (The stability function)

Let $L(b) = v(b, \beta) - v(1, \beta') = P(b) - Q(b - 1)$, where: $\beta = \{b, 1_{n-b}\}$, $\beta' = \{b', 1 - b'\}$, and $b' = b - 1$
L is named the stability function of the game.∎

If L is positive, then there is a singleton who has an incentive to join the coalition b. If L is negative, there is an incentive to free-ride on the coalition action. The stable coalition size is the one where no cooperating player is willing to defect and no free-rider is willing to join the coalition.

By definition, the free-riding function Q is equal to the non-cooperative payoff when $b = 2$, whereas the valuation function v is equal to the non-cooperative payoff when $b = 1$. In order to understand the mechanisms supporting a stable coalition, it is useful to draw the functions $P(b)$, $Q(b)$ and the resulting function $L(b)$ in three graphs that correspond to the three most likely situations: orthogonal free-riding and low fixed abatement costs (Figure 6.8), orthogonal free-riding and high fixed abatement costs (Figure 6.9) and non-orthogonal free-riding (Figure 6.10).

In the first situation, the game is characterized only by the positive externalities the coalition formation offers on external members; there is no feedback since there is no leakage. We see that the stability function $L(b)$ becomes negative for coalition sizes above b^*, which defines the stable coalition. If $b^* > 1$, the coalition structure is non-trivial and cooperation emerges endogenously and in a non-cooperative way.

The second situation shows that in presence of high fixed abatement costs a large coalition or even the grand coalition can appear as the equilibrium outcome of the non-cooperative coalition game. The profitability function $P(b)$ is now concave rather than convex. And the intersection between $P(b)$ and $Q(b - 1)$ may take place for values of b^* close to the size of population $(b^{*'})$ for $Q'(b - 1)$).

The last situation takes into account the possibility of leakage: here, cooperation may not be profitable if free-riders expand their own emissions to such a point that the abatement effort of cooperation is offset. For small coalitions, the function $P(b)$ is decreasing and then, when the coalition is larger, it increases and becomes positive for $b > b_m$. By

Figure 6.8   Stability function with orthogonal free-riding and low fixed abatement costs

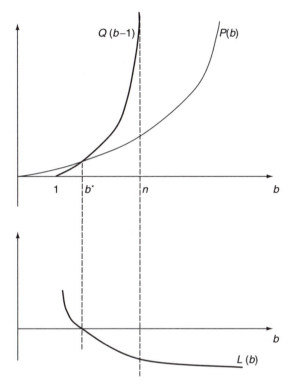

contrast $Q(b-1)$ is always increasing but concave. The economic mechanism behind the leakage effect usually exhibits decreasing returns. The resulting stability function is always increasing; if there is an intersection between profitability function and free-riding function at $b^{\#} > m$, then the grand coalition is stable. However it is necessary to design an incentive mechanism for pushing the number of cooperating players above b_m. Otherwise, the single equilibrium of the coalition game is the non-cooperative one. A possible incentive mechanism often proposed is 'issue linkage'. Barrett (1994) proposes linking environment negotiation to negotiation on trade liberalization, whereas Carraro and Siniscalco (1995) suggest linking them in negotiation on R&D cooperation (a survey on this question is in Carraro, 1997, Chapters 5 and 6).

The results obtained in the open membership environment game can be summarized in the following proposition (Carraro and Siniscalco, 1993, Barrett, 1994).

Figure 6.9 Stability function with orthogonal free-riding and high fixed abatement costs

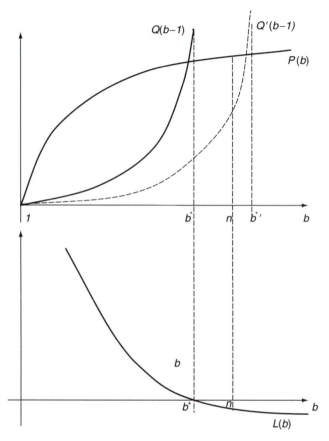

Let b^* be the largest integer lower than the value of b which satisfies $L(b) = 0$ and $L'(b) < 0$. For simplicity, let $b^* = 1$ when $L(b) < 0$ for all $1 \leq b \leq m$. The NE of a simultaneous single coalition game under the open membership rule is the following coalition structure:

- $\beta^* = \{b^*, 1_{n-b^*}\}$, when $1 \leq b_m \leq b^* < n$
- The grand coalition $b = n$, when $b^* \geq n$
- $\beta = \{1_n\}$, otherwise.∎

Notice that the symmetry assumption $A3$ implies that there is not a single NE in the game. Indeed the number of equilibria depends on the

Figure 6.10   Stability function with non-orthogonal free-riding

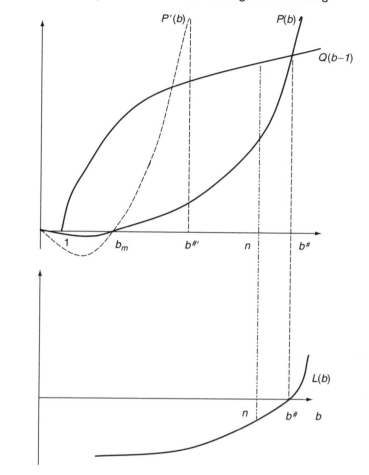

number of players (by symmetry, all sub-sets formed by b^* players can be an equilibrium). However, we can say that there is *one* NE if one refers to the typology of the equilibrium rather than to the players' identity in the coalition.

What lesson may be learned from these results ? First, the game structure which seems to reflect countries' interactions in international environmental negotiations is not a Prisoner's dilemma, but rather a Chicken game, in which at least two groups of countries coexist: signatories and defectors. Secondly, if free-riding is orthogonal, a stable coalition may emerge out of the two-stage game describing the situation.

Exclusive membership

In the exclusive membership game, players are not free to join an existing coalition. We have already seen (sub-section 6.4.2) that two situations may arise in this setting: in game Δ no player can join the coalition without the consensus of the existing coalition members, while in game Γ there are restrictions both on entry (as in game Δ) and on exit.

In the 'exclusive membership' game Δ (more simply named here 'exclusive membership' game), we need to define an *optimality* criterion: the coalition accepts a new country only if all its members would be better off in the larger coalition. Furthermore, in order to determine the new equilibrium coalitions, we need to slightly change the stability conditions.

Stability of coalitions in the exclusive membership game

A coalition is stable if and only if it is internally and externally stable. The definition of internal stability is unchanged. A coalition is externally stable if no singleton, *allowed to join the coalition*, would be better off by joining this coalition. We also need to introduce an additional feature: the case in which the valuation function is positively sloped and *monotonic* (with respect to the coalition size) rather than *humped-shaped*. In the monotonic case, above the minimum coalition b_m the valuation function is supposed to increase monotonically with respect to the member of cooperating players, while in the *humped-shaped* case there is an optimal size $\hat{b}$ at which the valuation function is maximized.

The results obtained in the exclusive membership game can be summarized in the following proposition (Carraro and Siniscalco, 1997).

Proposition 2 (Coalition formation in the exclusive membership game)

When the valuation function is monotonic, coalition members have no incentive to exclude other players from the coalition and the equilibrium structure of the game is thus the NE structure of the open membership game. When the valuation function is humped-shaped, the NE is the following coalition structure:

- $\beta = \{1_n\}$, when $b_m > b^*$
- when $b_m < \hat{b} \le b^*$, $\hat{\beta} = \{1_{n-\hat{b}}\}$ for all $b \le \hat{b}$; $\beta = \{b, 1_{n-b}\}$ for all $\hat{b} < b < b^*$ and $\beta^* = \{b^*, 1_{n-b^*}\}$ for all $b \ge b^*$
- $\beta^* = \{b^*, 1_{n-b^*}\}$, when $b_m \le b^* \le \hat{b}$ ∎

Hence, when the valuation function is humped-shaped, three group of countries may emerge: the countries which cooperate, those which would like to cooperate but are excluded from the agreement, and those which prefer not to cooperate (Figure 6.11). How to obtain a humped-shaped stability function? The simplest way is to suppose some coordination costs within the coalition, with such costs increasing with the coalition size. A less *ad hoc* approach is proposed by Carraro and Siniscalco (1997) where positive and negative R&D externalities are assumed to interact within the coalition.

Figure 6.11   Stability function with non-orthogonal free-riding and humped-shaped valuation function

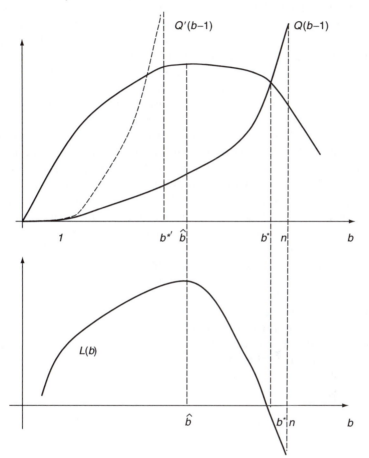

In the 'exclusive membership game Γ' (called more simply here 'coalition unanimity' game), no coalition can form without the unanimous consensus of its members. Players are not free either to join the coalition or to leave it. After a defection the coalition breaks up into singletons. Any defecting player's payoff is then the non-cooperative one.

Stability of coalitions in the coalition unanimity game
A coalition is stable if it is internally and externally stable. It is internally stable if it is profitable (i.e. if condition (6.9) holds), and it is externally stable if the same condition as in the exclusive membership game holds: that is, if no singleton allowed to join the coalition would be better off by joining this coalition.

These conditions are less stringent than the conditions required in the open membership game. It follows that the equilibrium stable coalition is generally larger (see Chander and Tulkens, 1995). The advantage of coalition unanimity stability is that, if players were able to coordinate their strategies for forming the coalition structure associated with the highest payoff, then the grand coalition would become the equilibrium outcome of the game. Yet, one can doubt the credibility of the threat which is implicit in this kind of rule. Why should the threat of breaking up into singletons be credible if countries have an incentive to form a coalition?

To summarize, the main conclusions that can be derived from the above analysis is that almost any coalition structure can be an equilibrium coalition structure on the game. In particular, by modifying the membership rules, we saw that stable coalitions of different sizes can appear at the equilibrium. The choice of the negotiation rules in international environmental agreements is thus crucial. If the goal is to maximize the number of signatory countries rather than the welfare of countries (notice that if the valuation function is monotonic, in fact these two purposes coincide), then the open membership rule could be preferred to the exclusive membership one. But if countries can commit to the coalition unanimity membership rule, then an even larger coalition can be achieved. Another important lesson of these theoretical works is that usually only a sub-set of countries is likely to sign an international environmental agreement (i.e. a partial coalition emerges at the equilibrium). We should emphasize that the recent history of environmental agreements (from Montreal to Kyoto) supports this theoretical result (Carraro and Moriconi, 1998, 30–1).

Appendix: Linear programming

- *Definition*   A linear program (P) is a problem of maximizing (or minimizing) a linear function (the *objective function*) subject to linear constraints. The most common form is:

$$\max \sum_j b_j y_j$$

s.t. $\sum a_{ij} y_j \leq c_i$, for all i

$$y_j \geq 0$$

The set of all points satisfying the constraints is the *constraint set* and the maximum of the objective function is the *value of the program* $P(v_P)$.
- *Duality*   Consider the linear program (D):

$$\min \sum c_i x_i$$

s.t. $\sum a_{ij} x_i \geq b_j$, for all j

$$x_i \geq 0$$

D is said to be the *dual* of P and x_i are the *dual variables*. Duality is in fact a reciprocal relation since P is also the dual of D.
- *Duality theorem*   Let the two linear programs P and D with solution y_j^* and x_i^*, respectively, then:

$$\sum_j b_j x_j^* = \sum_i c_i y_i^*$$

Bibliography

Aumann, R. J. (1959) 'Acceptable points in general cooperative *n*-person games', *Annuals of Mathematics Studies*, 40, 287–324.

Aumann, R. J. (1964) 'Markets with a continuum of traders', *Econometrica*, 32, 39–50.

Aumann, R. J. (1967) 'A survey of cooperative games without side payments', in M. Shubik (ed.), *Essays in mathematical economics* (Princeton: Princeton University Press).

Aumann R. J. (1989) 'Game theory', in J. Eatwell, M. Milgate and P. Newman (eds), *Game Theory – The New Palgrave: A Dictionary of Economics* (London: Macmillan; first published in 1987), 1–53.

Aumann, R. J. and J.H. Drèze (1974) 'Cooperative games with coalition structures', *International Journal of Game Theory*, 3, 217–37.

Aumann, R. J. and M. Maschler (1964) 'The bargaining set for cooperative games', in M. Dresher, L.S. Shapley and A.W. Tucker (eds), *Advances in Game Theory* (Princeton: Princeton University Press, 443–76.

Aumann, R. and R. Myerson (1988) 'Endogenous formation of links between players and coalitions: an application of the Shapley Value', in A.E. Roth (ed.), *The Shapley Value–Essays in Honor of Lloyd S. Shapley* (Cambridge: Cambridge University Press).

Aumann, R. J. and L. Shapley (1974) *Values of non-atomic games* (Princeton: Princeton University Press).

Barrett, S. (1994) 'Self-enforcing international environmental agreements', *Oxford Economic Papers*, 46, 878–94.

Bernheim, B.D., B. Peleg and M.D Whinston (1987) 'Coalition-proof Nash equilibrium: I and II', *Journal of Economic Theory*, 42, 1–12, 13–29.

Barrett, S. (1997) 'Towards a theory of international cooperation', in C. Carraro and D. Siniscalco (eds), *New directions in the economic theory of the environment* (Cambridge: Cambridge University Press).

Billera, L. J. and D.C. Heath (1982) 'Allocation of share costs: a set of axioms yielding a unique procedure', *Mathematics of Operations Research*, 7, 32–9.

Billera, L. J., D.C. Heath and J. Ranaan (1978) 'Internal telephone billing rates – a novel application on non-atomic game theory', *Operations Research*, 26, 956–65.

Bloch F. (1995) 'Endogenous structures of association in oligopolies', *Rand Journal of Economics*, 26, 537–55.

Bloch F. (1996) 'Sequential formation of coalitions in games with externalities and fixed payoff division', *Games and Economic Behavior*, 14, 90–123.

Bloch F. (1997) 'Non-cooperative models of coalition formation in games with spillovers', in C. Carraro and D. Siniscalo (eds), *New Directions in the Economic Theory of the Environment* (Cambridge: Cambridge University Press).

Bondareva, O.N. (1962) 'Teoriia iadra v igre n lits', *Vestniki Leningrad University, Mathematics, Mechanics, Astronomy*, 13, 141–2.

Bondareva, O.N. (1963) 'Some applications of linear programming methods to theory of Cooperative games' (in Russian), *Problemy Kibernetki*, 10, 119–39.

Buchanan, J. and G. Tullock (1962) *The Calculus of Consent* (Ann Arbor: University of Michigan Press).

Carraro, C. (ed.) (1997) *International Environmental Agreements: Strategic Policy Issues* (Aldershot: Edward Elgar).

Carraro, C. and F. Moriconi (1998) 'Endogenous formation of environmental coalitions', Fondazione Eni Enrico Mattei, Milan, mimeo.

Carraro, C. and D. Siniscalco (1993) 'Strategies for the internatioanal protection of the environment,' *Journal of Public Economics*, 52, 309–32.

Carraro, C. and D. Siniscalco (1995) 'Policy Coordination for sustainability; commitments, transferts and linked negotiations', in I. Goldin and A. Winters (eds), *The economics of sustainable development* (Cambridge, MA: Cambridge University Press).

Carraro, C. and D. Siniscalco (1997) 'R&D cooperation and the stability of international environmental agreements', in C. Carraro (ed.), *International Environmental Agreements: Strategic Policy Issues* (Aldershot: Edward Elgar).

Chander, P. and H. Tulkens (1995) 'A core-theoretic solution for a design of cooperative agreements on transfrontier pollution', *International Tax and Public Finance*, 2, 279–93.

Chatterjee, X., B. Dutta, D. Ray and K. Sengupta (1993) 'A non-cooperative theory of coalitional bargaining', *Review of Economic Studies*, 60, 463–77.

d'Aspremont,C., A. Jacquemin, J.J. Gabszewicz and J. Weymark (1983) 'On the stability of collusive price leadership', *Canadian Journal of Economics*, 16, 17–25.

Davis, M. and M. Maschler (1963) 'Existence of stable payoff configurations for cooperative games' *Bulletin of the American Mathematical Society*, 69, 106–8, abstract.

Davis, M. and M. Maschler (1965) 'The kernel of a cooperative game', *Naval Research Logistics Quarterly*, 12, 229–59.

Debreu, G. and H. Scarf (1963) 'A limit theorem on the care of an economy', *International Economic Review*, 4, 236–46.

Drèze J. and J. Greenberg (1980) 'Hedonic coalitions optimality and stability', *Econometrica*, 48, 987–1003.

Edgeworth, F.Y. (1881) *Mathematical Psychics* (London: Kegan Paul).

Gillies, D.B. (1959) 'Solutions to general non-zero-sum game', in A.W Tücker and D.R. Luce (eds), *Contributions to the Theory of Games, IV (Annals of Mathematical Studies Series*, 40) (Princeton: Princeton University Press), 47–85.

Greenberg, J. (1977) 'Pure and local public goods: a game theoretic approach' in A. Sandmo (ed.), *Public Finance*, (Lexington MAH: Health and Co).

Greenberg, J. (1994) 'Coalition structures', in R.J. Aumann and S. Hart (eds), *Handbook of Game Theory with Economic Applications*, 2 (New York: Elsevier), Chapter 37.

Gul, F. (1989) 'Bargaining foundations of Shapley value', *Econometrica*, 57, 81–95.

Harsanyi J.C. (1959) 'A bargaining model for the cooperative *n*-person game', in R.D. Luce and A.W. Tücker (eds), *Contributions to the Theory of Games IV (Annals of Mathematical Studies Series* 40) (Princeton: Princeton University Press).

Harsanyi, J. C. (1963) 'A simplified bargaining model for the *n*-person cooperative game', *International Economic Review*, 4, 194–220.

Harsanyi, J.C. (1977) *Rational Behavior and Bargaining Equilibrium* (Cambridge: Cambridge University Press).

Hart, S. (1985) 'An axiomatization of Harsanyi's nontransferable utility solution', *Econometrica*, 53, 1295–314.

Hart, S. and M. Kurz (1983) 'Endogenous formation of coalitions', *Econometrica*, 51, 1047–64.

Hart, S. and M. Kurz (1984) 'Stable coalition structures', in M.J. Holler (ed.), *Coalitions and Collective Actions* (Berlin: Springer-Verlag), 233–58.

Hart, S. and A. Mas-Colell (1989) 'Potential, value and consistency', *Econometrica*, 57, 589–614.

Hayek, F. (1976) *The Mirage of Social Justice, Law, Legislation and Liberty*, 2 (Chicago: University of Chicago Press).

Ichiishi T. (1981) 'A social coalitional equilibrium existence lemma', *Econometrica*, 49, 369–77.

Kannai, Y. (1992) 'The core and balancedness', in R. J. Aumann and S. Hart (eds), *Handbook of Game Theory with Economic Applications*, 1 (Amsterdam: North-Holland), Chapter 12.

Kreps, D. (1990) *Game Theory and Economic Modeling* (Oxford: Clarendon Press).

Kurz M. (1988) 'Coalition value', in A.E. Roth (ed.), *The Shapley Value – Essays in Honor of Lloyd. S. Shapley* (Cambridge: Cambridge University Press).

Lucas, W.F. (1992) 'Von Neumann–Morgenstern stable sets', in R.J. Aumann and S. Hart (eds), *Handbook of Game Theory with Economic Applications*, 1 (Amsterdam: North-Holland), chapter 17.

Luce, R.D. and H. Raiffa (1957) *Games and Dicisions* (New York: John Wiley).

Mas-Colell, A. (1989) 'Cooperative equilibrium', in J. Eatwell, M. Milgate and P. Newman, *Game Theory – The New Palgrave: A Dictionary of Economics* (London: Macmillan, First published in 1987), 95–102.

Maschler, M. (1992) 'The bargaining set, kernel and nucleolus', in R.J. Aumann and S. Hart (eds), *Handbook of Game Theory with Economic Applications*, 1 (Amsterdam: North-Holland), chapter 18.

Maschler M., J.A.M. Potters, S.H. Tijs (1992) 'The general nucleolus and the reduced game property', *International Journal of Game Theory*, 21, 85–106.

McLean, R. (2002) 'Values on non-transferable utility games', in R.J. Aumann and S. Hart (eds), *Handbook of Game Theory and Applications*, 3 (New York: Elsevier).

Mirman, L.J. and Y. Tauman (1982) 'Demand compatible equitable cost sharing prices', *Mathematics of Operations Research*, 7, 40–56.

Moulin, H. (1988) *Axioms of Cooperative Decision Making* (Cambridge: Cambridge University Press).

Moulin, H. (1995a) 'An appraisal of cooperative game theory', *Revue d'Economie Politique*, 105, 617–32.

Moulin, H. (1995b) *Cooperative Micro-Economics: An Introduction* (Princeton: Princeton University Press).

Myerson, R.B. (1977) 'Graphs and cooperation in games', *Mathematics of Operations Research*, 2, 225–9.

Myerson, R.B. (1991) *Game Theory – Analysis of Conflict* (Cambridge, MA: Harvard University Press).

Neyman, A. (2002) 'Values of games with infinitely many players', in R.J. Aumann and S. Hart (eds), *Handbook of Game Theory and Applications*, 3 (New York: Elsevier).

Nouweland A.V. (1993) *Games and Graphs in Economic Situations*, PhD dissertation, Tilburg University, The Netherlands.

Osborne, M.J. and A. Rubinstein (1994) *A Course in Game Theory* (Cambridge, MA: Mit Press), chap 13, 14.

Owen, G. (1977) 'Values of games with *a priori* unions', in R. Henn and O. Moeschlin (eds), *Mathematical Economics and Game Theory* (Berlin: Springer-Verlag), 76–88.

Owen, G. (1995) *Game Theory*, 3rd edn (San Diego: Academic Press), chapters 10 to 15.

Pegel, B. (1992) 'Axiomatizations of the core', in R.J. Aumann and S. Hart (eds), *Handbook of Game Theory with Economic Applications*, 1 (Amsterdam: North-Holland), Chapter 13.

Perry, M. and P.J. Reny (1994) 'A non-cooperative view of coalition formation and the core', *Econometrica*, 62, 795–817.

Peters, H.J.M. (1992) *Axiomatic Bargaining Game Theory* (Boston: Kluwer Academic publishers).

Ponssard J.P. (1978) *Bargaining Theory* (Berlin: Springer-Verlag).

Ransmeier, J.S. (1942) *The Tennessee Valley Authority: A Case Study in the Economics of Multiple Purpose Stream Planning* 2 (Nashville, TN: Vanderbilt University Press).

Ray D. and R. Vohra (1996) 'Binding agreements and coalition barganing', Boston University, mimeo.

Ray D. and R. Vohra (1997) 'Equilibrium binding agreements', *Journal of Economic Theory*, 73(1), 30–78.

Ray D. and R. Vohra (1999) 'A theory of endogenous coalition structure', *Games and Economic Behavior*, 26(2), 286–336.

Roemer, J.E. (1996) *Theories of Distributive Justice* (Cambridge, MA: Harvard University Press).

Roth, A. (ed.) (1988) *The Shapley Value – Essays in Honor of Lloyd Shapley* (Cambridge: Cambridge University Press).

Scarf, H.E. (1967) 'The core of an *n*-person game', *Econometrica*, 35, 50–69.

Scarf, H.E. (1973) *The computation of economic equilibria* (New Haven: Yale University Press).

Rubinstein, A. (1982) 'Perfect equilibrium in a bargaining model', *Econometrica*, 50, 97–109.

Selten R. (1981) 'A non-cooperative model of characteristic function barganing', in V. Bohm and H. Nachtkamp (eds), *Essays in Games Theory and Mathematical Economics in Honor of Oskar Morgenstern* (Mannheim: Bibliographisches Institut Mannheim), 131–51.

Shapley, L.S. (1953) 'A value for *n*-person games', in H.W. Kühn and A.W. Tücker (eds), *Contributions to the Theory of Games, II* (Princeton: Princeton University Press), 305–17.

Shapley, L.S. (1967) 'On balanced sets and cores', *Naval Research Logistics Quarterly*, 14, 453–60.

Shapley, L.S. (1969) 'Utility comparison and the theory of games', in G.T. Guilband (ed.), *La decision-agrigation an dynamique disorders de preference* (Paris: Editions du CNRS).

Shapley, L.S. (1973) 'On balanced games in without side payments', T.C. Hu and S.M. Robinson (eds), *Mathematical programming* (New York: Academic Press).

Schmeidler, D. (1969) 'The nucleolus of a characteristic function game', *SIAM Journal of Applied Mathematics*, 17, 1163–70.

Shenoy, P. (1979) 'On coalition formation: a game theoretical approach', *International Journal of Game Theory*, 8, 133–64.

Shubik, M. (1959) 'Edgeworth market games', in R.D. Luce and A.W. Tücker (eds), *Contributions to the Theory of Games, IV* (*Annals of Mathematical Studies Series*, 40) (Princeton: Princeton University Press).

Shubik, M. (1982) *Game Theory in the Social Sciences*, 1 (Cambridge, MA: MIT Press).

Sobolev, A.I. (1975) 'The characterization of optimality principles, in cooperative games by functional equations', *Mathematical Methods in Social Sciences*, 6, 150–65 (in Russ., Engl. summ.).

Telser, L.G. (1978) *Economic Theory and the Core* (Chicago: University of Chicago Press).

Thomson, W (1990) 'The consistency principle', in T.I. Chiishi, A. Newman, Y. Tauman (eds), *Game theory and applications* (Boston: Academic Press).

Thomson, W. (1994) 'Cooperative models of bargaining', in R.J. Aumann and S. Hart (eds), *Handbook of Game Theory with Economic Applications*, 2 (Amsterdam: North-Holland), chapter 35.

Thrall, R. and W. Lucas (1963) 'N-person games in partition function form', *Naval Research Logistics Quarterly*, 10, 281–98.

Von Neumann, J. and O. Morgenstern (1944) *Theory of games and economic behavior* (New York: John Wiley).

Weber, R. J. (1994) 'Games in coalitional form' in R. J. Aumann and S. Hart (eds), *Handbook of Game Theory with Economic Applications*, 2 (Amsterdam: North-Holland), chapter 36.

Winter, E. (2002) 'The Shapley Value', in R. J. Aumann and S. Hart (eds), *Handbook of Game Theory and Applications*, 3 (New York: Elsevier).

Yaari, M.E. (1981) 'Rawls, Edgeworth, Shapley, Nash: theories of distributive justice re-examined', *Journal of Economic Theory*, 24, 1–39.

Yi, S.-S. (1997) 'Stable coalition structures with externalities', *Games and Economic Behavior*, 20, 201–37.

Yi, S.S. and H. Shin (1995) 'Endogenons formation of coalitions in oligopoly', Working paper 95–2, Dartmouth College Department of Economics, Dartmouth.

Young, H.P. (ed.) (1991) *Cost Allocations: Methods, Principles, Applications* (Amsterdam: North-Holland).

Young, H.P. (1994) 'Cost allocation', in R. J. Aumann and S. Hart (eds), *Handbook of Game Theory with Economic Applications*, 2 (Amsterdam: North-Holland), chapter 34.

7 Evolutionary Games and Learning

7.1 Replictor dynamics and evolutionary stable strategies: the basic biological concepts

7.2 Extensions and generalizations to economics: evolution, rationality and efficiency

7.3 Learning models

7.4 Applications

Evolutionary games have been developed in biology and mathematics, notably by J. Maynard Smith and his collaborators and after them by many other researchers, including the Nobel prize in Economics, R. Selten. Evolutionary models have proven very helpful to study the behaviour of animals in various strategic contexts and to understand biological evolution. Now, these models are becoming popular among game theorists and the approach appears to be fruitful in the field of economics and business studies. One feels that the kind of adjustment dynamics studied by evolutionary games may be useful for discussing various types of economic issues where agents react slowly through emulation, imitation, or learning. Of course the kind of modelling suitable for applications in economics must be different from that used in biology. Even if managers, sellers and buyers, or other economic decision makers sometimes have very limited rationality, they can be expected to behave more rationally than birds or rats. It is then the introduction of *specific learning processes* that can bridge the gap between biological games and economic behaviour.

There is a particular reason why economists could now be interested in evolutionary models. Non-cooperative GT, as applied in economics, is facing two difficulties: first, in many economic problems, it is not entirely clear how a NE can be finally reached by the players and, second, when there are many equilibria, with different implications, it is important to understand how a particular equilibrium will eventually be selected. It happens that the dynamic adjustments described by evolutionary models may give interesting answers to both these questions. So, even though economic applications are still rare and some progress is still to be made in order to adapt the modelling, the path seems a very promising one to follow.

The present chapter will mainly develop the framework put forward to study biological games. Some applications to economic problems in the field of industrial organisation or international trade theory will be presented. Section 7.1 introduces to the basic concepts of Evolutionary Game Theory (EGT): the 'Replicator Dynamics' (RD) and 'Evolutionary stable strategies' (ESS) in both symmetrical and asymmetrical evolutionary games. Section 7.2 presents extensions of the basic concepts and discusses their relevance for economics. The relationship between RD, ESS and other equilibrium concepts is also presented in this section. In section 7.3, we present a brief introduction to learning models, both an older approach in the tradition of the Cournot adjustment model, and new developments which are designed to make EGT fit better traditional economic problems. Finally, section 7.4 will be devoted to a few examples of applications of the concepts of evolutionary games to economic issues.

7.1   Replicator Dynamics and evolutionary stable strategies: the basic biological concepts

The most interesting cases for the economist involve different populations of players. However, in order to keep things simple at first, let us introduce the RD and the concept of ESS by considering the case often studied in biology of a population of a single species, also called a homogeneous population, playing a symmetric game. Then, we will see how these concepts are used when there are more than one population.

In the single-population case, one studies the random matching of individuals who have the same set of strategies available and whose payoffs are entirely symmetric. Here a 'strategy' means a special behaviour and each individual is genetically programmed for playing a particular strategy. In biological games, a payoff may be interpreted as the number of offspring. It is also called 'fitness'.

Let us call $X = \{x_1, \ldots, x_i, \ldots, x_n\}$ the set of pure strategies available to the players, and $U(x, x')$ the payoff when one agent plays x and her (or his) opponent plays x'. In this chapter we will denote explicitly by m the mixed strategies.

7.1.1   The Replicator Dynamics

At one point in time there may be different fractions of the total population programmed to play a particular strategy. In order to study the evolution of these groups, admitting that only the fittest will survive, a type of dynamic adjustment must be imagined. It is common in biological games to use a kind of Malthusian dynamics, also called the RD.

According to the RD, the fraction of the population playing a particular strategy will increase if it performs better in terms of the fitness function than the population average. If a type of players gets less than the average payoff, then its percentage in the population will decrease.

There is a simple large population of agents playing the same symmetric game. In order to keep the presentation as simple as possible, the number of pure strategies is limited to two: x and x'. An extension to a larger number of strategies is straightforward.

Let n_t and n'_t be the number of agents, respectively, playing x and x' at time t and N_t the total population.

Let $s_t(x)$ denote the proportion of agents playing strategy x at time t:

$$s_t(x) = \frac{n_t}{n_t + n'_t} = \frac{n_t}{N_t} \tag{7.1}$$

Agents programmed for playing x have the expected payoff:

$$u_t(x) = s_t(x)u_t(x, x) + s_t(x')u_t(x, x') \tag{7.2}$$

The average payoff in the population is then:

$$\bar{u}_t = s_t(x)u_t(x) + s_t(x')u_t(x') \tag{7.3}$$

Starting from these assumptions, one can define several versions of the RD. The most common version in a continuous time is expressed in the following differential equation:

$$\dot{s}(x) = s(x)[u(x) - \bar{u}] = F(s) \tag{7.4}$$

This equation of replication describes the evolution process of populations programmed for playing the diverse strategies: in this case x and x'. It reflects the basic idea defining the RD: if strategy x is performing better than the average, the agents who play it will see their proportion increase in the total population.

There are different ways to obtain (7.4). We present two ways below, but if the the logic of the RD is understood, the reader may prefer to go directly to the numerical examples which follow.

A non-overlapping generations model of the Replicator Dynamics
(Van Damme, 1991)

In each period, agents are paired at random to play a symmetric game. Their payoffs correspond to their offspring who replace them in the next period. The number of players choosing each strategy depends on the payoffs in the previous play of the game.

If n_t players play x at t, then $n_t u_t$ players will play x at $t+1$. The expected number of players in period $t+1$ is:

$$n_t u_t(x) + n'_t u_t(x') = N_{t+1}$$

It is equal to $N_t \bar{u}_t$. The proportion of players choosing x in period $t+1$ is:

$$s_{t+1}(x) = \frac{n_t u_t(x)}{(n_t + n'_t)\bar{u}_t} = s_t(x)\frac{u_t(x)}{\bar{u}_t} \qquad (7.5)$$

In this discrete time model, the evolution of the population can be represented as:

$$s_{t+1} - s_t = s_t(x)\frac{u_t(x) - \bar{u}_t}{\bar{u}_t} \qquad (7.6)$$

Considering very short time periods allows us to write (7.6) as:

$$\dot{s} = s(x)\frac{u(x) - \bar{u}}{\bar{u}} \qquad (7.7)$$

Finally, a rescaling of time leads to the following equation:

$$\dot{s} = s(x)[u(x) - \bar{u}] \qquad (7.8)$$

which has the same solution trajectories as (7.7) and which is (7.4).

An overlapping generations model of the Replicator Dynamics (Binmore, 1992; Samuelson, 1997)

In the previous model, all agents were reproducing themselves at the same time and none of them could survive after reproduction. This assumption may apply to some kinds of animal species, but certainly not all. Moreover, it does not fit well the applications to economics, where we would like to have agents learning over time.

Now we assume that in each period of time of length τ, a fraction τ of the population reproduces itself. Payoffs of the game are again taken as representing offspring and each agent playing strategy x will give birth to $u_t(x)$ offspring at time t.

In period $t + \tau$, the number of agents playing strategy x is given by:

$$n_{t+\tau} = n_t + \tau n_t u_t(x)$$

The total number of agents next period is:

$$N_{t+\tau} = n_t(1 + \tau u_t(x)) + n'_t(1 + \tau u_t(x'))$$

The proportion of agents playing x next period is:

$$s_{t+\tau}(x) = \frac{n_{t+\tau}}{N_{t+\tau}} = \frac{n_t(1 + \tau u_t(x))}{n_t(1 + \tau u_t(x)) + n'_t(1 + \tau u_t(x'))}$$

or:

$$s_{t+\tau}(x) = \frac{s_t(x)(1 + \tau u_t(x))}{s_t(x)(1 + \tau u_t(x)) + s_t(x')(1 + \tau u_t(x'))}$$

Then, the evolution of the population can be represented as:

$$s_{t+\tau}(x) - s_t(x) = s_t(x) \frac{\tau u_t(x) - \tau \bar{u}_t}{1 + \tau \bar{u}_t} \tag{7.9}$$

Taking the limit $\tau \to 0$ in (7.9) gives:

$$\dot{s} = s(x)(u(x) - \bar{u})$$

which is again (7.4).

Example I

Consider the game of coordination described by the payoff matrix in Figure 7.1.

The players have two alternative strategies, x_1 and x_2. Call s the proportion of players programmed for playing strategy x_1. The player programmed for 1 will get:

$$u_1 = s.3 + (1 - s)2 = s + 2$$

Similarly:

$$u_2 = s.0 + (1 - s)4 = (1 - s).4$$

The average payoff is:

$$\bar{u} = s(s + 2) + (1 - s)(1 - s)4 = 5s^2 - 6s + 4$$

Figure 7.1   A coordination game

	x_1	x_2
x_1	3, 3	2, 0
x_2	0, 2	4, 4

Then the equation of replication $F(s)$ is:

$$F(s) = s[s + 2 - (5s^2 - 6s + 4)]$$

and finally:

$$F(s) = s(1 - s)(5s - 2)$$

The equation of replication can be represented graphically by the phase diagram in Figure 7.2.

It appears that, in such a game, if the proportion of players pro-grammed for playing strategy x is initially greater than $\frac{2}{5}$, the RD will increase it continuously, up to the point where everybody is playing it. Inversely, this percentage will fall to zero if the game starts at a level of s lower than $\frac{2}{5}$.

Notice that the RD has three steady states, that is points for which $F(s) = 0$: for $s = 0$, $s = \frac{2}{5}$ and $s = 1$. Are they all equilibrium points of the game? Clearly, one would not like to consider the point $s = \frac{2}{5}$ as an equilibrium, since a slight departure from it implies a continuous move towards $s = 0$, or $s = 1$.

This example shows how stability is important in the evolutionary approach. Let us now leave this particular example and get a more general view about the equilibrium definition.

Evolutionary equilibrium

In the evolutionary approach, equilibrium means not only a state of rest of the dynamical process (a steady state, or a fixed point of the function describing the dynamics), but also a certain form of stability of this rest point. More precisely, one can propose the following defin-ition.

Figure 7.2   Phase diagram of the RD in the coordination game

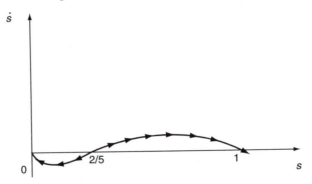

> **Definition 1 (*Evolutionary equilibrium*)**
>
> An evolutionary equilibrium (EE) is any asymptotically stable fixed point of the dynamical process of evolution (see Appendix 1 of this chapter, p. 379, for the definition of asymptotic stability).■

In the above example, a simple way to study stability is to consider the sign of the slope of function $F(s)$. When $dF(s)/ds < 0$, the steady state is stable. At points $s = 0$ and $s = 1$, the slope of the function $F(s)$ is negative; at $s = 2/5$, the slope is positive. These signs confirm that the former points are stable steady states, while the latter is not. In other words, $s = 0$ and $s = 1$ are EE of this game.

In Example 1 above the EE corresponds to a 'monomorphic' population, that is a population where everybody will play the same strategy (before any mutation brought by possible 'mutants'). We want to provide another example showing that the EE may also correspond to a polymorphic population.

Example 2

A good example is provided by the Hawk–Dove game. The members of a very large population are fighting for the use of a territory, or any other particular valuable scarce resource. V is the value of that resource for any member of this population. Individuals meet at random and can play one or the other of the two following strategies: behave like a Hawk (aggressively), or behave like a Dove (nicely). The Hawk is always ready to fight, the Dove will always avoid fighting. Every fight has a cost, noted C.

When a Hawk meets a Dove, the latter refuses the fight and leaves the place. Of course, the Hawk gets all the benefit. When two Doves meet, the payoff is shared pacifically, $V/2$ for each. Finally, when two Hawks meet each other, they fight until they get half of the value of the resource minus the cost of fighting, that is $(V - C)/2$. Figure 7.3 summarizes the game.

If one assumes a Malthusian dynamics, one gets the following equation of replication:

$$F(s) = s(1 - s)[s(V - C)/2 + (1 - s)V/2]$$

Figure 7.3 The Hawk–Dove game

	Hawk	Dove
Hawk	$(V{-}C)/2, (V{-}C)/2$	$V, 0$
Dove	$0, V$	$V/2, V/2$

where s is the percentage of the population playing Hawk. To be more precise, give numerical values to the parameters V and C; for instance: $V = 4$ and $C = 16$. Then:

$$F(s) = s(1 - s)(2 - 8s)$$

This equation has three roots: $s = 0$, $s = \frac{1}{4}$ and $s = 1$. The phase diagram is represented in Figure 7.4.

A simple look at the arrows describing the dynamics and the fact that $F'(s)$ at point $s = \frac{1}{4}$ is negative shows that this point is an EE. It is easy to check that this is the only EE in this game. So here the population is 'polymorphic' at equilibrium. There is a proportion of $\frac{1}{4}$ playing Hawk and $\frac{3}{4}$ playing Dove. The equilibrium can be interpreted either as a pure strategy equilibrium or as a mixed strategy equilibrium. In the latter case, we have to assume that individuals can be programmed for playing pure or mixed strategies.

The mixed strategy equilibrium is the only EE of this game. It is also the only symmetric NE (while there are also two asymmetric NE: Hawk, Dove and Dove, Hawk). We will see in the next sub-section that it has another stability property since it is an 'evolutionary stable strategy' (ESS) (see definition below).

Remark I

Of course, one may use many other ways to represent the evolution dynamics. One can, for instance, consider a *discrete* time rather than a *continuous* time dynamics. Unfortunately, this change can have dramatic effects on the results (see sub-section 7.2.2, the result obtained by Dekel and Scotchmer, 1992, showing that in a discrete time model the RD may not eliminate the strictly dominated strategies).■

Figure 7.4 Phase diagram of the RD in the Hawk–Dove game

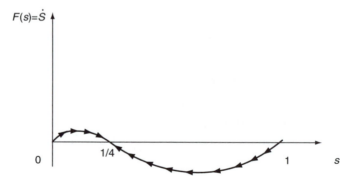

Remark 2

The s presented in (7.4) links the rate of growth of a strategy to its performance with respect to the average. But one can imagine other relationships. For example, the *instantaneous rate of change* of a strategy, instead of its rate of growth, may be related to the difference between the payoff from playing this strategy and the average payoff. Again, the assumption may make a difference (see, for instance, in Friedman, 1991). Other kinds of dynamics can still be envisaged for describing the evolution process. However, it is reasonable to require that they all verify a condition of compatibility with the fitness function (Friedman, 1991): the fitter strategies must grow compared to those which fit less well.■

7.1.2 Evolutionary stable strategies

A particular concept of equilibrium, called 'Evolutionary stable strategy' (ESS) has been proposed by Maynard Smith and Price (1973) in order to describe the stable state of the evolutionary process. The basic idea of ESS is to require that the equilibrium can 'resist' mutant invasion. While the RD is studying the dynamical property of a given strategy, the ESS concept focuses on a different issue: the study of possible mutations to unused strategies.

Suppose that the population is originally playing a strategy x, which can be a pure or a mixed strategy, and that a small percentage of 'mutants', say ε, play another strategy x'.

Definition 2 (Evolutionary stable strategy)

An ESS means that the incumbent population gets a higher payoff than the invaders when pairs of players are randomly chosen. Each player has a $(1 - \varepsilon)$ chance to meet someone playing strategy x and a probability ε to meet an invader. So the condition defining the ESS can be written:

$$u[x, (1 - \varepsilon)x + \varepsilon x'] > u[x', (1 - \varepsilon)x + \varepsilon x'] \qquad (7.10)$$

where ε is positive and sufficiently small ($0 < \varepsilon < \bar{\varepsilon}$).■

The above definition is sufficient to define an ESS, but it is common and useful to present an equivalent two-part condition. Notice first, using the linearity of expected utility, that:

$$u[x, (1 - \varepsilon)x + \varepsilon x'] = (1 - \varepsilon)u(x, x) + \epsilon u(x', x')$$

Then (7.10) can be rewritten:

$$(1 - \varepsilon)u(x, x) + \varepsilon u(x, x') > (1 - \varepsilon)u(x', x) + \varepsilon u(x', x') \qquad (7.10')$$

This inequality has to be verified only for values of ε close to 0. Hence for any $x' \neq x$:

(i) $u(x,\ x) > u(x',\ x)$

or

(ii) if $u(x,\ x) = u(x',\ x)$, then: $u(x,\ x') > u(x',\ x')$ $\qquad$ (7.11)

In condition (7.11), part (i) makes it clear that an ESS must be a NE. It means that when all players play x, it is unprofitable for any player to deviate and play x'. Part (ii) shows that ESS is a kind of refinement of symmetric NE. Even if strategy x cannot do better than x' against players programmed for x (that is, in a weak NE case), it can still win against strategy x' when opponents play x'.

Example I

A Prisoner's dilemma game is given in Figure 7.5. If the game is played only once, the DSE (D, D) also corresponds to an ESS. Clearly, with x for the strategy Defect (or 'Aggressive'), and x' for Cooperate (or 'Pacific'), and applying (7.10'), one gets:

$$3(1 - \varepsilon) + 6\varepsilon > 2(1 - \varepsilon) + 5\varepsilon$$

Now what would happen if the game were repeated many times without discounting, and if mutants were playing the so-called 'Tit-for-tat' (TFT) strategy'. It has been shown (see Axelrod and Hamilton, 1981) that the strategy (D, D) cannot resist the invaders.

A player programmed for TFT will eventually lose once against a player programmed for Defection, but thereafter will always also play Defection. On average (recalling that there is no discounting) over a large number of runs, she (or he) will get as much as the players who choose Defection at the first run, specifically a payoff of 3. So:

$u(TFT, D) = u(D, D).$

However, when they meet each other the mutants can perform better than when a player programmed for Defection meets them: respectively, on

Figure 7.5 A Prisoner's dilemma

	Cooperate (*C*)	Defect (*D*)
Cooperate (*C*)	5, 5	2, 6
Defect (*D*)	6, 2	3, 3

average 5 and 3 (that is because the mutants maintain a strategy of cooperation when the opponent does the same and switch to Defection when the opponent chooses this strategy). So, we also have:

$$u(D, TFT) < u(TFT, TFT).$$

Strategy D does not verify condition (7.11)(ii), and is not in this case an ESS.

Example 2

The payoffs of a coordination game are given in Figure 7.6.

This game has three NE: (x_1, x_1), (x_2, x_2), and the mixed strategy equilibrium $(m, m) = (\frac{1}{4}, \frac{3}{4})$. The first two are ESS, but the latter is not.

Let us check for the strategy (x_2, x_2), which provides a payoff of 1 for each player. The expected payoff of an individual playing strategy 2, when she (or he) has a $(1 - \varepsilon)$ chance of meeting someone playing the same strategy and a ε probability of meeting a mutant is:

$$(1 - \varepsilon)1 + \varepsilon.0 = (1 - \varepsilon)$$

The expected payoff of someone playing strategy 1 and facing the same distribution of opponents is:

$$(1 - \varepsilon)0 + \varepsilon.3 = 3.\varepsilon$$

Obviously, with a small value for ε, the former number is higher than the latter and condition (7.10') is met. The strategy (x_2, x_2) is an ESS. It is interesting to note here that the *inefficient* NE (x_2, x_2) may still appear as an equilibrium outcome of an evolutionary process.

By the same reasoning one can check that the strategy (x_1, x_1) is also an ESS. However the mixed strategy (m, m), although being a NE, is not an ESS. The strategy (m, m) can be invaded by a pure strategy x_1 or x_2.

Let us consider a population playing (m, m), and mutants playing x_2. We have:

$$u(m, m) = u(x_2, m) = \frac{3}{4}$$

Figure 7.6 A coordination game

	x_1	x_2
x_1	3, 3	0, 0
x_2	0, 0	1, 1

So we are typically in the case where condition (ii) of (7.11) must be considered. But precisely here the condition is not met:

$$u(m, x_2) = \frac{3}{4}, \text{ but: } u(x_2, x_2) = 1$$

so:

$$u(m, x_2) < u(x_2, x_2)$$

The mutants are doing as well as the incumbent population when they meet an incumbent but they perform better when they meet each other. Of course, mutants playing strategy x_1 will also invade a population playing (m, m).

Remark I

In some games there is no ESS. As Haigh (1975) has shown, the number of ESS is always finite, possibly zero.■

7.1.3 Neutral stability, evolutionary stable sets and robustness against equilibrium entrants

Neutral stability or weak ESS

In the formal definition of an ESS in 7.1.2, we used a strict inequality, but what happens if the mutant strategy can do as well against itself as the incumbent strategy does? In the latter case, mutants are called 'neutral'. The concept of a 'Neutrally stable strategy' (NSS) then is defined as an ESS with *weak* inequality.

Definition 3 (*Neutrally stable strategy*)

$x \in X$ is a NSS if for every strategy $x' \neq x$ there exists some $\bar{\varepsilon} \in (0, 1)$ such that for all $\varepsilon \in (0, \bar{\varepsilon})$ the following inequality is satisfied:

$$u[x, \varepsilon x' + (1 - \varepsilon)x] \geq u[x', \varepsilon x' + (1 - \varepsilon)x]■$$

This inequality can be rewritten as:

(i) $u(x, x) > u(x', x)$
(ii) if $u(x, x) = u(x', x)$ then: $u(x', x) \geq u(x', x')$

Obviously neutral stability is less demanding than evolutionary stability, since the condition guarantees here only that the mutants cannot do better than the incumbent population. Neutral stability is still a refinement of symmetric NE:

ESS ⊂ NSS ⊂ NE

Now, since neutral mutants can get as much as the incumbents, they may stay in the game. Hence, each neutral mutation will increase the share of neutral mutants in the total population. Such a progressive 'invasion' of the population by neutral mutants is called an 'evolutionary drift'. The problem is that at some point the evolutionary drift may destabilize the NSS. A new concept of stability defined on sets of NE (Thomas, 1985) is then useful in order to deal with this risk of destabilizing evolutionary drift.

Evolutionary stable sets

A *set* of symmetric NE strategies is called 'Evolutionary stable' (ES) if each strategy in the set can do at least as well against any close strategy x' as it can do against itself and if the mutant strategy also belongs to the set in the case of equal payoffs.

> **Definition 4 (*Evolutionary stable set*) (*Kandori*, 1997)**
>
> A closed set $X^* \subset X$ is ES in a symmetric two-player game if:
>
> (i)   each element of X^* is a NSS and
> (ii) $x \in X^*$, $u(x, x) = u(y, x)$ and $u(x, y) = u(y, y)$ implies $y \in X^*$ ∎

In other words, the evolutionary drift can never lead to an unstable point. At the border, the mutants would do strictly worse than the incumbent population.

Example

In the repeated Prisoner's dilemma, the TFT strategy is an NSS. However one can check that it does not belong to an ES set, since for TFT and C (cooperate) we have:

$$U(TFT, TFT) = U(C, TFT) \text{ and } U(TFT, C) = U(C, C)$$

There can be an evolutionary drift from TFT to C. Yet, C is not a NE, and hence not a NSS.

This example brings us to the interesting extension suggested by Swinkels (1992a). In economic applications one may want to consider that the agents, including the mutants, are smart enough to avoid trying stupid strategies against incumbent strategies. In the latter example strategy C is indeed very fragile compared to TFT. Even with weak rationality, an economic agent would hesitate before using C against TFT.

Equilibrium entrants and robustness to equilibrium entrants

Swinkels (1992a) argues that conditions on ESS might be too stringent in economic contexts. When players are firms it seems reasonable to restrict attention to mutant strategies that themselves fulfil a stability condition. In this line, Swinkels proposes a new stability concept, that he calls 'Robustness against equilibrium entrants' (REE) permitting us to consider only 'rational' mutations or experimentation and eliminate the 'stupid' ones. Assuming that the population share of mutants is ε, the post-mutation mixed strategy is: $\omega = \varepsilon x' + (1 - \varepsilon)x$. An entrant is called an equilibrium entrant if x' is a best reply to ω. But if x' is a best reply to ω, then a plan of invasion of mutants representing ε per cent of the population becomes self-enforcing. One may want to define situations where this risk does not exist, and this is precisely the objective of the REE.

Definition 5 (*Robustness against equilibrium entrants*)

A symmetric strategy profile (x, x) is REE if there exists some $\bar{\varepsilon} \in (0, 1)$ such that if $x' \neq x$ and $\varepsilon \in (0, \bar{\varepsilon})$ then x' is not a best reply to $\varepsilon x' + (1 - \varepsilon)x$:

$x' \notin BR[\varepsilon x' + (1 - \varepsilon)x]$ (where BR is the set of best responses).■

It can be shown that if a strategy is REE, it is also a best reply to itself, that is, it must be a NE. One can even go further (Swinkel, 1992a) and show that REE implies properness, thus being a particular refinement of NE (see sub-section 4.2.1 of chapter 4 for a definition of a proper equilibrium). Since REE is less stringent that ESS, we have the following inclusions of sets:

ESS $\subset$ REE $\subset$ NE

The motivations behind the Swinkels' stability concept are twofold. On the one hand, when all mutations are considered then some games can fail to have an ESS (see Remark 1 in sub-section 7.1.2). On the other hand, if some mutations are unplausible then the relationship between ESS and Nash refinements become less compelling if it does not persist in the presence of rational mutants. Note that although some games without ESS present strategies that are REE, the Swinkels' notion also fails to exist in some games.

An extension in terms of set-valued concepts is suggested by Swinkels (1992a) under the name: Equilibrium evolutionary stable sets (EES).

Definition 6 (*Equilibrium evolutionary stable set*)

A set $X^* \subset X$ is EES if it is a minimal closed non- empty set such that:

(i) X is a sub-set of the set of NE
(ii) for some $\bar{\varepsilon} \in (0, 1)$, if $\varepsilon \in (0, \bar{\varepsilon})$, $x \in X^*$, $x' \in X$ and $x' \in BR$
$(\varepsilon x' + (1 - \varepsilon)x)$, then:

$\varepsilon x' + (1 - \varepsilon)x \in X^*.$ ∎

The definition states that an EES set is a minimal closed set of symmetric NE such that the population can never be led out of X by a series of small equilibrium entries.

7.1.4 Asymmetrical evolutionary games

The previous sections dealt with single-population games. But, even if the payoff matrix is symmetric, an evolutionary game may easily show interesting asymmetries between the players. Maynard Smith (1982) raised the possibility that the animals could condition their behaviour on whether they are the 'row' or the 'column' player, that is to say that the strategies are then conditioned by the role played in the game (summarized by the phrases 'row and column'). Of course asymmetries can be worse still, payoffs being different between the row and the column players. In economics or business, the situations involve different kinds of players, in the sense that their available strategies are different and that they do not get identical payoffs from their participation in the game. If we want to model games with sellers and buyers, or incumbent firms and potential entrants, it is necessary to extend the evolutionary approach to multi-population settings. For reasons of simplicity, we will consider only the case of two different populations, but extensions to K populations ($K > 2$) is fairly possible.

Suppose that two large populations interact, the members of the first one being chosen randomly to meet also randomly chosen members of the second population. In order to avoid the difficulty coming from different speeds of adjustment, let us assume that the two populations are of equal size. The natural extension of the evolutionary model is then to consider a RD for each population. We have thus two replication equations:

$$\dot{s}_t^i(x) = s_t^i(x^i)[u_t^i(x^i) - \bar{u}_t^i] \quad i = 1, 2 \tag{7.12}$$

One can study the stationary points of the dynamics and verify the stability condition. A major finding in the multi-population case is that the mixed strategy profiles cannot be asymptotically stable.

One can also apply the ESS concept, although adapted to the multi-population context (see Weibull, 1995, section 5.1), and check whether the strategies are ESS or not. Since the members of a given population are now supposed to meet randomly members of a different population, the definition of an ESS given in (7.2) cannot any longer apply. A new definition of an ESS, allowing for asymmetric mutants, can be defined, as in Swinkels (1992b).

Another way to apply the concept of ESS is to symmetrize the game (see exercises 7.7 and 7.8). 'Symmetrizing' means that the player's role is chosen by Nature before the game starts. *Ex ante*, players do not know which role they will play and must then calculate their expected payoff under the assumption that they have an equal chance to be a row or a column player. An important result proven by Selten (1980) is that an ESS in such a symmetrized game is a *strict* equilibrium. Since a mixed strategy equilibrium by definition is not a strict equilibrium, mixed equilibria cannot be ESS of asymmetric games. On the other hand, one must notice that the 'symmetrization' of the game may work well for some games but may not fill many asymmetric games, the specific roles not being interchangeable (for a more complete discussion on this topic see Binmore and Samuelson, 2001).

Example I

A game of entry may oppose incumbent firms (player 1) and potential entrants (player 2). In order to maintain the assumption of large populations of players, one must imagine here a large number of incumbent firms, being in a position of local monopolies and many potential entrants, choosing randomly the location of their attack. The numerous possibilities of matching and the fact that two particular firms may meet only occasionally means that any reputational effect is negligible. What remains is that each entrant knows she (or he) is facing either an aggressive incumbent or a passive (accommodating) one. Similarly, the incumbent has only a probability on the chances of entry. Let p be the proportion of aggressive incumbents and q the proportion of potential entrants who actually enter.

The payoffs are given in Figure 7.7.

What is the RD for each category of player? For the local monopolies,

Figure 7.7   An entry game

	Enter	Do not enter
Aggressive	−1, −1	8, 0
Passive	3, 3	8, 0

We get:

$$\dot{p} = p[u_1^1 - \bar{u}^1]$$

where: $u_1^1 = q(-1) + (1-q)8 = 8 - 9q$
and since: $u_2^1 = 3q + (1-q)8 = 8 - 5q$
then: $\bar{u}^1 = p(8 - 9q) + (1-p)(8 - 5q) = 8 - 5q - 4pq$
and: $\dot{p} = p[(8 - 9q) - (8 - 5q - 4pq)] = p(1-p)(-4q)$
Therefore if q is positive, $\dot{p}$ is negative; which means that the percentage of incumbents playing aggressive is continuously decreasing.

Concerning the potential entrants, one gets by the same reasoning:

$$\dot{q} = q[u_1^2 - \bar{u}^2]$$

where $u_1^2 = 3 - 4p$ and $\bar{u}^2 = 3q - 4pq$
Then: $\dot{q} = q(1-q)(3-4p)$ and $\dot{q}$ is positive if $p < \frac{3}{4}$. In other words, the number of potential entrants who actually enter increases continuously if the proportion of aggressive local monopolies is lower than $\frac{3}{4}$.

The phase diagram in Figure 7.8 represents the dynamics of this example.

It appears clearly on the graph that the only stable point of the RD is the point corresponding to $q = 1$ and $p = 0$. The incumbent firms accommodate and the potential entrants do enter. Notice that the dynamical process has other stationary points: $(p = 0, q = 0)$, $(p = 1, q = 1)$, $(p = 1, q = 0)$ and $(p = \frac{3}{4}, q = 0)$. Among these four steady states, three are NE: two equilibria in pure strategies points: $(p = 0, q = 1)$, $(p = 1, q = 0)$, and the mixed strategy equilibrium $(p = \frac{3}{4}, q = 0)$. Yet only the equilibrium: $(p = 0, q = 1)$ is perfect. It is interesting to notice that it is also the EE of the game (the only asymptotically stable point of the dynamics). We will say more on the relationship between evolutionary equilibria and non-cooperative game equilibria in the next section.

Figure 7.8 Phase diagram of the RD in the entry game

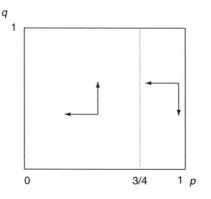

We must emphasize that the couple of strategies ($p = 0$, $q = 1$) also has the property of being an ESS (see exercise 7.7). In the end, the only SPE of this game is also an EE and an ESS. This correspondence will be investigated further later.

It is intriguing to see how players who do not chose rationally (they are just programmed) end up playing a SPE. A criterion like perfection seems to require a very strong intelligence of the game and a high capacity for computation, to solve for instance the backward induction type of calculation. Without any capacity for computation the players can find the same solution through an evolution process. The only drawback of the evolutionary approach is that the process takes time. In economic or business applications, the external conditions of the game may change rapidly. The evolutionary approach can be applied only for problems not characterized by rapidly changing environments (see Camerer, 1991, for a pessimistic view on this matter).

Example 2

We saw above that in the Hawk–Dove game the only EE was the mixed strategy: ($\frac{1}{4}$, $\frac{3}{4}$). Yet, what would happen if the game were played by two distinct populations? The mixed strategy is no longer an EE in this case.

Distinguishing two populations in this game means that there are two (large) groups of individuals who do not give the same value to the scarce resource: $V_1 \neq V_2$. Let us say that the scarce resource is a territory, and players 1 are residents, while players 2 are foreigners. So, normally, $V_1 > V_2$. For instance $V_1 = 6$, $V_2 = 2$, and as in the previous case, the cost of a fight is $C = 16$. Then the payoff matrix is as in Figure 7.9.

Now p is the proportion of residents playing Hawk and q is the proportion of foreigners playing Hawk. The Replication equations are:

$$\dot{p} = p(u_R - \bar{u}_R)$$

and

$$\dot{q} = q(u_I - \bar{u}_I)$$

where R is used for residents and I for invaders.
After some calculation, we get:

Figure 7.9 An asymmetric Hawk–Dove game

	Hawk	Dove
Hawk	−5, −7	6, 0
Dove	0, 2	3, 1

Figure 7.10   Phase diagram of the RD in an asymmetric Hawk–Dove game

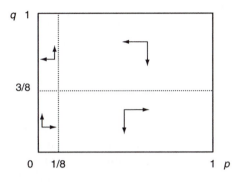

$$\dot{p} = p(1-p)(3-8q)$$

$$\dot{p} > 0(<0) \text{ if } q < \frac{3}{8}(>\frac{3}{8})$$

$$\dot{q} = q(1-q)(1-8p)$$

$$\dot{q} > 0(<0) \text{ if } p < \frac{1}{8}(>\frac{1}{8})$$

The dynamics can be represented by the phase diagram in Figure 7.10.

The RD shows two stable points $(p = 0, q = 1)$ and $(p = 1, q = 0)$. These are the EE of this game. All the players in a given population end up choosing to be Hawks while in the other population people choose to be Doves, depending on the starting point. No combination of Hawks and Doves can be maintained in the same population as an equilibrium of the evolutionary process. One can check that the two EE are also ESS (see exercise 7.8).

7.2 Extensions and generalizations to economics: evolution, rationality and efficiency

7.2.1 Connections between Replicator Dynamics, Evolutionary stable strategies and other equilibrium concepts

In the previous sections we have already underlined some connections between the evolutionary equilibrium concepts and the standard equilibrium concepts of non-cooperative game theory. When we defined an ESS, we stressed that it was a kind of refinement of symmetric NE. We also noticed that the ESS were stable stationary points of the dynamical process. In the present section, we want to give a more systematic review of all these connections.

For standard symmetric biological games, using bilinear fitness functions and Malthusian dynamics, there is a well-defined relationship between the different equilibrium points, which can be summarized by the following chain:

ESS ⊂ **EE** ⊂ **NE** ⊂ **FP**

where **ESS** is for Evolutionary stable strategy, **EE** for Evolutionary equilibrium (asymptotically stable steady states of the dynamics), **NE** for Nash equilibrium, and **FP** for the fixed point of the dynamical process.

Moreover, the last two inclusions can be generalized to any other kind of dynamics and for non-linear and multi-population fitness functions. The first inclusion cannot be so clearly generalized, because for certain types of dynamics, an ESS is neither a necessary nor a sufficient condition for the dynamic stability of a fixed-point of the dynamical process (see examples in Friedman, 1991).

For more precise results let us consider in turn the relationships between RD and NE and its refinements, then the relationship between ESS and the non-cooperative equilibrium concepts, and finally the relations between RD and ESS.

The Replicator Dynamics and non-cooperative equilibria

The RD has a simple relationship with NE. A first general proposition states that:

Theorem 1

If a strategy profile x^* is a symmetric NE, x^* is a stationary state of the RD

(for the proof see, for instance, Vega-Redondo, 1995, 53)∎

The converse of Theorem 1 need not be true. One can have stationary states of the RD which are not NE (this can happen if the steady state is an interior point in the simplex defining the frequencies of strategies). Theorem 1 says that symmetric NE are included in the set of steady states of the RD. A second proposition says that asymptotically stable steady states are a sub-set of NE.

Theorem 2

If a strategy profile x^* is an asymptotically stable steady state of the RD, then x^* is a NE. More precisely, it is a SPE

(see Weibull, 1995, Proposition 3.9, 39).∎

Let us turn now to the relationship between the ESS and NE and its refinements.

Evolutionary stable strategies and non-cooperative equilibria

Remember that an ESS is defined by:

(i) $u(x, x) > u(x', x)$

or:

(ii)   if $u(x, x) = u(x', x)$, then $u(x, x') > u(x', x')$

We have already seen that the first part of this definition is equivalent to saying that an ESS is a NE and that the second part says that an ESS has another property, something else which comes to be a form of refinement of NE. In fact it is a stronger refinement than the perfection criterion. One can establish the following results.

Theorem 3 (Bomze, 1986; Van Damme, 1991)

If a strategy profile x^* is an ESS, then x^* is a PTHE of the corresponding symmetric bilateral game. More precisely it is a PE.
(the definitions of a PTHE and a PE are provided in sub-section 4.2.1 of Chapter 4)∎

Remark I

Van Damme (1987) has shown that a PE in the agent-normal form of an extensive game is connected to the existence of a SE. We already noticed (sub-section 4.2.2 of Chapter 4) how demanding the concept of SE is in terms of rationality and complexity. Now, we see that agents with a minimal rationality and a very limited capacity of calculation find through evolution the complex equilibrium. However here our comments must be cautious, because very often extensive-form games do not possess an ESS, as a result of evolution drifts out of an equilibrium path. Yet the notion of a stable set of equilibria (see sub-section 4.3.3 of Chapter 4 for a definition of this notion) helps to solve the problem in this case. Indeed Swinkels (1992b) has been able to demonstrate that both backward induction and forward induction can be justified by evolutionary dynamics (for more details see Kandori, (1997).∎

At last, we can consider the relation between RD and ESS.

The Replicator dynamics and Evolutionary stable strategies

The RD describes the process of evolution of existing strategies, while the ESS looks at the possibilities of mutations. Nevertheless, the two instruments end up studying the stability of evolution. So, it is no surprise to find a strong relationship between the two. From the definition of an ESS and from Theorem 3 (p. 349), we know that ESS is a refinement of NE. From Theorem 1 (p. 348), we know that NE is a steady state of the RD. Then, it must be true that ESS are included in the set of Fixed points of the RD. What remains to be checked is the relationship between ESS and EE.

There is a result, a bit less general than the previous ones, but which still is verified for the most often used forms of the RD (see Friedman, 1991, for a discussion and several counterexamples).

Theorem 4 (Hofbauer, Schuster and Sigmund, 1979)

If the strategy profile x^* is an ESS, then x^* is an asymptotically stable steady state of the RD
(for the proof see for instance Vega-Redondo, 1995, 50).■

In general, the converse is not true. There are asymptotically stable points of the RD which are not ESS.

Example (Van Damme, 1991)

The game is described by the matrix of payoffs in Figure 7.11.

There is a unique symmetrical equilibrium in mixed strategies: $(\frac{1}{3}, \frac{1}{3}, \frac{1}{3})$, providing a payoff of $\frac{2}{3}$. However the strategy $(0, \frac{1}{2}, \frac{1}{2})$ can invade this equilibrium. The latter would give $\frac{2}{3}$ when confronted with the equilibrium strategy and $\frac{5}{4}$ when confronted with itself. Nevertheless the equilibrium is asymptotically stable. One can check that the Jacobian at equilibrium is:

$$\begin{pmatrix} 1/9 & -1/9 & -4/9 \\ -7/9 & -4/9 & 5/9 \\ 2/9 & -1/9 & -7/9 \end{pmatrix}$$

with eigenvalues: $\frac{1}{3}, -\frac{1}{3}, -\frac{2}{3}$.

Figure 7.11   A game for which the asymptotically stable points of the RD are not ESS

	x^1	x^2	x^3
x^1	0, 0	1, –2	1, 1
x^2	–2, 1	0, 0	4, 1
x^3	1, 1	1, 4	0, 0

Remark 2

It is interesting to figure out why the converse of Theorem 4 (p. 350) is not true. This result comes from the assumption about the kind of strategies that can be inherited in the RD. If only pure strategies can be inherited, then it is clear, as in Van Damme's example, that some strategies can be invaded, even if they are asymptotically stable steady states. The result changes if the RD is modified in order to authorize the possible inheritance of mixed strategies. In that case, there is total identity between an ESS and an asymptotically stable state of the RD (see Bomze, 1986; Hines, 1980; Vega-Redondo, 1995).■

One can easily check the consistency of Theorems 2, 3, and 4. Theorem 4 says that an ESS is an asymptotically stable fixed point of the RD. Theorem 2 says that such a stable steady state is a SPE. Taken together, Theorems 4 and 2 imply that an ESS is a PTHE (Theorem 3).

7.2.2   Evolution and dominance

Evolutionary models require a very minimal rationality for guiding the agents' choices. Nevertheless, we saw in previous sections that the result of evolutionary dynamics is often equivalent to the outcome of a non-cooperative game played by extremely rational agents.

Now, we know that rational agents must play 'rationalizable' strategies as defined by Bernheim (1984) and Pearce (1984) (see sub-section 4.1.2 of Chapter 4). So, dominated strategies must be eliminated, eventually through an iterative process. But, what will happen if agents are not really rational, as in the evolutionary approach? Will the evolution process lead to an elimination of dominated strategies? The problem is serious, because if such an elimination of dominated strategies seems highly desirable, it is not at all assured. The RD fuels the growth of a strategy providing a payoff greater than the average. The problem is that a dominated strategy may eventually give a higher payoff than the average.

The results obtained on this issue are rather reassuring, even if there are some examples of dominated strategies which may survive. The most often-quoted example of a dominated strategy which can survive has been proposed by Dekel and Scotchmer (1992).

The game is a version of the 'rock, paper, scissors' game (see sub-section 1.2.2 of Chapter 1), in which a fourth strategy D has been added. D is strictly dominated by a combination of the three first strategies, without ever been strictly dominated by any pure strategy among them. The payoffs matrix is given in Figure 7.12.

Figure 7.12   A version of the 'rock, paper, scissors' game

	R	P	S	D
R	1, 1	2.35, 0	0, 2.35	0.1, 1.1
P	0, 2.35	1, 1	2.35, 0	0.1, 1.1
S	2.35, 0	0, 2.35	1, 1	0.1, 1.1
D	1.1, 0.1	1.1, 0.1	1.1, 0.1	0, 0

A mix of the three first strategies, in equal proportions, strictly dominates strategy D (3.35/3 > 1.1). But for various proportions of strategies, the fourth one makes a higher than average outcome. For some kinds of RD, especially the discrete time RD used by Dekel and Scotchmer (1992), strategy D is not eliminated in the long run, except if it starts with a population exactly sharing the strategies R, S, and P.

Despite this sad example, the results obtained in more general frameworks, in continuous time RD, show rather a *general tendency of elimination of dominated strategies*. One can summarize these results as follows:

(i)   There is first a result due to Akin (1980): if a strategy is strictly dominated, the Malthusian dynamics starting from any interior initial point reduces the share of the population which plays it to zero.

(ii)   Introducing some notions of payoff monotonicity, several authors have proposed more general results. In particular Samuelson and Zhang (1992) show that if a pure strategy is eliminated by the process of iterative strict dominance (on the pure strategies), it cannot survive in a selection process verifying a property of 'dynamic monotonicity', that is if for all the interior points the strategies which have the highest current payoffs are also the strategies which grow more rapidly. This result can be extended to mixed strategies by using an adapted notion of payoff monotinicity (called 'aggregate monotonicity').

(iii)   An even weaker sufficient condition has been proposed by Hofbauer and Weibull (1996). This condition, called 'convex monotonicity' states that, for all interior points, if a mixed strategy m has a higher payoff than a pure strategy x, the former will have a higher 'growth rate' than the latter. Convex monotonicity is a necessary and sufficient condition for assuring that the selection dynamics get rid of the strategies which would be eliminated by strict iterative dominance, when all the strategies are initially present.

Remark 1

We have considered so far *strict* dominance and *strict* iterative dominance. As far as weakly dominated strategies are concerned, the RD and other evolutionary selection dynamics are not able to necessarily get rid of them.■

It finally emerges from this section that, for a large variety of selection processes, including the RD (which verifies convex monotonicity), the players behave as if they were rational and as if this rationality was common knowledge. Of course these results offer a supplementary reason to study the application of evolutionary games in economics and business.

7.2.3   Evolutionary stability and efficiency

We saw in Example 1 of section 7.1 (p 333) that the coordination game had two ESS, one corresponding to the inefficient NE (3, 3) and the other one to the efficient equilibrium (4, 4). The population ends up in one or the other of these equilibria depending on the starting point, that is depending on the initial percentage of players choosing x_1 or x_2. There is no particular guarantee of efficiency in this example. One can even notice that unfortunately in this case the basin of attraction (see definition in Appendix 1 of this chapter) of the efficient equilibrium is smaller than the basin of attraction of the other equilibrium. If each starting point is equiprobable on [0, 1], then in $\frac{3}{5}$ of the cases evolution will drive the strategies to the wrong (inefficient) equilibrium.

The evolutionary approach does not seem to be more reassuring on this issue than standard non-cooperative GT. But the works by Axelrod and his collaborators (Axelrod, 1984; Axelrod and Hamilton, 1981) and the experimental approach (see Chapter 8) tend to prove that agents can find some ways to learn more efficient ways to play games. Can the evolutionary approach find something similar?

One must then envisage a kind of 'pre-play communication' between the players. And indeed, several authors showed that some kinds of pre-play communication devices can lead to the efficient outcome in an evolutionary framework (see Matsui, 1991; Warneryd, 1991; Kim and Sobel, 1995; for the role of pre-play communication in the classical setting of non-cooperative games see sub-section 3.2.2 of Chapter 3).

In order to study the issue of the selection of an efficient outcome, let us introduce the concept of 'risk-dominance' (Harsanyi and Selten, 1988). Roughly speaking, a strategy may be called more or less 'risky', depending on the payoff it would permit us to obtain if the other player does not play the NE strategy. Pairs of strategies can thus be ranked according to the risks they involve for the players. A more formal definition is as follows.

Definition 7 (*Risk dominance*)

A pair of strategies is risk-dominant if each strategy is a best response to a mixed strategy of the other player that weights all the player's pure strategies equally.∎

Now, consider the game described by the payoff matrix in Figure 7.13. It is clear that the players should agree to play the efficient equilibrium (x_1, x_1). But strategy x_2 is risk-dominant, since x_2 is a best response to the mixed strategy $\frac{1}{2}x_1 + \frac{1}{2}x_2$:

$$\frac{1}{2}(0) + \frac{1}{2}(1) = 0.5 > \frac{1}{2}(3) + \frac{1}{2}(-100) = -48.5$$

So, it has a strong chance of being chosen. Can a pre-play communication be able to help the players choose the efficient strategy (i.e. the 'payoff-dominant' equilibrium)? According to standard non-cooperative GT, the answer is no.

A pre-play communication is dealt with by incorporating a supplementary stage to the game. In the first stage, the players announce their intention by sending a message. This message has no cost – it is cheap talk – in the sense that it does not influence the payoffs in the final stage of the game. In our example, the players announce their intention to play x_1 or x_2. The game so redefined (in its extensive form) is of course different from the original one. For instance, a strategy consisting in sending a message x_1, and playing x_2 in the next stage is a NE of the game. However, it can be shown that the set of equilibria obtained by various refinements of NE is perfectly identical to the one of the previous game.

The evolutionary approach is able to show how an efficient equilibrium may be reached. A population of players who play the strategy: message x_1 in the first stage and action x_2 in the second stage can be invaded by mutants who play the strategy: message x_2 in the first stage, and action x_1 in the second stage, if and only if message x_2 was sent in the first stage. Through this device, the mutant can choose the efficient strategy only if she (or he) is meeting another mutant. Facing a member of the incumbent population, she (or he) will play action x_2 as the opponent.

Figure 7.13   A game with strong losses if the other player deviates from the NE

	x_1	x_2
x_1	3, 3	−100, 0
x_2	0, −100	1, 1

It is easy to check that this strategy is able to yield a higher payoff for mutants than for incumbent members. Moreover, a population playing the efficient strategy cannot be invaded by other mutants. This strategy, sometimes called 'secret handshake' (Robson, 1990) is, however, not necessarily very strong. It rests on the assumptions that mutants can send a message not already utilized in order to be able to identify themselves mutually and that the members of the incumbent population do not react to the new message sent.

Imagine that each message is sent with a positive probability and that the incumbent players play x_2 whatever the message sent, then the mutants would have no means to identify themselves. We have then a 'babbling' equilibrium.

Another example showing the difficulties that may face the mutants is the following one (suggested by Kandori, 1997) (Figure 7.14).

If the incumbent population plays the strategy: message x_1 and action x_2, action x_3 otherwise, the mutants are punished when they announce x_2 (or x_3) and they cannot invade easily.

Remark 1

The evolutionary approach can help to promote efficiency only in the coordination game. When agents do not share the same opinion on the equilibrium that should be reached, the strategy seen above cannot be implemented.■

Remark 2

The difficulty in 'killing' some equilibria, like the babbling equilibrium, can be solved by using evolutionary drifts. In a babbling equilibrium, the choice of a message has indeed no importance whatsoever, since people will play the inefficient strategy anyway. So a drift may happen and after a sufficient accumulation of drift, some messages become unutilized (or rare enough) so that mutants can again find a way to identify themselves and invade the incumbent population.■

Figure 7.14 A game showing the difficulties faced by mutants

	x_1	x_2	x_3
x_1	3, 3	0, 0	0, 0
x_2	0, 0	2, 2	0, 0
x_3	0, 0	0, 0	1,1

> **Remark 3**
>
> The evolution towards an efficient solution is also possible if there can be a wrong perception of messages (see Bhaskar, 1994). In this case, the reaction of incumbents to a message usually not sent is not a NE.■

7.3 Learning models

In evolutionary games, as seen in previous sections, players are pro-grammed to play certain strategies. Even if one can add some elements which capture the fact that players may be a little bit smarter than animals (such as REE), the approach remains unsatisfactory to describe the behaviour of economic agents. We might expect that individuals learn something while playing the game, and behave accordingly.

We will now present a short review of different ways of studying learning games and we will note that for different versions of individual learning behaviour the aggregate outcome may result in some form of Replicator dynamics. One may distinguish three major types of learning games: routine learning, imitation and belief learning.

Routine learning is a process by which players modify their choice probabilities according to their recent experience of success or failure. This type of learning, also called the 'psychological stimulus response model' of learning, or 'reinforcement model', does not require any sophisticated behaviour. Agents are simply assumed to follow a rule of the type: 'what worked well in the past will work well in the future.' They only watch their own choices and payoffs, without any consideration for the choices and payoffs of their opponents.

Imitation of successful players can constitute another type of learning in a game. It is not very different from routine learning. However in this case, it is the success of *others* which influences the choice of probabilities of the players. We will see later in the section that both routine learning and learning through imitation can lead to some kind of Replicator dynamics.

The third type of learning is called '*belief learning*'. It is more complex than the previous ones. The general idea of belief learning is that the players use information about past choices and payoffs of *their opponents* to update their own beliefs about the choice of the other players in the current stage of the game. Of course, one may consider a variety of ways to model belief learning, depending on the learning rule assumed for each player.

In the original Cournot oligopoly (1838) the players base their beliefs on the rather naive assumption that the rivals will keep their outputs at the same level as in the last period. Assuming that the players have a long memory and take all the past observation into account leads to the learning rule called 'fictitious play'. An adaptive model of learning may keep the long-memory assumption but give more weight to the more recent observations. Finally the learning rule may represent more sophisticated behaviour, including Bayesian revision of beliefs and means for detecting eventual cycles or other regularities in the observations.

The main issues concerning learning are of course the evolution of the dynamic process generating the sequence of play. Does this process converge over time? If so, does it lead to a NE or one of its refinements?

7.3.1   Routine learning*

In psychology, individual learning has been studied by Bush and Mosteller (1955) as a process of reinforcement of actions which did well in the past. The same idea has been applied to describe how people learn in game experiments (see Roth and Erev, 1995, and sub-section 8.5.3 of Chapter 8). The model seems to fit well with observed behaviour, although much more must be learned about its mathematical properties.

Important results have been obtained by Borgers and Sarin (1997) concerning the link between this learning process and the replicator dynamics of EGT. The RD is a deterministic process in continuous time while the reinforcement process is stochastic and in discrete time. However, Borgers and Sarin show that in the limit, the stimulus–response process may converge in probability to the RD.

The game is played repeatedly by two players. At each date t, the agents use mixed strategies (m_t^1, m_t^2). The probabilities with which each pure strategy is used by an agent is updated according to the payoffs obtained previously. More precisely, call $p_{t+1}(x)$ the probability of playing the pure strategy x in $t+1$, Δ the time interval between two rounds, and $u_t(x_t)$ the payoff obtained at time t. Player i updates her probabilities in the following way:

$$\begin{cases} p_{t+1}^i(x) = p_t^i(x) + \Delta u_t^i(x_t)[1 - p_t^i(x)] & \text{if } x = x_t \\ p_{t+1}^i(x) = p_t^i(x) - \Delta u_t^i(x_t)p_t^i(x), & \text{if } x \neq x_t \end{cases} \tag{7.13}$$

Notice that the payoffs $u_t(x_t)$ are normalized to lie between zero and one, so that they can be interpreted as probabilities. It is clear from (7.13) that once a pure strategy is used, its probability of being chosen increases.

Borgers and Sarin study a continuous-time limit of this discrete time process. They assume that the game is repeated over a number of periods $t \to \infty$, and that $\Delta \to 0$; the 'real time' Δt is thus bounded. They compare this learning process with the RD starting at the same initial point, that is the same probability vectors of the mixed strategy m_0^1 and m_0^2.

They show finally that the trajectories converge to the point that the RD would have reached at the real time Δt, starting from the same initial point. However, one must notice that the asymptotic behaviour of the RD may differ from the asymptotic behaviour of the stochastic process. The reinforcement process converges to a pure strategy profile, while the RD may not do so (for instance, in the game of matching pennies).

7.3.2 Learning by way of imitation*

A simple evolutionary model linked to social learning and leading to the RD is developed below (borrowed from Gale, Binmore and Samuelson, 1985). The model is in discrete time, where each period has a length Δ.

At each period, each player keeps the previous strategy with probability $(1 - \Delta)$. With probability Δ, the agent compares her (or his) current payoff with an aspiration level called Ω. This level Ω is a random variable uniformly distributed on $[\ell, L]$. If by playing the current strategy a player gets more than Ω, she (or he) will keep on playing it. However, if this payoff is lower than Ω, she (or he) will choose another strategy at random. The probability that a given strategy is chosen is equal to the proportion of the population already playing it (imitation of other people's choices at random would give this probability).

Let $p_i(t)$ be the probability that Ω be higher than the payoff from strategy i for a player at time t. A proportion $p_i(t)$ of the players choosing i at time t are assumed to have an aspiration level higher than their payoff. They will change for a new strategy in exactly the same proportion as those strategies are played by the population of players.

From the previous assumptions, one gets:

$$x_i(t + \Delta) = x_i(t)(1 - \Delta p_i(t)) + \sum_{j \in s} \Delta p_j(t)x_j(t)x_i(t) \tag{7.14}$$

where $x_i(t)$ denotes the fraction of players who choose strategy i at time t. Calling $\Pi_i(t)$, the payoff from strategy i at period t one may notice that:

$$p_i(t) = \frac{(L - \Pi_i(t))}{(L - \ell)}$$

Replacing $p_i(t)$ in (7.14) and rearranging i gives:

$$\frac{x_i(t + \Delta) - x_i(t)}{\Delta} = x_i(t)\frac{\Pi_i(t) - \overline{\Pi}(t)}{L - \ell} \tag{7.15}$$

where $\overline{\Pi}(t)$ is the average payoff of all the players.

A continuous time version results from considering $\Delta \to 0$ in (7.15). Then:

$$\dot{x}_i(t) = x_i(t)\frac{\Pi_i - \overline{\Pi}}{L - \ell} \qquad (7.16)$$

It is clear then that the RD is a special case of (7.16) when the time scale is chosen in such a way that the constant term $(L - \ell)$ disappears.

Some noise can be introduced in the RD, if one assumes that each player ignores the learning process with a probability δ, at each period. Then in case of ignorance, the agent will give up her (or his) current strategy with probability Δ, without any consideration of the comparison with an aspiration level and she (or he) will choose at random a new strategy. Strategy i will then be chosen with probability θ_i.

Equation (7.14) becomes:

$$x_i(t + \Delta) = (1 - \delta)\left\{ x_i(t)(1 - \Delta p_i(t)) + \sum_{j \in s} \Delta p_j(t)x_j(t)x_i(t) \right\}$$
$$+ \delta\{x_i(t) + \Delta(\theta_i(t) - x_i(t))\} \qquad (7.17)$$

Again substituting

$$p_i(t) = \frac{(L - \Pi_i(t))}{(L - \ell)}$$

and considering the limit when $\Delta \to 0$, we get:

$$\dot{x}_i(t) = (1 - \delta)x_i(t)\frac{\Pi_i - \overline{\Pi}}{L - \ell} + \delta(\theta_i - x_i) \qquad (7.18)$$

And again, one can consider (7.18) as a special case of an RD equation, where the term $(L - \ell)$ is equal to one and the term $\delta(\theta_i - x_i)$ captures some noise in the learning process.

Of course the previous analysis can be generalized to several populations and different learning rules across the populations.(an application of the noisy RD is presented in the last section of this chapter).

7.3.3 Belief learning

Unlike routine learning and imitation, 'belief learning' has only an indirect influence on the players' behaviour. Past experience strengthens or weakens players' beliefs. More precisely, players use information about the past choices and payoffs of their opponents to update their own beliefs about the choices of their opponents in the current stage of the game. Then they are able to determine their optimal strategy (best response) to the expected choice of their opponents.

There are many ways to model the process by which each player updates her (or his) beliefs about the opponents choices. The basic idea of revising the beliefs about opponents' choices seem to require a higher level of sophistication in the learning rule than in the stimulus–response or the imitative learning models. However, the better-known models of belief learning assume only a very limited rationality for the players.

Cournot adjustment model

The oldest and most famous model of learning is the Cournot duopoly model itself. The model is the one described above (see sub-section 3.1.2 of Chapter 3), except that an adjustment process is added, as in the original work by Cournot.

There are two firms $i = 1, 2$, choosing at each period their optimal quantities so that there are best responses to the action chosen by the rival in the previous round. Calling x^1 and x^2 the pure strategy of firm 1 and 2, respectively, the best response dynamics is such that:

$$\begin{cases} x_{t+1}^1 = R^1(x_t^2) \\ x_{t+1}^2 = R^2(x_t^1) \end{cases} \tag{7.19}$$

where $R(.)$ is a best response function defined as $R^i(x^j) = \arg\max_{x^i} \Pi^i(x^i, x^j)$. A steady-state of (7.19) is a strategy profile x^* such that:

$$x^* = R(x^*)$$

Cournot adjustment can be illustrated by the diagram in Figure 7.15. Under reasonable assumptions about the slope of the best response functions, the dynamic process described by Cournot converges to an asymptotically stable point, which is the static NE. Here it is also a globally stable steady state (the basin of attraction is the entire space).

A simple way to check for the asymptotic stability is to compute the eigenvalues of the matrix:

$$DR(.) = \begin{bmatrix} 0 & R^{1'} \\ R^{2'} & 0 \end{bmatrix}$$

where $R^{1'}$ and $R^{2'}$ are the slopes of the R functions. The eigenvalues are

$$\lambda = \pm \sqrt{R^{1'} R^{2'}}$$

Figure 7.15 Adjustment in Cournot duopoly

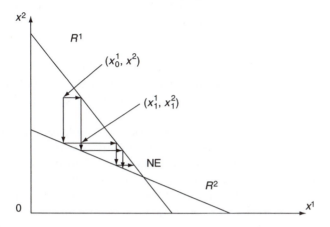

The absolute value of λ is smaller that 1 if the slope of R^2 is less than the slope of R^1. It is obviously true in Figure 7.15.

The Cournot adjustment may be considered as a learning model since each player makes a guess at the future move of his rival and reacts accordingly. However, the capacity of learning is very limited. Players remain myopic and assume that the opponent is simply going to repeat the previous move, while both of them actually change until the steady state is reached. If the players are smart enough, they should understand these changes and take them into account in the choice of the best response.

Several variants of the model have been proposed in order to turn the myopic expectation into an optimal behaviour. The Cournot model may get more strength as a learning model if players are allowed to make only alternating moves. Firms are locked-in for two periods, for example, because the decision bears on capital goods which can be replaced only after two periods. Then one gets the alternating move Cournot dynamics. Firm 1 chooses its capacity in periods 1, 3, 5... And firm 2 chooses in periods 2, 4, 6... They try to maximize the discounted sum of their per-period profit:

$$\sum_{t=1}^{\infty} \delta^{t-1} \Pi^i(x_t)$$

where δ is a discount factor, common to both firms. One can show again that the steady state of this process is asymptotically stable if the best response function R_1 is steeper than the best response function R_2.

Other variants of lock-in models have been proposed (see, for instance, Maskin and Tirole, 1988). However firms compute only their optimal actions and as in a static model do not really learn in the process.

Fictitious play

Another model of belief learning is known as the process of 'fictitious play'. Players believe that they face a stationary distribution of opponents' strategies. They do not know this distribution and eventually learn about it as the game is repeated over time.

Let us consider the simplest case of a two-player simultaneous-move game. Each player has a finite strategy space X and a payoff function $U(x)$. At each period the players revise their expectations about the distribution of opponents' actions and chose a best response accordingly. The process of updating the predictions is summarized by a weight function $K^i(x^j)$. The initial value K_0^i is given exogenously. Then the weights are revised by adding 1 to an opponent's strategy which is just being played:

$$K_t^i(x^j) = K_{t-1}^i(x^j) + \begin{cases} 1 & \text{if } x_{t-1}^j = x^j \\ 0 & \text{if } x_{t-1}^j \neq x^j \end{cases}$$

At date t, player i assigns to player j the following probability of choosing x^j:

$$\gamma_t^i(x^j) = \frac{K_t^i(x^j)}{\sum\limits_{\tilde{x}^j \in X^j} K_t^i(\tilde{x}^j)}$$

Based on this assessment of the distribution of opponents' actions, player i chooses a best response:

$$x_t^i = R^i(\gamma_t^i)$$

A simple example will illustrate the dynamic process. Consider the payoff matrix in Figure 7.16.

Now assume that the initial weights are (1, 2.5) and (2.5, 1) – that is, for instance, player A assigns first a weight 1 to player B's strategy 1 and a weight 2.5 to player B's strategy 2. Then the best responses are: A chooses strategy 2 and B chooses strategy 1. So the weights are revised and become: (2, 2.5) and (2.5, 2). So A will now choose strategy 2 and B will choose strategy 1 again. The weights become (3, 2.5) and (2.5, 3). Then A turns to strategy 1 and B turns to strategy 2. The weights become (3, 3.5) and (3.5, 3). A will choose 2 and B will choose 1, and so on.

Figure 7.16   A simple non-cooperative game

$$B$$

		1	2
A	1	3, 3	0, 1
	2	1, 0	2, 2

The key question about fictitious play is whether the process converges or not. There are sufficient conditions for fictitious play to converge. The following propositions have been established.

Theorem 5 (*Fudenberg and Levine, 1999*)

(i) If x is a strict NE and x is played at date t in the process of fictitious play, x is played at all subsequent dates; (ii) Any pure strategy steady state of fictitious play must be a NE.■

Theorem 6 (*Fudenberg and Levine, 1999*)

Under fictitious play, the empirical distributions converge if the stage game is 2×2 or zero-sum or is solvable by iterated strict dominance.■

Remark I

We should emphasize that, even if distinctions have been made in this chapter between evolutionary and learning models, the recent developments of the literature propose models that can be called 'evolutionary model of learning'. These models include at the same time considerations on the individual learning and rules belonging to the natural selection assumed by the evolutionary theory. For a detailed story of this promising area for future research see, for instance, Vignolo (2000).■

7.4   Applications

7.4.1   International trade and the internal organization of firms

In this section we will present the model developed by Friedman and Fung (1996) because it is, to our knowledge, the most interesting and empirically relevant application of evolutionary games in economics. The model was originally presented in a simple parametric version and in a more general and sophisticated version – we have chosen to give here only an intuitive presentation of the first version and we invite the readers to make a more thorough exploration of the original article.

The model is designed to discuss the issue, recently raised in policy debates, of the interaction between the trade environment and the internal organization of firms. In order to keep things simple, two basic modes of internal organization are distinguished, in accordance with the work of Aoki (1988, 1990) and others.

The first mode, denoted A, is called '*American*'. A set of stylized facts characterize this mode: (a) workers are specialized and narrowly classified; (b) decisions are centralized; (c) information flows from the top to the bottom; (d) buffer inventories are used to meet the fluctuation of demand The second mode of organization, denoted B, is called '*Japanese*'. It can also be identified by a series of typical facts and relationships: (a) job rotation is a usual practice; (b) lifetime employment may be provided to workers; (c) decisions are made and coordinated by shop-floor units; (d) the cost of inventories is minimized by 'Just In Time' (JIT) techniques; (e) banks and other corporations may participate actively in stockholding of firms.

It is generally acknowledged that the relative efficiencies of the two modes depend on the economic environment in which the firms operate (Aoki, 1990). More interestingly for our purpose, efficiency also depends on the proportion of firms using the other modes. The basic point here is that the average production cost of B falls when a larger proportion of firms choose this internal organization mode.

Friedman and Fung identify two sources of this externality: the *skimming* effect and the *network* effect.

Firm B must invest heavily in training their workers, in order to achieve job rotation, decentralization of decisions and lifetime employment. However wages are less linked to seniority in firm A. So, young workers in firm B may be interested in moving to firm A, where they might secure a higher wage. The larger the proportion of firm A, the higher the risk of such a 'skimming' effect of the best workers of firm B.

The network effect arises from the relationships between firms, their suppliers and their distributors. B firms develop strong ties with their various partners. Yet if the number of firms A, increases these ties may be loosened because B partners find alternative opportunities and get a stronger bargaining power.

Through these external effects the proportion of firms A influences the relative cost of production of firms B. Another kind of interdependence can be added in the demand side if the products of firms A and B are not perfect substitutes: it is called a 'glut' effect on output price.

The simple version of the model is a two-country model where there is in each country a fixed number of identical firms playing a Cournot game. These firms can also choose their best internal organization. The evolutionary (long-run) equilibrium is a steady state where firms have not any incentive to change to another mode.

A major outcome of the model is to compare the equilibria which can be reached in autarky and with international trade.

Autarky

In a single country, there are N firms. The number N must be large enough to avoid strategic choices of the organization mode. In biological evolutionary models N is a continuum of agents. Here the authors assume only $N \geq 2$. A parameter $s \in [0, 1]$ represents the percentage of firms choosing mode B: so sN firms choose mode B and $(1 - s)N$ choose mode A (of course, some restrictions on s are needed to have integers).

The cost structure is very simple: there are no fixed costs, c_A is the constant unit cost of firms A and $c_B - bs$ is the constant unit cost of firms B:

$$c_A > 0 \text{ and } c_B - bs > 0$$

The skimming and network effects operate through the parameter b (the relative costs of firms B decrease when s increases).

The inverse demand functions are:

$$P_A = \alpha_A - \beta X_A - \gamma X_B$$

and

$$P_B = \alpha_B - \beta X_B - \gamma X_A$$

where α_A, $\alpha_B > 0$, $0 < \gamma < \beta$ are parameters; P_A and P_B are the prices of A goods and B goods which are considered as substitutes; and $X_A = \sum_{i \in A} x_i$ and $X_B = \sum_{i \in B} x_i$ are the total outputs of firms A and firms B, respectively.

Each firm plays a non-cooperative game in quantities (Cournot) against all other firms. Each firm A chooses an output $x_A \geq 0$ to maximize its profit given by the profit function:

$$\Pi_A = [\alpha_A - \beta(x_A + X_{A-i}) - \gamma X_B]x_A - c_A x_A$$

where $X_{A-i} = X_A - x_A$. Each firm B has an identical profit-maximizing behaviour.

The unique symmetric equilibrium resulting from the first-order conditions of the problem gives the following output levels:

$$x_A = [(1 + sN)\beta\theta_A - \gamma sN(\theta_B + bs)]/\Delta$$

and

$$x_B = [(1 + (1 - s)N)\beta(\theta_B + bs) - \gamma(1 - s)N\theta_A]/\Delta$$

where:

$$\Delta = (1 + sN)(1 + (1 - s)N)\beta^2 - sN(1 - s)N\gamma^2$$
$$\theta_A = \alpha_A - c_A > 0$$

and

$$\theta_B = \alpha_B - c_B > 0$$

The short-run equilibrium corresponds to a given proportion of organization modes. The short-run profits are (see Appendix 1 of this chapter for more details):

$$\Pi_A = (x_A)^2\beta \text{ and } \Pi_B = (x_B)^2\beta$$

For given values of the various parameters and of the fraction s of firms B one can compute the profits Π_A and Π_B. Figure 7.17 shows the behaviour of Π_A and Π_B for s varying from 0 to 1 and for given values of the other parameters (number of firms, cost and demand parameters).

In this example, for $0 \leq \hat{s} \leq 0.5$ there will be in the long run an evolution towards mode A (since $\Pi_A > \Pi_B$). As in the general model of section 1 above, this evolution can be described finally be a differential equation

Figure 7.17 Profits profiles for different values of s (for given value of the parameters)

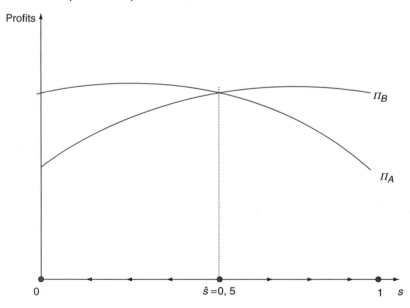

relating $\dot{s}$ (the rate of change of s) to all the environmental variables affecting firms' profitability.

It is clear, in Figure 7.17, that the steady state which corresponds to $\hat{s} = 0.5$ for which $\Pi_A = \Pi_B$ is unstable. A slight increase in s leads to a stable steady state where $s = 1$, all firms choose mode B in the long run. A slight decrease in s leads to the stable steady state $s = 0$, where all firms choose mode A.

Different values of the parameters would give other pictures of the relative levels of Π_A and Π_B. In all cases, however, the skimming and network effects tend to increase Π_B when s rises, while the 'glut' effect implies that an increase in s must have a depressive effect on the price of B products relative to A products. When the skimming and network effects dominate the glut effect, the profit function Π_B is upward sloping and its slope is steeper than the slope of the Π_A function. With the parameters leading to Figure 7.17, the EE is either all A or all B, depending on the starting point (historical accident!).

International trade

The model is then extended by adding a foreign country, similar to the domestic one in the sense that N^* firms (asterisks denotes foreign country variables) operate as Cournot competitors and can choose mode A or mode B for their internal organizations. We suppose that s^*N^* firms choose mode B, for $s^* \in [0, 1]$.

Now, using superscript d and e to denote production for the domestic market and for the exports, respectively, one can write the increased demand functions for domestic firms A and B:

$$P_A = \alpha_A - \beta(X_A^d + X_A^{*e}) - \gamma(X_B^d + X_B^{*e})$$

and similarly for $P_B(\cdot)$. There are also, of course, demand function $P_A^*(\cdot)$ and $P_B^*(\cdot)$ for foreign firms.

Profit maximization by domestic A firms now requires them also to choose between selling on the domestic market $x_A^d \geq 0$ or exporting $x_A^e \geq 0$. The profit function becomes:

$$\Pi_A = \lfloor \alpha_A - \beta(X_{A-i}^d + x_A^d + X_A^{*e}) - \gamma(X_B^d + X_B^{*e}) \rfloor x_A^d$$
$$+ \lfloor \alpha_A^* - \beta(X_A^{*d} + X_{A-i}^e + x_A^e) - \gamma(X_B^{*d} + X_B^e) \rfloor x_A^e$$
$$- c_A(x_A^d + x_A^e) - tx_A^e$$

where $t \geq 0$ is a parameter representing a tariff on exports or any other cost of selling abroad (any trade barrier). Mode B domestic firms have similar profit functions $\Pi_B(\cdot)$ and foreign firms also maximize profit functions $\Pi_A^*(\cdot)$ and $\Pi_B^*(\cdot)$.

Skimming and network effects are also present in the foreign country and these are captured in the cost function of foreign firms B through a parameter b^*, giving unit cost: $c_B^* - b^*s^* > 0$. All the other parameters could also differ between the domestic country and the foreign country (for simplicity Friedman and Fung, 1996, assume here that β, γ and t do not differ across countries).

Cournot equilibrium outputs $x_i^j(s, s^*)$ and $x_i^{*j}(s, s^*)$, where $i = A$, B and $j = d$, e, are presented in Appendix 2B of this chapter (for an explanation of the quadratic form of the profit function see Appendix 2A).

The (short-run) equilibrium profits are for domestic firms A: $\Pi_A(s, s^*) = (x_A^d)^2\beta + (x_A^e)^2\beta$ and similar expressions for Π_B, Π_A^* and Π_B^*. The interdependence of optimal values for mode A and mode B firms, at home and abroad, passes through the domestic effects (external effect and glut effect) and a transnational glut effect.

In long run, the signs of the profit difference $\Pi_D = \Pi_B - \Pi_A$ at home and $\Pi_D^* = \Pi_B^* - \Pi_A^*$ abroad orientates the adjustment dynamics.

Four different cases are presented in Figure 7.18.

Figure 7.18a represents the case where the trade barriers are too high to allow any amount of trade between the countries. We find again the autarkic equilibrium in each country so that the only stable steady states are either ($s = 0$ or $s = 1$) and ($s^* = 0$ or $s^* = 1$). Each corner of the square can then be an EE. The basins of attraction of each EE is separated by the lines $\Pi_D = 0$ and $\Pi_D^* = 0$.

In the situation represented in Figure 7.18 (b), there are no trade barriers ($t = 0$). As in Figure 7.18 (a), the square is divided in four regions by the loci $\Pi_D = 0$ and $\Pi_D^* = 0$. The domestic country is larger than the foreign country ($N = 20$, $\alpha_A = 220$ and $N^* = 10$, $\alpha_A^* = 110$). There are again four EE, but the basins of attraction for ($s = 0$, $s^* = 0$) and ($s = 1$, $s^* = 1$) are dramatically reduced. Those values of the parameters are chosen to represent a sort of stylized version of the US and Japan economies in a situation of free trade. Since by a pure accident of history Japan was in autarky at $s^* = 1$ and the US was at $s = 0$, the equilibrium with free trade is the EE (0, 1).

In Figure 7.18 (c), the situation corresponds also to $t = 0$, but asymmetries in size or other parameter values, such as transnational glut effects, turn the equilibria ($s = 0$, $s^* = 0$) and ($s = 1$, $s^* = 1$) into unstable steady states.

Finally, Figure 7.18 (d) represents a situation of free trade in goods and globalization of input costs. Now $c_A = c_A^* = \bar{c}_A$ and $c_B = c_B^* = \bar{c}_B$. The external effects (skimming and network effects) are also equalized. They are linked to the world proportion of B firms: $\bar{s} = \frac{Ns+N^*s^*}{N+N^*}$ and enter into the cost functions of B firms through a parameter $\bar{b}$: $\bar{c}_B - \bar{b}\bar{s}$. The EE are now symmetric: (0, 0) and (1, 1). The basins of attraction can be different, depending on the value of the parameters.

Figure 7.18   Phase diagram for different values of the parameters when countries are open to international trade

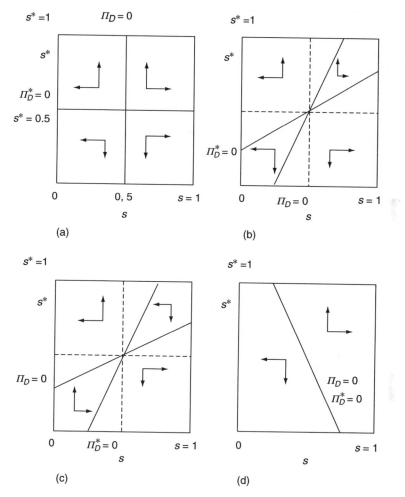

(a)

(b)

(c)

(d)

The evolution of the trade relations between the United States and
Japan can be described through the previous diagrams. Before the
opening of trade between the two countries, Japan and the United States
were, respectively, at $s^* = 1$ and $s = 0$ (point (0, 1) in Figure 7.18a. When
trade was open, the evolutionary forces tended to keep the organization of
firms as in autarky, that is at point (0, 1) in Figure 7.18b. But an extension
of free trade to inputs, that could be called complete globalization, would
destabilize the former EE and switch the equilibrium to the new EE (0, 0),
as shown in Figure 7.18 (d).

In other words the model has a *predictive power*: globalization can lead all firms in the world to select the same type of internal organization, and not necessarily the most efficient one.

The authors have tested the robustness of this result by varying the parameter values. They find that it holds under a wide range of values. They also proposed a more general model showing that the intuitive results obtained in the Cournot parametric model are indeed quite robust.

7.4.2 An evolutionary version of the 'chain-store' game

The famous 'chain-store' game, originally proposed by Selten, has already been presented above (see sub-section 4.4.1 of Chapter 4). Now we change the story a little in order to put it in an evolutionary framework.

There are two players: a monopoly and a potential entrant, each of them belonging to a large population. They are matched at random in an entry game. The idea of a population of monopolies may sound strange, but, we can interpret it as the large number of stores which constitutes the incumbent firm and each store has a local monopoly in one of m towns. On the entrant side, there is a large number of potential entrants, which will be matched at random with one of the m stores.

The game is presented below in extensive form (Figure 7.19a) and in strategic form (Figure 7.19b) with the following notations for the strategies: Entry (E), Stay Out (O), Cooperative (C), Aggressive (A).

Figure 7.19 The 'chain-store' game in both extensive form (a), and strategic form (b) (a ≥ 3)

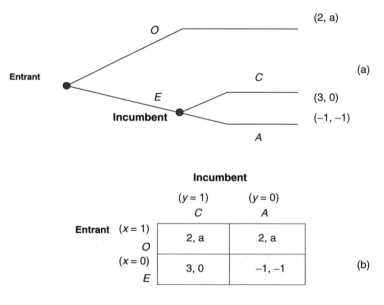

The NE of the game can be represented in Figure 7.20, in the space (x,y), representing the probabilities for the entrant and the incumbent, respectively, to play O and C. The game has a unique sub-game equilibrium at point S $(0,1)$, where the potential entrant actually enters (E) and the incumbent accommodates (C). There are also other NE (not SPE), where the monopoly chooses cooperation with a probability lower than $\frac{3}{4}$ and the potential entrant stays out. This set of NE is noted N on the graph and is represented by the line joining $(1, \frac{3}{4})$ to $(1, 0)$.

In order to be entirely in an evolutionary context in a two-population case, one can imagine that there are two chain-stores, each one with a large number of local monopolies. Before the start of the game there is not any competition between stores.

Now stores can be matched at random. A player called Nature intervenes at the beginning of the game to tell us which store will be in the position of the incumbent and which will be in the position of the entrant.

Let us call $\bar{x} = (x^1, x^2)$ a mixed strategy including x^1 when the player is in position 1 (entrant) and x^2 when it is in position 2 (incumbent). Similarly $\bar{y} = (y^1, y^2)$ is another mixed strategy.

The extensive form of the game is represented in Figure 7.21.

A mixed strategy $\bar{x} = (x^1, x^2)$ is an ESS if:

(i) $\Pi^*(\bar{x}, \bar{x}) \geq \Pi^*(\bar{y}, \bar{x}), \forall \bar{y}$
(ii) if $\Pi^*(\bar{x}, \bar{x}) = \Pi(\bar{y}, \bar{x})$ for every $\bar{y} \neq \bar{x}$, then $\Pi^*(\bar{x}, \bar{y}) > \Pi^*(\bar{y}, \bar{y})$

Let us check if the mixed strategy $\bar{x} = (E, C)$, which is the only PNE of non-cooperative game, is also an ESS:

$$\Pi^*(\bar{x}, \bar{x}) = \frac{1}{2}[\Pi_1(E, C) + \Pi_2(C, E)] = \frac{1}{2}[3 + 0] = \frac{3}{2}$$

Figure 7.20   Equilibria of the 'chain-store' game

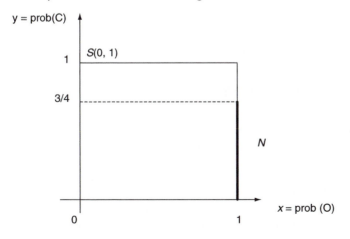

Figure 7.21   Extensive form of the evolutionary version of the 'chain-store' game

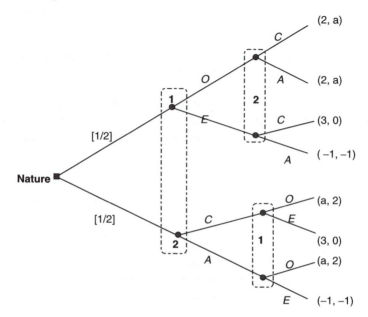

It is easy to verify that any mutant will get a lower payoff in a population where most of the players are choosing $\bar{x}$. For example, the strategy associated with the other NE of the game, $\bar{y} = (O, A)$ provides a payoff $\Pi^*(\bar{y}, \bar{x})$ equal to:

$$\Pi^*(\bar{y}, \bar{x}) = \frac{1}{2}[\Pi_1(O, C) + \Pi_2(E, A)] = \frac{1}{2}$$

Then: $\Pi^*(\bar{y}, \bar{x}) < \Pi^*(\bar{x}, \bar{x})$

This result is true for any $\bar{y} \neq \bar{x}$. Thus $\bar{x} = (E, C)$ is the only ESS of the game.

Strategies robust to equilibrium entrants

One can use a slightly different version of this game to give an application of the notion of REE suggested by Swinkels (1992a). We assume here that each of the two players has another strategy available, called 'innovation' (IN). A potential entrant may come with a product with entirely new characteristics, instead of entering directly into the incumbents' market. The innovation may not change the payoffs of the accommodating incumbent, (because the products are not good substitutes), but if the incumbent fears interference it may react by an aggressive pricing policy or by its

Figure 7.22 Extensive form of the modified 'chain-store' game

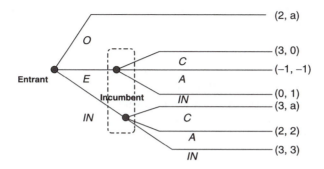

own innovation. The extensive and strategic forms of this modified 'chain-store' game are drawn in Figures 7.22 and 7.23, respectively.

With $a \geq 3$ there are two NE: (O, A) and (IN, C). The NE are not very different from the NE obtained previously. Yet now, neither of them is an ESS (in fact neither of them are *strict*).

Let us apply now the notion of REE. We saw above (sub-section 7.1.3) that a strategy profile is REE if there exists $\bar{\varepsilon} \in (0, 1)$ such that for any strategy profile $y \neq x$

$$y \notin BR[\varepsilon y + (1 - \varepsilon)x] \text{ for } \varepsilon \in (0, \bar{\varepsilon})$$

where BR is the set of best responses to the mixed population of mutants and non-mutants.

It is easy to verify that (O, A) and (E, IN) are not REE: (E, IN) can be destabilized by a rational mutant using (IN, IN). Let us call $w = \varepsilon(IN, IN) + (1 - \varepsilon)(E, IN)$ the strategy profile of the resulting population. Facing game w, the mutant strategy (IN, IN) belongs to the set of best responses since a mutant choosing IN against IN gets 3, and an innovating incumbent gets $2\varepsilon + 1$ against $\varepsilon IN + (1 - \varepsilon)E$. The profile (E, IN) cannot be REE. The same argument applies to the equilibrium (O, A) when confronted with a mutant (O, C).

Figure 7.23 Strategic form of the modified 'chain-store' game

		Incumbent		
		C	A	IN
	O	2, a	2, a	2, a
Entrant	E	3, 0	−1, −1	0, 1
	IN	3, a	2, 2	3, 3

Finally, the profile (IN, C) is REE. In other words, a potential entrant will not directly enter into the incumbent market but the latter agrees to let him develop a new market.

The standard Replicator dynamics

We have used so far the concepts of ESS and REE. What can be learned now from an application of the standard RD to the 'chain-store' game?

Let I be a large population of entrants and II a large population of incumbents. x_t is the fraction of potential entrants who stay out at time t (they play O), and $(1 - x_t)$ actually enter (they play E). y_t is the fraction of stores who accommodate at time t (they play C), and $(1 - y_t)$ actually fight (they play A). The payoff of an entrant choosing strategy $i = O, E$ is noted as Π_i when his opponent is chosen at random among the members of population II. Using the payoffs presented in Figure 7.19, one gets:

$$\Pi_0 = 2y + 2(1 - y) = 2$$

$$\Pi_E = 3y + (-1)(1 - y) = 4y - 1$$

And the average payoff of a member of population I is:

$$\bar{\Pi}_I(x, y) = 2x + (4y - 1)(1 - x)$$

The reader can check the corresponding values Π_j and $\bar{\Pi}_{II}$ for population II.
The standard RD equations are then:

$$\dot{x}_i = x_i(\Pi_i - \bar{\Pi}_I), \ i = O, E$$
$$\dot{y}_j = y_j(\Pi_j - \bar{\Pi}_{II}), \ j = C, A$$

The potential entrants who choose to stay out will evolve according to:

$$\dot{x} = x(1 - x)(3 - 4y) \tag{7.20}$$

and the incumbents who choose to cooperate according to:

$$\dot{y} = y(1 - y)(1 - x) \tag{7.21}$$

The dynamic system (1) − (2) is represented in Figure 7.24.

One can show that the SPE $S(0,1)$ is the unique asymptotically stable point of the dynamics. The set **N** of NE are local attractors (except for the limit point $(1, \frac{3}{4})$)

Figure 7.24 Phase diagram of the RD of the 'chain-store' game for particular values of the parameters

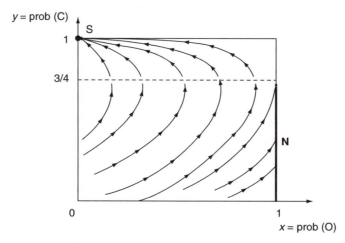

One important result of the standard RD is that the system may converge to a non-SPE. However this possibility must be considered with caution, especially because local attractors in **N** are only Lyapunov stable. Asymptotic stability is of course a much more reliable property. One way to 'test' the robustness of non-SPE as EE is to consider a noisy RD. If these potential EE can resist a continuous injection of (very) small fractions of all available strategies in the population, then they can be considered as serious candidates against the perfect equilibrium.

A noisy Replicator dynamics

Noise can be introduced into the RD as in the previous section. Let δ_I and δ_{II} be the mutation rates, respectively, of population I and population II. Newcomers in the population choose any strategy available i, without any sort of learning, with a certain probability θ_i. The RD equation for the potential entrants is now:

$$\dot{x}_i = (1 - \delta_I)x_i(\Pi_i - \bar{\Pi}_I) + \delta_I(\theta_i - x_i), \; i = O, E \qquad (7.22)$$

Similarly for the incumbent population:

$$\dot{y}_j = (1 - \delta_{II})y_j(\Pi_j - \bar{\Pi}_{II}) + \delta_{II}(\lambda_j - y_j), \; j = C, A \qquad (7.23)$$

It is rather difficult to determine the probabilities θ_i and λ_j. We will assume that there is a uniform distribution of strategies, so here

$\theta_i = \lambda_j = \frac{1}{2}$. With the payoff matrix given above (Figure 7.23) the system of RD equations is:

$$\dot{x} = (1 - \delta_I)[x(1 - x)(3 - 4y)] + \delta_I\left(\frac{1}{2} - x\right) \qquad (7.24)$$

$$\dot{y} = (1 - \delta_{II})[y(1 - y)(1 - x)] + \delta_{II}\left(\frac{1}{2} - y\right) \qquad (7.24')$$

The first equation describes the evolution of the fraction entrants playing strategy O (not enter) and the second describes the evolution of the fraction of incumbents playing C (cooperate).

Phase diagrams are presented in Figure 7.25 and Figure 7.26 respectively, for the case where the levels of noise are similar ($\delta_I = \delta_{II} = 0.01$) and the case where noise is more important in population $II(\delta_I = 0.01$, $\delta_{II} = 0.1)$. We observe that no point in **N** is local attractor when ($\delta_I = \delta_{II} = 0.01$) whereas a local attractor appears when (($\delta_I = 0.01$, $\delta_{II} = 0.1$).

This means that considering that population II is noisier than I in its selection process leads the system to create a point where the chain-store can build a reputation as a stable equilibrium.

Let us check the asymptotic stability of a point such as E in Figure 7.26. We have to consider the system (7.24)-(7.24′) when the mutation rates are close to zero (i.e. δ_I, $\delta_{II} \to 0$). Then, we define:

$$\phi = \frac{(1 - \delta_I)\delta_{II}}{(1 - \delta_{II})\delta_I}$$

Figure 7.25   Phase diagram for $\delta_I = \delta_{II} = 0.01$

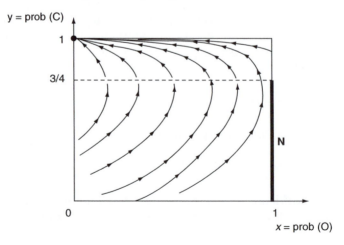

Figure 7.26   Phase diagram for $\delta_I = 0.01$ and $\delta_{II} = 0.1$

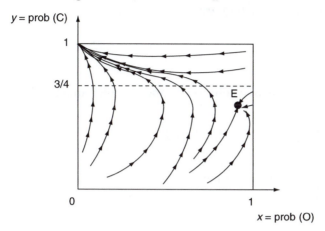

As δ_I, $\delta_{II} \to 0$, two cases must be taken into account:

Case 1: $\phi < \dfrac{1}{4 - 2\sqrt{3}}$

Case 2: $\phi > \dfrac{1}{4 - 2\sqrt{3}}$

These cases are connected with the alternative stories on the different levels of noise between the two populations. So, the first case can be seen as a situation where only the entrants are noisy, whereas the converse holds in case 2.

First of all one must take stationary points in the dynamical system (7.24)-(7.24'). Equalizing $\dot{x}$ and $\dot{y}$ to 0 gives:

$$-\delta_I(\tfrac{1}{2} - x) = (1 - \delta_I)[x(1 - x)(3 - 4y)] \tag{7.25}$$

$$-\delta_{II}(\tfrac{1}{2} - y) = (1 - \delta_{II})[y(1 - y)(1 - x)] \tag{7.26}$$

Dividing (7.26) by (7.25) and rearranging gives:

$$\phi = \frac{(1 - \delta_I)\delta_{II}}{(1 - \delta_{II})\delta_I} = \frac{y(\tfrac{1}{2} - x)(1 - y)(1 - x)}{x(\tfrac{1}{2} - y)(1 - x)(3 - 4y)}$$

We are looking for solution close to the set **N**, that has points corresponding to $x \to 1$, which gives:

$$\phi = \frac{-y(1-y)}{(1-2y)(3-4y)}$$

This equation has two solutions $\underline{y}$ and $\bar{y}$, which must satisfy:

$$\frac{1}{2} < \underline{y} < \frac{3-\sqrt{3}}{2} < \bar{y} < 3/4, \text{ when } \phi > \frac{1}{(4-2\sqrt{3})}$$

When $\phi < \frac{1}{(4-2\sqrt{3})}$, the equation has no solution satisfying $0 \le y \le 1$.

We can now make the following proposition.

Proposition I

Let $A(\delta_I, \delta_{II})$ be the set of asymptotically stable states of (7.24)-(7.24'), and consider $A^* = \lim_{(\delta_I, \delta_{II}) \to 0} A(\delta_I, \delta_{II})$ for ϕ given. Then, we can show that:

(i) In case 1, the set A^* presents a unique limit point, the SPE $S = (0, 1)$

(ii) In case 2, the set A^* presents two limit points, $S = (0, 1)$ and $(1, \underline{y})$ (a formal proof of this result is in Gale, Binmore and Samuelson (1995), who use the model in a structurally similar game).■

This result says that when $\delta_I > \delta_{II}$ a non-SPE (i.e. close to **N**) is asymptotically stable. This is because when almost all the entrants avoid entering on the monopoly market (i.e. when they play O), pressures leading incumbents to play C are low. Including noisy decisions on the part of entrants leads the system far from the strategy O and increases the probability that incumbents cooperate. In this case, the SPE is reached. However, as in the model the incumbents are also subject to noise, the population II includes players choosing C and players choosing A. Facing this mixed population, the best reply for an entrant is to play O. If this force is sufficiently strong, then it cancels the tendencies leading the system to the SPE. So, the incumbents in the chain-store stay with the mixed strategy and the strategy 'Stay Out' remains the best reply for the entrants.

Appendix I Elements of a dynamic system

(for more details see, for instance, Vega-Redondo, 1995)

- To write down a system of differential equations is a classical way to represent mathematically a deterministic dynamic process in *continuous* time This approach is used in evolutionary game theory. In this book are used only systems of *autonomous, first-order, ordinary* differential equations: the system does not depend on time, equations contain only first-order derivatives, and all derivatives are only derivatives with respect to time.
- Starting from an *initial point* x_0 the dynamic system is given by:

$$\dot{x} = f(x)$$

where $\dot{x} = (\dot{x}_1, \ldots, \dot{x}_k)$, and $x \in X$.

x is the *state vector* and X the *state space*. This system describes *trajectories*. A trajectory may converge or diverge.

- Except in pathological cases, a convergent trajectory is converging to a *stationary state* (or an 'equilibrium', a 'rest point', a 'fixed point') $\bar{x}$ given by:

$$\dot{x} = 0,$$

that is, $\bar{x}$ is such that: $f(\bar{x}) = \bar{x}$, for all $t > 0$

- The *basin of attraction* of a rest point R is the set of initial points from which the dynamic system converges to R.
- If the basin of attraction consists of every possible initial points, then the rest point is a *global attractor* (G). There are also *local* attractors (L_1, L_2) (Figure 7.27).

Figure 7.27 Stable equilibria of a dynamic system

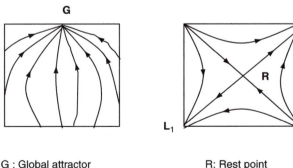

G : Global attractor

R: Rest point
L_1, L_2: Local attractors

- Global or local attractors are often said to be *globally or locally 'stable equilibria'* of the dynamic system.
- Local attractors often are asymptotic attractors. An *asymptotic attractor* is a rest point that lies in the interior of its basin of attraction. This implies that the rest point is not a boundary point of its basin of attraction, and so all trajectories that start near enough the rest point ended there.
- More formally, $\bar{x}$ is an *asymptotically stable equilibrium* if:

  (1)   It is Lyapunov stable, i.e. given any neighbourhood U_1 of $\bar{x}$ there exists another neighbourhood U_2 of $\bar{x}$ such that all trajectories with $x(0) \in U_1$ satisfy $x(t) \in U_2$, $\forall t \geq 0$.

  (2)   There exists some neighbourhood V of $\bar{x}$ such that all trajectories starting in V satisfy $x(t) \to \bar{x}$ as $t \to \infty$.

Appendix 2 The Model of Friedman and Fung (1996)

A   In the Cournot parametric model first proposed by Friedman and Fung (1996), the first-order condition for a representative firm is:

$$\frac{d\pi}{dx} = p - \beta x - c = 0$$

or:

$$x = \frac{p - c}{\beta}$$

Profits are thus of the form:

$$\pi = x(p - c) = x^2 \beta$$

The same logic applies in the open economy case:

$$\pi = (p^d - c)x^d + (p^e - c)x^e$$
$$= ((x^d)^2 \beta + (x^e)^2 \beta$$

B   Cournot equilibrium outputs in the case of international trade are:

$$x_A^d = \{\beta[\beta^2((1 - s^*)N^* + 1)(sN + s^*N^* + 1)$$
$$- \gamma^2(1 - s^*)N^*(sN + s^*N^*)]\theta_A^d - \beta^2\gamma sN\theta_B^d$$
$$+ \beta(1 - s^*)N^*[\gamma^2(sN + s^*N^*) - \beta^2(sN + s^*N^* + 1)]\theta_A^{*e} - \beta^2\gamma s^*N^*\theta_B^{*e}\}/\Delta$$

$$x_B^d = \{- \beta^2\gamma(1 - s)N\theta_A^d + \beta[\beta^2(s^*N^* + 1)((1 - s)N$$
$$+ (1 - s^*)N^* + 1) - \gamma^2 s^*N^*((1 - s)N + (1 - s^*)N^*)]\theta_B^d$$
$$- \beta^2\gamma(1 - s^*)N^*\theta_A^{*e} + \beta s^*N^*[\gamma^2((1 - s)N + (1 - s^*)N^*)$$
$$- \beta^2((1 - s)N + (1 - s^*)N^* + 1)]\theta_B^{*e}\}/\Delta$$

$$x_A^e = \{\beta(1 - s^*)N^*[\gamma^2(sN + s^*N^*) - \beta^2(sN + s^*N^* + 1]\theta_A^{*d}$$
$$- \beta^2\gamma s^*N^*\theta_B^{*d} + \beta[\beta^2(1 - s^*)N^* + 1)(sN + s^*N^* + 1)$$
$$- \gamma^2(1 - s^*)N^*(sN + s^*N^*)]\theta_A^e - \beta^2\gamma sN\theta_B^e\}/\Delta$$

$$x_B^e = \{ - \beta^2 \gamma (1 - s^*) N^* \theta_A^{*d} + \beta s^* N^* (\gamma^2 ((1 - s)N + (1 - s^*)N^*)$$
$$- \beta^2 ((1 - s^*)N^* + (1 - s)N + 1)) \theta_B^{*d} - \beta^2 \gamma (1 - s)N \theta_A^e$$
$$+ \beta [\beta^2 (s^* N^* + 1)((1 - s)N + (1 - s^*)N^* + 1) - \gamma^2 s^* N^* ((1 - s)N$$
$$+ (1 - s^*)N^*)] \theta_B^e \} / \Delta$$

Bibliography

Akin, E. (1980) 'Domination or equilibrium', *Mathematical Biosciences*, 50, 239–50.

Aoki, M. (1988) *Information, Incentives and Bargaining in the Japanese Economy* (Cambridge: Cambridge University Press).

Aoki, M. (1990) 'Toward an economic model of the Japanese firm', *Journal of Economic Literature*, 28, 1–27.

Axelrod, R. (1984) *Evolution of Cooperation* (New York: Basic Books).

Axelrod, R. and W. Hamilton (1981) 'Evolution of cooperation', *Science*, 211, 1390–6.

Bernheim, D. (1984) 'Rationalizable strategic behaviour', *Econometrica*, 52, 1007–28.

Bhaskar, V. (1994) 'Noisy communication and the fast evolution of cooperation', Center Discussion Paper, No. 94112, Tilburg University.

Binmore, K. (1992) *Fun and games* (Lexington, MA: D.C. Health).

Binmore, K. and L. Samuelson (2001) 'Evolution and mixed strategies', *Games and Economic Behavior*, 34, 200–26.

Bomze, I. (1986) 'Non-cooperative, two-person games in biology: a classification', *International Journal of Game Theory*, 15, 31–57.

Borgers, T. and R. Sarin (1997), 'Learning through reinforcement and replicator dynamics', *Journal of Economic Theory*, 77, 1–14.

Bush, R. and R. Mosteller (1955) *Stochastic Models of Learning* (New York: John Wiley).

Camerer, C. (1991) 'Does strategy research need game theory?', *Strategic Management Journal*, Special Issue, 12, 137–52.

Cournot, A.A. (1838) *Recherches sur les principes mathématiques de la théorie des richesses* (Paris: Librairie des sciences politiques et sociales, M. Rivière et cie) (English: N. Bacon (ed.), *Researches into the Mathematical Principles of the Theory of Wealth*. (London: Macmillan, 1897).

Dekel, E. and S. Scotchmer (1992) 'On the evolution of optimizing behavior', *Journal of Economic Theory*, 57, 392–406.

Friedman, D. (1991) 'Evolutionary games in economics', *Econometrica*, 59, 637–66.

Friedman, D. and K.C. Fung (1996) 'International trade and the internal organization of firms: an evolutionary approach', *Journal of International Economics*, 41, 113–37.

Fudenberg, D. and D.K. Levine (1999) *Theory of Learning in Games* (Cambridge, MA: MIT Press).

Gale, J., K. Binmore and L. Samuelson (1995) 'Learning to be imperfect: the ultimatum game', *Games and Economic Behavior*, 8, 56–90.

Gintis, H. (2000) *Game Theory Evolving* (Princeton: Princeton University Press).

Haigh, J. (1975) 'Game Theory and Evolution', *Advances in Applied Probability*, 7, 8–11.

Harsanyi, J.C. and R. Selten (1988) *A General Theory of Equlibrium: Selection in Games* (Cambridge, MA: MIT Press).

Hines, W.G.S. (1980) 'Strategic stability in complex populations', *Journal of Applied Probability*, 17, 600–10.

Hofbauer, J., P. Schuster and K. Sigmund (1979) 'A note on evolutionary stable strategies and game dynamics', *Journal of Theoretical Biology*, 81, 609–12.

Hofbauer, J and J. Weibull (1996), 'Evolutionary selection against dominated strategies', *Journal of Economic Theory*, 71, 558–73.

Kandori, M. (1997) 'Evolutionary game theory and economics', in D. Kreps and K. Wallis (eds), *Advances in Economics and Econometrics: Theory and Applications, Seventh World Congress of the Econometric Society*, 1 (Cambridge: Cambridge University Press).

Kim, Y. and J. Sobel (1995) 'An evolutionary approach to pre-play communication', *Econometrica*, 63, 1181–94.

Mailath, G.J. (1998), 'Do people play Nash equilibrium? Lessons from evolutionary game theory', *Journal of Economic Literature*, 36, 1347–74.

Maskin, E. and J. Tirole (1988), 'A theory of dynamic oligopoly 1: overview and quantity competition with large fixed costs', *Econometrica*, 56, 549–70.

Matsui, A. (1991), 'Cheap talk and cooperation in a society', *Journal of Economic Theory*, 54, 245–58.

Maynard Smith, J. (1974), 'The theory of games and evolution of animal conflicts', *Journal of Theoretical Biology*, 47, 209–21.

Maynard Smith, J. (1982), *Evolution and the Theory of Games* (Cambridge: Cambridge University Press).

Maynard Smith, J. and G.R. Price (1973), 'The logic of animal conflicts', *Nature*, 246, 15–18.

Pearce, D. (1984) 'Rationalizable strategic behaviour and the problem of perfection', *Econometrica*, 52, 1029–50.

Robson, A. (1990), 'Efficiency in evolutionary games: Darwin, Nash, and the secret handshake', *Journal of Theoretical Biology*, 144, 379–96.

Roth, A. and I. Erev (1995) 'Learning in extensive form games: experimental data and simple dynamic models in the intermediate term', *Games and Economic Behavior*, 8, 163–212.

Samuelson, L. (1997), *Evolutionary Games and Equilibrium Selection* (Cambridge, MA: MIT Press).

Samuelson, L. and J. Zhang, (1992) 'Evolutionary stability in asymmetric games', *Journal of Economic Theory*, 57, 363–91.

Selten, R. (1980), 'A note on evolutionary stable strategies in asymmetric animal conflicts', *Journal of Theoretical Biology*, 84, 93–101.

Swinkels, J (1992a), 'Evolutionary stability with equilibrium entrants', *Journal of Economic Theory*, 57, 306–32.

Swinkels, J. (1992b) 'Evolution and strategic stability: from Maynard Smith to Kohlberg and Mertens', *Journal of Economic Theory*, 57, 333–42.

Thomas, B. (1985), 'On evolutionary stable sets', *Journal of Mathematical Biology*, 22, 105–15.

Van Damme, E. (1991) *Stability and Perfection of Nash Equilibria*, 2nd edn (Berlin: Springer–Verlag).

Vega-Redondo, F. (1995) *Evolution in Games: Theory and Economic Applications* (Oxford: Oxford University Press).

Vignolo, T. (2000), *L'appariement stratégique dans les jeux evolutionnistes: une réponse au problème des équilibres multiples*, PhD, Université Montpellier 1, France (in French).

Warneryd, K. (1991) 'Evolutionary stability in unanimity games with cheap talk', *Economic Letters*, 36, 375–8.

Weibull, J. (1995) *Evolutionary Game Theory* (Cambridge, MA: MIT Press).

Weibull, J. (1999) 'What have we learned from evolutionary game theory so far ?', Working Paper, Stockolm School of Economics and the Research Institute of Industrial Economics, May.

8 Experimental Games

8.1   Some methodological remarks and first applications
8.2   Cooperation
8.3   Coordination
8.4   Bargaining
8.5   Learning and evolution
8.6   From experimental evidence to some new game theoretic modelling principles

We have seen in the previous chapters how GT can be applied to a series of economic problems. But it remains to be seen if the predictions of the game theoretic models are actually confirmed when the various games are played by real agents in controlled environments. From its early days, GT has actually largely developed alongside experiments, and a whole book could be devoted to this topic. Of course, these empirical tests do not have the same value for different researchers. Some of them think that GT has a 'descriptive' function, while others see it rather as a prescriptive body of knowledge. Whatever our view about the status of applied GT, it is useful to understand how people play the various types of games, and if the theoretical predictions can be verified in practice. This chapter will illustrate how game models have been tested by means of controlled laboratory experiments.

The experimental method, which has developed very rapidly since the 1970s, uses real people and puts them in situations that could be described as 'games'. Thus, the theoretical predictions can be tested by observing their behaviour. Of course, this technique is rather controversial since subjects' motivations may be difficult to control. Although we shall not discuss methodological issues at length, one should emphasize that testing games must be linked somehow or other to the distinction between the 'rationalistic' and the 'evolutive' approaches of GT presented in Chapter 1. Either we assume in experiments that subjects can make choices by deducing their opponents' behaviours from mental reasoning, or we let them play the same game several times in order to allow them time to learn. In other words, the results must be interpreted carefully, taking into account the fact that players may have learned by playing the same game several times (for overviews on methodological issues see Smith, 1982, 1994; Roth, 1988; Plott, 1990; Binmore,

1999; and for more critical viewpoints, Starmer, 1999, and Loewenstein, 1999).

It would be difficult to give here a full account of the numerous experiments which have been carried out, especially since 1990. Therefore, we have chosen to focus on problems for which experimental evidence is currently available. We will describe the main results and give their interpretation. We have also selected only some of the more representative experiments, so each problem will be illustrated only by two or three experiments. Other tests will be referred to in short remarks. In section 8.1, we introduce some methodological remarks explaining the purpose of experimental methods and their limits. We also present some applications to strictly competitive games (constant sum games and non-constant sum games), which were tested very early on. In section 8.2, we present experiments on 'cooperation' problems, which include not only experiments on the Prisoner's dilemma and public good provision, but also experiments in sequential games such as the centipede game. In these settings there is a conflict between individual rationality and collective interest: an outcome of the game always Pareto-dominates the equilibrium. Section 8.3 deals with 'coordination' problems, where there are several equilibria and the players have to select one of them. Section 8.4 is devoted to 'bargaining' problems, with first of all, experiments on the ultimatum bargaining game, that is one of the most tested game. Then, after other bargaining games testing strategic and the axiomatic solutions, some experiments on coalition games are briefly referred to. Section 8.5 deals with learning and evolution. When EGT is applied to economics, it is certainly correct and useful to interpret the evolutionary dynamics as a learning process. However, it is also important to study properly how individuals learn in playing games and what are the effects of various modes of learning. We describe first some recent experiments in an evolutionary framework, and we then present tests of learning processes in a more standard setting. Violations of game theoretic principles are not hard to find because all useful modelling principles are simplifications. The next step is to use the experimental evidence of failures as a means to suggest improvements to GT. In section 8.6, we review the substantial progress already made in two areas that concern first players' abilities, and secondly players' motivations.

8.1 Some methodological remarks and first applications

8.1.1 History and methodology

In the early 1960s, Rapoport and Orwant (1962) wrote: 'Literature on game experiments is rapidly becoming voluminous, but it is still possible to cover it in a single review.' More than thirty years later, GT has been widely developed and experiments in laboratories are so numerous that it is difficult to take into account all the results. The experimental method has proved to be successful in developing interactions and exchanges between theorists and experimenters; this method allows data to be collected in order to test theories. As GT is a way of simplifying more complex phenomena, it is generally easy to transfer it to the laboratory.

Games depend on initial parameters (preferences, beliefs, institutions...) that determine behaviours and give a prediction which depends on equilibrium concepts (NE, SPE, SE...) in non-cooperative games or on solution concepts (core, SV, ...) in cooperative games. By modifying these parameters, it is possible to carry out laboratory experiments in a controlled environment. Thus GT can be seen as a link between complex economic situations and more simplified laboratory situations (Plott, 1990).

The first experiments were conducted very early on, just after the publication of Von Neumann and Morgenstern's book. Dresher and Flood, for instance, tested the Prisoner's dilemma at the beginning of the 1950s (The results were reported in detail in Flood, 1952, 1958.) At this time, many experiments were conducted at the Rand Corporation. A conference in Santa Monica on 'experimental design on decision processes' attracted and influenced many authors, among them Simon, Shapley, Nash and Raiffa. Other experiments have followed in other areas directly linked to game theory, such as oligopoly theory. Yet it is only since the 1980s that experiments have become more numerous in economics, partly owing to the renewal of GT and microeconomic theory. Several empirical regularities have been observed, but many issues are still being discussed. In order to analyse all these results we decided essentially to present recent experiments. We also decided to focus mainly on classical 'toy games' or 'abstract games' rather than to report applied studies of games.

Before presenting the first experiments, it would be fruitful to recall briefly some methodological rules of the experimental method:

- *Reproduction* Experimental results must be reliable and experimental data must be easily reproduced by other researchers.
- *The experimenter's task* The experimenter should not be too subjective. Instructions should avoid terms such as 'loyal' or 'betray'. To compensate for this requirement instructions may become more complex. The experimenter should not interfere during the experiment. For this reason, it is best to remain anonymous.
- *Data analysis* Experimental results should be interpreted with care, especially but not only when aggregating individual data. For instance, three strategies chosen with the following frequencies by

two subjects – (0.4, 0.5, 0.1) and (0.4, 0.1, 0.5) – give the aggregated frequencies (0.4, 0.3, 0.3). Overall, the first strategy seems to have the higher frequency, although it is not the most frequent choice of any individual.

- *Subjects' motivation*   In order to avoid criticism about realism and to reduce variance, experiments must be conducted with monetary rewards. These rewards must satisfy several conditions: monotonicity, dominance, non-satiety, saliency and privacy (Smith, 1982). There are several ways to reward subjects. They can receive money, the amounts depending directly on their payoff from the experiment (score or tournament systems). They can be rewarded either for all their choices or just for one (chosen at random). They can all be rewarded or just a few of them (determined at random after the experiment).

- *The subjects' pool*   Subjects in experiments are generally students. Several factors have to be considered: gender, age, culture, experience, and so on.

- *Other recommendations*   Experimenters must be careful about the number of subjects (in order to avoid excess or lack of subjects for instance), about the length of the experiment (in order to avoid tiredness or boredom), and so on.

If these recommendations are followed, the experimental method works like any other empirical method: it tests theories, delimits their areas of validity and compares them. Experimental data can also suggest new theories in domains where existing theories have little to say.

In the following subsection we will deal with the topic of the first applications of the experimental method to GT. This concerns strictly competitive games, a very particular class of games which have occupied game theorists for several decades.

8.1.2   First applications: strictly competitive games

As mentioned in Chapter 2, strictly competitive games are those where players' preferences are totally opposed. What is interesting about this class of games is that Von Neumann's minimax theorem gives a unique prediction when mixed strategies are used. Instead of reporting the first experiments carried out in the 1960s and the 1970s, we will concentrate instead on two recent experiments on constant and non-constant sum games.

Constant sum games

In this setting, the first experiments reported negative results contradicting the minimax prediction. O'Neill (1987) conducted a new experiment by using the particular Roth and Malouf (1979) procedure. The purpose of this popular and convenient method is to control players' attitude towards risk.

According to this procedure, during the experiment subjects are paid in 'points' or 'tickets' rather than in cash, these points representing the probability of winning a prize in a lottery at the end of the experiment. For instance, if a player earns 400 points during the experiment, she (or he) has a probability of winning proportional to her (or his) payoff, say 0.4. At the end of the experiment, her (or his) monetary reward will be the result of the lottery draw. With this procedure, the expected utility function of a utility maximizer is linear in p, the probability of winning (regardless of any concavities or convexities the function might exhibit with respect to monetary earnings), and if p is a linear function of the payoff, then the expected utility is a linear function of the payoff (see exercise 86). It should be emphasized, however, that Roth and Malouf's procedure was severely criticized by Selten, Sadrieh and Abbink (1995) because it may actually lower the experimenter's control over the subjects' preferences.

This modification used by O'Neill seems to have provided different results which conform better to the minimax theorem. Yet, in this experiment, players repeated the same game 105 times with different opponents and Brown and Rosenthal (1990) have suggested that a correlation may exist among the choices made at different periods, and they remarked that incentives are certainly insufficient.

For this reason, Rapoport and Boebel (1992) have proposed a new game with five actions (Figure 8.1).

Incentives were higher and the authors used different payoffs for a win (*W*) or a loss (*L*). In treatment *A*, the winner receives 10 while the loser loses 6. In treatment *B*, the winner receives 15 while the loser loses 1. In this game, the mixed strategy minimax equilibrium consists of choosing the different actions with probabilities: ($\frac{3}{8}$, $\frac{2}{8}$, $\frac{1}{8}$, $\frac{1}{8}$, $\frac{1}{8}$). In this case, the first player wins with a frequency of 0.375 and the second player wins with a frequency of 0.625.

Figure 8.1 A constant sum game

		2				
		1	2	3	4	5
	1	*W*	*L*	*L*	*L*	*L*
	2	*L*	*L*	*W*	*W*	*W*
1	3	*L*	*W*	*L*	*L*	*L*
	4	*L*	*W*	*L*	*W*	*L*
	5	*L*	*W*	*W*	*L*	*L*

Experimental results on 120 decisions made by twenty players gave proportions near 0.4 and 0.6 in both treatments, but individual data differ from the minimax prediction. Nevertheless, this prediction does better than other alternative models such as random choice with a frequency of $\frac{1}{5}$ for each action, or a choice depending on possible wins with frequencies: $(\frac{1}{10}, \frac{3}{10}, \frac{2}{10}, \frac{2}{10}, \frac{2}{10})$. Results were: $(\frac{35}{120}, \frac{37}{120}, \frac{15}{120}, \frac{14}{120}, \frac{19}{120})$. Therefore, this experiment seems to validate partly the minimax theorem, since it is the theory that best fits the data.

Remark I

This result must be handled with care, since Mookherjee and Sopher (1997) applied the same tests to their data and were led to argue that their experiment does not support the minimax theory. But we may wonder whether these experiments are relevant for judging this theory. In accordance with the 'evolutive' viewpoint, we can argue that the only interesting question is whether subjects *learn* to play minimax strategies in repeated trials against changing opponents. In this perspective, Binmore, Swierzsbinski and Proulx (1996) have conducted an experiment that is sensitive to the learning issue and they found that, under such conditions, the mimimax theorem proved to be well supported.■

Non-constant sum games

Among constant sum games, the matching pennies game (see sub-section 3.2.1 of Chapter 3) has been studied in depth in the experimental literature. More recently, Ochs (1995) has tested some variants of this game including *non-constant* sum games (Figure 8.2).

The unique mixed strategy NE for player 1 in both games is $(m_1, m_2) = (\frac{1}{2}, \frac{1}{2})$, that is, she is choosing strategies (1, 2) with probabilities $(\frac{1}{2}, \frac{1}{2})$. However, for player 2, these probabilities are $(\frac{1}{2}, \frac{1}{2})$ in game A, $(\frac{1}{10}, \frac{9}{10})$ in game B and $(\frac{1}{5}, \frac{4}{5})$ in game C.

Experimental results at the aggregated level are difficult to interpret for reasons explained in the previous sub-section. However, it seems that player 1 actually chooses the first strategy with a frequency near 0.5. Some differences exist between game A and games B and C where this frequency

Figure 8.2 Non-constant sum games

A		2		B		2		C		2	
		1	2			1	2			1	2
1	1	1, 0	0, 1	1	1	9, 0	0, 1	1	1	4, 0	0, 1
	2	0, 1	1, 0		2	0, 1	1, 0		2	0, 1	1, 0

is higher. Similarly, player 2 chooses the first strategy with a higher frequency than predicted in games B and C.

The main explanation put forward by the authors is that players anticipate that their opponent will first choose more frequently one of the two actions, and then choose more frequently the other. This behaviour is directly linked to the existence of some learning effects, thanks to the repetition of the game and to the players' ability to consult their past choices and the resulting outcomes. It is now common that experiments are designed to test this type of learning in traditional GT. We will mention other interpretations of observed behaviour as forms of learning in later sections.

Other experiments have been designed to test formal models of learning. We will report them in the in section 8.5, in connection with experiments on EGT, which can also be interpreted as the result of learning in a context of limited rationality.

8.2 Cooperation

From now on we will refer to experiments on general games, i.e. games which are not strictly competitive, or games in which players' interests are not totally opposed. In this general setting, a 'cooperation' problem may arise when both players prefer an outcome which is not an equilibrium of the game. A classical example of two-player symmetric game illustrates this problem (Figure 8.3).

The typical matrix payoff is such that: $d > a > b > c$. Thus, (2, 2) is the unique NE, but (1, 1) Pareto-dominates the equilibrium. The problem is to find a way to cooperate in order to choose the better outcome (a, a).

Cooperation problems are very often illustrated by the Prisoner's dilemma game and the public goods provision game. The results obtained in this class of experimental games, generally drawn in a simultaneous-move structure, lead to controversial interpretations of the players' observed cooperative behaviour: do they reveal altruism or strategic reputation building behaviour? But cooperation problems exist also in

Figure 8.3 Cooperation problem in a symmetric game

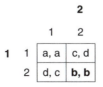

some sequential games (trust game, centipede game,...) in which the backward induction principle is supposed to apply.

8.2.1   Cooperation: altruism or strategic reputation building behaviour?

The Prisoner's dilemma game

There have been a lot of various experiments on the Prisoner's dilemma game since Flood (1952, 1958) (see sub-section 2.1.2 of Chapter 2, for a presentation of this famous game). We shall not deal here with the first experiments of the 1950s and the 1960s. They focused on the effects of communication, which seems to increase cooperative behaviour. Other experiments have tested the orientation of the instructions getting players to cooperate with others, or to behave selfishly. The main result of all the experiments is that one observes *some cooperation* both in one-shot games and finitely repeated games, and that the frequency of cooperation may be sensitive to some parameters; for instance, cooperation rates increase when the gains from cooperation increase (for a survey of these early experiments see Rappoport and Chammah, 1965).

More recently, Axelrod (1984) conducted simulations through a computer tournament and reached the conclusion that a cooperative strategy such as 'tit-for-tat' (TFT) could perform well (see sub-section 3.3.2 of Chapter 3 for a definition of a TFT strategy). This suggests that the Prisoner's dilemma could involve cooperation.

These conclusions have been taken into account by newer theoretical models such as Kreps *et al.* (1982). This model, based on incomplete information, predicts cooperation in a finitely repeated game by some *reputation effects* (see sub-section 4.4.1 of Chapter 4). Cooper *et al.* (1996) have proposed testing its predictions on the game in Figure 8.4.

In the *one-shot* game, predictions based on reputation cannot be maintained and cooperation should not be observed. However, in the *finitely repeated* game, the reputation model predicts some cooperation in the first periods followed by defections in the later periods.

The non-negligible observed rate of cooperation in the Prisoner's dilemma game have led some researchers to suggest another hypothesis concerning the 'altruism' of the participants, that is individuals whose utility increases with the well-being of other people. It may be possible to explain cooperation in both the one-shot game and the repeated game by

Figure 8.4   The prisoner's dilemma game

		2	
		1	2
1	1	350,350	1000,0
	2	0,1000	800,800

using a model based on altruism. Nevertheless, the latter does not explain either the variations during the repetition or the lack of cooperation at the end.

The results of the experiments have shown some cooperation in the one-shot games confirming the presence of 'altruistic' subjects, in a proportion estimated at 10 per cent by the authors. In the finitely repeated game, results show a higher rate of cooperation than in the one-shot game but that rate decreases over time. This result seems to validate the reputation model. Nevertheless, the observed level of cooperation is significantly higher than the predicted level and the dynamics is different. Finally, at the individual level, a large proportion of subjects behave in a manner that does not conform to the theory. For instance, some players cooperate in the last period or cooperate after a deviation. Therefore, although it explains the data better than altruism in the repeated game, the reputation model also seems unsatisfactory (Roth and Murninghan, 1978).

Remark 1

Other experiments have tried to test the prediction of the reputation model, such that the experiments carried out by Kahn and Murnighan (1993), in which simulated opponents were playing TFT with fixed probabilities, or by Andreoni and Miller (1996) or Cooper et al. (1996). These two last experiments show that the reputation model appears to be a good predictive model since subjects seem to build reputations for altruism. Yet, what is also interesting is the fact that some players are really 'altruistic' subjects, whereas the model only needs enough subjects to believe that such a motivation exists.■

Remark 2

Further experiments have shown that cooperation in the *one-shot* game should not be necessarily attributed to altruism. In a modified version of the one-shot game, where a subject is told what the other player has done, the cooperation rate is lower not only when the other defected but also when he cooperated. Thus *simultaneity* may explain the cooperation rate.■

Remark 3

Roth and Murnighan (1978) have tested an *infinitely* repeated version of the Prisoner's dilemma. They told players that the game would continue with a probability p. They observed that when p is high (0.5 or 0.9), players chose more frequently to cooperate than when p is low (0.1). However, even when p is high, the cooperation rate is only 36 per cent.■

Remark 4

Selten and Stoecker (1986) have studied learning effects in the Prisoner's dilemma game. They 'repeated' 25 times a repeated game (of 10 periods).

They observed cooperation in the first periods followed by a defection which appeared earlier on in the last 'repetitions' of the repeated game. The authors concluded that players first learn to cooperate in the early repetitions and then learn the strategic solution – with the backward induction argument – which is to defect earlier and earlier in the game.■

The public goods provision game

Are people selfish or cooperative in volunteering to contribute to public goods production? Such a question has been widely studied in experimental literature, with as many variations in procedures and treatments as there are research groups.

Let us look at a design sharing basic features used in most of the experiments. and which is easy to describe and understand (Ledyard, 1995, 112–13).

Four subjects are each given on endowment of $5. Each can choose to invest some or all of their endowment in a group project. Each will simultaneously and without discussion put an amount between $0 and $5 in an envelope. The envelopes are collected by the experimenter who will sum the 'contributions', double the amount and then divide this amount among the subjects. Here, the private benefit from the public goods is one-half the total amount of the contributions, which corresponds to what each subject receives from the group project. No one knows how much other people have contributed, but everyone knows the total amount of the contributions. Once this procedure has been implemented, the subjects are paid. In this standard experiment, the data collected are the amounts provided by the subjects.

The GT prediction for this problem is that no one will ever contribute anything. Each potential contributor will try to 'free-ride' on the others. In this experiment, it is a dominant strategy to choose $0. This is a 'public good problem' or a 'social dilemma' because the group would be better off if all subjects contributed the maximal amount of $5, each subject thus earning $10.

It should be noticed that this public good problem may be reduced to a standard Prisoner's dilemma by restricting subjects to allocations involving either all $5 or none of their total endowment to the group exchange.

What happens in a public good experiment? Analysis of the data shows that, as for the prisoner's dilemma game, the theoretical prediction is broadly invalidated. In many cases, some subjects contribute nothing, some contribute all their endowment and some prefer an intermediate choice and contribute less than $5. Generally, total contributions can be expected to correspond to an amount ranging from 40 per cent to 60 per cent of the group optimal provision. Thus, the results of the one-shot public goods game seem to show a wide range of behaviour, from pure selfishness to a completely altruistic behaviour.

As for the Prisoner's dilemma game, finitely *repeated* public goods games have been carried out. In this respect, Isaac, Walker and Thomas (1984) provides a new methodological framework which now is a standard setting.

In their game, player i's payoff can be written:

$$u_i = (D - m_i) + \frac{G}{n}\left(\sum_{i=1}^{n} m_i\right)$$

where:

$D_i = D$, $\forall i$: the endowment of subject i

m_i: subject i's provision for the public good

$\sum_{i=1}^{n} m_i$: the total provision of public good

$\frac{G}{n}(.)$: what each subject receives from the public good, i.e. the marginal *per capita* return (MPCR).

If each subject is thinking each stage of the game as a single-decision problem, she (or he) solves:

$$\max_{0 \le m_i \le D} u_i$$

For a subject who is not choosing her (or his) dominant strategy (free-riding), at least one of the following conditions must be verified:

- the agent is not selfish
- she (or he) perfectly understands the decision as a repeated game instead of a sequence of one-shot games
- she (or he) is learning to play the dominant strategy, thanks to the repetition of the game and through a trial-and error mechanism.

This setting allows one to make three assumptions about players' behaviour:

- strong free rider (SFR): $m_i = 0$
- weak free rider (WFR): $0 < m_i < D$
- cooperation: $m_i = D$.

When we add together the individual provisions, we get three global behaviours:

- aggregate SFR: $\sum m_i \approx 0$
- aggregate WFR: $0 < \sum m_i < D$
- aggregate cooperation: $\sum m_i \approx \sum D$.

Experimental data show that neither individual nor global assumptions are verified. Then, Isaac, Walker and Thomas (1984) propose to classify the various observed behaviours into five groups according to the values of $M_i = \dfrac{m_i}{D_i}$:

- complete FR: $M_i = 0$ per cent
- non-complete FR: $0 < M_i \leq 33.33$ per cent
- WFR: $33.3 < M_i \leq 66,66$ per cent
- incomplete cooperation: $66,6 < M_i < 100$ per cent
- complete cooperation: $M_i = D = 100$ percent.

The results of the experiment show that the WFR behaviour is the most frequently observed (51 per cent). Next comes SFR (30 per cent), and complete cooperation accounts for 19 per cent. If we include weak contributions ($M_i \leq 33,33$ percent) in the SFR class and consider strong contributions ($M_i \geq 66,66$ percent) as complete cooperation, the result is 44 per cent free-riders and 29 per cent cooperative agents. Moreover, periods and experiments are both of an heterogeneous nature. The 'experiment' involved eight groups, each one playing 10 times. The average contribution corresponds to 42.4 per cent of the potential total contribution. Furthermore, no particular behavioural assumption is verified; so, the authors can conclude that no stable behaviour was observed during the experiment.

To summarize, the experiment performed by Isaac, Walker and Thomas (1984) (which confirm many previous experiments on public goods) indicates that free-rider behaviour (strong and weak) remains dominant on the whole experiment, as much for an individual level as an aggregated level, and that, besides communication, the single factor that plays a strong positive effect on cooperation rates is the MPCR. On the other hand, people cooperate to a degree greater than would be implied by pure self-interest. However, the study shows that contributions toward public goods are not the result of 'pure altruism'. More complex motivations should be called for a more satisfactory interpretation of experimental data.

There is another possible extension for the apparent cooperation observed in public goods games, which is based on 'errors'. First, the fact that the dominant strategy corresponds to contributing nothing to the public good implies that any error will be an overcontribution. Therefore, since random errors cannot cancel out, they favour the cooperative interpretation. To avoid such a bias, Keser (1996) designed an experiment in which *partial* contribution was the dominant strategy, allowing overcontribution errors to be matched by undercontribution errors. However, the results clearly showed that the random error hypothesis cannot explain overcontribution in this environment. A more subtle explanation based on errors was provided by Anderson, Goeree and Holt (1998). Their central assumption is that subjects are more likely to make small cost errors than large cost errors, and that their errors are not independent but are 'strategic responses to errors of others' as described by the 'quantal response equilibrium' (see the second part of sub-section 8.6.1 for a presentation of this notion). These authors show that a logit equilibrium model combined with a small amount of altruism predicts most of the stylized facts observed in public goods experiments. An additional experimental test carried out by Willinger and Ziegelmeyer (2001) in order to explore the error hypothesis has obtained laboratory data which fit very well with this model (surveys on public goods experiments can be found in Ledyard, 1995; Palfrey and Prisbey, 1997; Holt and Laury 2002).

Remark 5

There exists a slightly different public goods game that consists of two stages. At stage 1 the game is identical to the standard game. At stage 2, each player is informed about the contribution vector and simultaneously imposes a costly *punishment* on the other player. The theory predicts for this two-stage game the same result as in the standard game without punishment: each player's optimal strategy is still given by $m_i = 0$. Since punishments are costly, players' dominant strategy at stage 2 is to not punish. Therefore, if selfishness and rationality are common knowledge, each player knows that stage 2 is completely irrelevant. Experiments on public goods games with punishment lead to an unambiguous rejection of the theoretical predictions. For instance in Fehr and Gächter's (2000) experiment, a large fraction of roughly 80 per cent of subjects cooperates fully.∎

Remark 6

As in experiments on Prisoners' dilemma games, a lot of experiments were devoted to measure reputation effects in public goods games. A particular design introduced by Andreoni (1988) was often used to identify the relative importance of altruistic behaviour and strategic reputation building behaviour. A 'partners' treatment, where the *same* small group of subjects plays a repeated public goods game is compared to a 'strangers' treatment, where subjects play this game in *changing* group formations.

For instance, in Keser and van Winden's (2000) experiment, one observes the following results: first, subjects in the 'partners' treatment contribute significantly more than subjects in the 'strangers' treatment; secondly, strangers' contributions show continual decrease, while partner's contributions fluctuate on a high level prior to decreasing in the final periods. The authors then interpret the subjects' behaviour in terms of 'conditional cooperation', which is characterized by both future-oriented and reactive behaviour. Notice this interpretation is thus opposed to the theories based on altruistic motives for giving, which imply *unconditional* cooperation (Andreoni and Miller, 1996, for instance).∎

8.2.2 Cooperation and backward induction in sequential games

Cooperation problems also arise in sequential games in which backward induction is used for solving the games. A first class of games corresponds to different sequential versions of Prisoner's dilemma.

The trust game and the sequential Prisoner's dilemma

The 'trust' game consists of two stages. At the first stage, player 1 can either 'trust' player 2 (T) or 'not trust' (NT). After observing player 1's choice, player 2 can 'honour' (H) or 'betray' (B) player 1's trust. 'Not trust' may be interpreted as an outside option of the game. The game tree is drawn in Figure 8.5, where payoffs are such that: $b > a > c > 0$.

Assuming rational and selfish players, application of sub-game perfection in this sequential asymmetric version of the Prisoner's dilemma ('trust' and 'honour' are 'cooperate', and 'not trust' and 'betray' are 'defect') leads to the prediction that player 1 never trusts. This result is rather paradoxical since equilibrium payoffs (c, c) are dominated by cooperative payoffs (a, a) (see, for instance, Berg, Dickhaut and McCabe, 1995, for a detailed description of properties of this game).

An experimental test of the trust game has been carried out by Bolle (1998), who used the special version of a trust game with variable reward: player 1 receives a given sum of money and she may trust player 2 by giving this sum; then player 2 gains twice the stake and may return a variable part. In this experiment, 76 per cent of subjects in the role of players 1 have decided to trust and they received about 50 per cent of the maximal payoff.

Experimental studies of sequential versions of the Prisoner's dilemma are reported in Bolle and Ockenfels (1990) and Clark and Sefton (1998). The results are in line with results on simultaneous Prisoner's dilemma and trust games: one observes a non-negligible rate of cooperation and this behaviour seems better regarded as reciprocation than pure altruism. On the other hand, there is strong evidence that we get more cooperation if players choose *sequentially* compared to the *simultaneous*-move structure (Watabe et al., 1996).

Figure 8.5 The trust game

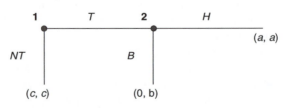

The centipede game

We have seen previously that the backward induction principle could lead to some paradoxical results in repeated sequential games such as the 'chain-store' paradox (see sub-section 4.4.1 of Chapter 4) or even in one-shot sequential games such as the centipede game paradox (see sub-section 3.4.3 of Chapter 3, and exercise 4). The latter game has been studied in particular by McKelvey and Palfrey (1992) who studied the two reduced versions drawn in Figures 8.6 and 8.7.

Equilibrium consists of the first player stopping the game at the first node in both examples. The solution comes from the use of backward induction: in the last period, player 2 will prefer to stop playing, knowing that, during the previous period, player 1 will also prefer to stop, and so on. However, it is clear that both players can reach higher payoffs if they continue the game after the third node. Thus, we have the same type of cooperation problem as in the Prisoner's dilemma or the public goods provision game. The experimental results of McKelvey and Palfrey (1992) show that players seldom stop at the first node, even though they hardly ever reach the last node. The frequencies with which they stop at each node are respectively: 0.07, 0.06, 0.2, 0.33, 0.25 and 0.08 in Figure 8.6 and 0.07, 0.36, 0.37 and 0.15 in Figure 8.7. The frequency with which they continue to the end are then 0.01 in Figure 8.6 and 0.05 in Figure 8.7.

These results suggest that players may act irrationally during the first periods in the hope their opponent will not maximize their chance (see

Figure 8.6 Centipede game A

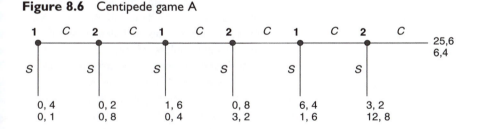

Figure 8.7 Centipede game B

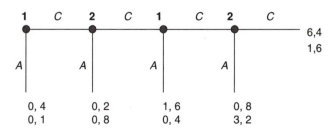

exercise 43 in Chapter 4). But it may be also that subjects may attribute a positive probability to encountering an altruistic person – that is someone who takes into account his opponent's payoff. In this case, even a selfish subject would prefer to continue playing in order to build up the reputation of an altruist. This works even if the proportion of altruistic people is very small. What is important is not the number of altruists but just the fact that *some* altruists do exist. It might also be possible to envisage, once again, incomplete information and reputation, just as in the Prisoner's dilemma.

Remark 7

Beard and Beil (1994) have also tested a sequential game introduced by Rosenthal (1981) in order to question the belief that non-SPE are always incredible. In this two-player extensive-form game of perfect information, a player (player A) can assure herself of a certain payoff $X > 0 by a secure action, or can allow a second player (player B) to fix her reward. In this latter case, player A's payoff is $1,000,000 or nothing, depending on player B's choice. Further, B has a small incentive to choose the action which results in A winning $1,000,000: he receives $1 instead of nothing. If player A chooses in the first move the secure action, player B's payoff is $Y > 0. Assuming that $0 < X < 1,000,000$, this game has one SPE leading to the payoffs: (1,000,000, 0). Rosenthal conjectured that, in some cases, player A would prefer the secure action when X was suitably large *but less than* 1,000,000. Beard and Beil (1994) find that nearly all subjects (97.8 per cent) in player B roles made choices that maximized their own payoffs, while secure choice behaviour occurred 54.5 per cent of the time when subjects play A role. Hence, these results provide strong evidence of Rosenthal's conjecture. Several competing explanations were proposed: first, that subjects are interpreting the game as involving incomplete information; second, that a psychological motive to control one's environment may produce secure play, subjects being induced to take an action *by the fear* of an irrational response or an envious behaviour. Notice that this experiment has to be contrasted with experiments on the centipede game, in which subjects are induced to take an action *in the hope* of an irrational response or an altruistic behaviour.■

Remark 8

We should emphasize that better results generally were obtained in laboratory experiments testing backward induction in *individual* decision problem (see Noussair and Olson, 1997; Noussair and Matheny, 1999; Aymard and Serra, 2001). Since this setting is perhaps more appropriate for isolating the predictions of backward induction, these results again seem to prove the role of social behaviour such as altruism, reciprocity or envy to explain the gap between experimental observations and theoretical predictions in experimental games.■

8.3   Coordination

Coordination problems arise when there is multiplicity of equilibria in the game. In a 'pure' cordination game players' interests are convergent; in other words they have the same preferences over the different equilibria. If there is a divergence, then we have an 'impure' coordination game.

Some classical examples of symmetric games illustrate these problems, whose typical payoff matrixes are drawn in Figure 8.8.

In these games, we assume: $a > b > c$. In the pure coordination game, there are two pure strategy NE: (1, 1) and (2, 2). The problem consists for players in finding a way to coordinate on the best outcome (a, a). In impure coordination games, such as the Battle of the Sexes game, there are also two pure strategy NE, but player 1 prefers (1, 1) whereas player 2 prefers (2, 2).

These classical examples can be complemented by many other cases with more than two pure strategy NE or with different payoffs for the out-of-equilibrium outcomes, such as in the matrix in Figure 8.9.

In this coordination game, players get security by choosing their second strategy. Yet, if we have $a > c > b$, the game of pure coordination – generally called in this case the 'Stag hunt' game – is such that players have to choose the *same* action to coordinate. If we have $b > c > a$, the game of impure coordination – generally called now the 'Chicken game' (or 'Hawk–Dove' in the biological literature and evolutionary games) – is such that players have to choose *different* actions in order to coordinate.

Pure coordination games have been widely studied by Schelling (1960). He used two-player games in which both players simultaneously have to

Figure 8.8   Coordination problems

Pure coordination   Impure coordination

Figure 8.9   General matrix of coordination games

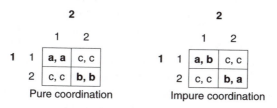

choose a strategy in the same set: for example to choose a positive number, to rank a set of three letters in the alphabet, to choose between 'heads' and 'tails', and so on. Subjects get positive payoffs only when they select the *same* strategy. If there are n strategies, the game has n pure strategy NE, among which any one among them can be the preferred one. The game is perfectly symmetric. Schelling noticed, however, that players often succeeded in coordinating. For instance, he found that 85.7 per cent of subjects has chosen 'head', which shows that labels of strategy are not indifferent. Some labels are more 'salient' than some others (number 1, alphabetic order, 'head', right hand, and so on). This explanation thus refers to the notions of focal point and saliency (see sub-section 3.1.3 of Chapter 3). Salience is a way for players to coordinate. But what makes a strategy more salient than another? We can distinguish at least two stages of salience: a first-order or 'non-rational' salience (no objective reason seems to explain why people select a particular strategy, but some labels are more attractive; cultural or social norms may also be put forward to explain this focalization), and a second-order or 'rational' salience (players maximize their expected utility taking into account their beliefs about the others' choices, but they think the others are making their choices according to the first-order salience).

Metha, Starmer and Sugden (1994) investigated Schelling's predictions about coordination by salience. Their experiment involved 20 questions, of which 10 involved 'real objects' (naming a flower, naming a year, and so on) and the 10 others involved abstracts objects. Subjects were randomly assigned to a group. In group 1, subjects were required to answer the question individually and were eventually paid if they would be randomly selected at the end of the experiment. In group 2, subjects had to answer exactly the same question, but they were told that they were randomly paired with another subject. Each question, for which the two subjects in a pair would give the same answer, would increase their amount points individually, and would be converted into cash at the end of the game. For each question the authors found that the number of categories of answers was lower in group 2, and the coordination index (the probability that two randomly selected subjects in the group provide the same answer) was higher in group 2. However, their experiment does not allow us to discriminate completely between second-order salience and Schelling salience, although they provide a strong case for the latter category.

More recently, several experimental studies in laboratories have investigated coordination games more deeply. Given the prominence of multiple equilibria, especially in recent macroeconomic games, it is clearly of interest to examine how individuals respond to this situation. Three questions readily come to mind: Are individuals able to coordinate upon one of the many equilibria? Will this be the Pareto-efficient equilibrium? How to explain the focus on a particular equilibrium? First we report classical experiments which have attempted to provide answers to these questions, and then some extensions testing factors increasing co-ordination through the existence of a pre-game interaction (for a more recent survey on coordination games see Cooper (1999).

8.3.1 Classical coordination games

These experiments were devoted to pure coordination games and to more general coordination games as well.

Pure coordination games

Van Huyck, Battalio and Beil (1990) have tested a game in which each player has to choose a number between 1 and 7 and receives a payoff depending on the minimum chosen by all the players. Formally, the pay-off is:

$$U = kM - rX$$

where M is the minimum chosen by the *group* and X is the number chosen by the *player*. Two treatments have been studied: $r = 0$ (treatment A) and $r > 0$ (treatment B).

Let us consider first a simple example in which two players have a choice between two actions. It may help to understand the game structure (Figure 8.10). In these two games, there are two NE: (1, 1) and (2, 2) if $k > r$. These equilibria are Pareto-rankable: (2, 2) yield higher payoffs for both players.

In Van Huych's experiment, parameters k and r have been chosen so that the payoffs for a player are those indicated in Figure 8.11 (game A, with $r = 0$) and in Figure 8.12 (game B, with $r > 0$) where the rows and the columns represent, respectively, the choice X of a player and the min-imum M chosen by the group.

In each game, there are seven Pareto-rankable NE on the diagonal. However, in game A, the choice of a number higher than the minimum does not have any effect on the player's payoff whereas in game B, there is

Figure 8.10 Coordination games' payoffs

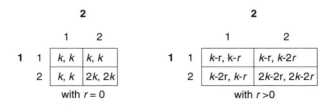

		2					2	
		1	2				1	2
1	1	k, k	k, k		1	1	k-r, k-r	k-r, k-2r
	2	k, k	2k, 2k			2	k-2r, k-r	2k-2r, 2k-2r
		with $r = 0$					with $r > 0$	

Figure 8.11   Pure coordination game A

Choice (X)	min. (M)						
	7	6	5	4	3	2	1
7	1,3	1,2	1,1	1	0,9	0,8	0,7
6	-	1,2	1,1	1	0,9	0,8	0,7
5	-	-	1,1	1	0,9	0,8	0,7
4	-	-	-	1	0,9	0,8	0,7
3	-	-	-	-	0,9	0,8	0,7
2	-	-	-	-	-	0,8	0,7
1	-	-	-	-	-	-	0,7

Figure 8.12   Pure coordination game B

Choice(X)	min. (M)						
	7	6	5	4	3	2	1
7	1,3	1,1	0,9	0,7	0,5	0,3	0,1
6	-	1,2	1	0,8	0,6	0,4	0,2
5	-	-	1,1	0,9	0,7	0,5	0,3
4	-	-	-	1	0,8	0,6	0,4
3	-	-	-	-	0,9	0,7	0,5
2	-	-	-	-	-	0,8	0,6
1	-	-	-	-	-	-	0,7

a penalty. For instance, in game *A*, if she (or he) chooses 5 and the minimum is 3, she (or he) receives a payoff of 0.9 as high as if she (or he) had chosen 3. Yet, in game *B*, she (or he) would receive a payoff of 0.7 instead of 0.9 if she (or he) had chosen 3. In this last game there is thus a *risk* for the players trying to coordinate on the most efficient equilibria (the choice of 7). In other words, in game *A*, the choice of 7 is a dominant strategy whereas it is not the case in game *B*. This class of symmetric coordination game, where there are multiple NE which can be Pareto-ranked, is sometimes called games of the 'weakest link type'. A strategy used by a single player in a given period can be interpreted as her (or his) *effort level* allocated to a joint production process whose production output is determined by the minimum effort player (Cooper, 1999, Chapter 2).

   In Van Huyck, Battalio and Beil's experiment, subjects played game *B* first (several times), then they played game *A*, before playing game *B* again. The results show that few subjects choose number 7 in game *B* and coordination failure is frequent. In this game, after repetitions, the choice of number 1 becomes predominant and there is less coordination failure. In game A, the choice of 7 is more frequent (84 per cent) and players coordinate better.

The main explanation of these differences is that in game A the choice of 7 is *less risky* whereas in game B, the maximin equilibrium (i.e. the choice of security strategies) consists in choosing number 1.

Recurrent features were also noticed:

(i)   The fact that subjects play game A again after playing game B does not improve coordination.

(ii)   The number of players is a crucial determinant for equilibrium selection. With only 2 players instead of 14 (the number of subjects in the first experiment), more coordination on the efficient equilibrium is reached. Thus, it seems that players assign probabilities on the potential choices of their opponents. When there are more players, the probability of coordinating on the efficient equilibrium is lower. On the other hand, when there are fewer players, the choice of the efficient equilibrium is less risky. Typically, when the number of players is 'sufficiently large', the average strategy choice tends to the less risky equilibrium of the constituent game.

(iii)   The dynamics is not the same in both games during the repetition. In game B, players who had chosen a number equal to the minimum increased their choices while players who had chosen a higher number decreased their choices. This did not improve the result. However, in game A, players who had chosen a higher number did not decrease their choices; so, the minimum increased.

Remark 1

Van Huyck, Battalio and Beil (1991) have conducted another experiment with payoffs depending on the *average* choice instead of the *minimum* chosen by the group. They observed that the dynamics are different in the sense that the history of choices is influenced by the first choice. Thus, players seem to use a 'precedence' criterion, and their past experience help them to select an equilibrium. Such a behaviour was allowed in the experiment by the possibility given to the players consulting the distribution of choices at the end of each period. In the same spirit, Crawford (1991) has proposed a learning model to explain these data. The idea is that players take into account their past experience and update their beliefs about others' choices.■

Other coordination games

Cooper *et al.* (1990) proposed to test games which they refer to as 'cooperation-coordination games'. In a first 3×3 symmetric game A

Figure 8.13   Cooperation–coordination game A

2

		1	2	3
	1	350,350	350,250	1000,0
1	2	250,350	550,550	0,0
	3	0,1000	0,0	600,600

Figure 8.14   Cooperation–coordination game B

2

		1	2	3
	1	350,350	350,250	700,0
1	2	250,350	550,550	1000,0
	3	0,700	0,1000	600,600

(Figure 8.13) there are two NE as in a standard coordination game, but a third outcome Pareto-dominates these equilibria.

In this game, outcome (3, 3) which is not a NE yields higher payoffs for both players than the two equilibrium outcomes (2, 2) or (1, 1). The game was repeated with random re-matching and the authors observed that players easily coordinate on one of the two NE, namely (1, 1). Yet, in a similar game B (Figure 8.14) the authors observed different results.

In this game, the selected equilibrium is now (2, 2). One explanation is that it corresponds to the best reply to the choice of the third strategy chosen by the opponent. In the same way, the selection of (1, 1) in game A may be explained by the fact that it corresponds to the best reply to this third strategy. What is surprising is that these outcomes correspond to *dominated* strategies.

One way to explain the potential selection of the third strategy by a player is to argue that it corresponds to the selection of the *Pareto-efficient* outcome of the game. Thus, an altruistic player, or simply one who wants to cooperate, may choose this strategy. However, an irrational player may also choose this strategy.

In order to discriminate between these two arguments the authors tested a third game C (Figure 8.15).

In this game, the best reply to the choice of the third strategy is strategy 1. The authors observed that the selected equilibrium is not (1, 1) but (2, 2). Therefore, the selection is not a best reply to an 'irrational choice'. Moreover (2, 2) Pareto-dominates (1, 1) and (3, 3). Hence the choice of the second

Figure 8.15 Cooperation–coordination game *C*

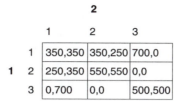

		2		
		1	2	3
	1	350,350	350,250	700,0
1	2	250,350	550,550	0,0
	3	0,700	0,0	500,500

strategy is the best reply to the choice of an opponent who wants to cooperate.

The main interpretation of these results suggests that players are *heterogeneous*; they may belong to different types (altruistic, selfish, and so on...), and subjects take them into account. This is a recurrent observation in experiments on game theory: it can be concluded that subjects often understand the game as a game with *incomplete* information and they may not have the same perception of the problem as the experimenter.

Many other experiments have tested coordination games, but they were generally devoted to the evaluation of factors increasing coordination.

8.3.2 Factors increasing coordination

What these factors have in common is the addition of a pre-game interaction. Thus, the game studied is slightly different, since it can be seen as a two-period game with the second period being the coordination game. What happens in the first period is rarely binding.

Pre-play communication

For example, Cooper *et al.* (1992) have tested the influence of pre-play communication (cheap talk) by allowing the exchange of messages announcing the strategy that will be played. In game *A* (Figure 8.13), they observed that one-way communication increased the selection of (2, 2) – which Pareto-dominates (1, 1) – to 67 per cent as opposed to 3 per cent without communication. However, *two-way* communication does not improve coordination. The explanation is that the two messages may differ; so it is better for both players not to take into account the opponent's message, nor the effect of their own messages. Moreover, two-way communications may lead to worse results. In fact, players often announced that they would choose the third strategy and rarely actually did so. Thus coordination failure is more frequent.

External advice

Another type of factor is the introduction of a referee who will advise players on moves before they start the game. Once again, these recommendations are not binding: players are not compelled to follow them. As we have seen before, this mechanism is of interest because it may help players to update their beliefs about their opponents' choices. Van Huyck, Battalio and Beil (1992) tested advice on the tree games A, B and C (Figure 8.16).

In game A, in which players had not received any advice, 40 per cent of the pairs of subjects had coordinated on one of the three NE. With a referee recommending one of these equilibria, the coordination is 98 per cent. Thus, by following the advice players increased their payoffs. In game B, without recommendation, 98 per cent of the pairs of subjects coordinated on the Pareto-efficient equilibrium (1, 1). With a referee recommending a Pareto-dominated equilibrium, the frequencies are 17 per cent for (3, 3) and 25 per cent for (2, 2); this evidence shows that subjects do not follow the advice when it is not in their interest. Finally, in game C, when no advice had been given to the players, 70 per cent of the pairs of subjects had coordinated on the symmetric equilibrium (2, 2); with a referee recommending an asymmetric equilibrium, the frequency is only 16 per cent.

Therefore this experiment shows that subjects usually follow the referee's advice except when there exists a Pareto-efficient equilibrium not advised by the referee.

Outside option

Another type of factors potentially increasing coordination is the introduction of an outside option. Typically, one player has the possibility of not playing the game by receiving a fixed payoff. If she (or he) decides to drop this outside option, then her (or his) choice will 'signal' her (or his) behaviour in the coordination game, i.e. she (or he) thinks she (or he) will obtain a higher payoff. This argument is directly connected to some interpretations of the forward induction concept (see Section 4.4, of

Figure 8.16 Coordination games with recommended plays

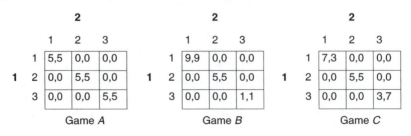

		2		
		1	2	3
	1	5,5	0,0	0,0
1	2	0,0	5,5	0,0
	3	0,0	0,0	5,5

Game A

		2		
		1	2	3
	1	9,9	0,0	0,0
1	2	0,0	5,5	0,0
	3	0,0	0,0	1,1

Game B

		2		
		1	2	3
	1	7,3	0,0	0,0
1	2	0,0	5,5	0,0
	3	0,0	0,0	3,7

Game C

Figure 8.17   Battle of the Sexes Game

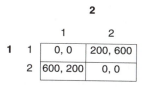

Chapter 4). Here, the decision to drop the outside option can be interpreted as the deletion of strategies dominated by this option in the coordination game.

Cooper *et al.* (1993) have tested an outside option of (300, 300) for the first player in the following Battle of the Sexes game (Figure 8.17).

Cooper *et al.* observed that when this option was not used, players coordinated 89 per cent of the time on (2, 1), namely the NE that yields a higher payoff for player 1. It is important to notice that the first strategy for player 1 is *dominated* by the outside option. Thus, if the first player does not use her option, both players know that she will not play her first strategy.

Similar results have been observed with an outside option of 100, which in this case does not dominate the first strategy. Hence, it seems that the sole presence of this option for player 1 gives him an advantage that leads players to coordinate on player 1's preferred equilibrium. The same behaviour can also be observed with sequential moves, with imperfect information or when player 1 is playing first.

Thus, the introduction of an outside option seems to have the same effect as one-way communication. It should be noted however that Brandts and Holt (1995) report contrasting results which show that it is only when it corresponds to the deletion of a dominated strategy that forward induction enables a particular equilibrium to be selected.

Remark 2

Brandts and McLeod (1995) also tested the influence of advice in games with two equilibria where only one is perfect. They observed that players always selected the perfect equilibrium even when the referee recommended the imperfect one. They also observed that these choices depend on the payoffs of the other outcomes (which determine the maximin), especially when the imperfect equilibrium Pareto-dominates the perfect one.■

Remark 3

Van Huyck, Battalio and Beil (1993) have conducted an experiment on the same pure coordination games presented above (Figures 8.11 and 8.12) but with an *auction* selecting the participants. In this case, they observed that the Pareto-efficient equilibrium (the choice of number 7 by players) was more often selected. The conclusion is that players have revised their beliefs about the opponents' choices and that this procedure has selected subjects with higher probabilities of choosing the number 7.■

Remark 4

So far we have not reported experimental results on signalling games, which are rather difficult to classify. Despite their particular involvement with cooperation problems, several properties (incomplete information, the use of a message and equilibrium refinements) relate them also to coordination problems where the question is which equilibrium to select. Among experiments on signalling games, Banks, Camerer and Porter (1994) have compared several refinement criteria: in particular, sequential equilibrium, intuitive criterion and divinity, (see sub-sections 4.3.1 and 4.3.2 of Chapter 4, for a definition of these refinements). Several signalling games have been tested; each one has two equilibria and one of the two is 'more refined' than the other. The results for one of these games are summarized in Figure 8.18.

The first observation is that subjects generally select a strategy leading to a NE in every game. The frequency of selection of NE is between 48 per cent and 95 per cent, depending on the game (76 per cent in Figure 8.18). Moreover, when subjects do not reach a NE, the reason generally is a coordination failure. For instance, player 1 selects a strategy leading to the more refined equilibrium whereas the other selects a strategy leading to the less refined one. Then both players try to coordinate on a NE but do not choose the same one.

The second observation is that subjects generally select the 'more refined' equilibrium, especially during the last periods. For instance, when there are two SE with only one that satisfies the intuitive criterion, they select this one with a frequency of 68 per cent. However, the selection of the more refined equilibrium is less obvious when refinements criteria are more restrictive. For instance, the selection of the more refined equilibrium is very clear for SE (as opposed to NE) or 'intuitive' equilibrium (as opposed to SE) but it is less clear for 'divine' equilibrium (as opposed to intuitive equilibrium).

Finally, it is also possible to compare subjects' behaviour in the various games and to observe some differences. For instance, the intuitive

Figure 8.18 Selection of each equilibria at the first and last periods (F-L)

	A	B	C	D
more refined	56%-76%	61%-71%	53%-68%	28%-38%
less refined		13%-24%	13%-4%	16%-8%
non Nash	44%-24%	26%-5%	34%-28%	56%-54%

A   Nash vs non-Nash; B   Sequential vs Nash;
C   Intuitive vs Sequential; D   Divine vs Intuitive.

equilibrium is selected with a frequency of 68 per cent in one game (last periods), whereas this frequency is only 46 per cent in another game, with a 38 per cent selection of the divine (and intuitive) equilibrium and a 8 per cent selection of the intuitive (and not divine) equilibrium. This last observation confirms results observed in many other experiments: generally subjects' behaviour is very sensitive to the game and its environment.■

8.4 Bargaining

This section deals with controlled laboratory experiments on bargaining problems. Pure bargaining games have been widely tested by various authors. First we shall present robust results on the ultimatum game, which has been tested as often as the Prisoner's dilemma game. The next sub-section overviews complementary results on strategic and axiomatic solutions. Finally, we give a few results on coalitional games.

8.4.1 The ultimatum game

The stylized facts

In the ultimatum game (see section 5.1 of Chapter 5), player 1 proposes a division $(X - S, S)$ of a sum X where $X - S$ is her share and S is the share of player 2. If player 2 accepts this proposition, each player receives her (or his) share. If he refuses, each player receives zero. The SPE of this game consists of the first player proposing a division $(X - \varepsilon, \varepsilon)$ where ε is the lowest share of X and for the second player accepting it. The idea is that player 2 will accept any *positive* amount since it is better than zero. Knowing that, player 1 will propose a division that gives player 2 the *minimum* amount.

The first experiments of this game, reported by Güth, Schmittberger and Schwarze (1982), have shown that the observed division is far from the equilibrium and is on average near the division (60, 40) when $X = 100$. Similarly, disagreements arise more frequently than expected (20 per cent of the cases). Thus, it seems that players 2 are ready to sacrifice a certain sum if they think the proposal is incorrect. It also seems that players 1 take it into account before making an offer.

The ultimatum game has intensively been studied. More than a hundred of experiments have been conducted on this game. Overviews of experimental results are presented in Thaler (1988), Güth (1995), Camerer and Thaler (1995) and Roth (1995).The behavioural regularities are quite robust and can be summarized as follows:

(i)   offers above 50, and offers below 20 are extremely rare
(ii) the modal offers lie in a range between 40 and 50

(iii) the rejection rate for offers below 20 is rather high, whereas offers close to 50 are practically never rejected.

Thus, the standard theoretical prediction implied by sub-game perfection is strongly rebutted by the stylized facts.

Several experiments were designed to test different interpretations of these results. We propose to classify them in three parts, depending on the procedure that was used. In the first category, experimenters have tried to modify institutional parameters in order to evaluate the robustness of the paradoxical results. In the second category, experimenters have modified the game structure and compared the results with the original game to draw conclusions about some factors explaining behaviour. Then, in the third category, experimenters have analysed generated data in the light of different models (expected payoff maximisation, learning, and so on).

Institutional environment

Instead of reporting one experiment, we will present briefly the main interpretation of different results. Most of them show that observed behaviours can be closer to predicted behaviours under certain circumstances:

- Some authors have distinguished between the subjects who understood the strategic solution of the game and the others. They observed that once those who did not understand have been removed, results are closer to the predictions. Nevertheless, results are controversial since the theory is not perfectly verified: results are only closer but sometimes not statistically significant.
- Most experiments use repetition of the game and players may earn money at different periods. It seems that subjects take this into account and when taking a decision on a proposal or a response, they may think of the next round, which distorted results.
- Most experiments are conducted with small rewards, i.e. the sum to be divided is about $10. A question that routinely comes up in discussions among specialists of experimental economics is whether a rise in the stake level will eventually induce subjects to behave in a self-interested manner. The surprising answer is that relatively large increases in the monetary stakes does not seem to change behaviour significantly (see, for instance, Cameron, 1999). Some experiments with extremely higher stakes, such as $10,000, report more selfish behaviour at least for some players. However, large segments of the population do not seem to be strongly concerned by this kind of issue. Of course, this kind of experiment is difficult to carry out because of its costs and most experiments use other procedures rather than standard payment of all subjects (grade points, rewarding of a selected subject, and so on).
- The selection of subjects may also affect results. If results are contrasted on gender effects, it seems that students in economics and children behave differently from others.

- The players' roles are generally attributed at random before starting the experiment. However, it is clear that the first player has an advantage and players 2 may dispute it. Some authors have proposed attributing roles after a game or after an auction, the winner being the first player in the ultimatum game. This procedure gives some kind of property rights to the first player that are not questioned by player 2. In this framework results seems to be closer to the prediction of GT.
- Some experiments have noticed the impact of presentation effects (framing effects) such as strategic/extensive form, percentage/money, and so on.
- Experiments on the ultimatum bargaining game generally try to remove any social context to avoid contamination effects. Thus, some protocol details have been used as treatment variables such as 'double-blind' anonymity, where the anonymity is introduced not only between subjects but also between subjects and the experimenter.
- Other experiments in psychology or sociology have re-introduced social relations between subjects – for instance, by allowing players to exchange messages, or by replacing the first player with a computer. Results show that emotions such as anger may partly explain player 2 behaviour. For instance, small offers accompanied by claims that they were fair were rejected more often than identical offers that were not accompanied by such claims.

Most of these results, even if they do help to explain some data, are not really helpful in answering the following question: do proposers behave according to *altruism*, that is an unconditional preference for sharing equally, or do they implement strategic moves in a context of incomplete information (*'strategic fairness'*), a behaviour owing to the fear that low offers will be rejected? The second category of experiments tries to find more direct answers to this question.

Experiments on modified versions of the standard game

There are several ways to modify the original game. Among the different modifications, three groups of experiments can be distinguished: (1) modifying player 2's veto, (2) increasing the number of players, and (3) introducing incomplete information about the pie.

Player 2's veto: the dictator game and other related games

One of the most famous examples of modification of player 2's role is the 'dictator game' introduced by Kahneman, Knetsch and Thaler (1986) and studied by Forsythe *et al.* (1994), Hoffman, McCabe and Smith (1996) and Eckel and Grossman (1998). This game is identical to the ultimatum game except that *player 2 cannot reject the division*. In other words, the task assigned to player 1 (the so-called 'dictator') is to divide an amount of money X between herself and player 2 (named here the 'receiver'). Player 1 can choose freely the division of the sum and player 2 has no choice to make, i.e. he has to accept any amount sent to him. The receiver's payoff is simply the amount S that has been sent by the dictator, while the dictator's payoff is given by the residual amount $X - S$. The dictator game allows us to separate the fear-of-rejection hypothesis from altruism since the responder' ability to reject the offers is removed.

With $X = 100$ for the pie, the stylized facts can be summarized as follows:

(i)   offers by the dictator larger than 50 are practically never observed
(ii) about 80 per cent of the offers are between 0 and 50, but compared to the ultimatum game, the distribution of offers is shifted towards 0
(iii) about 20 per cent of the dictator's offers are exactly 0, that is the amount predicted by backward induction.

Thus, the authors observed results which were different from previously observed divisions in the ultimatum game and closer to the standard theoretical prediction. Yet, it should be noticed that these results are not very robust with respect to treatment variations (for instance, increasing the social distance among participants of an experiment and the experimenter (i.e. double-blind treatment) increases the proportion of zero offers, and the precise distribution of dictator offers varies with 'framing effects') (Hoffman, McCabe and Smith, 1996; Hoffman *et al.*, 1996).

A general conclusion however can be drawn: in the ultimatum game, fear of rejection is part of the explanation for proposers' generous offers. Proposers do offer less when there can be no rejection; but this motive is not the entire explanation since many subjects still offer something in the dictator game. An additional result confirms us in this conclusion. In another experiment, player 2 was replaced by a charity organization, and the observed divisions then have been appreciably more equal in this setting. This result seems to show that the social context is significant, and fairness needs a social context.

Güth and Huck (1997) have studied other modifications of player 2's veto by testing two special games. In game A, player 2's decision affects only player 1's payoff. So, if player 2 decides to reject the division, he receives S, whereas player 1 does not receive anything. In game B, player 2's decision affects his own payoff: if he rejects, he does not receive anything whereas player 1 receives $X - S$. The results were significantly closer to an equal share in game A than in game B. That means that player 2's veto is taken into account by player 1. Thus, when this veto threatens her own payoff (like in game A), player 1 offers a more equal division. Moreover, the authors have observed that in game A, the results were more equal than in a standard ultimatum game, which means that the possibility of punishment by player 2 is an important feature of the game. The authors also observed that in game B, results were more unequal than in the dictator game. Some interpretations are that players 2 have to accept more often in order to avoid waste, or because if they don't have the possibility of punishing their opponent, they will behave more 'rationally'.

Further experiments have been designed in order to isolate pure altruism from positive reciprocity. The 'investment game' (Berg, Dickhaut and McCabe, 1995) is an interesting companion of the dictator game. Player 1 (an 'investor') receives an amount of money X that she can keep or transfer to player 2 (a 'trustee'). Then, the amount sent S ($0 < S < X$) is tripled by the experimenter. Player 2 is free to return anything between zero and $3S$ to player 1. If T is this counter-transfer, player 1's payoff is is $X - S + T$, and player's 2 payoff is $3S - T$. Notice that the investment game is essentially a dictator game in which the trustee dictates an allocation, but the amount to be allocated was created by the investor's initial investment. The investment game may also be interpreted as a trust game with variable degree of trust and variable degree of reward (see subsection 8.2.2 for a presentation of the trust game). Though the theoretical prediction is that player 2 will repay $T = 0$, experiments show that players 1 typically invest about half the maximum on average, and players 2 tend to repay slightly less than S, so that trust does not quite pay. Moreover, one observes that repay increases with S, which can be interpreted as 'positive' reciprocity.

The 'gift-exchange' game (Fehr, Kirchsteiger and Riedl, 1993; Fehr Gächter and Kirchsteiger, 1997) is another variant of the dictator game which enlightens the role of reciprocity in the enforcement of informal agreement or incomplete contracts. Player 1 (an employer) can offer a wage contract to player 2 (a worker) that stipulates a binding wage w and a desired effort level e. Player 2 may either take it or leave it. If he rejects, both earn nothing. If he accepts the wage offered, he is free to choose the actual effort level between a minimum e^m and a maximum level e^M. Player 1 always has to pay the offered wage irrespective of the actual effort level. Higher effort levels represent a higher profit for the employer and a higher cost for the worker. Thus, e^m gives the worker the highest payoff, but the highest profit for the employer is given at e^M. In this setting, selfish workers have no incentives to provide effort above e^m irrespective of the level of wage w. And employers who anticipate this behaviour will offer the smallest possible wage such that the worker just accept the contract. However, reciprocal workers will honour at least partly generous wage offers by choosing a non-minimum effort. This game is able to show to what extent employers do appeal to workers' reciprocity by offering high wages and to what extent workers honour this generosity. Experiments show that on average the offered contracts stipulate a maximum desired effort, the wage offered implies that the worker earn 44 per cent of the total income generated by a maximum effort, and a relative majority of the workers honour this generosity by putting forward extra effort above what is implied by purely pecuniary considerations.

More than two players

Another type of modification of the standard ultimatum game consists in including a *third player*. Güth and Van Damme (1998) introduced a third 'player' (or a third 'person') so that the division of player 1 is $(X - S - T, S, T)$ where T is the share of this third player. Players 1 and 2 are active while player 3 is an inactive dummy player. Three treatments were used. In treatment A, players 2 knew all shares before accepting or rejecting the division. In treatment B, they knew only their own share and in treatment C they only knew the third player's share. These treatments were used to check players' sense of fairness. The results showed that players 1 did not have a real sense of fairness since their proposals were unfair for the third player in treatment B where player 2 did not know how much this third player had received. Similarly, players 2 exhibited different behaviours when confronted by an unfair division when either their own payoff was the lowest or when it was the third player's payoff. Thus, neither the proposer nor the active responder seem to care about the well-being of the dummy.

These results confirm a conclusion reached in previous experiments: players' so-called 'fairness motives' disappear quickly in certain environments. Besides, if the third party is considered as 'active', the results change. For instance, in Knez and Camerer (1995) or Riedl and Vyrastekova (2002), experiments have been carried out with three active players and one of the main findings is that about half of the responders submit strategies that 'care' about the other responder. Therefore, in this setting, social comparison between responders matters.

Incomplete information about the pie

A third way of modifying the game is to introduce *incomplete information* about the sum to divide. The game is then similar to the ultimatum game (with the same equilibrium), except that one of the players does not know the amount of the sum to divide. Several procedures have been used. We report here two methods to introduce incomplete information.

In the simplest method, player 1 knows the sum to divide whereas player 2 is not informed. There are two traditional presentations. In the 'offer game', player 1 proposes a division (K, S) where K is unknown for player 2. In other words, she offers S to player 2 without any other information. In the 'demand game', player 1 offers a division (R, K), with $R = X - K$, where K is unknown for player 2. In other words, she demands R for himself from player 2.

Mitzkewitz and Nagel (1993) have tested these games with the 'strategy method', which consisted of asking players 2 to submit their plans of action for each possible proposal from players 1. In the offer game, the results were more and more unequal when the sum to divide was increased. For instance, when player 1 had to offer a share of, say, 100, her proposal in percentage of the total was higher than when she had to offer a share of 1,000. This behaviour shows that player 1 plays strategically. Similarly, in the demand game, the higher the sum to divide, the more equal the results, i.e. when player 1 has to demand for herself a share of 100, her proposal is higher in percentage of the total than when she has to demand a share of 1,000. Once again, player 1 behaves strategically. In both cases, she exploits her opponents' lack of information to obtain a higher payoff.

Kagel, Kim and Moser (1996) reached the same conclusion by using another environment. They introduced different conversion rates for points earned in the experiment. In some cases, one player only was informed about their values. Thus, when player 1 has to divide the sum of money, she has to take into account the conversion rates. For instance, if the rates are 0.1 for her payoff and 0.3 for her opponent's payoff, then a division (80, 20) yields payoffs of, respectively, 8 and 6 (that is more equal than the point division).

The authors observed that when player 1 is the only one informed, the division in points is more equal when she has the higher conversion rate than when it is the other way round. In other words, player 1 can afford to divide equally when she has a higher conversion rate since she will receive a higher payoff. Inversely, when she has a lower conversion rate, she has to divide less equally in order to receive a higher payoff. It is clear from this last observation that player 1 does not try to maximize collective welfare since the joint payoff could have been higher if she had proposed more to her opponent (whose conversion rate is higher). Moreover, when she has the higher conversion rates she rarely proposes an unequal division that could be justified by this sort of argument. So, this shows her fear of a rejection. When only players 2 know the values of the conversion rates, less disagreement is observed when they have the higher conversion rates than when it is the other way round. It seems that players 2 compare incomes when they decide to accept or to reject a proposal. Finally, the authors also observed that equal divisions in *points*, but unequal in *payoffs*, are more often rejected when both players know the conversion rates than when only player 2 knows them. Thus player 2 is kinder to player 1 when she has an 'excuse'.

All these results show that subjects play in a specific context and that the information they have is very influential for two reasons: it can help them to increase their payoffs if they behave strategically, and it can also lead them to follow equity principles more easily.

Remark 1

Many other experiments have tested some variants of modified games reported above. We summarize here some of them:

1   Bolton and Zwick (1995) have tested the so-called 'impunity game', which studies the influence of player 2's veto and the possibility of punishing his opponent. It seems that this possibility is a relevant factor to explain player 1's behaviour.

2   Güth, Huck and Ockenfels (1996) have tested a three-player ultimatum game where player 1 proposes a division $(X-S, S)$ to player 2. If he accepts, player 1 receives $X-S$ and player 2 receives S. If he rejects neither player receives anything. If player 2 accepts, he has to propose a division $(S-T, T)$ to player 3. This last player can accept and player 2 and player 3 receive $S-T$ and T, or reject and neither player receives anything. Thus, in this game, player 2 has two roles: proposer and respondent. Results seem to show some kind of 'reciprocity' since player 2 is more generous with player 3 when player 1 has been more generous with player 2.

3   Rapoport and Sundali (1996) and Rapoport, Sundali and Seale (1996) have studied an ultimatum game with incomplete information (offer game and demand game). They observed that when the uncertainty about the sum to divide is increased (formally the difference between the higher and the lower possible values), shares are more unequal, which means that players 1 really try to exploit any advantage to increase their own payoffs.

4   Another type of modification is related to the way subjects are rewarded. Carter and McAloon (1996) have tested an ultimatum game where the players' payoff depends on a 'tournament': both players 1 and players 2 are in competition with players who have similar roles. The authors observed more equal offers. This result can be due to the competition between players 2 who had to increase their acceptance threshold. Thus, in order to propose offers with higher probability of acceptance, players 1 have to reduce their share of the sum. Schotter, Weiss and Zapater (1996) also tested ultimatum and other games with tournament. Yet, only players 1 with the higher scores played a second game. Thus, the prize in the first game was a participation in a second game. Results were more unequal, which could be interpreted as the necessity for players 1 to 'survive'. For this reason, unequal results were more easily accepted since players 1 had an 'excuse'.■

Once again, these results show that *bargaining experiments are very sensitive to social context*. A way to conduct experiments in this area is to add a new controlled context and to study its effects. Another way to detect regularities is to analyse experimental data.

Data analysis

Different countries

One of the most famous results on the ultimatum game is provided by Roth *et al.* (1991). They studied behaviours in *different countries*: the United States, Japan, Yugoslavia and Israel. They noticed that offers were more unequal in two countries. If this was not due to a strategic behaviour from players 1, there should be no difference between players 2's behaviour in these countries and the other two. Or, there could be higher rejection rates in these countries with more unequal propositions. On the other hand, the authors observed less rejection in these countries. In other words, the same proposal leads to less rejection in these countries than in the other two.

One interpretation is that players 2 have a higher acceptance threshold and what is interesting is that this difference is reflected in players 1's behaviour. Thus, the higher the acceptance threshold, the more unequal are the shares proposed by players 1. It seems that players 1 try to maximize their *expected payoffs*.

One way to study that phenomenon more carefully is to calculate player 1's expected payoff for different offers. In this case, of course, we need to know the probability of rejection to do that. The authors used the observed frequency of rejection for different offers and produced the graph reproduced in Figure 8.19.

This graph represents player 1's expected payoff for different proposals in one of the four countries. The authors observed the same type of graphs in other countries with a main feature: the expected payoff has a maximum value for $S > 0$. What is most interesting is that this value is precisely the average observed proposal. In other words, it seems that players 1 do pretty well in maximizing their payoffs since, on average, they offer divisions very similar to the one that maximizes their payoff. This is particularly interesting since they do not know the frequency of rejection. They can only try to estimate it.

Figure 8.19 Expected payoff for player 1

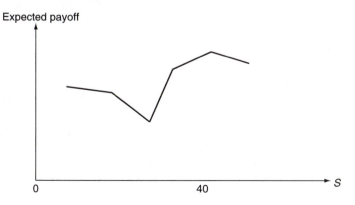

Learning

A second way to analyse data is to use *learning* models. The idea is to check and see if observed behaviour can be predicted. The main difficulty with this type of methodology is that it is often 'easy' to find a model which can explain experimental data in a particular game. However, it is often difficult to apply the same model to another game. Nevertheless, various authors have found simple models that work well in very different games, as we have seen previously. Here, we can complete them with the Mitzkewitz and Nagel's experiment (1994).

Briefly, they observed that players 1 proposed more equal division after a rejection and more unequal division after an acceptance. The interpretation is that players 1 try to maximize their payoffs. As there is an uncertainty about the opponent's acceptance or rejection, the repetition of the game is appropriate to help players 1. More generally, most experiments have shown that the minimum offer that players 2 can accept is around 20 and the maximum offer that players 1 can make is between 40 and 45. What is intriguing is that average offers are around 40. Thus, offers are closer to the player 2's preferred division. In other words, there is a way for player 1 to increase her payoff and repetition can be a possibility.

Remark 2

The unequal payoffs are an important feature of the ultimatum game. For this reason, authors have tried to see if other games with extreme payoffs can yield experimental data which conform better to the theory.

That is what Harrison and Hirschleifer (1989) have done with the 'best shot game'. In this game, player 1 proposes a quantity X to finance a public good. Player 2, once informed of the quantity X, has to propose a quantity Y. The public good is then produced in a quantity equal to the maximum value between X and Y. The player who proposed the highest quantity of the two has a payoff equal to her (or his) consumption of the public good (like the other player), minus her (or his) proposal (unlike the other player). The solution is for player 1 to propose $X = 0$. Experimental results were close to this prediction. Some authors explained it by out-of-equilibrium path behaviours. In the best shot game, the first player cannot increase her payoff when she deviates from $X = 0$ whereas, as we have seen above, in the ultimatum game, the expected payoff is increased when offers S are increased. However, other authors suggest that the reason is the incompatibility between equity and efficiency in the best shot game as opposed to the ultimatum game.

To answer this question, Prasnikar and Roth (1992) proposed another game: the 'sequential market game'. In this game, 9 buyers are in competition for proposing a division $(10 - S, S)$ to a seller. The equilibrium is for $S = 10$ or $S = 10$ less the smallest amount unit, i.e. $(1, 9)$. In this game, equity and efficiency are compatible: if all buyers propose $S = 1$, all players (including the seller) have an expected payoff of $1(\frac{1}{9} 9,1)$ and if the highest proposal is $S = 5$, the seller and the selected buyer have the same payoff of 5. Results of the experiment, however, have been very close to the theoretical prediction, which confirms the first interpretation: the out-of-equilibrium path behaviour is important in these games.∎

The ultimatum game is the bargaining game which has been the most widely tested in controlled experiments. However it is a very special case with specific properties. Studying this game is a good way to understand bargaining behaviour, but more general games contain other important features.

8.4.2 Some other bargaining games

As explained in Chapter 5, remember that there are two complementary ways to study bargaining games: the strategic and the axiomatic approaches. We present first some experiments on strategic models which generalize the ultimatum game and its variants

Further strategic models

Discount factor and number of periods

The ultimatum bargaining game is a particular case of an alternated offers model with only *one offer*. Therefore, it does not consider other parameters such as *discount factor*. Binmore, Shaked and Sutton (1985) have proposed testing a two-period game with a discount factor $\delta = 0.25$ and with $X = 100$. Thus, if player 2 rejects player 1's proposal, he will have to offer a new division of $X = 25$. The equilibrium consists for the first player to offer a division of the pie included in the interval: (74, 26), (76, 24). At the beginning, the results were close to (50, 50), contradicting the theory; but after repeating the game and changing the players' roles they were close to the theoretical prediction. Thus, the strategic model with alternated offers seems to be validated.

Nevertheless, several studies have tested the influences of the *value of the discount factor* and the *number of periods*. Among these laboratory experiments, we consider Ochs and Roth's experiment (1989) which put together a very large experimental design: the authors tested 8 games combining two values for the number of periods (two or three) and four structures of discount factors (0.4 or 0.6 for player 1 or player 2). The theoretical predictions are reported in Figure 8.20.

The authors observed that the results were close to the equilibrium prediction only in game A. For all the other games, the results were closer to the equal division than to the equilibrium. Moreover, they noticed that several offers that were rejected in the first period by player 2 were followed by counterproposals in which player 2 demanded *less* cash

Figure 8.20   Multistage bargaining games

Game	A	B	C	D	E	F	G	H
δ_1	0.4	0.6	0.6	0.4	0.4	0.6	0.6	0.4
δ_2	0.4	0.4	0.6	0.6	0.4	0.4	0.6	0.6
Periods	2	2	2	2	3	3	3	3
Equilibrium	59–41	59–41	39–61	39–61	76–24	84–16	77–23	65–35

than he had been offered. A significant number of players 2 were rejecting small shares of the relatively large sum available in the first period in favour of large shares of the much smaller sum available in the second period.

This observation needs some explanation. Obviously, that means that players 2's preferences cannot be directly measured by their monetary payoffs but they must include some non-monetary component, and this casts doubt on the methodology used to test the theory. Several interpretations are proposed. For instance, it is possible that income comparisons are present, as we have noticed in other games. Here, a player is not only interested in the amount of her (or his) payoff but also in her (or his) share of the sum and may desire to receive the highest share even if it is from a smaller sum. Yet, some experiments have shown that this kind of 'irrational' counterproposal is less frequent with a higher discount factor. Thus, the higher the price to pay for this behaviour (i.e. when the sum to be divided is very low), the more rational the players. This is also a typical observation from many other experiments (think of the Prisoner's dilemma, for example): the higher the cost, the less irrational the behaviour.

To summarize, even if some experiments with a fixed cost of bargaining instead of discount factor seem closer to the theory, most experimental results invalidate the theoretical prediction.

Outside options

Among strategic models of bargaining, there are some particular models with *outside options* (see sub-section 5.1.3 of Chapter 5). In these games, one player can quit the bargaining process and receive a fixed payoff of T. Several focal solutions are possible. Except for the conventional (50, 50) with $X = 100$, players can split the difference and receive $T + (100 - T)/2$ for the player with the outside option and $(100 - T)/2$ for the other player. Or, they can split equally unless $T > 50$ in which case, the player with the outside option receives T and the other receives the rest $100 - T$.

Binmore, Shaked and Sutton (1989) have tested games with an outside option. The main conclusion was that divisions were close to (50, 50) and that the outside option does not influence players' behaviour, especially when it leads its owner to a lower payoff than the equilibrium. For instance, if $T = 30$, a division (50, 50) yields a higher payoff than 30 and the outside option is not taken into consideration for the bargaining whereas a 'split the difference' solution would lead to a division (65, 35) more advantageous for the owner of the option.

Optional or forced breakdown

Inversely, in models with *optional or forced breakdown* results were closer to the theory (see sub-section 5.1.3 of Chapter 5). With optional breakdown, players can decide to stop the bargaining process at any time and receive breakdown payoffs: ($T1$, $T2$). With forced breakdown, the game can be terminated at random with a probability p, in which case players receive breakdown payoffs: ($T1$, $T2$).

Binmore *et al.* (1991) conducted an experiment with breakdown payoffs of (4, 36) in treatment A and of (4, 64) in treatment B. With the optional breakdown the equilibrium predictions are (50, 50) with treatment A and (36, 64) with treatment B. With the forced breakdown, they are, respectively, (34, 66) and (80, 20); this consists in splitting the difference between the rest of the sum and their payoffs. For example, in treatment A, the rest of the sum to be divided is $100 - 4 - 36 = 60$ which gives 30 to each player and final payoffs of 34 and 66 when we add their breakdown payoffs. Experimental results were in some way close to these predictions. In treatment A, divisions were very different with the forced or optional breakdown and these differences were in line with the prediction, i.e.: (36, 64) or (80 20), respectively. In treatment B, differences between forced and optional breakdown were smaller but still in the direction of the prediction.

Remark I

Many other experiments have tested strategic models of bargaining. They generally reproduced the results reported above. Among them, Bolton (1991) and Kahn and Murnighan (1993) have combined several parameters. The conclusions are generally identical. For example, when a player has an outside option of 90 with $X = 100$, players rarely reach agreement with shares above 90. Both (90, 10) and (50, 50) seems to attract players' attention and the average choice can be situated at about (70, 30). This observation leads us more directly to the notion of focal point which has been tested in axiomatic models.■

Axiomatic models

In axiomatic models of bargaining, the solution is determined by players' preferences and their attitude toward risk. Some results are similar to those reported in the previous paragraph, notably for focal points (a wide variety of experiments on bargaining behaviour is presented in Roth, 1987, 1995).

The basic setting for axiomatic bargaining experiments is as follows. There are two players which are told that both a large prize and a small prize are available. If the subject does not win the large prize, the small prize is automatically awarded (in the simplest experiments, the small prize is $0: the loser wins nothing). The large prize is awarded by a lottery at the end of the experiment. The large prize goes to the player holding the winning number. At the start of bargaining, there is a given number of lottery tickets on the table. The more lottery tickets a subject gets by bargaining, the greater that subject's chance of winning the large prize. The winning number is drawn by chance from the uniform distribution, so that each number is equally good. The tickets are converted in cash at the end of the experiment. Subjects bargain over how many of the tickets each will obtain. In case of disagreement, there is no lottery for the large prize, and each subject gets her (or his) small prize.

Roth and Malouf (1979) have observed that the division (50, 50) of $X = 100$ was observed when players can win identical prizes. However, when the prizes are different, results were different according to whether the players were fully or partially informed. In the case of full information, each player knew her (or his) own and her (or his) opponent's prizes whereas in the case of partial information, each player knew only her (or his) own prize. Two focal points seems to emerge: (50, 50) which yields equal probabilities and (20, 80) which yields equal expected payoffs if prizes are, respectively, 100 and 25. The average observation is in between these two points, which is far from the (50, 50) NBS prediction (see sub-section 5.2.1 of Chapter 5).

Roth and Murnighan (1982) have used different treatments to find out how information can influence players. In treatment A, one player is informed of the prize of the other player whereas in treatment B, she (or he) is also informed that her (or his) opponent knows that she (or he) is informed. There is 'common knowledge' in the sense that it is specified that both players receive exactly the same instructions. Four conditions were used for each treatment depending on which player was informed. One player had a $20 prize whereas the other has a $5 prize. With the first condition, neither knows her (or his) opponent's prize. With the second condition, the player who has the $20 prize knows the value of both prizes. With the third condition, the player who has the $5 prize knows the value of both prizes and with the fourth condition, both players know both prizes. The authors noticed that the division yielding equal expected payoff, here (20, 80), was a focal point when the player knew both prizes. When it was not the case, the (50, 50) division was predominant. This observation confirms the results obtained by Roth and Malouf (1979): the disagreement frequency varies according to the information given. When the player who has the $5 prize knows both prizes, the disagreement frequency is higher in treatment A. All these results show how important information is in bargaining.

Murnighan, Roth and Schoumaker (1988) have investigated the influence of players' attitude towards risk. They studied games with three lottery prizes: a high prize H, a low prize L and a disagreement prize D. Theory normally predicts that risk aversion is disadvantageous, except when the potential prize is lower than the disagreement payoff, i.e. when $D > L$. The authors first measured players attitude toward risk before playing the bargaining game, by making them fill in 'risky choice' questionnaires. They made a subject more risk-averse to play with a subject less averse to risk. If $D > L$ and as long as they have the same rewards, the player more averse to risk should obtain more than one-half of the sum to be divided. However, if $D > L$, she (or he) should obtain less than one-half. The experimental results showed that although the theory was partly confirmed (with more disagreements when $D > L$), most divisions were close to (50, 50). To avoid the effects of this focal solution, other experiments have been conducted with different prizes for the two players. Even if these experiments did not exactly confirm the theory, they tended that way: the player more averse to risk obtains a higher share when D is high than when D is low.

8.4.3   Coalition games

Coalition games will be dealt with in this sub-section. As mentioned in Chapter 6, this approach enables players to negotiate effectively and to form intermediate coalitions. As before, experiments are useful to determine which of the different solution concepts have better predictive power and to discover common features which have not been incorporated in existing theories. However, when we classically adopt cooperative games as framework, the methodological difficulties are harder since it is necessary to present the game to the subjects directly in terms of the coalitional (or characteristic) function (see sub-section 1.3.3, of Chapter 1 and sub-section 6.1.1 of Chapter 6). Thus, the interpretation of the results has to take into account their understanding of the game they are playing. Moreover, experiments have been conducted with different purposes as well as different experimental designs, subjects, and instructions. Comparisons are therefore very difficult to make. The main observation is that none of the solution concepts corresponds to the experimental observations.

A whole book would be necessary to make an exhaustive study of the main experiments. Rapoport (1970, 1990) or Kahan and Rapoport (1984) have studied most of the experiments on cooperative games. We will refer to those illustrative examples connected with methodological issues.

Maschler (1963) tested a 3-person-(0, 1)-normalized game (see sub-section 1.3.3 of Chapter 1) where:

$$v(\{1\}) = v(\{2\}) = v(\{3\}) = 0$$
$$v(\{1, 2\}) = v(\{1, 3\}) = v(\{1, 2, 3\}) = 90$$
$$v(\{2, 3\}) = 0$$

The unique outcome in the bargaining set is (90, 0, 0) where the first player receives the highest payoff (see sub-section 6.2.2 of Chapter 6 for a definition of the bargaining set). This prediction was observed during the first repetitions. But, after a while, the two other players decided to flip a coin. The winner negotiated with the first player whereas the other player was rejected. The observed outcome was close to (67.5, 22.5, 0) or (67.5, 0, 22.5) depending on the chosen player. The first player responded offering a slightly higher payoff to one of the two other players. Thus, the main observation is that the last results do not coincide with the theoretical prediction. However, players seemed to act very intuitively. What is important here is the process leading to this last result. All data seem significant in experimental works. It enables evaluations of missing items in the theory. Here, the bargaining set does not take into account the arguments described below. Maschler also noticed that – as in many other experiments referred to in previous sections – although the players were presented with a characteristic function, their perception of the game was different. The perceived values are in fact:

$$w(\{1\}) = 45$$
$$w(\{2\}) = w(\{3\}) = 0$$
$$w(\{1, 2\}) = w(\{1, 3\}) = w(\{1, 2, 3\}) = 90$$
$$w(\{2, 3\}) = 45$$

This methodological problem, namely that players do not have the same perception of the game as the experimenter, is indeed crucial, since it is often possible when data is not conform to find another game, that resembles the original game, and that gives a valid prediction.

Murnighan and Roth (1977) carried out an experiment with the following values:

$$v(\{1\}) = v(\{2\}) = v(\{3\}) = 0$$
$$v(\{1, 2\}) = v(\{1, 3\}) = v(\{1, 2, 3\}) = 100$$

Clearly, all players have the same opportunities except that players 2 and 3 cannot form a coalition without player 1. Thus, player 1 has an advantage in the form of a payoff of 100 for herself if a coalition is formed. 36 groups of 3 subjects played the game 12 times. In 95 per cent of the cases negotiations ended with coalitions {1, 2} or {1, 3}, and contrary to the prediction, player 1's payoff was generally much lower than 100. Of course, in more than 97 per cent of the cases, she received a payoff higher than 50, which means that the other players received less than she did.

These findings seem to be related to other experimental results on pure bargaining (sub-section 8.3.2) where we observed that subjects do not use entirely their bargaining power. In other words, when subjects have an advantage, they generally receive a higher payoff than their opponent, but it is not as high as the one predicted by the theory. Some authors would say that players are 'satisficing' rather than 'maximizing' (see Selten, 1987, and more generally, for satisficing principle and bounded rationality in decision theory, Simon, 1982).

A last example, dealt with by Raiffa (1982), raises further methodological issues. Raiffa tested the following game:

$$v(\{1\}) = v(\{2\}) = v(\{3\}) = 0$$
$$v(\{1, 2\}) = 118$$
$$v(\{1, 3\}) = 84$$
$$v(\{2, 3\}) = 50$$
$$v(\{1, 2, 3\}) = 121$$

This game was played with two different protocols for the negotiation: 'face to face' and communication via computer terminals. In the first case, 90 per cent of the games ended in a 3-person coalition whereas in the second, 91 per cent of the games ended in a 2-person coalition. Thus, it seems that the way subjects negotiate has a significant influence. For Raiffa (1982, 266), 'people probably find it easier to act tough if they are not looking at the other negotiators – if the others are anonymous. It's hard to squeeze out someone else from a coalition when that person is looking at you'. The average payoffs were 69, 40 and 10 for A, B and C in the first case and 49, 27.8 and 5.7 in the second case. They are 'relatively' close to the SV in the first case: (57.3, 40.3, 23.3) (see sub-section 6.3.1 of Chapter 6 for a definition of the SV). Moreover, the author noticed that if $v(\{1, 2, 3\}) = 126$(increase : +5), the core would be (76, 42, 8). Thus, 'a reasonable' solution could be (74.3, 40.3, 6.3), where one-third of 5 is deducted from each player's payoff. This solution also is 'relatively' close to the average payoffs in the first case, which are in fact intermediate between this solution and the SV. As noticed in other experiments, it is often hard to interpret results that differ from theoretical predictions, especially when there are two predictions and when the observed results are ranged between the two.

Many further examples of coalition games could be presented. Nevertheless, what is important to underline is that classical solution concepts are rarely good predictions, except in simple cases. It seems, as in most experimental games, that elements that have so far eluded experimental control are indeed significant. Moreover, coalition games are very special games and experimental tests on them raise many further questions on how players should communicate, and how time intervene, and so on.

It is because he expected pathological result in using backward induction in the Ultimatum game that Selten proposed the experiment to Güth in the first place. On the whole, what has been shown in all these experiments on bargaining is that Selten's premonition was right. As in cooperation problems, fairness motivations (reciprocity, altruism) may be advanced in bargaining problems in order to explain these anomalies, and one needs new models of individual preferences that incorporate a 'psychic', component or a taste for fairness. Section 8.6 deals among other things with this topic. But the relevance of learning processes for explaining experimental results is also largely put forward. The following section is devoted in part to this important question.

8.5 Learning and evolution

Evolutionary game theory (EGT) have proven useful for discussing the behaviour of animal species in strategic contexts. Chapter 7 has emphasized the advantages that could be drawn from transposing this approach to various fields of economics and business studies. However, in biology, players inherit the chosen actions from their parents, the more profitable actions leading to higher rates of reproduction. In economics, this process of Darwinian selection is replaced by some sort of learning and adjustment process. Experimental games create ideal situations to test the kind of strategic interactions which are best described by EGT. After setting out the major issues involved in such experiments, we will present some details on a few experiments and discuss the major results. When EGT is applied to economics and business, it is certainly correct and useful to interpret the evolutionary dynamics as a learning process. However, it is also important to study properly how people learn in playing games and what are the effects of various modes of learning on the process of adjustment. Experiments have been explicitly designed to deal with this issue. The last sub-section will be devoted to such experiments on learning in games.

8.5.1 Questions explored in experimental evolutionary games

For possible applications of EGT to laboratory studies, the experimental games must be such that two conditions be satisfied: (a) players do not try to influence other players' future actions; (b) the distribution of actions may change gradually over time. It is not hard to find a series of experimental situations in which these two conditions are satisfied. It is also interesting to vary the numbers of players or other conditions of the games in order to find the limits of applicability of EGT.

A traditional assumption in biological EGT is that the population is very large, which permits us to assume also that no player ever attempts to influence others' behaviours. But in applications to economics or business studies, one may want to adapt the large-number assumption. The only requirement is that players do not try to behave strategically as in the non-cooperative framework, that uses threats, promises or other strategic moves. In many interesting economic situations, a number of players no smaller than 4 or 5 may be enough to assure that the assumption of 'no attempt to influence other players' future actions' is actually valid (see for example Bresnahan and Reiss 1991, who found evidence that, in some industries, the entry of a third competitor in an incumbent duopoly may create a competitive structure equivalent to a large number of suppliers).

In an evolutionary context, the experiments will consist of repetitions of simple familiar games, such as the Prisoner's dilemma game, or a typical coordination game, played for instance by people paired at random in a single population. The very first kind of question raised in such experiments is whether after some periods an equilibrium is reached, which may be called a 'behavioural' equilibrium (BE), and which may or may not correspond to a NE of the corresponding non-cooperative game. Moreover, if EGT has any predictive power, the equilibrium reached after some periods should not only be a NE, but also, as we learned in Chapter 7, one of its refinements such as an Evolutionary Equilibrium (EE).

More specific predictions of EGT can also be tested while observing the process of convergence to an equilibrium. The rate of convergence may vary with different treatments, or environmental conditions. Various games, with different payoff structures have been tested.

Matching rules and information conditions have also been varied. Friedman (1996) examined two alternative procedures for matching players, respectively called random-pairwise (RP) and mean matching (MM). Under the RP protocol, players are paired at random independently in each period and receive their individual payoffs accordingly. Under the MM protocol, each player is matched against each possible opponent in each period and gets the average (mean) payoff. EGT suggests that convergence to a BE should be faster in the MM treatment than in the RP treatment.

Other variants concern the amount of historical information available. Under one protocol, the players may have no information about the game history (except what she (or he) can tabulate herself (or himself)). In the other treatment, players are informed about all the past moves. EGT suggests that convergence to a BE should be faster in the latter case.

Finally, treatments may be varied according to the population size. This dimension is crucial to test the limits of applicability of EGT. With a small number of participants in the game, each player may attempt to influence other players' future behaviour. For example, a player may have a 'Kantian' behaviour, that is 'act as they would like the others to play'. In that case, the large-number assumption would be violated in the sense that players would not respond only to their own current payoff differential.

8.5.2 Examples of experimental evolutionary games

Many simple games have been tested in an evolutionary environment. Van Huyck, Battalio and Gillette (1992) performed experiments on two-person divide-the-dollar game. Friedman (1996) tested a series of similar standard games, with two players and two strategies, and under the assumption of either a single population or of two distinct populations. Single population games include: Hawk–Dove (HD), Prisoner's dilemma (PD) and a Coordination game (Co). Hawk–Dove has also been experimented on in a two-population framework (HD$_2$) and in its three-strategy extension to the Hawk–Dove–Bourgeois game (see Chapter 7, exercise 7). Other two population evolutionary games tested by Friedman include a Buyer–Seller game, a Battle of the Sexes (BoS), and a game whose equilibrium can be found by IDE (Iterated Dominated Strategies, IDS). We will give here a brief account of the experiments on HD, PD, Co, HD$_2$, BoS and IDS.

Let us examine first the single population games.

Single-population games

We reproduce in Figure 8.21 the payoff matrices of the three standard games that Friedman (1996) tested in various experiments.

In HD, there are two pure strategies NE: (1, 2) and (2, 1) and a mixed strategy NE where players select the first strategy with probability $\frac{2}{3}$. This last equilibrium is an EE. In Co, there are two pure strategies NE: (1, 1) and (2, 2) and a mixed strategy NE where players select the first strategy with probability $\frac{2}{3}$. Only the two pure strategies NE are EE. In PD, (2, 2) is both the single NE and the EE.

Figure 8.21 Single-population experimental evolutionary games

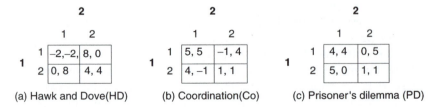

(a) Hawk and Dove(HD)   (b) Coordination(Co)   (c) Prisoner's dilemma (PD)

Friedman ran a series of experiments, each session consisting in numerous periods of strategic interactions among different groups of players. Groups were varied between 6 and 24 persons. The periods of interaction were split in runs of 10 or 16 periods (enough to allow some convergence to occur, but not too long to avoid boredom). As stated above, various treatments were proposed regarding the payoff functions, the matching rules and the amount of information available on the history of the games. We give below a summary of the main results.

Hawk–Dove game (single population)

The empirical data collected come from 156 runs. For example in session 3, Hawk–Dove was played by a single population of 12 persons, who interacted in several 10-period runs. Since there is a unique mixed strategy NE, also an EE (strategy 1 played with probability $\frac{2}{3}$), at equilibrium 8 individuals out of 12 should play the first strategy. To give a more specific example, in run 4 of this experiment, played in the condition of mean matching and no historical information, the actual play in each period is: 8, 6, 10, 6, 6, 10, 10, 8, 7, 7. Obviously there is some variance around the NE, but if one is ready to accept some behavioural noise, the band 8 ± 1 can be accepted as a success in reaching the equilibrium. In this run, the first period and the last three are in the band. A loose criterion and a tight criterion are proposed in order to assess the relative success of convergence toward a BE, a NE and an EE. Figure 8.22 summarizes the results for this particular game.

More detailed evidence shows that tight convergence is more frequent in the last periods. The EE is played frequently enough, especially with mean matching and when subjects were allowed to consult past moves (the game history). However there are some significant differences between players' behaviour. Some players always choose the first strategy while other players always choose the second strategy. Even if the aggregated result seems to conform to the mixed strategies, individuals do not properly randomize (see below for a discussion on this issue).

Coordination game (single population)

Evidence on this game bears on 116 different runs. The convergence percentages are summarized in Figure 8.23.

Figure 8.22 Convergence percentage in the Hawk–Dove game (single population)

Convergence criteria	BE	NE	EE
Loose	96.2	87.2	87.2
Tight	55	32.7	32.7

Figure 8.23 Convergence percentage in the coordination game (single population)

Convergence criteria	BE	NE	EE
Loose	98.3	69.4	41.8
Tight	79.7	40.5	25.9

In Co, there is a satisfactory rate of convergence toward a BE. But NE and EE get a relatively poor score of convergence. Fortunately, the treatments involving MM and information on past moves obtain better results. The same is true for the second half of the periods compared to the first half. This evidence is in full conformity with an evolutionary perspective.

It is interesting to note that the risk-dominant EE (2, 2) is less often selected than the payoff-dominant EE (1, 1), although the former has the larger basin of attraction. More precisely, the payoff-dominant EE appears 18 times according to the tight convergence criterion, while the risk-dominant EE appears only in 2 instances. According to the loose criterion, the respective appearances are 6 and 5. Another strange result is that the mixed strategy equilibrium which is not an EE is played relatively often. Behind this outcome, there is the behaviour of some players who either try to influence the other players' behaviour, or who simply have an altruistic behavior.

Prisoner's dilemma (single population)

Evidence on the Prisoner's dilemma game is given for 24 runs. Figure 8.24 gives the percentages of convergence.

The frequency of convergence is impressive, especially for the BE. Convergence to the NE – also EE – is less frequent if one applies the tight criterion, although 64.6 per cent is still a good percentage. The author also observed that the size of the population matters since with small groups – from 2 to 6 players – deviations are more frequent. In that case, players try to influence others' behaviours which does not fit with EGT assumptions. In fact, it is no surprise that EGT cannot be applied in strategic interactions involving a few players only. What should be

Figure 8.24 Convergence percentage in the Prisoner's dilemma game (single population)

Convergence criteria	BE	NE	EE
Loose	95.8	91.7	91.7
Tight	95.8	64.6	64.6

considered as more surprising is rather that above 6, a group is large enough for applying the theory successfully.

Two-population games

Figure 8.25 displays the payoff matrices of the three standard games which have been experimented on by Friedman (1996) in a two-population evolutionary context.

In HD_2 there are three NE: (1, 2), (2, 1) and a mixed strategy equilibrium ($\frac{2}{3}, \frac{2}{3}$,). Only the two pure strategy equilibria are EE of the game. In BoS, there are also three NE: (1, 1), (2, 2) and a mixed strategy ($\frac{1}{3}, \frac{3}{5}$). Only the two pure strategy are EE. Finally IDS has only one NE: (2, 1). This NE is also an EE.

As for the single-population games, experiments have been run in several sessions and with various treatments (matching rules, amount of information available).The main results are summarized in Figure 8.26, that displays the convergence data for the three games.

Figure 8.25   Two-population evolutionary games

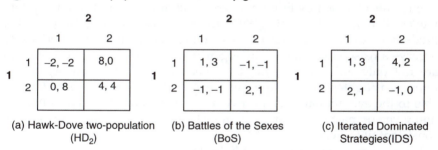

(a) Hawk-Dove two-population (HD_2) (b) Battles of the Sexes (BoS) (c) Iterated Dominated Strategies(IDS)

Figure 8.26   Convergence percentage in the three standard two-population games

Convergence Criteria	BE	NE	EE
(a) Convergence data for HD2 (based on 92half runs)			
• Loose criterion	98.9	81.5	26.1
• Tight criterion	52.2	16.3	14.1
(b) Convergence data for BoS (based on 128 half runs)			
• Loose criterion	93.0	75.8	56.3
• Tight criterion	61.7	40.6	39.1
(c) Convergence data for IDS (based on 60 half runs)			
• Loose criterion	91.7	30	30
• Tight criterion	35	10	10

HD_2 runs converged reasonably well toward a BE, which is close to a NE loose criterion. However, convergence toward the EE has much more noise (remember that there are two EE at opposite corners of the square). A rather more positive interpretation is that when the convergence appears to a NE on a tight account, then the point appears also to be an EE. This result is conform to the evolutionary theory.

BoS runs also display a significant rate of convergence toward a BE. Here convergence toward a NE and even an EE is remarkable. Friedman stresses also the fact that over the 52 half runs (40.6 per cent) that converged tightly to a NE, 50 actually converged tightly to an EE.

For IDS, the convergence record seems rather poor. However, one must notice that half the IDS runs used the 'random matching – no history treatment', for which convergence rates are low, in conformity with EGT. The author reports that when mean matching and information about the history of the game are introduced the convergence toward an EE was considerably improved, again in conformity with EGT.

Discussion

The results obtained by Friedman tend to confirm the tests made by Van Huyck, Battalio and Gillette (1992): the evidence generally supports the predictions of EGT. It does not take much longer than five periods to observe a reasonable rate of convergence toward a BE, and most of them are not only NE, but also EE, as expected. Moreover, convergence is improved (tighter and at a quicker pace) in the treatments more favourable to the evolutionary perspective: mean matching (MM) and information given on past moves of the game (Hist). All these results are globally consistent with EGT.

The evidence sheds some new light on an interesting issue concerning the stability of mixed strategy NE. Since the 1950s, experiments in game theory have showed the difficulty of obtaining convergence to a mixed equilibrium (see, for example, Rapoport and Orwant, 1962). Harsanyi (1973) shows that the stability of a mixed strategy equilibrium can be sustained through a 'purification' device, according to which mixed strategy NE are obtained by hetereogeneous choices among the players rather than by a true randomization by each individual player (see sub-section 3.2.1 of Chapter 3; see also Fudenberg and Kreps, 1993, where the idea is put in a learning framework showing convergence to a mixed strategy NE). The evidence collected by Friedman supports the 'purification' argument. Individual player data tend to confirm a preference for choosing pure strategies. For the group as a whole, in one-population games, one can observe a convergence to the interior EE, while this convergence does not appear as clearly in two-population games.

Concerning the so-called 'small-group effects', the data suggest that 6 may be considered as a significant threshold. When the minimum size of the group is above 6, a cooperative (or 'Kantian' behaviour, according to the expression used by the author) is seldom encountered. By contrast, this type of behaviour becomes considerably more frequent in experiments with groups of smaller size. It remains to verify to what extent these results can be generalized. However, they already bring some support to the optimistic views concerning the applicability of EGT to a variety of economic and business environments.

A last finding deserves further discussion, it concerns the conflict between 'payoff dominant' and 'risk-dominant' equilibria which may appear in coordination games. In the simple coordination games, such as the game Co tested by Friedman, the two corner NE are also EE, while the interior NE is not an EE. According to EGT, the risk-dominant EE $(2, 2)$ is most likely to be chosen in an evolutionary context since it has the larger basin of attraction (see Chapter 7 for a presentation of the concept of risk-dominance and the definition of a basin of attraction). An opposite theoretical analysis (Bergin and Lipman, 1995) suggests that an increase in the potential gains from cooperation should bias the convergence process toward the payoff dominant EE $(1, 1)$, even while holding constant the basins of attractions for the two EE. Friedman's observed data give some support to the later view. It seems that some players tried to influence others future actions by acting in a Kantian way, or that some of them had more simply an altruistic behaviour. More experiments are welcome on this type of issue. But as Friedman puts it: 'in some applications evolutionary game theory may have to be supplemented by a theory of trembles (or 'mutations') that allows for forward-looking attempts to influence others' behaviour' (Friedman, 1996, 24–5).

8.5.3 Learning in games

As we have learned in Chapter 7 (section 7.3) a very promising way of studying how people or firms play games in real life is to explore situations which are in between the extremely rational world of traditional non-cooperative game theory and the biological world of EGT. People learn how to play games certainly more quickly than animals. These learning abilities and procedures may converge more or less rapidly to NE or EE. This field of research is one of the most fruitful in modern GT and the experimental method already provides an invaluable input for further development in this direction.

Some experimental studies have already proven very useful in testing learning models. Roth and Erev (1995) have used a learning model to explain experimental evidence in extensive-form games. They used a routine learning model (see sub-section 7.3.1 of Chapter 7) where a player's behaviour is directly affected by experience. The probability of choice of a given action increases if this action has been successful in the past, i.e. has provided high payoffs to the players. Roth and Erev observe that the experimental data are very close to the model predictions. Boylan and El-Gamal (1993) have tested in nine laboratory game sessions the Cournot learning model and the fictitious play model (see sub-section 7.3.3). They found that the experimental data conform better to the fictitious play model. More recently, Cheung and Friedman (1997) have studied the dynamics of the adjustment process in experiments on some of the standard games tested by Friedman in the EGT framework (and presented in the previous sub-section).

In particular, learning models have been applied to the HD, Co, PD and BoS games, whose payoff matrices are presented in Figures 8.21 and 8.25.

We will present here a sketch of the theoretical framework used by the authors for discussing learning in strategic-form games. After a brief account of the experiments, we will give a summary of the main results.

A framework for studying the learning process

Given a stage game with specific payoff functions, a first set of actions by the n players will lead to a particular outcome. Each player may observe his payoff and possibly the other players' payoffs, depending on the institutional arrangements of the game. If the outcome does not correspond to the players' expectations, they will be prone to revise their beliefs about the other players' behaviour in case of repetition of this stage game.

Once the beliefs have changed, the actions may also change when the game is played again. This process should continue until the game reaches a NE, as predicted by GT. It is very important for applied GT to understand the conditions of convergence toward a NE (or an EE in an EGT framework) and the speed of convergence if it occurs at all.

The link between the observed outcome and the changes in beliefs is called a 'learning rule' and notated γ, whereas the link between beliefs and actions is called a 'decision rule' and represented by two parameters α and β.

If player i has observed the history of the game $S_{i1}, S_{i2}, \ldots, S_{it}$ and if he uses a discount factor γ_i on past evidence, he will have the following beliefs for period $t + 1$:

$$
\widehat{S}_{t+1} = \frac{S_{it} + \sum_{u=1}^{t-1} \gamma_i^u S_{it-u}}{1 + \sum_{u=1}^{t-1} \gamma_i^u}
\tag{8.1}
$$

Equation (8.1) allows us to treat as special cases the Cournot learning rule and the fictitious play rule. The Cournot rule assumes that player pay attention only to recent observations, whereas the fictitious play rule takes the current beliefs as the average of the previous observed actions. In (8.1), putting $\gamma = 0$ gives the Cournot learning rule, and putting $\gamma = 1$ gives fictitious play (current beliefs as simple averages of past observed actions). Cheung and Friedman call 'adaptive learning' the situations corresponding to $0 < \gamma < 1$. The decision rules relate beliefs to actions. They are based on differences in expected payoffs.

Cheung and Friedman propose a stochastic decision rule that is dependent on the expected payoff difference and on 'some persistent individual idiosyncrasies'. A parameter β_i represents player i's degree of responsiveness to the expected payoff difference. A parameter α_i represents the idiosyncratic tendency to play action 1. A perfectly rational player would follow only his assessment of the best response and would have an infinitely large positive β.

The model defines three parameters: the learning rule parameter γ and the two decision rules α and β, which can be estimated empirically after having observed individuals playing repeatedly a given stage game.

For example, the null hypothesis $\widehat{\alpha} = 0$ (unbiased choice) can be tested for α. The null hypothesis $\widehat{\beta} = 0$ (unsystematic choice) can also be tested. For $\gamma, \widehat{\gamma} = 0$ (Cournot) and $\widehat{\gamma} = 1$ (fictitious plays) are reference values.

Main results of the experiments

Laboratory procedures have been designed to test the 'three-parameters' learning models on various standard games. As in the case of experiments in the EGT framework, the authors have used a variety of payoff matrices (HD, Co, PD, BoS) and of institutional arrangements: MM as opposed to random matching, no information about the history of the game (other than what each agent can observe himself) as opposed to information about the past actions and outcomes.

Each session consisted in several runs (sequence of periods). In each run the institutional conditions were kept constant in order to allow the players to learn. The actions chosen by each player in each period of a run provided enough raw data to achieve statistical estimations of the parameters α and β (using logit or probit regression procedures). More sophisticated techniques were required in order to estimate the learning parameter γ.

We may summarize the main results as follows. The major conclusion is that the three-parameter model fits rather well with the experimental evidence. An important finding is that the players are *heterogeneous* (the authors show how useful is the estimation of the parameters on an individual basis as opposed to an estimation of the aggregate behaviour). Some players use a Cournot learning rule. Others follow the fictitious play rule. An intermediate category obeys an adaptive learning rule. The majority of the players can be clearly classified in these three groups and what is still more important, this classification is roughly invariant with the payoff functions (the various standard games). Other results are consistent with theoretical predictions. For example: γ generally decreases and, β generally increases in more informative environments. A general conclusion is also that the results tend to support the beliefs learning models over routine learning.

Remark I

There is a growing literature which is devoted to experimental tests of adaptive learning behaviours in traditional GT.

Camerer and Ho (1998) have designed an interesting experiment in which they merged belief-based learning and reinforcement learning. They studied several applications in order to assess learning parameters: constant sum games, median effort game, beauty contest (see sub-section 8.6.1 for a presentation of this game).

Bounmy, Willinger and Ziegelmeyer (2002) compared a global interaction treatment with a local interaction treatment (using a circle design) to study a simple coordination game with a payoff-dominant and a risk-dominant equilibrium. They expected to observe more coordination on the payoff-dominant equilibrium, but this was observed only for the specific parameter sets which corresponded to large basins of attraction of the risk-dominant equilibrium under global interaction. Furthermore, in contrast to Friedman's (1996) prediction, speed of convergence towards equilibrium is not faster under local interaction than under global interaction.

Battalio, Samuelson and Van Huyck (2001) is an example of a study that does not introduce a complete model of adaptive behaviour but checks on coordination failure in a close evolutive setting. They use a single-population continuous-time 'logistic response' and, assuming that the population is sufficiently large, the random individual choices are captured by a deterministic population equation. They compare three Stag-Hunt games (see section 8.3 for a definition of this pure coordination game). The games have the same best-response correspondence and the same expected payoff from the mixed equilibrium, but they differ in the incentive to play a best response rather than an inferior response. The expected earnings difference between the two actions is called the 'optimization premium'. One can think of this notion as describing the deepness, rather than the level, of the payoff function near the equilibrium. A larger optimization premium implies that the penalty for inferior play is larger. In each game, 'risk dominance' conflicts with 'payoff dominance' and selects an inefficient pure strategy equilibrium. The results show that changing the optimization premium influences players' behaviour. In particular, the risk-dominant equilibrium is more likely to emerge, the larger is the optimization premium. Thus, this finding provides evidence that there is more than best-response functions at stake when predicting human behaviour in laboratory experiments. More general analyses adopting this point of view will be developed in the next section.■

8.6 From experimental evidence to new game theoretic modelling principles

It is a well established fact in experimental economics that in competitive institutions market outcomes converge very well towards the outcome predicted by standard economic theory (see for instance Smith, 1982; Davis and Holt, 1993). Stylized facts collected through experiments on strategic interactions depict a very contrasting setting. When subjects' behaviour observed in laboratory experiments systematically differ from theoretical predictions, one needs explanations for what is observed and then extensions of formal GT to include these explanations. 'Behavioral' GT (Camerer, 1997), driven by experimental data, aims to describe *actual* individuals' behaviour, taking up a middle course between the rationalistic approach and EGT. Taking into account the learning processes in standard GT, thanks to adaptive learning models, is an important step in this perspective. In this section, we focus on two other areas where progress is being made (for an overview on behavioural GT, see Camerer, 2002).

Standard GT generally assumes very strong players' abilities to rightly understand the strategic situation and to calculate their best strategies. Yet, several experimental studies show that it is too strong an assumption: subjects' cognitive and instrumental rationality is bounded.

Traditional GT assumes in particular that rational players perceive a game clearly and consistently. Several experimenters, however, have found that different presentations of the same game problem have resulted in different patterns of behaviour. Of course, such 'framing effects' raise obvious design problems for an experimenter who has to decide how a game is to be presented through the instructions given to the subjects, but this anomaly also poses a challenge to game theorists. For instance, in a decision problem, individuals generally are more likely to take risk when outcomes are described as losses rather than as gains (see Tversky and Kahneman, 1992, for instance, for a presentation of this 'reflection' effect). A particular version of this effect may be observed in games. For instance, in bargaining problems, players seem more willing to risk disagreement if bargaining is over losses rather gains (Camerer *et al.*, 1993). In standard public goods experiments and repeated Prisoner's dilemmas, or in coalition games still, the literature suggests also that several framing effects (in a broad sense) may exist. A recent experiment has explicitly investigated the effects of framing effects on cooperation in a linear public goods game (Cookson, 2000). This study shows that aspects of presentation may have strong and replicable effects on experimental findings, even when care is taken to make the language and presentation of instructions as neutral as possible. Experimenters therefore should give careful consideration to potential framing effects, or explicitly test for them before making claims about validity of results.

Another plausible explanation of anomalies observed in experiments refers to biases in subjects' probability judgement. If players overrate the chance of good events, underrate the chance of bad events, and are overconfident of their own abilities, they may fail when assessing the likely consequences of their decisions. Several experimental studies have provided evidence for this overconfidence bias (see Camerer, 1997, for more details).

Moreover, it turns out that many principles of strategic reasoning widely used in GT require strong players' instrumental abilities and it would be interesting to look for the descriptive relevance of these principles. Iterated dominance, maybe, is one of the most subtle of these principles. Do individuals actually apply *all* the levels of iterated dominance when theoretical predictions require many levels? Asking this question is wondering about the 'deepness' of interactive rationality. In the same way, is it realistic to assume that individuals always are *certain* to play their best strategy when they make their choice? Maybe, allowing the possibility of errors on choices or uncertainty over payoffs is a more relevant assumption. The first sub-section will focus on these two last questions for which experimental evidence militates in favour of new bounded rationality principles.

On the other hand, as is the case in other parts of economic theory, GT is built on the assumption that people act selfishly and do not care about the well-being of other human beings. However, pure selfishness is obviously contradicted by the results of many experiments. Recently, several new 'models of social utility' have been designed in order to incorporate fairness motivations in addition to strategic behaviour. The second sub-section provides some typical examples of this flourishing literature.

8.6.1 Players' abilities: towards new bounded rationality principles

Several laboratory experiments were concerned with the deepness of players' interactive rationality or the precision in players' choices. They show that very often, some subjects fail to choose what the modelling principle predicts when many levels of iterated dominance are necessary, and taking into account errors in subjects' choices or 'noisy' introspection allows us to better explain experimental evidence.

Deepness of interactive rationality: the 'guessing' game (or 'beauty contest' game)

Application of iterated dominance, in many games, yields a unique outcome if enough steps of the iterative process are carried out. Experiments in laboratory may be very useful for assessing where the chain of iterated dominance reasoning breaks down.

An ideal tool for this purpose is the 'guessing' game, first discussed by Moulin (1986, 72) and studied experimentally by Nagel (1995). A typical guessing game is defined by the four following rules:

- There is a great number of players who simultaneously choose a number n from a closed interval $[0, 100]$
- The average of all these numbers is calculated
- A target is selected that is equal to a fraction p of the average
- The player who gives the closest prediction to the target wins a fixed prize (i.e. independent from p and the chosen number); ties are broken randomly.

This game is also called a 'beauty contest' (Camerer, 1997) because it captures the importance of iterated reasoning that J. Maynard Keynes (1936) described in his famous analogy for stock market investment. He speaks about a newspaper contest in which people guess what faces others will guess are most beautiful, and compares that contest with the stock market investment; 'professional investment may be likened to those newspaper competitions in which the competitors have to pick out the six prettiest faces from a hundred photographs, the prize being awarded to the competitor whose choice most nearly corresponds to the average preferences of the competitors as a whole' (1936, 156). Like people selecting the prettiest picture, each subject in the beauty contest game must guess what average number other subjects will prefer, then pick the fraction p of that average, knowing that everybody is doing the same as her (or him).

When $0 < p < 1$, the equilibrium strategy is to propose $n = 0$. The idea is that proposals higher than $100p$ will be immediately eliminated since the average cannot be higher than 100 and one cannot win by proposing a number higher than $100p$. Once these chosen numbers have been eliminated, all proposals higher than $100p^2$ will be eliminated for the same reason, and so on. Iterated application of dominance yields the unique IDE which is for everyone to pick out zero (that is also the unique NE of the game).

For illustration, let us assume that $p = 0.7$; numbers in the interval $[70, 100]$ violate first-order iterated rationality. If a player chooses a number below 70 and thinks everyone else will behave identically, then she (or he) can infer that the target will be below 0.7 (70), or 49, so that an optimal choice is in the interval $[0, 49]$. It follows that a choice between $[49, 70]$ is consistent with a player being first-order iterated rational, but not being sure others players are rational. If we continue this reasoning, we can infer that the next range of choices $[34.3, 49]$ is consistent with second-order rationality (players are rational and know that others are rational) but violates third-order rationality, and so on. Infinitely many steps of iterated

Figure 8.27 Iterated rationality in the guessing game ($n = 100$, $p = 0.7$)

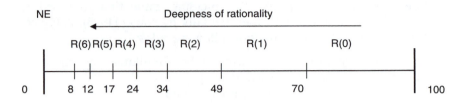

dominance leads us to pick zero. Hence, we see that number choices in this game reveal the deepness of rationality (see Figure 8.27 in which the level of iterated rationality is indicated by $R(i)$).

When $p = 1$, there are an infinity of equilibria in which everyone chooses the same number: we get a pure coordination game. And if $p > 1$, there are two equilibria; $n = 0$ and $n = 100$.

The results of Nagel's experiment can be summarized as following:

- nearly all the choices were integers
- for $p = \frac{1}{2}$ and $p = \frac{2}{3}$, 0 was never observed and only 6 per cent of the subjects chose a number $n < 10$.
- for $p = \frac{4}{3}$, only 10 per cent of the subjects chose $n = 100$, 99 or 1.

These findings show that deepness of interactive rationality is limited: subjects generally used no more than two steps of iterated dominance. Hence, instead of assuming that players apply iterated dominance through many levels, it should be more realistic to suppose in game models a limited number of iterations, which could be taken as a precise measure of the degree of players' bounded rationality.

Remark I

Further experimental studies on 'beauty contest' games have shown no substantial differences. Duffy and Nagel (1997) have replicated this experiment with the median, mean or maximum chosen in the group as the target number: they have observed higher choices only for the last target. Ho et al. (1998) have extended earlier findings in several ways. First, they draw a distinction between games with finite and infinite rationality thresholds (in the first, solving the games requires only a finite level of iterated reasoning whereas in the second, an infinite level is required); they prove that finite-thresholds games converge more quickly toward the equilibrium. Secondly, by using 10 rounds, with subjects receiving feedback after each round (and collecting eight times as much data), they get a fuller picture of learning. Two stylized facts are suggested by the test of various learning models: first, the data are consistent with the presence of adaptive learners who just respond to experience (level 10) and sophisticated learners who best respond to lower-level learners (level 11); second, usual 'belief learning' models (such that Cournot adjustment model and fictitious play) are rejected.■

Degree of randomness in decisions: the 'quantal response' function (or noisy introspection)

Allowing the possibility of errors on choice or uncertainty over payoffs means that, when players are seeking the strategy with the maximal expected utility, they are not certain to do so. With the purpose of capturing the degree of randomness in players' decisions, McKelvey and Palfrey (1995, 1998) introduce what they call a 'quantal response' function.

A convenient quantal response function is provided by the popular logit probabilistic choice rule which requires choice probabilities to be proportional to exponential functions of expected payoffs:

$$P(x_i) = \frac{e^{\lambda \pi(x_i)}}{\sum_i e^{\lambda \pi(x_i)}}$$

where $\pi(x_i)$ is the expected payoff of strategy x_i and λ is a constant that captures imprecision in choices. If $\lambda = 0$, then the player chooses equally often among all her (or his) strategies; all choice probabilities are equal regardless of payoff differences. But if λ goes to 1, small payoff differences have large effects, and the probability that the player selects one of her (or his) strategies with the highest payoff is 1 when $\lambda = 1$.

In this model, a 'quantal response' equilibrium (or 'logit' equilibrium) exists if players know how much randomness is the choice of others and take their decisions accordingly.

This stochastic approach allows us to explain several different behavioural phenomena. For instance, in the ultimatum game, a responder may be likely to reject a smaller proposal mistakenly, because it is a small mistake, and knowing this, rational proposers are not likely to make very uneven offers. The 'quantal response' approach also explains some experimental patterns in public goods provision and social dilemma game (Anderson, Goeree and Holt, 1998). The particular 'travellers' dilemma game' provides a good example of a game for which theoretical principles predict a unique equilibrium that is 'bad' for all concerned players and observed data are well explained by the 'logit' equilibrium (Capra et al., 1999).

The social dilemma is based on a story in which two travellers lose bags with identical contents, and the airline asks them to fill out claims independently, with the constraint that claims must be in some pre-specified range, for instance between $80 and $200. The travellers will be reimbursed if the claims are equal, but if claims are unequal the assumption is that the high claimant overstated the value, so both are reimbursed at the minimum of the two proposals. Moreover, the low claimant receives a reward (R) and the high claimant's reimbursement is reduced by a corresponding penalty (-R). For instance, if the claims are 99 and 100, then the minimum claimant is 99, so that the first person earns $99 + R$ while the second receives $99 - R$.

In this setting, everyone would have an incentive to 'undercut' the other's claim if it were known; it follows that the paradoxical NE corresponds to both claiming the lowest possible amount ($80 in this example). The remarkable feature of the travellers' dilemma game is that this argument does not depend on the size of the penalty/reward parameter R. But if R is low (i.e. cents), there is little risk in raising the travel claim while if R is large (say $50), there is considerable risk, so intuition suggests that claims will be higher with a low-penalty parameter. This intuition is confirmed in the laboratory experiments: the NE predicts well for high-penalty parameters, but the data cluster at the opposite end of the set of feasible claims when R is low. The logit equilibrium model explains data in both cases.

8.6.2 Players' motivations: the new 'social utility' models

In the previous sections we saw that in most games in which the predictions of theory can be directly tested through experimental methods (essentially in cooperation and bargaining problems), the cooperative outcome is observed much more frequently than is suggested by the equilibrium concepts. In contrast to what happens in experiments involving market institutions, where experimental evidence usually is consistent with standard notions of 'competitive' self-interest, these laboratory experiments appear to foster sharply different players' conduct.

'Altruism' has a long tradition in economics and had been used in particular to explain charitable donations or the voluntary provision of public goods (for instance, see Becker, 1974). So, it is not surprising that it was among the first psychological motivation given by experimenters for explaining anomalies in behavioural experiments. Altruism actually can explain *positive* acts to others players (for instance, giving in dictator games or voluntary contributions in public goods games), but it is clearly inconsistent with other observed behaviour, such that trying to retaliate and hurt other subjects even if this is costly for them (for instance in the ultimatum game or public goods game with punishment). Therefore, stylized facts cast doubt on the idea that people could care about payoff distribution in a way we would expect a 'purely altruist' would do. Generally people appear self-centred, albeit in a way that differs from the traditional rationalistic approach. 'Equity' or 'reciprocity', of a kind that differs from the standard strategic conception, are then proposed to explain players' behaviour in cooperation or bargaining games. Even for experiments done in an evolutionary setting, cooperative or 'Kantian' behaviour may explain data. Indeed 'there is a substantial controversy in the literature about what, if anything, connect these observations. The issue goes to the heart of what it is that experimental economics can hope to accomplish' (Bolton and Ockenfels, 2000, 166). Either no connection can be found among these various types of observed behaviour – and we are left with disjoint behavioural charts valid on a limited domain only – or common patterns can be proved and, in the latter case, experimental research offers a richer and wider appraisal of economic behaviour.

Several general models have been proposed in order to capture a large part of these observed subjects' motivations in controlled laboratory experiments. Among these new 'social utility models' (the terminology was proposed by Camerer, 1997), it is now common to distinguish two great variants. 'Intentionality' models (Rabin, 1993) posit that people want to be nice to whose who treat them fairly and want to punish those who hurt them, while 'distributional' models (Bolton and Ockenfels, 2000; Fehr and Schmidt (1999)) posit that people care about how their payoff stand compares to that of others in the final distribution. In the second approach, once the individual utility functions are modified in order to incorporate the other players' material payoffs, all agents are assumed to be perfectly rational; so, the traditional concepts of utility theory and GT can be applied. By contrast, in the first approach, since one assumes that players care about their opponents' intents, it is crucial to figure out how a player interprets other players' behaviour. Traditional GT cannot capture this requirement and the authors appeal to the framework of psychological GT. We present in this sub-section these two classes of new models whose goal is to provide a better formal description of experimental evidence by incorporating 'fairness' motivations in addition to classical strategic behaviour in GT.

The Rabin model: an intentionality model

'People like to help those who are helping them, and to hurt those who are hurting them' (Rabin, 1993, 1281). This phrase summarizes Rabin's thinking about fairness motivations that could be used to explain experimental evidence more clearly in many cooperation and bargaining problems (in the public goods game and the ultimatum game, for instance; see sub-sections 8.2.1 and 8.3.1). He develops a game theoretic framework for incorporating such an emotion into a broad range of economic models by emphasizing the role of *intentions* as a source of reciprocal behaviour.

This framework contains three stylized facts:

A People are willing to sacrifice their own material well-being to help those who are being kind (for instance, in the public goods game)
B People are adopting the same behaviour to punish those who are being unkind (for instance, in the ultimatum game)

C   Both motivations (A) and (B) have a greater effect on behaviour as the material cost of sacrificing decreases (for instance, in the ultimatum game again).

Rabin develops a 'fairness equilibrium' concept that includes these stylized facts. 'Positive reciprocity' is defined as a kind response to an action driven by fair intentions (A), while 'negative reciprocity' is defined as a hostile response to an action driven by unfair intentions (B). To formalize fairness, he modifies conventional game theory by allowing payoffs to be a function of players' *beliefs* as well as of their actions, and he builds a 'psychological game' in which players' subjective expected utility U_i depends on three variables (the concept of 'psychological game theory' was introduced by Geanakoplos, Pearce and Stacchetti, 1989):

a_i: the strategy chosen by player i
b_j: players i's beliefs about what strategy player j is choosing
c_i: player i's beliefs about what player j believes player i's strategy is.

In a first step the author gives the definition of two 'kindness functions' $f_i(a_i, b_j)$ and $\tilde{f}_j(b_j, c_i)$ which represent how kind i (hereafter named 'she') is *actually* being to j (hereafter named 'he'), and how kind i *thinks* j is being to her, respectively.
By definition:

$$f_i(a_i, b_j) = \frac{\Pi_j(b_j, a_i) - \Pi_j^e(b_j)}{\Pi_j^{\max}(b_j) - \Pi_j^{\min}(b_j)}$$

where $\Pi_j(b_j, a_i)$ is what player i gives to player j, with $\Pi_j^{\min} \leq \Pi_j \leq \Pi_j^{\max}$ and Π_j^e is an 'equitable' payoff defined as follows:

$$\Pi_j^e(b_j) = \frac{1}{2}[\Pi_j^{\max}(b_j) + \Pi_j^l(b_j)]$$

where Π_j^l is j's lowest payoff among points that are Pareto-efficient. Note that if the Pareto-frontier is linear, this payoff literally corresponds to the payoff that player j would get if player i 'splits the difference' with her among Pareto-efficient points. More generally, it provides a crude reference point against which to measure how generous player i is being to player j.

Hence, the function f_i captures how much more than or less than player j's 'equitable' payoff player i believes she is giving to player j.

The second 'kindness function' $\hat{f}_j$ represents player i's beliefs about how kindly player j is treating her:

$$\tilde{f}_j(b_j, c_i) = \frac{\Pi_i(c_i, b_j) - \Pi_i^e(c_i)}{\Pi_i^{max}(c_i) - \Pi_i^{min}(c_i)}$$

Notice that:

$$f_i = 0 \text{ if } \Pi_j = \Pi_j^e, \quad f_i > 0 \text{ if } \Pi_j > \Pi_j^e, \quad f_j < 0 \text{ if } \Pi_j < \Pi_j^e$$
$$\tilde{f}_j = 0 \text{ if } \Pi_i = \Pi_i^e, \quad \tilde{f}_j > 0 \text{ if } \Pi_i > \Pi_i^e, \quad \tilde{f}_i < 0 \text{ if } \Pi_i < \Pi_i^e$$

These two functions are normalized to take their values in $[-1, \frac{1}{2}]$.

In a second step, Rabin (1993) assumes that utility inputs are provided in two forms: material-based and fairness-dependent. These amount to a total utility:

$$U_i(a_i, b_j, c_i) = \Pi_i(a_i, b_j) + \tilde{f}_j(b_j, c_i)[1 + f_i(a_i, b_j)]$$

Π_i is the utility from material benefits, while the utility derived from the fairness of the outcome is represented by the product $\tilde{f}_j$ and $[1 + f_i]$. Both $\tilde{f}_j$ and f_i can be of either sign. If player i expects j to act kindly – $\tilde{f}_j > 0$ – then i is kind to j: $f_i > 0$. If player i believes that player j is treating her badly – $\tilde{f}_j < 0$ – then she wishes to treat player j badly: f_i low or $f_i < 0$. Therefore, the impact of fairness on i's total utility can either be positive or negative. Fairness considerations increase total utility if the signs match. But if both $\tilde{f}_j$ and f_i are negative, material losses usually outweigh psychic gains: $U_i(.) \leq \Pi_i(.)$.

Intuitively, if i thinks j is going to act fairly toward her, she is more likely to act fairly in return. When both act fairly, both derive positive 'psychological utility' from the exchange in addition to any material utility. By contrast, if i thinks j is going to act unfairly toward her, her incentive to act unfairly in return will be increased. In other words, acting fairly toward a partner who is unfair reduces the actor's materially based and psychologically based utility. And a player also receives psychological utility by acting selfishly towards one that acts selfishly towards her (or him). Generally the equilibrium where both agents act fairly is preferred.

In this setting, we can define a fairness equilibrium.

Definition I ('Fairness' equilibrium)

A pair of strategies (a_1, a_2) is a 'fairness equilibrium' if, for $i = 1, 2, j \neq i$:

$a_i \in \text{arg max}_a \, U_i(a_i, b_j, c_i)$

and:

$a_i = b_i = c_i.\blacksquare$

That means that a fairness equilibrium is a NE of the 'psychological game' and that an additional property holds: players' beliefs must be in conformity with players' actual behaviour

In the model, there are two types of outcomes which play an important role in many results: the so-called 'mutual-max outcome' and 'mutual-min outcome', where players mutually maximize or minimize each other's material payoffs. Furthermore each of the following definitions characterizes an outcome of the game in terms of the value of 'kindness' f_i induced by each of the players. An outcome is:

- strictly positive if $f_i > 0$, for $i = 1, 2$.
- weakly positive if $f_i \geq 0$, for $i = 1, 2$.
- strictly negative if $f_i < 0$, for $i = 1, 2$.
- weakly negative if $f_i \leq 0$, for $i = 1, 2$.
- neutral if $f_i = 0$, for $i = 1, 2$.
- mixed if $f_i f_j < 0$, for $i = 1, 2, i \neq j$

Using these definitions, Rabin (1993) then proves several propositions:

Proposition 1 Suppose that (a_1, a_2) is a NE, and either a mutual-max outcome or a mutual-min outcome. Then (a_1, a_2) is a fairness equilibrium.■

This result gives necessary conditions for a NE to be also a fairness equilibrium.

Proposition 2 Every fairness equilibrium outcome is either strictly positive or weakly negative.■

This second proposition characterizes which outcomes – eventually non-NE – can possibly be fairness equilibria.

These two propositions hold irrespective of the scale of the material payoffs. In contrast, further propositions hold when material payoffs are either arbitrarily large or small.

In particular it is proved that, for games with very small material payoffs, finding the fairness equilibria consists approximately in finding the NE in each of the two hypothetical games: (i) the game in which each player tries to maximize the other players' material payoffs, and (ii) the game in which each player tries to minimize the other players' material payoffs. That means that when the material payoffs are *small*, fairness motivations outweigh self-interest. In contrast, it can be proved that as material payoffs become *large* players' behaviour is dominated by material self-interest. Notably, players will play only NE if they get sizeable payoffs.

On the other hand, it would be interesting to look for a game in which all fairness equilibria yield *strictly positive* outcome. Rabin proves that, on the contrary, in every game there exists a *weakly negative* fairness equilibrium. Therefore, it is never guaranteed that people will part with positive feelings. This property implies a strong asymmetry in the Rabin model: there is a bias toward negative reciprocity.

To summarize, the Rabin model introduces a rather original idea of fairness in game models: an equilibrium is fair when players adopt the same behaviour, whatever that behaviour – hostile or kind. This notion of 'fairness' captures several important experimental regularities of behaviour. But it leaves out other issues. In particular, experimental data show that people's ideas of fairness are heavily dependent on *reference points*. Moreover, extending the model to more general settings will create issues that do not arise in the simple two-person strategic-form complete-information game. We shall present now models which partly overcome the weakness of the Rabin model.

Remark 1

Another disadvantage of Rabin's model is that it gives counterintuitive predictions if it is applied to the strategic form of a *sequential* game. For instance, in the sequential Prisoner's dilemma the model predicts that unconditional cooperation by the second mover is part of an equilibrium (i.e. he cooperates even if the first mover defects). Moreover, conditional cooperation by the second mover is *not* part of an equilibrium. The data of Watabe *et al.* (1996) show, however, that unconditional cooperation is virtually non-existent while conditional cooperation is the rule. Rabin's approach has been extended in interesting ways that do not share this disadvantage (Dufwenberg and Kirchsteiger, 1998; Falk and Fischbacher, 1999).■

Remark 2

One of the general implications of Rabin's model states that as material payoffs become large, the players' behaviour is dominated by material self-interest. However, Nelson (2001) has proved that if the relationship between material and fairness inputs is generalized, by not specifying how they interact while providing utility, fairness becomes a normal good as stakes move from very high to very very high. Using a utility function such that:

$$U_i(a_i, b_j, c_i) = v_i[\Pi_i(a_i, b_j), \tilde{f_j}(b_j, c_i)f_i(a_i, b_j)]$$

he shows that if payoffs are very very large, players' strategies will be dominated by fairness. A combination of experimental results (ultimatum game experiments carried out in the United States, the Slovak Republic and Indonesia) and charitable-giving data (natural dictator game played outside of the laboratory in United States) show how this augmented form of Rabin's value function is consistent with empirical evidence.∎

The Bolton–Ockenfels model: a relative payoff model

Rabin's approach assumes that, when taking their decision, individuals are not indifferent concerning *how* distributions come about: intentions matter when individuals are motivated by reciprocity considerations. A second class of social utility model focuses on distributional concerns. This distributional approach permits decision makers to be motivated not only by their own material gain, but rather by the final distribution of the material payoff.

In the Bolton–Ockenfels model – one of the most prominent models within this approach – individuals are assumed to be concerned not only about the absolute amount of money they receive but also about their *relative* standing compared to others. So, they formalize an idea (the 'relative income hypothesis') which has a long tradition in economics and which goes back at least to Veblen (1922).

The general model

Bolton and Ockenfels (2000) propose a simple model, called ERC, to denote the three types of behaviour reported from laboratory experiments that are captured by the theory: equity, reciprocity and competition (a first version was proposed in Bolton, 1991). Two main innovations are introduced.

First of all, the authors assume that, along with the pecuniary (or material) payoff, the *relative* payoff motivates people. According to the authors, fairness judgements are based on a kind of mental reference outcome, which itself is the product of complex social comparison processes. The relevance of such comparisons has been emphasized for a long time in social psychology and sociology. They borrow one key insight of this literature when assuming that relative material payoffs affect people's behaviour.

In the second place, contrary to Rabin's model, the ERC model is an *n*-person *incomplete*-information game, and it applies to games played in the extensive as well as the strategic form (the first version reported in Bolton, 1991, was a complete-information model).

The purpose of these authors is to show that their model is consistent with a wide number of experimental results where equity, reciprocity or competitive behaviours are usually called for in interpreting data.

The ERC model is concerned with *n*-person experimental games where players are randomly drawn from the population and anonymously matched. All payoffs are monetary: $y_i \geq 0$ for all i. Moreover, if a subject plays a game several times, she (or he) never plays with any particular subject more than once. Therefore each game can be considered as 'one-shot'.

Each player i is supposed to act in order to maximize the expected value of her (or his) 'motivation function':

$$v_i = v_i(y_i, \sigma_i)$$

where:

$$\sigma_i = \sigma_i(y_i, c, x) = \begin{cases} y_i/c & \text{if } c > 0 \\ 1/n & \text{if } c = 0 \end{cases}$$

is player i's *relative* share of the payoff, and:

$$c = \sum_{j=1}^{n} y_j \text{ is the total pecuniary payoff}$$

A motivation function is like a special expected utility function; the term tries to emphasize that v_i is a statement about the objectives that *motivate* behaviour during the experiment.

Three properties enable the motivation function to be characterized more clearly:

Property 1: Narrow self-interest

The function v_i is increasing and concave in y_i. Moreover, for a given σ_i, if $y_i^1 > y_i^2$, then player i chooses y_i^1. ∎

That means that the classical monotony property holds: 'more money is preferred to less.'

Property 2: Comparative effect

For a given y_i, the function v_i is strictly concave in σ_i, with a maximum around the allocation at which one's own share is equal to the average share $(1/n)$. ∎

This second property implies that the model refers to *equal* division as the *social reference point* for the players.

We saw previously that *heterogeneity* is an usual property of behaviours in many experimental games. The ERC model accounts for this property by assuming a trade off between accepting the reference point (i.e. the comparative effect) and trying to maximize personal gain (i.e. narrow self-interest). Each player is distinguished by how she (or he) solves this tension, which is captured by the thresholds at which behaviour diverges from the classical monotony property.

Two thresholds, r_i and s_i, are defined:
r_i is the solution of:

$$\max_{\sigma_i} v_i(c\sigma_i, \sigma_i), \; c > 0$$

s_i is implicitly defined by:

$$v_i(cs_i, s_i) = v_i(0, 1/n), \; c > 0, \; s_i \leq 1/n$$

where y_i is written as cs_i.

It should be incidentally noticed that for a two-person game, r_i represents the division that player i fixes in the 'dictator game', and s_i corresponds to i's rejection threshold in the 'ultimatum game' (see sub-section 8.3.1).

A third property provides an explicit characterization of the heterogeneity among players.

Property 3: Heterogeneity

Let f^r and f^s be density functions. For all c:

$$f^r(r|c) > 0, \; r \in \left[\frac{1}{n}, 1\right]$$

$$f^s(s|c) > 0, \; s \in \left[\frac{1}{n}, 1\right]. \blacksquare$$

Hence, the full range of thresholds is assumed to exist in the population.

The two-player model

Bolton–Ockenfels analyse the special two-player case in order to illustrate some key points of the general model. They consider the additively separate motivation function for player i:

$$v_i(c\sigma_i, \sigma_i) = a_i c \sigma_i - \frac{b_i}{2}(\sigma_i - 1/2)^2, \; a_i \geq 0, \; b_i > 0 \tag{8.2}$$

A player's type is characterized simply by a/b, the ratio of weights that are attributed to the pecuniary and relative components of v_i. It should be noted that strict relativism is such that $a/b = 0$, which implies: $r = s = \frac{1}{2}$. And strict narrow self-interest is the limiting case: $a/b \to \infty$, which implies $r = 1$ and $s \to 0$.

ERC equilibria

The ERC model makes equilibrium predictions that are intended to characterize the stable patterns. An 'ERC equilibrium' is defined as a PBE of the incomplete-information game solved with respect to player motivation functions and in which the player's r and s are *private* information while the densities f^r and f^s are common knowledge

Now we shall show how an ERC equilibrium can be calculated in some class of games and how the model is consistent with many of the observed patterns.

Reciprocity in cooperation games

In this class of games (Prisoner's dilemma, public goods, trust game,) deviation by strictly narrowly self-interested players from their equilibrium strategy implies a higher joint pecuniary payoff for the whole group, and enough contributions implies an outcome that is Pareto-superior to the equilibrium.

The ERC model can explain many of the reciprocal patterns observed in experiments on cooperation games. In these games, cooperation is explained by the interaction between players' heterogeneity and the scale of the payoffs, in particular the potential maximum gains resulting from cooperation.

Let us consider the standard one-shot prisoner's dilemma Figure 8.28 with $m \in [\frac{1}{2}, 1]$ the marginal per capita return (MPCR). We suppose that the players' motivation function is given by (8.2) where a/b describes the player's type. In order to understand why players choose to cooperate (P, P), we can explicitly consider the optimum decision rule for a player with type a/b.

Optimum decision rule of a player

P will be preferred to A if and only if:

$$\frac{a}{b} < \frac{p - \frac{1}{2}}{4(1 - m)(1 + 2m)^2} = g(m, p)$$

where p is the probability of cooperation from the other player.

What does this rule show? One sees that cooperation is dependent on the player's type, the value of the MPCR and the probability of cooperation of the other player (i.e. the proportion of cooperative players in the

Figure 8.28   Prisoner's dilemma payoff matrix

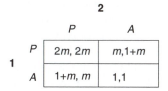

population). So, in this case, there is always an equilibrium in which nobody cooperates ($p = 0$), but there are also equilibria in which part of the population cooperates ($p > 0$).

Let us now consider the *sequential* version of the Prisoner's dilemma, in which player 2 chooses his strategy once he knows player 1's choice. In this setting we have to check two decision optimal rules of decision.

Player 2' s optimum decision rule

For player 2, P will be preferred to A if and only if:

(i) player 1 has chosen P
(ii) $a/b < g(m, 1)$

i.e. player 2 cooperates if and only if player 1 cooperates and he is motivated enough by the relative payoff. That means that the population of players 2 consists of players who don't cooperate and players who choose the TFT strategy.

Player 1's optimum decision rule

For player 1, P will be preferred to A if and only if:

(i) $-1 + m(1 + \hat{p}) > 0$

(ii) $\dfrac{a}{b} > \dfrac{1 - \hat{p}}{8(m\hat{p} + m - 1)(1 - 2m)^2}$

where $\hat{p} = \hat{p}(m) = F(g(m, 1))$ is the probability that player 2 responds cooperatively if player 1 cooperates. Hence, player 1 cooperates if and only if she is sufficiently motivated by pecuniary payoffs and the expected monetary net return of cooperation (i.e. the term $1 + m(1 + \hat{p})$ is positive). That means that a first mover who is interested in relative payoff can guarantee equal payoffs by playing aggressively (i.e. choosing A), since in this case the second mover will certainly play aggressively himself. Thereby, only if a first mover is sufficiently interested in her pecuniary payoff will she take the chance of being exploited in an attempt to 'trigger' cooperation from a second mover. Heterogeneity implies that the proportion of both first and second movers who cooperate increases with the MPCR. Even if $\hat{p}(m)$ is very small, a sufficiently high MPCR may incite the first mover to cooperate.

Several experimental studies support the view that potential efficiency gains and the propensity of others to cooperate (that is, in the ECR model, the marginal rate of substitution between pecuniary and relative payoffs) are major factors of cooperation in one-shot and sequential Prisoner's dilemma games or public goods provision games (see sub-section 8.2.1). In this framework, the ERC model is able to exhibit equity (a pure concern for distributive justice) and a kind of positive reciprocity, but for this latter motive there may be a potential confusion with the efficiency motive.

Equity in bargaining games

Again, in this class of game, the ERC model seems to provide theoretical predictions which are supported by experimental evidence. Bolton–Ockenfels derive results for a lot of games. We look at dictator and ultimatum games only (see sub-section 8.4.1).

(i) In the dictator game, remember that the dictator D distributes a pie of maximum size $k > 0$ between herself and a 'recipient'. The chosen division is represented by the pair (c, σ_D) with $0 \leq c \leq k$. The dictator's payoff is $c\sigma_D$ and the recipient's payoff is $c - c\sigma_D$. It can be proved that, for all dictator allocations, $c = k$, and $\sigma_D = r_D(c) \in [\frac{1}{2}, 1]$. On average, the dictator's giving is positive: $\frac{1}{2} < \bar{\sigma}_D < 1$.

   Several experimental tests have been devoted to this game (see sub-section 8.4.1). The results show notably that the precise distribution of dictator giving varies with 'framing effects'. The ERC model supports this heterogeneity, and the previous statement appears equally valid: dictators distribute the whole pie, almost always giving themselves at least half, and, on average, they keep less than the whole pie.

(ii) In the ultimate game between a proposer (P) and a responder (R), we represent the proposal as (c, σ_p), assuming that the size of the cake, $k > 0$, is common knowledge. We assume that if a responder is indifferent about accepting or rejecting (i.e. if $1 - \sigma_p = \sigma_p(c)$), then the responder always accepts the proposal. Bolton and Ockenfels (2000) prove that in this simple model the responder's ERC equilibrium strategy can be characterized as follows.

   For $c > 0$, the probability that a randomly selected *responder* will reject, $p(c, \sigma_p)$, satisfies the following conditions:

(1) $p(c, \frac{1}{2}) = 0$ and $p(c, 1) = 1$
(2) p is strictly increasing in σ_p over the interval $[\frac{1}{2}, 1]$
(3) for a given σ_p, p is increasing in c.

For all ultimatum proposals, the *proposer*'s behaviour is such that: $c = k$ and $\frac{1}{2} \leq \sigma_p < 1$.

Many experimental studies confirm these statements (see sub-section 8.4.1). Furthermore, in an experiment using the dictator and the ultimatum games, Forsythe *et al.* (1994) found that, on average, offers are higher in the latter than in the former. It is significant that the ERC model predicts this relationship, too. On average, $\bar{\sigma}_D > \bar{\sigma}_p$. In fact, no one offers more in the dictator game, and the only players who offer the same amount are precisely those for whom $r_i(1) = \frac{1}{2}$.

To summarize, we can conclude from the success of the ERC equilibrium that people do indeed behave strategically. The heterogeneous behaviour on the part of the same individual in such and such a context is the result of an opposition between her (or his) preference for selfish material gains and her (or his) preference for relative gains within the population.

In its form, the ERC model has, however, some limitations that Bolton–Ockenfels themselves identify: 'ERC is a theory of "local behavior" in the sense that it explains *stationary patterns* for relatively *simple games*, played over a *short time span* in a *constant frame*. Many important challengers for extending ERC have to do with the italicized phases' (Bolton and Ockenfels (2000, 189). In particular, incorporating learning requires a dynamic model. On the other hand, the definition of the social reference point in the model is perhaps too simple. Lastly, ERC raises the question of what constitutes the relevant reference group if more complex experimental games are considered. Unfortunately the same limits are present in the last model that is now examined.

The Fehr–Schmidt model: an inequity aversion model

The model proposed by Fehr and Schmidt (1999) is similar in spirit to the Bolton–Ockenfels model presented previously. What experimental evidence suggests is that many people resist unfair outcomes, but it would clearly be wrong to assume that *all* people are motivated by fairness considerations. The authors ask whether this conflicting evidence can be explained by a *single* model.

They claim that the answer to this question is affirmative if one accepts the following assumption:

Assumption: In addition to purely selfish people, there is a fraction of the population who is also motivated by 'self-centred inequity aversion'.

This assumption contains two elements. *Inequity aversion* means that people resist inequitable outcomes, i.e. they are willing to give up some material payoff to move in the direction of more equitable outcomes. But aversion is *self-centred* in the sense that people are interested only in the fairness of their *own* material payoff relative to the payoff of others.

The model

An individual is inequity-averse if she (or he) dislikes outcomes that are perceived as inequitable. But the question is, how do individuals perceive the fairness of outcomes? According to Fehr and Schmidt (1999), as well as for Bolton and Ockenfels (2000)), fairness judgements are based on a kind of *mental reference outcome* and they follow the same approach by assuming that the *relative* material payoffs affect people's well-being and behaviour. Indeed what differentiates the Fehr–Schmidt model and the Bolton–Ockenfels model is the way in which this idea is introduced.

How to determine the relevant reference group and the relevant reference outcome is ultimately an empirical question. In the laboratory, the reference group is simply the set of subjects playing against each other and the reference point is equality. Hence, they assume that *inequity* aversion can be approximated by *inequality* aversion.

Two assumptions characterize the model:

(i)   The population includes both selfish subjects, subjects who dislike being worse off in material terms than the other players in the experiment, and subjects who dislike being better off.

(ii) In general, subjects suffer more from inequality that is to their disadvantage than from advantageous inequality.

Consider a set of n players and let $x = (x_1 \ldots x_n)$ denote the vector of monetary payoffs (supposed to be common knowledge). The utility function of player i is given by:

$$U_i(x) = x_i - \frac{\alpha_i}{n-1} \sum_{j \neq i} \max\{x_j - x_i, 0\} - \frac{\beta_i}{n-1} \sum_{j \neq i} \max\{x_i - x_j, 0\}, \, i \neq j$$

(8.3)

with $\beta_i \leq \alpha_i$ and $0 \leq \beta_i < 1$.

In the two-player model the utility function can be simplified as follows:

$$U_i(x) = x_i - \alpha_i \max\{x_j - x_i, 0\} - \beta_i \max\{x_i - x_j, 0\}, \, j \neq i \qquad (8.4)$$

The second term of this relation measures the utility loss from disadvantageous inequality while the third terms measures the loss from advantageous inequality. The condition $\beta_i \leq \alpha_i$ expresses the idea that a player suffers more from inequality that is to her (or his) disadvantage. The condition $\beta_i \geq 0$ rules out the existence of subjects who like to be better off than others. The condition $\beta_i < 1$ means that it is very implausible that a subject's utility loss is very strong when the inequity is to her (or his) advantage. On the other hand, according to the authors, there is no justification on putting an upper bound on the parameter α_i.

Notice lastly that in the n-players' case, player i compares her (or his) payoff to all the other n-1 players' payoff. In this general model, Fehr and Schimdt (1999) normalize the disutility from inequality by dividing the second and third term of (8.3) by n-1. This normalization implies that the relative impact of inequality aversion on player i's total payoff does not depend on the number of players.

This model was applied to a lot of games including cooperation games, bargaining games and market games, among others. Like the ERC model, the Fehr–Schmidt model can explain both cooperative and non-cooperative behaviour in these games. In the presence of inequity-averse people, 'cooperative' (i.e. 'fair') as well as 'non-cooperative' (i.e.

'competitive') behavioural patterns can be explained in a coherent framework.

The main insight of this study is that 'the heterogeneity of preferences interacts in important ways with the economic environment' (Fehr and Schmidt, 1999, 818). More precisely, it is proved that the economic environment determines the preference type that is decisive for the prevailing behaviour in equilibrium. For instance, for the public goods game, a single selfish player is able to induce all other players to contribute nothing to the public good although the others may care a lot about equity. Conditions under which the existence of inequity-averse players in a population influences the equilibria of a game is the main result of the Fehr–Schmidt model.

Several objections can be raised concerning this model. First, as mentioned above, it rules out the existence of subjects who like to be better off than others. Clearly, such people exist. Fortunately, one can show that these subjects have virtually no influence on equilibrium. Secondly, as for the ERC theory, another set of questions concerns the choice of the reference group and of the reference outcome. For many laboratory experiments, the assumption in both the Bolton–Ockenfels model and in the Fehr–Schmidt model seems a natural starting point for determining the reference group. However, there may well be interactive situations in which, for instance, some agents have a salient position which makes them natural reference agents. Furthermore, it is likely that the social framework and the institutional environment in which interactions take place is significant. The choice of the reference outcome may also be a source of discussion. Finally, an obvious limitation of this model is that it cannot explain the evolution of the situation in time in the experiments discussed; a model that just focuses on equilibrium behaviour of players cannot explain the time path of the game.

The authors are fully aware of all those limitations and research in progress is trying to better understand and model individuals' observed behaviours in many games experiments.

Remark 3

Several other distributional models have been proposed in the literature (a recent survey may be found in Fehr and Schmidt, 2000). Each one focuses on a particular motivation: altruism (Andreoni and Miller, 1996, 2000); pleasure of giving (Andreoni, 1990, 1995, who call that a 'warm-glow effect'); envy (Kirchsteiger, 1994); altruism and spitefulness (Levine, 1998).

Other interesting approaches try to merge intention-based reciprocity and distributional equity. For instance, Falk and Fishbacher (1999) measure 'kindness' in terms of inequity aversion. An action chosen by player j is perceived to be kind by player i if it gives rise to a payoff for player i which is higher than *the payoff of player j* (and not in relation to the payoff of player i, as in Rabin's model). Charness and Rabin (2000) also propose a hybrid model in which players care about their own payoffs, and about a weighted average of the lowest payoff anybody receives (a kind of 'Rawlsian' or quasi-maximin component, by reference to the theory of justice developed by Rawls, 1971) and the sum of all payoffs (a kind of 'utilitarian' component). Their model has a hidden aversion to inequality through the emphasis on the lowest payoff; so, it incorporates a specific form of altruism. But, in addition, players are assumed to care also about the others' actions. These hybrid models allow us to better explain some data than the social utility model which focuses only on the role of fairness intention or the role of unfair outcomes. Yet, this increase in explanatory power comes at a cost because these theories are more complicated.■

Traditional GT, as most economic models, is based on a self-interest hypothesis that states that all people are exclusively motivated by their material self-interest. In recent years, experimental economics has gathered overwhelming evidence that systematically refutes this assumption. In this sub-section, we have described several recently developed models of fairness that maintain the rationality assumption but change the assumption of purely selfish preferences. Some authors, however, have reservations about this change in modelling players' motivations; they prefer to interpret observed behaviour in experiments as elementary forms of bounded rationality, coming back to learning models based on purely material preferences, such as the models presented above in section 8.5. For instance, Roth and Erev (1995) and Binmore, Gale and Samuelson (1995) try to explain the presence of fair proposals and rejections of low proposals in the ultimatum game by learning models which remain based on purely pecuniary preferences. We may doubt, however, the relevance of this viewpoint, although there can be little doubt that learning processes are very significant in real life and in laboratory experiments. In games such as the public goods, the trust game, the ultimatum or the gift exchange game, the setting is so simple that its is hard to believe that subjects make systematic mistakes by rejecting offers or rewarding generous proposals, even though they prefer not to act so. More interesting certainly is the approach which tries to merge models of learning with models that incorporate non-selfish motives (some explorations studies in this direction have been carried out: for instance, Cooper and Stockman, 1999; Costa-Gomes and Zauner, 1999).

Bibliography

Anderson, S., J. Goeree and C. Holt (1998) 'A theoretical analysis of altruism and decision errors in public goods games', *Journal of Public Economics*, 70, 297–323.

Andreoni, J. (1988) 'Why free ride? Strategies and learning in public goods experiments', *Journal of Public Economics*, 37, 291–304.

Andreoni, J. (1990) 'Impure altruism and donations to public goods: a theory of warm-glow giving?', *Economic Journal*, 100, 464–477

Andreoni, J. (1995) 'Warm-glow versus cold-prickle: the effects of positive and negative framing on cooperation in experiments', *The Quarterly Journal of Economics*, 60, 1–14.

Andreoni, J. and J. Miller (1996) 'Rational cooperation in the finitely repeated Prisoner's dilemma: experimental evidence', *The Economic Journal*, 103, 570–85.

Andreoni, J. and J. Miller (2000) 'Giving according to GARP: an experimental test of the rationality of altruism', University of Wisconsin and Carnegie Mellon University, mimeo.

Axelrod, R. (1984) *The Evolution of Cooperation* (New York: Basic Books).

Aymard S. and D. Serra (2001) 'Do individuals use backward induction in dynamic optimization problems? An experimental investigation', *Economic Letters*, 73, 287–92.

Banks, J., C. Camerer and D. Porter (1994) 'An experimental analysis of Nash refinements in signaling games', *Games and Economic Behavior*, 6, 1–31.

Battalio, R., L. Samuelson and J. Van Huyck (2001) 'Optimization incentives and coordination failure in laboratory stag hunt games', *Econometrica*, 69, 749–64.

Beard, R. and R. Beil (1994) 'Do people rely on the self-interested maximization of others? An experimental test', *Management Science*, 40, 252–62.

Becker, G.S. (1974) 'A theory of social interactions', *Journal of Political Economy*, 82, 1063–93.

Berg, J., J. Dickhaut and K. McCabe (1995) 'Trust, reciprocity and social history', *Games and Economic Behaviour*, 10, 122–42.

Bergin, J. and B.L. Lipman (1995) 'Evolution with state-dependent mutations', draft manuscript, Department of Economics, Queen's University.

Binmore, K. (1999) 'Why experiment in economics?', *Economic Journal*, 109, 16–24.

Binmore, K., J. Gale and L. Samuelson (1995) 'Learning to be imperfect: the ultimatum game', *Games and Economic Behaviour*, 8, 56–90.

Binmore, K., A. Shaked and J. Sutton (1985) 'Testing non-cooperative bargaining theory: a preliminary study', *American Economic Review*, 75, 1178–80.

Binmore, K., A. Shaked and J. Sutton (1989) 'An outside option experiment', *Quarterly Journal of Economics*, 104, 753–70.

Binmore, K., P. Morgan, A. Shaked and J. Sutton (1991) 'Do people exploit their bargaining power? An experimental study', *Games and Economic Behavior*, 3, 295–322.

Binmore, K., J. Swierzsbinski and C. Proulx (1996) 'Does minimax work? An experimental study', *ELSE Discussion Paper*, UCL.

Bolle, F. (1998) 'Rewarding trust: an experimental study', *Theory and Decision*, 45, 83–98.

Bolle, F. and P. Ockenfels (1990) 'Prisoner's dilemma as a game with incomplete information', *Journal of Economic Psychology*, 11, 69–84.

Bolton, G.E. (1991) 'A comparative model of bargaining: theory and evidence', *American Economic Review*, 81, 1096–1136.

Bolton, G.E. and A. Ockenfels (2000) 'ERC: a theory of equity, reciprocity and competition', *American Economic Review*, 90, 166–93.

Bolton, G.E. and R. Zwick (1995) 'Anonymity versus punishment in ultimatum bargaining', *Games and Economic Behavior*, 10, 95–121.

Bounmy, K., M. Willinger and A. Ziegelmeyer (2002) 'Global versus local interaction in coordination games: an experimental investigation', Working paper, BETA, Strasbourg (France).

Boylan, R. and M. El-Gamal (1993) 'Fictitious play: a statistical study of multiple economic experiments', *Games and Economic Behavior*, 5, 205–22.

Brandts, J. and C. Holt (1995) 'Limitations of dominance and forward induction: experimental evidence', *Economics Letters*, 49, 391–95.

Brandts, J. and B. McLeod (1995) 'Equilibrium selection in experimental games with recommended play', *Games and Economic Behavior*, 11, 36–63.

Bresnahan, T.F. and P.C. Reiss (1991) 'Entry and competition in concentrated markets', *Journal of Political Economy*, 99, 977–1009.

Brown, J. and R. Rosenthal (1990) 'Testing the minimax hypothesis: a reexamination of O'Neill's game experiment', *Econometrica*, 58, 1065–81.

Camerer, C. (1997) 'Progress in behavioral game theory', *Journal of Economic Perspectives*, 11, 167–88.

Camerer, C. (2002) *Behavioral Game Theory: Experiments on Strategic Interaction* (Princeton: Princeton Unversity Press).

Camerer, C. and Fehr, E. (2002) 'Measuring social norms and preferences using experimental games: a guide for social scientists', Institute for Empirical Research in Economics, University of Zurich, Working Paper, 97 (forthcoming in Henrich, Boyd, Bowles, Camerer, Fehr, Gintis and McElreath (eds), *Foundations of Human Sociality – Experimental and Ethnographic Evidence from 15 Small-Scale Societies*).

Camerer, C. and T.H. Ho (1999) 'Experience-weighted attraction learning in normal form games', *Econometrica*, 67, 827–74.

Camerer, C., E. Johnson, T. Rymon and S. Sen (1993) 'Cognition and framing in sequential bargaining for gains and losses', in K. Binmore, A. Kirman and P. Tani (eds), *Contributions to Game Theory* (Cambridge, MA: MIT Press).

Camerer, C. and R. Thaler (1995) 'Ultimatums, dictators and manners', *Journal of Economic Perspectives*, 9, 209–19.

Cameron, L. (1999) 'Raising the stakes in the ultimatum game: experimental evidence from Indonesia', *Economic Inquiry*, 37, 47–59.

Capra, C.M., J.K. Goeree, R. Gomez and C.A. Holt (1999) 'Anomalous behaviour in a traveller's dilemma', *American Economic Review*, 89, 678–90.

Carter, J. and S. McAloon (1996) 'A test for comparative income effects in an ultimatum bargaining experiment', *Journal of Economic Behavior and Organization*, 31, 369–80.

Charness, G. and M. Rabin (2000) 'Social preferences: some simple tests and a new model', University of California at Berkeley, mimeo.

Cheung, Y.W. and D. Friedman (1997) 'Individual learning in normal form games: some laboratory results', *Games and Economic Behavior*, 19, 46–76.

Clark, K. and M. Sefton (1998) 'The sequential Prisoner's dilemma: evidence on reciprocal altruism', University of Manchester, mimeo.

Cookson, R. (2000) 'Framing effects in public goods experiments', *Experimental Economics*, 3, 55–79.

Cooper, D.J. and C.K. Stockman (1999) 'Fairness, learning and constructive preferences: an experimental investigation', Case Western Reserve University, mimeo.

Cooper, R.W. (1999) *Coordination Games* (Cambridge: Cambridge University Press).

Cooper, R.W., D. Dejong, R. Forsythe and T. Ross (1990) 'Selection criteria in coordination games: some experimental results', *American Economic Review*, 80, 218–33.

Cooper, R.W., D. Dejong, R. Forsythe and T. Ross (1992) 'Communication in coordination games', *Quarterly Journal of Economics*, 107, 739–71.

Cooper, R.W., D. DeJong, R. Forsythe and T. Ross (1993) 'Forward induction in the Battle-of the-Sexes games', *American Economic Review*, 83, 1303–16.

Cooper, R.W., D. Dejong, R. Forsythe and T. Ross (1996) 'Cooperation without reputation: experimental evidence from Prisoner's dilemma games', *Games and Economic Behavior*, 12, 187–218.

Costa-Gomes, M. and K.G. Zauner (1999) 'Learning, non-equilibrium beliefs, and non-pecuniary payoff uncertainty in an experimental game', Harvard Business School, mimeo.

Crawford V. (1991) 'An evolutionary interpretation of Van Huyck, Battalio and Beil's experimental results on coordination', *Games and Economic Behavior*, 3, 25–59.

Crawford V. (1997) 'Theory and experiments in the analysis of strategic interaction', in D.M. Kreps and K.F. Wallis (eds), *Advances in Economics and Econometrics: Theory and Applications – Seventh World Congress*, 1 (Cambridge: Cambridge University Press), 206–42.

Croson, R. (1996) 'Information in ultimatum games: an experimental study', *Journal of Economic Behavior and Organization*, 30, 197–212.

Davis, D. and C. Holt (1993) *Experimental Economics* (Princeton: Princeton University Press).

Duffy, J., and R. Nagel (1997) 'On the robustness of behaviour in experimental 'beauty contest' games', *Economic Journal*, 107, 1684–700.

Dufwenberg, M. and G. Kirchsteiger (1998) 'A theory of sequential reciprocity', Discussion Paper, CentER, Tilburg University.

Eckel, C. and P. Grossman (1996) 'The relative price for fairness: gender differences in a punishment game', *Journal of Economic Behavior and Organization*, 30, 143–58.

Eckel, C. and P. Grossman (1998) 'Are women less selfish than men? Evidence from dictator experiments', *Economic Journal*, 108, 726–35.

Falk, A. and U. Fischbacher (1999) 'A theory of reciprocity', Working Paper, 6, Institute for Empirical Research in Economics, University of Zurich.

Fehr, E. and S. Gächter (2000) 'Cooperation and punishment in a public goods experiment', *American Economic Review*, 90, 980–94.

Fehr, E., S. Gächter and G. Kirchsteiger (1997) 'Reciprocity as a contract enforcement device: experimental evidence', *Econometrica*, 65, 833–60.

Fehr, E., G. Kirchsteiger and A. Riedl (1993) 'Does fairness prevent market clearing? An experimental investigation', *Quarterly Journal of Economics*, 153, 437–60.

Fehr, E. and K.M. Schmidt (1999) 'A theory of fairness, competition and cooperation', *Quarterly Journal of Economics*, 114, 817–68.

Fehr, E. and K.M. Schmidt (2000) 'Theories of fairness and reciprocity – Evidence and economic applications', Working Paper prepared for the invited lecture session on Behavioral Economics at the 8th World Congress of the Econometric Society, Seattle.

Flood M. (1952) 'Some experimental game', Research memorandum RM-789, RAWD Corporation, June

Flood M. (1954) 'Game-learning theory and some decision-making experiments', in R.M. Thrall *et al.* (eds), *Decision Processes*, 139–58.

Flood M. (1958) 'Some experimental games' *Management Science*, 5, 5–26.

Forsythe, R., J. Horowitz, N. Savin and M. Sefton (1994) 'Fairness in simple bargaining experiments', *Games and Economic Behavior*, 6, 347–69.

Friedman D. (1996) 'Equilibrium in evolutionary games: some experimental results', *Economic Journal*, 106, 1–25.

Friedman, D. and S. Sunder (1994) *Experimental Methods: A Primer for Economists* (Cambridge: Cambridge University Press).

Fudenberg, D. and D. M. Kreps (1993) 'Learning mixed equilibria', *Games and Economic Behavior*, 5, 320–67.

Geanakoplos J., D. Pearce and E. Stacchetti (1989) 'Psychological games and sequential rationality', *Games and Economic Behavior*, 1, 60–79.

Güth, W. (1995) 'On ultimatum bargaining experiments – a personal review', *Journal of Economic Behavior and Organization*, 27, 329–44.

Güth, W. and S. Huck (1997) 'From ultimatum bargaining to dictatorship: an experimental study of four games varying in veto power', *Metroeconomica*, 48, 1262–79.

Güth, W., S. Huck and P. Ockenfels (1996) 'Two-level ultimatum bargaining with incomplete information: an experimental study', *Economic Journal*, 106, 593–604.

Güth, W., R. Schmittberger and B. Schwarze (1982) 'An experimental analysis of ultimatum bargaining', *Journal of Economic Behavior and Organization* 3, 367–88.

Güth, W. and E. Van Damme (1998) 'Information, strategic behavior and fairness in ultimatum bargaining: an experimental study', *Journal of Mathematical Psychology*, 42, 227–47.

Harrison, G. and J. Hirshleifer (1989) 'An experimental evaluation of weakest link/best shot models of public goods', *Journal of Political Economy*, 97, 201–25.

Harsanyi, J. (1973) 'Gamesworth randomly distributed payoffs: a new rationale for mixed strategy equilibrium points: *International Journal of Game Theory*, 2, 1–23.

Ho, T.H., C. Camerer and K. Weigelt, 'Iterated dominance and iterated best response in experimental "p-Beauty contest"', *The American Economic Review*, 88, 947–69.

Hoffman, E., K. McCabe, K. Shachat and V. Smith (1996) 'Preference, property rights and anonymity in bargaining games', *Games and Economic Behavior*, 7, 346–80.

Hoffman, E., K. McCabe, and V. Smith (1996) 'Social distance and other-regarding behavior in dictator games', *American Economic Review*, 86, 653–60.

Holt, C.A. and Laury, S.K. (2003) 'Theoretical explanations of treatment effects in voluntary contributions experiments', in C.R. Plott and V. Smith (eds), *Handbook of Experimental Results* (Amsterdam: North Holland).

Isaac, R.M., J.M. Walker and S. Thomas (1984) 'Divergent evidence on free-riding: an experimental examination of possible explanations', *Public Choice*, 43, 113–49.

Kagel, J., C. Kim and D. Moser (1996) 'Fairness in ultimatum games with asymmetric information and asymmetric payoffs', *Games and Economic Behavior*, 13, 100–10.

Kagel, J. and A. Roth (eds) (1995) *A Handbook of Experimental Economics* (Princeton: Princeton University Press).

Kahan, J.P. and A. Rapoport (1984) *Theories of Coalition Formation* (Hillsdale, NJ: Erlbaum).

Kahn, L. and K. Murnighan (1993) 'A general experiment on bargaining in demand games with outside options', *American Economic Review*, 83, 1260–80.

Kahneman, D., J.L. Knetsch and R. Thaler (1986) 'Fairness as a constraint on profit seeking: entitlement in the market', *American Economic Review*, 76, 728–41.

Keser, C. (1996) 'Voluntary contributions to a public good when partial contribution is a dominant strategy', *Economic Letters*, 50, 359–66.

Keser, C. and F. van Winden (2000) 'Conditional cooperation and voluntary contributions to public goods', *Scandinavian Journal of Economics*, 102, 23–39.

Keynes, J.M. (1936) *The General Theory of Interest, Employment, and Money* (London: Macmillan).

Kirchsteiger, G. (1994) 'The role of envy in ultimatum games', *Journal of Economic Behavior and Organization*, 25, 373–89.

Knez, M.J. and C.F. Camerer (1995) 'Outside options and social comparison in a three-player game experiments', *Games and Economic Behavior*, 10, 65–94.

Kreps, D., P. Milgrom, J. Roberts and R. Wilson (1982) 'Rational cooperation in the finitely repeated Prisoner's dilemma', *Journal of Economic Theory*, 27, 245–52.

Ledyard, J. (1995) 'Public goods: a survey of experimental research', in J. Kagel and A.E. Roth (eds), *A Handbook of Experimental Economics* (Princeton: Princeton University Press).

Levine, D. (1998) 'Modelling altruism and spitefulness', *Review of Economic Dynamics*, 1, 593–622.

Loewenstein, G. (1999) 'Experimental economics from the vantage-point of behavioural economics', *Economic Journal*, 109, 25–34.

Maschler, M. (1963) 'The power of a coalition', *Management Science*, 10, 8–29.

McKelvey, R. and T. Palfrey (1992) 'An experimental study of the centipede game', *Econometrica*, 60, 803–36.

McKelvey, R. and T. Palfrey (1995) 'Quantal response equilibria for normal form games', *Games and Economic Behavior*, 10, 6–38.

McKelvey, R. and T. Palfrey (1998) 'Quantal Response equilibria for extensive form games', *Experimental Economics*, 1, 9–41.

Metha, J., C. Starmer and R. Sugden (1994) 'The nature of salience: an experimental investigation of pure coordination games', *American Economic Review*, 84, 658–73.

Mitzkewitz, M. and R. Nagel (1993) 'Experimental results on ultimatum games with incomplete information', *International Journal of Game Theory*, 22, 171–98.

Mookherjee, D. and B. Sopher (1997) 'Learning and decision costs in experimental constant-sum game', *Games and Economic Behavior*, 19, 97–132.

Moulin, H. (1986) *Games Theory for Social Sciences*, 2nd rev. edn (New York: New York University Press).

Murnighan, K. and A. Roth (1977) 'The effects of communication and information availability in an experimental study of a three-person game', *Management Science*, 23, 1336–48.

Murnighan, K., A. Roth and F. Schoumaker (1988) 'Risk aversion in bargaining: an experimental study', *Journal of Risk and Uncertainty*, 1, 101–24.

Nagel, R. (1995) 'Unraveling in guessing games: an experimental study', *American Economic Review*, 85, 1313–26.

Nelson, W.R. (2001) 'Incorporating fairness into game theory and economics: comment', *American Economic Review*, 91, 1180–83.

Noussair C. and K. Matheny (1999) 'An experimental study of decisions in dynamic optimization problems', Working Paper, Purdue University.

Noussair C. and M.A. Olson (1997) 'Dynamic decisions in a laboratory setting', *Southern Economic Journal*, 978–92.

Ochs, J. (1995) 'Games with unique, mixed strategy equilibria: an experimental study', *Games and Economic Behavior*, 10, 202–17.

Ochs, J. and A. Roth (1989) 'An experimental study of sequential bargaining', *American Economic Review*, 79, 355–84.

O'Neill B. (1987) 'A non-metric test of the minimax theory of two-person games', *Proceedings of the National Academy of Sciences*, 84, 2106–9.

Palfrey, T. and J. Prisbey (1997) 'Anomalous behavior in public good experiments: how much and why?', *American Economic Review*, 87, 829–46.

Plott, C. (1990) 'Will economics become an experimental science?', *Southern Economic Journal*, 57, 901–19.

Prasnikar, V. and A. Roth (1992) 'Considerations of fairness and strategy: experimental data from sequential games', *Quarterly Journal of Economics*, 107, 865–88.

Rabin, M. (1993) 'Incorporating fairness into game theory and economics', *American Economic Review*, 83, 1281–302.

Raiffa, H. (1982) *The Art and Science of Negotiation* (Cambridge, MA: Harvard University Press).

Rapoport A. (1970) *N-Person Game Theory* (Ann Arbor: University of Michigan Press).

Rapoport A. (1990) *Experimental Studies of Interactive Decision* (Dordrecht: Kluwer Academic Press).

Rapoport, A. and R. Boebel (1992) 'Mixed strategies in strictly competitive games: a further test of the minimax hypothesis', *Games and Economic Behavior*, 4, 261–83.

Rapoport, A. and A.M. Chammah (1965) *Prisoner's Dilemma: A Study in Conflict and Cooperation* (Ann Arbor: University of Michigan Press).

Rapoport A. and C. Orwant (1962) 'Experimental games: a review', *Behavioral Science*, 7, 1–37.

Rapoport, A. and J. Sundali (1996) 'Ultimatums in two-person bargaining with one-sided uncertainty: offer games', *International Journal of Game Theory*, 25, 475–94.

Rapoport, A., J. Sundali and D. Seale (1996) 'Ultimatums in two-person bargaining with one-sided uncertainty: demand games', *Journal of Economic Behavior and Organization*, 30, 173–96.

Rawls, J. (1971) *A Theory of Justice* (Cambridge, MA: Harvard University Press).

Riedl, A. and J. Vyrastekova (2002) 'Social preferences in three-player ultimatum game experiments', CentER Working Paper, 2002–05, Tilburg University.

Rosenthal, R.H. (1989) 'Games of perfect information, predatory pricing and the chain store paradox', *Journal of Economic Theory*, 25, 92–100.

Roth, A. (1986) 'Laboratory experimentation in economics', *Economics and Philosophy*, 2, 245–73.

Roth, A. (1987) 'Bargaining phenomena and bargaining theory', in A. Roth (ed.), *Laboratory Experiments in Economics: Six Points of View* (Cambridge: Cambridge University Press).

Roth, A. (1988) 'Laboratory experimentation in economics: a methodological overview', *Economic Journal*, 98, 974–1031.

Roth, A. (1995) 'Bargaining experiments', in J. Kagel and A. Roth (eds), *Handbook of Experimental Economics* (Princeton: Princeton University Press).

Roth, A. and I. Erev (1995) 'Learning in extensive form games: experimental data and simple dynamic models in the intermediate term', *Games and Economic Behavior*, 8, 163–212.

Roth, A. and M. Malouf M. (1979) 'Game-theoretic models and the role of information in bargaining', *Psychological Review*, 86, 574–94.

Roth, A. and K. Murnighan (1978) 'Equilibrium behavior and repeated play of the Prisoner's dilemma', *Journal of Mathematical Psychology*, 17, 189–98.

Roth, A. and K. Murnighan (1982) 'The role of information in bargaining: an experimental study', *Econometrica*, 50, 1123–42.

Roth, A., V. Prasnikar, M. Okuno-Fujiwara and S. Zamir (1991) 'Bargaining and market behavior in Jerusalem, Ljubljana, Pittsburgh and Tokyo: an experimental study', *American Economic Review*, 78, 806–23.

Schelling T. (1960) *The Strategy of Conflict* (Cambridge, MA: Harland University Press).

Schotter, A., K. Weigelt and C. Wilson (1994) 'A laboratory investigation of multiperson rationality and presentation effects', *Games and Economic Behavior*, 445–64.

Schotter, A., A. Weiss and I. Zapater (1996) 'Fairness and survival in ultimatum and dictatorship games', *Journal of Economic Behavior and Organization*, 31, 37–56.

Selten, R. (1987) 'Equity and coalition bargaining in experimental three-person games', in A. Roth (ed), *Laboratory Experimentation in Economics: Six Points of View* (Cambridge: Cambridge University Press).

Selten, R., A. Sadrieh and K. Abbink (1995) 'Money does not induce risk-neutral behavior, but binary lotteries do even worse', *Theory and Decision*, 46, 213–52.

Selten, R. and R. Stoecker (1986) 'End behavior in sequences of finite prisoner's dilemma supergames: a learning theory approach', *Journal of Economic Behavior and Organization*, 7, 47–70.

Simon, H.A. (1982) *Models of Bounded Rationality* (Cambridge, MA: MIT Press).

Smith, V. (1982) 'Microeconomic systems as an experimental science', *American Economic Review*, 72, 923–55.

Smith, V. (1994) 'Economics in the laboratory', *Journal of Economic Perspectives*, 8, 113–31.

Starmer, C. (1999) 'Experimental economics: hard science or wasteful tinkering?', *Economic Journal*, 109, 5–15.

Straub, P. and J. Murnighan (1995) 'An experimental investigation of ultimatum games: information, fairness, expectations and lowest acceptable offers', *Journal of Economic Behavior and Organization*, 27, 345–64.

Thaler, R.H. (1988) 'Anomalies: the ultimatum game', *Journal of Economic Perspectives*, 2, 195–206.

Tversky, A. and D. Kahneman (1992) 'Advances in prospect theory: cumulative representations of uncertainty', *Journal of Risk and Uncertainty*, 5, 297–323.

Van Huyck, J., R. Battalio and R. Beil (1990) 'Tacit coordination games, strategic uncertainty and coordination failure', *American Economic Review*, 80, 234–48.

Van Huyck, J., R. Battalio and R. Beil (1991) 'Strategic uncertainty, equilibrium selection principles and coordination failure in average opinion games', *Quarterly Journal of Economics*, 106, 885–911.

Van Huyck, J., R. Battalio and R. Beil (1993) 'Asset markets as an equilibrium selection mechanism: coordination failure, game form auctions and forward induction', *Games and Economic Behavior*, 5, 485–504.

Van Huyck, J., R. Battalio and A. Gillette (1992) 'Credible assignments in coordination games', *Games and Economic Behavior*, 4, 606–26.

Van Huyck, J., R. Battalio, S. Marthur, A. Ortmann and P. Van Huyck (1992) 'On the origin of convention: evidence from symmetric bargaining games', Texas A&M Working Paper, 92–05.

Veblen, T. (1922) *The Theory of the Leisure Class – An Economic Study of Institutions* (London: George Allen & Unwin, first published 1899).

Von Neumann, J. and O. Morgenstern (1944) *Theory of Games and Economic Behavior* (New York: John Wiley).

Watabe, M., S. Terai, N. Hayashi and T. Yamagishi (1996) 'Cooperation in the one-shot Prisoner's dilemma based on expectations of reciprocity', *Japanese Journal of Experimental Social Psychology*, 36, 183–96.

Willinger, M. and A. Ziegelmeyer (2001) 'Strength of the social dilemma in a public goods experiment: an exploration of the error hypothesis', *Experimental Economics*, 4, 131–4.

Name Index

Abbink, K.   389
Abreu, D.   132
Akerlof, G.   xx
Akin, E.   352
Anderson, S.   396, 443
Andreoni, J.   393, 397, 458
Aoki, M.   364
Aristotle   239
Arrow, K.   52, 228–9, 234–5
Aspremont, C. d'   37, 59, 86, 137, 235, 294
Aumann, R.J.   1, 2, 3, 5
Axelrod, R.   96, 132–3, 338, 353, 392
Aymard, S.   400

Bagwell, K.   133
Banks, J.   171, 179, 410
Barrett, S.   312, 315, 317
Barry, B.   239
Battalio, R.   403, 404–5, 408, 409, 430, 434, 438
Beard, R.   400
Becker, G.S.   44
Beil, R.   400, 403, 404–5, 408, 409
Bellman, R.   39
Benoit, J.P.   96, 133
Berg, J.   398, 415
Bergin, J.   435
Bernheim, B.D.   144, 259, 351
Bertrand, J.   2, 73, 119, 120
Bhaskar, V.   356
Billera, L.J.   310
Binmore, K.   2, 5, 6, 7, 9, 44, 74
Blackburn, K.   188
Bloch, F.   296, 297, 298, 300, 302, 303, 311
Boebel, R.   389
Bolle, F.   398
Bolton, G.E.   418, 423, 445, 450, 458
Bomze, I.   349, 351

Bondareva, O.N.   265, 266, 324
Borda, J.C de   49
Borel, E.   2
Borgers, T.   58, 357
Bounmy, K.   438
Boylan, R.   435–6
Brandenburger, A.   84, 90, 145
Brander, J.   110, 114, 120
Brandts, J.   171–3, 409
Bresnahan, T.F.   429
Brown, J.   389
Buchanan, J.   257
Bulow, J.   114
Bush, R.   357

Camerer, C.   346, 410, 411, 416, 438, 439, 440, 441, 445
Cameron, L.   412
Capra, C.M.   443
Carraro, C.   311, 312, 315, 317, 320, 322
Carter, J.   418
Chammah, A.M.   392
Chander, P.   311–12, 322
Charness, G.   459
Chatterjee, X.   303
Cheung, Y.W.   436–7
Cho, I.K.   171, 177, 179, 195, 202
Clark, K.   398
Clarke, E.H.   55–9
Cookson, R.   439
Cooper, D.J.   459
Cooper, R.W.   392, 393, 403, 404, 405, 407, 409
Costa-Gomes, M.   459
Cournot, A.A.   2, 120, 356, 360–2, 364–5, 367, 368, 370, 381

Dasgupta, P.   54, 74, 83, 143, 240
Davis, D.   439
Davis, M.   259, 271, 273, 282

Debreu, G.   264
Dekel, E.   84, 90, 145, 336, 351-2
Dickhaut, J.   398, 415
Dixit, A.   110, 118, 129, 132, 133
Dockner, E.   107
Donze, J.   195
Drèze, J.H.   260, 282, 288, 289, 290, 291-2, 294, 295, 296, 297, 300
Duffy J.   442
Dufwenberg, M.   449

Eaton, J.   120
Eckel, C.   413
Edgeworth, F.Y.   2, 73, 208, 261, 264
Erev, I.   357, 435-6, 459

Falk, A.   449, 458
Farqharson, M.   34, 58
Fehr, E.   397, 415, 445, 456-9
Fershtman, C.   107
Fischbacher, U.   449, 458
Fishburn, P.C.   213
Fleubaey, M.   236
Flood, M.   387, 392
Forges, F.   86, 90
Forsythe, R.   413, 455
Friedman, D.   429, 430-1, 433-4, 435, 436-7, 438
Friedman, J.   95, 134, 233
Friedman, M.   9
Fudenberg, D.   6, 8, 222, 225, 363, 434, 463
Fung, K.C.   363, 364, 368, 381-2

Gächter, S.   397
Gale, I.   358, 378
Gale, J.   459
Gauthier, D.   239
Geanakoplos, J.   114, 446
Gerard-Varet, L.A.   59
Gibbard, A.   53-4
Gillette, A.   430, 434
Gillies, D.B.   261
Glicksberg, I.L.   83
Goerce, J.   396, 443
Goldin, C.   9, 9344
Green, E.   134
Green, J.   54, 58
Greenberg, J.   257-8, 294

Greif, A.   9
Grossman, G.   120
Grossman, P.   413
Grossman, S.J.   170, 179
Groves, T.   55-9
Gul, F.   84, 257
Güth, W.   411, 414, 416, 418, 428

Haigh, J.   340
Hamilton, W.   338, 353
Hardin, G.   33
Harrison, G.   420
Harsanyi, J.C.   xx, 2, 5, 11, 75, 85, 242, 353, 434
Hart, O.   127
Hart, S.   257, 279, 282, 285, 289, 290, 291-2, 295, 299, 300, 301, 302
Hayek, F.   257
Heath, D.C.   310
Hines, W.G.S.   351
Hirshleifer, J.   420
Ho, T.H.   438, 442
Hobbes, T.   239
Hofbauer, J.   350, 352
Hoffman, E.   413, 414
Holmstrom, B.   127
Holt, C.   171-3, 396, 397, 409, 439, 443
Horwell, J.D.   130
Huck, S.   414, 418
Hume, D.   33, 239
Hurwicz, L.   50-1

Ichiishi, T.   297
Isaac, R.M.   395-6
Israel   419

Johansen, L.   76

Kagel, J.   417
Kahan, J.P.   425
Kahn, L.   393, 423
Kahneman, D.   413, 439
Kalai, E.   236-8, 239
Kamien, M.I.   107
Kandori, M.   341, 349, 355
Kannai, Y.   264
Kant, I.   239
Kennan, J.   130
Keser, C.   396, 397

Keynes, J.M. 441
Kim, C. 417
Kim, Y. 353
Kirchsteiger, G. 415, 449, 458
Klemperer, P. 114, 155
Knetsch, J.L. 413
Knezs, M.J. 416
Kohlberg, E. 170, 171, 175, 185, 187
Kolm, S.C. 236
Kreps, D.M. 3, 6, 15, 217–18, 392, 434
Krishna, V. 96, 133
Krugman, P.R. 110
Kühn, H.W. 13, 38, 86
Kurz, M. 288, 289, 290, 291–2, 295, 296, 299, 300, 301, 302

Laffont, J.J. 54, 58
Laury, S.K. 397
Laussel, D. 114–16, 130
Ledyard, J. 394, 397
Lensberg, T. 239
Leonard, R.J. 2
Levine, D. 363, 458
Lewis, D.K. 5
Lipman, B.L. 435
Locke, J. 239
Loewenstein, G. 386
Lucas, W. 270, 296
Luce, R.D. 30, 34, 92, 144, 236, 259, 278

McAfee, P. 56, 155
MacAloon, S. 418
McCabe, K. 398, 413, 414, 415
McDonald, I.M. 244
McKelvey, R. 399, 443
McLean, R. 285
McLennan, A. 170
MacLeod, B. 409
McMillan, J. 56, 129, 155
Mailath, G. 179
Malcomson, P. 244
Malour, M. 389, 424
Marks, R. 97
Maschler, M. 259, 271, 273, 274, 276, 279, 282, 283, 425–6
Mas-Colell, A. 252, 256, 257, 279, 282
Maskin, E. 59, 83, 96, 362
Maskin, H. 54
Matheny, K. 400

Matsui, A. 353
Maynard Smith, J. 8, 329, 337, 343
Mertens, J.-F. 86, 170, 171, 175, 185, 187
Metha, J. 402
Milgrom, P. 126, 176, 190
Miller, J. 393, 397, 458
Mirman, L.J. 310
Mirrlees, J. xx
Mitzkewitz, M. 417, 420
Mongin, P. 235
Montet, C. 114–20
Mookherjee, D. 390
Morgenstern, O. 1, 2, 13, 20, 251, 269, 287, 387
Moriconi, F. 311, 312, 322
Moser, D. 417
Mosteller, R. 357
Moulin, H. 235, 253, 257, 275, 280, 281, 283, 441
Muller, E. 54, 59
Murnighan, K. 393, 423, 424, 425, 426
Muthoo, A. 232
Myerson, R. 54, 59, 152, 160–1

Nagel, R. 417, 420, 441, 442
Nash, J.F. xx, 2, 80, 81, 204–5, 387
Nelson, W.R. 449
Neyman, A. 287
Noussair, C. 400
Nouweland, A.V. 293

Ochs, J. 390, 421
Ockenfels, A. 445, 458
Ockenfels, P. 398, 418
Okuno-Fujuwara, J. 179
Olson, M.A. 400
O'Neill, B. 388, 389
Orwant, C. 386, 434
Osborne, M.J. 6, 8, 94, 97, 106, 283
Owen, G. 44, 83, 107, 233, 268, 280, 289, 290, 292

Palfrey, T. 397, 399, 443
Pearce, D. 106, 144, 145, 351, 446
Peleg, B. 259
Perry, M. 170, 179, 303
Peters, H.J.M. 230, 236, 238, 281
Plott, C. 385, 387

Porter, D. 410
Porter, R. 134
Possel, R. de 2
Postlewaite, A. 179
Potters, J.A.M. 282
Prasnikar, V. 420
Price, G.R. 337
Prisbey, J. 397
Proulx, C. 390

Rabin, M. 445–50, 459
Raiffa, H. 30, 34, 92, 144, 236–8, 259, 278, 387, 427
Ransmeier, J.S. 306, 308
Rapoport, A. 386, 389, 392, 418, 425, 434
Rasmusen, E. 127, 177
Rawls, J. 235, 239, 459
Ray, D. 296, 297, 303
Reiss, P.C. 429
Reny, P.J. 303
Reynolds, S. 107
Riedl, A. 415, 416
Riezman, R. 130, 133, 134
Riley, J. 184, 199
Roberts, J. 176, 188, 190
Roberts, K. 236
Robson, A. 355
Roemer, J.E. 236, 239, 281
Rosenthal, R. 108, 389, 400
Rotemberg, J. 133
Roth, A. 229–30, 278, 357
Rothschild, M. 176
Rousseau, J.-J. 239
Rubinstein, A. 6, 8, 94, 97, 106, 283, 303

Sadrieh, A. 389
Safra, Z. 240
Saloner, G. 133
Samuelson, L. 159, 332–4, 352, 358, 378, 438, 459
Sarin, R. 357
Satterthwaite, M.A. 53–4, 59
Savage, L.J. 20
Scarf, H. 264, 268
Schelling, T. 7, 75, 109–10, 401–2
Schmeidler, D. 274
Schmidt, C. 2
Schmidt, K.M. 445, 456–9

Schmittberger, R. 411
Schotter, A. 418
Schoumaker, F. 425
Schuster, P. 350
Schwarze, B. 411
Scothmer, S. 336, 351–2
Seale, D. 418
Sefton, M. 398
Selten, R. xx, 2, 303, 389, 393, 427, 428
Sen, A. 226
Serra, D. 400
Shaked, A. 213, 214, 220, 421, 422
Shapley, L.S. 2, 17, 24, 387
Shenoy, P. 295–6, 299, 300
Shin, H. 300, 301
Shubik, M. 44, 251, 253, 264, 275, 276
Sigmund, K. 350
Simon, H.A. 387, 427
Siniscalco, D. 312, 315, 317, 320
Smith, M.A.M. 110–11
Smith, V. 385, 388, 413, 414, 439
Smorodinsky, M. 236–8
Sobel, J. 171, 177, 179, 353
Soboloev, A.I. 282
Solow, R.M. 244
Sopher, B. 390
Sorin, S. 106
Spence, M. xx, 110, 176, 184, 188, 195, 196
Spencer, B. 110, 114, 120
Stacchetti, E. 446
Stackelberg, H. Von 2
Staiger, R. 133
Starmer, C. 386, 402
Stiglitz, J.E. xx, 176
Stockman, C.K. 459
Stoecker, R. 393
Sugden, R. 402
Sundali, J. 418
Sutton, J. 213, 214, 220, 421, 422
Swierzsbinki, J. 390
Swinkels, J. 341, 342, 344, 349, 372

Tan, T.C.C. 145
Tauman, Y. 310
Thaler, R. 411, 413
Thomas, B. 341
Thomas, S. 395–6
Thomson, W. 236, 239, 240, 281

Thrall, R.   296
Tijs, S.H.   282
Tirole, J.   6, 8, 222, 225, 242–3, 362
Tucker, A.W.   32
Tulkens, H.   311–12, 322
Tullock, G.   257
Tversky, A.   439

Van Damme, E.   161, 173–5, 331–2,
    349, 350, 351, 416
Van Huyck, J.   403, 404–5, 408, 409,
    430, 434, 438
van Winden, F.   397
Veblen, T.   450
Vega-Redondo, F.   348, 350, 351,
    379–80
Vickrey, W.   xx, 55–9, 152
Vignolo, T.   363
Ville, J.A.   2
Vohra, R.   296, 297, 303
Von Neumann, J.   1, 2, 13, 20, 44, 80,
    251, 269, 287, 387, 388
Vyrastekova, J.   416

Walker, J.M.   395–6
Walliser, B.   5
Warneryd, K.   353

Watabe, M.   398, 449
Weber, R.J.   253
Weibull, J.   344, 348, 352
Weintraub, E.   2
Weiss, A.   418
Werlang, S.R.C.   145
Whinston, M.D.   259
Willinger, M.   397, 438
Wilson, R.   15, 133, 155, 162, 165, 167,
    188, 190, 192
Wolfstetter, E.   125
Wolinsky, A.   240

Yaari, M.E.   285
Yi, S.-S.   294, 299, 300, 301, 311, 316
Young, H.P.   236, 279, 281, 305, 307

Zamir, S.   205
Zapater, I.   418
Zauner, K.G.   459
Zermelo, E.   2
Zeuthen, F.   2, 242
Zhang, J.   352
Ziegelmeyer, A.   397, 438
Zwick, R.   418

Subject Index

acceptance threshold (in the ultimatum game)   419
α-characteristic function   252
additivity   278, 279, 289, 291
   see also superadditivity
adverse selection   127, 152, 177
advertising game   78–80, 82, 86
agent normal form   158–9
alternating offers in finite and infinite horizon bargaining games   211–18
altruism   392–7, 400, 413–15, 428, 435, 444, 458–9
apex game   279
assessment equilibrium   161–4, 165
asymptotic
   attractor   379, 380
   model ('equivalence principle')   264
   stable equilibrium   380
attractor   379, 380
auction   151–5, 409
   as Bayesian games   151–2
   common value   56
   first-price sealed-bid auction   152–5
   optimal   152
   Vickrey   55–6, 152
   coalitions: cooperative and non-cooperative games   252, 255, 258, 259, 260, 265, 271, 282, 283, 285–7, 288, 289, 290, 291–2, 293, 295, 296, 297, 299, 300, 302, 310
   non-cooperative games with complete and perfect information   84, 86, 90–1, 94, 97, 109
Aumman–Drèze theorem   290
Aumann–Shapley prices   310
Aumann–Shapley value   285–7
automata theory   97
axiomatic bargaining theory   *see* bargaining

axioms
   β-value   289–90
   CS value   290–2
   egalitarian solution   288–9
   experiments   423–5
   Nash bargaining solution   227–9
   Nash equilibrium   142–3
   Nash program   239–42
   Raiffa–Kalai–Smorodinski solution   236–8
   sequential bargaining   213
   Shapley value   277–80
   Shapley value and pre-nucleolus   282
   solution concepts   256

babbling equilibrium   355
backward induction   37–9
   and forward induction   171–5
   experiments   400
   in individual decision experimental games   398–400
   and Stackelberg games   100–1
   sub-game perfect equilibrium   97–100
balanced game collection of weights   265, 267–8
bargaining   74, 411–28
   axiomatic models   226–42, 423–5
   coalition games   425–8
   discount factor and numbers of periods   421–2
   equity   455–6
   experimental games   439, 444, 445, 457
   non-cooperative to cooperative games   206–46; applications 242–6; Nash program and axiomatic models   226–42; strategic games   207–26

non-cooperative   240-1
non-cooperative under incomplete
    information   222-6
optional/forced breakdown   423
outside options   422-3
pure   249
sequential bargaining (and Nash
    bargaining solution)   241-2
set   228, 271-3, 275, 283, 288;
    generalization to NTU games   270
solution; egalitarian   238; Nash
    226-31; Raiffa–Kalai–Smorodinski
    236-8
ultimatum game   411-21
basin of attraction   379
Battle of the Sexes game   66-7, 79,
    173
experimental games   401, 409, 430,
    433, 434, 436, 437
Bayes' rule   223, 224, 225
non-cooperative games with
    imperfect or incomplete
    information   150, 162, 165-7,
    178-9, 193, 197
Bayesian
approach   90-1
decision theory   31
equilibrium   11, 54, 58, 59, 141,
    142-55, 168; auctions   151-5; and
    Nash equilibrium   146-51; perfect
    Bayesian   164-5
game   85, 152; common prior
    belief   150-1   see under beliefs,
    extensive   176; in strategic
    form   150; signalling   174-84,
    195-203   see signalling game
inference   164
players   161
rationality   31, 146
β-characteristic function   252
'beauty contest' game   440-3
beer-quiche game   179-84
behavioural equilibrium   429
behavioural strategies   85-6
beliefs
consistency with strategies   165-6
mixed strategies   83-5
rationalizability   144-6
system   161

Bergson–Samuelson social welfare
    function   235
Bertrand
case   119
duopoly model   10, 82
equilibrium   71-3, 106-7, 130
game   193, 194
Nash equilibrium   117
paradox   73
best response function   64
best shot game   420
bilateral monopoly   242-4
bi-matrix game   104
binding agreements   258
Binmore
bargaining: non-cooperative to
    cooperative games   213, 231, 239,
    240
evolutionary games and
    learning   332-4, 358, 378
experimental games   385, 390, 421,
    422, 423, 459
non-cooperative games with
    imperfect or incomplete
    information   143, 155, 162, 179-84
biology   329-30
Bolton–Ockenfels model   450-6, 458
Bondareva–Shapley theorem
    (core)   266
bounded rationality   76, 356   see
    under rationality
β-stability   302
burden sharing rule   312
burning money game   173-5
Buyer–Seller game   430
β-value   289-90, 291, 295

cartels   294
centipede game   108-9, 399-400
'chain-store' game   188-9, 190-2,
    370-8
chance move   147, 149
characteristic function   23, 251
cheap talk games   177
cheating   134
Chicken game   319, 401
Clarke mechanism   57
closed-loop   107
coalitional-form game   22-6

coalitions   22–6, 276, 312, 313–22,
    425–8
  complementary   282
  cooperative and non-cooperative
    games   248–32; applications
    304–22; cooperative games,
    interpretation and classification of
    solution concepts in   255–8;
    domination approach: core and
    related solution concepts   260–76;
    formation   258–60; general
    properties   249–54; linear
    programming   323; valuation
    approach: Shapley value and
    extensions   276–87; see also
    endogenous coalition structures
    and formation of coalitions
  excess   271
  experimental games   439
  partial   312
  stability   293–6
  structure   259–60, 271
  structure value   290
  unanimity game   321–2
Coasian dynamics   225
common beliefs   see under belief
common knowledge   5, 37, 84,
    143–6, 151
communication   392
  direct   74
  indirect   75
  pre-play   86, 353–4, 403, 407
competition   450
  for the first move   100
  imperfect   83
  perfect   151
  for the second move   101
  see under strictly competitive
competitive equilibrium   264–5   see
    under equilibrium
complete information   96, 207,
    208–11
  axiomatic framework   142–4
  experimental games   449, 450
  and non-cooperative games with
    imperfect or incomplete
    information   141, 144, 146, 149,
    150, 151, 165, 188, 197
  voting games   47–9

see also non-cooperative games
    with complete and perfect
    information
Condorcet effect   48, 49
consistency   119, 162–3, 165–7, 183,
    259, 277, 281–2
contraction   229
constituent game   92, 127–30
contests   74, 206
continuation game of repeated game
    162, 168–70
continuous-time model   106
continuum model ('equivalence
    principle')   265
convex game   254, 270, 282, 283
convexity   135–6, 254
cooperation   2–3, 188, 339, 341,
    391–400
  altruism/strategic reputation
    building behaviour   392–7
  backward induction in sequential
    games   398–400
  'cooperation' problem   391
  experimental games   395, 407, 434,
    439, 444, 445, 449, 453, 454, 457
  structure   293
  see also bargaining: non-cooperative
    to cooperative games; coalitions
coordination   155, 333–4, 339, 353, 355,
    401–11, 431–2
  by exterior entity   75–6
  devices   87–91
  experimental games   407, 408, 429,
    430, 435, 438
  factors increasing   407–11
  indirect   86
  problem   401
  pure coordination games   403–7
  symmetric   404
core   260–9, 274–5, 280, 282–3, 287–8,
    294–6, 307, 427
  convergence theorem   264
  equivalence principle   264–5
  existence   265–8
  extension to NTU games   268–9
  imputation and domination
    principle   261–4
  Shapley value, relationships in
    non-atomic games   287

stability   295–6
correlated equilibrium   86–91
  coordination devices   87–91
cost-sharing games   304–10
  multipurpose reservoir
    problem   305–10
  standard model   304–5
cost-sharing rule   56
counter-objections in coalitional
    games   257, 273, 283
Cournot
  adjustment model   12, 360–2, 433
  duopoly   10, 82, 101–2, 112
  equilibrium   106–7, 114, 116, 130
  learning model   436
  learning rule   437
  –Nash equilibrium   68–71, 117
Crawford, V.   6, 9, 177, 405
credible threats   221–2, 256, 257
  see also repeated games and credible
    threats or promises
CS value   291, 292

D_1 criterion   179
decision
  nodes   15
  rule   436, 437, 453–4
  theory   4, 31
definition of game theory   1–2
demand game   416–17, 418
dictator game   413–16, 444, 449, 452,
    455
differential games   106, 107
differentiated goods duopoly
    model   116–20
direct agreements   255
direct communication   74
direct mechanisms   53
distributional models   445
'dividing the dollar'   208–9, 233–6
divine criterion   179, 410–11
division game   208–9
dominance
'dominance solvable game'   35
  iterated dominance   34–7, 172
  mixed strategy   36–7
  risk dominance   75, 353–4, 438
  strict   30
  strict dominance   30, 36, 105, 168

weak   36, 200–1, 203
dominant strategy equilibrium   29–34,
    53–5
  definition   29–31
  efficiency   32–4
  existence   31
domination approach: core and related
    solution concepts   260–76
  core   260–9
  like-core solution concepts   269–76
  valuation approach, relationship
    with   283
δ-stability   301, 302
duality   323
dummy player condition (null player
    condition)   277, 279
duopoly   68
  Bertrand   71–3
  Cournot   68–71
  entry deterrence   110–14
  Stackelberg   101–3
  strategic investment in duopoly
    116–20
dynamic games   see under game
dynamic programming   38–9

ε-cores   263–4
education, Spence's model   195–203
efficiency   32–4, 277, 420, 454
  relative   289, 290
  see also under evolutionary games and
    learning
egalitarian solution   226, 235, 238–9
Eichberger, J.   15, 186
elimination of dominated strategies,
    see dominance, iterated dominance
empiricism   9
endogenous coalition structures and
    formation of coalitions   287–304
  generalities   287–96; reason for
    formation   289; stability   293–6;
    value   289–93
  non-cooperative games with
    externalities   296–304
entry deterrence: multinational
    firm   110–14
entry game   344, 345
envelope theorem   115
environmental coalitions   311–22

coalitional game 313–22
games 311–13
envy 400
equilibriating processes 76–7
equilibrium
in beliefs 83–5
domination 185
refinements 200–2
equity 255–6, 275, 420, 444, 450, 454,
455–6, 458
equivalence principle 264–5
ethics 7
evolution *see* learning and evolution
evolutionary
approach 346
drift 341, 355
equilibrium 334–7, 429
equilibrium entrants and
robustness 342–3
neutral stability or week (ESS) 340–1
stable sets 341
stable strategy (ESS) 337–40,
348–50, 370–2
see also evolutionary games and
learning
evolutionary games and
learning 329–82
applications 363–78; 'chain-store'
game 370–8; international trade
and internal organization of
firms 363–70
asymmetrical 343–7
dynamic system, elements of 379–80
extensions and generalizations to
economics: evolution, rationality
and efficiency 347–56;
dominance 351–3; evolutionary
stability and efficiency 353–6;
Replicator Dynamics and
Evolutionary stable
strategies 347–51
Friedman–Fung model 381–2
learning models 356–63
replicator dynamics 330–47
evolutive, interpretation of an
equilibrium 6–9, 385
exclusive membership games 300–1,
319–20
experimental games 385–459

bargaining 411–28
cooperation 391–400
coordination 401–11
history and methodology 386–8
learning and evolution 428–38
new game theoretic modelling
principles 439–59
strictly competitive games 388–91
extensive-form game 13–17
extensive-form game
agent normal form 158
behavioural strategy 85–6
chance move 17–18, 147–50,
166
external stability 269, 294

fair game 81
fairness 416, 450, 456, 459
equilibrium 446, 447–8, 449 *see also*
Rabin model
Fehr–Schmidt model 456–9
Feldstein pricing 304
fictitious play model 357, 362–3, 433,
436, 437
finite horizon bargaining game
211–13
finite game 14, 81, 92, 105, 132–4, 158,
161, 167, 186
finite horizon 92, 211–13
finite repetition 92, 96, 132–4, 392
see also finite horizon
firm-union bargaining over wage and
employment 244–6
first theorem of welfare
economics 264
fitness function 331, 337, 348
fixed point theorem 67–8, 82, 137
focal equilibrium 209
focal-point principle 7, 75, 97, 134,
402
folk theorem 45, 94–7, 106, 132 *see also*
perfect folk theorem
formal representations of games 13–26
coalition-form games 22–6
extensive-form games 13–17
partition function-form game 296
strategic-form games 17–22
forward induction 170–88
and backward induction 171–5

signalling games, formalizations
      in   175–84
stable sets of equilibria   185–8
framing effects   414, 439–40, 455
free-riding   33, 313–19, 321, 395–6
   evolutionary games and
      learning   337, 348, 350, 363, 364,
      368, 381–2
   non-cooperative games with
      complete and perfect
      information   96, 107, 110, 115, 119
   non-cooperative games with
      imperfect or incomplete
      information   146–51, 152, 165, 167

game form   51
game tree   15, 18, 21, 212, 218, 219
   experimental games   398
   non-cooperative games with
      complete and perfect
      information   98, 103–4, 108, 109
   non-cooperative games with
      imperfect or incomplete
      information   162, 163, 171, 187
Gibbard–Satterthwaite theorem   54–5
Gibbons, R.   152
gift-exchange game   415, 459
Glicksberg theorem   83
global attractor   379, 380
grim strategy   95
Groves–Clarks–Vickrey
      mechanism   55–8
'guessing' game   440–3

Harsanyi
   coalitions: cooperative and
      non-cooperative games   249, 252,
      281, 284, 285
   non-cooperative games with
      imperfect or incomplete
      information   141, 142, 146, 147,
      151, 165, 167
Hart–Kurz theorem   292
Hart–Mas–Colell theorem   282
Hawk–Dove game   335–6, 346–7
   experimental games   401, 430, 431,
      433, 434, 436, 437
hidden actions: moral hazard   120–7
horse game (Selten)   107–8

Hurwicz's diagram   51

ideal point   237–8
imitation   356, 358–9
impatience in bargaining game   241–2
imperfect information   103, 107, 108,
      165, 409
   and perfect information   14, 21
   perfect and imperfect recall   14
   perfect Bayesian equilibrium   164–5
   perfect trembling hand
      equilibrium   156–9
   proper equilibrium   160–1
   subgame perfect equilibrium   103–5
   sequential equilibrium   166–7
   see also non-cooperative games with
      imperfect or incomplete
      information
implementation theory
   cooperative solution concepts   257
   direct mechanism   52
   dominant strategy
      implementation   53–5
   Groves–Clarke–Vickrey
      mechanism   55–9
   mechanism design   50–3
   public decision-making   49–59
   welfare economics   50
impunity game   418
imputation   261–4, 269–75
incentive compatibility
      constraint   123, 125, 126, 194–5
incentive mechanism   317
incomplete information   96, 108, 109,
      133, 207, 222–6, 416–18
   experimental games   392, 400, 407,
      413, 418, 450, 452
   voting games   46–7
   see also non-cooperative games with
      imperfect or incomplete
      information
independence of irrelevant
      alternatives   228–9
individual rationality
   bargaining solution   227
   core   261
   Shapley value   see under Shapley
   stable set   see stable set
industrial organization   100–3, 269

inequity aversion model   456–9
inessential games   291–2
infinite game   73, 83, 105, 167, 393
infinite horizon   92, 213–18
infinite repetition   130–2, 393
   see also infinite horizon
information   4–6
   asymmetric   120, 123–4, 175–6, 177,
      184, 188, 190
   exchange   100
   experimental games   431, 432, 433,
      434
   private   149, 150, 176, 177, 184, 453
   sets   158
   symmetric   122–3
   see also complete; imperfect;
      incomplete; perfect
intentionality model   445–50
internal organization of firms   363–70
internal stability   269, 294
   see under stability
international trade   363–70
intuitive criterion   202–3, 410–11
invariance   227–8, 238
investment game   415
irrationality   108, 156, 188, 190
iterated dominance   34–7

job market game   195–203

Kakutani theorem   67–8, 137
   see also fixed point theorem
Kantian behaviour   430, 434, 435,
      444–5
kernel   273–6, 280, 283, 288
Kreps
   non-cooperative games with
      complete and perfect
      information   75, 85, 96, 133
   non-cooperative games with
      imperfect or incomplete
      information   162, 165, 167, 171,
      177, 179, 188, 190, 192, 195, 202
Kühn theorem   86
Kühn–Tücker multipliers   126

λ-transfer value   284
learning   420–1
   adaptive   437, 438, 439

belief   356, 359–63
   and evolution   428–38; questions
      explored   428–30; single-
      population games   430–3;
      two-population games   433–4
   models   356–63, 459; belief
      learning   359–63; learning by way
      of imitation   358–9
   routine learning   356–8
   rule   436, 437
   see also evolutionary games and
      learning
Lebesgue measure structure   265
like-core and solution concepts
      269–76
   bargaining set   271–3
   kernel   273–6
   nucleolus   274–6
   stable sets   269–71
linear programming   267, 323
logit equilibrium   433–4

machine game   97
Malthusian dynamics   348
market games   457
Markov strategy   106
Marshall–Lerner conditions   128
'matching pennies'   80
matrix game   21
maximin strategies   40, 42, 43, 45
mean matching   429, 434
mechanism design   50–9
   see also implementation theory
mental equilibrium processes   76
minimax theorem   42–4, 252, 388, 389,
      390
mixed strategy   19–20
   behavioural strategies   85–6
   definition and interpretation   80–3
   equilibrium in beliefs   83–5
mixed strategy equilibrium   80–6
   and correlated equilibium   90
   mixed strategy   19–20
monotone likelihood ratio
      condition   126
monotonicity   208, 238, 298, 352
moral hazard   50, 120–7, 289
motivation function   451, 452, 453,
      454

optimal decentralized decisions   31,
   34, 41, 43, 44, 46, 49, 58
multinational firm   110–14
multipurpose reservoir problem
   305–10
multistage bargaining games   422
multivalued solution concept   281
mutual knowledge   5, 84, 143
Myerson
   coalitions: cooperative and
      non-cooperative games   249, 256,
      278, 285, 293, 299, 300
Myerson value   293

n-person   281, 304
   bargaining model   249, 250, 251, 253
   cooperative game   269
Nash bargaining solution   211, 219,
   226–36, 244, 254
Nash behaviour   65
   characterization of bargaining
      problem   226–7
   Nash axioms   227–9
   Nash products: regular and
      generalized Nash solutions
      229–32
   risk aversion: 'dividing the dollar'
      233–6
   variable threat games   232–3
Nash demand game   240–1
Nash equilibrium   63–80
   and Bayesian equilibrium   146–51
   Bertrand equilibrium: price
      competition   71–3
   'closed loop'   106
   Cournot–Nash equilibrium: quantity
      competition   68–71
   definition   63–7
   existence   67–8
   failures: non-existence, multiplicity
      and inefficiency   78–80
   justification and selection   73–7
   'open-loop'   106
   strict   64
   symmetric   68, 336, 340
Nash product   252
Nash program   207, 213, 257
Nash program and axiomatic models
   226–42

Nash bargaining solution   226–36
   strategic and axiomatic approaches,
      relationships between   239–42
Nash–Cournot equilibria   111, 114
Nash–Roth theorem (bargaining
   solution)   230
Nash theorem (equilibrium)   67
Nash theorem (solution)   233
nature   124, 344, 371
   non-cooperative games with
      imperfect or incomplete
      information   147, 149, 150, 151,
      166, 176, 179, 181, 183, 193, 196
   see also chance move
negotiation   3, 74, 206, 250, 260, 263
   pre-play   74–5, 90, 132, 176
   see also bargaining
new game theoretic modelling
      principles   439–59
   players' abilities   440–4
   players' motivations': new 'social
      utility' models   444–59
non-atomic games   285–7
non-constant sum games   390–1
non-cooperative approach   207, 211,
   213, 214
non-cooperative behaviour   65, 76
   see also Nash behaviour
non-cooperative equilibria   349
non-cooperative games   2–3, 347, 348,
   363, 365, 371, 429
   experimental games   435, 457
   see also bargaining; coalitions;
      optimal decentralized decisions
non-cooperative games with complete
      and perfect information   62–137
   applications   109–34; sequential
      games and strategic
      commitment   109–20
   convexity   135
   correspondences   136–7
   extensions: randomization and
      correlation   80–91
   fixed point theorems   137
   Nash equilibrium   63–80
   repeated games   91–7
   sub-game perfect equilibrium
      97–109
   topological concept, basic   135

non-cooperative game of coalition
formation 296–304
partition function form-games
296–8
stability and valuations 299–304
non-cooperative games with imperfect
or incomplete information
141–203
applications 188–203; repeated
games with incomplete
information: reputation
effects 188–92; signalling
games 192–203
Bayesian equilibrium 142–55
forward induction 170–88
perfectness 156–61
sequentiality 161–70
non-existence 63, 78–80
non-overlapping generations model of
the Replicator dynamics 331–2
normal-form game 17
see also strategic-form game
normative approach 236, 255–6
notation xxvi
NTU game and Shapley value 284–5
nucleolus 274–6, 282
extension to NTV games 275
normative interpretation 274
relationships with bargaining set,
core and kernel 274
null player condition 290

objections 256, 257, 271–3, 276, 283
bargaining set 271–3
kernel 273–6
nucleolus 274–6
Shapley value see Shapley
stable set 269
offer game 416–17, 418
oligopoly 133
see also duopoly
one-shot game 392–3
open-loop 106–7
open membership games 300–1, 315,
322
optimal decentralized decisions
28–59
applications 45–59; implementation
theory and public decision-

making 49–59; voting
games 45–9
backward induction 37–9
dominant strategy equilibrium
29–34
iterated dominance 34–7
safety first rule 39–45
optimization premium 438
orthogonal games 253
out-of-equilibrium
action 184
beliefs 200
messages 177–8, 179
outside option games 218–22,
408–11, 422–3
overlapping generations model of the
Replicator dynamics 332–4
overtaking criterion 94
Owen value 280

Pareto
domination 33, 95, 99
experimental games 391, 406, 407,
408, 409
efficiency (optimality) 32, 33, 42, 50,
58, 79, 132, 253, 261, 262, 264, 281
bargaining: non-cooperative to
cooperative games 227, 228,
229–30, 238, 239
experimental games 402, 406, 408,
409, 446
frontier 231, 232, 233, 245
inefficiency 59, 63, 78, 80, 86, 99,
159, 281
participation constraint 122, 125, 126
partition function-form game 296–8,
312, 313
'partner' treatment in
experiments 397
payoff function 16
of repeated games 92–4
perfect folk theorem 106
perfect information 141, 189, 199, 400
see also non-cooperative games with
complete and perfect information
perfect recall 86
perfect trembling hand
equilibrium 156–9
perfectness 156–61, 167, 170

proper equilibrium – strict   159
see also perfect trembling hand
    equilibrium and
perturbed games   157,158,159,167,187
player partition   16
players' abilities   440-4
players' motivations': new 'social
    utility' models   444-59
  Bolton–Ockenfels: relative payoff
      model   450-6
  Fehr–Schmidt: inequity aversion
      model   456-9
  Rabin: intentionality model   445-50
pooling equilibrium   177, 184, 194,
    195, 198, 199-200, 203
portfolio management game   192-5
possible worlds   155
'potential'   279
see also Shapley value
pre-bargaining   282
preference profiles   52, 53
pre-imputation   261, 272, 274, 280
pre-kernel   282
pre-nucleolus   282
principal–agent model   50, 120-7
Prisoner's dilemma   32-4, 338, 341,
    392-4, 432-3
  experimental games   387, 391,
      394-5, 397, 400, 422, 429-30, 436-7,
      439, 449, 453-4
  non-cooperative games with
      complete and perfect
      information   65, 79, 91-2, 94-5,
      127, 129
  sequential   398
promises   188
see also repeated games and credible
    threats or promises
proper equilibrium   160-1
psychological game   446, 447, 448
public decision-making   see
    implementation theory and public
    decision-making
public goods provision game   391,
    394-7, 399, 420, 433, 439, 444-5,
    453-4, 458-9
punishment   132, 134, 397
purification of mixed strategy
    equilibrium   85

'quantal response' function   443-4
quantity competition   68-71

Rabin model   445-9, 458
Raiffa–Kalai–Smorodinsky
    solution   226, 236-8
Ramsey–Boiteux pricing   304
Ranann, J.   310
Rand Corporation   387
randomization   81, 86, 88-9, 182,
    223-5, 443-4
see also extensions: randomization
    and correlation
rational expectation equilibrium   76
rationalistic interpretation of
    equilibrium   6-9, 155, 385
rationality   4-6, 211, 228, 230
  Bayesian   31, 146
  bounded   76-7, 440-4
  full   76
  group   261, 266, 277, 279, 280
  rationalizability   144-5
    correlated   145
  group condition   271
  individual   227, 261, 262, 266, 271
  interactive   440-3
  sequential   162, 163, 164, 165, 166,
      167, 183-4
  strategies   144-6
see also under evolutionary games and
    learning
reciprocity   400, 415, 418, 428, 444, 450,
    454, 458
  negative   446, 449
  positive   446
reduced game property   281
refinements   7, 97, 155-6, 170
  evolutionary concepts   336, 340, 342,
      349
  forward induction   170, 179
  in extensive-form games   156
  in strategic-form game   156
  perfectness   156
  sequentiality   161
  sub-game perfection   97
relative payoff model   450-6
  equity in bargaining games
      455-6
  ERC equilibria   452-3

relative payoff model *cont.*
　general model　450–2
　reciprocity in cooperation
　　games　453–4
　two-player model　452
repeated games　91–7, 393
　application-tariff game　130–2
　and credible threats or
　　promises　127–34
　constituent game　127–30
　definition　91–4
　finite repetition　132–4
　infinite repetition　130–2
　folk theorem　94–7
　mixed strategy　84
　perfect folk theorem　106
　subgame perfect equilibrium　106
　with incomplete information:
　　reputation effects　188–92
replicator dynamics　330–51, 352–3,
　　356–9, 374–6
　asymmetrical evolutionary
　　games　343–7
　evolutionary equilibrium　334–7
　non-overlapping generations
　　model　331–2
　overlapping generations
　　model　332–4
　relationship with ESS and other
　　equilibrium concepts　347–51
reputation effects　188–92, 392–3, 397,
　　400
revelation principle　54, 125, 152
Riley equilibrium　199, 201, 202, 203
risk　425, 444
　aversion　125, 233–6
　-dominance　353–4, 438
　-neutral　125, 152, 173, 234
robustness (against equilibrium
　　extracts)　342–3
rock, scissors, paper game　21–2, 23,
　　351–2
　experimental games　385, 389, 393,
　　411, 419, 420, 421, 423, 424, 425,
　　426, 435–6, 459
Roth–Malouf procedure　389, 424
　bargaining: non-cooperative to
　　cooperative games　211–18, 220,
　　221–2, 226, 240, 241–2

theorem　213
Rubinstein theorem　213

saddle-point　43, 44
safety-first rule　39–45
　security strategies　39–41
　security strategies in strictly
　　competitive game　42–5
saliency　402
satisficing principle　427
Scarf–Shapley theorem　268
scoring method　49
screening game　176, 177
secret handshake　355
security strategies in strictly
　　competitive game　42–5
self-interest　448, 449, 459
　narrow　451, 452, 453
Selton
　evolutionary games and
　　learning　329, 344, 353, 370
　non-cooperative games with
　　complete and perfect
　　information　75, 103, 105, 107–8
　non-cooperative games with
　　imperfect or incomplete
　　information　156, 158, 185, 188
semi-pooling equilibrium　176
separable costs remaining benefits
　　method　308
separating equilibrium　176, 194–5,
　　198, 199, 201, 203
sequential bargaining　241–2
sequential equilibrium　165–70, 179,
　　197–9
　and perfect Bayesian
　　and trembling hand perfect
　　equilibrium　167
　assessment　162
　belief system　161
　consistency　166
　equilibrium　167
　example　168
　existence　167
　refinements　170
　sequential rationality　162, 166
sequential games　303, 398–400
sequential games and strategic
　　commitment　109–20

entry deterrence: multinational
firm 110–14
hidden actions: moral hazard
120–7
repeated games and credible threats
or promises 127–34
strategic investment in differentiated
goods duopoly model 116–20
strategic trade policy 114–16
sequential market game 420–1
sequentiality 161
see also perfect Bayesian equilibrium;
sequential equilibrium
sequential rationality see sequential
equilibrium
Shapley
coalitions: cooperative and non-
cooperative games 254, 265, 266,
268, 285–7, 310
theorem 278
Shapley value 12, 256–7, 260, 307–8,
427
application: cost-sharing
games 304–10
axiomatic characterization 277–8
relationship with other solution
concepts 280–3
generalization for NTU games
284–5
see also valuation approach: Shapley
value and extensions
signalling games 50, 86, 127, 173,
175–84, 192–203, 222
beer–quiche game 179–84
continuous 184
experimental games 410
intuitive criterion 177–9
job market game 195–203
portfolio management game 192–5
single-crossing condition 184, 196–7,
202, 203
single-population experimental
evolutionary games 430–3
skimming effect 364–5, 367–8
social choice rule 51, 52–3, 54, 55,
57, 58
social coalition equilibrium 297–8
social conventions 75
social dilemma game 433

'social utility' models 444–59
social welfare function 206, 235, 312
Bergson–Samuelson 235
solution concept (for cooperative
games)
bargaining games (bargaining
solution) 227
coalition games 255
'domination' versus 'valuation'
approaches 256–7, 283; see also
core, stable set, bargaining
solution, kernel, nucleolus,
Shapley value, Owen value,
Myerson value, Aumann–Shapley
value, β-value, Aumann–Dreze
Value, CS value
'split the difference rule' 221, 231–2,
241, 245, 423
stability 293–6, 299–304, 316–19, 321,
343
α, β, γ, δ stability 301–2
coalition unanimity game 321–2
coalition structures 293
exclusive membership 320–1
coalition structure in games with
valuations 293–302
equilibrium refinements 179
neutral 340–1
open membership game 316–19
stable sets 269
stable equilibrium, individual 294
stable sets 185–8, 269–71, 288
Stackelberg duopoly model 10,
101–3
Stackelberg equilibrium 100–3, 106–7,
115
Stag–Hunt games 401, 438
stage game 92
stand alone cost condition 306
stand alone stability 316
state variables 106, 107
state–space strategy 106
stationary state 379
steady-state interpretation of
equilibrium 8
'stranger' treatment in
experiments 397
strategic commitment see sequential
games and strategic commitment

strategic bargaining games 207–26
  indeterminacy or extreme Nash
    equlibria and complete
    information 208–11
  non-cooperative theories of
    bargaining under incomplete
    information 222–6
  'outside option' games 218–22
  Rubinstein model: alternating offers
    in finite and infinite horizon
    games 211–18
strategic-form game 19
strategic-form games 17–22, 23
strategic investment in differentiated
    goods duopoly model 116–20
strategic reputation building
    behaviour 392–7
strategic trade policy 114–16
strategy 17
  behavioural 85–6
  dominated 29
  dominant 30
  in Bayesian games 150
  mixed 19, 80–4
  pure 17
  security 39
  strictly dominant 30
  strong security 41
strict Nash equilibrium 64
strictly competitive games 388–91
  constant sum games 388–90
  non-constant sum games 390–1
sub-game perfect equilibrium 97–109
  backward induction 97–100
  general games 103–9
  Stackelberg equilibrium:
    application in industrial
    organization 100–3
superadditivity 208, 253, 254, 266, 280,
    292–3, 299
symbols xxvi–xxvii
symmetric games 391, 401
symmetry 228, 229, 238, 239, 277, 279,
    289, 291

tariffs 127–8, 129, 130, 133, 134
Tennessee Valley Authority 306–10
terms of trade 128, 134

threats 188
  see also repeated games and credible
    threats or promises
three-person bargaining model 250
time equilibriating processes 76–7
Tirole
  non-cooperative games with
    complete and perfect
    information 107, 110, 115, 119
  non-cooperative games with
    imperfect or incomplete
    information 146–51, 152, 165, 167
tit-for-tat 96, 132–3, 338, 341, 392,
    393, 454
top-dog strategy 115
topological concept, basic 135
toy game 108
Tragedy of the Commons 33
transferable utility 251, 253–4, 268–71,
    273–5, 284, 288, 296, 298
  coalitional games 23, 24
travellers' dilemma game 433–4
trembles 167
trigger strategies 95, 134
trust game 398, 453, 459
truthful implementation 53
two-player, zero-sum game 42
two-population experimental
    evolutionary games 433–4
ultimatum game 209–11
  experimental games 411–21, 428,
    433, 444–5, 449, 452, 455, 459; data
    analysis 419–21; institutional
    environment 412–13; modified
    versions of standard game
    413–18; stylized facts 411–12
undefeated equilibrium 179
upper semicontinuity 137
utilitarianism 235

valuation 152–3, 256–8, 299–304
  approach: Shapley value and
    extensions 276–87;
    characterization 277–8;
    extensions 284–7;
    interpretation 278; in games of
    coalition formation with
    externality 299; relationship
    between Shapley value and other

solution concepts   280–3; Shapley
    value   276–80
  function   314, 316, 320, 321, 322
  symmetric   312
value   42–3
  coalitional game   439
  strictly competitive game   ??
  Aumann–Shapley value of non-
    atomic games   285–7, 310
  β-value (Aumann–Dreze value)
    289–90
  CS value   290
  of a coalitional structure   289
  λ-transfer value   284
  Owen value   280
  Myerson value   293
  NTU Harsanyi value   284
  NTU Shapley value   284–5
  private (in auctions)   56
  Shapley value   276–9
  zero-sum game   42, 44, 81
variable threat games   232–3

VNM utility functions   124
Von Neuman theorem   44
  see also minimax theorem
voting
  games   45–9
  paradox   48

Walrasian auctioneer   75
Walrasian equilibrium   264, 265
weighted majority game   25
welfare/welfarism   50, 129, 131, 226,
    236
winner's curse   56
worth of players coalitions   45

γ-stability   301, 302

zero-sum games   42, 43, 44, 45, 66, 80,
    81, 101